BLACK ARTS, BLACK MUSLIMS

BLACK LIVES IN THE DIASPORA: PAST / PRESENT / FUTURE

BLACK LIVES IN THE DIASPORA: PAST / PRESENT / FUTURE

EDITORIAL BOARD

Howard University
Clarence Lusane, Rubin Patterson, Nikki Taylor, Amy Yeboah Quarkume

Columbia University
Farah Jasmine Griffin, Frank Guridy, Josef Sorett

Black Lives in the Diaspora: Past / Present / Future is a book series that focuses on Black lives in a global diasporic context. Published in partnership with Howard University's College of Arts and Sciences and Columbia University's African American and African Diaspora Studies Department, it builds on Columbia University Press's publishing programs in history, sociology, religion, philosophy, and literature as well as African American and African Diaspora studies. The series showcases scholarship and writing that enriches our understanding of Black experiences in the past, present, and future with the goal of reaching beyond the academy to intervene in urgent national and international conversations about the experiences of people of African descent. The series anchors an exchange across two global educational institutions, both located in historical capitals of Black life and culture.

Cisco Bradley, *I Hear Freedom: The Great Migration, Free Jazz, and Black Power*

Isis Barra Costa, *Imagining the Past, Remembering the Future: Forms of Knowledge in the Afro-Brazilian Diaspora*

Nicole M. Morris Johnson, *The Souths in Her: Black Women Writers and Choreographers and the Poetics of Transmutation*

Jamall A. Calloway, *Imagining Eden: Black Theology and the Search for Paradise*

Wendell H. Marsh, *Textual Life: Islam, Africa, and the Fate of the Humanities*

For a complete list of books in the series, please see the Columbia University Press website.

BLACK ARTS, BLACK MUSLIMS

Islam in the Black Freedom Struggle

ELLEN McLARNEY

Columbia University Press

New York

Columbia University Press
Publishers Since 1893
New York   Chichester, West Sussex
cup.columbia.edu

Copyright © 2026 Columbia University Press Ellen McLarney
All rights reserved

Cataloging-in-Publication Data is available from the Library of Congress.

ISBN 9780231219419 (hardback)
ISBN 9780231219426 (trade paperback)
ISBN 9780231562683 (ebook)
ISBN 9780231565509 (pdf)

LCCN 2025037393

Cover design: Elliott S. Cairns
Cover image: Ademola Olugebefola

GPSR Authorized Representative: Easy Access System Europe, Mustamäe tee 50, 10621 Tallinn, Estonia, gpsr.requests@easproject.com

FOR BRUNO,
pareja de mi vida

IN THE MOST HOLY NAME OF ALLAH, THE BENEFICENT, THE MERCIFUL

The *basmallah*—written in Arabic in Marvin X's own hand—opens his collection *Black Man Listen: Poems and Proverbs* published by Broadside.

>   this constant prayer
>   i give, is mine, and the eye thought you would see . . .
>
>   keeping the world natural
>   changing the nature of
>   moving in the actual spirit, it's the time
>   ing
>   the
>   ri-
>   thum
>
>   in the constant gorgeous
>   reenactment of God re-
>   creating
>   himself.
>
>   —LeRoi Jones, "Salik," *Black Art* (1966)

CONTENTS

Acknowledgments xi

THE OPENING

Prelude. الاطلال (al-Atlal): Poetic Tracings of the Past   3

1. "Constant Conscious Striving": Jihad of the Pen and the Black Arts Movement   22

PART I: ANTICIPATING THE BAM

2. Nation in a Nation in a Nation: The Islamic Counterpublic and the Black Arts   51

3. Science's Fictions: Yakub and the Black Arts   70

PART II: MALCOLM X AND BLACK ART

4. Music in the Message: Malcolm X's Gospel Truth   101

5. "Flame Feeding Flame": The Literary Malcolm X   124

PART III: BLACK STUDY AND BLACK LIFE

6. "Fly to Allah": Marvin X's Fugitive Life and Black Study   149

7. The Barakas in New Ark: The Homeplace of Black Art   178

8. "blk/visions for blk/lives": Sonia Sanchez's Rebirth in Islam   207

Coda. 360° of Islamic Audiovisualities: Revolution and Evolution   240

......

Notes   263

Bibliography   319

Index   349

ACKNOWLEDGMENTS

I want to first thank the BAM artists who shared their knowledge, life stories, archives, writings, and artwork. They opened their homes and introduced me to their extended families. Marvin X took me under his wing; had me sit with him at his Academy of da Corner; showed me around Oakland and Marin City; took me on a poetry tour from Durham to Philadelphia, Brooklyn, and Newark with his grandson James Rhodes; and introduced me to his family. Amina Baraka welcomed me numerous times to her home, showed me around Newark, introduced me to her children and grandchildren, and took me to the Shani Baraka Women's Resource Center. Malika Iman graciously gave me a copy of her book and provided permission to quote her father's poetry. Sonia Sanchez invited me to talk with her in her home and on her porch, introducing me to her sons Mungu and Morani. Askia Muhammad Touré's partner, Jacqueline McRath, gave me encouragement when I needed it most. Ademola Olugebefola invited me to the Dwyer Cultural Center, talked to me for hours, and gave me permission to reproduce his art. Abdul Rahman's daughter Sultanah Rahman shared pictures, stories, friends, and family (including her daughter and grandson). Hortense "Bunnie" DuVall spoke to me at a key moment just the day after her husband Taiwo DuVall Shabazz passed on to the next world, on Eid al-Fitr. الله يرحمه.

Several main scholars have been intellectual guides for this project: Hisham Aidi lived down the hall in International House when I first returned from the Peace Corps in Morocco; Samy Alim and I first met as graduate students in Ramzi Salti's Arabic class at Stanford; Jamillah Karim was finishing her doctorate in Religion at Duke when I first arrived in 2003, and she returned many times to share her bright spirit and intellect; Edward E. Curtis IV, an assistant professor at UNC when we first met at Ebrahim Moosa's home, gave encouragement at key points; Jeanette Jouili has been my scholarly twin and spirit sister; Zain Abdullah welcomed me to Newark, showed me around, and took me seriously; Youssef Carter came to speak in my Black Muslims class while still a graduate student at Berkeley and became a friend, colleague, and professor at UNC; Suʻad Abdul Khabeer presented on *Muslim Cool* at Duke and gave me feedback on the book's chapter about Sonia Sanchez; Sylvia Chan-Malik presented on *Being Muslim* at Duke's Kenan Institute for Ethics; Michael West and Dara Walker invited me to write about Malcolm X for their Black Power volume and to Penn State for the centennial of Malcolm X's birth; Solayman Idris has been my collaborator and intellectual and spiritual brother; Maurice Hines was one of the pioneers of the ar-Razzaq project; amina wadud has always been generous with her time, intellect, and mentorship; Ula Taylor treated me kindly at the ASALH conference; and R. A. Judy brought his dazzling erudition to Duke and our ASALH panel on "Islam and Black Art." These people all made this work possible during the many times I profoundly doubted my right and ability to do justice to this work.

I owe profound thanks to the editors and journals who published early conceptualizations of this work: the inestimable Barbara Ransby, editor of *Souls*; Tavia Nyong'o and Jennifer Stoever at *Social Text*; the editors of the African American Intellectual History Society's journal *Black Perspectives*; and Reynaldo Anderson, who included me and my coauthor Solayman Idris in his special issue of *The Black Scholar*, "Africology and the Rise of Afrofuturist Studies." Stephen Finley gave me encouragement on the chapter "Science's Fictions," which is profoundly indebted to his scholarship. The curator Myrah Brown Green helped connect me to Weusi artists Ademola Olugebefola, Taiwo DuVall Shabazz, and Abdul Rahman. Professor Jontyle Robinson, the first curator at Spelman College Museum of Fine Art and Tuskegee University's Legacy Museum, imparted her bright spirit, keen insights, and friendship. I am also grateful to the Schomburg Center for Research in Black Culture for providing access to their invaluable resources.

I cannot thank Brother Joshua Salaam and Imam Abdul Hafeez Waheed enough. They have been guides, friends, mentors, teachers, and family every step of the way. Brother Joshua, Duke's Muslim Chaplain, grew up in my hometown, Kansas City, and went to school down the street from my house. At that time, Islam was (thousands of) miles from my consciousness, only a list of the five pillars in my Catholic school textbook. Our paths converged through our mutual commitments to Islam as our different odysseys led us to the same place.

I also want to thank Imam Ronald Shaheed of Masjid Ash-Shaheed mosque in Charlotte and Samaiyah Faison of the Mary Lou Williams Center for Black Culture at Duke. I want to especially thank my colleague Professor Mbaye Lo for the inspiration of his scholarship and tireless dedication. I also owe thanks to my other colleagues in the Arabic program—Maha Houssami, Badr Badr, Saadbou Cheikh Abdi Vall, and Amal Boumaaza—whose goodwill and support have buoyed me, and Omid Safi, a spiritual and intellectual guide and friend. He began the Muslims in America project with Duke Arts and the Doris Duke Foundation for Islamic Arts and then graciously handed it over. And the 2015 conference "The Legacy of Malcolm X: Afro-American Visionary, Muslim Activist" he organized as director of the Duke Islamic Studies Center brought together "The Global Malcolm," "The American Malcolm," and "The Muslim Malcolm."

I extend thanks to the Doris Duke Foundation for Islamic Art for supporting the Building Bridges: Muslims in America project and to all the scholars, artists, musicians, poets, and filmmakers who took part in spreading knowledge about the Islamic art of the African diaspora—Maimouna Youssef, Sasa Aakil, Saadiya Bashir, Oddisee, Tariq Touré, Amir Sulaiman, Dua Saleh, Alsarah & The Nubatones, Brother Ali, Youssef Carter, Rashida James-Saadiya, Richard Brent Turner, Su'ad Abdul Khabeer, and Hisham Aidi. Thanks to Brian Valentyn and Julie Maxwell, tireless warriors whose labor and organization brought these artists to schools and the community. Thanks to Abbas Rattani, Yusuf Siddiquee, and Shimul Chowdhury for the collaboration on the Al-Hamdu / Muslim Futurism conference and exhibit. They brought joy, love, and spirit every step of the way.

Thanks to the Office of the Provost at Duke for supporting the "Islam and Racial Justice in the American South" project with Professor Mbaye Lo (and especially for the support of Vice Provost Abbas Benmamoun). Thanks to Kenny Dalsheimer for collaborating on the *Moonchild: The Life and Music of Yusuf Salim* concerts at Hayti Heritage Center and for his important work on the documentary film.

Profound thanks are due to the John Hope Franklin Humanities Institute for organizing the manuscript workshop for this book—Ranji Khanna and Sylvia Miller for spearheading it, Sohail Daulatzai, Edward E. Curtis IV, Youssef Carter, Rashida James Saadiya, Juliane Hammer, and Mark Anthony Neal for helping shepherd this project in its earlier stages. I also owe miriam cooke, Bruce Lawrence, Carl Ernst, and Charles Kurzman my gratitude for their mentorship and leadership over the years and their support of this project. Michael Sells has been a guiding light of spirit and poetry since we first visited the shrines of Shaykh Abd al-Aziz al-Mahdawi and Abu Abdullah al-Kinani in Tunis.

I owe sincere gratitude to Mark Anthony Neal, who took time to meet with me repeatedly as I conceptualized this project, giving me invaluable insights and encouragement, despite my trepidation. Komozi Woodard generously gave of his time, speaking to me at length and giving advice. Professors J. Kameron Carter, Meta DuEwa Jones, David Grundy, Titsi Jaji, Michael Muhammad Knight, Adriane Lentz-Smith, Richard Powell, James Smethurst, and Joseph Winters all provided feedback at key points, as did Patrick Bowen. Professors Grundy and Smethurst directed me at a key moment early in the manuscript, just as they were paying tribute to Askia Muhammad Touré's *Songhai!* in a special issue of *Paideuma: Modern and Contemporary Poetry and Poetics*.

Thanks to my editor Alyssa Napier for being unfailingly dependable every step of the way; to the Black Lives in Diaspora: Past/Present/Future series and their editorial board; to Eric Schwartz for meeting with me at ASALH and bringing this manuscript to Columbia; and to Mary Bagg for her editorial help and amiability.

The roots of this project go back to my study of Francophone African literature in high school and deepened with continued study in college at Brown. I applied to the Peace Corps to go to West Africa, ultimately being posted in Morocco for two years where I lived, learned, and taught. Wanting to deepen and formalize my knowledge of Arabic, Islam, and the Middle East, I applied for a PhD program at Columbia where I studied literature—theory with Edward Said, Arabic literature with Magda al-Nowaihi, and African and Caribbean literature with Maryse Condé يرحمهم الله. I owe Maryse Condé a deep debt of gratitude for her mentorship and for making Black Studies, the Caribbean, and West Africa a critical part of my graduate education. Living at the edge of Harlem, different Islams were all around me, including the Malcolm X project at Columbia, awakening my consciousness. My first year at Duke I began a project called "Local Islams," partly funded by Harvard's Pluralism Project and the Kenan Institute for Ethics, to develop a service-learning course in which students worked in the different local Muslim communities. They tutored at the al-Iman school, helped found the Mariam Clinic for low-income women (Muslim and otherwise), and volunteered at the Durham History Hub's project on ar-Razzaq Mosque, the former Nation of Islam Muhammad's Mosque No. 34.

Thank you to Candis Watts Smith (Kenza) for traveling this student-teacher journey with me from Arabic to Egypt to Durham and for encouraging me in this project since its earliest beginnings in the Local Islams project. Thank you to Nashua Oraby for being part of the Local Islams project and becoming a friend, sister, and always a spiritual inspiration. I also want to acknowledge and thank several key students: Iyesha and Ezra Belgrave, Seliat Dairo, Antonio de Jesús López, Shadee Malaklou, Hadeel Hamoud, Razan Idris, and Ibtihaj Muhammad. Razan sent copies of Samy Alim's *Roc the Mic* and Marvin X's *Somethin' Proper* while I was in Argentina on a Fulbright in 2018. I embarked on this project with sincere intention and ask forgiveness for any errors, mistakes, or lack of judgment.

The greatest gratitude goes to my entire extended family (KC shout out!) but especially my mother Martina, father Patrick, sister Megan, and brother Michael for always supporting my path. Thank you to my husband Bruno and to my children—Nico the engineer, Mateo the philosopher intellectual, and Catalina the artist athlete—for giving me a life of love, supporting my journeys, always being there for me, and teaching me the meaning of true happiness. Bruno, *pareja de mi vida*, you make life worth living.

The Opening

PRELUDE

الاطلال (AL-ATLAL)

Poetic Tracings of the Past

Key poets of the Black Arts Movement (BAM) who converted to Islam—Lawrence Edward Graham, Marvin Jackmon, LeRoi Jones, Sylvia Robinson/Wilson, Sonia Sanchez, Rolland Snellings, Ronald Stone, and Joseph Washington—took the names Ahmed Akinwole Alhamisi, Marvin X, Amiri Baraka, Amina Baraka, Sonia 5X/Laila Mannan, Askia Muhammad Touré, Yusuf Rahman, and Yusef Iman. They used Islamic words, language, writing, references, scripture, signs, and symbols to describe the emergence of a new consciousness and to give expression to their commitments to Islam—in poetry, plays, anthologies, essays, interviews, autobiographies, parables, pamphlets, music, films, and visual art.

Black Arts, Black Muslims explores these artists' commitments to Islam and the ways in which they helped (re)define Black art, an Islamic poetics, and a Black Muslim aesthetics in the struggle for racial justice in the United States and transnationally. Their cultural production draws on certain formal elements to root their work in the Islamic tradition: Islamic words and expressions in Arabic like *as-salaamu alaykum*, *bismillah*, *Allahu akbar*, *al-hamdulillah*, and *jihad*; references to Islamic scripture and verses from the Qur'an; visual depictions of Islamic architectural forms and symbols like the crescent star; Islamic clothing such as the fez, skullcap, and headwrap; and Arabic sometimes written in the poet or artist's hand. Temporal markers situate their writing and publication in Islamic time, according to the *hijri* calendar; and locations in places like Harlem, Chicago, Newark, Detroit, and Oakland connect to (other) geographies in the Muslim world, such as Timbuktu, Songhai, and Mecca. These Islamic framings, and the interjection and eruption of Islamic terms, teachings, and language, serve to disrupt the Eurocentric orientation of American letters and center the contributions of people of color—and of Muslims—so formative to Western culture. Black life and Islam are frequently thought to reside "beyond the dominion of the West," writes Alexander Weheliye in his essay "Black Studies and Black Life." "One significant way to disassemble the coloniality of being in Western modernity is to continually insist on just how fundamental black [and Muslim] life is to this terrain."[1]

Islamic words and concepts function as a language or code for raising the dead, speaking to secret societies, communicating with the initiated, and creating a sense of sacred community. These poets draw on the deep, fertile roots of "African American esoterica and expressive cultural forms," Meta DuEwa Jones writes in *The Muse is Music*; they "read, revise, and recite works by their artistic ancestors in order to maintain connections to the past while taking pleasure in their returns to and revisions of historical memory." These rituals of recital—these recitations—reconstitute cultural artifacts through "riffs, remembrance, and improvisatory revision," writes Jones.[2] *Black Arts, Black Muslims* explores the citation and re-citation of key elements of the Muslim tradition in the BAM, as practitioners riff, remember, and improvise on an inherited Islam, revised under a set of historical conditions far in time and space from their origins. An Islamic consciousness came to permeate American and African American popular culture and poetics, in bebop and hip hop, jazz and rap, calypso and ska, and in the wide cultural production of new generations of American Muslims and Muslim-adjacent creatives. This Islamic consciousness became not only a sign of protest, but also an ethos—and ontology—alternative to the unethical racial inequality of the dominant culture of the white, bourgeois, implicitly Christian, American public sphere. The cultural creatives of the BAM envisioned themselves reviving and resurrecting Islamic elements already present in African American culture—an indigenous Islam at the foundations of American culture—its forcible subjugation imparting Muslim practices with their character of defiance, protest, and rebellion against the dehumanizing conditions of racial capitalism. Through processes of resurrection and revivification they also forged radically new aesthetic forms that were Islamic, African American, African diasporic, and American, combining elements of Asian, Moorish, Indian, Native American, Latin American, and Caribbean cultures. Rather than "reproducing or replicating what came before it," writes Tina Campt in *A Black Gaze: Artists Changing How We See*, the Islamic art and poetics of the BAM instead "creates new beginnings, . . . cycles of return that create new formations and new points of departure," through "a practice of attunement."[3]

BAM writers understood Islam as an integral part of the African American cultural, spiritual, and intellectual heritage brutally suppressed under slavery and in its aftermath, one that survives through fragments and vestiges.[4] Islamic signs, expressions, and writing carry talismanic-like properties of protection, functioning as coded communication; they are emblematic of their own long survival over historical time and geographical space. In *Black Chant*, Aldon Lynn Nielson describes how BAM writers recuperated fragments of the past, recollecting a "history of fractures," through an "excavation, restoration, and rereading" of languages, symbols, and literacies.[5] The time-traveler narrator in John Akomfrah's Afrofuturist film *The Last Angel of History* talks about a "poet figure" conducting an archaeological dig, finding fragments and fossils: "If you can put those elements together, you'll crack that code and it will give you the keys to the future."[6] The Afro-Asiatic religion of Islam provided one of the keys to that code, through the very survival of Black knowledge of the Islamic past.

Black Arts practitioners see their poetry, music, and art as tapping into those codes to resurrect knowledge of self and past, to live it in the present, and to create communities of the future. Though the European Christian world tried to wipe out Islam in both Europe and the Americas, Islam left traces all over the Americas, Sylviane Diouf observes in *Servants of Allah*.[7] Other scholars write about these vestiges as "hidden transcripts," "cryptography," or "flashes of the spirit" in the rubble of history.[8] "Muslim 'survivals' and 'continuities,' would become critical to twentieth-century social movements," write Hisham Aidi and Manning Marable in *Black Routes to Islam*, retentions that became "raw material for their ideological and cultural repertoires."[9] Twentieth-century movements like the BAM leveraged Islamic concepts—such as jihad—to their struggles against the white power structure, the bourgeois public sphere, white representations in the publishing industry, and the dominance of Euro-American modes of knowledge production. The jihad that they envisioned is defensive, but also an active struggle to overthrow the structures of oppression and build a new society, partly imagined and articulated through BAM as the cultural arm of Black Power. Islamic words, signs, symbols, and language function like "an amulet or a mantram with which to unlock an 'other world,'" writes Peter Lamborn Wilson in *Sacred Drift*.[10] To interpret these "esoteric idioms of the Black Atlantic" we require a *"poetics of discovery."* This poetics, or what R. A. Judy calls "poiesis in Black" is my focus in this book.[11]

Black Arts, Black Muslims explores how BAM practitioners deployed Islamic knowledge toward cultivating an Islamic aesthetics for new generations of Muslims. They did so through Afro-Asian and African American referents that reinvigorated critical elements from the Islamic past, incorporating them into contemporary art forms to revive—and give expression to—Islamic commitments and modes of identification. They reinvent and reimagine the Islamic poetic and literary tradition in the context of racial subjugation in the Americas, drawing on (what are understood as) sonic retentions from the past in music and language, reenvisioning an Islamic aesthetics resurrected in the West (the "sunrise in the West"). In so doing, BAM artists reignite some of the oldest debates in Islamic cultures about the nature of literary and poetic innovation (*bid'a*), the relationship of creativity to religion, and the lyrical quality of the Qur'an in relation to—and distinct from—poetry and music. Since the earliest Muslim communities, these arts have thrived as an integral aspect of Islamic cultures. Remembering (*dhikr*) has always been at the heart of the Islamic poetic—and mystical—tradition, as one of its most important formal elements. The poet traveler mourns over remains of the past, reconstructing the ruins (*al-atlal*) of the present with the fullness of poetic memory. What was initially a yearning for the beloved at the ruins of an abandoned campsite became a dominant trope in Islamic poetics and a metaphor for the poet-devotee's distance in time and space from the origins of the Muslim world in Mecca. The searching for something lost but not forgotten expressed the poet's passionate desire for reunion with the beloved divine, partly through return to the core of an early Islam in the spiritual center of the Muslim world.[12] Scholars understand these poetic conventions as functioning ritualistically, indicative of not just a distance from Mecca but also of a gap, or a *barzakh*, between this world and the next—a break or a silence traversed only through a feat of imagination or devotion or through dreams or death and resurrection. This gap can also be bridged through recitation of the Qur'an, Islamic expressions like *Allahu akbar*, *al-hamdulillah*, the *basmallah*, and the ninety-nine names of God.[13]

Instead of a broken genealogy, artists of the BAM engaged in a process of what Lorenzo Thomas calls the "reclamation" of the "lost souls" of the pre-slave Black past—of which Islam was but one iteration alongside others like the Yoruba, Akan, Serer, Bantu, and Edo religions. Drawing on a Yoruban and Islamic framework (and referencing Du Bois), Solayman Idris writes that slavery stole the souls of Black folks. His book *Star Logic* seeks to address "cultural eclipses and ruptures" by "(re)creating alternative time-space paradigms, allowing a break with the Gregorian calendar that was imposed over Orun's Afro Arabic Islamic lunar calendar with the slave trade."[14] Through their poetic journeys, new generations of cultural creatives have revived and reinvigorated Islamic cultural forms already embedded in the African American literary tradition, reinterpreting them for new cycles of struggle against oppression. Rather than remaining frozen in time, the Islamic identification in BAM cultural production juxtaposed different temporalities and modes of spatial orientation, performing "a dizzying back-and-forth toggle in time." In their work on race and performance, Soyica Diggs Colbert, Douglas Jones, and Shane Vogel describe this juxtaposition as a dramatic technique that warps time, disrupts dominant modes of (linear) representation, and makes the familiar uncanny. This uneven layering of multiple temporalities functions as a form of restoration, they write, "as repair or mending—of what has been forgotten, overlooked, misremembered, suppressed, dormant, or denied," thus challenging "the historical negation of populations" and offering "cultural workers in the present a useful past."[15] Elijah Muhammad characterized this as a resurrection of Islamic knowledge—suppressed, negated, and denied—providing a conceptual conduit for seeking, accessing, and reinhabiting Islamic cultural forms, practices, and beliefs. These modern Islamic cultural forms were also unprecedented, creating something radically new and different than what came before, not just reviving and resurrecting, but innovating for new contexts and for new media forms.

Most scholars agree that the "Islam brought by the enslaved West Africans has not survived. It has left traces; it has contributed to the culture and history of the continents; but its conscious practice is no more."[16] For the Islam brought by enslaved West Africans to grow and survive, Diouf asserts, it would have had to expand vertically through transmission to children and horizontally through conversion. There were nearly insurmountable barriers to that kind of transmission in the Reconstruction era, but Islam did grow in the twentieth century, both through conversion and transmission. The children were not necessarily biological descendants, but these relationships were oftentimes configured as kinship, through brotherhoods and sisterhoods, ancestors and descendants. In her essay "Meditations on the Legacy of Malcolm X," Angela Davis talks about "the political descendants of Malcolm" who have transformed his legacy into "a forward-looking impetus for creative political thinking."[17]

Black Arts, Black Muslims is about the aesthetic descendants of Malcolm X and (other) Muslims from the African diaspora in the Americas. Amiri Baraka constructed an intellectual and spiritual genealogy between Malcolm X and the BAM in his new introduction to *Black Fire*, published in 2013 during the Black Lives Matter protests of the murder of Trayvon Martin. He calls the contributors "Malcolm's sons and daughters" and the anthology "a powerful document of that time & of the BLM in overview historically and yet it focuses on aspects of the struggle still very much in evidence today."[18] These political and aesthetic descendants were many: the Organization of Afro-American Unity; the Revolutionary Action Movement founded by Max Stanford (who later converted and took the name Muhammad Ahmad); contributors to Margaret Burrough's and Dudley Randall's poetry collection *For Malcolm*; John Henrik Clarke's anthology *Malcolm X: The Man and His Times*; Joe Wood's *Malcolm X: In Our Own Image*; and Rita Edozie and Curtis Stokes's *Malcolm X's Michigan World View*; the founders of Malcolm X Liberation University; the Malcolm X project at Columbia University; and the many scholars, biographers, documentary filmmakers, artists, and musicians interpreting and reinterpreting Malcolm X's life and significance. These were the "children of Malcolm X," the living "afterlife of Malcolm X."[19]

My book is about those sons and daughters and about their children, who carried on that legacy of Islam by constructing genealogies that did not just go back in time but traveled in space, envisioning other kind of futures and other kinds of spaces for Black art and Black life. *Black Arts, Black Muslims* chronicles how a violently suppressed tradition reemerged via vitally meaningful modes of expression in African American Islamic movements and cultural production. These retentions were not necessarily passed down in a linear fashion but were rather reinterpreted and reinvented through a kind of bricolage—"nothing less than the reclamation of a buried history . . . wrest[ing] a certain rogue redemptive potential," Sofia Samatar observes in "Toward a Planetary History of Afrofuturism."[20] These artists drew out forms of Black knowledge already integral to, but sometimes sublimated in the Islamic tradition—a "Bilalian consciousness" that future generations of scholars and creatives would (further) cultivate in Islamic scholarship. Scholars, thinkers, and writers of the BAM developed a hermeneutic that has worked to interpret and reinterpret the role of Islam in the struggle for Black political determination, but also the role of Blackness in the global Muslim community, in the early Muslim community, and in Islam as a religion.

BAM poets, musicians, artists, and intellectuals understood their Islamic commitments as indicative of an Eastward orientation—toward the African continent, Asia, and broader transnational solidarities with the Third World. Though oftentimes understood as Black nationalist, BAM artists just as often envisioned a nonwhite art as broadly catholic, encompassing different creeds, colors, and ethnicities. Calling the Nation of Islam (NOI) "Black nationalist" is a misnomer, argues Stephen Finley, since these organizations embraced nonwhite identities and ethnicities, as did the Moorish Science Temple of America (MSTA) and the Ahmadiyya. In the Circle Seven Koran of the MSTA, for example, the chapter on the "Divine Origin of the Asiatic Nations," counts the Moors, Egyptians, Arabians, Japanese, Chinese, Hindus, Mexicans, Brazilians, Argentinians, Chileans, Colombians, Nicaraguans, Salvadorans, and Turks as Muslims and as Asians. Similarly, "Turkish people, Chinese, Japanese, Filipinos, those of Pakistan, Arabs, Latin Americans, Egyptians and those Asiatic Muslims and non-Muslim nations. All black American or non-whites are welcomed" to meetings of the NOI, its leader Elijah Muhammad declared in 1963, banning whites after being extensively harassed by the FBI in a 1963 meeting in Flint, Michigan.²¹ Finley also argues that reducing the NOI to a political entity obscures its religious meanings—and its efforts to reclaim "black bodies from the discursive white normative gaze."²² These modes of identification with Islamic and Moorish nations like the MSTA and the NOI forged membership in different kinds of communities, reconfiguring racialized notions of citizenship and its connection to whiteness, as well as to Christian—and middle class—forms of belonging.

African American (and) Islamic epistemologies provided alternative frameworks to the Eurocentric cultural histories perpetuated by American educational institutions and the predominantly white, implicitly Christian, bourgeois public sphere. BAM practitioners drew on and experimented with Islamic knowledge systems and cultures alongside Egyptian, Yoruban, Indian, Asian, African, Caribbean, and Latin American ones. Islamic knowledge provided a set of literacies interpreted as historically oppositional to European, Christian, Western epistemologies, despite their overlapping legacies. BAM practitioners envisioned these cultural systems as a way to cure the West of its moral and ethical ills, among them, the European conception of itself as the center and pinnacle of knowledge and civilization. Claiming "the centrality of blackness to the creation of the occident is as important as it is necessary for the particular decolonizing critique developed within black studies," writes Wehiliye. Black life is not just a "parochial, ethnographic phenomenon," but the very "history of Western civilization."²³ Introducing alternative knowledge pathways helped challenge the parochialism of the American educational system—not just with respect to the world but with respect to its own history—and its relationship to Mexico, Latin America, Native Americans, African Americans, the Islamic world, Africa, Asia, and its own immigrant communities. These were the very peoples the NOI and MSTA identified as "Muslim."

The poetry, music, and cultural production of the BAM shaped (re)emerging Islamic commitments, functioning as a hermeneutic for exploring a Black Atlantic Islam, Islam's role in Black life in America, and the centrality of Blackness to the Islamic tradition. The BAM's appeal to and adaptation of an Islamic aesthetics, along with a seemingly limitless palette of references to non-European African American, African, Asian, Moorish, and Indian cultural and religious traditions, produced a heterogeneous Black Muslim art and poetics. This Islamic American aesthetics expanded the limits of American art by incorporating latent and conscious Islamic elements configured within the history of African American cultural production. It also furthered narrow conceptions and understandings of Islamic art and poetry, reorienting these arts among minority populations in the West. Like African American Islamic movements, Black Muslim cultural production drew out and emphasized elements of Blackness from deep within the Islamic tradition, via figures such as Luqman and Bilal ibn Rabah. These emphases read racial justice in(to) the origins of Islam, a hermeneutic taken up in later scholarship.[24] BAM practitioners built on the work of these movements, furthering their mission of decolonizing the mind, self-determination, economic struggle, and Black knowledge. They helped raise consciousness about the centrality of Blackness in Islam, decolonize Islam as an Arab religion (as with the *shu'ubiyya* movement previously), and reinvigorate possibilities for racial justice in Islam—possibilities not yet fulfilled, but reenvisioned by new generations of Black Muslims in Chicago, Detroit, New York, Newark, Philadelphia, Oakland, and throughout the diaspora.

ISLAMIC MIXED MEDIA IN THE BAM

BAM anthologies, music, poetry, drama, essays, and the Black press formed a multimedia network disseminating Black art and knowledge, functioning not just pedagogically, but also collectively as a celebration of a multivocal Black aesthetics that spoke in different registers, genres, and voices. BAM poets, thinkers, and dramatists drew on the Islamic intellectual tradition as an alternative knowledge system challenging the racialized underpinnings of a Euro-Western humanism. They leveraged the legacy of the Islamic tradition as one among many Afro-Asian intellectual, cultural, and spiritual traditions, with the aim of radically reenvisioning not just Western cultural aesthetics, but also its ethics and epistemologies. BAM artists reimagined, reconceptualized, and recreated Islamic art and aesthetics for new generations, through new kinds of media, visual art, and sonic landscapes.

Black Arts, Black Muslims explores cultural artifacts from the BAM, focusing on how they operated on multiple sensory planes through different media—in visual art, poetry, drama, music, film, autobiography, parables, pamphlets, children's literature, and essays. Such works created a kind of surround effect that aimed to awaken the mind and senses. These "technologies of sensation" enabled the circulation of new forms and definitions of Islamic practice and belief in the context of racial struggle during the 1950s, 1960s, and 1970s. The various media in which these forms of Islamic identification circulated helped create a sense of "embodied forms of participation in extended communities joined in imagination, feeling, affinity, and affect," through a kind of "synthesis of religion and media."[25] They helped shape a discursive community that communicated through a common set of Islamic referents embedded in the African American tradition—referents understood to be both vestiges of the past and reclamations of a new identity, an African American Islamic identity, but also a transnational diasporic identity connecting with the larger Muslim Third World. The Islamic media of the BAM was both sonic and visual, operating via auditory forms like music, poetry recordings, and albums; in print media like newspapers, magazines, pamphlets, broadsheets, poetry collections, and anthologies; and in visual media like photography, film, graphic design, and visual art. These various forms of mediation created "technological forms and modes of practice whereby religion, politics, and aesthetics [were] folded into one another ... an architecture of circulation and representation that in turn creates the pragmatic context for modes of practice."[26] Margo Natalie Crawford describes the BAM's mixed and multimedia approach as a kind of "counter-literacy," a form of reading, teaching, and knowledge production that radically innovated on the sterility of white cultural forms. It was also a mode of liberation, breaking free from white representations through a "black aesthetics unbound."[27]

In the cultural production of the BAM, there is a specific focus on what Sun Ra called "tone poems" and "sound images," "pivoting planes" of sound and sight, a "mirror that you must hear/Vibration," bringing out the visuality of the word, the orality of writing, the musicality of language, and the poetry of music.[28] Sun Ra interpreted the pivoting planes in esoteric terms as mediating between this world and the next, the material and spiritual, and the earth and cosmos. Though Sun Ra was not Muslim, he incorporated Islamic signifiers into his dress, poetry, and performances; claimed that the NOI used his ideas; and said that he was kin to Elijah Muhammad.[29] The imagery of "tone poems" and "sound images" suggests what Michael Sells calls the "sound vision" that is "brought out and cultivated in Qur'anic recitation," as well as in the Islamic art of the Qur'an as scripture.[30] Sun Ra's use of "tone poem" in reference to both his music and poetry emphasizes the sonic dimensions of poetic recitation, as well as the poetic dimensions of music, in addition to playing on the "visual and audial significations of the word tones" that simultaneously suggest a mood, color, and skin tone.[31] "Sound visions" and "tone poems" convey how aspects or dimensions of the Islamic tradition surface in the African American poetic and musical traditions, through echoes of what W. E. B. Du Bois called "a message [that] is naturally veiled."[32] This is what Su'ad Abdul Khabeer refers to as "a sonic religious genealogy" that is "part of a long historical trajectory in which Muslims of

African descent use the arts, specifically music and poetry, as a means of spiritual training and education and for cultural expression."[33]

Black Arts, Black Muslims explores how BAM artists excavated elements of a dismantled Islam, reassembled them in new aesthetic forms, paid tribute to ancestors, but also reread and reinterpreted Islamic signs, symbols, and beliefs through their own creative processes.[34] BAM artists re-created an American Islam in hostile territory, constructing a new Islamic language for the context of the struggle for Black liberation. They drew on Arabic and Islamic expressions embedded in an African American vernacular, bringing out the Islamic dimensions of African American language, culture, and history. The "overall cultural style" in which the *deen* (religion) is articulated is indicative of Islam's cultural versatility and adaptability.[35] Muslim elements mingle with the Yoruban, Eygptian, Moorish, Swahili, and African American, creating a polyvocality that orients this cultural production toward Africa, Asia, and the East, breaking out of what Amiri Baraka calls the "strait jacket of American expression" and bringing what Julian Mayfield calls "salvation . . . in escaping the narrow national orbit—artistic, cultural, and political—and soaring into the space of more universal experience."[36]

SPECULATIVE RETURNS AND CRITICAL FABULATION

The BAM's reappropriations of Islam had an orientalist edge—the headwraps and fezzes, crescent stars and moons, Islamic expressions and Arabic writing, and geographical references to places in the Muslim world (Timbuctoo, Mecca, Medina, Morocco, Egypt, Songhai)—but they also seem to possess talismanic like qualities of protection. They do not function as a colonial fetish as European orientalism did, through fantasies of penetration, domination, and appropriation. Rather, the BAM's Islamic imagery and references become a means of healing psychic alienation from natal roots and transforming collective trauma through what Michelle Commander calls "speculative returns" that have revolutionary potential. These returns are also restorative and redemptive, functioning as "a means of allaying dispossession." The Islamic cultural production of the BAM helped "reimagine history; engage with the imagined fantastic, spiritual memories within."[37]

The BAM's African American Islamic imaginary fashioned a genealogical narrative through a process of critical fabulation that reconstructed, bridged, and healed silences and omissions in the historical record, germinating "in the immense gaps in the archival vestiges of racial slavery."[38] In a discussion of Saidiya Hartman's concept of critical fabulation, Weheliye cautions against reading critical fabulations as either historical fact or imagined fiction, but rather as a way "to call attention to the violence of the lacunae in ways not possible through either a 'detached' historiographic lens or the allegedly 'freer' fictional imagination."[39] Critical fabulation "germinates" within the gaps or breaks in the archive, through a vacillation—or what BAM artists call "vibration"—between historiography and a speculative imagination; between past, present, and future; between what has been lost and what has been recuperated (in the language of the NOI).[40] These diasporic Muslim identities are rooted in historical fact revivified and reconceptualized to create social change, but also to reclaim forms of African cultural identity a priori to the alienating experience of deterritorialization and enslavement.[41] In *Afro-Fabulations*, Tavia Nyong'o describes "the agonistic black diasporic productivity of ethnic fictions" that creates a "'conceptual galaxy' beyond Western humanism." He asks: "Is ethnicity accurately understood as that which the US slave is natally alienated from and must reclaim via a diasporic trajectory? Or has a certain troping of black ethnicity always been constitutive to how blackness emerges into in/visibility?"[42] The reclaiming of a Black diasporic Muslim identity and ethnicity in BAM cultural production helped make an Islamic blackness visible out of the silences, lacunae, gaps, and breaks in the archive, giving voice to an Islam silenced under slavery and in its aftermath. BAM artists and writers situated their commitments to Islam and forms of Islamic (and Afro and Asian diasporic) knowledge systems agonistically, in opposition to, and against, Euro-American epistemologies. They also situated these identities in opposition to the integrationist ethos of the civil rights movement and the Southern Christian Leadership Conference and the middle-class values of the Black bourgeoisie, as what Nyong'o calls "a blackness that is *internally differentiated and differentiating*"). These kinds of agonistic (or insurrectionary) Black Muslim ethnicities emerged in conjunction with "*particular modes of knowledge production*"—particularly in the battle to assert Black epistemologies and Black studies.[43]

MALCOLM X AS DISCURSIVE CATALYST

Malcom X was a discursive catalyst for the reclamation of Islam, through the artistic alliances that he cultivated during his life and the extensive cultural production that sprang up in his wake. He was, as Geneva Smitherman says, "a master of signifying."⁴⁴ Malcolm X navigated multiple media simultaneously, projecting his voice and message on radio and television, in newspapers and magazines, in speeches and sermons, in debates and interviews—an intellectual and rhetorical presence amplified through music, poetry, literature, film, and scholarship.⁴⁵ While in the Nation of Islam, Elijah Muhammad monitored his contact with the many artists, intellectuals, and activists that gathered around him; his break with the NOI freed him up to develop these friendships as he traveled abroad to Ghana and on the hajj and established the Organization of Afro-American Unity. The call and response between Malcolm X and BAM artists sparked a public dialogue about Islam, Black nationalism, and the role of Black art—the "sonic religious genealogy" deployed for "spiritual training and education" that Abdul Khabeer references.⁴⁶ These creative expressions found their fullest flowering after Malcolm X's death in the outpouring of grief that inspired anthologies like Dudley Randall and Margaret Burrough's *For Malcolm* (1967) and John Henrik Clarke's *Malcolm X: The Man and His Times* (1970), but also the "Malcolm poem" that became, along with the "Coltrane poem," the BAM's elegiac form.⁴⁷ The mourning and grief for these two figures gave expression to a longer history of loss.

Black Arts, Black Muslims explores the creative alliances Malcolm X cultivated, friendships that catalyzed the BAM's own interpretation of Islam in African American life and culture. Islam was "deeply connected to numerous diverse and even contradictory elements of African American culture," writes Patrick Bowen, reflecting "the religion's pervasiveness and widespread influence."⁴⁸ African American cultural identification with Islam transcended the strict parameters set by the NOI—as well as the strictures set by other forms of Islamic orthodoxy on music, poetry, and visual art.⁴⁹ These art forms flourished throughout the Muslim world despite or because of doctrinal limits on cultural production, sometimes interpreted as expressions of spiritual transcendence, like in Sufi poetry and music. Some of the BAM artists discussed here abandoned their identification with Islam because of the NOI's prohibitions of artistic expression (like Sonia Sanchez and Amina Baraka) or because of certain kinds of interpretation of Islam, such as those regarding gender relations and the place of women (like Amina and Amiri Baraka). But Islamic cultural production continued to flourish through the emergence of hip hop in the 1980s and the resurgence of Malcolm X in the 1990s during the era of mass incarceration, the war on drugs, and expanded policing. This included important films released on Malcolm X: Woodie King's *Death of a Prophet: The Last Day in the Life of Malcolm X* (1981), Spike Lee's *Malcolm X* (1992), John Akomfrah's *Seven Songs for Malcolm* (1993), and Orlando Bagwell's *Malcolm X: Make It Plain* (1994). But key books also had their place the resurgence, most notably (among others): James Cone's *Martin & Malcolm & America* (1991), Carson Clayborne's *Malcolm X: The FBI File* (1991), Joe Wood's anthology *Malcolm X: In Our Own Image* (1992), Karl Evanzz's *The Judas Factor* (1992), Amiri Baraka's *Malcolm X: Justice Seeker* (1993), Heshaam Jaaber's *I Buried Malcolm* (1993), and Michael Eric Dyson's *Making Malcolm* (1996).[50] Malcolm X's own journey charted a path for navigating forms of racial oppression through Islam, but the journey cut short at its prime left many unresolved questions that were taken up in the BAM and its aftermath, an imaginary of what might have become and of the meaning of his legacy. Questions of what Malcolm X might have become and the meaning of his legacy have been raised again and again in the hip hop generation and with the turn to Sunni Islam, as cultural creatives continued to grapple with the spiritual and political legacy of Islam in America. They also re-created this legacy through a new vision of the Islamic past and an Islamic future, rereading it for new generations.

METHODS, DISCIPLINES, FIELDS

Music, poetry, and drama are sometimes interpreted as antithetical to Islamic orthodoxy, though these forms have played critical roles in elucidating an Islamic ethos throughout history and across the diverse geographical and cultural landscape of the *umma*. My analysis interprets the Islamic cultural production of the Black Arts Movement as improvisations that riff on tradition and its claims to authenticity, through remembrance (*dhikr*), but also as reinterpretation, renovation, restoration, reclamation, and perhaps most importantly for the Islamic tradition—recitation.[51] The Islamic cultural production of the BAM can be situated within the tradition of Islamic art, poetry, and music, just as the Islamic tradition is itself connected geographically, historically, ritualistically, scripturally, and culturally to the African diaspora: from the first hijra to Aksum in Abyssinia; the figure of Luqman in the Qur'an; the first muezzin Bilal ibn Rabah; and the spread of Islam across the African continent. *Black Arts, Black Muslims* is situated at the nexus of Black Studies and Islamic Studies, African American and Islamic cultural production. In this book I orient Black Muslim cultural production in Islamic Studies; and center Islam in the study of the Black Arts Movement. The BAM was a pivotal moment between (re)emergent expressions of Islamic faith of early African American Islamic movements and the outpouring of vibrant Black Muslim cultural production in contemporary poetry, literature, and music. An impressive body of work by scholars like Suʻad Abdul Khabeer, Hisham Aidi, Samy Alim, Sylvia Chan-Malik, Sylviane Diouf, Michael Muhammad Knight, Mark Levine, Felicia Miyakawa, James Spady, and Richard Brent Turner have explored expressions of Islamic commitments in music: in blues, heavy metal, hip-hop, and jazz.

I use a cultural studies approach to explore the personal, spiritual, and ethical dimensions of the Islamic art, poetry, and music of the BAM, as well as its politics of protest. Larry Neal wrote of the BAM that its aesthetics were "predicated on an Ethics."[52] The Islamic tradition has a long history of leveraging cultural production, or what is known as *adab*, toward developing ethical subjectivities, a tradition that the BAM helped reinvent and reimagine in the struggle for racial justice and a more ethical society. Through Muslim American poets, musicians, and writers of African descent, *Black Arts, Black Muslims* engages in a process of reckoning, consciousness raising, and recuperation of Black Muslim history and Islamic arts in the Americas.

In each chapter I explore the spiritual and aesthetic dimensions of the Islamic cultural production in the BAM but also focus on how Muslim beliefs and faith functioned as protest: against scientific racism and medical discrimination (chapter 2); police brutality (chapter 3); colonial domination and economic oppression (chapter 4); Eurocentric education (chapter 6); violence against Black life (chapter 7); and discrimination against Black women (chapter 8). BAM production extends beyond protest literature to embody spiritual visions of a new world, created by reimagining language, aesthetics, media, cultural forms, and ways of being. In that sense this art was revolutionary—a new aesthetic turn— "and when you have light giving, revolutionary, spiritual [art], that light travels and it strikes you in your mind, and it causes your mind to rotate like the earth, causing you to think differently . . . As-Salaam-Alaikum."[53]

Black Arts, Black Muslims builds on my doctoral training at Columbia University in African literatures and literatures of the Caribbean and African diaspora with the author Maryse Condé, and also my training in North African and Islamic literatures. It grows out of my work on American Islam and engagement with the Muslim community in North Carolina: the service-learning project "Local Islams" coordinated through the Pluralism Project at Harvard and Kenan Institute for Ethics; the "Black Muslims and Racial Justice in the American South" project organized with my colleague Professor Mbaye Lo, which included a conference on "Islam, Slavery, and the American South"; and collaboration with Kenny Dalsheimer on his documentary film *Moonchild* about the life and music of Durham jazz musician Yusuf Salim. This included two concerts of Salim's music at the Hayti Heritage Cultural Center that I helped organize as director of the Duke Islamic Studies Center in collaboration with North Carolina Central University's Jazz Studies program, featuring musicians and vocalists Gary Bartz, Nnenna Freelon, Eve Cornelious, Rachiim Ausar-Sahu, Chip Crawford, Lois Deloatch, and Adia Ledbetter. I developed the book in tandem with the "Black Muslims in America" project I helped curate in conjunction with Duke Arts and the Duke Islamic Studies Center, supported by the Doris Duke Foundation for Islamic Art's Building Bridges initiative. We brought Black Muslim poets and musicians like Maimouna Youssef, Sasa Aakil, Saadiya Bashir, Oddisee, Tariq Touré, Amir Sulaiman, and Dua Saleh to Durham public schools including Hillside (where the BAM artist Elizabeth Catlett once taught), Durham School of the Arts, and the School for Creative Studies. They also performed at Black-owned businesses in Durham like the Black-author bookstore Rofhiwa Book Café, as well as other organizations like Girls Rock and the Pinhook.

Black Arts, Black Muslims builds on more than six years of fieldwork, interviews, and archival research with BAM elders, beginning with my own tutorial in Black study with Brother Marvin X at his Academy of da Corner. When I first traveled to Oakland to meet Marvin X, we drove up to Marin City to celebrate Juneteenth at a street fair of Black vendors where he set up his mobile school, displaying his library, archive, and archival materials. The Juneteenth celebration featured an exhibit commemorating Black history, with a poster of Marcus Garvey that quoted his words about "emancipation from mental slavery" alongside another poster of Carter Woodson's *Mis-Education of the Negro*—the Africa World Press 1990 edition featuring Adjoa Jackson Burrowes's drawing of a woman with a padlock on her head.

The following spring, I accompanied Marvin X on a poetry tour up the East Coast, driving Marvin and his grandson James Rhodes (son of Marvin's daughter Nefertiti) to poetry readings at the Black Muslim Atlantic Symposium at Duke; at Shakespeare & Co. in Philadelphia with Lamont B. Steptoe; on WBAI radio in Brooklyn; and at the 360° Poetry Night on Halsey Street in downtown Newark—the former headquarters of the Women's Political Union of New Jersey. In Philadelphia, we had dinner with Marvin's ex-wife Nisa and their granddaughter at Atiya Ola's Spirit First Foods and also visited Sonia Sanchez at her house in Philadelphia. I would later return to Sonia Sanchez's house after the pandemic, visiting on her porch with my sixteen-year-old son Mateo.

In Brooklyn, Marvin, James, and I visited the *Muslims in Brooklyn* exhibit at the Brooklyn Historical Society (now the Center for Brooklyn History) organized by Zaheer Ali, which featured oral histories and an installation by artist Kameelah Janan Rasheed. We traveled uptown to Harlem to meet with Malika Iman, daughter of Yusef Iman, who gave me a copy of her book *Intimate with the Ultimate: Memoirs and Tribute to Family and Political, Cultural, Spiritual Activists*. We then headed to Newark, spending time at Amina Baraka's house. I interviewed Amina Baraka over the course of five years (visiting in 2019, 2020, 2022, and 2024) and spent extensive time with her as she showed me around her house and Newark. She took me to the memorial commemorating the Newark uprisings in 1967; to the Shani Baraka Women's Resource Center, named for her daughter Shani killed in a domestic abuse incident; and to Newark City Hall with statues of Newark's first Black mayor Kenneth Gibson and of George Floyd. Amina read aloud poems from her anthology *Confirmation*, which she coedited with Amiri. She introduced me to her sons Obalaji and Amiri Jr., showed me pictures, told me stories, and gave me recordings. I interviewed the artist Ademola Olugebefola of the Weusi Collective in New York; he invited me to the Dwyer Cultural Center in Harlem he founded, where he recounted stories about Muslim artists like Taiwo Shabazz, Abdullah Aziz, and Abdul Rahman, who illustrated collections of BAM poets.

I later reconnected with Marvin just after his eightieth birthday. He took me on a tour of the Oakland of his childhood and showed me numerous Black Panther sites: the BAM Business District, the Dr. Huey P. Newton Foundation, Women of the Black Panther Party Mural and Museum, the Black Panther affordable housing complex, and the Oakland Museum. All these people provided me with access to archival materials, supplementing research I did in the archives at the Schomburg Center for Research in Black Culture.

My analyses of the BAM's Islamic cultural production is interdisciplinary and comparative, putting three main bodies of scholarship into conversation: (1) the Black Arts,[54] (2) Black Muslims in America,[55] and (3) contemporary Islamic cultural production (music, poetry, and art).[56] The aim is exploring a vibrant body of Islamic popular culture circulating through new media technologies and via mass education—in the United States, across the Muslim world, and throughout the globe—reinterpreting Islam for new generations. These cultural forms foster a Muslim ethos that is interpreted in local contexts, but that also seeks community with the larger *umma*.

Black Arts, Black Muslims draws on several main texts that explore the relationship of BAM with what Sohail Daulatzai calls the "Muslim International, as it employed Islam and Islamically themed symbols and ideas in their radical Black cultural practices of the time."[57] In addition to the primary texts of the BAM, this scholarship includes: H. Samy Alim's essay "360 Degreez of Black Art Comin at You: Sista Sonia Sanchez and the Dimensions of a Black Arts Continuum" published in *B. Ma: The Sonia Sanchez Literary Review* in 2000 and expanded into a chapter in his book *Roc the Mic Right*; Melani McAlister's article "One Black Allah: The Middle East in the Cultural Politics of African American Liberation, 1955–1970" later expanded into a chapter in *Epic Encounters*; Sohail Daulatzai's seminal *Black Star, Crescent Moon* (2012), which explores the relationship between the Muslim international and the Black liberation struggle; and Sylvia Chan-Malik's book chapters "Islam and the Arts in the US" (2012) and "Cultural and Literary Production of Muslim America" (2014), as well as her *Being Muslim: A Cultural History of Women of Color in American Islam* (2018). Patrick D. Bowen's chapter "A Cultural Revolution" in his *History of Conversion to Islam in the United States* is an incredibly informative exploration of "how Islam itself was, in a real sense, truly converting black culture," as a result of the influence of Islam, Islamic groups, and Islamic movements on Black cultural life. Islamic elements have always existed as a substrata in African American life, but were revivified and reinvigorated for Black liberation struggles in the mid to late twentieth century.[58] Daulatzai's "cultural history of Black Islam, Black radicalism, and the Muslim Third World in the post–World War II era, when Black freedom struggles in the United States and decolonization in the Third World were taking place" pays close attention to the Islamic cultural production in the BAM.[59] He shows how the BAM challenged "white-dominated ideas about art and literature" through "radical breaks from white or Western ideas about art and aesthetics," envisioned as emancipation from "Western values and standards."[60] *Black Star, Crescent Moon* explores the transnational solidarities between the Muslim world and the Black liberation movement, but this book focuses specifically on the cultural production of the BAM that functioned as a kind of *da'wa*, as a call or invitation.

Other important works on music and Islamic culture—but not focusing specifically on the BAM or literary, dramatic, or poetic production—have also been key interpretive tools: Hisham Aidi's *Rebel Music: Race, Empire and the New Youth Culture* (2014); Su'ad Abul Khabeer's *Muslim Cool: Race, Religion, and Hip Hop in the United States* (2016); and Richard Brent Turner's *Soundtrack to a Movement: African American Islam, Jazz, and Black Internationalism* (2021). Chapters by Moustafa Bayoumi and Fatimah Fanusie critically emphasize the centrality of music to the Islamic revival in the United States, as does Sylvia

Chan-Malik's chapter on "Cultural and Literary Production of Muslim America."[61] This project draws inspiration from R. A. Judy's deployment of an Islamic hermeneutics toward analyzing Black poetics and "the relationship between language, perception, and imagination as a technology of life ... where the poetic and sociality meet." Judy writes about the BAM's "insistence on a radical aesthetic alterity," and how Muslim signs, symbols, and language expressed that cultural and historical alterity.[62] Rather than ontological difference, these motifs are deeply embedded in a spiritual, ethical, and cultural way of life and survival.

My book builds on these scholars' formative insights—about BAM poetics and language shaping the emergence of hip hop; about BAM writers formulating a distinctly Muslim American literature; about the impact of jazz and a jazz poetics on the poetry of BAM artists and on BAM conversions to Islam; about the affective (and artistic) dimensions of this Black Muslim insurgency; and about how the Black liberation struggle connected to the broader transnational struggles of the Third World through Islamic practices, teachings, and imaginaries. Throughout this book I focus on the catalytic role of Islamic cultural production in the Black Arts Movement: its function as a mode of protest alternative to the Christian-inflected civil rights movement; its roots in earlier cultural and religious movements; its relationship to the political projects of Black Power and Black nationalism; and its connection to the development of Black Studies. Moreover, *Black Arts, Black Muslims* examines how Islamic consciousness, practice, and study helped reconceptualize the nature and role of Black art, develop new visions of Islamic art, and interpret and disseminate different forms of American Islam. Most importantly, these cultural media circulated the message of Islam as a form of *da'wa*, or proselytization, as a call to Islam, but also as a jihad of the self and pen.

The Islamic consciousness of the BAM planted seeds for the flourishing of contemporary generations of cultural workers whose poetry, music, and film continue to draw on the Islamic tradition—culturally, spiritually, and politically. *Black Arts, Black Muslims* closely examines African American (and) Islamic literature, poetry, music, and visual art; the conceptualization of their roots in Muslim survivals; and their political, ethical, and spiritual dimensions. Black art, writing, and music amplified the ethos of African American Islamic movements through their circulation in popular culture, but also helped formulate an Islamic aesthetics for the context of the struggle for racial justice in the United States and the Americas.[63] This cultural production reinvigorated—and reinterpreted—a long tradition of Islamic art, poetry, and music that functioned as a call (*da'wa*) to Islam—for which Bilal's performance of the call to prayer (*adhan*) became the exemplar. The lyrical quality of the call to prayer is emphatically understood in the Islamic tradition to *not* be music; cultural creatives through time wove Islamic elements like the call to prayer into poetry, music, and writing, as a mode of popular interpretation (or *tafsir*) of Muslim tradition, Muslim practices, and Islamic teachings. Black Muslim creatives revived, renewed, and reinterpreted the art, music, and poetry of Islamic tradition and the African diaspora, adapting it to New World struggles. Their work reawakened and furthered the impulse toward racial justice in Islamic thought and scholarship, renewing a hermeneutic already present in the tradition.

CHAPTER 1

"CONSTANT CONSCIOUS STRIVING"

Jihad of the Pen and the Black Arts Movement

I wanted to be an artist, but Allah took my heart and tuned it for the Jihad of this Age.

—Askia Muhammad Touré, "Notes from a Guerilla Diary (for Marvin X and Che Guevara)," *Songhai!*

From the East, we marched, the Armies of the Jihad, speaking a New Tongue, the Language of the Jihad.

—Larry Neal, "Jihad," *Black Boogaloo (Notes on Black Liberation)*

Black Arts Movement (BAM) writers developed a sense of verbal jihad that not only challenged white supremacist narratives but also served as a hermeneutic for interpreting—and reinterpreting—the Islamic tradition in the struggle for racial justice in the United States and transnationally. BAM poets like Sonia Sanchez, Amiri Baraka (LeRoi Jones), Yusef Iman (Joseph Washington), Larry Neal, Marvin X Jackmon, and Askia Muhammad Touré (Rolland Snellings) developed an understanding of cultural revolution as a jihad of the pen and of the tongue—as a struggle against the violence inflicted on Black life and culture. These poets understood this struggle as a means of decolonizing the mind and as resistance against the brainwashing effects of Eurocentric schooling. They were informed by Nation of Islam teachings about "knowledge of self" and the NOI's advocacy of self-defense, as well as by Qur'anic conceptions of the struggle for knowledge as an integral aspect of jihad in the path of God. They connected these struggles to larger movements for decolonization, citing the work of Frantz Fanon and his own analysis of the role of the *mujahidin* and *mujahidat* in the Algerian war of independence—as warriors for both political self-determination and psychological liberation.[1] Similarly, BAM writers and their intellectual descendants developed a conception of jihad for justice alongside their conceptualizations of jihad as armed struggle. Fanon grappled with how the Algerian warriors for independence reinterpreted Muslim custom and practice for the context of political and psychological struggle, though he did not see religion as an effective revolutionary tool.

Neither Elijah Muhammad, Malcolm X, nor Frantz Fanon spoke or wrote about jihad, but Black Arts Movement writers did. BAM poets developed a concept of jihad as a means of fighting against the hegemony of racialized European epistemologies, drawing on Islamic (and other alternative) knowledge systems as counter-pedagogies, especially in the BAM's fight for Black Studies. They understood the ethical struggle for racial justice as a jihad of the self or spirit—the greater jihad alongside the lesser jihad of armed struggle. These poets supported the idea of armed struggle and self-defense: through work in organizations like the Revolutionary Action Movement (RAM), they actively waged jihad of the pen and jihad of the tongue in their writings, recordings, and cultural activism. Askia Muhammad Touré envisioned revolution as connected to the "struggles of colonized people around the world," writes Robin D. G. Kelley in *Freedom Dreams*. Kelley takes the title of his chapter "Roaring from the East"—and the book itself—from Touré's 1965 essay "Afro-American Youth and the Bandung World," which explores the influence of "uprisings and revolutions in Africa, Asia, and Latin America" on the RAM. The founder of RAM, Max Stanford, also converted to Islam, taking the name Muhammad Ahmad.[2] Touré led RAM's "literary arm," along with the BAM poet and theorist Larry Neal; he was also a member of the Umbra Workshop, considered a BAM precursor, and a founding member of Baraka's Black Arts Repertory Theatre School (BARTS).[3] These poets created an intellectual poetic matrix that mobilized Black art and an Islamic aesthetics for consciousness-raising and education, one that spanned the East and West Coasts and helped establish Black Studies as a discipline. This was part of their jihad for knowledge, one that drew on Black American, Islamic, and African diasporic literacies, woven into their vernacular poetics.[4] BAM poets banded together—around the time of their conversions—to establish the first Black Studies program at San Francisco State College in 1967 where Sanchez, Baraka (then LeRoi Jones), and Touré (then Rolland Snellings) taught and where Marvin X was a student. They established a communal collaborative network that moved between different microcommunities in San Francisco, Oakland, Philadelphia, Newark, Brooklyn, and Chicago, cultivating on the ground grassroots mobilization that circulated through their cultural production.

Theorists across the Muslim world revived the concept of jihad for the era of independence and decolonization movements in key texts: Abu al-A'la al-Maududi's *Al-Jihad fi-l-Islam* (Jihad in Islam, 1927) in India; Hasan al-Banna's *Risalat al-Jihad* (Message of Jihad, 1930) and Sayyid Qutb's *Ma'alim fi-l-Tariq* (Signposts on the Path, 1967) in Egypt; as well as 'Ali Shari'ati's *Jihad ve Shahadat* (Jihad and Witnessing, 1967) and Ayatollah Ruhollah Khomeini's *al-Jihad al-Akbar* (The Greater Jihad, 1978) in Iran.[5] Conceptualizations of jihad in the Black Power and Black Arts movement emerged in late 1960s in a parallel set of discourses that drew connections with transnational liberation movements. BAM writers talked about jihad in anthologies like Amiri Baraka and Larry Neal's *Black Fire*; in poems like Larry Neal's "Jihad" and Gaston Neal's "Personal Jihad"; in plays like Baraka's *A Black Mass*; in essays like Askia Muhammad Touré's "Jihad!: Toward a Black Nationalist Credo"; and in the different political pamphlets, poetry, drama, albums, and anthologies issued by Amiri and Amina Baraka's Jihad Productions.[6] Muslim women like Ni'mat Sidqi in *Jihad fi Sabil Allah* (Jihad on the Path of God, 1975), Zaynab al-Ghazali in *Nazarat fi Kitab Allah* (Perspectives on the Book of God, 1994), Sonia Sanchez in her poem "Ima Talken Bout the Nation of Islam" (1971), and amina wadud in *Inside the Gender Jihad* (2006) also developed a concept of jihad against gender, racial, and colonial oppression.[7] In her chapter in the critical anthology *The Black Woman* (1970), Francee Covington rereads women's political action in the Algerian war of independence through the lens of Black struggle in the United States and in Harlem specifically—comparing and contrasting their struggles.[8]

The hip-hop linguist Samy Alim calls poets of the BAM like Baraka, Sanchez, Marvin X, and Touré "verbal mujahidin" who engage in a "jihad of the tongue, or a *jihad bi-l-lisaan*, which also includes *jihad bi-l-qalam*, or jihad of the pen." Alim draws on interpretations of jihad from deep within the Islamic tradition, situating this BAM poetics as the precursor to a hip-hop hermeneutics that understands the jihad of the tongue as "discursive struggle" and "weapons of mass culture."[9] Arguing that the "Nation-conscious wisdom" of hip-hop grew out of the BAM's Muslim consciousness, Alim builds on earlier analyses of the jihad of the word in Black Muslim cultural production, like in Juan M. Floyd-Thomas's article "A Jihad of Words: The Evolution of African American Islam and Contemporary Hip-Hop." In *Islam in the African-American Experience*

(1997), Richard Brent Turner argues that the crypto-writings, amulets, talismans, and teachings of African Muslims enslaved in the Americas constituted a jihad of the word that was later taken up in the proselytization work of the Ahmadiyya and Malcolm X.[10]

In the foreword to his anthology *Black Fire* edited with Larry Neal, Amiri [Ameer] Baraka describes jihad as a kind of *ijtihad*, a striving of the intellect to throw off shackles on the mind, an emancipation from mental slavery.[11] He calls the contributors of the volume "wizards, bards, the *babalawo*, the *shaikhs*, of Weusi Mchoro" engaging in "the constant conscious striving (jihad) of a nation coming back into focus." He refers to these "founding Fathers and Mothers, of our nation" as religious scholars (*babalawo* in Yoruba and *shaykhs* in Arabic) and to their art (*weusi mchoro* in Swahili) as "Black design."

> Throw off the blinds from your eyes
> The metal pillars of Shaitan from your minds
> Find the will of the creator yourself where it was[12]

"Throwing off the blinds from your eyes" poetically references Nation of Islam teachings about being "blind, deaf, and dumb," a metaphoric characterization of how Eurocentric education shuts off knowledge about African American history, culture, and language. Being "blind, deaf, and dumb" also invokes verses of the Qur'an—"it is not the eyes that are blind, but the hearts in the chest" (22:46 but also 17:72, 5:71, 47:23, 35:19—as well as biblical passages that Elijah Muhammad so often quoted in his speeches and writings, casting them in an Islamic tone. The "pillar of Shaitan" references the ritual of the hajj, the pilgrimage where pilgrims throw stones at the pillars of the devil. By calling them "metal pillars," Baraka turns the imagery into a kind of mental prison. Baraka's "pillars of Shaitan" superimposes ritualistic elements from the hajj, Arabic language of "Shaitan" for Satan, and allusions to the NOI's language of devils. He also connects these writers' creativity to the creator, through their own vision quest.

BAM writers and poets saw the jihad of the self as a process of political and psychological liberation, through the jihad of the pen—what the scholar amina wadud calls a "jihad for justice," with the struggle for "justice and full human dignity" being "essential to the divine order of the universe."[13] BAM poets and writers understood music, poetry, and art as a life drive giving expression to the fundamental humanity denied by the enslavers and the colonizers—the heart and soul of creativity beating back against necropolitics of racism.[14] BAM writers connect their artistic creation to a sense of divine justice and what Fanon calls "supernatural power."[15] Jihad in BAM cultural production is "an insurgent ethical, political, and religious framework in which 'Islam' facilitates holistic practices of... liberation and spiritual awakening," writes Sylvia Chan-Malik, referring to Sonia Sanchez's poetry during the time she identified as Muslim. Chan-Malik calls this Muslim women's "affective insurgency," arguing that Islam provides "a set of racial, religious, and gendered affective practices of Black liberation."[16] BAM poets saw *jihad al-nafs*, the jihad of the spirit, self, soul, and psyche, as a form of psychological and spiritual struggle for "self-determination."[17]

Presses like Jihad Productions, Songhai, Third World Press, Broadside, and New Pyramid Productions published and circulated writings, "insurgent creative activity on the margins of the mainstream ensconced within bludgeoning new infrastructures." These "black infrastructures for intellectual activity" were "organically linked with Afro-American cultural life," writes Cornel West in "The Dilemma of the Black Intellectual."[18] The jihad for justice—of the pen, self, tongue, and armed struggle—was also a fight to construct institutional spaces envisioned as refuges free from the poisoning effects of racial oppression and discrimination.[19] The Barakas called Newark the "New Ark," listing New Ark as the place of publication of Jihad Productions in homage to both Sun Ra's Myth Science Arkestra and to reports that Noble Drew Ali also called the city New Ark.[20] Baraka's documentary film *The New-Ark* (1968), made after his conversion to Islam in 1967, opens with the Islamic call to prayer, a recitation of *al-fatiha* (the opening chapter of the Qur'an), and the actors from his play *A Black Mass* reciting their lines in the street. In a voice over, Baraka talks about Black art as a means of fighting the "white death context."[21] In an interview published the following year in *Negro Digest*, Baraka responds to a question Marvin X asks about "Islam [as] a political ideology" for the Black community. It functions, Baraka says, as a "unifying principle—the collectivizing principle—to withstand the deathblows that white America is seeking to put on him ... the onslaught of white America ... these are the things that will mean survival."[22]

Baraka's *A Black Mass*, which reinterprets the Nation of Islam's Yakub teaching, ends by repeating over and over the Muslim expression "ism-al-azam" (the "greatest name" of God) and the narrator saying, "Let us declare the Holy War. The Jihad."[23] In her interpretation of the play, Melani McAlister observes that "the call for *Jihad* (Arabic for righteous struggle or Holy War) becomes a religious and moral response to the problem of evil, the answer of the present to the history presented in the play. The language of Islamic militancy is mobilized for black militancy; religious struggle and racial struggle are made one."[24] McAlister notes the influence of Islam and Islamic symbolism on the BAM, a discussion Sohail Daulatzai extends in *Black Star, Cresent Moon*, calling the BAM "a site for the Muslim International, as it employed Islam and Islamically themed symbols and ideas in their radical Black cultural practices of the time."[25]

BAM poets (like Baraka, Touré, Neal, and Sanchez) wrote about jihad as a struggle for survival in the face of the necropolitics of white racial terror, but they also wrote about spiritual struggle as a creative life force. A few months after the performance of *A Black Mass* in Newark (in May 1966), Baraka (then still LeRoi Jones) published a series of columns in *DownBeat* magazine highlighting performances by musicians like Sun Ra, Pharoah Sanders, and Marion Brown at Newark's Jazz Arts Society. These articles reorient the focus on the death urge of the white devil depicted in *A Black Mass*, instead emphasizing the musicians' "consciously Spiritual Music," which he calls a "Life Force" as they "try and *become* one of the creative functions of the universe." In one key passage, he uses language evocative of *jihad al-nafs*. The word *nafs*—meaning self, psyche, or spirit—is etymologically, phonetically, and semantically connected to the word *nafas*, denoting "breath." Baraka reflects on the "soul as *anima*, spirit (*spiritus*, breath), as that which carries breath or the living wind. We are animate because we breathe. And the spirit which breathes in us, which animates us, which drives us, makes the paths by which we go along our way and is the final characterization of our lives. . . . There is no life without spirit."[26] His language also evokes the concept of *jihad fi sabil Allah*, jihad on the path or way of God, as he writes about making "the paths by which we go along our way . . . the final characterization of our lives." He conceptualizes the spirit of Black music and art as inspiration, breath, anima, and life counteracting what he calls the poison gases of argon blue eyes, an image that simultaneously evokes both the Nation of Islam's blue-eyed devils and the poison gases of Zyklon B (or Prussian blue) used by the Nazis in World War II. The poison gases epitomize racial evil as "anti-life" and as a form of necropolitics, and jihad as a fight for life.[27] This fight for life, this jihad for survival, is also a "sign of solidarity, spiritual oneness, cultural unity, and political struggle," a kind of kinship expressing continuity between "ancestral spirits, . . . the embodied spirits of Black Arts Movement poets esteemed as elders and griots," and the rap and hip-hop inflected spirit of young poet-performers, as Lorrie Smith characterizes the performance of Black spirit work across generations.[28]

The BAM poet Rolland Snellings describes performing this kind of spirit work across generations. Just after his conversion to Islam, he wrote "Jihad!: Toward a Black National Credo" during the month of Ramadan. The article, in *Negro*

Digest, was one of his first to be published under Askia Muhammad Abu Bakr el-Touré, his new Muslim name invoking the leader of the Songhai dynasty and the Muslim ancestors of the West African diaspora in the Americas. In "Jihad!" Touré writes that he is "moving to re-establish the broken links with my Racial Ancestors, while maintaining a Revolutionary Black Awareness of the modern world. Moving Eastwards—towards Mother Africa and Holy Mecca—in these young years of Black Awareness, heeding the Call of the World Spirit, I come, I come. Striding forward, striving in a Great Jihad of Collective Be-ing."[29] He roots the essay in Islamic time, dating it according to the *hijri* calendar A.H. 1388 during Ramadan (November/December 1968). Touré describes how his commitments to Islam converged with his understanding of himself as a "revolutionary intellectual" and a poet, realizing "a full and complete existence" and becoming "truly free" by bringing his life and work, teaching and activism, poetry and writing into harmony.[30] "Now, thanks to my continued striving (jihad) and growth, I have returned to myself: I no longer shun the 'poet' in me, for now I see a greater, deeper definition of poet (and artist) in the Eastern sense"—one modeled on "the great priests of ancient Egypt & Ethiopia, the Black Magi of ancient Persia and Elam, and the learned Shiekhs of Timbuctu."[31]

The eastward orientation was toward a political ideology of decolonization, independence, and self-determination, but also an ethical, epistemological, and aesthetic shift in consciousness. BAM writers orient this within both the African American and the Islamic tradition, as scholars Lorenzo Thomas and James Smethurst observe of BAM writings in general and Touré's work in particular. This dual tradition, writes Thomas, stems from the "African cultural impulse that created both traditions."[32] In "Jihad!" Touré calls for decolonization but also a "Spiritual Internal Revolution which will create 'new people,' . . . a 'Revolution' which will follow in El Hajj Malik El Shabazz's (Malcolm X's) footsteps to relink Afro-America with the Afro-Asian East; a 'Revolution' which will restore the Mind and Soul of the Black man to his Ancestral rhythms and Ancient Spirituality. . . . It is as though an African Nation were rising here in the West."[33] Tapping into an Afro-Islamic substratum permeating African American language and culture in conscious and subconscious ways, Touré, like other artists, musicians, and poets of the BAM, used keywords and symbols to access a history buried by Eurocentric epistemological violence and white racial oppression, fragments of religious, linguistic, and cultural practices that together function to reconstitute, reclaim, and revive lost histories. Touré calls for brothers and sisters to return to "their true Religion" through a process of "Easternization, or Re-Africanization," but also through "the Vibrations of Allah in the atmosphere" and a self-conscious exploration of this "Path."[34]

LOVING YOUR ENEMY

The concept of jihad directly challenged the passive resistance of the civil rights movement and Martin Luther King Jr.'s doctrine of "loving your enemies," taken from Luke 6:27–29 and Matthew 5:44. After King's home was dynamited at the beginning of the Montgomery bus boycott in January 1956—with his daughter and wife inside—he told an angry crowd *not* to take up weapons, saying: "He who lives by the sword will perish by the sword.... We are not advocating violence. We want to love our enemies. I want you to love our enemies. Be good to them. Love them and let them know you love them."[35] Both Elijah Muhammad and Malcolm X directly criticized this teaching by responding publicly in print, but also by developing a moral language for standing up to white racial violence. In his book *The Supreme Wisdom* (1957), Elijah Muhammad pointedly referred to the same biblical verses, arguing that the injunction to "love your enemies, bless them who curse you, pray for those who spitefully use you, turn the other cheek to those who slap you" is "another poison addition of the slavery teaching of the Bible."[36] Malcolm X launched an analogous critique in his "God's Angry Men" columns in the *New York Amsterdam News*, just after the brutal police beating of Johnson X Hinton in April 1957. "Our own religious leaders were teaching us to love, be patient, understanding, forgiving, 'turn-the-other-cheek' to the cruel white Christian slave master, who was holding a Bible in one hand and the Lyncher's Rope in the other."[37] King would respond to the critique less than three weeks later, debating with Malcolm X in the public sphere. On May 17, 1957, at the Prayer Pilgrimage for Freedom in Washington, DC, King preached against "a philosophy of Black supremacy" in his "Give Us the Ballot" speech, citing the same biblical passage of "turning the other cheek."[38] King included the Prayer Pilgrimage speech in his 1963 book *Strength to Love*, as "loving your enemies" became a cornerstone of King's philosophy articulated in key sermons and writings.[39] His public exchange with Malcolm X was part of a longer debate between the two about the nature of resistance and self-defense in the face of white racial terror.[40]

In the aftermath of Malcolm X's assassination, Baraka (still LeRoi Jones) started the BAM independent press Jihad Productions in "New Ark." Among Jihad's first publications was Yusef Iman's collection *Something Black Dedicated to the Millions of Black Brothers and Sisters in the West* (1966), which opens with one of the BAM's most famous poems, "Love Your Enemy." Larry Neal and Amiri Baraka included "Love Your Enemy" in *Black Fire*—and it would also be played over a loudspeaker as part of the Metropolitan Museum of Art's 1969 exhibit

Harlem on My Mind.⁴¹ The poem is a portrait of white racial terror during the civil rights movement in 1963: police attacking protesters with fire hoses and dogs in Birmingham and the bombing of the 16th Street Baptist Church that killed Addie Mae Collins (age 14), Denise McNair (11), Carole Robertson (14), and Cynthia Wesley (14). It explicitly references King's essay "Loving Your Enemies" in *Strength to Love*.⁴² That year (1963) Iman joined the Nation of Islam with his wife Dara Aireen after a long affiliation with Marcus Garvey's Universal Negro Improvement Association and African Communities League (UNIA-ACL). The following year they both joined Malcolm X's Organization of Afro-American Unity (OAAU), and it was Malcolm X who translated the poet's "slave name" Joseph Washington to the Islamic Yusef Iman: Joseph being the slave who became governor of Egypt in Jewish, Christian, and Muslim scriptures; and Iman meaning "belief."⁴³ Dara became close friends with Betty Shabazz, later continuing her education at Medgar Evers College where Sister Betty was an administrator. After Malcolm X's assassination, Yusef and Dara joined LeRoi Jones's Black Arts Repertory Theatre School in Harlem in 1965 and his Spirit House Movers and music group, The Jihad, after Jones moved back to Newark.⁴⁴ In 1966, Iman acted the part of the Black magician Nasafi in the Newark production of *A Black Mass* at Proctor's Theater. A true "renaissance man," Iman published several collections of poetry, circulated numerous pamphlets, wrote plays, performed as a musician and vocalist (with The Jihad, the Wrens, and the Sparrows), and acted in the theater and the movie *Death of a Prophet: The Last Day of Malcolm X*.⁴⁵ This experimental film—narrated by Ossie Davis, starring a young Morgan Freeman as Malcolm X, and featuring a soundtrack by Max Roach—depicted Malcolm X's everyday life "as a series of moments," but with a consciousness of his death hovering over it.⁴⁶

Iman's "Love Your Enemy" critiques the civil rights mantra to turn the other cheek, juxtaposing images of white racial terror against Black life. The poem riffs on the rhetoric of Elijah Muhammad and Malcolm X, as well as Louis Farrakhan's "A White Man's Heaven Is a Black Man's Hell." Farrakhan's song and Iman's poem are both readings and interpretations of NOI teachings, but also contrapuntal responses to pacifism in the struggle for Black freedom.

> Brought here in slave ships and pitched overboard.
> Love your enemy
> Language taken away, culture taken away
> Love your enemy
> Work from sun up to sun down

Love your enemy
Last hired, first hired
Love your enemy
Rape your mother
Love your enemy
Lynch your father
Love your enemy
Bomb your churches
Love your enemy
Kill your children
Love your enemy
Forced to fight his Wars
Love your enemy
Pay the highest rent
Love your enemy
Sell you rotten food
Love your enemy
Forced to live in the slums
Love your enemy
Dilapidated schools
Love your enemy
Puts you in jail
Love your enemy
Bitten by dogs
Love your enemy
Water hose you down
Love your enemy
Love,
Love,
Love,
Love,
Love, for everybody else,
 But when will we love ourselves?[47]

Iman's Islam becomes an alternative to the Christian prescription of passive resistance, as it was in Malcolm X's writings. The repetition of the word "enemy" and the violence of the imagery emphasizes white racial terror, but also the incredible dissonance of the word "love," in this context, as a means of counteracting such a degree of hate. The poem functions as a multilevel critique as well as an account of historical violence against Black life—the slave trade, forced labor, sexual violence against Black women, lynching, redlining, incarceration, and educational inequality. Jihad Productions published the poem on a poster graphically illustrating the poem's description of violence against Black women, an image that also depicts the making of the white devil out of this moral violence, allegorically described in the NOI's Yakub teaching that Baraka reinterpreted in *A Black Mass*.

Similar critiques of "loving your enemy" were levied in writings from other parts of the Muslim world, like in Ahmad A. Galwash's two-volume *The Religion of Islam: A Standard Book* published multiple times between 1940 and 1978 in New York, Cairo, Lahore, Delhi, and Isfahan. The volume is a sourcebook for "standard" Sunni practices in Islam, and it comments on issues of racial discrimination and inequality in the United States. Galwash describes the political organization of Islam as distinguished by "equality of rights."[48]

> Even a slave was admitted as a brother from the very moment of his conversion and the highest dignitary in the state thought it no dishonor, to partake of his repast with him. Nor in the place of worship were suffered artificial differences between man and man: the high and the low, the prince and the peasant, the rich merchant of Mecca and the roaming Bedouin of the desert, stood shoulder to shoulder in the presence of their common Deity. This equality and fraternity was, and is even today, the key-note of Islam and the secret of its power as a world religion.... Tribes and races, hitherto a war with one another, were, in the embracing fold of Islam, welded into one nation.[49]

His next section discusses the use of force in Islam, or jihad, arguing that Muslims could not adhere to the Christian maxim "love your enemy" in the face of "all sorts of ruthless tortures and merciless butcheries." "When it is a sin to resist evil," Galwash writes, "the natural consequence is the abject toleration, or rather encouragement, of all sorts of nefarious designs and natural courses." Peace is the Muslim watchword, a "highly practical ideal" compared to the Christian injunction "love your enemy." After "long years' persistent persecution," he insists, "when all peaceful measures had failed and proved unavailing, ... it would not have been right to act upon the Gospel verdict 'Love your enemies and do good to them who hate you,' and thus to allow the enemies of Islam to revel in the wholesale massacre of harmless worshipers of the one true God."[50]

JIHAD OF EDUCATION

"Love Your Enemy" offered a poetic critique of King's passive resistance and an advocacy of self-defense and militancy against white violence and oppression, as Iman and others in the BAM effectively waged a jihad of the pen as a form of cultural revolution. They envisioned this jihad as an intellectual struggle to disseminate alternative forms of knowledge and build alternative educational institutions. The Barakas' Jihad Productions operated via multiple media, as a complete sensory experience and a holistic mode of disseminating the message through grassroots communications systems and homespun Black institutions. Jihad Productions operated on a sonic, written, and visual level, issuing not just poetry collections and plays, but also recordings of spoken word poetry performances ("Black Art"), jazz poetry, experimental bebop (*Sonny's Time Now*), R&B (*Black and Beautiful*), and plays (*A Black Mass*). It produced educational manuals (*Mwanamke Mwananchi [The Nationalist Woman]*) and posters and broadsheets ("Jihad," "Love Your Enemy," *Black Bird: A Parable for Black Children*); magazines and newspapers (*The Cricket* and *Jihad News*); and reproductions of revolutionary African texts like Ahmed Sékou Touré's *Afrika and Imperialism* and Julius Nyerere's *Ujamaa: The Basis of African Socialism*. The Barakas formed autonomous institutions, envisioning them as a form of "incipient sovereignty" in Newark's urban core—what Russell Rickford calls "a step toward formal self-determination" through "the creation of grassroots enterprises able to remain separate from the state and existing power apparatuses."[51] They built "parallel institutions" like Spirit House and the African Free School in Newark similar to other Black Power institutions that "offered a means of pursuing self-reliance, meeting social needs, and conveying moral and political principles." As Rickford observes, the founders of alternative schools like the Uhuru Sasa Shule in Brooklyn, the African Free School in Newark, and Ron Karenga's US School of Afroamerican Culture in Los Angeles "yearned to politicize black residents of core cities, but they also wanted the children of such territories to become fully literate and conscious of the world as it was and as it might be."[52] These kinds of schools built on longer traditions of Black study and expanded on earlier institutions like the NOI's University of Islam schools.[53] In the Muslim world, a "parallel Islamic sphere" developed under the conditions of colonial secularism and secular modernity, creating a kind of Islamic counterpublic that similarly became a mode of resistance against Euro-American cultural dominance.[54]

Yusef Iman, his wife Dara Aireen, and their family were key contributors to the Barakas' Spirit House in Newark; they were also active in "The East," a community cultural center located on the border of the Bedford-Stuyvesant and Fort Greene neighborhoods in Brooklyn. The East was founded by Jitu Weusi (Leslie Campbell), a high school teacher who was ultimately dismissed when he campaigned for Black Studies in the Brooklyn school system. He led a coalition of African American teachers and students that founded their own community school, the Uhuru Sasa Shule as an educational arm of The East. (Cultural events featured at The East included the " 'Black Experience in Sound,' a series of performances by avant-garde jazz artists" like The Last Poets, Pharoah Sanders, Max Roach, Sun Ra, Archie Shepp, and McCoy Tyner—who were either Muslim or experimented with Muslim forms of identification in their music, practices, and performances.)[55] The Uhuru Sasa Shule ("Freedom Now School" in Swahili) was "designed to train children in both traditional academic subjects and black nationalist principles."[56] Yusef and Dara Iman had a "tremendous impact" on the development of The East, its founder Jitu Weusi acknowledged in an interview with the scholar Kwasi Konadu. Iman was "such a central figure that many of the cultural protocols and practices of The East and Uhuru Sasa—such as marches, oaths, songs, and other elements—were products of his creativity."[57] The Iman family operated a branch of The East called "The Mid-East" in their own neighborhood Brownsville in Brooklyn.

Iman's cultural creativity is archived at the Schomburg Center for Research on Black Studies at the New York Public Library, with illustrated art/poem books like his *Weusi Alfabeti* (Black Alphabet) primer for the Uhuru Sasa Shule, the anthology *The Young Black Poets of Brooklyn*, and a series of illustrated poems self-published as educational pamphlets.[58] *Young Black Poets of Brooklyn* lifts up the writings of Brooklyn youth connected to The East; it was illustrated by Jim (Seitu) Dyson, one of the founders of The East, and published by The East's radical newspaper/magazine *Black News* (Agitate-Educate-Organize). His language drew on writings by Elijah Muhammad in *Muhammad Speaks* that called for unity in the face of genocide and focused on race preservation, through criticisms of race mixing, birth control and abortion, same sex relations, and women not performing their "natural" womanly / motherly / domestic roles. The literature warns against racial genocide, annihilation, and extermination with graphic illustrations of police brutality, war, lynching, and rape, showing prisons as concentration camps for the extermination of Black people.[59] In her book about her family, the Imans' daughter Malika remembers how Yusef would show

FIGURE 1.1 Image illustrating Yusef Iman's *Extermination or Unification*.
Malika Iman

films for the children to study, like *The Battle of Algiers*, teaching that "we had to be ready and prepared for the ungodly and put 'Jihad (Holy War) on their head.'"[60]

"JIHAD! A BLACK NATIONAL CREDO"

Even before Rolland Snellings converted to Islam and took the name Askia Muhammad Touré, his poetry referenced jihad of the sword, like in "Song of Fire," first published in *Umbra* in December 1963 and later included in *Black Fire*. The poem talks about a jihad of the sword through the words "Allah / will send his flaming sword a 'whistling / through the 'chosen land' . . . (Fire!) / will cauterize the Racist Plague!" The dedication of "Song of Fire"—"(for Africa, Asia, Latin & Afro-America—the Wretched of the Earth)"—pays tribute to Fanon but also to Malcolm X's sense of the Black revolution "sweeping white supremacy out of Africa, Asia, and Latin America, . . . even now manifesting itself also right here among the black masses."[61] "Song of Fire" was first published around the time Malcolm X gave his famous speech, declaring: "The black revolution, which is international in nature and scope, is sweeping down upon America like a raging forest fire. . . . Here in America, the black revolution (the 'uncontrollable forest fire') is personified in the religious teachings, and the religious works, of the Honorable Elijah Muhammad."[62] The poem, which translates Malcolm X's speech into poetry but also into song, like Max Roach did in his 1956 track "Mr. X," begins as an elegy for the four girls killed in the bombing of the 16th Street Baptist Church in Birmingham the previous September, an elegy similarly woven into Yusef Iman's "Love Your Enemy" with the lines "Love your enemy / Bomb your churches / Love your enemy / Kill your children." In "Song of Fire," Snellings simultaneously mourns the victims of the 1960 Sharpeville massacre that killed sixty-nine protesters, including ten children. He interweaves the two protests—and the two massacres—through reference to Max Roach's "Tears for Johannesburg" in the following lines: "Tears that weep for shattered Sunday schools / are lost / like diamonds leaving ebon hands among the dark / South African sands: / lost-lost . . . and never found! / Save your tears! Save your anguished cries!"[63] The poem is a battle cry, calling not for tears but for fire, in a way that also echoes James Baldwin's *The Fire Next Time* (1963), itself structured through reference to hymn ("no more water, the fire next time!"). "Song of Fire" operates on layered political and rhetorical registers, juxtaposing white violence against Black lives at home and abroad, connecting the voices of Fanon and Malcolm, doing so through reference to the Max Roach and Abbey Lincoln's protest album *We Insist! Max Roach's Freedom Now Suite* (1960). The poem remembers the dead, doing so through jazz prosody, as Meta DuEwa Jones observes when she writes that jazz poetry in the BAM "often performs as a vehicle for hearing the dead speak."[64] Through "Song of Fire," he raises the spirits by remembering them, performing a kind of spiritual ascension or resurrection.

Touré published two collections of poetry just after his conversion: *Juju (Magic Songs for the Black Nation)* (1970) and *Songhai!* (1972). Both extend his earlier experimentations with poetry as music, engaging in a process of citation and recitation of musical and intellectual ancestors, "Scientists and Prophets, Scholars and Sages, / Philosophers and Myth-making Priests. / Garvey and DuBois, Langston and Booker T., / Bessie and Satchmo, Bird and Lady Day, / Malcolm and

Elijah, Otis and Aretha— / and John Coltrane."⁶⁵ Each poem in *Juju* pays tribute to a jazz composition and musician, as the poetry musicalizes his poetic language and verbalizes the music in what Amiri Baraka called "speech musicked."⁶⁶ The visual / sonic / written / symbolic "meta-language" of Islam infuses both collections—art with Islamic symbols by Weusi artists Ademola Olugebefola, Bilal Farid, and Abdul Rahman; Islamic language like *tauhid* "the oneness of God" / *as-Salaam Alaikum* / *al-hamdulillah* (praise be to God); citations of the Qur'an and hadith; and dating by the *hijri* calendar. *Juju* opens with Ben Caldwell's "Islamic Vision," a poem that describes symbolically representing "Allah's universe" with an "unswerving... sense of justice and peace," a Black fire burning "the white evil" of the devil. The collection's dedication includes hadith and verses from the Qur'an about "fighting in the way of God" (4:76); pays tribute to enslaved people of African descent who planned armed insurrections like the "fallen prophets" Nat Turner, Denmark Vesey, and Gabriel Prosser; and pays homage to Black leaders and creatives like Marcus Garvey, W. E. B. Du Bois, Malcolm X, and John Coltrane. The dedication also quotes Jimmy Stewart's essay "Revolutionary Black Music" published in the Jihad Productions' journal *The Cricket*: "Black music is the accompaniment of the vision of the Black Nation we are bringing to reality, with Blk poets and singers and playwrights constructing new Black poetry and musics for the Black Nation."⁶⁷ *Juju* envisions poetry as "the Living Word" vibrating through breath and song, the sound of "Ancestors singing," a ritual that creates a "living link of connection to the Racial Ancestors" through "ISLAM:... my Vision, my Song."⁶⁸

"Song," writes Touré's fellow Umbra poet Lorenzo Thomas, "is the very basis of Touré's poetry.... It was song through which Africans enslaved in actual chains in these Americas preserved our history and expressed their various selves. A song is breath entranced by thought... as breath, a song is Life."⁶⁹ Thomas calls this a "program of reclamation" performed by the BAM, "a labor of reclaiming the lost souls of black folk" through spirit work. The title *Juju* plays on the Nigerian and West African musical tradition juju, but also juju as a kind of Black magic—and on the Black Arts Movement association of Black Arts with Black magic, as a conjuring or necromancy, a raising of the dead and revival of the ancestors. The title *Juju* engages in a process of citation and re-citation of the African American musical tradition—of saxophonist Wayne Shorter's album *Juju* (1964) and Archie Shepp's *The Magic of Ju-Ju* (1965).⁷⁰ Shorter recorded *Juju* in August 1964 with Muslim McCoy Tyner (piano), Elvin Jones (drums), and Reggie Workman (bass)—at the tail end of his four-year tenure with the Muslim musician Art Blakey's Jazz Messengers. In December 1964, Tyner and Jones recorded *A Love Supreme* with John Coltrane. After Gary Bartz took Shorter's place with Blakey's Jazz Messengers, Bartz's NTU Troop recorded their own album *Juju Street Songs* (1972). This sonic landscape framed the publication of Touré's *Juju*, in 1967, in a call and response between the bebop and the poetics. Touré's *Juju* also paid tribute to Jamaican Lebert Bethune's poetry collection *Juju of My Own* (1965), whose title poem would be published in Amiri Baraka and Larry Neal's *Black Fire*, alongside Touré's three poems "Sunrise!!," "Mississippi Concerto," and "The Song of Fire," all structured as songs. Bethune filmed Malcolm X on his 1964 visit to Paris, just months before his assassination; footage that he made into his short film *Malcolm X: The Struggle for Freedom* (1967) and that was later reused in Woodie King Jr.'s 1981 film *Malcolm X: Death of a Prophet* (in which Yusef Iman appeared).[71] These juju compositions were spirited responses to colonial writings about juju as "jungle magic," like the British colonial administrator Frank Hives's writings on juju in Nigeria and James H. Neal's writings on juju in Ghana.[72]

The title poem of Touré's *Juju* is "Juju (for John Coltrane, a Black Priest-prophet)." It begins with a subsection called "The Opening," a literal translation of *al-fatiha*, the first chapter of the Qur'an, which is recited in Muslim prayer. Each poem pays tribute to a jazz composition and musician, as the poetry riffs on the music, verbalizing the music, and making the poetic language music. Throughout the poem are words of praise almost like a refrain, ending with a kind of incantation of tribute to Coltrane's "A Love Supreme" repeated again and again, and the *al-hamdulillah* translated to English:

> PRAISE BE TO:
> ALLAH:
> who brought us Malcolm and Elijah
> and reopened Islam like a Flaming Torch[73]

The flaming sword of Touré's earlier "Song of Fire" from 1963 has now become a "flaming torch" of the Black priest prophets Coltrane, Malcolm X, and Elijah Muhammad leading the way. He frames them as God-sent, even though Touré's commitments soon moved to Sunni Islam. Touré signs the poem with his Muslim name and the date in the *hijri* calendar. The poem "Tauhid" that follows uses the same title as Pharoah Sanders's jazz track "Tauhid," a word that refers to the Islamic doctrine of the "oneness" of God. It begins with an injunction to "Reach with hungry Black minds towards that bright Crescent Moon . . . Eternal Beauty Cosmic Rhythms / flowing/ in the sound of Pharoah's horn . . . Reach into the Womb of Time, past aeons of chains, / to find your Afro-Soul, that holy part of you connecting / Harlem to the roots of Timbuctoo . . . Cosmic Order: Allah's Love vibrating."[74] Touré

FIGURE 1.2 Illustration by artist Abdul Rahman of the Weusi Collective in Harlem. "Allahu Akbar" written in Arabic emanates from John Coltrane's horn, like a call to prayer. The sketch illustrates Askia Muhammad Touré's poem "Juju" in his collection *Songhai!*

Sultanah Rahman

structures nearly all his poetry with reference to music; his poems, writes Thomas, are "very nearly song."[75]

Margo Natalie Crawford describes the mixed media of the BAM as accentuating "the flows and ruptures between the visual, sonic, and the written staged as a meta-language," constituting a kind of multisensory "counter-literacy" that brought together writing, reciting, and visual art.⁷⁶ The BAM visually and sonically articulated this meta-language through Muslim keywords and expressions, like *tauhid, jihad, salaam alaikum, Allahu akbar, al-hamdulillah*, written and drawn in Arabic, recited in poetry, exclaimed in protest, and rendered through music. This multimedia approach is very much in the spirit of Islam: at the heart of the Qur'an's double meaning of reading and recitation and the Islamic tradition's visual elaboration of the scriptural message. These multisensory, multimedia BAM projects, instead of being deaf, dumb, and blind, were vitally alive through knowledge of Black (and) Muslim history. The poet/author/scholar Sofia Samatar refers to this multimedia sampling of elements from the Black past as a form of bricolage or "remixology, . . . nothing less than the reclamation of a buried history" through "the excavation of the past" that helps construct "visions of what is to come."⁷⁷

Touré's 1972 *Songhai!* poetry collection is structured as a double album with four "sides" illustrated by the artist Abdul Rahman, who was part of the Weusi Collective in Harlem that founded the Weusi Nyumba Ya Sanaa Gallery. *Songhai!* opens with an epigraph of verse 3:104 from the Qur'an about "a nation calling" (*yad'uun*) to Islam, with the first pages numbered according to the Arabic alphabet rather than Roman numerals. The first poem is "The Call (A Solo From the West)," flanked by Abdul Rahman's illustration for "Side 1: Rhythm and Blues." It shows a muezzin issuing the call to prayer from a minaret in an urban landscape suggesting Harlem, the place name Touré marks whenever he signs and dates his name in the text. "The Call (A Solo from the West)" interprets music as a form of *da'wa*, but it also evokes the musicality of the *adhan* (call to prayer)—and both as calling up the spirit.⁷⁸ This is a jihad of *da'wa*, the call to Islam through jihad of the tongue, of words, and of the pen, using print media, music, and art as a means of proselytization and "mobilizing Islam."⁷⁹

Evoking the call to prayer and the call to Islam, "The Call" also echoes LeRoi Jones's earlier poem "S.O.S.," published before he took the name Amiri Baraka in summer 1967. It is included in the short (twenty-page) collection *Black Art* (1966), the third work published by Jihad Productions. "S.O.S." reads like an urgent call for help radioed over the airwaves, but it is also an invitation to join the cause:

> Calling black people
> Calling all black people, man woman child
> Wherever you are, calling you, urgent, come in
> Black People, come in, wherever you are, urgent, calling
> you, calling all black people
> calling all black people, come in, black people, come
> on in.⁸⁰

The *Black Art* collection includes the poem "Salik," which uses Sufi terminology to refer to a disciple traveling on the path of truth, speaking to the awakening of Jones's consciousness at the time. These poetics anticipate the later work of Tariq Touré, whose poem "The Call" is also about *da'wa* and *adhan*. A short film of Tariq Touré reciting the poem opens with the call to prayer and Touré bowing in prayer in a mosque—Allah lit up in green neon. The prayer sequence is spliced with scenes of the poet wading in the water fully clothed, an Islamic "wading in the water" simultaneously referencing baptism, ablutions, and fugitivity. The visual imagery of Tariq Touré's poem suggests the water of the Black Atlantic and the prayer direction that points toward Mecca, as well as Africa and the Middle Passage. The echoes between these poets and the Islamic past construct a jagged genealogy partly through their plays on language and naming, but also through their multimedia calls to ritual prayer in Islam.

As this BAM poetry engages deeply with African American oral and poetic traditions it also uses Islamic language as a call to arms—for a restoration and a revival of what has been lost, stolen, buried, and denied. The musicality within (and of) the Islamic tradition is something that has been long contested and debated, yet it has been an integral part of Islamic societies and cultures through time, whether through the lyricism of Qur'an recitation, Sufi *dhikr* (chanting or "remembrance" of God), or poetry put to music to make song. In her book about the sonic landscape of African American jazz poetry, Meta DuEwa Jones writes about African American poets returning to poetic traditions, reinterpreting and revising them through struggle and creative adaptation, as a record of "literary, musical, and cultural traditions"—but also of religious and spiritual ones. Their improvisations "renovate tradition's rituals of recital."[81] These poetics and their sonic forms expand the Islamic tradition, explorations necessitated by the distance from their origins in time and space. It is a process of renewal and revival—of something the white power structure literally tried to kill off—forms of life, worship, and ritual practice, as well as customs, languages, and modes of being. Reinhabiting those forms took a feat of imagination, but also an excavation that these BAM practitioners labored to perform, not only through the erection of structures, institutions, and media but also through performances and languages fit for the task they set out for themselves. Their creations are testament to the efficacy of the media of their message, a jihad that has resonated through time to the hip-hop generation that Samy Alim calls "verbal mujahidin" who use "weapons of mass culture."[82] BAM poets, writers, and musicians engaged in their own processes of interpretation, reinterpretation, and revivification—reclaiming roots, creating community, and teaching knowledge. Teaching and education became an integral aspect of this process, recuperating not only a lost past, but suppressed knowledge systems, epistemologies, and languages.

SONIC AND VISUAL JIHAD

In her 1971 poem "Ima Talken Bout the Nation of Islam," Sonia Sanchez envisions jihad as a Black Muslim insurrection.

> ima talken about Muslim men and women on the move
> like a fire travellen down a fuse . . .
> ima talken about a nation
> ima talken about a black muslim
> insurrection, (don't you hearrrRRRR it?)
> ima talken about a nation
> ima talken about a jihad like
> the world ain't never seen.
> (can you seeeEEE it?)[83]

The poem epitomizes the BAM aesthetic, moving sensorily between reading and recitation, the sonic and the graphic. With the vernacular "talken bout," Sanchez directly poses questions to her readers/listeners/audiences, asking if they can "seeeEEE" the jihad and "hearrrRRRR" the sound of the insurrection "thumpen like drums" against skin, as she says in the poem, like a heart, a song, a harmony, a voice, a message. The message resonates through the formal dimensions of her poetic form, the beat-like repetition, the talking like rapping, the elongated questions that are like calls to the cause. The poem was published simultaneously in both audio and print—on Sanchez's Smithsonian Folkways album *A Sun Lady for All Seasons* and as a broadsheet by the small independent Black press, New Pyramid Productions, in Chester, Pennsylvania. Both publications were mixed media collaborations with BAM visual artists including photographer Bilal Farid and Ademola Olugebefola of Harlem's Weusi Collective. In Farid's photograph of Sanchez and her two young sons Morani and Mungu Weusi, Emory Douglas's 1970 "Free Huey" poster can be seen in the background, with its image of a barefoot, gun-toting militant shedding tears for the incarcerated Black Panther. Sanchez sits patiently in the foreground, her young twins fussing in her arms, her head wrapped in a style different from the naturals she wore in portraits for her earlier publications. That same year, Farid's photography also graced the cover of the Last Poets' "jazzoetry" album *This is Madness* (1971), as well as Touré's poetry collection *Songhai!* published the following year.[84]

In *A Sun Lady for All Seasons*, Sanchez also included a poem "To Fanon," titled in response to the Ghanaian author Ayi Kwei Armah's article "Fanon: The Awakener," published in *Negro Digest*. (Armah himself moved to Algeria in 1962 just after independence to work for the radical journal *Révolution Africaine*.) In her poem, Sanchez writes about destroying "the BEAST / that enslaves us" through "WAR. DISCIPLINE. LEARNEN."[85] In "Ima Talken Bout the Nation of Islam," jihad is identified with the violence of "insurrection" and "fire travellen down a fuse"—decolonization by "cannon fire" as Frantz Fanon wrote in his essay "On Violence"—violence colored by "the exploitation of the colonized by the colonizer." In *Discours sur le colonialism* (1950), Fanon's teacher Aimé Césaire wrote about how colonization "brutalizes and degrades" the colonizer, awakening "buried instincts to covetousness, violence, race hatred, and moral relativism."[86] Similar critiques were leveraged in the heart of the BAM, like in Larry Neal's essay "The Black Arts Movement," which comments on this moral hypocrisy: "Even though Western society has been traditionally violent in its relation with the Third World, it sanctimoniously deplores violence or self-assertion on the part of the enslaved. And the Western mind, with clever rationalizations, equates the violence of the oppressed with the violence of the oppressor."[87] Self-defense was an integral aspect of Black Power, Black nationalism, and the NOI, but the BAM, as the "spiritual sister of Black Power," also understood this struggle in psychological and intellectual terms, as Fanon did in his writings about the Algerian war of independence and the *mujahidin* and *mujahidat*. The events of the war "steeping Algeria in blood ... are the logical consequence of an abortive attempt to decerebralize the people," he wrote in his resignation letter from the Blida-Joinville psychiatric hospital in December 1956.[88] He called the armed fight of the *mujahidin* and *mujahidat* against undemocratic political representation in their own country a struggle of "disalienation." The *mujahidin* and *mujahidat* fought on the streets and in the countryside, but also on discursive terrain—to reclaim selves from the alienating effects of French rule over Algeria and from a French educational system that suppressed the Arabic language, the religion of Islam, and any traces of Arab, Islamic, or Algerian forms of knowledge and culture. In a parallel struggle, artists and intellectuals fought by mobilizing "all that popular energy" through processes of signifying and resignification of the colonizer's dominant narratives about the colonized—but also of the Islamic tradition for the context of new kinds of struggle.[89]

For the cover of Sonia Sanchez's broadsheet *Ima Talken Bout the Nation of Islam*, Ademola Olugebefola provided artwork infused with signs of Islam and

Egypt: the word Allah written in Arabic at the center of a sun, rays emanating outward; the crescent star shining through a keyhole window, a classic motif in Islamic architecture; a woman and man in Muslim clothing, wearing a Nation of Islam–like head covering and a fez, respectively; the pyramids of Egypt emblazoned with two ankhs, the Egyptian "key of life," and a God's eye shining like a star. Olugebefola centers the Islamic tradition through the centering of the calligraphic Allah written in his own hand above the crescent star. But he also situates the men and women of the Nation of Islam squarely inside Islamic cultural and religious tradition, not outside or at its edges.[90] Sanchez closes the poem by calling it a "prayer" and by praising God with the Islamic expression "al-Hamdulillah."[91]

This poem about the NOI epitomized the BAM's multimedia collaboration by bringing together diverse communities of cultural creatives and collective pedagogies: Olugebefola from the Weusi artist collective, Emory Douglas from the Black Panther Party (who did the cover for Sanchez's *Home Coming*), photographers Bilal Farid and Merrill A. Roberts, New Pyramid Productions Press, and Smithsonian Folkways. At the time, Sanchez was teaching Black Studies at Rutgers and at Manhattan Community College and was on the cusp of joining the Nation of Islam. She was also a part of Amiri Baraka's Black Arts Repertory Theatre School in Harlem and the Barakas' Spirit House in Newark, joining various groups to further Black Studies through community organizations, arts collectives, and movement schools. She taught at the Downtown Community School in New York City, in the first Black Studies program at San Francisco State (with Amiri Baraka, Ed Bullins, Marvin X, Sarah Fabio, Askia Muhammad Touré, Nathan Hare, and others), at the University of Pittsburgh (with Etheridge Knight), and later at Amherst College, Temple University, and the University of Pennsylvania.

Sanchez's commitments to Black study dovetailed with her commitments to Islam. In 1971, alongside "Ima Talken Bout the Nation of Islam," she published the anthology *three hundred and sixty degrees of blackness comin at you* through the 5X Publishing Co.—referring to the name Sonia 5X, which Sanchez took when she joined the NOI.[92] Most accounts date her conversion to the following year, but her literary and poetic language attests to her identification with Islam and the NOI during this earlier period.[93] The anthology collected writings from a workshop she taught at the Countee Cullen Library in Harlem. The "three hundred sixty degrees" of the title signifies "knowledge of self" in the *Supreme Mathematics* of the Five Percenter Lessons: 120 degrees of knowledge, 120 degrees of wisdom, and 120 degrees of understanding. 360 degrees also refers to zero or the cipher: "from knowledge to understanding, back to knowledge."[94] Another collection she also published in 1971, *It's a New Day (poems for young brothas and sistas)*, opens and closes with the greeting "As-Salaam-Alaikum." The collection included artwork by Olugebefola, dotted with crescent stars and joyous imagery of Muslim families singing in unison. One poem "We're not learnen to be paper boys (for the young brothas who sell Muhammad Speaks)" describes Islam as a route to knowledge of self, through the voices of the brothers selling the NOI newspaper:

> our route is the mind of blk people.
> ... spreaden the
> knowledge of self and truth.
> Let us recite out loud our blk/ praises to Elijah Muhammad
> Let us recite out loud our blk/ love for our selves.[95]

In these poems, jihad is armed insurrection, but also a jihad of the mind, or a kind of *ijtihad*.

These reinterpretations of jihad in the BAM also epistemologically impacted the interpretation of the Islamic tradition. Just after "Ima Talken Bout the Nation of Islam" was released on *A Sun Lady for All Seasons*, a student at the University of Pennsylvania named Mary Teasley took a writing class with Sonia Sanchez. Both women converted about the same time—Sanchez joining the Nation of Islam and Teasley Sunni Islam, taking the name amina wadud; wadud remembers reading all of Sanchez's works and being "definitely INSPIRED by Dr. Sanchez's spirit."[96] She would go on to publish the important work of feminist exegesis *Qur'an and Woman: Re-Reading the Sacred Text from a Woman's Perspective* (1999) and another work titled *Inside the Gender Jihad: Women's Reform in Islam* (2006). Like Sanchez, wadud uses jihad to write about struggle for justice. Her book outlines the fight for "justice and full human dignity" through teaching and learning, establishing collectives, and a new kind of hermeneutics.[97] The collectively authored, public access anthology *A Jihad for Justice* furthered this vision through a collaborative working in tandem in tribute to wadud's contribution and legacy. The scholarship, hermeneutics, poetry, and personal testimony in *Jihad for Justice* expanded wadud's intervention through the contributors' own intersectional analysis of racial and gender justice in Islam.

By redefining the idea and concept of jihad, wadud aligns with contemporary reinterpretations of Islamic ideas and concepts, partly through the process of a revivified *ijtihad*, or "independent reasoning," a word closely connected to the word "jihad," but a reflexive jihad, a jihad of inner intellectual struggle to interpret and understand the meaning of Islamic scripture and teachings. Her

FIGURE 1.3 Cover of Sonia Sanchez's broadsheet *Ima Talken Bout the Nation of Islam* with artwork by Ademola Olugebefola—the word Allah written in Arabic calligraphy centered in a sun rising in the East. The image is framed by a keyhole window emblematic of Islamic architecture.

Ademola Olugebefola

Qur'an and Woman is very much a feat of *ijtihad* as she struggles with the meanings of key verses and passages of the Qur'an that talk about women and their rights, roles, and responsibilities. In a sense, wadud opened up the door of *ijtihad* to a flood of new feminist exegeses and hermeneutical approaches to reading and rereading the Qur'an. Her work, and approach, is part of a long tradition of interpreting and reinterpreting Islamic scripture, but also of defining and redefining the jihad of spiritual and intellectual struggle, an aspect of "global jihad" (or *ijtihad*) that has received far less recognition in popular consciousness or scholarship. In this respect, wadud is a pioneer, but as a *mujtahida* she is also carrying on a longer tradition of interpreting and reinterpreting the Islamic tradition for new contexts of struggle, as Sanchez and so many others did for the BAM.[98] Though Sanchez ultimately left the NOI because of the constrictions they placed on her cultural work, she tapped into an Islamic poetics, an Islamic hermeneutics, and an Islamic art that she furthered through her own creative struggle. As wadud comments, "She made a compelling case about substance over form when talking about her experience with the NOI. . . . She might have even used the phrase 'the spirit of prayer,' . . . so I got the sense that she learned from what she had been taught and then kept learning."[99]

PART I
Anticipating the BAM

CHAPTER 2

NATION IN A NATION IN A NATION

The Islamic Counterpublic and the Black Arts

> *La lutte de libération nationale s'est accompagnée*
> *d'un phénomène culturel connu sous le nom de réveil de l'Islam.*
>
> —Frantz Fanon, *Les damnés de la terre*

> *As one of the oldest containers for Black identity . . . Islam functioned as a formal system of governance, as a producer of subjects and a figure of sovereignty.*
>
> —Achille Mbembe, *Critique of Black Reason*

In the epigraph to his chapter "Sur la culture nationale" in *Les damnés de la terre*, Frantz Fanon quotes Sékou Touré's presentation at the second Congrès des écrivains et artistes noirs held in Rome in 1959: "Il ne suffit pas d'écrire un chant révolutionnaire pour participer à la révolution africaine, il faut faire cette révolution avec le peuple. Avec le peuple et les chants viendront seuls et d'eux-mêmes" (To participate in the African revolution, it's not sufficient to write a revolutionary song, this revolution must be waged with the people. With the people, the songs will come on their own by themselves.)[1] Fanon first presented a version of the chapter at the same 1959 Congress of Black Writers and Artists where Touré presented—an indictment of Negritude's poetic and literary valorization of a precolonial Black past, as insufficient to the national struggle for independence, but also irrelevant to and disconnected from it. He argued that the fetishization of precolonial history is essentially derivative of the attitude and culture of the colonizer. *Les damnés de la terre* was published a few days before Fanon's own death in November 1961, on the eve of Algeria's independence in March 1962, and after seven long years of a brutal war. "On National Culture" reflects on the relationship between the anticolonial movements on the African continent, the sit-in protests in the United States, and the African diaspora in the Americas. Fanon explores the commonalities—and differences—in their mutual struggles to shake off the political, economic, and psychological legacy of colonialism, economic exploitation, and slavery.

Fanon writes about the revival of Islam in the Arab world, reflecting on "Black-African or Arab-Islamic" modes of reasoning, "a cultural phenomenon commonly known as the awakening of Islam."[2] He was ambivalent if not dismissive about the revolutionary potential of religion, and of Islam, in the fight for decolonization, independence, and national sovereignty. This chapter examines how Islam became a means (among several means) of expressing Black nationalism in the United States, shaping an alternative political imaginary articulated partly through reference to the Black past, but also through solidarities with transnational independence movements. Despite his ambivalence, Fanon grappled with Islam's role in decolonization, something also critical to Sekou Touré's conceptualization of a postcolonial national identity in Guinea—as a bulwark against the psychic incursion of European colonialism but also as a blueprint for political and personal sovereignty. As Achille Mbembe observes in *Critique of Black Reason*, Islam is "one of the oldest containers for Black identity.... Islam functioned as a formal system of governance, as a producer of subjects and a figure of sovereignty." Despite the diversity of different traditions, interpretations, and readings of Islam, "one element united the different traditions: the privilege that they accorded to faith in determining the relationship between identity, politics, and history.... With laws of religion defining the modes of belonging and exclusion, the observance of religious precepts (how to live morally in the eyes of God) became the condition of admission into an imagined nation whose physical and symbolic borders encompasses a wide-ranging community of believers."[3] The BAM tapped into the "awakening of Islam" as a critical dimension of postcolonial nationalist mobilization, a "figure of sovereignty," a mode of "belonging," "an imagined nation," and a key to buried elements of African religion in Black American cultural life.

This chapter reflects on the Black nationalism of the BAM and the role of an Islamic counterpublic within—and beyond—the Black counterpublic. BAM artists and writers mined the fertile terrain of the preslave past to help construct visions of a liberated future and to forge connections with Third World nationalist movements (also) shaking free of the yoke of European domination. The Islamic nation in the Black nation destabilized the monolithic hegemony of "the black experience" but also expressed how Blackness is othered in the Eurocentric imaginary.[4] The Black Muslim nationalism of the BAM articulated "a blackness that [was] *internally differentiated and differentiating*" through an attunement to Black diversity and a vision of alternative Black ethnicities, religious forms, cultures, languages, and modes of national belonging.[5] Black Muslim nationalisms built on earlier forms of Black nationalism—conceptualized by leaders like Martin Delany, Marcus Garvey, and W. E. B. Du Bois, and by Muslim and Muslim-identifying figures like Dusé Mohamed Ali, Satti Majid, Abdul Hamid Suleiman, Sufi Abdul Hamid, Noble Drew Ali, and Wallace Fard Muhammad.[6] Religious diversity became a way of celebrating ethnic and racial diversity—with the 1893 World's Fair in Chicago, the accompanying World's Parliament of Religions, and the founding of The Ancient Egyptian Arabic order Nobles Mystic Shrine of North and South America and Its Jurisdictions (the Black Shriners). Black religious diversity was chronicled in works like the Jamaican Harlem Renaissance writer Claude McKay's *Harlem: Negro Metropolis* (1940) and Arthur Huff Fauset's *Black Gods of the Metropolis* (1944). As Jim Crow segregation crystalized—legally, politically, economically, culturally, and socially—Black religious identity became a means (among other means) of expressing alternative forms of belonging.

The Islamic inflections in Harlem Renaissance cultural production—and a correlating African American awakening (or "resurrection") of Islamic consciousness—anticipated the Black (Muslim inter-) nationalism of the BAM in all its diverse instantiations and interpretations. McKay devoted a chapter of *Harlem: Negro Metropolis* to the labor organizer Sufi Abdul Hamid, an "Oriental philosopher" and "a mystic" who "delved into the mysteries of occultism, mixing together a hash of Hindoo, Persian and Chinese religions." Sufi Abdul Hamid was convinced by "a group of Negro Moslems in Chicago" to pursue "the more serious work of job campaigning."[7] Despite the way he "thundered" on his stepladder on 135th and Fifth Avenue, "reaching large masses of his people and articulating their hidden thoughts," he was also deceiving them with the "mumbo-jumbo" of his mystical spirituality. McKay finds it "odd to listen to him all tricked out in his Oriental toggery," but Sufi Abdul Hamid's preaching of economic self-determination was key to his Black nationalism, which was also expressed through what McKay called oriental religion and a doctrine of "do for self."[8]

The labor leader Sufi Abdul Hamid became a central character (named Abdul Sufi Hamid) in Ishmael Reed's BAM novel *Mumbo Jumbo* (1972), which parodies the conservatism of Elijah Muhammad and the NOI, as well as other monotheistic religions (the "Atenists"), critiquing their stern attitude to the arts, music, and dance. *Mumbo Jumbo* explores the Islamic elements in African American culture—and the African American elements in Islam—uncovered (or rediscovered) in a process of self-education about the Black past. Abdul Sufi Hamid talks about how he was self-taught, learning a new language through "transliteration and translation of hieroglyphics":

> I had no systematic way of learning but proceeded like a quilt maker, a patch of knowledge here a patch there but lovingly knitted, . . . the way I taught myself became my style, my art, my process. . . . I am building something the people will understand. This country is eclectic. The architecture the people the music the writing. The thing that works here will have a little bit of jive talk and a little bit of North Africa, a fez-wearing mulatto in a pinstriped suit. A man who can say give me some skin as well as Asalamilakum.[9]

Both Claude McKay of the Harlem Renaissance and Ishmael Reed of the BAM are critical of Sufi Abdul Hamid and of Abdul Sufi Hamid's (respective) identification with Islam. Yet both authors acknowledge the popular appeal of their coded language giving expression to difference—whether hoodoo, Hindu, Russian, or Turkish—the "mumbo jumbo of African fetishism and Oriental philosophy" in McKay's words.[10] Figures like Sufi Abdul Hamid used Islamic names, dress, forms of worship, and aesthetics to evoke what Mbembe calls the alterity of the *"African sign,"* but also "a formal system of governance, as a producer of subjects and a figure of sovereignty."[11]

Earlier conceptions of Black nationalism during the Harlem Renaissance (the "New Negro Arts Movement" or the "Negro Renaissance") reverberated in the BAM—especially W. E. B. Du Bois's understanding of Black art's role in giving expression to the nation in a nation.[12] BAM artists picked up on the Islamic (and orientalist) motifs in the Harlem Renaissance that expressed a sense of cultural and aesthetic alterity, but also a different kind of national belonging and identity. The BAM theorist Margo Natalie Crawford writes about how "Harlem Renaissance writers anticipated the BAM, and some of those anticipatory visions shaped the more militant tones of the Harlem Renaissance," though the BAM insisted on "being 'Black,' not 'Negro.'" Crawford analyzes Marita Bonner's play *The Purple Flower* (1926), calling it an "uncanny anticipation of the rhetoric and radicalness of the BAM" that presaged the BAM's "performance of aesthetic warfare (the rage against the white aesthetic)" and "warfare against white power."¹³ Crawford argues that the play's imagery of white devils anticipated the teachings of the Nation of Islam (NOI), founded a few years later. She calls the play "a profound anticipation of the Black Arts and Black Power movement theorizing about the need to create a 'nation within a nation' as colonized space is transformed into black space." These geographies became key to the conceptualization of BAM institutions as refuges for Black life, informed by "a deep awareness ... that when oppression has penned you in you must claim your own space in order to breathe."¹⁴

Identification with Islam helped articulate the concept of a nation within the nation, drawing on Black nationalism's transnational dimensions that sought to transcend "the narrow national orbit—artistic, cultural and political—and soaring into the space of more universal experience."¹⁵ This identification was both deep and wide; it was historical and geographical; it reached across spatial divides and back in time.¹⁶ The transnational modes of identification of the Moorish Science Temple of America (MSTA) and the NOI connected their adherents to Asia, Africa, and Morocco, as did the Ahmadiyya's strategy of transnational decolonization. These American Muslim movements sought self-determination, independence, and sovereignty as "a Black nation within a nation," calling for full citizenship rights, as their counterparts in Morocco and India were doing in Africa and Asia. Islamic signs, symbols, and language(s) became code for initiation into wider brotherhoods and sisterhoods; conceptualized as outside—and in opposition to—the dominant modes of representation perpetuated in the bourgeois, Christian, Euro-American, and largely white American public sphere. Islamic modes of belonging expressed both difference—and alienation—from mainstream white America and Christianity. But this Islamic identification also forged membership in different kinds of communities in which adherents claimed full citizenship and full humanity not recognized in the white public sphere.

AN ISLAMIC COUNTERPUBLIC IN THE BLACK COUNTERPUBLIC

There were gestures to Islam in the seminal Harlem Renaissance text "Harlem: Mecca of the New Negro," a special issue of the journal *Survey Graphic*, later expanded to become *The New Negro* anthology edited by Alain Locke (1925).¹⁷ *Survey Graphic* used the word "Mecca" just after the opening of the Mosque of Mecca Temple in New York City in December 1924—the "Parent Temple" of the

Shriners (Ancient Arabic Order of the Nobles of the Mystic Shrine) first established in 1872. The Black Shriners, the Ancient Egyptian Arabic Order Nobles Mystic Shrine also had their own Mecca Temple, but in Washington, DC, established just after the organization's founding in 1893.[18] At the time of the special issue's publication, the white Shriners had (however ironically) sued the Black Shriners for appropriating "their" Islamic and Egyptian regalia, insignia, signs, symbols, and language, with the US Supreme Court ultimately deciding in favor of the Black Shriners in 1929. Calling Harlem the Mecca of the New Negro (re)claimed this Islamic (and orientalist) imagery—as not owned by the white Shriners but as an integral to the patrimony of the African diaspora in the West.

Earlier Black nationalist movements like Marcus Garvey's Universal Negro Improvement Association and African Communities League (UNIA-ACL) considered Islamic modes of identification in the organization's anthem while deliberating an official religious affiliation.[19] Islamic organizations emerged alongside the UNIA and the NAACP, as did African American masonic organizations, fraternal brotherhoods, secret societies, and women's organizations. These critical institutions of Black civil society "came into existence alongside and complementary to African American churches but also, like the churches, provided symbolic, ideological, and organizational resources for African Americans to resist racism and find their way through contested terrain of American civil society."[20] The MSTA drew on the Islamic language, symbols, names, and clothing of the Black Shriners, but also developed specifically nationalistic frames of reference by using the Moroccan (Moorish) flag, identity cards, and an embassy.[21] They developed their own sense of citizenship and national belonging—as African Americans were systematically disenfranchised from rights of full citizenship and political participation. During the same period in the 1920s, the Ahmadiyya connected their anticolonial conceptions of self-rule and self-determination to racialized political justice, ideas that gained substantial traction in 1920s Chicago. Organizations like Prince Hall and the Shriners catered mainly to the middle class, but the Ahmadiyya, MSTA, and NOI attracted "more recent arrivals" from the Great Migration.[22] Islamic identification in the twentieth-century urban North spread among the disenfranchised underclass, making available brotherhoods and sisterhoods to those ineligible for membership in the NAACP and Prince Hall, imparting a sense of national belonging, citizenship, and civic participation.[23]

African American religious communities flourished during and after the Great Migration, as African Americans created "competing and complementary black ethnicities" through a "transnational consciousness" that drew on a range of "diverse and vibrant ethnic identities."[24] The formation of an uprooted and disenfranchised Black working class in the North provided fertile ground for the Islamic modes of identification that emerged in the 1920s and 1930s, alongside the Black nationalist Pan-Africanism of Marcus Garvey and Dusé Mohamed Ali.[25] Segregation within the Christian church and the "deradicalization of the Black Church" led to the "dechristianization of Black radicalism."[26] The Ahmadiyya movement developed a critique of white mainstream Christianity, as well as racism in the United States, as missionaries worked toward "a new vision of a global Pan-Islamic alliance in which Indian nationalism and Pan-Africanism were linked in a potent multi-racial synthesis of anti-imperialist and anti-Christian religious and political ideas."[27] These Islamic movements enabled their adherents to imagine alternative kinds of citizenship as well as alternative kinds of nationhood—converts to the Moorish Science Temple were known to show their national identity cards to people "telling them that Noble Drew Ali had liberated black people from the curse of European influence."[28] These Islamic movements self-consciously called for the revivification of Islamic elements through a process of excavation that included education and knowledge about African American roots in Islamic societies and cultures and the routes by which these cultures were forcibly relocated to the United States.[29] Along with the NOI (in particular), these movements performed a remarkable feat of redefining an African American Islamic culture, observes Sherman Jackson. They connected Islam "with the masses of Blackamericans via the creation of a long-sought alternative modality of American blackness," he writes, and in the process, "Blackamerican popular culture was profoundly reshaped."[30]

Under conditions of a dominant Christian public sphere and a Protestant ethic hostile to signs of Islam, early Islamic proselytizers like Noble Drew Ali and Wallace Fard Muhammad drew on key Islamic signs, symbols, practices, and language in their teachings—elements of both an Islam indigenous to the United States and transnational identification with the Muslim International.[31] Signs of a suppressed Islam persisted in American culture and society, sustained in the "active, vibrant, and compelling" presence of formerly enslaved Muslim communities in places like South Carolina and Georgia (where Elijah Muhammad was from).[32] Michael Gomez describes their ongoing presence as a "cultural transmogrification to survive," strengthening the Islamic heritage as a result of an "ideological restructuring."[33] Noble Drew Ali's Moorish Science Temple constituted the

> beginning of a qualitatively different trajectory in the history of modern, religiously based African American social movements. His ideas reflect the quintessential convergence of Islam, Islamism, Freemasonry, New Thought,

Rosicrucianism, anticolonialism in its critique of European imperialism, and nationalism in the rejection of American racism. Having once formed a coherent stream, subsequent rivulets flowing from the conceptual world of Noble Drew Ali, in the form of organizational principles and philosophical legacies, remain and inform until this day.[34]

Sherman Jackson argues that these early Islamic proselytizers drew on "traditional Blackamerican culture," whereas Gomez argues for a continuity of Islam in traditional Blackamerican culture—in language and names, cuisine, folk traditions, dress, and writings sublimated in cultural practices sometimes not readily identifiable as Muslim traditions. In addition to the traces of these retentions, Islamic movements raised consciousness about this history, consciousness of Islamic beliefs, scripture, practices, teachings, language, and culture, forms of knowledge buried and lost but still alive and present in African American and American culture. These organizations provided frameworks for disseminating knowledge but also spaces for living them.

Islamic groups that emerged in the 1920s and 1930s formed a subaltern counterpublic within the Black counterpublic, as nations within the Black nation within the nation.[35] These organizations had their own doctrines, rituals, and spaces; literature, newspapers, and catechisms; schools, teaching materials, and curricula; dress, headgear, and insignia. They cultivated an Islamic aesthetic that was alternately Moorish, Asiatic, Egyptian, and South Asian. Institutions, publications, and spaces gave shape to an Islamic counterpublic, but also an Islamic aesthetics that drew on transnational signifiers sometimes identified as "alien" in the context of American cultural life. African American Islamic organizations produced their own literature that circulated among its members as tools of proselytization and provided educational opportunities for learning beyond the narrow confines—and racist contours—of state-sponsored education. The first issue of the Ahmadiyya's journal *The Moslem Sunrise* included Arabic script of Islamic expressions like the *basmallah*, but also phonetic transcriptions of verses from the Qur'an that could be recited—in Arabic—by English speakers who could not read Arabic script.[36] Following these teachings on the Qur'an and others on the hadith was a didactic poem teaching basic principles of Islamic practice and belief. It used Arabic-Islamic words like *zikr* (i.e., *dhikr*) to talk about "remembrance of God," a "reminder" about an original Islamic self. Like speaking in tongues, the Islamic Arabic expressions from the Qur'an helped express a different kind of subjectivity, an Islamic identity that became, in the language of the NOI, a means of tapping into a lost language and self. The Arabic language signified difference, but linguistic difference understood as sacred.

During this period of reemergent modes of Islamic identification in the early twentieth century, thriving art, literature, culture, and intellectual production coalesced as a key part of the Black counterpublic, alongside new kinds of political associations and modes of religious identification. Because of the "formal expulsion of African Americans at the end of the nineteenth century from official spheres of public discourse," African Americans struggled "to reinsert themselves into the channels of public discourse" through "an active counterpublic" that included fledgling civil rights organizations, journals, literary circles, Black academics, and the Black church. "The blossoming of black organizational forms in the political, economic, and social arenas, when combined with the outburst of the Harlem renaissance, led to a strengthening of the Black counterpublic and increased the pressure for African-American inclusion, both in official discourses as well as oppositional publics," writes Michael Dawson in his book *Black Visions*.[37] The art of the Harlem Renaissance played a critical role in opening up a space for debate about "race, culture, and society" and for the "norms and values of black culture... in American civic life."[38]

Part of the Black struggle over representation centered on issues of ownership—of publishing houses, presses, journals, newspapers, music companies, and educational institutions. The Harlem Renaissance sought to formally codify the ephemera of Black life, in the recordings by the Fisk singers, W. E. B. Du Bois's statistics and archival work, Zora Neale Hurston's intensive work to record Black folklore and narratives of Black life, and Paul Dunbar's vernacular poetry. These efforts faced herculean structural obstacles that were economic, structural, and political, problems of funding, access to libraries and materials, leisure time to pursue scholarship and make art, and the lack of circulation of recordings and publications to the broader public.[39] Since the means of cultural production were largely white owned, the circulation of Black art sometimes meant the representation of Black life for white audiences, through a kind of translation that structurally propagated double consciousness.

The organizational infrastructure of the Black counterpublic gave political voice to this nation within a nation, as did "Black representational space," through burgeoning modes of intellectual, poetic, and literary expression. The nature of this cultural expression became the subject of extensive debate between leading intellectuals in the 1920s—in dueling essays by Du Bois, Alain Locke, George Schuyler, and Langston Hughes concerning the nature of Black art, poetry, and music. Analyzing Du Bois's "Criteria for Negro Art," Darby English argues that the production of "black images" were essential to survival under conditions of extreme duress in the 1920s and 1930s, with the reemergence of the Ku Klux Klan, rise of the eugenics movement, expansion of Jim Crow, surge in lynchings, and economic disenfranchisement that disproportionately affected Black Americans during the Great Depression. In this "violently riven context" of Jim Crow, "an American vocabulary of 'black representation' had to develop." Correlating race and culture, he writes, "was a life function, a matter of survival." Though English argues that the conditions of Black art have changed in the contemporary world, BAM poets, artists, and writers themselves responded to the "violently riven context" of the civil rights and Black power eras—the bombing of the 16th Street Baptist Church; assassinations of Malcolm X, Martin Luther King, and Medgar Evers; and brutal suppression of Black protest and dissent.[40] It is a struggle that continues into the twenty-first century with ongoing violence against Black lives.

"BLACK ART HOKUM"

Intense debate erupted in the public sphere over the nature of Black art following the 1925 publication of *The New Negro*: George Schuyler's "Negro-Art Hokum," Langston Hughes's "The Negro and the Racial Mountain," and W. E. B. Du Bois's "Criteria for Negro Art," the latter culminating a series published in *The Crisis* on the theme "The Negro in Art: How Shall He Be Portrayed?" The Schuyler-Hughes debate in *The Nation* centered on the role of both class and religion in Black art, but also the issue of difference versus norms in creative production. Schuyler advocated for middle-class (Western European Christian) standards while denigrating "low" art, specifically the "contributions of a caste in a certain section of the country"—like spirituals, sorrow songs, blues, rag time, and jazz. He criticized the fetishization of "Negro rustics and clowns . . . as authentic and characteristic Aframerican behavior."[41] Hughes in contrast celebrated the "low-down folks, the so-called common element, and they are the majority—may the Lord be praised! . . . Their joy runs, bang! into ecstasy. Their religion soars to a shout . . . They furnish a wealth of colorful, distinctive material for any artist because they still hold their own individuality in the face of American standardizations."[42] Black art, Hughes argues, is the art of the people—what Douglas A. Jones calls "the Black below" and Fred Moten and Stefano Harney, "the undercommons."[43]

Schuyler's "Negro-Art Hokum" ridiculed the "non-existent . . . great renaissance of Negro art," writing that, "as for the literature, painting, and sculpture of Aframericans—such as there is—it is identical in kind with the literature, painting, and sculpture of white Americans: that is, it shows more or less evidence of European influence."[44] He argues that immigrants and "Aframericans" are "indistinguishable from the mass of Americans" after being exposed to the same social forces—such as schools, politics, advertising, moral crusades, restaurants, cars, films, literature, media, clothing, language—in a remarkable disavowal of systemic racism, the concept of a "nation in a nation," and non-European art in the Americas. Schuyler declares that Black and white Americans read "the same Bible" and belong to "Baptist, Methodist, Episcopal, or Catholic church." Whereas Schuyler flattened the landscape of American religious life, the Harlem Renaissance anthropologist Arthur Huff Fauset would later chronicle its diversity in *Black Gods of the Metropolis* (1944), a book that included chapters on the Black Jews and the MSTA. Fauset's book built on Claude McKay's 1940 *Harlem: Negro Metropolis* but shifted the language from "Negro" to "Black, "anticipating" the BAM.[45]

Schuyler's erasure of aesthetic and religious diversity—but also of race and class—was underscored in his much-criticized comment that "the Aframerican is merely a lampblacked Anglo-Saxon . . . subject to the same economic and social forces that mold the actions and thoughts of the white Americans." Anything else, he argues, is "a peculiar art . . . rejected with a loud guffaw by intelligent people," what he refers to as "Negro-art hokum."[46] Schuyler's references to minstrelsy charges the artists of the Harlem Renaissance as caricaturing, fetishizing, and essentializing "the 'peculiar' psychology" of Black life.[47] Schuyler deployed imagery from minstrelsy at a time when Black face performers like Al Jolson were reaching the height of fame. Jolson appeared in theater performances and talking films like *Bombo* (1921) (in which he played a slave to Christopher Columbus), *A Plantation Act* (1926), and *The Jazz Singer* (1927). Hughes's spirited retort "The Negro and the Racial Mountain," published in *The Nation* the following week, reversed the charge of the "Aframerican [a]s merely a lampblacked Anglo-Saxon," calling Schuyler (without naming him) "a self-styled 'high-class' Negro . . . aping of things white."[48]

The BAM embraced "Negro-Art Hokum" as the "Black Arts" of the Black masses, opposing it to the bourgeois values Schuyler espoused as the norm, his characterization of Black art as minstrelsy, and his flattening of religious life to Christianity. The BAM launched scathing critiques of the class dimensions of bourgeois white art, following in the path of the leftist intellectuals of the 1950s and 1960s—like those associated with Paul Robeson's *Freedomways*, the Committee for the Negro in the Arts, the American Society of African Culture, the Harlem Writers Guild, the Umbra Workshop, Revolutionary Action Movement, and Fair Play for Cuba. BAM artists played on Schuyler's conception of Black art as "hokum" (hocus pocus), instead identifying it with "the alchemy of Black," Black magic, or what they called i-*magi*-nation.[49]

BLACK ART AND BLACK MAGIC

The Black Arts as Black magic runs through BAM texts—like the "magicians" in LeRoi Jones's play *A Black Mass* and Larry Neal's poem "The Narrative of the Black Magicians," both composed just after Malcolm X's assassination. (Neal closes the poem with the date "Spring—1965 a painful season.") Both works—Jones's play (written before he became Amiri Baraka) and Neal's poem—imagine forms of religious alchemy entailing "the production of a black religion of liberation" that decolonizes "the 'blackness' invented by the modern project of religious racist colonization."[50] Both works do so through "Black religious aesthetic production" that draws on sound—Jones's *A Black Mass* includes Sun Ra's Myth Science Arkestra, and Neal's "Narrative" describes the jazz prosody of "deep wails of saxes, "the voice of Malcolm," and "searing waves of sound."[51] "The Narrative" poetically narrates an African American (Muslim) history partly through the Islamic practices and faith revivified by figures like Malcolm X. It charts an Eastward orientation: not just of return—temporally and geographically—but also a ritualistic turn toward the East in the Muslim prayer. Several times in the poem Neal evokes the dawn prayer facing "Eastward" as "morning eyes strain for the horizon." When the Black (Arts) magicians head northward to "strange cities" (in the Great Migration), "they mouth that language awkwardly in an eastern / blueness. / faces under the timeless sky. their sky"—lines suggest the recitation of verses of the Qur'an during Muslim prayer, but also a certain alienation and distance. The poem moves through "memories out of our private and collective past," from "the shores of home," the Middle Passage, enslavement, slave rebellions, the Underground Railroad, the Great Migration, the Scottsboro Boys trial, urbanization, and gentrification, culminating with the voice of Malcolm X.[52] Neal writes of facing east—as an aesthetic, a spiritual practice, and a form of rebellion, but also as an inner spiritual transformation and a cosmic one, a turning "from the west, turn inward eyes on themselves, / control the black cosmos."[53]

Margot Crawford brilliantly writes about Neal's poem, arguing that his chant-like repetition of the phrase "form child" and the word "form" represents "one of the most lucid examples of the BAM's understanding of form as the antiformulaic.... Sound, for Neal, becomes a prime way of breaking the boundary between form and formlessness.... Purposeful plays with poetic formlessness become one way of representing the 'free jazz' of blackness ... tied to the black aesthetic."⁵⁴ The BAM also breaks with the form of the "western cultural aesthetic" and, more importantly, with the "ethics" of "western society" (as Neal writes in his "Black Arts Movement" essay). The Black (Arts) magicians face eastward where "Ancestor faces form on the film of our brains. / form our contours out of deep wails of saxes. / form in the voice of Malcolm. / form child." Neal describes a rebirth through an aesthetic and spiritual return, through an ocean of "searing waves of sound."⁵⁵

Neal's poetry uses sound, music, jazz, and blues as "a challenge to linear ideas of history and temporality," writes Carter Mathes.⁵⁶ In Neal's unpublished manuscript "Black American Music," he calls for avoiding "labels like 'old' and 'new' music. Mainly because Afro-American music is not historically linear, but rather it is multi-directional. It goes back & forth in time . . . The music is informed by the past & present. It is time itself rather than any particular time. It is non-matrixed always in motion & free."⁵⁷ Mathes describes Neal as "furthering an expansive phenomenological perspective," drawing on "music, phenomenology, and ideas of the supernatural to help reframe black aesthetics." He talks about Neal as analyzing "abstract, expressionistic sound" as improvisational—and opposing "Western conceptualizations of musical sound," thus highlighting the need for "listeners to reorient themselves in relationship to distortions of time and space," partly though "tonal memory."⁵⁸ These are the temporal dimensions of Black nationalism critiqued by Fanon, an Islamic revival that looks simultaneously to the past and the future. Neal's jazz poetry envisions the spatial dimensions of this form of identification, an eastward orientation through the dawn prayer and through the figure of Malcolm X. These spatial and temporal dimensions of Black nationalist identification with Islam create an "ideological bridge" between past and future and between African Americans and the Muslim world.

The jazz prosody of the BAM drew on earlier modes of experimentation in the Harlem Renaissance, as poetic forms evolved in tandem with new modes of musical expression over the twentieth century. BAM writers converting to Islam followed in the footsteps of jazz musicians in the 1940s and 1950s and patterned their poetics on these musicians' jazz aesthetic.⁵⁹ As Lorenzo Thomas argues, BAM writers saw "jazz as a significant social critique of an oppressive social structure" and explored "a spiritual dimension of jazz that can be compared to an almost religious fervor." They saw jazz musicians as "not merely the custodian of an authentic folk culture or even the conscious avant-garde artist," but as leaders "of rebellion against postwar conformity and the spiritual agent of the politically powerless."⁶⁰ James Smethurst similarly observes that the BAM sought to theorize "the relationship of the African American artist and his or her formal practices to the black community (or nation)." Among these was the relationship between poetry and music—"the formal rhythms, emotions, gestures, and other elements of performative style were significantly rooted in gospel and the R&B vocal-group style that later became known as doo-wop as well as in new thing jazz"—particularly in the poetry of Askia Touré, Larry Neal, Yusef Rahman, Amiri Baraka, and Sonia Sanchez, some of the main BAM poets who converted to Islam; though Neal did not, Islamic references permeate his writing. "A sort of bop sensibility predominated in which jagged rhythms and anaphoric fragments of sentences and phrases resembled the riffs of bop improvisation," Smethurst writes.⁶¹

LeRoi Jones's essay "The Changing Same," written in 1966—before he converted and changed his name to Amiri Baraka—is a companion piece to Neal's poem "The Narrative of the Black Magicians." Jones riffs on the ideas in Neal's poem, the two pieces speaking back to each other about Black history, culture, identity, and religion through poetry and music. Both the essay and the poem describe changing forms of religious tradition channeled through music and "searing waves of sound." Jones talks about how "the older religiosity falls away from the music, but the deepest feel of spirit worship always remains" through a self-conscious concern about God, which he says is why so many beboppers have become Muslim. It is "Wisdom Religion" that "wants to change forms" and does so in the new music, though "the Black religious roots are still there. This form is as old as Black religious gathering in the forests of the West ... and connects straight on into Black free-Africa."⁶² He writes about the "social consciousness" of musicians like Coltrane, Albert Ayler, Pharoah Sanders, and Sun Ra, calling them "God-seekers": "black musicians who are or say they want to be 'Spiritual Men' (some of the boppers embraced Islam), or else they are interested in the Wisdom Religion itself, i.e., the rise to the spirit. It is expanding the consciousness.... They are interested in the *unknown*. The mystical."⁶³ "Changing Same" is LeRoi Jones's BAM version of W. E. B. Du Bois's "Sorrow Songs," where Du Bois talks about the remnants of "phrases of a dimly understood theology" coded into new forms of music that "have displaced the older sentiment," though "once in a while we catch a strange world of an unknown tongue."⁶⁴ The BAM tried to catch the strange world of that unknown tongue, as Larry Neal writes, mouthing "that language awkwardly."⁶⁵ The power of the aural and recited word in Islam reverberates through these works as echoes and traces of something lost but not erased.

BLACK NATIONALISM AND THE BAM

Fanon's reflections "On National Culture" emerged in conversation with kindred debates about Black art and Black nationalism taking place at the same time among African American intellectuals.[66] BAM had its roots in anthologies, festivals, and conferences that brought together Black writers and intellectuals who debated the nature of Black art—members of the Committee for the Negro in the Arts (1949), the Congresses of Black Writers and Artists (1956 in Paris / 1959 in Rome), the American Society of African Culture (1959 in New York), the World Festival of Negro Arts (1966 in Dakar), the Black Writers Conferences at Fisk University (1966), and the Afro-American Festival of the Arts (1966 in Newark)—conferences and festivals that were variously policed and infiltrated by the FBI, CIA, and US Information Agency. The First Negro Writers Conference in 1959 was a stateside version of the meeting in Rome, resulting in the publication of *The American Negro Writer and His Roots*. It brought together some of the most important writers of the generation, such as Lorraine Hansberry, Langston Hughes, Julian Mayfield, John O. Killens, John Henrik Clarke, Sarah E. Wright, and Sarah Fabio, writers who were the immediate precursors to the Black Arts Movement. Their writings, discussions, and collaborations reflected deeply on the role of Black art in the new Black nationalism (and the role of Black nationalism in the new Black art)—and would be included in some of the BAM's most important anthologies like Dudley Randall and Margaret Burroughs's *For Malcolm: Poems on the Life and Death of Malcolm X* (1967), Amiri Baraka and Larry Neal's *Black Fire* (1968), and Addison Gayle's *The Black Aesthetic* (1972).[67] They forged close alliances with Malcolm X, engaging with him both before and after his break with the Nation of Islam. They were listening to his speeches and reading his writing, turned on and tuned in to what he had to say.

Malcolm X, who read Du Bois in prison, talked about the "downtrodden and oppressed masses" as "a nation within a nation." In a speech at the Harvard Law Forum in 1961 he said that the "prophetic figure" Elijah Muhammad was chosen "from among the lowly, uneducated, downtrodden and oppressed masses, among the lowest element of America's 20 million ex-slaves.... The Christian world has failed to give the black man justice.... Thus the black masses are turning away from the church back to the religion of Islam."[68] Using Marx's understanding of religion as the opiate of the masses, he talks about "shaking off the drugs or narcotic effects of token integration promises," critiquing the Southern Christian Leadership Conference as selling "integration" to pacify the Black masses to keep them from revolting. Later that year, John Henrik Clarke interviewed Malcolm X for an article published in *Freedomways*. He connected the reemergence of Black nationalism to Islamic groups like the Nation of Islam and the Muslim Brothers—as C. Eric Lincoln did in his 1961 book *The Black Muslims of America* and E. U. Essien-Udom would do the following year in his book *Black Nationalism*.[69] Partly a response to and an analysis of the rise of the Nation of Islam as a Black nationalist organization, publications like Lincoln's and Essien-Udom's grappled with the NOI's Islamic consciousness as an expression of Black nationalism, but also as an Islamic revival, the "cultural phenomenon known as the awakening of Islam" that Fanon critiqued as nostalgia and enchantment. Malcolm X framed Elijah Muhammad's message as mobilizing the Black masses, a revolutionary nationalism that connected with larger struggles in Dar al-Islam, Asia, Africa, and also, across the Americas. In "The New Afro-American Nationalism," Clarke interpreted the NOI as a "latter-day version of the Garvey Movement, with a new sounding dogma which is basically the same.... The Black Muslims in the United States have created what is essentially a proletarian movement."[70] Lincoln and Essien Udom would make similar arguments about these movements as forms of political Islam.

The BAM, with its emphasis on the spirit, revised this characterization of African American Muslim groups as purely social and political movements, insisting on the spiritual and even mystical dimensions of their cultural revolution. BAM artists described a sense of conjuring up the spirit—using the idea of Black Art as Christianity's antithesis but also as the antidote to Christianity's more nefarious dimensions as a tool of colonial and racial domination. Clark's essay connects the New Afro-American nationalism to the protests at the UN of Patrice Lumumba's assassination in March 1961—protests that brought together various political, literary, and intellectual constituencies that catalyzed the Black Arts Movement.[71] The Muslim Brotherhood and the NOI were blamed in the popular press for these protests—and two of the protest's organizers, Maya Angelou and Abbey Lincoln (who herself later converted to Islam), tried to forge an alliance with Malcolm X in its aftermath. LeRoi Jones participated in these protests and wrote about them in his 1962 essay "'black' is a country," which reflects on a reemergent Black nationalism and connects it to larger struggles for decolonization and independence. "The black man has been separated and made to live in his own country of color, ... forced for hundreds of years to inhabit the lonely country of black.... The Negro's struggle in America is only a microcosm of the struggle of new countries all over the world," Jones wrote.[72] His related essay, "the myth of a 'negro literature,'" also published in 1962, argued that Black literature did not connect with Black protest in the way that Black music did—through its powerful "fusion between African musical tradition and the American experience, as a highly personal version of Black life in America."[73]

The Black nationalist "'black' is a country" and the Black arts "the myth of a 'negro literature,'" were both included in Jones's collection of essays *Home*, published in 1966 when he returned home to Newark and began distributing albums, poetry, and writings through Jihad Productions. *Home* concludes with an essay reflecting on "the legacy of malcolm x, and the coming of the black nation." Jones talks about Malcolm X "as statesman from a *nation*. An oppressed Black Nation 'laying' in the Western Hemisphere," liberated by a "'universal' Islam" and "Black National Consciousness," and calls for "the sovereignty of nations, the sovereignty of culture, the sovereignty of race, the sovereignty of ideas and ways 'into' the world."[74] He traces this Black national consciousness from Garvey to Elijah Muhammad to Malcolm X ("as the accretion of his spiritual learning, ... energies of historic necessity and the bursting into flower of a National Black Cultural consciousness")—a lineage that Larry Neal would similarly chronicle in his famous essay, "The Black Arts Movement."[75] Jones's later poem "It's Nation Time" (1970), first published by Haki Madhubuti's Third World Press, was recited to music on a 1972 Motown album. By then, he had changed his name to Imamu Amiri Baraka. In the poem he writes: "Christ was black / krishna was black shango was black / black jesus ... / Shango budda black / hermes rasis black / moses krishna / black ... / and we are the same, all the blackness from one black allah."[76]

BLACK ART AND SURVIVAL

In his afterword to the BAM anthology *Black Fire*, Larry Neal grappled with the historical roots of the new Black nationalism—an "emotional history" that Malcolm X interpreted. Malcolm's ideas were "a synthesis of Black nationalism's essential truths as derived from Martin Delany, Du Bois, Garvey, the honorable Elijah Muhammad, Fanon, and Richard Wright." Drawing an analogy between Malcolm and a horn musician, Neal wrote that Malcolm delivered this interpretation in "a particular cadence," as "Malcolm started 'blowing'—started telling the truth in a manner only a deaf man would ignore." Writing about Black separatism, Neal observed that there was "peace in the separation," gesturing to Islam's morphological connection to the word "peace," but then commented on this "sense of haven found most often in the poetry."[77] Neal charted his own genealogy of the Black nationalism of the BAM, writing about the "ghosts of ... Nat Turner, Martin Delany, Booker T. Washington, Frederick Douglass, Malcolm X,

Garvey, Monroe Trotter, Du Bois, Fanon, and a whole panoply of mythical heroes from Br'er Rabbit to Shine. These ghosts have left us with some very heavy questions about the realities of life for black people in America."[78]

Malcolm X read Du Bois during his own self-education at Norfolk Prison Library, not far from where he grew up in Roxbury, Massachusetts. In a speech delivered at the Harvard Law Forum in 1961, Malcolm talked about the "downtrodden and oppressed masses" as "a nation within a nation."[79] While at Harvard (Du Bois's alma mater), he paid tribute to Du Bois's 1933 essay "A Negro Nation Within a Nation." The essay drew on the work of Martin Delany (who was accepted to Harvard but then rejected) and especially on Delany's conception of "a nation within a nation." Delany used the phrase in his 1852 *Condition, Elevation, Emigration and Destination of the Colored People of the United States*, in which he wrote about oppressed minorities that took no part, or only a restricted part, in the body politic because of "the deprivation of political equality with others."[80]

Through reference to the political, economic, educational, and religious effects of Jim Crow segregation, Du Bois's "A Negro Nation Within a Nation" called for a separate economy, educational system, government, and culture. He wrote the essay just after resigning from the NAACP (during the Great Depression), advocating for self-determination as the path to "the economic and cultural salvation of the American Negro." Du Bois explores a concept of Black nationalism partly through his emergent identification with Marxism, as he seems to call for revolution: economic independence through the organization of "a cooperative State," leveling economic classes and racial barriers, and "intensified class and race consciousness as will bring irresistible force rather than mere humanitarian appeals."[81] His vision is not far from Malcolm X's later call for Black revolution, nor from Elijah Muhammad's vision of the Black nation as economically self-sufficient. Du Bois's analysis of and vision for a Black separatism emerged chronologically about the same time as the NOI was founded. Despite the divide between these two leaders—in terms of religion, education, and class—they were united in a pan-African, pan-Asian vision of the economic, social, and cultural unity of the "Black masses." Like Malcolm X would later, Du Bois called on Black artists to "dramatize and beautify the struggle," arguing against waiting for "the salvation of a white God." The stakes, he wrote, are nothing short of "the survival of colored folk in the world and the building of a full humanity instead of a petty white tyranny."[82]

The conception of Black art mobilizing Black political consciousness (and vice versa) was at the core of the Black Arts Movement, though BAM writers and artists saw themselves as more radical than figures like Du Bois from the Harlem

Renaissance, more connected to the struggles of the people. Neal, in his classic essay "The Black Arts Movement," calls the BAM "the flowering of a cultural nationalism" suppressed since the Harlem Renaissance though it "failed to take roots, to link itself concretely to the struggles" of the Black community, "to become its voice and spirit."[83] Neal draws on the language of Du Bois's "A Negro Nation Within a Nation" to characterize the Black nationalism of the BAM—though he attributes the language to Elijah Muhammad and Marcus Garvey. "Implicit in the Black Arts Movement," he writes, "is the idea that Black people, however dispersed, constitute a *nation* within the belly of white America. This is not a new idea. Garvey said it and the Honorable Elijah Muhammad says it now. And then there is the struggle for Black survival."[84] Like Du Bois, Neal sees Black art as a struggle for survival: "It is clear that the question of human survival is at the core of contemporary experience. The Black artist must address himself to this reality in the strongest terms possible." He concludes the essay writing that "Afro-American life and history is full of creative possibilities" and that these possibilities are part of "the struggle for Black survival. If art is the harbinger of future possibilities, what does the future of Black America portend?"[85] Du Bois posed a similar question in "A Negro Nation Within a Nation" when writing about "the highways of future expansion. They will survive, but on what terms and conditions?"[86]

CHAPTER 3

SCIENCE'S FICTIONS

Yakub and the Black Arts

It is the ongoing event of an antiorigin and an anteorigin, replay and reverb of an impossible natal occasion, the performance of the birth and rebirth of a new science, a phylogenetic fantasy that (dis)establishes genesis, the reproduction of blackness in and as (the) reproduction of black performance(s). It's the offset and rewrite, the phonic irruption and rewind . . . casting of effect and affect in the widest possible angle of dispersion.

—Fred Moten, *In the Break: The Aesthetics of the Black Radical Tradition*

The book of Science Fiction might be more revolutionary than any number of tracts, pamphlets, manifestoes of the political realm.

—Ishmael Reed, *Mumbo Jumbo*

The Nation of Islam's Yakub teaching is an allegorized description of a historical reality of scientific racism, medical experimentation on human subjects, eugenics discourses and practices, and obstetric violence against Black women. The teaching has several versions and iterations in different NOI documents, texts, articles, and speeches. The Southern Poverty Law Center has called the teaching the NOI's "bizarre and fundamentally antiwhite theology, or more appropriately its mythology."[1] The SPLC means mythic in the sense of a "false idea or belief," but the Yakub teaching is also a way of "conveying the early history of a people or explaining natural or social phenomenon, typically involving supernatural beings or events."[2]

The teaching's central figure is the scientist Yakub who created the blue-eyed Devil (and the white race) by destroying the black "germ" of the original Black people, separating out the brown "germ," and "grafting" it "into a white" germ on an island called Pelan (the biblical Patmos) in the Aegean Sea.[3] As an allegory, the teaching describes a eugenics campaign of genocide, whitening the Black race through scientific experimentation, and breeding the white race through the selection of lighter, brown-toned babies. Stephen Finley calls the teaching a form of *"theological phenomenology*, a term that describes Elijah Muhammad's practice of *description* and meaningful *interpretation*. That is, the story of Yakub describes intense and overwhelming white racial terror in multiple forms and then offers a definitive response, in the mythology of Yakub, about the meaning of black suffering."[4]

This chapter explores the legal, scientific, and cultural context of the emergence of the NOI's Yakub teaching by looking at the circulation of eugenics discourses in popular culture and popular science, particularly in the 1920s and the 1930s. Science espoused strange fictions about breeding, miscegenation, and racial purity, fictions depicted in literature, film, magazines, newspapers, radio—and theology.[5] Scientific theories about race and social Darwinism permeated popular culture and popular science, like the *To-day and To-morrow* series published between 1924 and 1931. Theories of eugenics directly impacted medical practices and scientific experimentation but also shaped federal and state laws in the decades leading up to World War II. Some of these laws included the Supreme Court decision upholding forced sterilization (1927), antimiscegenation laws ratified in all but seven states, and immigration bans (1924). In this chapter, I contextualize how the Yakub teaching functioned as a hermeneutic of eugenics discourses: the teaching is a rereading of representations of race in popular culture and pseudoscientific literature of the time, coinciding with alternative interpretations of race that emerged during the time of the Harlem Renaissance. By reinterpreting, reversing, and critiquing scientific fictions of white supremacy, the Yakub teaching created a counter-narrative resisting the representational violence inflicted on Black bodies and minds. Using science fiction as a "reading practice" for interpreting the Yakub teaching allows us to examine the historical context of fictions of science and science fictions.[6] My argument is *not* that the teaching is sci-fi, but rather that sci-fi opens up possibilities for understanding the teaching's interpretation of scientific fictions—sci-fi is what Stephen Finley calls a *"hermeneutical necessity"* for understanding NOI teachings. Finley analyzes NOI's teachings about the Mother Plane as a

UFO, arguing that sci-fi as a hermeneutic is critical to understanding their messages about cosmic alienation, flight, other worlds, and emancipation.[7] Sci-fi offers a window for understanding how the NOI countered some of the most nefarious myths about race circulating in popular science and popular culture—NOI theologies that were then, in turn, taken back up in popular culture and, particularly, in Black art.

The science-fiction sensibility of NOI teachings has been analyzed by scholars like Michael Lieb, Stephen Finley, and Edward E. Curtis IV, and noted as well by Patrick Bowen, Michael Muhammad Knight, and Claude Clegg.[8] NOI references, symbols, and teachings have become integral to Afrofuturist cultural production—most notably in the figure of the Mothership—Sun Ra's Arkestra, Parliament's *Mothership Connection*, John Akomfrah's *Last Angel of History*, Jamika Ajalon's short film *Locations of the M/othership: Black Women as Future Archetype of Resistance*, the ending of the 2019 Black Panther movie that shows the landing of a Mothership in Oakland, Jenn Nkiru's REBIRTH IS NECESSARY, and Oakland Museum of Art's "Mothership: Voyage Into Afrofuturism" exhibit.[9] In the 2022 *Muslim Futurism* exhibition, Samira Idroos's "The Force is Female" (2020) textile art weaves a UFO/Mothership into traditional prayer rug floral motifs, speaking of prayer as a mode of spiritual transport. This work interweaves traditional Islamic art forms (of the prayer rug) and conceptions of spiritual ascension with sci-fi notions of UFOs. NOI references to the Mother Plane circle back to Islamic ritual practice and prayer envisioned as a mode of taking flight, one connected to notions of ascension, transcendence, and transport to other worlds. Representations of the Mother Plane surface and resurface in Afrofuturist cultural production as vehicles and agents of mental, spiritual, physical, and temporal transport.

While the Mother Plane gives material form to flight and fugitivity—and to the concept of transport to other lands and other worlds in time and space—the Yakub teaching speaks of white terror and the inhumanity of eugenics, medical racism, and experimentation on human subjects. The teaching calls for reclaiming knowledge and science—and knowledge of Islam—as a means of countering a history of unethical and inhumane practices and reversing the damage inflicted. The artist Safiyah Cheatam explores this kind of "countermemory" in her MFA thesis project, which chronicles Black Muslim history in the United States through "a mundane Afrofuturist lens" and draws on Sofia Samatar's argument about "the labor of countermemory." [10] Building on Cheatam and Samatar's invaluable insights, alongside Alondra Nelson's article about the representation of biomedical experimentation in *A Black Mass*, I read the Yakub teaching as a counterhistory that details the physical and psychological effects of medical racism and eugenic pseudoscience on Black lives and bodies. Science-fiction literature from the Harlem Renaissance and the Black Arts Movement—namely George Schuyler's *Black No More* (1931) and Amiri Baraka's *A Black Mass* (1965)—provide interpretive tools ("hermeneutical possibilities")—for understanding the teaching and also for how it figured in critical understandings of Black Arts as reversing the deadening effects of inhuman (and inhumane) forms of Western "scientific" knowledge.[11] The theology of the Yakub teaching is a mode of race-reading as true as—or even truer than—science's myths. Or, it can be read as what Sun Ra calls "myth science."

A BLACK MASS AND MYTH SCIENCE

LeRoi Jones wrote *A Black Mass* in the aftermath of Malcolm X's assassination. He had moved uptown and founded the Black Arts Repertory Theatre School (BARTS) in Harlem in response to Malcolm's call for establishing a "cultural center in Harlem" that would conduct workshops in theater, music, writing, painting, film, and Black history. The charter of the Organization of Afro-American Unity (OAAU) called for cultural revolution: "We must recapture our heritage and our identity if we are ever to liberate ourselves from the bonds of white supremacy. We must launch a cultural revolution to unbrainwash an entire people. . . . Armed with the knowledge of our past, we can with confidence charter a course for our future. Culture is an indispensable weapon in the freedom struggle. We must take hold of it and forge the future with the past."[12] Although written in the offices of BARTS in Harlem, *A Black Mass* was first performed in Proctor's Theater in Newark in May 1966 after Jones moved home, with Sylvia Wilson performing the role of Tiila. After the Newark uprisings in 1967, Jones and Wilson would marry, taking the names Amiri and Amina Baraka. In 1968, the Barakas issued the play as an album through their Jihad Productions publishing house, featuring the voices of Yusuf Iman, Amina Baraka, and the music of Sun Ra and His Myth Science Arkestra. The following year, the mainstream publisher Bobbs-Merrill published the play in Baraka's collection *Four Black Revolutionary Plays: All Praises to the Black Man* (1969). The play was a kind of cultural catalyst to the BAM—held up by Larry Neal as an exemplar of the BAM ethos in two of his most important critical essays, both published in 1968: his "Black Arts Movement" essay in *The Drama Review* and the afterword to *Black Fire*, the volume he edited with Baraka.[13] In the afterword, Neal calls for a Black literature that achieves a sense of "collective ritual" in the way Black music operates as ritual. *A Black Mass* achieves that, Neal argues, as does the music and poetry of Sun Ra.[14]

Sun Ra's sonic interpretation of the Yakub teaching brings out the origins story's "myth-science" dimensions, but the music also functions as a kind of proto-Afrofuturist reading of Yakub. The music of Sun Ra and His Myth Science Arkestra is written into the script at key junctures: in the description of the setting (soft peaceful music that then fills the room swelling and screeching), in the climactic emergence of the white beast ("Sun-Ra music of shattering dimensions"), and as the women shriek "Sun-Ra songs."[15] Sun Ra's "myth science" opens up "hermeneutical possibilities" for interpreting the Yakub teaching, riffing on its Afrofuturistic, sci-fi dimensions that Finley sees as so necessary to its meaning.[16] The play is infused with a sci-fi ethos, with the stage set in a scientists' laboratory with futuristic tones (or what Sun Ra might call *Cosmic Tones*):

> Jet blackness, with maybe a blue or red-violet glow. Soft peaceful music (Sun-Ra). Music of eternal concentration and wisdom.... Three Black Magicians. They are dressed in long exquisite robes, one with skullcap, one with fez, one with African hat (fila). The outline of some fantastic chemical laboratory is seen, with weird mixtures bubbling, colored solutions (or solutions that glow in the dark).... Signs in Arabic and Swahili on the wall. Strange drawing, diagrams of weird machines.[17]

This passage seems to refer to Sun Ra's "Sun-Organ," which lit up colors of the spectrum with low notes ("deep blues and dark colors") and high notes ("oranges and yellows") in what Sun Ra called a "tone poem."[18] Sun Ra also called his musicians "tone scientists"—and here, they interpret the Yakub teaching, reading it as a kind of theology of tone.[19] In his biography of Sun Ra, John Szwed calls Sun Ra the "silent partner" in Baraka's "consciousness of the possibilities of playing the spoken word against the written.... To young black poets he provided a means for releasing the words from the page, and for relocating them in the conventions of black instrumental and ritual performance."[20] Baraka clearly modeled *A Black Mass* on Elijah Muhammad's description of Yakub in *Message to A Blackman in America*, published in November 1965, around the time he wrote the play. Like Louis Farrakhan's *Orgena* (first performed in 1959), this was a different kind of musical, Black performance, theater, and drama that critiqued the whitening of Black art as a form of violence against Black life.

In August 1966, following the first performance of *A Black Mass* in Newark the previous May, Jones published an essay in *DownBeat* magazine about performances by Sun Ra, Marion Brown, and Pharoah Sanders at the Jazz Arts Society in Newark. He wrote about their music in mystical spiritual terms and used the NOI language of blue-eyed devils living in caves. But he also framed his analysis in sci-fi terms, talking about space and spaceships, as a metaphor for resurrection or the afterlife. Jones wrote that the Arkestra uses knowledge of "Wisdom Religion" toward "actual evolution through space, not only in space ships, but of the higher principles of humanity, the progress after the death of the body."[21] Baraka would later reflect that *A Black Mass* brought out the "otherworldliness" of the Yakub teaching through the "outness" of Sun Ra and His Myth Science Arkestra.[22] He observed how aspects of their aesthetic collaboration illuminated historical dimensions of the teaching—a "mythologized history" whose facts they "scientifically" illuminate: "The collaboration between word and music... both connect and extend each other with a dramatic gestalt of Myth-Science music and the mythologized history deepens our emotional perception of what is being told... it even projects a rationale that's more scientifically based, 'search-lighting' some evasive facts of human history."[23] The play uses what Kodwo Eshun terms *sonic fiction* as a way of exploring a painful past, looking at it as something strange and (what the Southern Poverty Law Center called) bizarre, but also as something inhuman/e. Confronting it is also a way of getting free of it. The science fiction tone of *A Black Mass* brings out the dystopian elements of the history the Yakub teaching describes—and the Afrofuturistic aesthetic and philosophy signaled by Sun Ra charts a path out of the madness. Afrofuturism transmits "hope across the transhistorical feedback loop," the scholar Isiah Lavender writes in *Afrofuturism Rising*, "a charged impulse representing the desire for life, liberty, and knowledge... reverberat[ing] across time and space, linking past, present, and future."[24]

Both Sun Ra and Louis Farrakhan recounted experiences of transport in UFOs—Sun Ra to Saturn and Farrakhan when he was at the top of a mountain in Mexico near the ruins of a temple of Quetzalcoatl. Farrakhan described meeting Master Fard Muhammad and Elijah Muhammad in the Mother Wheel, evoking elements of the Prophet Muhammad's night journey (*isra'*) and his ascension (*mi'raj*) into heaven where he meets other prophets. Finley speculates on the account's relationship to popular science fiction and film, like H. G. Wells's *The War of the Worlds* (1895–97). But he shuts down this line of analysis, not wanting to question—or cast aspersion on—the authenticity of Farrakhan's report.[25] Similarly, my aim is not to question the truth of Farrakhan's journey, nor to trace direct lines of influence between science fiction and NOI teachings, but rather to explore science fiction as an exegetical tool for interpreting NOI teachings. The teachings speak back to dominant scientific paradigms that permeated popular culture at the time and offer an alternative kind of "myth science," epistemologies rooted in—and drawing on—Black knowledge and the experience and history of scientific racism. This "counter-science" dismantles dominant discourses, unraveling them by going back to their epistemological premises, and unmaking subjectivities forged through "positivity in the human sciences." Britt Rusert calls this a form of "fugitive science"—a means to "critique racist science and to mobilize scientific knowledge," creating "rich speculative terrain."[26] In this chapter I explore the "fugitive science" of the NOI through the "dynamic scientific engagements and experiments of black writers, performers, artists, and other cultural producers who mobilized natural science and produced alternative knowledges in the quest for and name of freedom." This cultural production, writes Rusert, "profoundly meditate[s] on the category of the human itself"—but also on what being humane means in relation to our collective sense of humanity.[27]

The Yakub teaching—and *A Black Mass*—meditates specifically on the inhumanity of scientific racism, especially with respect to medical ethics. It critiques social Darwinist concepts of evolution unfolding according to a progressive linear hierarchy by inverting its logic, depicting it as a form of regression and dehumanization. In two key essays published in 1968, Larry Neal held up *A Black Mass* as emblematic of the ethos of the BAM.[28] His essay "The Black Arts Movement" called for reevaluating and reordering Western cultural ethics and aesthetics, its "alien sensibility," and its "anti-human nature." The BAM, he writes, is

> an ethical movement. Ethical, that is, from the viewpoint of the oppressed. And much of the oppression confronting the Third World and Black America is directly traceable to the Euro-American cultural sensibility. This sensibility, anti-human nature, has, until recently, dominated the psyches of most Black artists and intellectuals.... It is this natural reaction to an alien sensibility that informs the cultural attitudes of the Black Arts and Black Power movement; ... it is a profound ethical sense.[29]

Neal cites Aimé Césaire, evoking Césaire's understanding of colonial domination as a form of dehumanization through the inhumanity of the colonizer, a "brutalization" that is effectively the colonizers' rapaciousness, violence, racism, and moral relativism. The Yakub teaching represents the inhumanity of white oppression, as knowledge metamorphoses into ignorance and human into beast along a continuum of racialization that creates whiteness as a form of evil. "Race itself was a monster if ever Americans conceived one," observes Bruce Dain, "but a monster hidden in their minds."[30]

A Black Mass is a type of passion play allegorically dramatizing the historical realities of scientific racism, eugenics practices, and medical experimentation. The science fiction elements serve as a means of portraying the strange fictions of scientific racism and moreover, the horrors of its practices that had real, material consequences for Black lives.[31] Informed by Isiah Lavender's scholarship on race and science fiction, I also seek to study "the specific overlaps of history and imagination with proper seriousness as they relate to human experience" with particular attention to "the development of scientific racism through literary, scientific, and cultural discourses."[32] Sf provides a way of interpreting both the Yakub theology and the history it depicts: scientific myths about race propagated by eugenics discourses and practices. Through the figure of the "beast," the teaching also reflects on the monstrosity, barbarity, and immorality of these practices—by turning social Darwinism upside down and making racial whiteness the nadir of devolution.

YAKUB'S BLACKGROUND

A number of scholars, like Bowen, Clegg, and Finley, speculate on the relationship between sf literature, film, and radio and NOI teachings about the Mother Plane. Clegg draws connections between the NOI founder Fard Muhammad's contention "that there was intelligent life on Mars" and cultural representations of life in other worlds in film and literature (like H. G. Well's *War of the Worlds*).[33] Other sf works circulated at the time of the NOI's founding have echoes and reverberations in the Yakub teaching, like George Schuyler's *Black No More* (1931) and the film *Island of the Lost Souls* (1931) based on Wells's *Island of Dr. Moreau* (1898). *Black No More* tells the story of the Black scientist Dr. Julius Crookman, who devises a procedure for turning Black people white, opening maternity wards and hospitals with the specific objective of whitening brown babies from mixed race relationships—a story with uncanny echoes in the Yakub teaching. Isiah Lavender identifies *Black No More* as forming what he calls the "blackground" of sf as a genre, a term he coins "to define the embedded perceptions of race and racism—intended or not—in Western sf and criticism. 'Blackground' brings race and racism to the foreground of science fiction as it relates to the critical discussion of the black/white binary." Lavender's book *Race in American Science Fiction* links "social concepts such as miscegenation and passing for white with a variety of classic sf motifs," with the aim of examining "the pervasiveness of race in sf."[34] More importantly, Lavender demonstrates how the racialized texts and subtexts of literary and cultural production shape scientific racism and vice versa.

Black No More: An Account of the Strange and Wonderful Workings of Science in the Land of the Free (1931) is set in the "future"—in 1934—which is also the date of the NOI's "Lost Found Muslim Lessons" that include the Yakub teaching. Schuyler's *Black No More* can be situated alongside other key Harlem Renaissance texts like James Weldon Johnson's *Autobiography of an Ex-Colored Man* (1912/1927), Jessie Fauset's *Plum Bun* (1928), and Nella Larsen's *Passing* (1929)—fictionalized memoirs that thoughtfully analyzed the mortal dangers and psychological trauma of navigating the color line, although *Black No More* satirized them.[35] These literary texts formed the "blackground" of the Yakub teaching and the NOI's theorization of the eugenicist dimensions of racial mixing. These Harlem Renaissance texts also formed the "blackground" of what would become the BAM, as writers took up and reinterpreted the Yakub teaching, like Baraka did in *A Black Mass*. My analysis draws on Margot Natalie Crawford's understanding of how the Harlem Renaissance (HR) anticipated the BAM, shaping the HR's "more militant tones." "Harlem Renaissance texts that can almost pass as Black Arts texts pivot on the conceptual edge" of the HR, she writes, "an edge of this cultural movement that was not fully formed and that approached the aesthetic theory and practice of BAM."[36] The theoretical back and forth in time that Crawford describes is at the heart of sci-fi as a genre, a technique that the Yakub teaching deploys. The story is projected back in time 6,600 years and grapples with the origins of the Lost Found Nation of Islam, but it also reflects the historical context of its formulation in the early 1930s: discourses about race circulating in popular science and popular culture and Fard Muhammad's own dialogues with Elijah Muhammad.

Harlem Renaissance literary texts about passing grappled with the nature of Black art and its relationship to the white literary mainstream, appearing as sometimes anguished reflections on literary debates of the time about the nature of Black art and literature. Critical BAM cultural production like *A Black Mass* was forged in these earlier cultural-theological debates about race, miscegenation, and eugenics, but also about Black art versus white art, assimilation versus separation, Black cultural specificity versus the white mainstream, middle class values versus the Black below, and high versus low art. I explore the Yakub teaching's embeddedness in the historical context of scientific fictions about race, but also in science fiction literature about race. Schuyler's *Black No More* formed part of the "blackground" of the Yakub teaching, as did the colonial racism in mainstream sci-fi fiction like H. G. Wells's *Island of Dr. Moreau* and its Hollywood film adaptation *Island of the Lost Souls*.[37] Sun Ra and Amiri Baraka's collaboration on *A Black Mass* orchestrated their own reading of the Yakub teaching through a sci-fi lens, picking up on the "more militant tones of the Harlem Renaissance." But they also kicked off the BAM with a celebration of Black art in the streets of Harlem—a BARTS parade down 125th Street led by Sun Ra and His Myth Science Arkestra.

POPULAR SCIENCE AND EXPERIMENTATION ON HUMAN SUBJECTS

The Yakub teaching uses the word "germ" as it was used in late nineteenth- and early twentieth-century scientific writings that understood heredity as passed through what they called the "germ plasm," a term referring to August Weismann's theory that hereditary information is carried in the "germ cell," meaning gametes like egg cells and sperm cells.[38] In the early twentieth century, eugenicists adopted concepts of the "germ plasm" thinking that characteristics of "degeneracy"—like crime, mental health, depression, learning disabilities, disease, and illness (or of social "degeneracy" like prostitution, sexual promiscuity, and even rape and incest)—were passed on via germ cells. Believing that such "characteristics" represented a kind of "reversion or atavism of a bestial ancestor of humanity," eugenicists argued for restricting the reproduction of "degenerate elements of society" through sterilization and/or institutionalization.[39] Michigan, where Elijah Muhammad and his wife Clara lived between 1923 and 1934— and where they first met Fard Muhammad in 1931—passed laws allowing forced sterilizations in 1913, 1923, and 1929, policies that disproportionately targeted African Americans.[40] Estimating from data where race was reported, 18 percent of the patients were African American, though they constituted only 3.5 percent of the population, and 13 percent were mixed race, totaling nearly 30 percent of the number of sterilizations.[41] Forced sterilization became legal in 1927 with the Supreme Court case *Buck v. Bell*. Some of the main supporters of sterilization laws were eugenicists like Dr. John Harvey Kellogg, president and founder of the "Race Betterment Foundation" in Battle Creek, Michigan, an organization that held conferences in 1914, 1915, and 1928 coinciding with the ratification of the sterilization laws. Moreover, euthanasia of newborn infants was a known practice, "in hospital jargon of the times, they were 'set aside' . . . to live or die," writes Jeffrey Hodges, whose MA thesis argues that "Michigan's policies did provide a legal basis for much of what the Nazis would proceed to carry out."[42]

Elijah Muhammad, né Elijah Poole, joined the NOI (then the Allah Temple of Islam) in 1931, becoming a "hundred percent convert" and a close companion of Fard, training to become a minister.[43] According to NOI teachings, Fard taught Elijah Muhammad the story of Yakub during this time in the early 1930s. The

Yakub teaching comes from sections of the NOI's foundational catechism the *Supreme Wisdom Lessons*, specifically the two "Lost Found Muslim Lessons" dated February 20, 1934, "presented as Fard Muhammad's examination of his student Elijah Muhammad." Both lessons were "said to have been given privately to Fard's leading minister Elijah Muhammad"—teachings born out of their private conversations, confidences, and mutual understandings.[44] Although Elijah Muhammad attributes the teaching to Fard, Michael Muhammad Knight notes that "the text of the Lessons reaches us exclusively through Elijah's mediation," meaning that there is no independent verification of their origins and exact dating.[45]

The dating, whether historically factual or theologically embedded in the catechism, conceptually situates the teaching in 1934. Knight observes that the catechism "evinces a thriving marketplace" of ideas "that informed the movement's early context. *The Supreme Wisdom Lessons* speak to this world, often drawing on intellectual trends, familiar themes, and imagery accessibly within a context such as 1930s Detroit."[46] Knight argues that the *Lessons* should be read in this context, "reflecting a setting in which the fundamental argument of eugenics discourses" and the era's prominent assumptions about human societies as breeding labs.[47] Knight focuses on the esoteric influences on NOI teachings (as do other scholars like Bowen and Solayman Idris) and eugenic theosophical speculation about race. But the teaching also reflected aspects of Fard's own experience with experimentation on live human subjects known as vivisection. While Fard was in prison at San Quentin between 1926 and 1929, the prison's chief surgeon Dr. Leo Stanley was performing grafting experiments on inmates. Stanley, a vocal eugenicist, sterilized about six hundred inmates during his time at San Quentin, but also conducted horrifying experiments grafting testicles—of animals like rams, goats, deer, and boars, as well as executed prisoners—onto living inmates.[48] The "first glandular implantation" was performed after the African American prisoner Fred Miller was executed in 1927—when Fard would have been in prison.[49] Stanley used needles to inject "'strips of fresh testicle,' mashed to the consistency of toothpaste" into the abdomen of the inmates, believing that crime grew out of "glandular defects" in the "germ-plasm."[50] These science experiments created their own stranger than fiction fictions about race, and also about mental health, sexuality, and disabilities. These scientific fictions were also historical realities with elements of horror.

In the 1920s—while Fard was at San Quentin—the surgical and medical wards were in the same building (Building 22) as the prison library and education center, meaning that Stanley's activities were in close proximity to any books, scientific knowledge, or self-education available to the inmates.[51] In his early 1938 article about the NOI, Erdmann Beynon writes that Fard suggested writings like Hendrik van Loon's *Story of Mankind* (1921) to his followers, something that Patrick Bowen explores in his *History of Conversion to Islam in the United States*. More likely, Fard was recommending H. G. Wells's hugely popular and widely circulated *A Short History of Mankind* (1925)—a book that talks about early ("primitive") priests as scientists.[52] In the chapter "The First True Men," Wells writes how "at the very outset of the known human story, mankind was already racially divided into at least two main varieties," black and brown, talking about the brown as "tall and big brained," the way Yakub is described.[53] The Yakub teaching echoes some of Wells's key passages about human differentiation into races, especially his description of how "brownish people" with ancestors in Asia evolved to

> a more blond variety of men with blue eyes, . . . branching off from the main mass of brownish people, a variety which many people now speak of as the Nordic race. In the more open regions of northeastern Asia was another differentiation of this brownish humanity; . . . in the south of Asia were remains of the early negroid people. The central parts of Africa were already a region of racial intermixture. Nearly all the coloured races of Africa to-day seem to be blends of the brownish peoples of the north with a negroid substratum.[54]

Wells expanded on these theories of racial evolution in *Science of Life* (1930), written with Julian Huxley, the evolutionary biologist who was also vice president and president of the British Eugenics Society, brother of the science fiction writer Aldous Huxley. (Aldous Huxley's *Brave New World* [1932] was initially composed as a parody of Wells's *Men Like Gods* [1923].) Wells and Huxley's chapter "How Individuals Originate" synthesized evolutionary debates about racial characteristics and heredity circulated at that time. The chapter included sections on grafts and the "germ cell" of the "germ plasm." The "germ plasm," they write in their chapter "The A B C of Genetics," "shifts now and then and changes, and the race alters a little," causing mutations in "pure" genetic lines.[55] In the same chapter, they explore eugenicist Charles Benedict Davenport's work on miscegenation that attempted to "provide statistical evidence for biological and cultural degradation following interbreeding between white and Black populations."[56] Davenport, the director of the Station for Experimental Evolution and the Eugenics Record Office, advocated for both immigration restrictions and sterilization of "genetically inferior" races.[57]

The Yakub teaching reversed white supremacist understandings of biological and cultural degradation. It proffers what Lavender calls alternative histories of "cultural memory of past events" that use science fiction as a means "to expose and combat racism."[58] In Alondra Nelson's analysis of *A Black Mass*, she argues that "historical atrocities linking race and biomedical research have sedimented in the collective memory of African American communities.... *A Black Mass* could be described as crystallizing African American attitudes about scientific experimentation."[59] She writes specifically about the Tuskegee syphilis experiments that began in 1932 and were exposed in 1972. Yet other experiments had already been conducted in New York in 1912 by the scientist Hideyo Noguchi, who injected orphans and hospital patients with syphilis. Noguchi was working at the Rockefeller Institute for Medical Research, one of the leaders in eugenics research, around the time that John D. Rockefeller established the Bureau for Social Hygiene preoccupied with sexually transmitted diseases and prostitution. As part of his research, Noguchi injected both children and adults with syphilis at locations on Randalls Island across the Harlem River that included a children's hospital and asylum for juvenile "idiots," as well as a house of refuge for youth with criminal histories. He also injected patients at the Good Samaritan Dispensary in the lower East Side of Manhattan, a neighborhood at the time largely inhabited by "Hebrews."[60] (Hideyo Noguchi was a colleague of Yusaburo Noguchi—the Japanese scientist whose claim that he could turn Blacks white was satirized in Schuyler's *Black No More*.) The strangeness and cruelty of these science experiments—the injection of sexually transmitted diseases into children, grafting of glands onto prisoners, and forced sterilizations—are gruesome testaments to science gone awry.

SCI-FI, POPULAR CULTURE, AND YAKUB

In Patrick Bowen's book on the African American Islamic Renaissance, he speculates on possible sources for early NOI teachings, focusing mainly on theosophical and theological sources, but also on science fiction ones like Wells's *War of the Worlds*.[61] There are "specific overlaps of history" with these teachings "as they relate to human experience" and specifically to medical racism.[62] The Yakub teaching itself reads like science fiction—with its mad scientist conducting experiments on human subjects (vivisection) with the aim of breeding a new race. But it also references actual legal policies and medical practices through its terminology and vocabulary of grafting, breeding, birth control, and the "germ" of racial identity. It draws on the vocabulary of eugenics discourses, but also depicts historical *practices* of forced sterilization, grafting, and experimentation on human subjects. The teaching portrays miscegenation and racial mixing as diluting racial purity and propagating a sickly, degenerate "breed," characterizing whiteness as weak, sick, and evil, as the d/evil.

In 1929, the Japanese biologist Yusaburo Noguchi returned from his "jungle studies" in Brazil claiming that he could change the "racial characteristics of human beings" through "electrical nutrition and glandular control . . . beginning when the patient was a child." An article in the *New York Times* reports that not only could Noguchi change racial color on "the physical side, but in the mental as well," as in the case of "underdeveloped children . . . with distinct mental deficiencies."[63] The report circulated in a number of different newspapers, including the *Pittsburgh Courier*, where the writer George Schuyler had a column and where Elijah Muhammad would later publish his own column "Mr. Muhammad Speaks."[64] The news note formed the basis of *Black No More*. Its preface included an account of Noguchi's claim alongside a disturbing letter written by an electrical engineer to the NAACP that called for experiments to remove pigment from Black skin. The book's title refers to skin lightening treatments and specifically Ida White-Duncan's hair straightening product "Kink-No-More."[65] Noguchi's claim—and Schuyler's dramatization of that claim—came at a time when the Japanese were forging alliances with African American groups within the United States, including with the NOI, seeking to "organize the colored people" toward the "unification of all the darker people of the world."[66] In this context, Noguchi's claims would appear to be going in the wrong direction and as a betrayal of the cause, more indicative of the Japanese's growing interest in ideas of racial hierarchies that led them into World War II.

Black No More dramatizes the historical details of Noguchi's visit to the United States—his newspaper conference and nonsensical claims of using "electrical nutrition and glandular control" as the reductio ad absurdum of the eugenics movement's premises.[67] Schuyler's use of sf as a tool of satire—and satire as a tool of sf—brilliantly work in tandem to parody scientific racism. Schuyler imagines Noguchi as the Black scientist Dr. Junius Crookman who creates a "devilish machine" able to turn Blacks white, including mixed-race newborns.[68] The name "Crookman," suggests the eugenicist F. G. Crookshank, author of *The Mongol in Our Midst: A Study of Man and His Three Faces* (1924), a book that compared anatomical and physiological similarities of the "Mongol Race (true Orientals)" and "so-called Mongolian imbeciles," as well as the "kinship between the gorilla and the Negro, the chimpanzee and Semites, and the orangutan and Orientals. It is an important milestone in the 'medicalization of eugenics' . . . and scientific racism," writes Michael Kohlman.[69] Books like these published in the popular British *To-day and To-morrow* book series demonstrate "the futuristic accuracy (or fantasy) of classic science fiction."[70] *Black No More* is a seminal but neglected text of the Harlem Renaissance, writes Lavender, analyzing "social concepts such as miscegenation" that are linked to "a variety of classic sf motifs."[71]

Scholars of the NOI speculate on the influence of Wells's *War of the Worlds* on NOI conceptions of the Mother Plane. His *Island of Doctor Moreau* (1898) describes, much like the Yakub teaching, how a scientist on a remote island fashions a hybrid race (called Beast people in the novel) through a brutal process of grafting and experimentation on living beings (known as vivisection). In 1932, Hollywood studios made the novel into a science fiction horror film *Island of the Lost Souls*, following releases of *Frankenstein* and *Dr. Jekyll and Mr. Hyde* in 1931. Dr. Moreau is modeled after the French scientist François Magendie, whose experimentations on live animals in the late nineteenth century led to the emergence of the antivivisection movement. In the novel the Beast people are barely concealed depictions of the colonized as half human and half animal—a colonial allegory of an incomplete civilizing mission carried out by a cast of characters—a shipwrecked narrator, a magician scientist ruling the island, his accomplice, and a Caliban-like manservant, all straight out of Shakespeare's *The Tempest*. Wells describes the Beast people as "simian" black- and brown-faced devils with "negroid" features.[72] The Beast Folk on the island include, among others, Leopard Man, Ape Man, Wolf Woman, and Panther Woman. (While running a contest to search for the starlet to play the Panther Woman in the film, a Detroit contestant appeared on stage at different Detroit theaters for three weeks in a row—where both Elijah Muhammad and Fard Muhammad were living at the time.) When the Beast Folk revert to their animal state in *The Island of Dr. Moreau,* they start to crawl on all fours and eat their food raw, as in the Yakub teaching. In prison with Fard at San Quentin was the serial killer and child rapist Gordon Stewart Northcott, who authorities called "Ape Man," purportedly because of the thick hair that covered his body.

In his American Museum in New York, P. T. Barnum displayed African Americans with vitiligo and albinism, calling them "Leopard Men" like the Leopard Man character in *Island of Doctor Moreau*, and joining part of a longer racist history of exhibiting "Negroes Turning White."[73] Schuyler's *Black No More* retells and critiques this history as sci-fi, partly through the character of Dr. Crookman who studied "skin diseases" in Germany, including "a nervous disease known as vitiligo" that "removes skin pigment and sometimes turns a Negro completely white."[74] In New York, where Schuyler lived, the Dreamland Circus on Coney Island displayed a "leopard man" in 1930, just before he published *Black No More*.[75] Other literary and experimental texts of the era played on Wells's concept, like the book *Black Magic* (1928), a fictionalized memoir by the eugenicist Nazi collaborator Paul Morand. Morand's chapter "Panther-Man" in *Black Magic* is a thinly disguised racist mockery of W. E. B. Du Bois at the Second Pan-African Congress in Brussels in 1921. It describes a visit by a "Dr. Lincoln" to the Museum of the Belgian Congo where, captivated by the experience, he transforms into a panther. The Black Panther imagery would later be reclaimed as an emblem of freedom and justice—first through the Lowndes County Freedom Organization's snarling black panther logo it used to advocate for voters rights in Alabama, then through Jack Kirby's Black Panther character, then through the Black Panther Party formed by Huey Newton and Bobby Seal in Oakland, and then through the Black Panther film franchise. The Black Panther imagery would also be reappropriated and transformed in the Afrofuturist work of Black Kirby, Stacy Robinson, and Jack Jennings who "through established aesthetics and classic comic noir ... deconstruct, recreate, sample, remix, and restructure Jack Kirby's imagery and flip the script on a White male dominated culture," creating "a quasi-graphic-gumbo of AfroFuturism, Hip Hop, souped-up bricolage, digital-ocular hacking, insanely esoteric meta-references, and outrageous formal experimentations."[76]

The Yakub teaching can be situated in a tradition of "African diasporic cultural production" that "engages in imaginative practices of worlding from the perspective of a history of blackness's bestialization," as Zakiyyah Iman Jackson writes in *Becoming Human: Matter and Meaning in an Antiblack World*. The teaching engages in these kinds of "practices of worlding" through a theology that identifies white racialization as a process of bestialization. It constructs what Jackson calls "a critical praxis of being, paradigms of relationality, and epistemologies that alternately expose, alter, or reject ... the racialization of the human-animal distinction found in Western science and philosophy." It introduces "dissidence into philosophical and scientific frameworks that dominate definitions of the human."[77] The white "Ape Man" at San Quentin, as well as the white "Panther Woman" in the *Island of Lost Souls* suggest whites engaging in "dangerous crossings" (in Claire Jean Kim's words) with animals. The *Island of Dr. Moreau* is a metaphor for colonialism, but it also allegorizes racial mixing as the creation of animal-human hybrids through vivisection or experimentation on live subjects. Although Wells's racist allegory dehumanizes the colonized, it is ultimately a story about the inhumanity of the colonizer, about how colonialism's racial capitalism subjugates, exploits, and taints the animal world as much as the human. Fard directly experienced this inhumanity at San Quentin: through Leo Stanley's experiments injecting animal tissue into humans, and through the white "Ape Man," Gordon Stewart Northcott, who inflicted brutal crimes on children.

In 1929, Schuyler published a pamphlet titled "Racial Intermarriage in the United States" advocating his own solution to the problem of the color line—just after marrying Josephine Cogdell, a white heiress from Texas. *Black No More* was published in 1931, the year his daughter Philippa was born, a child prodigy of the piano who experimented with passing herself, changing names and identities between Europe and the United States.[78] In *Black No More*, Dr. Crookman writes that his sociology teacher believed there were only three ways to solve the "Negro problem": "To either get out, get white or get along," words that would later inform the title of Jordan Peele's sci-fi horror film *Get Out*, a meditation on similar themes of racial mixing, medical racism, experimentation on human subjects, and white brainwashing.[79] Lavender argues that *Black No More* "is a powerful critique of the racial hierarchy of American society and our preoccupation with skin color and concepts of racial purity and white supremacy." Using this strategy," Lavender says, Schuyler "makes an explicit science fictional account of race and racism in American culture" that suggests "a strong conviction about the arbitrary—even worthless—nature of race from a scientific standpoint."[80] Others read Schuyler's book as "assimilationist," representing what Langston Hughes called the "urge to whiteness" in the classic essay he wrote responding to Schuyler's "Negro-Art Hokum." In *Racechanges*, Susan Gubar argues that Schuyler's novel "views the demise of blackness as the only viable solution for African Americans," effectively functioning "as a form of genocide, threatening to annihilate all African Americans."[81]

Black No More, *Island of the Lost Souls*, and the Yakub teaching all function as exegeses of transnational eugenics discourses and practices that circulated as both popular science and popular culture. The Black scientist who develops "Black-No-More as [a] device of the Devil," opens maternity wards to whiten babies, and uses nurses, doctors, and ministers to carry out his project—all have echoes in the Yakub story. Both the teaching and the novel reference unethical practices of experimentation on human subjects. The Yakub teaching was formulated in the midst of this science fiction cultural production: Schuyler's *Black No More*, the film *Island of the Lost Souls* (based on Wells's *Dr. Moreau*), as well as the stranger-than-fiction scientific claims of Yusaburo Noguchi, the grafts of Leo Stanley, and Noguchi's classmate Hideye Noguchi's syphilis injections predating the Tuskegee experiments. These fictions of science (and science fictions) were likely less direct influences or "sources" (in Bowen's words) than part of the historical reality and cultural context of the teaching's emergence. They were realities treated and analyzed in the popular culture of their time, as facts made fictions and fictions made facts. The Yakub teaching described crimes of medical racism and bioscientific experimentation, experiences of racial terror that "were unspeakable," though "these terrors were not inexpressible," Paul Gilroy writes in *The Black Atlantic*.[82]

A BLACK MASS AND GENOCIDAL VIOLENCE AGAINST BLACK LIFE

Baraka's *A Black Mass* dramatizes the science fiction elements in the Yakub teaching for the BAM era, although it was written before he embraced Islam. The play also portrays the strange and disturbing history of scientific experimentation on Black bodies: eugenics projects to limit the births of Black babies; sterilization policies and laws, forced and otherwise; and unethical experimentation on human subjects like the Tuskegee syphilis experiment, but also the earlier experiments of the two Noguchis. In Lavender's *Race in American Science Fiction*, he explores how science fiction popularizes scientific theories by making them understandable to a general public without extensive knowledge of science. "Sf's vision," he argues, "concerns the cultural and philosophical consequences of technological advancement and scientific progress." It enriches "our understanding of Western society's violent past." Science fiction continually frames "ideas of race through invoking the cultural influence of science" even while "always questioning the cultural moment. It occupies a privileged position from which it is capable of attuning its readership to the intersections of scientific theory, technological development, and social conventions," particularly with respect to issues of race, though this remains a sublimated aspect of sci-fi only recently theorized in the work of Lavender and others.[83]

A Black Mass functions as an allegory of white genocide against Black life and of white violence against Black women—something key scholars like Alondra Nelson, Werner Sollors, and Melani McAlister have noted.[84] Nelson developed this analysis in conjunction with her own work on medical discrimination, genetics, and race in the United States, seeing *A Black Mass* as a commentary on "the racial stakes of bioscientific experimentation."[85] Her article "*A Black Mass* as Black Gothic: Myth and Bioscience in Black Cultural Nationalism" was published after the seminal special issue on Afrofuturism she edited for *Social Text*. The article grapples with Baraka's vision of scientific racism and genocidal eugenics, interpreting the play as "a narrative about bioscience and race" and "the laboratory power relations that typify the history of racial science."[86] The play, she argues, portrays the history of scientific experimentation on Black bodies as it is "sedimented in the collective memory of African American communities."[87]

The Yakub teaching both appropriates and inverts eugenics discourses, subverting them by reversing their racial assumptions. But the teaching also stakes a claim to scientific knowledge—knowledge of the original people of science—gesturing to the historical role of Islamic knowledge in developing science and math, but also the corruption of that knowledge when stripped of its ethical bases. It critiques the racial dimensions and genocidal elements of eugenics practices that represent a corruption of scientific knowledge—racial differentiation that evolved in European societies partly through their confrontation with Muslims and Jews during the Reconquista, Inquisition, and Crusades. The Yakub teaching allegorically depicts the monstrosity of eugenics programs, their experimentation on live human subjects, and their use of forced sterilization. Elijah Muhammad's *Message to the Blackman*, published just before Baraka wrote *A Black Mass*, "outlines the story of Yakub in far greater detail than any of the movement's [earlier] catechisms," writes Edward E. Curtis IV in an essay on the science fiction elements in NOI teachings. The Yakub teaching evokes "parallels between German *rassenhygiene* (racial hygiene) and racist eugenics program in the United States" and specifically, the forced sterilization of Black women.[88] It is well known that these programs provided the basis of some of the scientific experiments and eugenics practices developed in Nazi Germany.[89] Yakub's "final solution for the black race," Curtis observes, "reflected some of the most horrific applications of science and technology in the 20th century."[90] He hypothesizes that the Yakub teaching was developed in the aftermath of the holocaust because of its references to a "cremator," but scholars recognize that different versions of the teachings developed over time.[91]

Message to the Blackman was published just after the legalization of birth control (for married couples) in the June 1965 Supreme Court decision in favor of Planned Parenthood. The book—and NOI doctrine—describes birth control as a plan of white people to "destroy" Blacks and keep them "from being a nation through our women, as Pharaoh attempted to destroy Israel by killing off the male babies of Israel at birth. . . . The same goes for the so-called Negroes and the slave-masters' children. The slave-masters envy their once-slaves' future and want to destroy it."[92] The NOI saw birth control as part of a eugenics program to limit the reproduction of the Black race at a time when Black bodies "constantly faced the threat of violence" and women were subjected to forced sterilizations.[93] Opposition to birth control is detailed in issues of the NOI newspaper *Muhammad Speaks*, as well as in chapters like "Birth Control Death Plan!" and "Plan to Destroy Our Race" in *Message to the Blackman*. The NOI viewed birth control, family planning, and abortion as forms of racial genocide.[94] In *Women, Race, and Class* (1981), Angela Davis argues that birth control became suspect among the Black community in a climate of eugenicist campaigns to limit Black births through sterilization and other means—and also became a major premise of the "cultural nationalist line against birth control" that the movement "deemed genocide."⁹⁵

The making of the white beast inverts eugenics discourses of white supremacy and racial theories of social Darwinism, depicting a regression from Black to white, from knowledge to ignorance, from human to animal. But it is also an ethical commentary on racism as a form of moral degeneracy—reflected in the inhumanity of the oppressor. The chapter "The Making of the Devil" in *Message to the Blackman* describes a devolution "into the family of wild beasts—going upon all fours; eating raw and unseasoned, uncooked food; living in caves and tree tops, climbing and jumping from one tree to the other. Even today, they like climbing and jumping. The monkeys are from them. Before their time, there were no such things as monkeys, apes and swine."⁹⁶ (In *Dr. Moreau*, the "Law" given by the scientist to the Beast Folk includes two main rules—that they must not go upon all fours or eat raw food.) If *Dr. Moreau* can be read as an incredibly racist allegory of the colonial project, the Yakub teaching depicts the dehumanization of Euro-American racial hierarchies. In the words of Aimé Césaire, colonialism "dehumanizes even the most civilized man," "brutalizes" the colonizer "in the true sense of the word," degrades him to "covetousness, violence, race hatred, and moral relativism," a "howling savagery" that poisons Europe. The colonizer, Césaire writes, "gets into the habit of seeing the other man as an animal, accustoms himself to treating him like an animal, and tends objectively to transform himself into an animal." Using words that echo NOI language—or that NOI language echoed—Césaire writes about trickery and the demon of Hitler that inhabits the colonizer, as he drains the colonized of their essence and smashes their religions.⁹⁷

A Black Mass brings out the Yakub teaching's message about the dehumanizing effects of biomedical experimentation, social Darwinism, and eugenics. This inhumanity is what the play calls a "projection of anti-humanity; ... the mirror image of creation, turned and distorted, given power."⁹⁸ The play describes this kind of thinking as being "against humanity ... and beyond human feeling. A gross distortion of the powers of righteousness." After Jacoub creates the beast in the play, the Black magicians say that it is "the substitution of thought for feeling. A heart full of numbers and cold formulae. A curiosity for anti-life, for the yawning voids and gaps in humanity."⁹⁹ The beast is an absence "of feeling, of thought, of compassion ... the twisted thing a man would be, *alone* ... without his human soul." The Black magicians ("scientists" in the NOI) implore the women to sing "Sun-Ra songs" "against this sucking death," using language of "sucking wind" from the song *Strange Fruit* ("Here is a fruit for the crows to pluck

/ For the rain to gather, for the wind to suck"). Speaking collectively as a chorus, they sing: "The earth is alien. Our mothers are sick. The world... is choking us." The white beast is antilife and antihumanity, a monster that has no heart, soul, feeling, or compassion. "THIS THING WILL KILL," says the Black magician Nasafi, "IT WILL TAKE HUMAN LIFE... BECAUSE IT HAS NO REGARD FOR HUMAN LIFE."[100]

BLACK MAGIC AND RAISING THE DEAD

The Yakub teaching is not only an allegory about the creation of the white race through pseudoscientific theories of racial differentiation—and a reflection on the corruption of scientific knowledge—but it is also about the necropolitics of white violence against Black bodies, women, and children. Achille Mbembe coined the term "necropolitics" in a 2003 essay that discussed how modern states function on the basis of "the sovereign right to kill," partly through the "subordination of everything to impersonal logic and the reign of calculability and instrumental rationality." These are features of the dehumanization of a purely technical industrial world that sees its victims as "savages," thereby legitimizing their lack of sovereignty, whether in the form of colonial occupation, enslavement, class oppression, or discrimination based on gender and sexuality.[101] Eugenics, as practiced in science and law, is a way of defining who deserves—and who is denied—full citizenship and full sovereignty, but also the right to life. It was coded into immigration restrictions against nonwhite and non-European Asians, Africans, and Latin Americans, but also into practices like forced sterilization and experimentation on human subjects. Mbembe argues that biopower functions "through dividing people into those who must live and those who must die. Operating on the basis of a split between the living and the dead, such a power... presupposes the distribution of human species into groups, the subdivision of the population into subgroups, and the establishment of a biological caesura between the ones and the others,... what Foucault labels with the term *racism*.... In the economy of biopower, the function of racism is to regulate the distribution of death and to make possible the murderous functions of the state."[102]

NOI teachings vigilate against racism's necropolitics—through Nation discourses of nationhood, sovereignty, and a "land of our own"—claiming justice, freedom, and equality as sovereign rights essential to life. NOI theologies aim to reverse the deadening effects of state necropolitics through what Elijah Muhammad repeatedly referred to as resurrection from a "mentally dead condition," from being "brainwashed" by white definitions and awakening to the knowledge of Islam as the religion of people of Afro-Asian descent in the Americas. He insisted, again and again, that this salvation and resurrection—and judgment—did not come *after* the death of the body, but in this life. "I am offering you LIFE eternally," writes Elijah Muhammad in *The Supreme Wisdom*, "and our enemies are offering you slavery and death."[103] Elijah Muhammad describes social death and its psychological (and physical) impact on Black lives as the effects of a racialized necropolitics: a mental status imposed by white definitions and a material status imposed by the structural racism of American society. In a 1964 interview for the San Francisco radio station KQED, Elijah Muhammad said that the mission of his teachings was giving life to the dead. He also spoke in terms of citizenship, arguing that white Americans, the slave masters, "have never made us citizens, and under law we cannot be made citizens. We could never be citizens as stated in their first slavery courts.... We are in alien country. We are aliens and not citizens."[104]

Around the time *A Black Mass* was first performed at Proctor's Theater in Newark in 1966, the writer and poet Henry Dumas interviewed Sun Ra at Slugs' Saloon in New York. In the interview, Sun Ra talked about the politics of citizenship in the "necropolis" and connected the word "negro" to "necro": "The black man is under the name of death. He carries it around with him. The word negro. It is the same as the word necro. The g and the c are interchangeable according to cosmic mathematics. It is an equation. A negro equals a necro. The sound of one is in the other. In the Greek necro means dead body. Necropolis is a city of the dead. Once you accept the name without checking into things, then you are automatically a citizen of the city."[105]

Sun Ra's words seem to draw on NOI teachings about "mentally dead so-called Negroes," but Sun Ra claimed that the Black Muslims took their ideas from *him*, specifically his connection of the words "negro" and "necro" as meaning "death." Sun Ra and his manager Alton Abraham, who cofounded El Saturn records together, circulated pamphlets and broadsheets in Chicago's Washington Park just off 54th Street, only a few blocks from the Moorish Science Temple of America (MSTA) headquarters on Wabash Avenue. In a 1986 interview, longtime Arkestra member John Gilmore said that the Black Muslims took their ideas from Sun Ra, who told them, "Negro meant 'dead body' and it came from a word 'necromancy.' He told them about interchangeable g's and c's and other grammar, that's when they started giving themselves x's. They were filtering information from some of Sun Ra's papers."[106] Sun Ra's influence on the Black Muslims—and vice versa—is further explored in books by John Szwed, Graham Lock, John Corbett, Brent Hayes Edward, and William Sites.[107]

It is generally assumed that the "Black Muslims" Sun Ra influenced (or that influenced him) were NOI, but they may have (also) been MSTA.[108] The MSTA circulated the negro/necro connection in their catechism *Koran Questions for Moorish Children* before Herman "Sonny" Blount first visited Chicago in his senior year of high school, where he performed with his music teacher John "Fess" Whatley's band.[109] Sun Ra's later pamphlet "Jesus said, 'Let the Negro bury the Negro'" is structured as a series of questions and answers, much like the MSTA's *Koran Questions*, which connects the words "Negro" and "Black" to death.[110] In the pamphlet Sun Ra writes: "Unfortunately for the Negro the word Negro means dead body.... The Cemetery itself is named after the word Negro: Necropolis or City of the Dead.... Negro means dead body; ... if you like death and like being one of the Living dead then call yourself a Negro and continue to be rejected by the world as firstclass citizens."[111] Sun Ra might have picked up these ideas from the MSTA as it circulated in Chicago's cultural and religious ether, regenerating them in his own work. In his book about Sun Ra, Szwed observes that Elijah "Muhammad's idea that 'Negro' = 'death' Sonny felt was his own. He had discovered that Roger Bacon's book on ceremonial magic was called *De Nigromancia*, and he found in etymology books that the Middle English 'nigromancie'

FIGURE 3.1 Richard Saunders photographed Malcolm X in Harlem's Temple No. 7 in August 1963, titling this image "Deconstructing 'Negro.'"

Richard Saunders / Pictoral Parade / Archive Photos / Getty Images

had been formed by folk etymology from the Latin 'nigro' and had been substituted in Middle Latin for 'necro' (dead)."[112] Necromancy is the art of "raising the dead," but it is also "Black magic," one of the Black Arts. *A Black Mass* calls the Black scientists of the NOI teaching "Black magicians," or necromancers, interpreting the role of the Black artist as raising the dead and giving life to what Larry Neal called "dead ideas."[113]

In Dumas's interview, he uses NOI language, asking Sun Ra: "If the citizens of a necropolis are dead, how does one resurrect them?" Sun Ra answers: "through music and myth."[114] *A Black Mass* employs the "myth science" of Sun Ra's Myth Science Arkestra to riff on and revise the Yakub teaching, just as the Yakub teaching itself "revises" the standard texts of Islam in ways that many decried as heretical, but others saw as an Islamic revival for the particular context and conditions of racial oppression in the Americas. Elijah Muhammad created what Larry Neal called for when writing his "Black Arts Movement" essay—a separate symbolism and mythology, with the aim of radically reordering the ethics, epistemologies, and theologies of the Western cultural aesthetic.[115] These poets draw on what Michael Muhammad Knight calls "Muslim practices [that] contributed to what could be called African magic in the Americas," talismans and healing prayers provided by Muslim holy men that are "secret tunnels" and "holes in the fences" of "Islamic authenticity [and] 'orthodoxy.' "[116]

In the foreword to his 1968 anthology *Black Fire* edited with Larry Neal, Baraka describes BAM writers and poets using words that suggest a conjuring, but also an uprising and resurrection: "We rise, as we rise (agin). By the power of our beliefs ... These are the wizards, the bards, the *babalawo, shaikhs* of Weusi Mchoro." He uses Swahili words for "Black art," connecting it to Black magic ("wizards") but also to the holy men (*babalawo*) and religious scholars (*shaikhs*) of both Yoruban and Islamic West African religious traditions. He uses Arabic and Swahili, as the Black magicians do in the opening of *A Black Mass*. Larry Neal's afterword to *Black Fire* similarly calls for Black artists to be Black magicians, alchemists converting the dross of the world into glimmers of future worlds. He calls for a Black literature that achieves, like Black music, a sense of "collective ritual, but ritual directed at the destruction of useless, dead ideas, ... a ritual that affirms our highest possibilities." He calls for a "new sense of literature as a *living* reality" and for Black literature to perform the ritualistic function that Black music plays in "the collective psyche." He asks for the artists to "be a kind of priest, a black magician, working juju with the word on the world."[117] "Human beings are magical," Sylvia Wynter writes: "Bios and Logos. Words made flesh, muscle, and bone animated by hope and desire, belief materialized in deeds, deeds which crystalize our actualities."[118]

Baraka's later works *Answers in Progress* and "Rhythm Travel" would further explore the Afrofuturist potential of Black space, as would Askia Muhammad Touré in his collection *Songhai!*, which envisioned future cities and worlds. Writing about "Rhythm Travel," Paul Youngquist observes that "Baraka's work intersects with the brazenly sci-fi elements of free jazz, from Sun Ra's Astro-blackness to Ornette Coleman's *Science Fiction Sessions*. In the hands of these black artists, science fiction gets 'musicked,' to apply a phrase Baraka uses to describe poetry that recapitulates the disruptive sounds of bebop."[119]

"RIFFS, REVISIONS, AND REMEMBRANCES"

In *A Black Mass*, Baraka and Sun Ra engaged in a process of creative adaptation of the Yakub teaching, just as the Yakub teaching itself creatively improvises on the Islamic tradition "as an authenticating convention." In *Music Is the Muse*, Meta DuEwa Jones writes about the "formally experimental aesthetics developed" in jazz poetry, "improvisatory performances that alter the slant of tradition as an authenticating convention."[120] The artists engage in a "process, an act of struggle and creative adaptation."[121] Although Jones comments on the ritualistic function of jazz poetry, *A Black Mass* is a jazz play—performing the Yakub tradition and "planting roots in African American esoterica and expressive cultural forms and mores"[122] She describes this as a process of reading, revising, and recitation; "riffs, revisions, and remembrances . . . in order to maintain connections to the past while taking pleasure in their returns to and revisions of historical memory." *A Black Mass* performs what Jones calls the "ceremonial and communal function" of musically informed Black poetry, through "rituals of recital."[123] Here, it is a recital of the Yakub teaching, but it is also a passion play written in the aftermath of Malcolm X's assassination, an interrogation of white violence against Black life, an allegory of racialization, and a representation of obstetric and reproductive racism against Black women and children.

The Yakub teaching is an origins story about "the creation of the Original People on Earth, Mars, and Venus" seventy-six trillion years ago, a story about the past with futuristic science fiction elements, even as it speaks to the cultural context of its formulation.[124] The science fiction of *Black No More*, the NOI's Yakub teaching, and *A Black Mass* rework "Western conceptions of history and time" through "a dizzying back-and-forth toggle in time, in which subjects experience multiple temporalities simultaneously or out of joint," creating theater that is "closer to ritual than drama," write Soyica Colbert, Douglas Jones, and Shane Vogel.[125] *A Black Mass* stages the Yakub teaching as ritual, a conjuring up of the "original Black scientists" who become, in the play, Black magicians or necromancers who use Black art to resurrect the lost Nation of Islam through knowledge of the Black past. This kind of theater performance has "the capacity to warp or subvert the familiar and dominant through restorations—as repair or mending—of what has been forgotten, overlooked, misremembered, suppressed, dormant, or denied," write Colbert, Jones, and Vogel. It "can challenge the historical negation of populations and offer cultural workers in the present a useful past."[126]

Both Baraka and Sun Ra were poets and philosophers as well as theorists of music and its relationship to (the expression and construction of) race, identity, and belonging. Both believed in music—and poetry's—power of transport and its power to give life and raise the dead. Their collaboration on *A Black Mass* merges performance, drama, experimental jazz music, and critical race theory. Both interpreted Black art as a kind of necromancy, performances of rituals of recital to "raise the dead," but also to bring the past into the future through the present—and in doing so, enact a restoration. These fugitive pedagogies create what Sun Ra calls "alter-destiny / destinies" that go beyond the past, present, and future and reach outward beyond the possible.[127] Marvin X's *Resurrection of the Dead*, like *A Black Mass*, also ritualistically dramatized NOI teachings about the restoration of an Islamic identity, religion, and language that had been forgotten, suppressed, dormant, and denied. This resurrection connects an Islam of the past to a resurrected Islamic consciousness in the present, as a way of countering its suppression, but also, armed with this knowledge, charting an alternative course to the future. Marvin X staged *Resurrection of the Dead* in collaboration with Sun Ra when they were both teaching in Berkeley's Ethnic Studies Department in 1971 (and Sun Ra was teaching "Black Man in the Cosmos"). Forging Black Studies along with Amiri Baraka, Sonia Sanchez, Askia Muhammad Touré, and Marvin X—their own conversions converged with their understanding of Islam as providing epistemological bases for knowledge of self, beyond and against the Eurocentric bases of Western educational forms.

In the preface to his poetry collection *Black Magic* (1969), Baraka writes about the "deathurge of this twisted society, . . . the concept of hopelessness and despair, from the dead minds and dying morality of Europe. There is a spirituality always trying to get through, to triumph, to walk across these dead bodies like stuntin for disciples, walking the water of dead bodies Europeans call their minds."[128] Though the name LeRoi Jones is on the cover of the book, published by the mainstream press Bobbs-Merrill, the preface is signed with *As Salaam Alaikum* and his Islamic name Ameer Baraka.

Baraka constantly riffed on the philosophy and method of Sun Ra, just as they both riffed on Islamic signs and symbols in their poetics and performances. Baraka not only called Newark New Ark, but also the title of his 1971 book *Raise, Race, Rays, Raze* echoes the name of Sun Ra's first band The Cosmic Rays.[129] Throughout his life, Sun Ra punned on "rays," like in his poem "The Black Rays Race." The poem puns on tones and shades of meaning and sound: "See how the black rays of the black race / Have touched the immeasurable wisdom / ... See the unlimited freedom of the black rays."[130] In his essay on Sun Ra's poetry, Brent Hayes Edwards talks about the "epistemological work" of Sun Ra's Afrofuturism, forcing us to "alter our conception of what 'the inhabitants of this planet' can be. It 'races,' but more *razes* and *raises*, as Ra might say, the potential of the human."[131] Critics like Edwards, drawing on Duke Ellington, connect Sun Ra's destabilization of the concept of race through reference to the "space race" as a vision for a better future beyond the material exigencies of this world. Sun Ra's sense of a "space race" was connected to his understanding of Black people as a "sun people" in the solar system, invoked through the Egyptian sun god Ra, Sun Ra's adopted name Le Sony'r Ra [the sunnier Ra?], and the name everyone called him by, Sonny. Another Sun Ra poem "When Angels Speak" elaborates on the motif of cosmic flight by talking about music as an angelic language that makes myth not just audible but visible as "rays of darkness": "Wavelength infinity ... / Synchronizing the rays of black darkness/ Into visible being ... / Dark Living Myth-world of being."[132] Sun Ra's own homophonic, punning style plays on the word "rays" in the verse "synchronizing the rays of black darkness," destabilizing and reimagining "race" as "rays" in the poiesis of his tone poem.[133] Frequencies, vibrations, and wavelengths become modes of tapping into the esoteric language of the cosmos and the planets, like rays in the darkness. Through multiple layers of referentiality—to sound and sight, wavelengths and rays, visibility and invisibility—Sun Ra interprets the sensory power of music as a way of giving life to the blind, deaf, and dumb who do not see, hear, or understand.[134] His "tone poems" and "sound images" held up a "mirror that you must hear."[135]

The sci-fi, Afrofuturistic cultural production of the BAM functioned as a hermeneutic for interpreting the effects eugenics policies, white racial violence, and medical racism on Black life. Baraka's collaboration with Sun Ra on *A Black Mass* is often seen as one of the movement's founding texts, as they interpreted the Yakub teaching in what might be called a "tone theology," a way of reading and rereading the teaching's message about race and racism through "visual and audial significations of the word tones" operating "at the border between shade and sound."¹³⁶ The NOI's Yakub teaching forms the "blackground" of *A Black Mass*, just as the violence of scientific fictions about race formed the blackground of the NOI teaching and of Harlem Renaissance texts, like *Black No More*, that anticipated the BAM. The teachings of the NOI call for the alternative knowledges of fugitive science, performing a labor of counter-memory through knowledge of the Black past, but also charting trajectories to future political imaginaries. In Amiri Baraka's essay "Black Art, Nationalism, Organization, Black Institutions," published in *Raise, Race, Rays, Raze*, he wrote that "to be a black artist is to go back in time for the purpose of developing and defending what we need in the present for the future."¹³⁷ These BAM imaginaries provided conceptual and material space for catalyzing and realizing these futures, partly through what has become a thriving body of Afrofuturist literature, music, and visual art that emerged parallel to and in tandem with this BAM production—like the writings of Samuel Delany and Octavia Butler, who started publishing right around this same time alongside the music of Parliament, Funkadelic, and their *Mothership Connection*. John Akomfrah's *The Last Angel of History* (1996) charts a genealogy of this cultural production, with the narrator talking about excavating fragments of the past to find the keys to the future. A newer generation of Muslim artists and writers, including Safiyah Cheatam, Khaalidah Muhammad-Ali, Angel Nafis, and Vanessa Taylor, have built on this legacy and reenvisioned Afrofuturism "as a framework that recognizes Black suffering and critiques present day afflictions, while demanding for the interrogation and reexamination of the past." It is a history of ancestors and Black American Muslims who came before, developing what Taylor "the original tenets of the liberation theology that would drive movements" before she was born.¹³⁸ Cheatam worked as a curatorial research assistant on *Afrofuturism: A History of Black Futures*, an exhibit at the Smithsonian's National Museum of African American History and Culture. One of the opening images of the book published in conjunction with the exhibit shows Renée Cox's Afrofuturistic photograph *The Signing*, which reinterprets Howard Chandler Christy's painting of the founding fathers, *Scene at the Signing of the Constitution of the United States*.¹³⁹ Instead of George Washington, Cox stands in her own bright purple dress—the founding fathers now Black men and women, including West African Muslims, as she tells and retells the story of the American polity from its original framers, interpreted by Cox as peoples from the African diaspora.

"If we want freedom, justice, and equality," Elijah Muhammad wrote in *Message to the Blackman in America*, "we must look for it among ourselves and our kind, not among the people who have destroyed and robbed us of even the knowledge of ourselves, themselves, our God, and our religion."[140] In his speeches and writings, Elijah Muhammad repeatedly referred to knowledge of Islam as a resurrection from a "mentally-dead condition" being "brainwashed" by white definitions, an awakening to "knowledge of self and kind"—knowledge of where you come from. Though he uses a theological frame and an exhortatory tone of warning, Elijah Muhammad's Black nationalist rhetoric also employs a vocabulary of citizenship (civil) rights, human rights, and legal personhood (justice). He always connected freedom, justice, and equality to the cosmic imagery of the Sun, Moon, and Stars, signs of Islam woven into the signature fezzes that he always wore.[141]

PART II
Malcolm X and Black Art

CHAPTER 4

MUSIC IN THE MESSAGE

Malcolm X's Gospel Truth

It was as though the song had been there all the time and he knew it and aroused it.

—Ralph Ellison, *Invisible Man*

Many jazz musicians had been telling me about the growing, disciplined members of Elijah Muhammad's straightbacked legions. And they had talked about this tall, lean prince of the Nation of Islam, this Malcolm X, who was one hell of a soloist.

—Nat Hentoff, "Remembering Malcolm"

Then we began to hear Malcolm, the black voice skating and bebopping like a righteous saxophone solo—mellow truths inspired by the Honorable Elijah Muhammad, but shaped out of Malcolm's own style, a style rooted in black folk memory, and the memory of his Garveyite father.

—Larry Neal, "New Space/The Growth of Black Consciousness"

In one of the climactic scenes in Ralph Ellison's *Invisible Man* (1952), the narrator leads a funeral procession through the streets of Harlem in honor of a friend slain by the police. In a confrontation presciently suggestive of the police killing of Eric Garner over sixty years later, the narrator's friend, peddling wares on the street, is confronted by the police and killed for that "crime." The funeral procession in *Invisible Man* turns into an uprising led by a Marcus Garvey-like West Indian black nationalist Ras, a name evoking Ras Tafari, who became the Emperor of Ethiopia Haile Selassie, symbol of decolonial diasporic Black nationalism. Ellison describes the making of a mass movement as someone begins singing "There's Many a Thousand Gone," a euphonium joins in, and the narrator launches into his speech, "the pattern of [his] voice upon the air," as "zoot suiters, hep cats, men in overalls and poolhall gamblers step into the procession." Ellison writes, "It was as though the song had been there all the time and he knew it and aroused it."[1] Ellison's dramatization of the 1943 Harlem uprisings in *Invisible Man* prefigures later protests that catalyzed the Black Power era—Birmingham in 1963, Harlem in 1964, Watts in 1965, Newark and Detroit in 1967—each precipitated by police violence. In his autobiography, Amiri Baraka wrote about how music "took on special significance and meaning" in the urban uprisings of the 1960s, as artists reflected "the rising tide of the people's struggles ... 'Dancing in the Streets' was like our national anthem...[it] spoke to us of Harlem and the other places, then Watts and later Newark and Detroit."[2]

Through the speeches and writings of Malcolm X, this chapter explores the prehistory of Black Power protest against police brutality—in the sonic dimensions of his sermonic oratory rooted in the protest tradition of Black music. In 1957, five years after the publication of *Invisible Man*, Malcolm X engaged in a process of "arousing the song" in his own writing. He wove lyrics into his rhetorical technique and literary style, drawing on spirituals like "Steal Away" and "Shout All Over God's Heaven," gospel like "How Long, oh Lord, How Long," and blues like "Motherless Children" in a series of articles he wrote for the *New York Amsterdam News*. The first article in the series was published April 27, 1957, the day after he orchestrated a protest of the police beating of Johnson X Hinton, who himself tried to intervene in the police beating of another man.[3] Hinton was a member of the Nation of Islam (NOI) Temple No. 7 in Harlem where Malcolm X was minister, and Malcolm X negotiated Hinton's release to the hospital while NOI and Harlem residents gathered in protest outside the police precinct. Later, the Nation of Islam helped Hinton sue, winning "the largest police brutality judgement that New York City ... ever paid" at the time.[4]

The first installment of Malcolm X's "God's Angry Men" column is dated the day after Hinton's beating. This chapter explores these writings as a lens into the early development of his rhetorical technique and public presence. It specifically looks at Malcolm X's use of music in his message, testifying to the depth and breadth of his knowledge of the African American musical tradition, but also his attunement to the songs galvanizing the civil rights movement and the popular music being recorded on vinyl, circulated on the radio, and played on jukeboxes. He bent the lyrical dimensions of the Black sermon, not only to his own preaching but also away from their Christian roots and (back) toward Islam. Though used in a secular setting, in the *New York Amsterdam News*, the tone of the writings are sermonic *da'wa* (the "call" to Islam or "proselytization") precisely at a time when Malcolm X was fishing for converts as minister of Temple No. 7 in Harlem. Malcolm X weaves what Hortense Spillers calls threads of music from the fabric of the history that is the African American sermon, but in the service of the NOI and Islam, rather than Christianity.[5] (Or, as Amiri Baraka writes in his famous essay "The Changing Same," this "signifying and rhythm pounding, this form is as old as Black religious gatherings in the forests of the West . . . and connects straight on into Black free-Africa."[6]) Malcolm X reclaims that history—the sermon as music and the music as sermon—drawing out the Islamic tones coded into the hymns' history. But he also goes further, using the music as a critique of Christianity and Christian preachers "whose doctrines only proved them to be puppets and tools for the slave master."[7] At a time when spirituals and gospel were becoming instrumental to the civil rights movement, Malcolm X leverages this music as a critique of Martin Luther King in particular (though not mentioning him by name), even as he adapts some of King's most effective rhetorical tools. He appears to be trying out King's speaking style, which wove spirituals and gospel music into his preaching, as well as the moral tenor of his political activism. As the narrator in the *Invisible Man* notes, the songs are protest, but they also go beyond protest to "something deeper," what Malcolm's speeches, sermons, and writings of this time talk about as knowledge "of our own glorious history, our own religion, our own God."[8]

In his "God's Angry Men" columns, Malcolm X repeats the words "White Man's Heaven Is Black Man's Hell" almost like a chorus at the end of each paragraph, words that would become the title and refrain of a song recorded by Louis X, later Farrakhan. Released on vinyl in 1960—and performed at Carnegie Hall on December 24, 1960, in Farrakhan's musical *Orgena*—the lyrics poetically and musically paraphrase Malcolm's words in his June 1 and June 8, 1957, articles.[9] The columns are written in a forceful, fire-and-brimstone tone of sermonic warning, almost as a jeremiad, a tone Louis X replaces with rhyming verses melodically strummed on guitar and piano to a calypso beat on the bongos. This was a remarkable example of Farrakhan putting Malcolm X's words to song (or, Malcolm X channeling an early, unreleased version of the song into his writing). It was a kind of call and response between Malcolm, Farrakhan, and Elijah Muhammad, as Malcolm X drew on Elijah Muhammad's words and teachings in his writings and speeches, just as Louis X drew on Malcolm X and Elijah Muhammad. This call and response resonated even further, as these ideas and teachings circulated among NOI members, potential recruits, and the broader public—in newspapers and magazines, on records and juke boxes, on television and radio, in streetcorner preaching and mass gatherings.[10] It helped constitute an Islamic counterpublic within the Black counterpublic, a Nation of Islam within the Black nation within the nation.[11]

Louis X's music expanded the sonic dimensions of Malcolm X's writing, as he modeled himself on Malcolm and interpreted the cadences of his speech in his own way. Farrakhan attributed his conversion to hearing Malcolm X speak in July 1955. "I never heard any man talk like that. I was convinced that this was where I wanted to be, ... hearing Malcolm and then becoming a student and really a disciple of Malcolm," Farrakhan told Henry Louis Gates Jr. in an interview. Malcolm X "had a tremendous impact on my life." Farrakhan had heard Elijah Muhammad speak on an earlier occasion, but "wasn't thoroughly convinced."[12] After converting, Louis X studied under Malcolm X in his assistant minister class in early 1956; was soon appointed a Fruit of Islam captain at Temple No. 11 in Boston, and was later appointed minister. The young Farrakhan studied, worked, and served under Malcolm "enough time for him to incorporate Malcolm's oratorical style into his own," writes Manning Marable.[13] When Gates asks Farrakhan if he knew he would become a preacher and lead his flock, he answers by talking about music and how he learned to speak: "Because my mom had put the violin in my hand at five years of age, I gradually learned to play this instrument, and I began to speak, go with the music."[14] In "White Man's Heaven Is a Black Man's Hell," Farrakhan put Malcolm X's writings and speech—as well as Elijah Muhammad's teachings—to music, an intervention that would fuel the music and poetry of the Black Arts Movement and its inheritor, the hip hop generation, through continual sampling of his words and speeches.

The song and the column speak to the dynamic relationship between the sermonic tone of Malcolm X's writing, his oratorical style, and the music he references. But the song and the column also testify to the dynamic relationship between Farrakhan and his mentor Malcolm X—and how they communicated between each other through music, but also with ever wider audiences through their rhetorical prowess patterned on the preaching tradition and its own symbiotic relationship to the musical tradition. Malcolm X and Farrakhan use their voices as "a marvelous instrument," how James Weldon Johnson describes the musicality of the African American sermon in *God's Trombones*. The effect amplifies the human voice and gives expression to a "wide and varied range of emotions."[15] Hortense Spillers describes the African American sermon as both poetry and music, calling it "a *mezclada* of elements which combine musical patterns (including jazz-like syncopation and blues overview)."[16] Through a process of musical citation and recitation, these preachers deploy the vocal instrumentality of the Black religious tradition—and the Islamic tradition—toward spreading their message. But they also riff on, revise, and remember longer traditions that they rework through what Meta DuEwa Jones calls "rituals of recital."[17] The Islamic tradition has its own rituals of recitation that function as performative hermeneutics marked by differentiation and variation in vocal tones, as well as innovation (however contested "innovation" has been in the Islamic tradition). But innovation has functioned within the Islamic tradition, and continues to function, as a key element in literary and poetic creativity.[18] In the case of African American Islam, this innovation has been an adaptive mechanism for the survival of "fragments and traces" of Islamic practices under conditions of severe duress.[19]

Farrakhan expands on the musicality of these religious traditions—and the religiosity of the musical tradition—to include the calypso from his own Caribbean roots in St. Kitts and Jamaica; he shared those roots with Malcolm X (whose own mother was from Grenada) and Marcus Garvey (who he mentions with reverence in his interview with Gates).[20] He did so at a time when Harry Belafonte's 1956 *Calypso* album, and his "Day-O (The Banana Boat Song)" was enjoying unprecedented commercial success—and Belafonte was becoming one of Martin Luther King's most faithful soldiers in the civil rights movement. Harking from the tradition of a call and response work song, Belafonte turned "Day-O" into pop. "White Man's Heaven Is a Black Man's Hell" is a retort to "Day-O" and Belafonte's newfound fame alongside Elvis, but the song also confronts the civil rights movement and King (the "preacher" in the lyrics). More broadly, however, it critiques Christianity as the religion of the "white slavemaster," a religion instrumentalized in colonial domination.[21] In "White Man's Heaven Is a Black Man's Hell," Farrakhan draws on calypso's tradition of anticolonial critique: singing about the slave trade, the wresting of the land from the Native Americans, and European economic exploitation of Asia, Africa, China, India, and the Middle East.[22] "White Man's Heaven Is a Black Man's Hell" would travel back to the Caribbean, remixed and reinterpreted in Prince Buster's ska version in the late 1960s, after Prince Buster converted to Islam and joined the NOI in 1964, the year he befriended Muhammad Ali. By slightly altering the words to specifically reference Jamaica's own history of slavery and European exploitation of natural and human resources, Prince Buster reinterpreted the song for the context of Jamaica's anticolonial struggle. Citing and reciting Malcolm and Farrakhan, Prince Buster engages in his own kind of archival practice, through Malcolm's "God's Angry Men" column and Farrakhan's song, and through the story and history of Islam in the Americas recounted through music.

Through "celebratory, ritual performances," Paul Gilroy writes in *There Ain't No Black in the Union Jack*, "these singers did not simply provide a soundtrack for the political actions of their soul sisters and brothers"; they also transmitted struggles for racial justice across the diaspora through music.[23]

"MUSIC, BROTHER, IS OURS": THE CALL TO ISLAM

Malcolm's pre-NOI lifestyle of Lindy dancing, zoot suiting, house robbing, and cocaine sniffing become part of the morality tale and redemption narrative constructed in *The Autobiography*, perhaps with Alex Haley's guidance, to document a life Malcolm leaves behind for the austerity of the Nation of Islam. On his first night in Harlem ever, after riding the train from Boston, he visits landmarks like the jazz bar Small's Paradise, the Apollo, the Braddock Hotel, and the Savoy Ballroom, seeing (almost improbably in one night!) Jay McShann, Walter Brown, Dizzy Gillespie, Billy Eckstine, Billie Holiday, Ella Fitzgerald, Dinah Washington, and Lionel Hampton, some of whom became good friends.[24] The *Autobiography* testifies to the deep influence of music on Malcolm, through his euphoric and exuberant participation in the music scene while later working Small's. (Even the name "Small's Paradise" resonates with the critique in "White Man's Heaven Is a Black Man's Hell," as Malcolm ends up hellishly incarcerated for drug dealing and stealing in pursuit of the high life with his white girlfriend.) In Haley's treatment, the vibrant music fades from the scene with Malcolm's asceticism after his conversion, even though the conversions of jazz musicians and musicians like Farrakhan testify to the close relationship between the music scene and the Black Muslims. One of Malcolm X's letters in prison, written after his conversion, credits Elijah Muhammad with guiding him out of "this Hellish Darkness, Lighting us our Path to Paradise."[25]

Music was closely woven into Malcolm X's earliest engagement with Islam and the Nation of Islam, from his time in prison, to his early *da'wa* (his "call," through outreach and proselytization) in Boston, to his rise in Temple No. 7 in Harlem. In letters written just after his conversion, he talks intimately about jazz music in spiritual terms, as a way of articulating his commitment to Islam. In a letter dated March 9, 1950—one of the first known instances of him signing his name with an "X"—he talks about music as a way to "soothe the soul." Addressed to a Muslim brother Raymond (likely Raymond Sharrieff, who would become the Supreme Captain of the Fruit of Islam), the letter crescendos with an existential reflection on the mystical capacity of music to shape the soul into a song.

Music, Brother, is ours ... it is us ... and like us it is always here ... surrounding us ... like the infinite particles that make up Life, it cannot be seen ... but can only be felt ... Like Life!!! No, it is not created ... but like the never-dying Soul ... eternally permeated the atmosphere with its Presence ... ever-waiting for its Master ... the Lordly Musician ... the Wielder of Souls ... to come and give it a Temple ... mould it into a Song. Music without the Musician is like Life without Allah ... both being in need of the house ... a home ... The Temple ... the Complete Song and its Creator. Yes, Brother, Allah is Truly God!![26]

The prose is structured more like a poem through the rhythmic breaks of his prolific ellipses—something like what Meta DuEwa Jones observes in her analysis of the dashes and ellipses as formal poetic elements in John Coltrane's handwritten liner notes for *A Love Supreme*. "Blessed Be His Name. Thought waves—Heat Waves—ALL vibrations—ALL PATHS Lead To God. His way—It is Lovely—IT is Gracious IT is merciful."[27] She calls the script "a unique form of 'spirit writing' that has roots in Africanist-derived practices of graphic inscription. I would call his expressively punctuated manuscript hand his *soul-post*."[28] Malcolm X, recently converted, reaching out beseechingly for guidance from and connection to his Muslim brothers, uses music and musical poetic metaphors to express his newfound faith.

Though Malcolm's letter insists on his allegiance to the NOI, his rumination has resonance with the philosophy of the Indian Sufi musician Hazrat Inayat Khan, whose *Notes from the Unstruck Music* (1923) was republished in 1948. One of the aphorisms in the book, for example, says: " 'When the soul is attuned to God, every action becomes music.' Because God is the perfection of harmony.... Time and tune produce music and the attunement to vibrations and rhythms results in music, the music of life itself."[29] Such works would not have been available in the prison library, but both Malcolm X and his friend, accomplice, and fellow inmate Malcolm Jarvis ("the other Malcolm") describe receiving visits, prayer books in Arabic, and "privileged information" from an Indian Muslim, Abdul Hameed, who Jarvis says was Ahmadiyya and Malcolm says was "orthodox."[30]

Jarvis and Malcolm X met Abdul Hameed in Boston before going to prison; Jarvis introduced himself "as a young musician and trumpet player." When Jarvis visited him for the first time, Abdul Hameed presented him with a lecture and a concert of classical music, afterward introducing him to "books on Oriental history and philosophy from both India and Egypt. He also showed me some books on harmony and music composition and theory.... I knew I had to introduce Malcolm.... After meeting Malcolm, Abdul took great interest in us and spent many hours teaching us." Jarvis later acknowledged that Abdul "was instrumental" in both Malcolm's and his life.[31] In a July 1949 letter to Abdul Hameed Jarvis included a poem nearly identical to the passage in Malcolm's later letter to Brother Raymond, but signed by "Red Little," aka Malcolm Little, though Malcolm had already begun signing other letters, like one to his brother Philbert with "As Salaam Alaikum."[32]

From his earliest days as a Muslim, Malcolm understood music as a tool of proselytization. He writes about jazz musicians who had converted to Islam as a bridge between his old life and his new path, giving expression to his newfound commitments, but also spreading the message through music. In a March 12, 1950, letter responding to Brother Raymond, he pleads with him to identify those in the music business who are Muslim, and specifically members of the Nation of Islam, so he can let his fellow inmates know. "The musicians' leanings, religiously and otherwise," he writes, "tend to sway the leanings of the youth."[33] He observes that many of the musicians belong to the Ahmadiyya movement, but he wants to know "how many and which ones . . . belong to ours, under Mr. Elijah Muhammad."[34] He expresses fear about the "temptations of that life and its memories," vowing to steer clear "unless I know the fellows are brothers, . . . so I ask you the ones who are for the Truth." Apparently, Brother Raymond did not answer his questions about music, because Malcolm X writes a second time inquiring in a postscript about the musicians' allegiances to Islam. Despite his misgivings about reconnecting with his former life of "drink, dope and . . . the lures of night life to create some sort of peace within ourselves," he reminisces about his contacts and friendships in the music scene, Sonny Stitt, Milt Jackson, Lionel Hampton, Al "Soul" Hayse, and Dinah Washington ("my ace girl").[35] He asks whether "Diz" (Dizzy Gillespie) was a Muslim and if "B" is a Muslim. "B" most likely refers to Billy Eckstine, known as Mr. B: the Billy Eckstine Orchestra was an incubator for jazz musicians like Ahmad Jamal (Frederick Russell Jones), Sahib Shihab (Edmund Gregory), and Art Blakey (Abdullah Ibn Buhaina). Or, it may refer to Blakey who converted to Ahmadiyya Islam by 1947 and in 1948 founded the Jazz Messengers, "an Islamic brotherhood of bebop artists, . . . African American artists who had converted to the Ahmadiyya Muslim community."[36] Gillespie was portrayed in a 1948 *Life* magazine photograph seemingly prostrate in Muslim prayer, with the caption purposefully misleading in this respect: "Mohammedan leanings are shown by many bebop musicians, some of whom have actually turned Mohammedan, interrupt rehearsals at sunset to bow to the east. Here Dizzy bows to Mecca from his Hollywood apartment."[37] In his letters to Brother Raymond, Malcolm X twice inquires whether Sonny Stitt, who had just recorded "All God's Chillun: Got Rhythm," was Muslim.[38]

When Malcolm was released from prison, he translated his belief in music's power of persuasion—and its spiritual energy—into strategy. As minister in Detroit, Boston, Philadelphia, and Harlem, he brought jazz musicians into the fold, often at the expense of the Ahmadiyya movement. His "God's Angry Men" column and his *Autobiography* testify to his sense of music's potential to spread the word, and its role in *da'wa*.

After his release from prison, Malcolm X "fished" for converts in the jazz scene, first in Detroit where he was appointed minister in Temple No. 1 and then, in 1953, in Boston's Temple No. 11, building on the presence of Islam already circulating in the jazz community through proselytization of both the Ahmadiyya and the NOI.[39] Malcolm X developed a rhetorical style that "picked up on the cadence and percussive sounds of jazz music," Manning Marable argues.[40] Hisham Aidi—who worked on the Malcolm X project with Marable—similarly argues that "Malcolm X's speaking style was influenced by the big-band sounds of the 1940s, and in turn, this fiery Muslim leader's rhetorical cadences would influence jazz artists like Coltrane, who Amiri Baraka dubbed 'Malcolm in the New Super Bop Fire.'"[41] But jazz musicians were also listening to Malcolm X and channeling him into their compositions, in a kind of call and response between Malcolm and the musicians, between Islam and jazz. One of Max Roach's first albums, *Max Roach + 4*, includes the track "Mr. X." Roach attended Manhattan School of Music until 1953, and in 1954 Malcolm X was appointed minister of Harlem's Temple No. 7, only a few blocks away from the school. Roach, who also became Muslim, tuned in to other Islamic frequencies as well, recording the track "Däähoud" with Clifford Brown in 1954—a tribute to Talib Dawud, a mutual friend. Dawud, a jazz trumpeter, founded and led the Muslim Brotherhood USA in the early 1950s, helped establish the Islamic and African Institute in Philadelphia with J. A. Rogers and Mahmoud Alwan, and connected with Sheik Nasir Ahmad and Imam Abdul Raheem's International Muslim Brotherhood in Harlem.[42] Max Roach's musical interpretation of the vocal instrumentality of Malcolm X would become a full-blown genre of music incorporating Malcolm X's speeches and writings, most notably in jazz and hip hop, but also in calypso, reggae, and ska, as well as pop music by Beyoncé and Megan Thee Stallion.

Another musician listening attentively to Malcolm X at Temple No. 7 in Harlem was Louis Eugene Walcott. From the age of six, Walcott trained as a violinist but later began playing the ukulele and calypso music in clubs under the stage name "the Charmer" and "his Afro-Rhythm Boys." After Walcott joined the NOI, however, Elijah Muhammad "disallowed music."[43] Over time, that policy would change from when the followers of Elijah Muhammad "totally shunned music," as Abdul Basit Naeem would write in 1967, leading to what Naeem called a "new outlook on music." But that policy would be lifted, his article says, with the release of "White Man's Heaven Is a Black Man's Hell."[44] Despite writing for *Muhammad Speaks*, and being close with Elijah Muhammad, Naeem himself does not seem entirely clear on the nature of NOI policy, writing in the article that Elijah Muhammad may have "removed or relaxed" the ban on music and wondering if Muhammad will clarify the reasons for this.[45] In a *New Yorker* article titled "The Music of Malcolm X," Hisham Aidi observes that "music for emancipation is permissible."[46]

Under Farrakhan, music became an integral part of the NOI's mission—and one of its most powerful tools for spreading the message. Under Elijah Muhammad, he eventually recorded other songs like "Chains" and "Black Gold." "Music, like truth, is the essence of my life," he has said, "People really don't know Farrakhan, they don't fully know the soul of a man—and I think that can be expressed through music."[47] Echoing the lyrics from Pharoah Sanders's "Hum-Allah Hum-Allah Hum-Allah," he says, "music is a universal language."[48] After becoming the head of the NOI, he gave concerts playing Mendelssohn in 1993, spearheaded the hip hop summit in June 2001, and released his *Let's Change the World* box set in 2018, with songs featuring Snoop Dog, Chaka Khan, and Bach. Music is not *haram*, Su'ad Abdul Khabeer writes in her book *Muslim Cool*, but part of an "Afro-diasporic Islamic genealogy."[49]

"GOD'S ANGRY MEN": ROUSING SONG

Malcolm X began writing his "God's Angry Men" columns in response to an article published in in the *New York Amsterdam News* titled "Mr. X Tells What Islan [*sic*] Means." The first installment of his column included several corrections to the "Islan" article, as well as an editorial note saying that "in the interest of fair reporting, [the newspaper] asked Mr. Malcolm X to explain his faith to its readers in his own words."[50] The April 20, 1957, "Islan" article quoted Malcolm fiercely criticizing Martin Luther King Jr., saying that "Reverend" had become a title of "scorn and ridicule" thanks to religious leaders "teaching us to love, be patient, understanding and forgiving (turn-the-other-cheek) to the Slavemasters."[51] Several articles in that same issue of the *New York Amsterdam News* were devoted to the civil rights movement, including an announcement that King would receive the Social Justice Award of the Religion and Labor Foundation for his role in the Montgomery bus boycott. The front page featured an exposé of Harry Belafonte and his new white wife, Julie Robinson, who he married only one day after divorcing the mother of his children, his Black wife Marguerite Byrd. (Belafonte himself first met King during the bus boycott, contributing funds to support the cause.) The article on Belafonte was scathing: "wondering why a man who has waved the flag of justice for his race so strongly could suddenly turn from a Negro wife to a white wife.... Racial identity is something to be worn with a badge of pride. Certainly Harry wore his thusly."[52] The article mocked him for acquiring a white wife along with his newfound fame and fortune. Malcolm X's first article in the "God's Angry Men" series picked up the thread of this argument, criticizing both King and Belafonte even without naming them. The images and arguments he used would become part of the lyrics of "A White Man's Heaven Is a Black Man's Hell"—namely Malcolm's argument that integration into a "white heaven" is actually a form of mingling with "the wicked race of white Christians who had enslaved us." Referring to Belafonte, he wrote that Christians "worship the artificial, false beauty of the slave master's pale, leprous looking women ... diseased, sickly creatures ... no regard whatsoever for the feelings and the well-being of our own women, neither in public nor in private."[53]

As Malcolm X developed his own rhetorical style and public presence, he experimented using lyrics in his writing, in ways analogous to how King and other preachers engaged spirituals and the gospel music tradition in their speeches and sermons. During a time when music was nearly banned by the NOI—and gospel was becoming a critical instrument of the civil rights movement—Malcolm X wove gospel, blues, and spirituals into his "God's Angry Men" column of June 1, 1957. He leveraged the songs as a critique of King's embrace of "love your enemy," but also to raise consciousness about "the God (Allah) and religion (Islam) of our foreparents."[54] Malcolm used the music's coded references to evoke the spiritual and religious dimensions of the struggle against racial injustice and for freedom, but in an Islamic framework rather than a Christian one. Claiming the spiritual, gospel, and blues traditions for the Nation, he orchestrated what Carter Mathes, in his book *Imagine the Sound*, calls "the ritualistic convergence between writing and sound," arguing that "sonic forms offer means of accessing the inchoate political possibility within black expression."[55] Malcolm X also reinterpreted—and reclaimed—the music for a different kind of protest against white racial terror, preaching flight and resistance, rather than integration and loving your enemy. He bent the spirituals and gospel blues away from their Christian roots and (back) toward the Islamic tradition—anticipating a connection more recent scholars have drawn between the Islamic tradition (the call to prayer, for example) and the blues.[56]

Malcolm X again fiercely criticized King, calling him, without naming him, "the Number One tool of the white slavemaster, ... the black preacher who preached the slavemaster's Christian doctrine: 'Love your enemies.'" This teaching was invented, he wrote, "by the white slavemaster himself, and it was designed to make better mental slaves of the so-called Negroes, and therefore the black preacher of such false doctrine was the best tool of the slavemaster against the black pastors' very own kind."[57] Exactly two weeks prior—on the May 17, 1957—King had quoted "love your enemies" from Matthew 5:43 in a speech delivered at the Prayer Pilgrimage for Freedom in Washington, DC. In the immediate aftermath of the brutal police beating of Johnson X Hinton, King's call for passive resistance must have appeared as an affront to Malcolm X. In addition, King directly critiqued the Nation in his Prayer Pilgrimage speech, calling for rejecting "a philosophy of black supremacy."[58] That same (June 1) issue of *New York Amsterdam News* also included an article titled "King Emerges as Top Negro Leader," which must have rankled. An early instantiation of the March on Washington, the Prayer Pilgrimage aimed to pressure the Eisenhower administration to enforce the *Brown v. Board of Education* decision on its third anniversary. Organized by Bayard Rustin, Ella Baker, A. Philip Randolph, Adam Clayton Powell, and King, it was also attended by Rosa Parks, Harry Belafonte, Paul Robeson, Sidney Poitier, Roy Wilkins, and Charles Diggs. Hymns were sung throughout as in a prayer service, between sermon-like speeches and Mahalia Jackson's performance of the spirituals "I've Been Buked and I've Been Scorned" and "Keep-A-Trustin."[59] King would return to the imagery of "loving your enemies" a few months later in November, when he returned to Montgomery in the aftermath of the bus boycotts, preaching at the Dexter Avenue Baptist Church.[60] This message was remarkable, especially because the bus boycott had been met with intense and violent backlash—the Ku Klux Klan lynching of Willie Edwards and the bombing of five Black churches. But just as Malcolm X consciously spoke to King's teachings, so King must have been conscious of the Black nationalist critique of him and his teachings.

Malcolm used the lyrics of the gospel song "Steal Away" to talk not just about fugitivity, but also about the clandestine practice of African religion and the suppression of "knowledge of the God (Allah) and religion (Islam) of our foreparents" under slavery. "When we wanted to pray to our God (the one God, ALLAH), we had to 'steal away' . . . to keep the Christian Slavemaster from hearing us. White Man's Heaven . . . Black Man's Hell."[61] "Steal Away" was the anthem of the Montgomery bus boycott—and Belafonte, who raised funds for the protesters, later recorded the song. Malcolm X used "Steal Away" to talk about religious freedom—"a message not just about the escape to physical freedom but also about the quest for religious liberty," as the NBC radio show

Freedom's People described the spiritual in 1942.⁶² He used the spiritual to talk about fugitive pedagogies—with implicit reference to NOI teachings about separation rather than integration.⁶³ The song had been recorded by the Fisk University Jubilee Singers, but also by the Soul Stirrers (who also performed in jubilee style). Mahalia Jackson would perform the song with Nat King Cole on his television program in 1957 and Sam Cooke would record it in 1960.⁶⁴ In *Souls of Black Folk*, Du Bois called "Steal Away" "the song of songs" of the "many songs of the fugitive."⁶⁵

Malcolm's column focused on the issues of education, knowledge, and teaching that were part of the Prayer Pilgrimage's call to enforce desegregation of the schools. The NOI had long had their own school system, the University of Islam, where students were taught religious doctrine alongside reading, writing, and math. The April 20 *New York Amsterdam News* interview with Malcolm X mentioned the University of Islam as the "solution" to these issues of segregation, through a pro-Black curriculum tailored toward NOI culture and Black history, as students read texts like J. A. Rogers's *One Hundred Amazing Facts About the Negro* and John Hope Franklin's *From Slavery to Freedom*.⁶⁶ In one letter to the *Baltimore Afro-American*, Elijah Muhammad urged people to "awake from that dumb teaching the white man gives you"—teachings propagated by "so-called Christian preachers."⁶⁷ In his "God's Angry Men" column, Malcolm X described how white slavemasters suppressed knowledge under slavery, so that "our children, with no one to teach them, no one to open their eyes, grew up blind, (mentally) in gross darkness (ignorance), . . . 'mother gone, father gone, motherless children saw a hard time.' White Man's Heaven is Black Man's Hell." Malcolm X again used that final line as a chorus to close out paragraphs that function almost like stanzas. He extended his engagement with music to the blues, weaving in lyrics from Blind Willie Johnson's gospel blues song "Motherless Children," which had first been recorded in 1927 under the name "Blind Pilgrim" but was just rereleased by Folkways in 1957.⁶⁸ In Johnson's lines there are echoes of Malcolm X's own life story, of losing his mother to a psychiatric institution and being raised by his sister: "Well, some people say that sister will do, when mother is dead. . . . Nobody treats you like a mother will." Malcolm referred to Johnson's actual blindness in the column, but also to the poverty he suffered as a "motherless child," reportedly blinded by his stepmother with lye.⁶⁹

Through biblical motifs (in Exodus 4:11 and Isaiah 42:18, for example)—and allusions to Johnson's blindness—Malcolm portrayed Black Americans as "God's people" fallen into the clutches of "beast-like people, who robbed them deaf, dumb, and blind and then made slaves of them (Daniel 1)." He quoted directly from Elijah Muhammad's *The Supreme Wisdom: Solution to the So-Called Negroes' Problem* (1957) to describe how God "declared that we were without the knowledge of self or anyone else, and had been made blind, deaf and dumb by this white race of people, and that we must return to our people, our God (Allah) and His Religion of Peace (Islam)." Through these references, Malcolm gave musical expression to Elijah Muhammad's teachings about being "blind, deaf, and dumb," teachings rooted in both the Bible and the Qur'an.[70] Louis X's song revisited Malcolm's language, as well as *The Supreme Wisdom*, with the lyrics: "Why are we called Negroes? Why are we deaf, dumb, and blind?" It was a conversation, or a call and response, circulating among these leaders, but also with the civil rights movement and the African American musical tradition. Malcolm X interpreted the music, claiming it for Islam rather than Christianity and tracing its roots to other genealogies of protest, fugitivity ("separatism" in NOI teachings), and knowledge of self.

The reverberation of these gospel blues songs and spirituals functioned as a contrapuntal critique of both the civil rights movement and Christianity, even as Malcolm X tuned in to their rhythms. "The Christian Slavemaster" he writes, "made up a 'new religion' (Christianity), and put Jesus' name on it to fool us, telling us we would get our heaven (Freedom) after we die, 'way up yonder in the sky'...'after we die.' While at the same time our slavemaster himself was getting his heaven on earth, now, in this life. White Man's Heaven Is Black Man's Hell." Here Malcolm X drew on lyrics from the gospel song "When the Roll Called Up Yonder," sung as part of Billy Graham's "New York Crusade," which had begun only two weeks before on May 15, 1957, and continued for a full sixteen weeks.[71] In July King accepted Graham's invitation to join him at the pulpit and deliver the opening invocation.

Malcolm's analysis brings out the subtext of "When the Roll Called Up Yonder" written by the white evangelist James Milton Black. It was recorded that year by Carl Smith, for his *Sunday Down South* album, and by Jimmy Dean on his *Hour of Prayer* album. It was also performed on the radio and television show *Singing Time in Dixie* by the gospel quartet The Statesmen that had previously recorded on the "White Church" label, and had been sponsored by Dixie Lily Flour.[72] The lyrics allude to the day of reckoning and the promise of "home beyond the skies": "Let us labor for the Master from the dawn till setting sun / Let us talk of all his wondrous love and care / Then when all of life is over and our work on earth is done / The roll is called up yonder."[73] The (false) promise of heaven after a hell of toil became the essence of both Malcolm X's critique in the article and Farrakhan's in "A White Man's Heave Is a Black Man's Hell": "The preacher...told us of a heaven way up in the sky / That we can't enjoy now, but rather after we die."[74] Yet Malcolm X and Farrakhan were also playing fugitive spirituals like "Steal Away" and blues songs like "Motherless Children" against white-composed gospel songs, performing an analysis of the racial politics coded into the songs and their messages.

Malcolm used the songs as proselytization, as he envisioned doing with jazz while in prison, but now targeting a population different from the prison youth he mentions in the letter. In 1957, Malcolm was "fishing" for converts for his Temple No. 7 in Harlem—targeting Adam Clayton Powell's Abyssinian Baptist Church, Pentecostal churches, and "little evangelical storefront churches."[75] In the *Autobiography*, Malcolm X describes the Christian churches as "by far the best 'fishing' audience of all, by far the best-conditioned audience for Mr. Muhammad's teachings.... Southern migrant people who would go anywhere to hear what they called 'good preaching,' ... shaking and rattling and rolling the gospels with their guitars and tambourines." He elaborates on a "whole circuit of commercial gospel entertainers who have come out of these little churches in the city ghettoes or from down South. People such as Sister Rosetta Tharpe, The Clara Ward Singers, and there must be five hundred lesser lights of the same general order. Mahalia Jackson, the greatest of them all, she was a preacher's daughter in Louisiana."[76] The "God's Angry Men" column wove lyrics from "Oh Lord, How Long" sung by The Famous Ward Singers in 1957—a group with both Baptist and Pentecostal members. (The lead singer, Clara Ward, was the companion of Aretha Franklin's father C. L. Franklin and was one of Aretha's most important mentors.) Malcolm X quoted from "Oh Lord, How Long" that expresses the frustration of waiting for freedom: "Seeing the blood roll down the naked backs of our fathers, and of our brothers and our sons, ... seeing our wives, our daughters and our sisters raped and ravished by the wicked slavemaster right before our eyes,... we wondered: 'how long, oh Lord, how long?' White Man's Heaven Is Black Man's Hell."[77] He referenced contemporary gospel music that grew out of some of the earliest recorded slave songs, citing music from deep within the African American musical tradition.[78] But he also created, in concert with Farrakhan, a new musical tradition, through lyrics that would become song (or that were already song). Malcolm situated his writing and preaching in this tradition, even as he and Farrakhan reinterpreted the tradition through a different kind of music (in this case calypso), and different lyrics (based on NOI rather than Christian theology). Their reinterpretation and reinvention of an older tradition, for another time and place, functions like an analogy for Malcolm, Farrakhan, and Elijah Muhammad's reinterpretation of the Islamic tradition, as they drew on elements coded into the fabric of history but revivified for a different era of struggle against racial oppression.

In Malcolm X's column, his letters from prison, and his later speeches, music shaped not only his literary and rhetorical, but also his spiritual and political sensibility. It came from his mother's own religiosity as a Seventh Day Adventist, his later apprenticeship at Small's Paradise and the Apollo, and his study in prison where he read W. E. B. Du Bois's *Souls of Black Folk* (1903). Carter Mathes, reflecting on the book's last chapter, "The Sorrow Songs," calls Du Bois a writer who "imagined the power of sound as a form of resistance to racial subjection in the United States from the earliest transcriptions of black experience in the Americas." What the words mean, Mathes says, may resonate less "than the historical consciousness projected through the tonal memory of the music."[79] This "tonal memory" is rooted in West African musical styles, scholars like Sylviane Diouf argue, with melisma, glissandos, nasality, and elongated notes that are "characteristics of reciting and singing in the Islamic world," as well as the "high lonesome complaint" of the holler, the slider technique, and the use of string instruments. She sees "a direct link with specific Islamic practices that survived in the Americas, such as prayers, the recitation of the Qur'an, Sufi chants, and the call to prayer.[80] Du Bois calls this the "strange world of an unknown tongue," words and music of an older "theology" that has been displaced. This is what Farrakhan's lyrics refer to as he sang of being "stripped of our name, our language, our culture, our God, and our religion." That language, culture, and religion did survive, argue Diouf, Du Bois, and Mathes, in the "tonal memory" but also in ritual practices. In his May 25, 1957, column, Malcolm called for "rejoining the ranks of our darker brothers and sisters of the East, whose ancestral faith is the age-old religion of Islam, the true religion of dark mankind, the true religion of our foreparents"— and he did so by defining and explaining the meanings of the Arabic words Islam, Muslim, and salaam, making familiar, intelligible, and known that world and that tongue.[81] But he also tapped into that "true religion of our foreparents" through another language, one more commonly known and understood: the language of music.

Malcolm composed these writings in his own musical style, with ellipses that indicate pauses in the flow of the delivery for impact, the chorus "White Man's Heaven Is Black Man's Hell" repeated after each paragraph, and a process of musical citation and re-citation. In the last installment of the column, on June 8, the music abruptly disappeared, replaced with a surplus of biblical citations and quotes and a more strident tone, suggesting censure from Elijah Muhammad and prohibition of the music. Did Elijah Muhammad object to Malcolm X engaging with the music, too closely emulating the civil rights movement's rhetorical and political use of gospel and spirituals, straying too far from NOI guidelines, or shining too bright? What kind of rhetorical music might Malcolm have made without Elijah Muhammad's censure and strict discipline? Or, would Malcolm X have become the speaker/preacher he was without Elijah Muhammad leading him (back) to Islam? Malcolm forged many friendships with artists and musicians, despite Elijah Muhammad's strict discipline.[82] His close relationships with artists, intellectuals, writers, and musicians were rooted in an understanding of the role of cultural revolution in political change.[83] His later speeches and alliances give a sense of what he might have been and might have become. But others, too, have taken his words far and wide, in music, poetry, film, and scholarship.

Farrakhan has woven music into his preaching over the course of his career, culminating in his "Swan Song," a six-hour sermon delivered on Saviours' Day in 2022.[84] Through a process of musical citation and recitation, these leaders honed their vocal instrumentality as public speakers, but also reinterpreted the struggle for newer contexts.[85] Music also spread the word, as spiritual practice and healing, historical memory and remembrance, politics and protest. In *Music is the Muse*, Jones writes about musical-poetic "riffs, revisions, and remembrances" that function as acts of creative adaptation renovating "tradition's rituals of recital as powerful sites of alterability" infused with "a sense of the sacred."[86] Just as Diouf describes enslaved Muslims in the United States renovating the Islamic tradition's rituals of recital—recitation of the Qur'an, Sufi chants, the call to prayer, and prayer itself—under extreme forms of racial oppression, so Malcolm X reclaims that renovated tradition through his own process of "struggle and creative adaptation." The music can be understood as a metaphor for how the Islamic tradition functioned "as an energizing, inspirational base," rather than a "closed canon."[87] Music became a vehicle for tapping into—and giving expression to—Islamic "'survivals' and 'continuities'" that were "critical to twentieth-century social movements," write Hisham Aidi and Manning Marable. These survivals and continuities were both actual and imagined, becoming "raw material for their ideological and cultural repertoires."[88]

Malcolm X, as well as the Muslim jazz musicians he wanted to connect with, riffed on the Islamic tradition's "rituals of recital as powerful sites of variation," even if the alterations that they performed were oftentimes critiqued as beyond the pale of Islamic orthodoxy.[89] Elijah Muhammad was clearly ambivalent about the role of music, not only in the NOI, but also with respect to the larger Islamic tradition, explains Abdul Basit Naeem. This sense of the powerful variations on rituals of recital resonates with scholarly speculation about the roots of blues and jazz in West African Qur'an recitation, the call to prayer, and Sufi *dhikr* (remembrance and recitation of sacred words and texts).[90] Even if substantiating this historical genealogy may be impossible, these imagined links nourished visions of connections to an Afro-Asian Islamic past, the resurrection of a suppressed tradition, the "'dead' who would be raised from the 'grave,'" as Malcolm X writes in his column.[91]

MUSIC IN THE MESSAGE: CALL AND RESPONSE

Malcolm X and Louis X engaged in a literary musical call and response at a time that the civil rights movement was deploying gospel songs and spirituals toward mobilizing their message for Black liberation. Despite Malcolm X's intense critique of King and the civil rights movement, he sampled some of the same songs in his writings, using them strategically to speak both about and against their objectives and methods. Despite different beliefs, religious orientations, and approaches to resistance, King, Malcolm X, and Louis Farrakhan put music to their message, weaving it into their speeches, sermons, and writings. Or, as Public Enemy would say, themselves reinterpreting "A White Man's Heaven Is a Black Man's Hell" as "White Heaven / Black Hell" on their 1994 album *Muse Sick-n-Hour Mess Age*, music was in their message.

The words—and the music—live on through a call and response "from one context to another context, from one social collective to another, from one generation to another generation," carrying the power of the different contexts in which they were uttered.[92] This literary-musical call and response creates a dialogue that "traverses generational lines" from W. D. Fard to Elijah Muhammad to Malcolm X to Louis Farrakhan to W. D. Muhammad.[93] It is also an "excavation and a restoration" of an Islamic past through a "recollection of a history of fractures."[94] In their signifying of the Islamic tradition, these leaders engage in their own processes of interpretation and reinterpretation, vision and revision, transformation and reconfiguration. They engage in a hermeneutics that uses NOI theology to interpret the African American experience, just as they use the African American experience to interpret Islam. Malcolm X, Louis Farrakhan and Public Enemy code music into their message (or their message into their music) through what Henry Louis Gates calls a "principle of repetition and difference," a "practice of intertextuality... in the Afro-American formal literary tradition," epitomized by blues, jazz, the spirituals, and gospel.[95] Emphasizing

Gates's point, T. J. Anderson writes that this call and response across generational lines engages "in a continual process of (re)vision ... transformation and reconfiguration."[96]

Malcolm's words, speeches, and writings have been sampled, cut, mixed, and remixed, and interpreted across musical genres and styles. Resonating through time and space, they have been coded into music, song, lyrics, and poetry, woven into the fabric of not just African American—but also Islamic—cultural life. Malcolm drew on the lyrical dimensions of the African American religious tradition, even as he reinterpreted the relationship between Black music and Black protest through the lens of Islam. His speeches, writings, and words had a profound impact on Black music, not just jazz and hip hop, but also calypso and ska. His words have been interpreted in jazz compositions like Max Roach's "Mr. X" (1956); Archie Shepp's "Malcolm, Malcolm Semper Malcolm" (1965) and "Poem for Malcolm" (1969), which function like elegies; electronic music like Keith Leblanc's "Malcolm X, No Sell Out" (1983); operas like Anthony Davis's *X: The Life and Times of Malcolm X* (1985); hip hop like Lakim Shabazz's "Black is Black" (1990), Gangstarr's "Tons o Gunz" (1994), Ghostface Killah's "Malcolm" (2000), and EastSide K-Boy (+Kendrick Lamar)'s "Malcolm X" (2021); Salaam Remi's jazz "Black on Purpose Intro" (2020); and pop like Beyoncé's "Don't Hurt Yourself" (2016) and Megan Thee Stallion's (2020) performance on *Saturday Night Live*. The *SNL* performance sampled a speech Malcolm gave in the immediate aftermath of the 1962 killing of Ronald Stokes, a member of Temple No. 27 in Los Angeles, shot in a confrontation with the police. In his famous speech asking, "Who taught you to hate the color of your skin?" (a response to the 1959 television documentary about the NOI, *The Hate That Hate Produced*), Malcolm X also spoke about Black women: "The most disrespected person in America is the Black woman. The most unprotected person in America is the Black woman. The most neglected person in America is the Black woman." Megan Thee Stallion sampled these words in her performance, referencing another cycle of police violence against Black lives, the police shooting of Breonna Taylor, also unarmed and innocent, like Ronald Stokes.[97] But it also referenced the gun violence she herself suffered at the hands of her partner. Public Enemy, Beyoncé, and Megan Thee Stallion are what Baraka calls "Malcolm's sons and daughters."[98] Malcolm's teachings have traversed generations and contexts, but also circulated in ever wider publics through music and popular culture—revived and reinvented to confront new cycles of violence against Black life.

"White Man's Heaven Is a Black Man's Hell" traveled back to the Caribbean, remixed and reinterpreted in Prince Buster's ska version in the late 1960s, produced after he converted to Islam and joined the NOI in 1964. Taking the name Muhammad Yusef Ali, he established a mosque above his record store where he and Jimmy Cliff held prayer meetings. Harassed for his beliefs, he was charged with "possessing prohibited literature" when found with a copy of Elijah Muhammad's *Message to the Blackman*, which had been banned under Prime Minister Hugh Lawson Shearer. Prince Buster (Cecil Bustamente Campbell) recorded two tracks, "Message to the Black Man, Chpt. 1 & 2" (also named "White Man's Heaven Is a Black Man's Hell, Pt. 1 & 2"), the first version closer to Farrakhan's original and the second riffing on the lyrics for the specific but analogous context of Jamaica—white European colonialism and economic exploitation, displacement and genocide of native peoples and enslaved Africans, and a brutal African slave trade. Prince Buster founded the label "Islam" alongside his earlier label "Voice of the People," producing tracks like "Islam," "The Prophet," "The Message," and "Black Power" that articulated his Islamic commitments alongside his political critiques, commitments that he wove into his recordings and performances. These tracks and others were later compiled into the 2019 album *Africa-Islam-Revolution*, accompanied by "A Rock Steady & Reggae Manifesto" as liner notes.

In the liner notes, Prince Buster lays claim to being the inventor of ska. Though the origins are (undoubtedly) disputed, he is recognized as one of ska's originators. Ska, writes the music critic Heather Augustyn, is "a voice of the people, a blend of all that had come before. This music brought together the jazz of the clubs, the R&B of the yards, the drums of Africa, the mento and calypso, the indigenous forms in all their sound and display."[99] His own "White Man's Heaven Is a Black Man's Hell" sonically looped back to the song's origins in calypso through its descendant ska and via transnational flows of people and sound, but it also looped back to the East, Africa, and Islam, as in the song's lyrics. Its origins were also Malcolm X's words in the "God's Angry Men" column, in Farrakhan's song, and in the teachings of Elijah Muhammad in the 1965 *Message to the Blackman in America*. In *Muslim Cool*, Su'ad Abdul Khabeer talks about the "sampling technique in which a selected piece of music is looped to play over and over as part of the creation of a new piece of music; . . . the loop extends and returns, not in closure but in a cypher," as a communal space of regeneration— and as "a metaphor of the linkages" between Islam and the African American cultural tradition. This "looped musical sample defined by sonic repetition and variation," Abdul Khabeer writes, "is a site of critical continuity and change."[100]

In *Imagine the Sound*, Carter Mathes writes about how "the political and aesthetic qualities of sound resist these implicit and explicit perpetuations of white supremacy as they are narrated and enacted across the bodies of black Americans ... the sonic becomes a mode of aesthetic and political resistance against external and internal oppression."[101] Building on the work of scholars like Robin D. G. Kelley, Hisham Aidi, and Richard Brent Turner—who have explored Malcolm X's deep engagement with (and impact on) jazz—I look in this chapter at Malcolm's engagement with spirituals, gospel, and blues. Other important scholarship like Zaheer Ali's "Malcolm X Mixtape" project at Columbia and the work of Su'ad Abdul Khabeer, Samy Alim, Sohail Daulatzai, Graeme Abernethy, James Spady, Turner, Aidi, and others explore Malcolm X's influence on hip-hop,[102] although his words, writings, and speeches were also woven into calypso and ska.

Public Enemy reinterpreted "White Man's Heaven Is a Black Man's Hell" on their track "White Heaven / Black Hell"—using the language of Malcolm X's column and Louis X's song—a track issued on their 1994 album *Muse Sick-n-Hour Mess Age* ("Music in Our Message"). They released the album in the midst of an incredible resurgence of cultural production around Malcolm X, in the aftermath of the beating of Rodney King, and on the eve of Farrakhan's Million Man March. "White Heaven / Black Hell," engages in its own process of musical citation and recitation that revises even as it remembers through powerful new versions of earlier verses. Public Enemy invokes these earlier struggles for the era of mass incarceration and the war on drugs: "This is for the ones on the corner / This is for the ones in the cell."[103]

Public Enemy invokes these struggles against police brutality for a new generation, speaking of their cyclical nature, the "intransigent fungibility of structures of racism," explains Dylan Rodriguez, writing himself in the context of Black Lives Matter.[104] The album came out in the midst of the ratification and signing into law of President Clinton's $30 billion "Violent Crime Control and Law Enforcement Act" in September 1994. The law instituted mandatory sentencing and life sentences for some three-time offenders, leading to the rise of mass incarceration and what Michelle Alexander has called the New Jim Crow. When Clinton was running for election in summer 1992, he proposed putting a hundred thousand new police officers on the streets, garnering the endorsement of the National Association of Police Officers, who were later involved in the drafting of the law. The album cover of *Muse Sick-n-Hour Mess Age* by Marvel inker Michael (Hernandez) Bair presciently depicts the stakes of the bill with a joint-smoking skeleton, wearing a red, yellow, and green tam and earphones, pointing a gun at his skull. On the table in front of him is a book with "LAW" written on it and a package of marijuana—signifying the crime bill, the war on drugs, and its victims. On either side of the skeleton are a Klansman and what looks like Bill Clinton as a presidential candidate. Although the original album cover shows a police officer in crosshairs, the visual effect makes the viewers the targets of the police. Later "clean" versions of the album erased the critique of police violence, with the image of the police in crosshairs shrunk, the references to the war on drugs and the crime law removed, and the skeleton eliminated, replaced with a photograph of the band members under the Manhattan Bridge. References connecting Bair to the image likewise have been scrubbed from public representations of his own career in comics, probably because it would compromise his place in the Marvel universe. Even without knowing the specific connection of Farrakhan's song to Malcolm's critique of police brutality in "God's Angry Men," Public Enemy implicitly understood its history.

Despite being cut down in his prime, Malcolm X's words, speeches, and writing have lived on through a constant stream of citation and re-citation in music, poetry, film, and scholarship. Public Enemy's 1990 "Fight the Power" sampled—and scrambled—Malcolm's words from his 1963 "Message to the Grassroots" speech, where he calls for revolution, criticizing the civil rights activists for locking arms and singing "We Shall Overcome." "You don't do that in a revolution," says Malcolm, "you're too busy swinging." But Chuck D and Flavor Flav make the music the revolution, rapping "y'all swingin' / while I'm singin' givin' whatcha gettin' . . . / while the Black band's / Sweatin' and the rhythm-rhyme rollin!'"[105] Malcolm would also revise himself. After his break with the NOI, he returned to his earlier understanding of music in his prison letters, as emblematic of a spiritual and intellectual harmony needed to build a new society. Fifteen years later, he again used language evocative of Hazrat Inayat Khan's mysticism, in one of the final speeches of his life: his January 24, 1965, speech "On Afro-American History" presented at the Audubon Ballroom where he would be assassinated one month later. In the speech, he used music as a metaphor for building and balance. "Rhythm is mathematics, harmony is mathematics. It's balance. . . . But when you are in tune with yourself, your very nature has harmony, has rhythm, has mathematics," he said, "You can build. . . . You play music by ear. You dance by how you're feeling. And you used to build the same way."[106]

Malcolm X's words, writings, and speeches spread sonically, interpreted through music, living on as they circulate and recirculate in a loop, back and forth in time. Malcolm X drew on Elijah Muhammad's rhetoric and teachings in his writings and speeches—just as Louis X drew on Malcolm X's and Elijah Muhammad's words (and Prince Buster drew on Farrakhan, Muhammad, and Malcolm)—sowing ideas and teachings among Nation members, potential recruits, the broader public, and across the African and Muslim diaspora. A dialogue played out, not only between Malcolm X's writing and Farrakhan's song but also with the larger Black musical tradition, the longer Islamic tradition, and the wider Umma. The column's, as well as the song's, repeated emphasis on origins, specifically Islamic origins, weaves the music and preaching into these intertwined traditions, calling out to them. Reinforcing the message via multiple media, these writings, speeches, and music function as protest and preaching, as a "soundtrack to the movement." As both Ellison and Malcolm X remark, it also functions as some kind of magic where "the dead rise up and walk again," awoken by song. Music, as Malcolm wrote in his letter from prison, is "Like Life!!!"[107]

CHAPTER 5

"FLAME FEEDING FLAME"

The Literary Malcolm X

a spark brought from nothing . . .
Stone rubbed against stone
Upon the thirsty grass,
Dried and baked by a burning son . . .
Then suddenly: flame.
Flame feeding flame.
. . . Now, nothing is the same.

—Sun Ra, "Saga of Resistance," *Black Fire*

The nightmare that opens *The Autobiography of Malcolm X* is of a house on fire, Malcolm's X "earliest vivid memory" of being "suddenly snatched awake into a frightening confusion of pistol shots and shouting and smoke and flames. . . . Our home was burning down around us."[1] This traumatic formative moment becomes the starting point of the narrative, the threat of white racial terror against Black life framing his first memories. The scene—Malcolm's pregnant mother standing amid the chaos of the burning house, her small children around her and a baby in her arms, facing the threat of the Klan—frames Malcolm's baptism by fire. This nightmare of the house on fire is what Saidiya Hartman calls "an original generative act," what she describes as a birth into consciousness of racialization "equivalent to the statement 'I was born.'"[2] It is a moment of deracination through loss of home, destruction of property, and by the end of the opening chapter, loss of father, mother, brothers, and sisters. The apparatus of the state—police, legal system, social services, even the firemen sent to (not) put out the fire—works systematically to dismantle family and home. "Nightmare," the *Autobiography*'s first chapter, is about the specter of that night, but also about the denial of basic rights to property ownership and self-determination, the foundations of the American dream and citizenship in a capitalist democracy.

In the *Autobiography*, Malcolm X (or Alex Haley) remembers recounting this childhood memory to an audience at Michigan State University in East Lansing, not far from where he had grown up—and where the house had been burned down.[3] The story Malcolm X told in the speech, however, was not of his own house burning down, but the parable of the master's house catching fire—the life story mingling with the parable and vice versa.[4] The memory of his mother famously brought Malcolm X's life story tumbling out of him, in "stream-of-consciousness reminiscing" that removed subconscious blocks on his mind and led him to reconnect with her after twenty-five years, bringing her home from the asylum where she had been institutionalized.[5] The parable of the house burning down would become one of Malcolm's most famous rhetorical interventions.[6] Malcolm had written and spoken about fire as retribution from as early as his "God's Angry Men" articles in 1957, writing that God would destroy the slave master with an "unquenchable fire" and would save "His People from the lake of fire."[7] A few months later, he similarly wrote in the Los Angeles *Herald-Dispatch* about Islam "sweeping through Black America like a 'flaming fire,' under the Divine Guidance of Messenger Elijah Muhammad."[8] But not until January 1963 did he develop the image of the master's house on fire as a parable for the relationship between the "House Negro and the field Negro." That same month, James Baldwin published *The Fire Next Time*, in which he posed the question: "Do I really *want* to be integrated into a burning house?"[9] Malcolm and Baldwin engaged in a call and response that grew out of their public meetings and dialogues—on WBAI radio and on the television program *The Open Mind* in April 1961. *The Fire Next Time* grew out of a conversation or dialogue between Baldwin and the "Muslim movement," as he drew on the language of Malcolm X, Elijah Muhammad, and Louis Farrakhan. Baldwin quoted "White Man's Heaven is a Black Man's Hell" in the middle of the essay, gave an account of the impact of Malcolm X's speeches, and described in detail his private meeting with Elijah Muhammad in Chicago. With *The Fire Next Time*, Malcolm's ideas—and the teachings and theology of what Baldwin calls the "Muslim movement"—began to flow into the literary sphere, though Malcolm X had already been long engaged with artists, writers, musicians, and intellectuals.

Malcolm X's relationship with artists, intellectuals, and activists, writes Peniel Joseph, was "an unlikely alliance" rooted in "a long history of black radicalism" and an understanding of "artistic rebellion as the cultural arm of a political revolution."[10] Despite Elijah Muhammad's ambivalent attitude toward cultural production, Malcolm developed an agenda for the politics of cultural reproduction—one that planted the seeds of BAM, rooted in the organizing, activism, and writings of the leftist writers and intellectuals of his time. Malcolm's "friendships with popular artists and musicians in the 1940s made him comfortable around cultural and literary figures," writes Joseph: "His outreach to New York City's leading black artists and intellectuals stretched the limits of acceptable behavior within the Nation."[11] In addition to debating the leaders of the civil rights movement, he met at Ossie Davis and Ruby Dee's home with intellectuals connected to the Harlem Writers Guild—a meeting that included Julian Mayfield and Lorraine Hansberry—most likely in late 1961.[12] He attended Davis's play *Purlie Victorious*; met with Maya Angelou and Rosa Guy after they protested Patrice Lumumba's assassination at the UN; debated James Baldwin and hung out with him; talked on the phone with Paule Marshall; visited Shirley Graham Du Bois, Sylvia Boone, Mayfield, and Angelou in Ghana; and attended Hansberry's funeral only weeks before his own.[13] More formal alliances developed after Malcolm X severed ties with the Nation of Islam in 1964, when he formed the Organization of Afro-American Unity (OAAU), whose charter Malcolm X wrote with Harlem Writers Guild pioneers John Henrik Clarke and John O. Killens. The document's last section is devoted to outlining the role of "Culture" and "cultural revolution to un-brainwash an entire people" as a means of liberation from "the bonds of white supremacy." The OAAU charter draws on NOI language (about white supremacy and brainwashing) despite Malcolm's break with the organization, purposefully and mindfully using NOI teachings to engage the cultural sphere. It calls for the establishment of a cultural center with workshops in the arts, film, creative writing, painting, theater, music, and Afro-American history—"Culture," it says, "is an indispensable weapon in the freedom struggle."[14]

One of the most quoted lines in *The Fire Next Time*—"Do I really *want* to be integrated into a burning house?"—grew out of (and personalized) a statement Lorraine Hansberry made during "The Negro in American Culture" a panel discussion hosted by WBAI radio on January 10, 1961. "There are tones of Negro nationalism articulated in a far more sophisticated and pointed way than years ago. The question is openly being raised today among all Negro intellectuals and among all politically conscious Negroes: Is it necessary to integrate oneself into a burning house?"[15] Hansberry, along with the other panelists—Baldwin, Langston Hughes, Alfred Kazin, Emile Capouya, and Nat Hentoff—had been discussing Black art, the representation of Black life, and the role of the Black writer, when she questioned the value of integrating into the literary mainstream of American letters. But the Cuban revolution and anticolonial independence movements across the globe were also on her mind, and she connected these revolutionary movements to the self-determination of the Black nationalism reemerging in the early 1960s. Hansberry also seemed to be implicitly referencing Malcolm X as a politically conscious Black intellectual—and his own fiery rhetoric about the United States as a "house of bondage"—something he had talked about with Bayard Rustin on WBAI radio only a few months earlier.[16]

Hansberry's words circulated among a cadre of Black intellectuals in the early 1960s. They became one of the defining images of Black radicalism, but also of Black art. Just after the WBAI panel discussion, Baldwin directly quoted Hansberry in "The Negro Assays the Negro Mood," an article published in the *New York Times Magazine*, but without citing her.[17] The "burning house" query then made its way into "Letter from a Region of my Mind" and *The Fire Next Time*—leading Martin Luther King to attribute the comment to Baldwin. Similarly, Malcolm X developed his own imagery of the master's house on fire after the comment circulated on WBAI, in the *NYT Magazine*, and in the *New Yorker*. Though Baldwin, Malcolm X, and King all seem to quote Hansberry in their references to "integrating into a burning house," her own contribution to this debate has not been acknowledged or cited. As her biographer Imani Perry observes: "Lorraine remains in their shadows, although she was key to them and they to her."[18]

Through the eschatological—but also revolutionary and insurrectionary—image of the burning house, this chapter traces the roots and routes of this rhetorical trope, exploring an "insurgent genealogy" of the image.[19] Its circulation among these politically conscious Black intellectuals testifies to the power of the conversation between them—one that played out as a feedback loop that was both debate and "tag team assault on white supremacy," a process of sampling that was tribute and reinterpretation, a sermonic call and response that preached a liberation theology.[20] At a critical juncture in the early 1960s, this dialogue expanded the dimensions of the Black counterpublic, amplifying its critique of the white public sphere and bourgeois values—with Black fire signifying insurrection, rooted in a longer tradition of black protest.[21] It is well known that the Black Arts Movement grew out of Malcolm X's influence, speeches, and rhetorical style. But Malcolm X also listened to, read, and engaged with the leftist intellectuals of his time through imagery that they sampled from each other and used to powerful effect in the American public sphere, on radio, on television, in newspapers and journals, in interviews, and in debates and speeches at universities and in public lecture halls. Just as Malcolm X so clearly influenced the intellectuals of his time, they also influenced him—in ways that both dovetailed and diverged from the teachings of Elijah Muhammad.

The words "integrating into a burning house" have lived on through a call and response between politically conscious Black intellectuals, in a dialogic transfer from person to person, "from one context to another context, from one social collective to another, from one generation to another generation," carrying the power of the different contexts in which they were uttered.[22] Rooted in a longer tradition of Black protest—like the Harlem Renaissance journal *Fire!!*—the language of fire was threaded through James Baldwin's *The Fire Next Time* (1963), Amiri Baraka and Larry Neal's seminal Black Arts Movement anthology *Black Fire* (1968), and later critical interventions like Cornell West's *Black Prophetic Fire* (2015). It became integral in Black Arts Movement poetry and thought, symbolizing a torching of the bourgeois values of the white public sphere—and the flourishing of a radical poetics of a Black counterpublic.[23] The imagery of the burning house has continued to inform new generations of Black creatives, thinkers, and writers: The Fire This Time Festival, Jesmyn Ward's edited volume *The Fire This Time* (2016) dedicated to Trayvon Martin; Amir Sulaiman's visual poem *Laying Flowers, Setting Fires* (2020); Kim McMillon and Kofi Antwi's *Black Fire This Time* (2022) anthology, and Meshell Ndegeocello's music performance "No More Water / the Fire Next Time" (2022).[24] Malcolm X's use of the image of fire on several occasions of police brutality—after the beating of Johnson X Hinton (in 1957) and the death of Ronald Stokes (in 1962)—suggest the reasons for its ongoing salience as protest of the violence against Black life. In 2013, Black Classic Press reissued *Black Fire* only months after George Zimmerman's acquittal for killing Trayvon Martin. In a new introduction, Amiri Baraka called the anthology a document of its time, "of the BLM in overview historically and yet it focuses on aspects of the struggle still very much in evidence today." The book represents a united front "against white supremacy & submissive 'integration into a burning building' (as Malcolm and Dr. King both told us)."[25] The image of integrating into a burning house circulated widely through the Black Lives Matter protests, as emblematic of the problems inherent in the white value structure, of police brutality, racialized violence, and the prison industrial complex—but always attributed to Baldwin, King, and Malcolm X.[26]

The misattribution of Hansberry's words testifies to her "invisibilization and erasure" as a "radical producer of knowledge." She has been written out of histories of Black radicalism, something both her biographers, Imani Perry and Soyica Diggs Colbert, have worked to redress.[27] Hansberry played a seminal role in fostering a "creative, liberation-focused, and generally radical political-intellectual practice" at a pivotal moment in the early 1960s, as Black nationalist consciousness fueled a revolution of values, shored up by a flourishing of Black writings that laid the foundations of Black Studies as a discipline.[28] Like the "spark" in Sun Ra's "Saga of Resistance," Hansberry's words were "flame feeding flame."[29]

BLACK WRITERS AND "INTEGRATION IN THE HOUSE OF BONDAGE"

The 1961 WBAI panel discussion "The Negro in American Culture" is a remarkable literary conversation on the relationship between Black art, life, and politics on the cusp of the Black Arts Movement, in the midst of the civil rights movement, and during the reemergence of Black nationalism. With good reason, the words from that intervention have echoed through time, recycled again and again, through what Henry Louis Gates Jr. calls "intertextuality . . . in the Afro-American formal literary tradition."[30] Malcolm X may have been listening to the panel discussion, since he had just appeared on WBAI and would again a few months later in a debate with James Baldwin. Bits and pieces of the discussion filtered into his own speeches, interviews, and writings that year.[31] What is certain is that Malcolm X engaged with the leftist intellectuals and literary figures of his time, in both public conversations and private dialogues. "Malcolm X provided a model of how one might be an intellectual and an artist (especially an artist with language) and a political radical," writes James Smethurst. "He presented a vision of black freedom linked to generations of black radicalism . . . and to new liberation movements and the new independent nations of Africa and Asia."[32] But these artists and intellectuals also clearly influenced him and the development of his thought.

Hansberry's criticism of "integrating into a burning house" on WBAI radio came at the height of her career. The film version of *A Raisin in the Sun*, starring Sidney Poitier and Ruby Dee, was about to premiere (in May 1961), and the Broadway play had received a glowing critical reception and was broadly popular. Yet her success was double-edged, leading some critics to interpret the play as a dramatization of middle class, bourgeois dreams of integration.[33] Yet such an analysis misinterprets the radical politics coded into the play, her insistence on Black characters, her advocacy of the working class, her intellectual tutelage under W. E. B. Du Bois and Paul Robeson, and membership in the Communist Party.[34] *A Raisin in the Sun* (1959) drew on autobiographical elements from her own family's traumatic experience buying a house in a white neighborhood governed by racially restrictive covenants, leading to a Supreme Court case challenging such covenants. At the end of the play, as at the end of the Hansberry's court case, the family moves into the house in the white neighborhood. Perry describes the experience as "a harrowing story," with Hansberry, her mother, and her siblings living "under siege. Outside their door a howling white mob lay in wait," hitting, spitting on, and cursing them on their way to school. "In truth," writes Perry, "the Hansberry experience was not unique."[35] The scene resonates with the opening chapter of Malcolm X's *Autobiography*; "Nightmare" similarly describes a harrowing attack on the family home by a howling white mob. Both works reflect on the Black home as a kind of refuge, the difficulty of property ownership in the face of racial discrimination, its effects on survival, and its crushing impact on dreams.

In his own analysis of the play, Amiri Baraka recognized the radicalness of Hansberry's intervention. The play clearly summed up the Black liberation movement at a moment of transition, he argues, just as "Malcolm X, 'the fire prophet,' emerged as the truest reflector of black mass feelings." *Raisin in the Sun*, Baraka writes,

> is the accurate telling and stunning vision of the real struggle.... We thought that Hansberry's play was part of the 'passive resistance' phase of the movement, which was over the minute Malcolm's penetrating eyes and words began to charge through the media with deadly force. We thought her play was 'middle class' in that its focus seemed to be on 'moving into white folks' neighborhoods.... We missed the essence of the work—that Hansberry had created a family on the cutting edge of the same class and ideological struggles as existed in the movement itself and among the people.[36]

As a mea culpa of sorts, Baraka retracts his earlier criticism of *Raisin in the Sun*, acknowledging Hansberry's radical politics in tandem with those of Malcolm the fire prophet. Although Malcolm X and Lorraine Hansberry came from very different backgrounds, they circulated in overlapping circles, developing a shared understanding of the transnational dimensions of the struggle for economic and racial self-determination. Both used the image of the burning house as a metaphor for revolt against the structures of racial capitalism—calling for building a house of your own in a system that connects citizenship rights to property.[37]

The WBAI discussion revolves around the metaphor of American letters as a house, developing earlier theorizations of Black art and its relationship to the literary mainstream of white literature (as in the writings of W. E. B. Du Bois and

Langston Hughes).³⁸ In the WBAI discussion, Hughes elaborates on this metaphor specifically through reference to *Raisin in the Sun*, saying that despite all the "differences and difficulties, *this is our house*." This comment is a remarkable example of Gates's later understanding of intertextuality and call and response in the African American literary tradition: Hughes interprets Hansberry's play, which takes as its title a line from Hughes's book-length poem *Montage of a Dream Deferred* (1951). The panelists engage in a remarkable literary dialogue about the hypocrisies of the American dream, exemplified by the dream house. But they are also engaging in a metaphorical—or allegorical—discussion about Black writers' contentious relationship to a house that has placed them in a subordinate position. The WBAI panelists talk about the work of William Faulkner and his representation of Black characters as exemplifying this problem. Baldwin notes that Faulkner surely never sat in the kitchen of an African American home, though African Americans have been sitting in white kitchens for generations. Baldwin observes the limits of what white Americans are able to know about not only Black life but also the realities of *American* life and the American dream. Extending the metaphor of the house of American letters, Baldwin quotes a French idiom: " 'If you want to know what's happening in the house, ask the maid.' And it occurred to me that in this extraordinary house, I am the maid."³⁹ By making himself the "maid" in the house of literature, Baldwin comments on the position of Black authors (with reference to the gendered subordination of Black women). But Baldwin also casts a queer eye on his own position within the structural mechanisms of the white value system, openly acknowledging his gayness through coded language. His—and Hansberry's—non-normativity creates what he calls "a very great advantage" with respect to the literary mainstream of white cultural production. And Hansberry responds that Black Americans' "intimacy of knowledge . . . of white Americans does not exist in reverse."⁴⁰

The panelists turn to discussing what the moderator Nat Hentoff calls the urge to assimilate and the "desire for equality within the white value-structure." Hentoff asks: "Has there been enough questioning of this in Negro writing?"⁴¹ Baldwin and Hansberry are both indignant, if not incredulous, recognizing how much Black literature has questioned the urge to assimilate—something that Langston Hughes's famous essay "The Negro and the Racial Mountain" explicitly explored. Baldwin's response ended up in *The Fire Next Time*, as he himself questions Hentoff, "Equal for what? . . . What makes you think I *want* to be accepted?" His tone suggests a rejection, not just of the white value-structure but also of heteronormativity. He and Hansberry finish each other's ideas and sentences, functioning as a "marvelous tag team, their ideas bouncing back and forth, rapid-fire," as Perry says in her biography of Hansberry.⁴²

"Into this?" says Lorraine Hansberry.

"Into this," affirms Baldwin.

"Maybe something else," says Hansberry.

"It's not a matter of acceptance or tolerance," says Baldwin. "We've got to sit down and rebuild this house."

"Quickly," says Hansberry.

"Very quickly," says Baldwin, "And we have to do it together.["]43

Their discussion centers on the insight of Black writers into the realities of American life—and the lack of reverse consciousness in white literature—imbuing Black art with its inherently political nature ("a consequence of structures of racism that have historically marginalized access to the means of cultural production").[44]

In the WBAI discussion, the literary critic Alfred Kazin talks about the values of freedom and equality that the United States purports to espouse versus the reality of how American society is actually structured. Kazin calls it an "enormous comedy of American pretensions"—hypocrisy that is "the central fact about our moral history. And the conflict in the American heart . . . comes out of a constant tension between what this country is ideally supposed to mean and what it actually has been as such. The problem has become more and more catastrophic and dangerous because of the growing world anxiety about possible world annihilation. Suddenly you begin to realize that people who don't treat their fellow citizens well are, in a sense, *building up a bonfire* for everyone else, as is likely to happen in Africa before our generation is over."[45] Kazin connects struggles over economic and racial inequality in the United States to global struggles for decolonization in Asia and Africa in the Cold War era—talking about a bonfire of racial and economic inequalities feeding revolutionary movements.

The insight of Black writers into the hypocrisies and paradoxes of American life is what Hansberry, a student of Du Bois, understands as a double consciousness.[46] For Hansberry, this insight fuels a political consciousness stripped of its falseness, imparting a certain truth value in literature, partly through faithful representation of the realities of Black life—in marked contrast to the mainstream of the white public sphere.[47] Hansberry argues that this is the prerequisite for any kind of serious writing, saying that she cannot imagine "a contemporary writer any place in the world today who isn't in conflict with his world. . . . If he was any kind of artist, he had to be." But Black writers and artists are "doubly aware of conflict because of the special pressures" they face in America.[48] This double consciousness about the realities of life in the United States, the panelists argue, makes not just great Black art, but great art.[49] Good art, says Hansberry, is informed by "social awareness, social intelligence ... social passion. And one must not ever try to divide the two."[50]

The social intelligence of double consciousness is also rooted in tensions between the "masses and the mainstream," between "high" and "low" art, the white, bourgeois public sphere and the Black counterpublic. The panelists are attuned to the economic struggle at the heart of these modes of cultural production as it intersects with representations of race—especially with regard to questions of ownership—not just of intellectual property, but also of presses, journals, and publishing houses (a discussion cut out of the transcript published in *CrossCurrents*).[51] The class dimension was especially critical for Hansberry, who had worked for Paul Robeson's journal *Freedom*, studied at the Communist-affiliated Jefferson School for Social Science with W. E. B. Du Bois, and joined the Communist Party as well as the Labor Youth League.[52] Hughes himself had been accused of being a communist and was forced in 1953 to testify before Senator Joseph McCarthy. He said to the committee that, at one point in his life, he "believed in the entire philosophies of the left, ... including socialism, communism, Trotskyism."[53] The panelists refer to this class struggle in leftist terms—as between the masses and the mainstream—with Hughes quoting at length from Julian Mayfield's essay "Into the Mainstream and Oblivion," which itself drew directly on language from the Marxist journal *Masses and Mainstream*, published in New York between 1948 and 1963. Mayfield observes that the Black writer has the special "insight of the stranger in the house, placing him in a better position to illuminate contemporary American life as few writers of the mainstream can. This alienation should serve also to make him *more sensitive to philosophical and artistic influences that originate beyond our national cultural boundaries*."[54]

Mayfield's essay questions the value of integrating into the literary mainstream—and the passage that Hughes quotes at length in the WBAI discussion speaks directly to this issue. American literature is plagued by what Mayfield calls "the vacuity of the American mainstream, ... the façade of the American way of life," the false consciousness described by Baldwin and Hansberry. The Black writer "owes it to the future of his art to analyze the contents of the American mainstream to determine the full significance of his commitment to it. He may decide that, though the music sweet, he would rather play in another orchestra.... The Negro writer may conclude that his best salvation lies in escaping the narrow national orbit—artistic, cultural, and political—and soaring into more universal experience."[55] Coded into this conversation about Black literature and Black art is a wider discussion about other modes of identification with the African diaspora and the Bandung world. Mayfield was already living in Puerto Rico with his wife, Ana Livia Cordero, and would later go into exile in

Ghana. His essay was originally presented at the First Negro Writers Conference in 1959, organized by the American Society of African Culture, envisioned as a stateside instantiation of the Congresses of Negro Writers and Artists in Paris (1956) and Rome (1959) organized by *Présence Africaine*. The AMSAC conference brought together what Mary Helen Washington characterizes as "an embattled internationalist Left ... determined to advance black cultural and political self-determination."[56] Only days before the Broadway premiere of *Raisin in the Sun*, Hansberry delivered the conference keynote, although it would not be included in the collected essays *The American Negro Writer and His Roots* (1960).[57] Mayfield's essay also critiqued the concept of the American dream versus the American reality lived by the "masses," arguing that the Black writer "sings the national anthem *sotto voce* and has trouble reconciling the 'dream' to the reality he knows."[58] Mayfield was riffing off of Langston Hughes's *Montage of a Dream Deferred* (1951), just as Hansberry did in the title and epigraph of *Raisin in the Sun*. Malcolm X's own speeches about the American nightmare picked up on this critique of the American dream; Martin Luther King would himself intervene in this discussion with his "I Have a Dream" speech at the 1963 March on Washington, pushing back against Malcolm's concept of the nightmare. But in a later 1967 interview on NBC News "After Civil Rights: Black Power," King admitted that "the dream I had has in many points turned into a nightmare."[59]

This was not just a literary critique, but an economic one as well. Mayfield was a member of the Communist Party and the leftist Committee for the Negro in the Arts. In October 1960, he wrote about Cuba as the solution to the race problem in *Fair Play for Cuba*—connecting the struggle for racial justice to anti-imperialism in not just Cuba, but also in Vietnam, Korea, and Puerto Rico.[60] When Hansberry made her comment about the necessity of "integrating into a burning house," she did so in direct reference to Mayfield ("in Mayfield's statement that you read just now, there are tones of Negro nationalism, articulated in a far more sophisticated and pointed way than years ago"). She urges the panelists to be mindful of larger political questions ("real and true things existing in the consciences of Negroes today"); she talks about anticolonial movements abroad and the Cuban revolution, connecting them to Black struggle in the United States. She specifically cites the United States's upholding of colonial occupation with its abstention from the UN resolution 1514, "Declaration on the Granting of Independence to Colonial Countries and Peoples" less than a month earlier (on December 14, 1960) and its vote against Algerian independence in the UN's GA/Res 1573 on December 19, 1960.[61] She also talks about Fidel Castro's warm reception in Harlem when the Cuban delegation visited the UN in September 1960, when he moved uptown to stay at the Theresa Hotel and met with

Black leaders like Robert F. Williams and Malcolm X.[62] Hansberry's comment about the "burning house" connected "politically conscious Black nationalist intellectuals" to struggles for independence, decolonization, and revolution—linking "black nationalism with Pan-African internationalism in a way that pointed straight toward Black Power."[63] This is something Hansberry talked about in her keynote speech at the First Negro Writers Conference in March 1959: "the ultimate destiny and aspirations of the African people and twenty million American Negroes are inextricably and magnificently bound up together forever."[64]

The transnational solidarities between the Black liberation movement and anticolonial freedom struggles was a political perspective that Hansberry and Malcolm X shared. (Malcolm X talked about the Black liberation movement coming together "in the spirit of Bandung" at the Harlem Freedom Rally in summer 1960.)[65] The comment about the burning house, and Hansberry's tribute to the new wave of Black nationalism, suggests that she had tuned in to Malcolm X's rhetoric—and may have been listening to him in his own appearance on WBAI a few months earlier or reading his articles published in the *New York Amsterdam News*.[66] Hansberry and Malcolm X circulated each other not only via print media, but also on the radio and in person. The same month that Malcolm X met with Castro in Harlem (in September 1960), he and Lorraine Hansberry both served as orientation leaders for John F. Kennedy's Airlift Africa program.[67] Malcolm X also appeared on WBAI on November 6, 1960, just two months before Hansberry's panel discussion, in a debate with the civil rights activist Bayard Rustin. Malcolm criticized the idea of "integration in the house of bondage" and compared Elijah Muhammad to Moses leading the "Black masses" in an exodus out of captivity.[68] He also talked about Islam spreading like "wildfire" across the globe—citing a *New York Times* article that linked the rise of the Ahmadiyya movement in the United States to Islam in Nigeria, just after Nigeria's independence in October 1960.[69] Malcolm X would develop the image of the master's house—using the "house of bondage" to reference slavery, but also to draw analogies between citizenship rights and property—and the exclusion of the "Black masses" from full citizenship through the denial of "a land of their own."[70]

Both Hansberry and Malcolm X were students of W. E. B. Du Bois. Hansberry's critique of integration invoked not only the Black nationalist separatism of the Nation, but also of Du Bois and his later embrace of political, economic, and cultural separatism, communism, and decolonization. Malcolm X himself read Du Bois in prison and would later visit Shirley Graham Du Bois, Mayfield, Sylvia Boone, and Maya Angelou in Ghana.[71] Malcolm X used Du Bois's language of a "nation within a nation" in his speeches, language that would also appear in

Elijah Muhammad's speeches and writings, including *Message to the Blackman in America* (1965).[72] Malcolm X conceptualized the class dimensions of racial oppression in dialogue with Elijah Muhammad, but also in close conversation with the radical activists and intellectuals of his day—ones who saw economic equality as the path to racial justice. He developed close relationships with Robert F. Williams, Julian Mayfield, Max Stanford, and the labor leader A. Philip Randolph. (In summer of 1961, Randolph invited Malcolm X to be a part of a "Working Committee for Unity of Action.") Their connections with "the decolonizing nationalisms of the Third World—and with Cuban socialism in particular—illustrate the ideological richness of the African American Left," writes Rafael Rojas in his own analysis of their relationship.[73] Malcolm X also cultivated a close relationship with Williams, inviting him to speak at Temple No. 7 in 1959 and funneling funds toward his work as head of the NAACP in Monroe, North Carolina.[74] Williams had secured the release of two boys (ages seven and nine) convicted for kissing a white girl in the "kissing case" in Monroe (1959); helped desegregate the Monroe pool (1961); provided refuge for the Freedom Riders (1961); and did armed battle with the KKK when the police refused to provide protection. Julian Mayfield also worked closely with Williams in Monroe—and they both fled into exile in 1961 after being accused of kidnapping a white couple they had given refuge to in the midst of the Freedom Rides—Williams to Cuba and Mayfield to Ghana.

Mayfield also developed a close relationship with Malcolm X—and appears to have met with both Malcolm and Hansberry at Ossie Davis and Ruby Dee's house in Mount Vernon—while he was a fugitive, sometime in October or November of 1961 before going into exile.[75] (He would not return from exile until after Malcolm X's death.) Davis describes the meeting as taking place while his play *Purlie Victorious* was showing on Broadway (between September 28, 1961 and May 13, 1962); he recalled Hansberry rebuking Malcolm X for an article he wrote, criticizing her and other Black leaders for their interracial relationships, published on October 1, 1961, in the inaugural issue of *Muhammad Speaks*.[76] Mayfield acquired his passport in New York City on September 11 and his visa from the Ghanaian Consulate in New York on November 8.[77] The meeting shows Malcolm X's close engagement with these literary figures and civil rights leaders long before his break with the NOI, as they worked in tandem to secure fugitive justice for Mayfield and Williams. When visiting Mayfield in Ghana, Malcolm X may have paid tribute to Mayfield's own critique of the American dream in a speech presented at the University of Ghana, "For the twenty million of us in America who are of African descent, it is not an American dream; it's an American nightmare."[78]

THE FIRE NEXT TIME AND
THE MASTER'S HOUSE ON FIRE

Just after the WBAI panel, Baldwin quoted Hansberry in an article he wrote about the 1961 demonstrations at the UN protesting the assassination of Patrice Lumumba. Only one week after the WBAI panel discussion, Lumumba was assassinated in the newly independent Congo with the help of the CIA, retribution for an alliance struck with the Soviet Union to defend against Belgian supported secessionists. When the news of Lumumba's assassination finally broke a month later, a coalition of Black leftist organizations planned demonstrations at the United Nations, disrupting Adlai Stevenson's inaugural address as US representative. Joining the protests were writers, artists, intellectuals, and activists like Sarah E. Wright, Calvin Hicks, Robert F. Williams, Maya Angelou, Abbey Lincoln, Rosa Guy, Daniel Watts, Askia Muhammad Touré [still Rolland Snellings], and Amiri Baraka [still LeRoi Jones] from the Harlem Writers Guild, On Guard for Freedom, the Umbra Workshop, the Cultural Association for Women of African Heritage, and the Liberation Committee for Africa. Snellings and Jones first met at the protest, forming key alliances that brought together an informal coalition of Black leftist organizations catalyzing the emergence of the Black Arts Movement, fostering "new links between a disparate group of New York-based intellectuals, activists, and artists."[79] In his article about the protests—and about decolonization in the Congo, Cuba, the United States, and the UN—Baldwin revisited Hansberry's questions about the necessity of integrating into a burning house, structuring his argument around her analysis of the allure of the Cuban revolution for the Black freedom movement and other independence movements on the African continent. Published in the *New York Times Magazine* on March 12, 1961, Baldwin's article "A Negro Assays the Negro Mood" explicitly invoked something that Hansberry had implicitly evoked: the intellectual power of Black nationalism and the Black Muslim Movement. The article laid out some of main arguments Baldwin would raise in *The Fire Next Time* connecting the Muslim movement to larger transnational struggles for racial and economic justice. ("This searching disaffection has everything to do with the emergence of Africa. 'At the rate things are going here, all of Africa will be free before we can get a lousy cup of coffee' "—a direct quote of Malcolm X's interview with Eleanor Fischer. Or, was Malcolm X citing Baldwin? It's hard to know since the date of the interview is uncertain.)[80] In "A Negro Assays the Negro Mood" Baldwin borrows the imagery from Hansberry's comments in the WBAI interview without naming her—just as he would in "Letter from a Region in My Mind": " 'I am not at all sure,' states one prominent Negro, who is *not* a Muslim, 'that I *want* to be integrated into a burning house.' "[81]

Only twelve days after the publication of Baldwin's article about the Black Muslims in the *New York Times Magazine*, Malcolm X revisited his earlier image of the "house of bondage," talking about it catching on fire. "This wicked old house," he said at the Harvard Law School on March 24, 1961, "is going to collapse or go up in smoke." In the speech, he also characterized Elijah Muhammad as a leader of "the lowly, uneducated, downtrodden and oppressed masses, among the lowest element of America's 20 million ex-slaves." Using Marxist imagery of Christianity as an opiate of the masses, he said: "The black masses are shaking off the drugs, or narcotic effect of the token integration promises.[82] He also drew on Du Bois's language of Black America as a "nation within a nation," ideas Du Bois developed in his later advocacy of separatism that got him expelled from the NAACP.[83]

Soon after, Baldwin and Malcolm X appeared together in two back-to-back appearances on radio and television. One of these was also on WBAI radio, an April 25, 1961, discussion of the sit-in movement versus the Black Muslims. The other was a panel discussion on the television show *Open Mind* about the Black Muslim movement, an appearance that led Elijah Muhammad to invite Baldwin to his home in Chicago. That meeting that became the central focus of "Letter from a Region of My Mind" published in November 1962. In May of that year, Malcolm X developed the image of the burning house in a speech delivered after the police shooting of Ronald Stokes and six other members of Muhammad's Temple No. 27 in Los Angeles. In the speech, he said: "If the white man is not ready to clean his house up, he shouldn't have a house. It should catch on fire. And burn down."[84]

The Fire Next Time developed the burning house imagery of both Hansberry and Malcolm X, again quoting her almost directly without citing her: "Hence the question: Do I really *want* to be integrated into a burning house?"[85] The fire of moral retribution, insurrection, revolution, and racial justice structures the essay as a whole, closing with the warning to "end the racial nightmare."[86] The evocation of the American nightmare is a direct tribute to Malcolm X, who had used the image in a debate with James Farmer at Cornell in March 1962 and published in the journal *Dialogue* in May 1962, just before the police killing of Stokes: "What to them is an American dream to us is an American nightmare, and we don't think that it is possible for the American white man in sincerity to take the action necessary to correct the unjust conditions that 20 million black people here are made to suffer morning, noon, and night."[87] The nightmare became an integral part of Malcolm's rhetorical tools, one that ultimately led James Cone to develop his own understanding of King and Malcolm X's differing theologies in terms of the American dream versus the American nightmare.[88] "The American dream that has become something much more closely resembling a nightmare," writes Baldwin, "on the private, domestic, and international levels."[89] And "Nightmare" became the title of the *Autobiography*'s opening chapter, with Malcolm's earliest memory of his house being set on fire recounting the origins of his racialized consciousness.

The Fire Next Time analyzed the ideological and rhetorical power of Elijah Muhammad, Malcolm X, and Louis Farrakhan. But Malcolm X and Elijah Muhammad also adapted language from *The Fire Next Time*. In *Message to the Blackman in America*, published after Malcolm X's assassination in 1965, Muhammad talks about "the warning of destruction of the wicked world by fire the next time is made clearer to those whom that fire will destroy."[90] The month *The Fire Next Time* was published (January 1963), Malcolm X developed the image of the master's house on fire as an analysis of the class dynamics of racial oppression in US society, between the Black bourgeoisie and the Black masses. In two main speeches, one at Michigan State University on January 23 and the other at the University of Pennsylvania on January 25, he recounted the parable of the "house Negro and the field Negro"; it would become one of his fiercest rhetorical interventions, an image that has circulated widely.[91] "When the house started burning down, that type of Negro would fight harder to put the master's house out than the master himself would. But then you had another Negro out in the field, ... the masses—the field Negroes were the masses. They were in the majority. When the master got sick, they prayed that he'd die. If his house caught on fire, they'd pray for a wind to come along and fan the breeze."[92]

Malcolm X revisited the parable of the master's house on fire numerous times during 1963 in some of his most famous speeches: "Message to the Grassroots" in Detroit in November and "God's Judgement of White America" in early December—just after the March on Washington, the bombing of the 16th Street Baptist Church, and John F. Kennedy's assassination. In "God's Judgement of White America," delivered less than two weeks after JFK's assassination, he pays direct tribute to the gospel refrain in *The Fire Next Time*.

> Like the flood in Noah's day, revolution drowns all opposition, or like the fire in Lot's day, the black revolution burns everything that gets in its path. America is the last stronghold of white supremacy. The black revolution, which is international in nature and scope, is sweeping down upon America like a raging forest fire. It is only a matter of time before America herself will be engulfed by the black flames, these black firebrands.... Here in America, the black revolution (the 'uncontrollable forest fire') is personified in the religious teachings, and the religious works, of the Honorable Elijah Muhammad.

Malcolm X deploys the apocalyptic imagery of his earlier speeches to talk about decolonization and "the black revolution (the 'uncontrollable forest fire') ... the real black revolution that has already swept white supremacy out of Africa, Asia, and is sweeping it out of Latin America, ... and is even now manifesting itself also right here among the black masses."[93] But he also talks about the revolution in terms of the capitalist versus "the Communist world and the Socialist world—Eastern world and Western world—Oriental and Occidental world—dark world and white world." It is the end of time for the Western, European, Christian world, with God preparing a lake of fire to cast the wicked oppressors into the burning flame. In the midst of these speeches, Andrew Hill recorded his jazz album *Black Fire*, the title Amiri Baraka and Larry Neal would use for their 1968 anthology *Black Fire*. It was language that Archie Shepp would similarly use in his 1965 album *Fire Music*, which included the elegy "Malcolm, Malcolm Semper Malcolm."[94] These speeches and this imagery helped give expression to the "passion and rage and rebellion and love ... [of] the young Black intellectuals and revolutionaries of that time"—in both music and poetry.[95]

The call and response between Hansberry and Malcolm X played out in public and private, in her WBAI comments about politically conscious Black intellectuals and Black nationalism, in his critique of her in *Muhammad Speaks*, and in their meetings at Ossie Davis and Ruby Dee's house. Ultimately, Malcolm developed his own class critique of the structures of racial inequalities through the image of the master's house on fire, connecting it to the concept of Black revolution spreading across the world like a wildfire. Taking up elements of Hansberry's critique shows how "black women radicals shaped Malcolm X's trajectory ... [and] also contributed to his understanding of black internationalism," Ashley Farmer remarks in her article "The Many Women Mentors of Malcolm X."[96] The leftist intellectuals and writers of Malcolm X's time clearly impacted his own revolutionary philosophy in ways sometimes overtly at odds with Nation of Islam policy, but the dialogue between them helped pave the way for the Black Arts Movement in the wake of his assassination. By then, Lorraine Hansberry would be gone.

BLACK FIRE AND BLACK ART

The imagery of Black fire became one of the most salient images threaded through the cultural production of the Black Arts Movement. In *The Autobiography of LeRoi Jones*, Amiri Baraka talks about how Malcolm's "cold class analysis" in the parable of the master's house on fire "dug into me, cutting both ways," giving voice to things he had "not even thought, but felt." "What it meant to my life immediately was words in my head coming out of my mouth."⁹⁷ Throughout his career, Baraka's work paid tribute to Malcolm X, calling the contributors to *Black Fire* the sons and daughters of Malcolm X from "the generation that came up after Jimmy Baldwin."⁹⁸ Among these sons and daughters were Rolland Snellings who, like Jones, would convert to Islam, changing his name to Askia Muhammad Touré (in reference to one of the rulers of the Songhai Empire in West Africa). Both poets would play catalytic roles in the emergence of the Black Arts Movement and also, the first Black Studies program at San Francisco State. They first met at the protest against Lumumba's assassination at the UN, a moment that brought together disparate activist intellectual circles that would coalesce as the decentralized organizations and coalitions of the Black Arts Movement. Touré's [Snelling's] poem "Song of Fire" was published just after Malcolm delivered his "God's Judgement of White America" speech, its refrain "(Fire!)" evoking the speech's apocalyptic tone and imagery.

> Allah
> will send his flaming sword a 'whistling
>   through the 'chosen land' . . .
> (Fire!)
> will cauterize the Racist Plague!⁹⁹

But the poem's dedication to Africa, Asia, Latin and Afro-America also directly references the language of Malcolm X's speech. "Song of Fire" was published just after another poem Touré [Snellings] wrote titled "Floodtide," as the two poems in tandem evoke Baldwin's and Malcolm's imagery of flood and fire. The literary critic Lorenzo Thomas argues that the image of fire is always used "in the sense of greater knowledge being awakened in us."¹⁰⁰ Histories of the Black Arts Movement situate its emergence in the aftermath of Malcolm X's assassination when Baraka [LeRoi Jones] moved uptown to Harlem to found the Black Arts Repertory Theatre School (BARTS). Others, like Thomas, argue that its roots are earlier—in a longer genealogy—extending back to the Umbra Workshop (of which Touré [Snellings] was a member) and the Harlem Writers Guild, whose members included, among others, Hansberry and other Malcolm X confidantes, like Mayfield, John O. Killens, John Henrik Clarke, Ossie Davis, Ruby Dee, Maya Angelou.¹⁰¹ Only weeks before his own assassination, Malcolm X attended Hansberry's funeral, approaching Davis for an introduction to Paul Robeson. Writing about Black arts activism,

Rebeccah Welch describes Hansberry as a "historical bridge between two generations of black radicals often deemed distinct."[102]

After Malcolm X's assassination, Touré [Snellings] published an essay about Malcolm X in *Liberator*, calling him "Malik, the Fire Prophet, God's anger cast in glowing copper, burning the wicked of the earth with his flame."[103] "Song of Fire" would later be included in *Black Fire*, along with other poems, like Marvin X's "Burn, Baby, Burn" about the Watts riots, which explicitly reference the parable of the slave master's house on fire.[104] "Burn, Baby, Burn" became the chorus and title of Jimmy Collier and Frederick Douglass Kirkpatrick's civil rights anthem, explicitly referencing *The Fire Next Time* but also the idea of the American nightmare: "If I can't enjoy the American dream, won't be water but the fire next time."[105] Stokely Carmichael sang the song while starting a small bonfire in his hotel room. In Paris for an antiwar conference, he was on the cusp of deportation, having been stripped of his passport traveling to Cuba.[106]

The anthology *Black Fire* brought together the epistemological foundations of the revolutionary tradition in Black literature, as a body of intellectual treatises by thinkers, writers, activists, and poets. The pieces were assembled from myriad important publications and publishers from the time, growing out of earlier anthologies like *For Malcolm* (1967) and *Anthology of Our Black Selves* (1966), but also the even earlier *American Negro Writer and His Roots* (1960).[107] They helped establish the field of Black Studies as "an invitation to create, think, and struggle [that] is nothing less than a modality of revolt and is at best a catalyst for remaking/unmaking the world."[108]

This chapter traces the roots and routes of the metaphor of the burning house, how it circulated as a symbol of the American nightmare, a "prophetic prelude to the fiery black awakening of the 1960s," and ultimately, an emblem of revolution, retribution, and regeneration.[109] I chart an "insurgent genealogy" of the leftist poets and intellectuals who laid the foundation for a "creative, liberation-focused and generally radical political-intellectual practice," a "black fire" later articulated in BAM essays, poetry, drama, music, and art.[110] Though Hansberry was one of the roots of this flourishing, one that flowered over time through a myriad of different branches of Black radical thought and creative expression, her seminal contribution has been eclipsed by other figures. The image of America as a burning house conceptually shaped the long struggle for Black liberation in debates about Black nationalism and civil rights, separation and integration, informing scholarship like Gerald Horne's *Fire This Time: The Watts Uprising and the 1960s* (1995); Taylor Branch's *Pillar of Fire: The King Years* (1998); and Sean Patrick O'Rourke and Leslie K. Pace's *Like Wildfire: The Rhetoric of the Civil Rights Sit Ins* (2020). In the Bible, the pillar of fire guided the exodus of the Israelites out of captivity in Egypt into a new land (Exodus 13:21–22)—and

Branch begins the first chapter with the Los Angeles police shooting of Stokes and six other members of the Nation of Islam mosque there.[111]

The burning house became a central point of reference in the call and response between Hansberry and Baldwin, King and Malcolm, and future generations of Black radical thinkers. The image has also been key to class analyses of the relationship between the mainstream and the masses, the bourgeoisie and the working class, property owners and the propertyless—and their differing investments in the American dream (as a dream house). The trope of the burning house grew concretely out of their lived experiences and the material violence experienced by their families whose home were attacked and threatened with fire by "howling white mobs." The trope of the burning house also reflects how citizenship rights are connected to property ownership in a racial capitalist system—and how revolution incinerates that connection seeking equal citizenship rights for rich and poor, Black and white.[112] The image of the "burning house" has had enduring salience in the long struggle for Black freedom: in the Harlem Renaissance journal *Fire!!*; protests against the CIA's role in Lumumba's execution, and Williams's Monroe campaign in 1960 and 1961; the police shooting of Ronald Stokes in 1962; the Birmingham campaign, March on Washington, and bombing of the 16th Street Baptist Church in 1963; the assassinations of JFK, Malcolm X, and King; and the violence against Black lives protested by the Black Lives Matter movement. Baldwin himself talked about the burning house in the immediate aftermath of King's assassination but attributed the metaphor to Stokely Carmichael. Asked about integrating into a burning house in an interview with *Esquire*, he bitterly remarked: "I think Stokely's right when he says that integration is another word, you know, the latest kind of euphemism for white supremacy. No, I don't want to be integrated into this house or any other house, especially not this burning house. I don't want to become . . . like you. You, the white people. I'd rather die than become what most white people in this country have become."[113] During the Ferguson uprisings, the NOI newspaper the *Final Call* published an article "Integrating into a Burning House," with Jineea Butler writing: "Burning house? What was the burning house Dr. King was referring to? Does the burning house resemble Ferguson, Mo.?"[114]

LAYING FLOWERS, SETTING FIRES

In his autobiography *My Song* (2011), Harry Belafonte recounts talking with Martin Luther King Jr. a week before his death, after a meeting with Amiri Baraka in Newark left him shaken. Belafonte recalls King saying: "We fought hard and long. . . . But what deeply troubles me now is that for all the steps we've taken toward integration, I've come to believe that we are integrating into a burning house."[115] King made an analogous comment in the NBC News interview "After Civil Rights: Black Power" filmed at the Ebenezer Baptist Church in 1967, which ended with an allusion to the first chapter of Malcolm X's *Autobiography*. Asked about Black Power's rejection of white, bourgeois values, King calls for a "restructuring of the architecture of our society where values are concerned," speaking specifically about militarism and economic exploitation in the context of the war in Vietnam. "These young people are saying that there must be a revolution of values in our country. As Jimmy Baldwin said on one occasion, what advantage is there being integrated into a burning house? I feel that there is a need for a revolution of values in America . . . the dream that I had has in many points turned into a nightmare."[116] The comment about integrating into a burning house, for which Hansberry was once less cited than Baldwin, has also been widely attributed to King, seen as a hallmark of his later thought more critical of militarism, the war in Vietnam, economic inequality, and poverty.[117]

In his visual poem *Laying Flowers, Setting Fires*, the poet musician Amir Sulaiman samples three overlapping, connected riffs: audio of James Baldwin's voice, taken from the January 10, 1961, panel discussion on WBAI radio "The Negro in American Culture" ("to be a Negro in this country and to be relatively conscious is to be in a state of rage"); the "After Civil Rights: Black Power" interview with King, where he questions the integrating into a burning house (attributing the comment to Baldwin), and Dave Chapelle talking about the 8 minutes and 46 seconds Derek Chauvin kneeled on George Floyd's neck. By mixing these samples, Sulaiman connects the WBAI discussion about Black art and Black nationalism to Black Power and Black Lives Matter, paying tribute (laying flowers) to those who have gone before, even while setting fires to the architecture of structural racism. Sulaiman's "trueandlivingmedia" refers to the film as a "poetic view into black love and the ever-present threat of violence and actual violence leveled against black people in America. It is both love poem and eulogy." The film seemingly begins as a funeral, focusing on a coffin adorned in flowers, with women and girls dressed in white milling about, but then the women and girls emerge from the coffin, suggesting a kind of resurrection or revival.[118]

Sulaiman engages in a broad range of citational and re-citational practices, sonically and visually summoning the Islamic tradition, opening the film with the Arabic letter *baa* that stands for the *basmallah*, the invocation of God's name, and with him whispering the *basmallah*. He also samples Malcolm X's speech from his January 23, 1963, speech at Michigan State University, where he develops his parable of burning down the master's house—but that he remembers, in the *Autobiography*, as him telling the story of his own house burning down. Did Sulaiman know the connection between the WBAI panel discussion, *The Fire Next Time*, Malcolm's parable of the house burning down, and King's later thought, his dream that had in many respects turned into a nightmare? Or did he just know the hi/story anyway, a history already coded into this poetics, imprinted through what Hansberry calls three hundred years of experience that led to a certain kind of art? Or did the art itself already see, know, and represent this hi/story as an ancestral legacy of living in the house of bondage? Rather than using the master's tools to dismantle the master's house, as Audre Lorde would say, Sulaiman envisions a fire of justice and redemption, but also laying the flowers of commemoration, planting seeds, and remembering roots.[119] Angela Davis calls this new generation "the political descendants of Malcolm" that have transformed his legacy into "a forward-looking impetus for creative political thinking."[120] But they are also the descendants of other creative progenitors—like Hansberry and Mayfield—and many more who came before.

PART III
Black Study and Black Life

6

"FLY TO ALLAH"

Marvin X's Fugitive Life and Black Study

Runnin was religion
Runnin was sanctuary
Runnin was prophecy

—Tariq Touré, *2 Parts Oxygen: How I learned to Breathe*

Black Arts Movement pioneer Marvin X Jackmon made a life dedicated to Black study in spaces rooted in community outside the walls of the institutional bases of power, whether educational, military, or religious. Though these institutions have repeatedly tried to silence and expel him, he continues to teach at his Academy of da Corner, setting up a table in places like downtown Oakland, the Berkeley Flea Market, and Marin City, and distributing conscious literature to whoever happens by—people he knows from the Black freedom movement, young people on the street, and emergent poets. He tirelessly self-publishes and disseminates writings through his printer, website, and newsletters; at poetry readings and public lectures; in leaflets and pamphlets; in books and collections of poetry; in essays and articles. This chapter chronicles Marvin X's struggle to establish a space for Black Studies at the margins of formal institutions but inside community, in the face of expulsion from the US educational system and ostracization from the commercial publishing industry.

When Marvin was an English major on the verge of failing out at San Francisco State College in 1965, his literature professor encouraged him to write. He composed *Flowers for the Trashman*, which the SFSC Drama Department staged later that year. The journal *Black Dialogue* published the play, as did Amiri Baraka and Larry Neal in their seminal 1968 anthology *Black Fire* along with two of his poems.[1] After Marvin's teachers told him to "tone down" his writing, he dropped out of SFSC and founded the Black Arts West Theater on Filmore and Turk in San Francisco. In the midst of the campaign for Black Studies at SFSC these new spaces became gathering places for the free expression of Black art, performance, and study. Alternative institutions like Marvin X's Black Arts West Theater and Black House (both in San Francisco) "reflected a shared concern with creating new spaces for black art, essentially an atmospheric ethics of space connected to black expression, . . . a new type of performance space . . . representative of an ethical movement."[2]

In "Black Study, Black Struggle," Robin D. G. Kelley writes about how spaces for alternative study were critical to developing a vision of Black Studies "as a vehicle for collective transformation and an incubator of knowledge." Organizing and reading as a community, political study groups were a "lifeblood—both on and off campus." Drawing on Stefano Harney and Fred Moten's understanding of "fugitive study" and the "undercommons," Kelley writes about seeking, creating, and establishing communities and knowledge systems outside the university, to escape its oppressive structures rooted in ties to the military industrial complex.[3] This chapter explores Marvin X as student, scholar, writer, teacher, and poet and how he was relentlessly and mercilessly ejected from the educational system for speaking up, but also how he fled its strictures in search of a space of free expression, despite how impossible that quest seemed to be. Perhaps more importantly, Marvin fled from service in American wars taking not just an ethical stance but also a religious one, refusing to fight as a conscientious objector. "Some people want to run things, other things want to run," write Harney and Moten. "If they ask you, tell them we were flying. Knowledge of freedom is (in) the invention of escape, stealing away in the confines, in the form, or a break. This is held close in the open song of the ones who are supposed to be silent."[4]

Marvin X's writings poetically document his fugitivity from the Eurocentric university, American educational system, and Euro-American structures of knowledge and his quest for other spaces, homes, and geographies for Black study. Marvin X's autobiography *Somethin' Proper* is about his literal and metaphorical homelessness within systems of sanctioned knowledge: as he creates his own intellectual home in the undercommons; independently publishes, disseminates, and circulates his writings; and forms his own institutions and structures of teaching and learning. *Somethin' Proper* is also about Marvin getting something of his own, his fair share, something for himself. The autobiography reflects on his campaign for the first Black Studies program at San Francisco State, his conversion to Islam, and his dismissal from teaching positions at McClymonds High School, Oakland City College, and Fresno State College for engaging with radical Black thought. He was expelled from school after school as both a student and a teacher for experimenting with what Black Studies might look and sound like and for speaking in the language of his students. He dropped out of SFSC just as agitation for Black Studies was heating up, becoming the secretary of Black House, later the headquarters of the Black Panthers, and founding his Black Arts West Theater in San Francisco. He was later thrown out of Black House by the Panthers for his embrace of cultural revolution (versus armed revolution).

Losing his student status meant that Marvin was drafted into the army in the middle of the Vietnam War. So he fled the draft, emigrating to Canada, where he joined other Muslim communities, broadening and deepening his knowledge of Islam through exposure to Sunni, Shi'a, and Sufi communities. It was then that he began writing poetry and drama that drew on Islamic language as a way of signaling "covert social spaces as a means of building and maintaining community, ... [as] an enduring force within the African-American diaspora."[5] In his poetry, he describes his flight as rooted in the African American narrative tradition of fugitivity northward toward freedom, but also in the Islamic tradition of escaping oppression through emigration, or *hijra*. Instead of fighting in Vietnam, he became an "artistic freedom fighter."[6] Marvin X calls his flight to Canada as a convert and a conscientious objector "flying to Allah," as his Islamic commitments took him on a path of "fugitive study." Marvin would eventually be on the street, though still teaching, albeit in alternative spaces, giving him another kind of education.[7]

After joining the Nation of Islam, Marvin X took the name El Muhajir (the "emigrant") etymologically connected to the word *hijra*. His writings from that point speak allegorically of "flying to Allah"—a "Black bird" escaping from a mental cage. Marvin X quotes verses from the Qur'an, writes words in Arabic script, and translates concepts into and from Arabic while also drawing on NOI teachings about "mental death." He develops a new kind of language, a vocabulary, a lexicon that gives voice to his heightened political consciousness and moral conscience. His conversion was intimately connected to his flight from conscription into the army and the war in Vietnam, as he sought conscientious objector status and faced jailtime because of it. But he also sought out pedagogies, epistemologies, and knowledge systems alternative to the Eurocentric schooling that marginalized his own voice and suppressed knowledge of Black geographies, histories, cultures, and languages. The language of the NOI framed this knowledge as a resurrection from the mental death imposed by epistemological violence and erasure. In Marvin X and Faruk's 1969 interview "Islam and Black Art," Amiri Baraka commented that Islam is a means of withstanding "the deathblows that white America is seeking to put on" Black people, as both a spiritual and political philosophy.[8] As Larry Neal wrote of the BAM, it is "a struggle for Black survival."[9]

Mohja Kahf sees Muslim authors of the Black Arts Movement as "Prophets of Dissent" who carry out a "deliberate espousal of an aesthetic that has Islamic roots." She closes her exploration of Muslim American diasporic literature by calling for others to "do work in areas I have left aside in this brief initial exploration."[10] Answering that call I consider Marvin X's extensive oeuvre as a whole: plays and theatrical productions; collections of poetry, proverbs, and parables; published articles and essays; an autobiography; and numerous lectures and interventions. Through a close reading of six main works he wrote right after becoming Muslim—poetry collections *Sudan Rajuli Samia* (1967), *Fly to Allah* (1969), and *Black Man Listen* (1969); the parable *The Black Bird* (1968); the book of proverbs *Son of Man* (1969); and the short play *Resurrection of the Dead* (1969)—I explore his development of a poetic language that gives expression to a Black American Islamic aesthetics. Marvin X's autobiography *Somethin' Proper* (1998) provides testimonial context for these writings, along with a series of interviews I conducted with him: in Oakland, Berkeley, Marin City, Durham, Brooklyn, and Newark; at his Academy of da Corner; and on pilgrimage to visit Sonia Sanchez in Philadelphia, Malika Iman in Harlem, and Amina Baraka in Newark. I consider these writings alongside archival resources provided by Marvin X, along with his papers at the University of California, Berkeley's Bancroft Library.

Marvin X draws on a consciously Muslim American literature, and on what Kahf calls "the Afrocentric Islamic aesthetic of the Muslim authors in the Black Arts Movement."[11] He engages as well with the broad creative possibilities of African American life and history, situating it in reference to Afro-diasporic language, culture, and religion. He codes his poetry with Arabic and Islamic words, expressions, and script. Even if sometimes incomprehensible to the uninitiated, it becomes a cipher, "a performance of knowledge" that interpolates other histories within local ones.[12] This Islamic literacy functioned as it did historically, as "alternative histories and definitions of histories" and as a way of keeping Islamic knowledge and practice alive, even under conditions of duress.[13] These forms of knowledge and writing performed what Larry Neal called "a radical re-ordering of the western cultural aesthetic" by forging new histories and purifying "old ones by fire." An Islamic idiom fused with a Black American one helped create alternative linguistic possibilities that were both new and old, lost and found, "new discursive grammars" that "imagine and inhabit multiple temporalities" and geographies.[14]

In the first of his Islamic publications, *Sudan Rajuli Samia / Black Man Listen* (1967), Marvin uses Arabic and Islamic language to reorient his poetry in a different linguistic, aesthetic, and epistemological paradigm, signaling a different kind of English, identity, and poetics. He introduces the self-published, hand-typed broadsheet by calling for the poet "to listen to the music and language of his people," but also to create "a new language, ... a Holy Language" that gives expression to the spiritual, moral, and ethical dimensions of the struggle for racial justice.[15] Marvin uses Arabic writing and language as the "lingua franca of the Islamic intellectual tradition," for its "symbolic power" and its "semiholy character and value."[16] In his famous essay on the BAM, Larry Neal describes a "new spirituality" from the perspective of the oppressed, "produced by the upheavals of the colonial world of which Black America is part." But he also talks about deconstructing white aesthetics along with white ethics.[17] The Arabic and Islamic elements root this poetry in the African tradition, "revealing and reveling in the suppressed Africanity of international modernism," formally reinserting this diasporic consciousness by using the "registers of modernist language innovation" that include polyglossia and the juxtaposition of different languages. This poetic technique functions as "a means of revealing the canon of international modernism to itself in a postmodern, postcolonial rupture," argues Aldon Nielsen in *Black Chant*.[18] "Dispersed and hidden fragments of coherent cultural systems" provide "a space for a syncretic African-based spirituality or diasporic consciousness," observes Harryette Mullen in her essay "African Signs and Spirit Writing."[19] Marvin X relentlessly insists on an Islamic pluralism that is culturally and theologically diverse, encompassing but refusing to be confined to Ahmadiyya, Nation of Islam, Sunni, Shi'a, or Sufi Islam(s). But he also uses Arabic and Islamic language to open up the suffocatingly closed space of aesthetic practice dominated by the Eurocentric textualism disseminated in state-sponsored educational systems.

NOI concepts of being "mentally dead" and of "mental slavery" took on new salience in reference to Marvin X's addiction to crack cocaine in the 1980s and

1990s.[20] Describing addiction as mental slavery in his play *One Day in the Life* (1996), he deployed writing and religion to fight his way toward emancipation from the prison of substance abuse. His autobiography opens on the road to recovery, described as a homecoming to his family and a "road to Mecca." These writings speak of his near social death in the grips of crack cocaine for over a decade in the 1980s and 1990s; and they characterize his emergence from addiction as a resurrection. In the introduction to Marvin X's *How to Recover from the Addiction to White Supremacy: A Pan African 12-Step Model for a Mental Health Peer Group*, the Black Studies pioneer Nathan Hare describes Marvin X as having a "PhD in Negrology . . . issued by the University of Hardknock's College of Hell, based on twelve years of research, independent study, and practicum in unlettered social laboratories throughout the United States."[21]

"MY REAL DEGREE WAS IN BLACKNESS"

Marvin X received an associate of arts degree in sociology from Oakland City College in 1964, "but my real degree was in blackness," he says, "through independent study with the brothers and sisters at OCC." Two of those brothers were Bobby Seale and Huey Newton, who Marvin X then introduced to Eldridge Cleaver. When graduating from OCC, his English professor advised him to "get into black studies—it would be the wave of the future."[22] After enrolling in San Francisco State College (now University), he joined the Negro Students Association, which soon became the first Black Students Union in the United States, partly through the campaigning of the activist Mar'yam Wadi, or Maryanna Waddy, daughter of the painter Ruth Waddy.[23] In *Somethin' Proper*, Marvin X uses Nation of Islam language to criticize the word "Negro," saying that Wadi helped lead him out of his "negrocity, i.e., a state of death, necro (something dead)," a form of white brainwashing or "mental death."[24] The Black Student Union (BSU) began agitating for a Black Studies program leading to the establishment of the first department of Black Studies in the United States.[25] In fall 1966, the BSU at SFSC "launched a Black Arts and Culture series within the Experimental College, which stood as an exemplar of what Black studies might offer," with both LeRoi Jones and Sonia Sanchez teaching courses. BSU president Jimmy Garrett taught a course titled "The Mis-education of the Negro," based on Carter Woodson's 1933 book calling for Black intellectuals' engagement in the Black community. "The activists at San Francisco State were extraordinarily creative and resourceful," writes Martha Biondi. "Like the Black Panther Party, they built their own programs. They did not just advocate instituting a Black studies department, for example, they created one." This "cultural richness and empowerment" was the "foundation for new consciousness and identity."[26] The aim was not just to desegregate but also to challenge the epistemological foundations of the American educational system grounded in Eurocentric texts, cultures, and languages.[27] The fight for Black Studies, Marvin writes, "would involve blood, sweat, and tears, literally.... We were not only challenging the college, but the society, the state. Challenging the view that we were deaf, dumb, and blind so-called negroes, tools and fools of the white man, domestic colonial subjects, servile, to be placated with crumbs from the master's table."[28]

In 1967, SFSC hired Nathan Hare, recently dismissed from Howard University for his radical politics, which included authoring a "Black University Manifesto" and participating in a series of campus protests that involved the Student Nonviolent Coordinating Committee and the Revolutionary Action Movement.[29] He had also brought Muhammad Ali to campus, just after his refusal of the draft, though the administration locked the auditorium to try and prevent him from speaking.[30] Hare would ultimately be fired from SFSC as well for participating in the "Third World Strike" in 1967 and 1968 when students made demands for the Black Studies program and protested the Vietnam War. In the midst of the strike, Hare wrote a "Conceptual Proposal for a Department of Black Studies," advocating for the "important ingredient of motivation growing out of collective community involvement" as a "cultural base" to "increase communication, interpersonal contact, knowledge and sociopolitical awareness." It called for a Black community press, Black journalism, Black communications, a "Bureau of Black Education," a Black information center engaging in research, and outreach aimed at Black children. In the proposal, he lamented the students who dropped out because of racial discrimination in their studies, the subject matter, and the "racist textbooks." Hare could have been talking about Marvin Jackmon when he spoke about students who pass the test of "verbal facility" but "drop out of college or flunk out (often one way of dropping out)" as he reflected on "how schooling becomes complicit in and serves as a site of Black material and psychic suffering."[31] Hare called for organizing "a black textbook and syllabi writing corps ... in an effort to escape the confines of perfunctory learning and utilize the laboratory of life."[32]

After being dismissed from San Francisco State, Hare went on to found *The Black Scholar: A Journal of Black Studies and Research*. Its first issue focused on "The Culture of Revolution," with contributions by Eldridge Cleaver

("Education and Revolution"), John Oliver Killens "(The Artist and the Black University"), Roosevelt Johnson ("Black Administrators and Higher Education"), and a review of Sidney F. Walton Jr.'s *The Black Curriculum: Developing a Program in Afro-American Studies*. *The Black Scholar* would become a major forum for the exploration of the meaning and aims of Black Studies and the state of Black Education.[33] Hare eventually changed fields to clinical psychology, publishing *The Miseducation of the Black Child* (1991) with his wife Julia Hare, drawing on Carter Woodson and advancing an agenda to "educate every black man, woman and child."[34]

In March 1967, the month the BSU submitted a ten-point proposal for Black Studies, Jackmon converted to Islam, describing the "mosque as coming to him" through the artists, intellectuals, and activists he encountered at his Black Arts West Theater. Other, key pioneers of Black arts like Sonia Sanchez and Amiri Baraka (then still LeRoi Jones) circulated in this milieu, with Sanchez teaching at SFSC at the time and Jones visiting in 1967 with Amina Baraka (then still Sylvia Wilson), who was pregnant with their first child, Obalaji. Baraka converted later that summer as would Sanchez in the early 1970s. At the Black Arts West Theater Marvin began studying Islam and Arabic with Ahmadiyya Muslim Ali Sharif Bey, who gave Marvin the Arabic name Nazzam al-Fitna, words that mean "organizer of chaos" or "harmonizer of conflict."[35] The Black Arts West Theater building had been previously occupied by Alonzo Harris Batin, who had served time with Eldridge Cleaver in San Quentin. Batin "taught us savage artists Islamic civilization," Marvin X wrote, introducing them to the Nation of Islam and Islamic knowledge, ideas, language, and texts. Batin was the "Black Arts West guru who recruited us to the Nation of Islam," Marvin X said, "while Ali Sharif Bey exposed us to Ahmadiyya Islam, Arabic, Urdu, and Islamic literature, Ibn Khaldun, and Sufi Poets." In an interview, Marvin X talked about how he studied Islam in San Francisco with the Black Arts West Theater crew: Carl Boissiere, Duncan Barber, Hillery Broadous, and Ethna X Hurriyah (her Islamic name meaning "freedom"). Yet the Black Arts West artists would ultimately find themselves on the margins, even of the already unorthodox Nation of Islam, since they "could not accept the NOI discipline" as they fought for artistic freedom at its edge.[36] Black Arts West Theater became a space for dissident culture, "resistance to the dominant culture that took the form of religious heterodoxy," a "pariah intelligentsia."[37] In a militantly fugitive way, Marvin lived on the margins of institutions and their strictures, becoming stateless—literally renouncing his citizenship—and later, becoming homeless.

Recalling those study groups at Black Arts West—fifty years later at the 360 Poetry Night with Justice event in Newark—Marvin talked about the study of

African consciousness, Black consciousness, revolutionary consciousness. On our own. We were self-motivated. We studied books on the African revolution like Frantz Fanon's *Wretched of the Earth*. We studied the Cuban Revolution, Fidel Castro's court speech *History will Absolve Me*. We studied South African Nelson Mandala, what was going on in Sharpeville with the Sharpeville massacre. We studied Kwame Nkrumah's *Dark Days in Ghana* and *Neo-Colonialism: The Last Age of Imperialism*, Patrice Lumumba and what was going on in the Congo. We studied Ho Chi Min about the Vietnamese revolution. We studied the Chinese Revolution. As artists, what did Mao say? What he says in his excellent essay "On Literature and Art." You should read that essay if you want to know what a revolutionary artist should do. All art reflects one class or another. Either the oppressed or the oppressor class. It helped us in the Black Arts Movement to define our aesthetic, what we were about. What we were about, the Artistic Freedom Fighter.[38]

Alternative institutions and organizations, publishing presses, and journals like *Black Dialogue, Soulbook*, and the *Journal of Black Poetry* were organs of the flourishing of the Black Arts Movement in the Bay Area. "You see, it's not just an intellectual struggle," Sylvia Wynter observes of Black Studies, "You could call it a psycho-intellectual struggle. Then you could understand why in the '60s it wasn't just a call for Black Studies; it was a call for Black Aesthetics, it was a call for Black Art(s), it was a call for Black Power."[39]

During this period of agitation for Black Studies, the Black Panthers turned on the cultural revolutionaries in the Black Arts Movement for being insufficiently committed to armed protest. Marvin was ejected from Black House in San Francisco, becoming a kind of fugitive even within the Black Power movement for his embrace of cultural revolution.[40] Around the time he was drafted into the army, during the Vietnam War, Marvin sought refuge in the Nation of Islam. "I joined the army I wanted to join," he wrote, referring to his conversion to Islam and membership in NOI, "to fight the battle the way I wanted to fight."[41]

Marvin X converted after the antiwar magazine *Ramparts* sent him to interview Muhammad Ali about his refusal of the draft. Their meeting at Elijah Muhammad's house in Chicago echoes James Baldwin's visit to Elijah Muhammad in *The Fire Next Time*. Baldwin reflects on the possibility of becoming Muslim: "For where else, after all, could I go? I was black, and therefore a part of Islam." Baldwin demurs (looking forward to meeting some white devils for a drink on the other side of town), but Marvin does join the NOI at Muhammad's Mosque No. 26 in San Francisco becoming Marvin X, "X slave, X n*****,

X tool and fool, X, true name unknown, X, mystery, X, lost/found socalled negro—no longer lost, now found, finally."[42] He is paraphrasing Muhammad Ali's famous words: "There was no way in hell I was going to Vietnam or round the corner for America, the Great Satan! ... Ain't no Vietcong called me a n*****, raped my mama, lynched my daddy, brought my foreparents here on slave ships, through the Middle Passage."[43] Marvin's words echo Muhammad Ali's and Muhammad Ali's echo Elijah Muhammad's words echoed in Yusef Iman's "Love Your Enemy," published by Jihad Productions in 1966—the poem that critiques the love-your-enemy ethos of the civil rights movement. But Iman also reflects on loving the enemy in a time of war.

> Brought here in slave ships and pitched overboard.
> Love your enemy
> Language taken away, culture taken away ...
> Love your enemy
> Rape your mother
> Love your enemy
> Lynch your father ...
> Love your enemy
> Forced to fight his Wars[44]

These layers of intertextuality, of call and response between poets, dissidents, religious leaders, and conscientious objectors "refigure" the signification of "key canonical topoi and tropes received from the black tradition," creating a "web of filiation."[45] These different texts from the Black radical intellectual tradition, Elijah Muhammad's writings and speeches, Yusuf Iman's poetry, Muhammad Ali's speeches and interviews, and Marvin X's autobiography, speak back and forth to each other. They reinterpret the Christian teaching "love your enemy" as peace with the Vietnamese in the face of American violence. Iman, Ali, and Marvin X drew on the conceptual lexicon of the NOI in their own critiques of the US wars abroad, creating a discursive universe parallel to the Christian, as well as the language of the Southern Christian Leadership Conference.

Muhammad Ali's resistance to the draft inspired Marvin X's conversion to Islam as he readied himself for "a different kind of battle," referenced through the Qur'an verses (22:39, 2:190-91, 2:216) that open his poetry collections.[46] Marvin was an "artistic freedom fighter" waging a jihad of the pen, but he also stood in a line of conscientious objectors: not just Muhammad Ali, but also Elijah Muhammad and Wallace Fard Muhammad before him, all of whom faced jail time for their refusal to fight in America's wars. In a poem in his collection

Fly to Allah, Marvin writes that "he wouldn't kill his brothers / For his enemy."[47] He flees institutionalized state violence—the army, but also the university and its own forms of discursive violence. But his creative commitments to the free expression of Black art put him in tension not only with the school system but also with the institutions of Black Power and the Nation of Islam. He became a fugitive on multiple fronts.

HIJRA AND FUGITIVITY

Marvin X fled to Toronto in the summer of 1967—flunked out of SFSC, kicked out of Black House, and forced to leave Black Arts West. He pursued what Jarvis R. Givens calls a "fugitive pedagogy" through modes of experimentation with different "ideas about teaching and learning."[48] When Marvin later took a name that referred to that fugitivity—El Muhajir (the emigrant)—it spoke to his "flight" from the army and to Allah, as well as his search for knowledge giving expression to his emergent Islamic consciousness, what he described as a new language. He also became a fugitive from the university that wanted him to "tone down" his language, "tone down" his message, "tone down" his writing—not only the "loud" tone of his voice and the noise he was making for political change and the language of his radicalism, but also the tone of his Blackness in the context of the white educational system and other state institutions like the army.[49] Flight became the leitmotif of Marvin's journey, one he framed in terms of hijra (emigration), a duty for Muslims "whenever their faith and practice were at risk in their own lands," whenever they were "oppressed in their own lands or unable to perform their religious obligations."[50] The name "al-muhajir" denotes someone who forsakes his own land to take up residence in another country, referring to those who emigrated (and pledged to fight) with the Prophet Muhammad from Mecca to Madina in 622, the first year of the Muslim *hijri* calendar. In the Islamic tradition, there is also an earlier hijra—to the African continent.

Marvin X explored a different kind of fugitive pedagogy: fleeing conscription in the army, war in Vietnam (*fitna*), and formal institutions of state-sponsored higher education and their relation to the military-industrial complex.[51] He renounced his US citizenship at the American Embassy in Toronto, becoming stateless and precariously outside formal institutions. But Marvin X kept his intellectual life alive and thriving by writing, studying, and exploring new terrains and languages; he used Islamic literacy to chart a path toward freedom, in ways he saw as analogous to the way Islamic literacy and Arabic writing sometimes functioned in rebellions of African Muslims enslaved in the Americas. Writing in Arabic sometimes became of mode of communication between insurgents, an emblem of citizenship in other nations, and a tool of abolition.[52] The formerly enslaved 'Abd al-Rahman Ibrahima ibn Sori used his Arabic-language writing skills to claim a "Moorish" citizenship, demand emancipation, and seek return to his homeland Futa Jallon.[53]

Between 1967 and 1969 Marvin X published three collections of poetry permeated with his Islamic commitments—*Sudan Rajuli Samia* (1967), *Fly to Allah* (1969), and *Black Man Listen* (1969)—dedicating each, respectively, to "the Asiatic Black Peoples of North America. My beloved Brothers and Sisters, I say to you, submit to Allah, the Best Knower"; to Elijah Muhammad; and to "the Nation of Islam and all Asiatic Black peoples here in the hells of north america." The collections include verses from the Qur'an, Arabic words and Islamic expressions, and Arabic script carefully rendered in Marvin X's own hand. The publication trajectory follows Marvin X to Canada and back, with the publication of *Sudan Rajuli Samia* in Burlington, Ontario, *Fly to Allah* in Marvin X's home town of Fresno, and *Black Man Listen* in Detroit by Dudley Randall's Broadside Press, one of his only books issued by a commercial publishing house. The books recycle and revise poems and motifs, speaking to each other and to other texts, whether canonically Islamic (the Qur'an), NOI (*Message to the Blackman*), or historical (Edward Wilmot Blyden), situating his writing in reference to multiple traditions.

The self-published, hand-typed broadside *Sudan Rajuli Samia*, priced at $1 apiece, is both poetry collection and political pamphlet comprising a statement of Marvin X's beliefs, a poetic rendering of his conversion to Islam, a chronicle of his flight to Toronto, and forms of experimentation with his emergent knowledge of Arabic. Marvin X uses Arabic for the title and an Arabic name, Nazzam Al Sudan, for the byline, which he translates as "the black organizer/poet"; he calls the press by the Arabic name Al Kitab Sudan ("the black book"), orders the pages with the numbers written out in transliterated Arabic, and provides a glossary of key Arabic terms, like those of kinship (father, sister, and brother) and "white devil." In his introduction, Marvin X uses Arabic, Islamic, and NOI terms to describe the poet as a priest "of the Holy Tribe of Shabazz. Baraka-llah. As-Salaam-Alaikum." "The poet must listen to the music and language of his people. He must express their collective rhythm. The poet is their servant. He records the mythology of his people, his brother and sisters, (*akhi wa akatun*)," Marvin X writes, translating the words brother and sister into Arabic. "He knows their heartbeat."[54] He fuses an Islamic idiom with a Blackamerican one, simultaneously consolidating communities of imagined kinship and creating alternative linguistic possibilities in his poetic production.

The errors in the formal Arabic—like in the title, the translations, and some of the transliterations—reflect Marvin X's self-study outside the strictures of formal education at the Black Arts West Theater with Alfonso Batin, and in Toronto with friends from Jordan, Egypt, Sudan, and the Gulf. While in Toronto, he was offered a scholarship to the Islamic University of Omdurman in the Sudan, but could not accept it because he no longer had a passport.[55] Marvin X taught Arabic to his friends and his children—and his son Darrel Patrick Jackmon (Abdul Ibn El Muhajir) studied Arabic at UC Berkeley, majoring in Near Eastern Studies; at the University of Damascus on a Fulbright; and at Harvard's Graduate School in Middle East Studies.[56] He both formalized his own study and brought his Islam into these institutions of higher learning.

For Marvin, Arabic and the language of Islam shape what Jarvis Givens calls the "hidden curriculum" of a "fugitive pedagogy," a kind of "learning that becomes a means of escape." In the volume *The Future is Black: Afropessimism, Fugitivity, and Radical Hope in Education*, the editors write about how education has possibilities "as a site of fugitivity, of *hope*, of escape, and as a space within which to imagine an emancipation yet to be realized."[57] The Arabic words in "Al Fitnah Muhajir," the final poem of *Sudan Rajuli Samia*, describe Marvin's emigration to escape the war (*fitna*) by taking the plane (*tayyarah*), crossing the border, and flying to freedom. The words "Bismillah!" (In the name of God!) open the poem as well as his journey. Other Arabic and Islamic phrases are threaded throughout, greetings of peace and an exclamation of Allahu Akbar, Marvin X reading the Qur'an on the plane, "Ayat al-kursi / The verse of knowledge" (2:255).[58] "Al Fitnah Muhajir" is also included in *Fly to Allah* but with a different title "The Underground Railroad: Revisited"—explicitly comparing fugitivity from slavery to the flight from oppression that was the hijra. This Islamic lexicon helped shape Marvin X's creative outpouring, as he tapped a knowledge system functioning as protest, but also a community bound together via a set of shared signs, symbols, words, and languages. The Afro-Asian, Eastern, non-European language of Islam became one of the most important elements of the marriage between Black Religion and Islam, Sherman Jackson observes in *Islam and the Blackamerican*, "language being perhaps the most important and deeply missed of all the casualties of the American slave experience."[59] The Arabic also functions like a hidden transcript, a dissident language illegible to the dominant power structure.

"The Underground Railroad: Revisited" in *Fly to Allah* adds a verse from the Qur'an that refers to hijra: "And whoever flees in Allah's way, he will find in the earth many a place of escape and abundant resources. And whoever goes forth from his home fleeing to Allah and His Messenger, then death overtakes him, his reward is indeed with Allah. And Allah is ever Forgiving, Merciful" (4:100).[60] This set of verses in the Qur'an discusses fighting, war, and flight, those who emigrate in the "path of God... to God and his messenger," and the "oppressed of the earth" (*al-mustadaʿifin fi al-ard*) who live in a kind of "hell as a home," urging believers to seek refuge because "God's earth is wide enough for you to emigrate" (4:97).

Marvin's poem "Fly to Allah" opens both *Sudan Rajuli Samia* and his later collection *Fly to Allah*. The poem riffs on Louis Farrakhan's famous song "A White Man's Heaven Is a Black Man's Hell," the motifs in Yusef Iman's "Love Your Enemy," and NOI teachings about knowledge of self. The Eurocentric education of the American school system is described as a form of brainwashing and imposed ignorance through its elision of what Carmen Kynard calls "alternative histories and definitions of literacies."[61] "Fly to Allah" draws on Elijah Muhammad's language in *Message to the Blackman*:

> We were blind,
> Deaf and dumb,
> Lowest of the low,
> No name, no tongue, no mind
> Deaf, dumb, and blind
> Hated self and kind
> Loved enemy to death
> Fly to Allah![62]

Marvin X would rework the poem in *Fly to Allah*, juxtaposing Qur'an verses (2: 190–91) with the NOI language to reference concepts of self-defense and jihad as a means of fighting oppression. He extends that Islamic language to other transnational struggles, like in the poem "Ernesto Che Guevara" to salute Che as a brother and a fallen comrade—"Salaam, Akhi Jihad/Salaam" ("peace, my brother in struggle, peace")—quoting again from the Qur'an (2:156). Marvin codes these decolonial struggles into his Islamic language and also connects the Muslim international to revolutionary Cuba.[63]

The transcriptions of Arabic are sounds that can be read, but they can only be understood by the initiated. This creates a kind of speech community within a speech community, with Arabic and Islamic language nestled within Black American linguistic histories. Suʿad Abdul Khabeer describes how this process of acquiring "religious terminology in ritual speech" becomes "a means of expressing newer worldviews and rearticulating older worldviews and forms of sociality."⁶⁴ Weaving Islamic and Arabic words and expressions into his writings, Marvin X improvises on the ritualistic performance of what Fred Moten calls "idiom(atic difference)" as a kind of philosophical writing that "re-members," enacts, and "re-enacts" community, nation, and race not just through an "originary creativity," but through a free generativity. Moten explores this "old-new language" as an echo of the unremembered that is like a wound, a form of "aural remembrance," "the dream of another universality," and "the vision of an old song."⁶⁵ Marvin X invokes what Moten calls a *metalanguage* that he ritualistically performs in his poetry, a reawakening, a remembering, a reverting, an idiomiatic (and poetic) difference, and another name. The old-new language "constitutes not only its own metalanguage but its own truth," a truth of the brutal suppression of Islam and other African religions, of the systematic oppression of African Muslims through deracination, but also the life forms, cultural practices, spiritual life, and modes of expression that continue to thrive.⁶⁶

In Marvin X's poem "Harlem Queen" (in *Fly to Allah*, 1969), he uses the Arabic name Malika, meaning "queen" to speak in dual registers—one English and the other the *salaam* (peace) of Islam that he includes in the poem through the greeting "As-Salaamu-Alaikum." The "peace / in her face / a sadness too" invokes glimmers of "her past," coded into the poem through references to queens like the biblical and Qur'anic Sheba and the Egyptian Cleopatra. But the queen also references Black Power queens, the "Malaika" of Ron Karenga's US School of Afroamerican Culture in Los Angeles and Amiri Baraka's Committee for a Unified Network.⁶⁷

> There was peace
> in her face
> A sadness too
> I wondered about her past
> Her history was in her walk
> Was she Sheba
> Or Cleopatra
> She was herself
> And she knew she was Black . . .
> I taught her another tongue:
> Alif, ba, ta, tha, jim, ha, kha. . . .
> But she wouldn't speak it . . .
> Baraka-llah Malika
> As-Salaamu-Alaikum.⁶⁸

As Abdul Khabeer observes, "the sociolinguistic meanings of Arabic words can be related to both a religious (Islamic) context and parallel meanings found within the context of broader African American culture."[69] These Arabic words replace the English, she argues, to more meaningfully describe social realities.

Marvin X's poetic process reflects the way Islamic language is coded into Black American vernaculars, but also how Black Muslims are integral to Islamic history and culture.[70] He translates phrases like "Black Power" into Arabic as "qadir sudan" epitomizing this "old-new language." He carefully renders Arabic transcription of central Islamic invocations like *Allahu akbar* and *bismillah al-rahman al-rahim* and key Arabic words and phrases in place of English ones. In *Black Man Listen*, an entire poem, "The Origin of Blackness," is written in transliterated Arabic words with their English translations in alternating lines.

> Sudan la al lawn
> Black is not a color.
> Lawn kuli min sudan
> All colors come from Black
> Sudan al harakat
> Black is a rhythm . . .
> Ka umma sudan
> Your mam is Black
> Ka abu sudan
> Your father is Black . . .
> Hurriya
> Freedom.
> Adil
> Justice.
> Musawat
> Equality.[71]

The poem exemplifies, albeit through the Arabic tradition, what Henry Louis Gates Jr. identifies as the repetition and revision of the Black tradition to create a parallel literary universe, what he describes as a "double-voiced text" that talks to other texts, becoming "a joyous proclamation of antecedent texts," whether here, with the Qur'an, or with *Message to the Blackman*.[72] Aldon Nielson calls this "a recollection of the history of fractures. Excavation, restoration, and rereading must proceed simultaneously."[73]

In Toronto, Marvin X met "brothers from Jordan, Egypt, Sudan, and the Persian Gulf" for the Friday prayer service connecting with a transnational Muslim community. Among those brothers was Hussain al-Shahristani, who would become the deputy prime minister of Iraq.[74] The brothers questioned Marvin's identification with the Nation of Islam and Elijah Muhammad as the Last Messenger, saying that they would not trade their collection of Islamic knowledge, hadiths, and commentary on the Qur'an, or books of Islamic law, for *Message to the Black Man*. Marvin X responded with a verse from the Qur'an: "*Lakum dinukum wa liya din*!" (You have your religion and I have mine, 109:6), writing that "Elijah's ideas were not foreign to Islam or beyond the pale of Islam.... Listen up, ... all Muslim nations have their own traditions, prophets, saints, saviors, holy cities, sacred mosques, etc. The North American African Muslim needs knowledge of his African Islamic tradition, so he can stop his pathetic identification with Arab Islam. Arabs have no monopoly on Islam." He writes that Elijah Muhammad's soul passed into "the soul-force of Iran's Imam Ayatollah Khomeini, who adopted Elijah's definition of America as The Great Satan or Devil, and established a Nation of Islam."[75] Through his rhetorical arguments, Marvin X connects a global Islam with "traditional Blackamerican culture," redefining "both that culture and its relationship to the dominant culture," writes Sherman Jackson, "forging in the process a new, alternative modality of blackness that was both identifiably 'Islamic' *and* American."[76]

Although Marvin X dedicated his poetry to Elijah Muhammad and repeatedly paid tribute to him as a messenger of Allah, Elijah Muhammad sent Marvin X a letter asking him to give up poetry and telling him to speak in the "plainest way to get the truth" rather than in a symbolic language full of metaphor.[77] When Marvin X returned to the United States, the Nation of Islam suspended him because of an extramarital relationship with a childhood friend from California, Ethna Wayat (Hurriyah), the Muslim sister who led him into the NOI. He remained on the edges of even the NOI, chastised by Elijah Muhammad for his poetry, and put on probation for his behavior. But this position at the edge of formal institutions of Islamic knowledge enabled him to embrace unorthodox readings of Islamic doctrine—and in some senses, reinvent a tradition of poetry that had long been integral to Islamic culture but often stood in creative tension with formal institutions of Islamic learning. Marvin found his own creative impulses in tension with educational institutions (at SFSC, in Oakland, and in Fresno), the institutions of Black Power like the Black Panthers and Black House, and the Nation of Islam itself. He continued to experiment with different ways of being Muslim, in practice and in poetry, resisting circumscription by various orthodoxies and epistemologies, creating at their interstices. Marvin X's Islamic language is what Moten calls a "free" almost "anarchic... generativity; a reconceptualization or out-from-outside reinstrumentalization of idiom that allows an improvisation." He struggled to free himself from what Amiri Baraka called the "strait jacket" of Euro-American expression "*sans* blackness" even while also facing the censorship of Elijah Muhammad and the Black Panthers.[78]

Marvin X's later poem "Oh, Ancestors Speak to Me, Digame por favor" is emblematic of that improvisation and reconceptualization—on not just a poetic and idiomatic level, but also a doctrinal one. The poem begins with the word "speak," like in the NOI newspaper *Muhammad Speaks*, but also the injunction *iqra'* (recite!) in verse 96:1 in the Qur'an. The poem pays tribute to Ali Sharif Bey, Marvin's mentor from the Black Arts West Theater, by also speaking in Spanish.

> speak
> digame
> Ali Sharif Bey
> speak Islam
> Sunni Shia Ahmadiyya Sufi
> Nation of Islam
> speak
> polytheism Islam
> Tell me
> black stone rejected
> corner stone
> we black stone
> rejected despised
> socalled Negro[79]

This multiple polyglossic, polyphonic Islam simultaneously speaks the language of the NOI, the Ahmadiyya Islam of Ali Sharif Bey, the Sufi poetry of Ibn Arabi, and the BAM poetry of Amiri Baraka. Baraka's 1972 poem "Ka 'Ba" similarly paid tribute to the black stone of the Kaaba in Mecca, asking, "What will be the sacred words?"[80] Marvin X's reference to the Kaaba interconnects these various streams of Islamic faith with this cornerstone of Muslim ritual practice (like the pilgrimage and prayer), but it also evokes the foundational role of African Muslims in early Islam like the Ethiopian Bilal ibn Rabah, the first muezzin to issue the call to prayer from the Kaaba.

Upon returning from exile in Canada, Marvin X traveled to Harlem, which he calls the "Mecca" of Black Arts. In *Fly to Allah*, "Al Hajj Harlem" frames this as pilgrimage but also as Black study in the "Mecca of the west": "I have studied / The theory & practice / Of Blackness / in this University / Of Harlem / Greater / Than Timbuctu! / . . . Mecca of the west / I am moved . . . / To be here / A star / In Allah's Heaven / As-Salaam-Alaikum / Wa rah-matu-llah! / Wa barakatuh."[81] In New York, he was exposed to Sufism, Sufi poetry, and mystical philosophy and the work of Islamic thinkers like Abu Hamid al-Ghazali, Jalal al-Din Rumi, and Hazrat Inayat Khan. "Poets, artists, and musicians," Marvin X wrote, "are in the front ranks of the Sufis. When I arrived in Harlem, I would be introduced to Sufi Islam—actually, I would become a Sufi. Logically, with my eclectic background, I had no choice, it was natural." Marvin developed a philosophy of Islamic aesthetics, arguing that "art is the celebration of Allah. We create to celebrate the Creator, to acknowledge His power and glory, which is our own. To celebrate Allah is . . . to put ourselves in harmony with eternity, with the living, the dead, and the yet unborn." In his *Somethin' Proper*, he writes that "music is Allah talking" and drama is "an instrument of Allah."[82] All Muslim artists," Marvin X would later write in his *Black Bird News & Review*, "drift toward the Sufi Way."[83]

FLIGHT AND THE BLACK BIRD

Marvin X's 1968 *The Black Bird* is a parable for children, illustrated by an image of a blackbird sitting in a cage with the door open. Although the cage catches on fire, the bird refuses to leave: "The cage door was always open, but the little bird wouldn't come out. He loved the cage, he had been in it so long." *The Black Bird* interprets elements from Malcolm X's speech "Twenty Million People in a Political, Economic, and Mental Prison" delivered in January 1963 that recounted a parable about the "house Negro" who refuses to leave the master's house, which is on fire.[84] Malcolm X delivered the speech in the midst of efforts to desegregate the military, schools, and housing.

In September 1963—between the March on Washington and the bombing of the 16th Street Baptist Church—Nina Simone released her song "Blackbird" with hauntingly prescient lyrics: "Why you wanna fly, blackbird? / You ain't ever gonna fly." The song was her reinterpretation of a Clarence Bernard Jackson and James Hatch song from the 1961 musical *Fly Blackbird*, about the civil rights movement and the Greensboro sit-ins. In October 1963, Malcolm X would echo the imagery of a bird taking flight in another speech at the University of California, Berkeley, apparently drawing an analogy between himself and a bird for the first time. Having been asked *not* to talk about Islam, said: "It's like telling a bird to fly without his wings."[85]

One month later, on November 10, 1963, Malcolm X recounted the parable of the master's house on fire in his Detroit speech "Message to the Grass Roots." He described the house slave who refused to take flight, preferring to live with the master (referencing the desegregation of housing and neighborhoods) and eating the master's food (referencing the sit-in protests at lunch counters).[86] The allegory also directly described the violence against the integration movement—like at the University of Mississippi in Fall 1962 and the University of Alabama in summer 1963. Malcolm X's allegory is also about psychological violence perpetuated against young minds as they struggle for representation—both political and epistemological. It is based on Malcolm X's own experiences in all white schools, being discouraged by his white teacher from being a lawyer, his self-education in prison, and the awakening of his Black consciousness in the NOI. The allegory is as much about slavery and class as the politics of education and knowledge—and for Malcolm the allegory reflects on the lived experience of incarceration that became an analogy for a "mental prison."

Malcolm's speeches and Marvin X's parable riff off *The Fire Next Time* published earlier that year—in which Baldwin characterized the United States as a burning house—not only because of the racial situation but also because of American wars against independence movements abroad and against decolonization.[87] "Freedom is the fire that burns away illusion," Baldwin wrote in his 1959 essay "Nobody Knows My Name." "Any honest examination of the national life shows how far we are from the standard of human freedom with which we began."[88] This "Black prophetic fire" cleansing the United States of its structures of injustice would become one of the most important images of the BAM, like in Marvin X's 1965 poem "Burn, Baby, Burn," written after the Watts uprisings in 1965, a poem Larry Neal and Amiri Baraka included in *Black Fire*.[89]

Marvin X's *The Black Bird* is a pedagogical tool for Black study that urges the new generation to escape from "mental cages." It was printed as a broadsheet by the Barakas' Jihad Productions and read at the 1968 Black Power conference in Philadelphia. Marvin X would later name his own independent publishing house Black Bird Press. The parable alludes to Marvin's own fugitivity as a conscientious objector and the very real possibility of a prison sentence, but it is also about the strictures of the state educational system and the white literary mainstream. Julian Mayfield, another literary and political exile, published "Into the Mainstream and Oblivion" just before (also) fleeing to Canada and then to Ghana with his Puerto Rican wife, the physician Ana Livia Cordero—along with a flood of other African American emigrant artists and intellectuals (as documented in Kevin Gaines's *African Americans in Ghana*). Mayfield's essay begins by questioning America's wars abroad ("colonial war[s] in Africa," the Korean War, and implicitly Vietnam), observing that the Black writer "sings the national anthem *sotto voce* and has trouble reconciling the 'dream' to the reality he knows. He walks the streets of his nation an alien." The Black writer, Mayfield argues, may be better off at the margins. "He is indeed a man without a country" writes Mayfield. "And yet this very detachment may give him the insight of the stranger in the house, placing him in a better position to illuminate contemporary American life as few writers of the mainstream can. This alienation should serve also to make him more sensitive to the philosophical and artistic influences that originate beyond our national cultural boundaries."[90] In Marvin X's own melancholic exile, his route to freedom through the *tayyarah* (airplane) that is his underground railroad, he laments the lived experience described by Mayfield, stripped of citizenship rights, a man without a country, walking the streets an alien. Both writers escaped from the burning cage into another kind of freedom.[91]

By elaborating on Malcolm X's own parable of the house on fire, Marvin X uses figurative language from other Black texts as a rhetorical strategy, drawing on not only Malcolm X's speeches but also the longer African American literary, poetic, and musical tradition. The parable engages in what Henry Louis Gates Jr. describes as "motivated Signifyin(g), in which the text Signifies upon other Black texts, in the manner of the vernacular ritual of 'close reading.'" Marvin X underscores his relation to Malcolm X's, like "black jazz musicians who perform each other's standards . . . not to critique these but to engage in refiguration as an act of homage."[92]

The following year Maya Angelou published her autobiography *I Know Why the Caged Bird Sings* (1969), drawing on the imagery of the caged bird from Paul Laurence Dunbar's poem "Sympathy" at the suggestion of jazz singer and civil rights activist Abbey Lincoln.[93]

> I know why the caged bird beats his wing
> Till its blood is red on the cruel bars;
> For he must fly back to his perch and cling
> When he fain would be on the bough a-swing;
> And a pain still throbs in the old, old scars

> And they pulse again with a keener sting—
> I know why he beats his wing!
>
> I know why the caged bird sings, ah me,
> When his wing is bruised and his bosom sore,—
> When he beats his bars and he would be free . . .[94]

Dunbar's wife Alice explained the material conditions that gave rise to the poem—"iron grating of the book stacks in the Library of Congress" where Dunbar worked "suggested to him the bars of the bird's cage."[95] This insight into Dunbar's poetic labors, as he shelved books of other writers, speaks of his financial struggles for literary independence, as well as his fight for an education cut short by poverty. In *Oak and Ivy*, a collection that mixes vernacular with standard registers, Dunbar writes about a little bird coming down to his window trying to call notice to his song, as he urges his readers to "Keep pluggin' away" though "there'll be lots of sneers to swallow, / There'll be lots of pain to bear." He calls for "birds of peace and hope and love Come fluttering earthward from above."[96] The bird free in nature mirrors Dunbar's own poetic labors yearning to be free.

Marvin X's development of the blackbird motif, in the parable and later in his independent publishing house Black Bird Press, evokes the longer tradition of poetry and music that has taken the blackbird at its center as a rhetorical strategy, using figurative language from the vernacular tradition to signify upon other texts. His Black Bird Press provided an escape from mainstream commercial publishing, giving voice to ideas and language outside its parameters, as Marvin X struggled to make ends meet by selling his works on the street. Paying tribute to Malcolm X's speeches and words, Marvin X constructed a poetics of Malcolm X—"through a process of repetition and revision . . . fundamental to black artistic forms."[97] The blackbird is what Henry Louis Gates Jr. describes as ritualistic homage through the reconfiguration of signs, performing an act of communal bonding through storytelling—and also through music, poetry, and literature.

Marvin's self-published *Black Bird* was also a kind of reclamation the year that the Beatles recorded their own song "Blackbird" (1968), however ironically released on their *White Album*. The following year, Third World Press published Carolyn Rodgers's collection of poems *Songs of a Black Bird* alongside Angelou's *I Know Why the Caged Bird Sings*.[98] The blackbird motif migrated from its (unacknowledged) roots in the *Fly Blackbird* musical to Nina Simone's "Blackbird" to the Beatles to Marvin X, Maya Angelou, and Carolyn Rodgers, and later to

Beyoncé's reinterpretation in her 2024 "Blackbird." These modes of revision play out as a kind of call and response or dialogue about the interpretation and reinterpretation of color, tone, Blackness, and race.

Henry Louis Gates Jr.'s own collection *Thirteen Ways of Looking at a Black Man* (1997) itself reworked Wallace Steven's 1917 poem "Thirteen Ways of Looking at a Blackbird" by using it to explore different ways of seeing Blackness. Gates actually begins the book with recollections of Black Muslims selling the NOI newspaper *Muhammad Speaks* on the street when he was a student at Yale in 1975. His reinterpretation of the "blackbird" motif would in turn be reinterpreted by Morgan Parker in her "Thirteen Ways of Looking at a Black Girl" and Tony Lopez's "13 Ways of Looking at a Paloma Negra." This form of pastiche, Gates argues, dramatically extends "the modes of revision available to writers in the tradition and reveals that acts of formal revision can be loving acts of bonding rather than ritual slayings."[99]

Marvin would be imprisoned upon his return to the United States but when released would go on to obtain his MA at San Francisco State, open his Black Educational Theater, and teach in Berkeley's Ethnic Studies program in 1972 with Sun Ra. Marvin X called Sun Ra "the example of the artist as holy man and scientist. Some of us came to realize, finally, the need to be holy. The theatre was our temple, the audience our congregation. There was to be no difference between theatre and church. In the ritual theatre we attempted to create, the audience must join the action. Revolutionary black art must be about the business of national liberation, about freedom, justice and equality."[100] He also returned to his home town to teach Black Studies at Fresno State College, but Governor Ronald Reagan barred him from the classroom, as he did with Angela Davis at UCLA. Marvin tried to hold classes anyway, but a restraining order was issued against him. When he took his classes offsite to the Christian Community Baptist Church, the state threatened to withhold funding from their community center.[101] Marvin X was out of work, a teacher without students, a classroom, or a school. "To try and stop me from teaching," he told the *Fresno Bee*, "is like trying to stop the sun from shining." He was also facing trials on two fronts: in federal court in San Francisco for evasion of the draft and in district court in Fresno. "I was only twenty-five, still a child, but had to battle the courts, the police, racist administrators and professors and red neck KKK farm boys."[102] Marvin X fled again, this time to Mexico, joining the artist Elizabeth Catlett, another vivid interpreter of Black life and a refugee from a small-minded and narrow school system (Hillside High School in Durham, North Carolina, where she taught between 1935 and 1937). Her art, too, vividly portrays fugitivity, as with her well-known print of Harriet Tubman. Harney and Moten talk about this kind of dispossession, exile, and statelessness as "being together in homelessness," an "undercommon appositionality" in which there is "a society of friends where everything can fold in dance to black, in being held and flown, in what was never silence."[103]

ADDICTION AND MENTAL SLAVERY

After publishing four collections of poetry in the 1970s and early 1980s, Marvin would go silent for nearly fifteen years, experiencing a kind of social death through addiction to crack cocaine. Sylvia Wynter, in her "Black Studies Manifesto" (1994), describes social death by observing how knowledge systems validate life forms as "human" but also constitute life forms, tying *bios* to *logos*, narrative forms that reward certain kinds of life and punish others. Referencing Carter Woodson's *The Mis-Education of the Negro*, she comments on the ways in which narrative systems are linked to biochemical systems of reward and punishment—governing consciousness and forms of knowledge that make us human, but also shaping how we "experience ourselves as human"[104] Wynter talks about narrative systems that make Blackness a signifier of symbolic death, embedded in the material reality of the death of Black lives, through state violence and health outcomes, but also through systems of poverty and educational inequity that limit the possibilities of Black life.

Marvin X's autobiography *Somethin' Proper* begins in recovery and reconciliation as a mode of confession and repentance. The opening chapter, "Road to Mecca," describes traveling to his daughter's wedding. Beginning at the end, the anachronistic organization initially makes it hard to follow where the narrator is going. Only after reading the book in its entirety—and traveling the duration of Marvin X's journey—does it become clear how he breaks the chains of the social death of addiction by connecting life to words, *bios* to *logos* through poetry, drama, and autobiography. *Somethin' Proper* tells the story of Marvin's childhood, upbringing, family, friends, collaborators, schooling, conversion, teaching, writing, and activism. It also tells the story of addiction as mental slavery—first recounted in Ed Bullins's play *Salaam, Huey Newton, Salaam* about Marvin X and Huey Newton's relationship, their addiction to crack, and Newton's murder. They both identify each other as teachers of the other, Black Power of the Black Arts and the Black Arts of Black Power. (As Huey Newton says in Bullins's script, "Many of our comrades came through [Marvin's] black theatre.") The play is a stark portrait of the fate of two leaders and crack "as the last weapon in the devil's arsenal for the Black nation"—a form of "chemical warfare" for the destruction of the Black community.[105] In the postscript to *Somethin' Proper*, Marvin X writes that the book started off being about Huey Newton, material that Ed Bullins took and published as his own, since "I guess he thought that I was lost to crack and I wasn't coming back."[106]

Marvin X incorporated *Salaam, Huey, Salaam* into his own semiautobiographical play about addiction, *One Day in the Life*. In the play he reflects on other kinds of slavery, other kinds of prisons, alluding to *One Day in the Life of Ivan Denisovich*, Aleksandr Solzhenitsyn's novel detailing the brutal fight for survival in a Soviet gulag, and the reduction of revolutionary ideals to "bare life," as a "politicized form of natural life," or "life exposed to death, especially in the form of sovereign violence."[107] The prison in Marvin's play, though, is crack. "Crack," one of the characters says, "is worse than slavery." Marvin draws on Islamic motifs of finding the right path, NOI motifs about the devil, and recovery programs at Black churches, as he tries to claw his way out of addiction, struggling against what he calls "the devil crack." The character of the Christian preacher helping Marvin X uses religious language that echoes NOI imagery from Louis Farrakhan's famous speech, delivered at Mosque Maryam on November 3, 1996, "Crack-Cocaine: The Great Conspiracy to Destroy the Black Male."[108] Farrakhan's argument about government indifference to crack-related deaths in Black America would be argued in scholarship like Michelle Alexander's *The New Jim Crow*, a book that rested on the table of Marvin X's Academy of da Corner. In *One Day in the Life*, the preacher calls crack "an evil demon. Crack is Satan himself.... Oh, this crack is a wicked devil. Crack is worse than slavery ... The crack slave is a pitiful slave.... That wicked devil crack cocaine destroyed your family." Crack is worse than slavery because the "crack slave" does not care about "his God or his family, his woman or his children.... He don't care about nothing."[109]

Marvin's point is driven home in this work, and in his autobiography, through key references to his children who frame the addiction scenes—and the scenes of his recovery. There is a scene of Marvin cashing in the bus ticket to his mother's funeral for crack and another of him missing his daughter's valedictorian address; those heartrending memories are wedged between other glimmers of hope in community life, children and family, and religion. The first act of the play is filled with nightmarish images of addiction and closes with Marvin X calling out to Allah for help. Instead, the Devil enters through the door, saying: "You're going to be my slave ... and I'm going to toss you straight down to hell. Just make the wrong slip and I'll have you forever," words that make Marvin crawl on the floor. But then his son Abdul appears to him in a dream and implores Marvin to "fight the devil, Dad, don't submit." The scene is even more wrenching with the knowledge that Abdul died by suicide in 2002. Marvin dedicated his 2004 collection of essays *In This Crazy House Called America* to the memory of his son Abdul Ibn El Muhajir (Darrel Patrick Jackmon) writing "a beautiful mind is a terrible thing to lose," which echoes the slogan of the United Negro College Fund "a mind is a terrible thing to waste." Abdul's very name speaks of being a "slave of God" and "son of he who emigrates" or flees, in the case of Marvin X, the fugitive engaging in Black study. Abdul's intellectual and scholarly accomplishments are highlighted in the dedication, as well as in the collection itself and the play. In the play, Abdul outlines how Marvin taught him the Arabic alphabet and then how he went on to major in Arabic and study in Egypt and Syria. I am "the fruit of your creation," Abdul says, although Marvin responds that Abdul went further in these "revolutionary things," as a son should.[110] Darrel is testimony to the movement that Marvin helped spearhead for Black Studies, changing the landscape of the American educational system through struggles to incorporate Black history, students, faculty, arts, and religion. But his tragic death looms over the play.

Marvin's children stand like angels in the play and in his other work, exhorting him toward recovery and toward his revolutionary agenda of "fighting for our people." "But now," says Abdul, "you've got to fight for your own soul. Fight the devil, Dad, don't submit to him." The second act begins with a letter from Marvin X's daughter Nefertiti, who he describes as sharing his religious fire, his religious conviction. Although she is a Christian, she uses Islamic and Qur'anic language urging Marvin to "submit to God and Him alone," echoing the *shahada*, the declaration of faith and the first pillar of belief in Islam.

RESURRECTION AND RECOVERY

Just after his conversion, Marvin X wrote a very short dramatic work titled *Resurrection of the Dead*. The play functions as a performative interpretation of NOI teachings about the resurrection, similar to how Amiria Baraka's *A Black Mass* interprets the Yakub teaching. Elijah Muhammad, in *Message to the Blackman in America*, refers to a "mental resurrection of the black nation" and an awakening from the deceptions of the "slave masters."[111] Resurrection is one of the Nation of Islam's five "principles of belief," a reinterpretation of the five pillars of Islamic faith that integrates Christian (and Islamic) concepts of resurrection. *Resurrection of the Dead* is a performance of rising from symbolic death through conversion to Islam.[112]

The play, put to drum music "(Milford Graves style)," is structured in four movements, beginning with a terrible vision of Black life reduced to abjection, as "dead bodies in the hells of North America." The play's third movement describes a purification through a "new language" "the pure Black tongue, the voice of Allah in the Person; Allahu Akbar! Sami allahu-lil-man hamida! Rabbana-la-ka-l-hamd."[113] This work was performed in 1972 at Marvin's Black Educational Theater in San Francisco as a "ritual-myth dance drama" accompanied by Sun Ra's Arkestra, with dancers throwing off their chains and dancing free. The interpretive performance of the work with experimental music by Milford Graves, Juju, and Sun Ra's Arkestra at different times, melded sound, words, and music to dramatize NOI teachings in mythopoetic terms. Like Baraka in *A Black Mass*, Marvin X uses Islamic and Arabic phrases to create a ritual-like performance dramatizing an emergence into new life, language, and sound. After Marvin X emerged from a twelve-year addiction to crack cocaine, *Resurrection of the Dead* was staged at Warm Daddy's in Philadelphia to commemorate the publication of his collection of essays *In this Crazy House Called America* (2002). Writing became part of his recovery and the performance of *Resurrection* took on new meaning in the midst of the crack epidemic and mass incarceration.

At the beginning of *Somethin' Proper*, Marvin X writes about selling newspapers on the streets in San Francisco when he was homeless. He chronicles the reasons for his homelessness: fired from teaching for reading his poems in class, for sending students to the library to read Amiri Baraka and Larry Neal's anthology *Black Fire*, for refusing to fight in Vietnam. He taught in schools from elementary to college, hoping to "make Oakland a better place for all its citizens ... until they ran me out." By introducing students to Black Arts poetry and prose, he tried to turn them on to a different kind of literature "in their language [that] deals with themes relevant to their life style. At least use their language as a starting point, and move on from there."[114] *Somethin' Proper* describes Marvin's literal and metaphorical homelessness within systems of sanctioned knowledge, and how he creates his own home in the undercommons by teaching on the street, at community events, and at the market, shaping his own institutions, his own structures of dissemination, and telling his own stories to whoever stops by. In *The Undercommons: Fugitive Planning and Black Study*, Stefano Harney and Fred Moten discuss writing in the language of the colonizer (drawing on Frantz Fanon) describing it as its own kind homelessness, with this radical being beside itself of blackness, its off to the side, off on the inside, out from the outside imposition. The standpoint, the home territory, *chez lui* ... among his own, signifying a relationality that displaced the already displaced impossibility of home. Can this being together in homelessness, this interplay of the refusal of what has been refused, this undercommon appositionality, be a place from which emerges neither self-consciousness nor knowledge of the other but an improvisation.... Not simply to be among his own; but to be among his own in dispossession, to be among the ones who cannot own, the ones who have nothing and who, in having nothing, have everything.... What is the sound of this patterning? What does such apposition look like? In the absence of amenity, in exhaustion, there's a society of friends where everything can fold in dance to black, in being held and flown, in what was never silence.[115]

In "Road to Mecca," the opening chapter of Marvin's autobiography, he describes his efforts to get home to his daughter's wedding, back to his family and his birthplace, tracing his journey on Amtrak from Seattle to Fresno. He characterizes the journey as the end of his flight, from being drafted into the army, from being chained by addiction, from formal institutions of knowledge production. The reunion with his child, the celebration of the marriage, and the family photographs become a document and a testament to his recovery. If Islam seems to have charted a path for his flight, his escape, it also charted a road to recovery, resurrection, and reunion.

THE AMERICAN MISEDUCATION SYSTEM

In summer 2019 Marvin X set up his Academy of da Corner at a Juneteenth commemoration in Marin City, California, with a table offering "conscious literature,"[116] archival materials, journals, newspapers, pamphlets, and photographs; books like Nathan and Julia Hare's *The Miseducation of the Black Child* and Michelle Alexander's *The New Jim Crow*; and copies of his most recent book, *Notes of an Artistic Freedom Fighter*. The Juneteenth celebration was on Drake Avenue, a strip of poverty in one of the wealthiest areas in the nation, at a community center located between the administrative offices of the Sausalito Marin City School District, the Marin City Recovery Center (formerly the Harriet Tubman House), and public housing projects designed by a Frank Lloyd Wright associate in the 1960s. In the midst of the strike for Black Studies at San Francisco State in 1968, Marin City launched Project Breakthrough at the Harriet Tubman House, with the aim of giving "academic opportunity" to "underserved students" toward "equitable access to higher education."[117]

A few years earlier, in 1964, the Congress for Racial Equality organized a school boycott in Marin City to bring attention to continuing "Negro and white discontent with de facto segregation" in the aftermath of *Brown v. the Board of Education*.[118] But sixty-five years after the US Supreme Court's decision, in summer 2019, the Justice Department released a report of its two-year investigation into the Sausalito Marin City School District, arguing that it had "knowingly and intentionally maintained and exacerbated" racial segregation. The school district encompasses two towns on different ends of the economic spectrum: Sausalito's median family income is $186,000 and Marin City's is $39,000.[119] The Justice Department report ordered a(nother) plan of desegregation. The Harriet Tubman House, where the Juneteenth ceremony was being held, was formerly an educational center for low-income students, aiming to provide more equal educational opportunities. Today it is part of the Marin City Health and Wellness Center providing substance abuse, addiction, and recovery services.

In the ceremony kicking off the Juneteenth event, one of the organizers, Oshalla Diana Marcus, passed around a heavy chain to the audience, asking them to imagine what it was like to be shackled not only on the ships. She poured water from a calabash over the chains to symbolize the Middle Passage, reading the names of community members, both young and old, who had died that year. Most of the community was attending a funeral for one of those youths—an honor student who had got caught in a wave and drowned. The organizers symbolically buried the chain after the ceremony, "to leave the suffering behind and to continue to live." When the elders of the community were called to the stage, Marvin X stood up to speak. "We broke the chains of four hundred years of slavery but we still have chains on our mind. How did Kunta become Toby? We need to get Toby back to Kunta," he said, referring to Alex Haley's *Roots*.[120] An educational display at the celebration walked attendees through the history of slavery, Juneteenth, and the quest for emancipation. One poster featured Adjoa Burrowes's sketch of a Black woman with a padlock on her head, an image on the cover of the Africa World Press edition of Carter Woodson's *The Mis-Education of the Negro*. Another poster of Marcus Garvey featured a quote from his famous 1937 speech in Nova Scotia, Canada—what later became the lyrics of Bob Marley's "Redemption Song"—"We are going to emancipate ourselves from mental slavery because whilst others might free the body, none but ourselves can free the mind. Mind is your only ruler, sovereign."[121]

CHAPTER 7

THE BARAKAS IN NEW ARK

The Homeplace of Black Art

the world it gives birth to is the beautiful quranic vision

—Imamu Amiri Baraka (LeRoi Jones), "Study Peace," *Spirit Reach*

In the climactic scene at the center of Amiri Baraka's *The Autobiography of LeRoi Jones* (1984), police are beating him[1] with guns and nightsticks. Blood runs hot over his head, face, hands, and clothes as he screams "Allahu Akbar. Al Homdulliah [*sic*]!" The scream is a cri de coeur at the heart of the Newark rebellion between July 12 and 17, 1967, making him "feel an absolute kinship with the suffering roots of African American life." In his confrontation with police brutality, Baraka writes: "This was it, the real America, the America of slavery and lynching."[2] The scream, Fred Moten reflects, is resistance to extreme subjugation, a sonic signifier of the visual spectacle of racial terror. Moten begins his book *In the Break* with the scream that opens the *Narrative of the Life of Frederick Douglass*; in *Scenes of Subjection*, Saidiya Hartman describes this "primal scene of torture," "passing through the blood-stained gate" of American history, as a birth into a kind of kinship.[3] Moten describes the scream as giving birth, despite all odds, to "tonal and grammatical fissures that mark the space of ... political agency and theoretical intervention."[4]

The Muslim exclamation "God is Great! Praise God!" became a primal scream of life and kinship in the face of a genocidal state violence threatening Black life—expressions that were used as protection while Muslims were being attacked by police.[5] Both Moten and Hartman interpret the scream in Frederick Douglass's narrative as an evocation of a birthing—of a life born into the anguished consciousness of racial terror, yet born with a "knowledge of freedom." Moten notes the echoes in Abbey Lincoln's scream in "Triptych: Prayer/Protest/Peace" on *We Insist: Max Roach's Freedom Now Suite* (Roach and Lincoln also became Muslim).[6] Baraka's scream literally saves him, delivering him from death at the hands of the police, seemingly through his invocation of divine protection at a catalytic moment of persecution. Baraka identifies two main triggers for the uprisings: white political and institutional control of majority Black Newark and "constant incidents of police brutality," including the beating of cab driver John Smith and a police raid of a Muslim home.[7] Police brutality sparked the Newark uprisings, as it had with the Watts rebellion in 1965 and would in Detroit a few weeks later. Baraka writes about how the political situation in Newark was "living proof" of the need for "black political determination," "self-sufficiency," and "doing for self," drawing on the political lexicons of the Nation of Islam, Black Power, and Black nationalism. "What I had screamed while they were trying to kill me [was] 'Al-Homdulliah!' [sic] All Praise the Power of Allah, the Power of Blackness. I felt transformed, literally shot into the eye of the black hurricane of coming revolution. I had been through the fire and had not been consumed."[8]

In the aftermath of the Newark uprisings, Baraka began living Islam as "a total form, a total way of looking at the world," by taking a new name, abstaining from smoking and from drinking alcohol, praying, and engaging with Islamic thinkers and ideas.[9] In the *Autobiography* he writes about his Islamic commitments; about turning Spirit House, where they lived, into a *jama'at* or a prayer space where they held Qur'an recitations and prayers.[10] The documentary film he made during this time, *The New-Ark*, opens with the Islamic call to prayer broadcast out of Spirit House and actors Barry Wynn and Yusuf Iman reciting their lines from *A Black Mass* in the street. At the end of the scene, they all pile into the Volkswagen bus that Baraka and Wynn were riding in when stopped by the police during the uprisings.[11] This chapter explores Baraka's cultural restructuring of Newark as a New Ark—as a "vessel or sanctuary that protects against extinction" or a "place of protection, security, refuge, asylum."[12] Baraka would use the name NewArk for Jihad Productions, for the documentary film *The New-Ark*, and for a local newspaper *Black NewArk* he and his wife Amina published in the late 1960s.[13] The New Ark, the new covenant, pays tribute to Sun Ra and His Myth Science Arkestra, who recorded "The Futuristic Sounds of Sun Ra" at Newark's Medallion Studios in 1962. But the name also paid tribute to reports that Noble Drew Ali founded the Moorish Science Canaanite Temple there in 1913 and called the city "New-Ark."[14] Nation of Islam (and Moorish Science Temple of America) conceptualizations of Black Muslim separatism and the Black family informed their construction of Spirit House and "New Ark" as Black political geographies, and as sites of safety from violence against Black lives, though Amiri identified with Sunni Islam and Sufism and Amina left the Nation of Islam when Malcolm X was assassinated.

Baraka's writings helped crystalize a Black Muslim ethos in the BAM, one he situated in alternative "moral geographies" that articulated a "black consciousness and politics based on the teachings of Islam." This chapter expands on insights by scholars like Melani McAlister, Sylvia Chan-Malik, and Ammar Abduh Aqeeli who explore how Baraka's writings contributed to developing an African American Muslim literature in the period of Black Power mobilization in Newark in the late 1960s and early 1970s.[15] Baraka mobilized a Muslim consciousness in his art and activism in Newark by performing *A Black Mass* there in May 1966, disseminating materials through Jihad Productions, setting up Spirit House at 33 Stirling Street, organizing the Committee for Unified Newark (CFUN) around key issues like elections and housing, and publishing writings infused with Islamic imagery. He described his epiphany during the uprisings as the culmination of his earlier activism and what he called a new awakening as he began to "agitate and propagandize ... raised up to another notch in intensity" during a time of "mystical focus" in his life. Not until he returned to Newark, Baraka wrote, did he begin "to get serious about Islam in terms of a spiritual philosophy, rather than just a connective tissue with political activism."[16]

The Barakas forged a homeplace by building key institutions in the heart of the Black Arts and Black Power movements, institutions that functioned as sites of political mobilization and loci of cultural production. They reenvisioned Newark as a Black political geography, campaigning out of Spirit House for Black leaders of majority Black Newark—ultimately succeeding in electing Kenneth Gibson as mayor, a job their own son Ras Baraka would take over in 2010. The Barakas built Spirit House as a homeplace and a site of resistance, as both a material space and a psychic one. It was an "everyday space of blackness," but also the headquarters of Black Power organizing and Black Arts cultural production in Newark.[17] Black Power women "engaged in battles around home-, family-, and neighborhood-based issues," writes Rhonda Williams about the "politics of resistance," creating "physical, symbolic, and relational spaces ... to politicize and transform communities plagued by economic disadvantage, social alienation, and highly destructive racial-gender ideologies that routinely constrict the political empowerment of their inhabitants."[18]

Spirit House at 33 Stirling Street in Newark was the Barakas' living space, but also a center for community organizing, cultural production, and political mobilization. Its name was inspired by music like Albert Ayler's *Spirits* (1964), *Spiritual*

Unity (1964), and *Spirits Rejoice* (1965). When the Barakas later moved to South 10th Street, they held concerts and performances in their basement, calling it Kimako's Blues Café after Amiri's sister, who was murdered in New York City in 1984. Communal spaces for Black art that overlapped with the Barakas' living space were also conceived as a home supporting "the struggle for Black survival," as Larry Neal said in his classic essay on the BAM. "The question of human survival is at the core of contemporary experience. The Black artist must address himself to this reality in the strongest terms possible."[19] Other institutions Amina Baraka founded and ran—like the African Free School, the grocery cooperative Duka Ujamaa, United Sisters ("a nationalist women's study group"), and a childcare collective—were critical sites for Black Power mobilization, but also for sustaining daily life.[20] The African Free School and the United Sisters were key institutions for conceptualizing Black study and developing pedagogies for both children and adults. The Shani Baraka Women's Resource Center, located today down the street from the Baraka home, was named for their daughter who was killed along with her girlfriend Rayshon Holmes in a domestic violence incident.

FIGURE 7.1 Amina Baraka teaching at the African Free School in the documentary *The New-Ark* (1968).

Amina Baraka

Institutions like these provide spaces of safety and refuge from violence against Black life, and specifically Black women, yet they also function as sites of memorial and remembrance.

In the *Autobiography* Baraka describes the kinship at the heart of the Black Arts and Black Power movements in Newark and the New Ark as a kind of rebirth into an Islamic consciousness that fused his identity with his new name, his union with Amina, and the birth of their first child Obalaji. This kinship was grounded both in constructed communities and in actual extended family networks, as they worked in tandem to build political and cultural spaces for Black life in the city. This chapter looks at how the Barakas' family life and homeplace rooted the Black Arts and Black Power movements in actual lived spaces, even as they struggled with a gendered division of domestic and literary labor. Both Amiri and Amina struggled to define and redefine that division of labor through their mutual literary work in the BAM and their political organizing in the Black Power movement. Both used their literary and poetic production to interrogate the political and cultural dynamics of family and community and profoundly reshaped the political and cultural life of Newark, doing so amid the surge in Black feminist writings, activism, and consciousness during the 1970s and 1980s.

The Barakas understood their family, Spirit House, and the New Ark as Black political geographies that were both sites of resistance and refuges. This convergence of forces was precipitated by the Newark performance of *A Black Mass* in May 1966, in which Sylvia Wilson played one of the main roles, bringing her together with LeRoi Jones. Moten calls this event of "antiorigin and anteorigin, replay and reverb of an impossible natal occasion, the performance of a birth and rebirth ... the reproduction of blackness in and as (the) reproduction of black performance(s)."[21]

HOME

Moten describes the move from Greenwich Village up to Harlem and back to Newark as a "return": "When Baraka split—from the Village, from interracial 'romance' and (black) 'bohemian' lifestyle, from other, former selves (in)to other, new ones—he attempted (by way of complex 'return') to move away from a particular structure of thought."[22] The *Autobiography* describes him stepping away from the white intellectual and social circles he'd been part of in Greenwich Village. His "focus had gotten much whiter," through his literary work—and his children—with wife Hettie Jones (with whom he coedited the literary journal *Yugen: a new consciousness in arts and letters*) and with mistress Diane DiPrima (with whom he coedited the literary journal *The Floating Bear*).[23] Using language from *A Black Mass*, he writes: "It was not, ever, that I consciously desired not to be black or the brown consciousness tied irrevocably to the *black mass soul*—I had just . . . gotten isolated to the extent that almost all my closest friends, the people I saw every day, were white!"[24] In March 1964, his play *Dutchman* was performed at the Cherry Lane Theatre, dramatizing a white woman who tries to seduce a Black youth on the subway, but ends up killing him. After the play received critical attention—and ultimately won an Obie—he reread the play to try and understand its meaning, realizing that he had "set in motion some symbols from out of my own life."[25] His play *The Slave* was also performed that year, foreshadowing his separation from Hettie. Its dramatic arc is about a Black "would-be revolutionary who splits from his white wife on the eve of a race war, [it] was what Nellie called 'Roi's nightmare.' It was so close to our real lives, so full of that living image."[26] During this time, he began engaging with a "new blacker circle" of musicians, artists, and militants, a "heavier black circle . . . fueled by reality," tuning in to the new music of Archie Shepp, Marion Brown, Sonny Murray, Cecil Taylor, Albert Ayler, Thelonius Monk, John Coltrane, Miles Davis, Pharoah Sanders, and Sun Ra. He describes the music as "the reaching searching cry for freedom and life that not only took the music in a certain direction, but that direction was a reflection of where people themselves, particularly the African American people, were going. It is no coincidence that people always associate John Coltrane and Malcolm X, they are harbingers and reflectors of the same life development."[27]

Not long after he returned to Newark, Jones met Sylvia Wilson. Born Sylvia Robinson, she grew up in the heart of Newark on Howard Street after her family migrated from North Carolina, but spent weekends and summers in Harlem with her grandmother. As a teenager, she hung out in the downtown Village arts scene, listening to then emergent jazz greats like Coltrane, Max Roach, and Abbey Lincoln. She attended Newark Arts High School but dropped out after becoming pregnant, married Walter Vernon Wilson, and raised their children Vera and Wanda. Sylvia joined the NOI after hearing Malcolm X speak at the Rickory Theatre in 1958 but left after his assassination. She sent Vera and Wanda to the NOI's University of Islam school in Newark, later the Sister Clara Muhammad school, "because it was the only Black education around."[28]

She chafed against the NOI's restrictions as a dancer and an artist, but also because she embraced communism.

One of the first times LeRoi saw Sylvia, she was performing at the Jazz Arts Society in Newark with the Yusuf Rahman (Ronald Stone), "dancing while he read his swooping jazzical lines."[29] What poetry did Rahman read that night? There are few records of his work, except radio archives and the two-poem broadsheet *Alhomdullilah!*.[30] Rahman also published a poem titled "Transcendental Blues" in Baraka and Larry Neal's anthology *Black Fire*, a poem about "ALLAH's song" that calls for an "expanded consciousness... into a new peaceful & blissful Jesus-like hue Nirvana in infinite Tao-blue smelling eternal ALHOMDULLILAH."[31] Following the poetry reading was a performance by Pharoah Sanders, Marion Brown, and Rashied Ali. (Sanders and Brown were just off recording John Coltrane's *Ascension* in February 1966.) In his February 1966 "Apple Cores #4" column in *DownBeat* magazine, Baraka (writing as Jones) talked about that evening and described Sanders's command of "his lyric timbre even when he is screaming, his control of the horn with his breathing; ... all were visibly moved and shaken by the experience. At the height of the music, the moaning and screaming came on in earnest. This is the ecstasy of the new music. At the point of wild agony or joy, the wild moans, screams, yells of life, in constant change."[32] Was that evening at the Jazz Arts Society, when he saw Sylvia perform, a prelude to his Islamic consciousness—awakened by the scream of Pharoah Sanders's horn and Yusuf Rahman's *al-hamdulillah*?

In the "Apple Cores #4" column, Jones described Rahman's poetry that evening as "a revelation," "speech musicked," and "love poems... turned very consciously by the woman thing. The black woman, i.e., how to get her back with us."[33] But the column does not explicitly mention Sylvia, though she was one of the founders of the Jazz Arts Society in 1963 (known as the "Loft" then the "Cellar"). Amiri later recognized the Jazz Arts Society in the *Autobiography* as Amina's "own cultural work... in and around Newark, against much heavier odds," comparing it to what they were trying to do with the Black Arts Repertory Theatre School (BARTS) in Harlem—except that he identifies a "black working-class underpinning" as the "intellectual and philosophical basis for their efforts."

> It was hooked up objectively to the same kind of thing we were doing at the Black Arts. In those cities like Newark, grim industrial towns in the real world, these kinds of projects are necessarily smaller but at the same time tougher and blacker.... People must fight to bring art to a place like Newark.... And so she

had a whole life as cultural worker in Newark that paralleled what we were trying to do at the Black Arts in many ways.... The unwavering focus of responsibility, especially as it relates to the African American people, was what the whole of the Black Arts movement was about. People like Sylvia, in the Newarks all over North America, had had that sense of focus and responsibility because, finally, there was much more of a black working-class underpinning for what they were doing. Such an intellectual and philosophical basis for their efforts was a given.[34]

The Jazz Arts Society functioned as an alternative space outside the commercial mainstream of the white-run recording industry and clubs regulated by cabaret cards. The "do it yourself" approach of a cooperative jazz club "would be a revolution on the jazz scene," he wrote in *DownBeat* about a month after he saw Sylvia's performance at the Jazz Arts (in March 1966). "But there are very few people strong enough to see such a program through."[35] Amina was one of those people, following through with founding institutions of the DIY revolution, institutions that were both "conceptual" spaces.[36] These kinds of early Black Arts cultural institutions created safe spaces for the free expression of Black art, creating what Carter Mathes calls "alternative spaces for existence that challenge the hegemony of apartheid terror." Such institutions reflected "a shared concern with creating new spaces for black art, essentially an atmospheric ethics of space connected to black expression."[37]

Sylvia and LeRoi would later hook up while rehearsing *A Black Mass* in the loft of the Jazz Arts Society. Sylvia played the role of Tiila, and Jones's pregnant girlfriend Olabumi Osafemi played the role of Olabumi. A few months after its May 1966 performance of the play at Proctor's in Newark, Osafemi died from a pulmonary embolism—and the baby did not survive—a frightening fulfillment of the play's (and the Yakub teaching's) message about medical racism and obstetric violence against Black women. As the Black magician Jacoub experiments with "his final solution" in the play, the lights go out and the women scream: "Our mothers are sick. The world... is choking us."[38] It was in this context that LeRoi and Sylvia came together, what she would later describe as life affirming in the face of the loss of life of mother and child.

In his next Apple Cores column—in August 1966—Jones wrote about another performance of Pharoah Sanders and Marion Brown at the Jazz Arts Society, this time with Burton Greene. He describes Sanders and Brown "screaming us into spirit" through "a consciously Spiritual Music. That is, we mean to speak of Life Force and try to *become* one of the creative functions of the universe."³⁹ In October, Sanders recorded his album *Tauhid* (an Islamic term meaning "oneness of God") at Van Gelder Studios in Englewood Cliffs, New Jersey. Sylvia and LeRoi's first son Obalaji was born the following May, little more than a year after the performance of *A Black Mass*, bringing what Baraka calls "mystical focus" to his life.⁴⁰ Just after the uprisings, in August 1967, they were married in a Yoruba ceremony conducted by Nana Oserjeman.⁴¹ Hajj Heshaam Jaaber, known for mentoring—and burying—Malcolm X after his break with the NOI gave the Barakas their new names, to which Amiri would append the honorific Imamu indicating Muslim leadership and giving him "metaphysical elevation."⁴²

Baraka first used the expression "Alhomdulillah!" to describe the Newark rebellion in his 1968 essay "Newark—Before Black Men Conquered," published in *Black NewArk*, and later in his collection of essays *Raise, Race, Rays, Raze* (1971).⁴³ That same year, Yusuf Rahman published his broadsheet *Alhomdulillah!* speaking to a kind of intertextuality between Rahman's poetry and Baraka's account of his experience as he riffs off Rahman, who was a teacher at Newark Arts High School where Amina had been a student. The following year, Pharoah Sanders put the words *al-hamdulillah* to music on his track "Hum-Allah-Hum-Allah-Hum-Allah"—the lyrics "Hum-Allah-Hum-Allah-Hum-Allah" chanted, sung, and yodeled by the vocalist Leon Thomas. Sanders's tenor saxophone crescendos into what sounds like a screeching scream at the song's climax—the poet and the musician echoing each other and speaking each other's language—as they trace a musical and poetic call and response through the Islamic language of praising God. Sanders's track and Baraka's *Autobiography* also riff off Abbey Lincoln's scream in "Triptych: Prayer/Protest/Peace," reinterpreting the scream as an expression of protest that mingles with the *al-hamdulillah*'s expression of prayer or praise. Baraka describes the scream as "yells of life" and a "Life Force."⁴⁴ "Hum-Allah-Hum-Allah-Hum-Allah" was recorded in October 1969, the month President Richard Nixon threatened war with the Soviet Union over Vietnam by flying warplanes loaded with nuclear weapons to the edge of Soviet territory. The lyrics call for peace, playing on the etymological connection of the word "Islam" to peace, as Leon Thomas sings: "Peace is a united effort for coordinated control. Peace is the will of the people and the will of the land. With peace we can move ahead together. We want you to join us this evening in this universal prayer. . . . Let loving never cease. Hum-Allah, hey, Hum-Allah, yeah, Hum-Allah, hey."⁴⁵ These BAM musicians and poets use the Islamic language of *al-hamdulillah*, of praising God, to simultaneously invoke prayer, protest, and peace. But they also chart what Su'ad Abdul Khabeer calls "a sonic religious genealogy, . . . a long historical trajectory in which Muslims of African descent use the arts, specifically music and poetry, as a means of spiritual training and education and for cultural expression."[46]

NEWARK UPRISINGS: "SUFFERING CRUEL PERSECUTION—POLICE BRUTALITY"

In *The Autobiography*, the cry of "Allahu Akbar. Al-Hamdulillah" becomes a birth into a sense of kinship in the "New Ark," sealing LeRoi and Sylvia's relationship. The scene is performed doubly—as a death of his former self consumed in the heat of the uprising and as a (re)birth. As blows from the policeman's pistol rain down on Jones's head, he begins to lose consciousness and his entire body is covered in "wet hot blood." "I was already being removed from conscious life. I was being murdered and I knew it."[47] In this moment of near death, and the extinguishing of his consciousness, this primal scream seems to save him, turning the passage into a kind of revival. People around him begin to shout at the police, "You're killing them. Motherfucking bastards, stop it." The murderous intent of the police manifests itself anew in the precinct when the police chief smiles "poisonously" (Jones's archenemy Dominic Spina). But Jones defiantly declares: "I'm alive. You didn't kill me."[48] Jones's reckoning with the genocidal consequences of being Black in America continues when he is transferred to the hospital, treated by a doctor he describes as "some primitive Gestapo butcher." The doctor sews Jones up without anesthetic, threatening that he'll never write poetry again.[49] This scene in the *Autobiography* sutures life to words, but also connects the cry of LeRoi Jones to Amiri Baraka, who is literally born out of the uprisings. The birth-like dimensions of this deliverance are underscored when LeRoi marries Sylvia and they are given the names Ameer (later Amiri) and Amina Baraka.[50] Discarding one genealogy, they forge another.

Though Obalaji was born only a few weeks earlier, Sylvia Wilson runs barefoot and distraught into the hospital where Jones is handcuffed to his wheelchair. "Are you going to kill me now?" she yells at the policemen.[51] Writing about this moment in the *Autobiography* Baraka articulates his feelings of "absolute kinship with the suffering roots of African American life," epitomized by the mother standing in protest against the police. During the uprisings, the police shot a kid named James Rutledge thirty-nine times. On July 20, just days after the uprisings, the Black Power Conference was held in Newark and Jones, recently released from jail, convened a press conference at Spirit House with Rutledge's mother present.[52] In photographs of the press conference, Jones, his head still bandaged from the beating, calls for UN intervention, evoking the Civil Rights Congress 1951 "We Charge Genocide" petition to the United Nations, as well as "Malcolm's correct dictum that the black struggle in the US was the struggle of a non-self-governing people against genocidal oppressors." He distributes photographs of Rutledge's "brutal murder," summoning images of lynching, the figure of Emmett Till, and the longer genealogy of state violence against Black life.[53]

Running the gauntlet of the institutional racism governing, disciplining, and punishing Black life, Jones is transferred from police station to hospital to prison where National Guardsmen and state policemen ("straight out murderers") are on a shooting spree. Thinking he will not survive the night, he writes what he calls a "parting statement," which he titles "From the Book of Life," and addresses it to his wife and son (and daughters, in parentheses) as a letter, like the letters written to Elijah Muhammad by those who wanted to join the NOI and have their names written in the NOI's "Book of Life."

Dear Wife

Dear Son (also my daughters)

Life Life LIFE is what we want. We want life more desperately than anyone. But where is it? There is no life without *honor*! *We* must choose the way we live. Under what laws and under what Gods! Our rule will be just . . . because we *feel* (the need for) justice (dear wife you taught me) we understand the demand all Allah-God's creatures make for justice.[54]

At the moment of his arrest and incarceration Jones conceptually aligns his path with Malcolm X's life story. He passes through a dungeon-like valley of darkness that he describes as an inferno populated by devils—similar to Malcolm X's transformation in prison from "Satan," the title of the central chapter in *The Autobiography of Malcolm X* recounting Malcolm's experience in prison. Baraka realizes, relentlessly, that his middle-class status separates him from Malcolm, but he traverses the distance to solidarity with the "black masses" partly through shared experiences of police brutality, prison, conversion, and redemption—but also through his union with Sylvia. He stops drinking and smoking, like Malcolm X stopped eating pork and smoking cigarettes after his conversion in prison—an emblem of his commitment, but also of the bodily reconfiguration of an Islamic self through Islamic ritual practice. Malcolm's brother promises him that this is the way out of prison.[55]

The struggle against police brutality was a principal element of the Nation of Islam's "Program and Position" outlined in Elijah Muhammad's *Message to the Blackman in America*. In the chapter "What Do the Muslims Want," Muhammad calls for freedom, justice, and equality, the freeing of incarcerated Muslims, and "an immediate end to the police brutality and mob attacks against the so-called Negro throughout the United States."[56] In the book's first pages, he writes about "suffering cruel persecution—police brutality" and devils that "have always persecuted and killed the righteous. But the time has at least arrived that Allah (God) will put an end to their persecuting and killing the righteous (the black nation)."[57] In an earlier book Muhammad already denounced police monitoring of the early Nation of Islam, the killing of Ronald Stokes on April 27, 1962, and the police use of dogs to attack civil rights protestors—images that were widely disseminated in the American public sphere.[58] Referencing the shooting of Stokes and six other Muslims in Los Angeles in *Message to the Blackman*, he chides his readers for loving "an open enemy" despite the fact that "night and day they are out seeking a chance to beat and kill you."[59] About six months after the Stokes killing, James Baldwin published "Letter from a Region in My Mind" in which he specifically discusses Black Muslim resistance to police brutality as jolting African Americans into "a kind of intelligence of hope." He describes the "silent intensity" of audiences listening to Black Muslims speak on 125th Street and 7th Avenue. "What these men were saying about white people I had often heard before," he writes, but what distinguished them from other street corner preachers was "the behavior of the police ... because they were afraid," because power "had shifted out of their hands."[60]

In the mobilization around Amiri Baraka's trial in the aftermath of the uprising, Baraka is called a "political prisoner" and flyers and pamphlets call for protest of "the EXTERMINATION of ANOTHER BLACK LEADER." Other flyers show the image of Baraka handcuffed to the wheelchair in the hospital, blood running down his bandaged head. The pamphlets include poems that seem to be from Amina to Amiri: they are included in quotations, nestled in Amiri's poem "All in the Street," and later published in Baraka's 1972 collection *Spirit Reach*. These letter/poems reference the temporal and spatial dimensions of a "sonic religious genealogy" in poetry: "'Love I hear you from way cross the / sea ... in East Africa ... Arabia ... / Reconstructing the grace of our long past.'" Amiri responds to Amina in the poem in a vision of collective action, divine inspiration, and creative imagination.

> Time space manifest into the unity of
> the creator ...

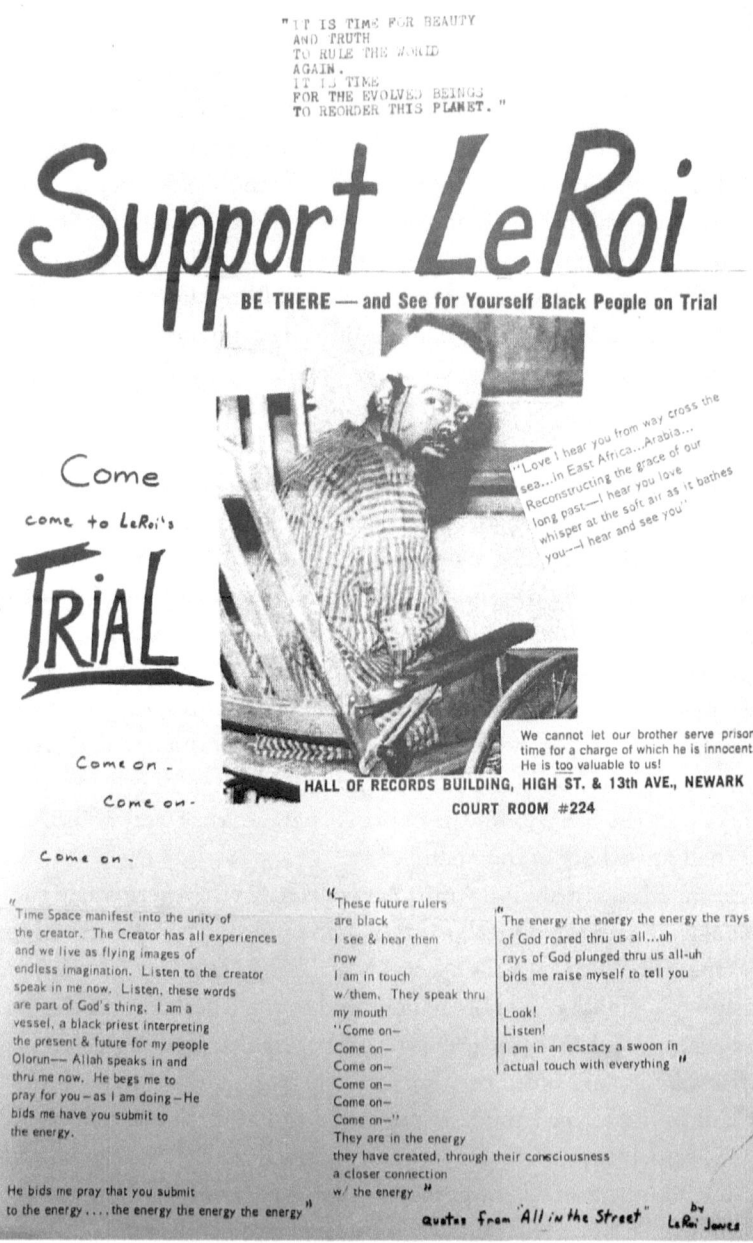

FIGURE 7.2 Leaflet circulated when Baraka went to trial after the Newark uprisings, featuring a picture of Baraka bandaged, bleeding, and sitting in a wheelchair after being beaten by the police. It includes new poetry that would later be published in his collection Spirit Reach, saying: "Allah speaks in and thru me now."

Amina Baraka

> we live as flying images of
> endless imagination. Listen to the creator
> speak in me now. Listen, these words
> are part of God's thing. I am a
> vessel, a black priest interpreting
> the present & future for my people
> Olorun—Allah speaks in and
> thru me now ...
> The energy The Energy the energy the rays
> of God roared thru us all ... uh
> rays of God plunged thru us all-uh[61]

In this verse the sounds of "all ... uh" (Allah) and "us all" merge, even as Baraka code switches with the Yoruban Olorun, mixing African divinities, channeling their energies in his speech and words, collapsing time and space "into the unity of the creator." In the poem the reference to "part of God's thing" is communal ("us all ... uh") and pluralistic ("Olorun—Allah"), musical ("hummers and oobeedah scatters obbbeeoobbee dah") and vernacular (feel it ... huh?), spiritual and mystical ("flying images of / endless imagination"). Baraka plays on Sun Ra's punning on "race" as "rays," writing about the "rays of God [that] plunged thru us all-uh." "All in the Street" is also a vision of giving birth to the future through the process of creation—a vision "grown swollen in the center / of the earth ... past the disease / of the cracker ruled present."[62]

One of Jihad Productions' first publications, *Something Black*, includes poems that contrast with Baraka's vision of new birth for the future by giving voice to the violence in Black life. Yusef Iman's "Lord Make Me Understand" uses the names of the four girls killed in the 16th Street Baptist Church ("Cynthia/Addie/Denise/Carole") to frame the verse as a prayer addressed to God.[63] Other poems riff on biblical imagery of the valley of death, composed as poem/prayers, like "Show me Lord, Show me," "Soul Food," "Revelation," and "Confession." The collection closes with "Searching for an Answer," reflecting on a life of "Lynching, / Bombing, / Discriminations, / Segregations, / Assassinations, / A life without Freedom, Justice, or Equality ... Why / Why / Why." Iman extended his reflections on the genocidal dimensions of white racial violence in a series of graphically illustrated pamphlet/broadsheets that he self-published in 1972 through Uhuru Sasa: *Organize and unify, unify and organize, unify or die, die*; *Extermination or Unification*; *Annihilation or Separation*; and *Genocide or Unify*. The pamphlet *Extermination or Unification* begins with the line "genocide with the help of churches," showing an image of a Black "preacher" calling on people to forgive while a policeman holding a cross kneels on a Black man's back, strangling him.[64] The pamphlet/poems declare genocide by police brutality, war, and lynching, and show prisons as concentration camps. (The images' aesthetics suggest illustrations by Jim "Seitu" Dyson for The East's *Black News: Agitate, Educate, Organize*—like Seitu's full page black and white image of white police beating a crowd of Black (protesters?) laying on the ground bleeding and unconscious.[65]) The pamphlets talk about genocide by rape, dope, alcohol, race mixing, birth control, abortion, and same sex relations—with a Black nationalist focus on heteronormativity as race preservation. The literature reflects a fear of racial genocide, annihilation, and extermination by violence, but also the representational violence inflicted in the publishing mainstream.[66]

In the poem "Love Is the Presence of No Enemy" Baraka plays on Iman's "Love Your Enemy," but reconfigures its Afro-pessimistic poetics by envisioning what it looks, feels, and sounds like to experience love existing freely. The poem describes Newark as an idyll, as Amiri walks down the street on a "blue summer" evening with Obalaji and Amina (pregnant with Ras), "aaaahhhs in harmony love."[67]

> waves in the evening
> soft voice chanting
> purple in the air where the colored folks
> live
> aaah so lovely to be
> free of ugly-nature
> free of death and greed
> rising expanding to be the father of Ras
> and Obalaji
> husband
> to the beautiful
> Amina
> all the world inhales, in its blue perfection ...
> Our love is here its grown so full. Our hearts from Be have
> become what they must be. Be. we say, for the coming revelation ...
> BE, we say to the epoch of
> tomorrow. And tomorrow is now.[68]

The poem proffers love, family, children, music, harmony, and summer as antidotes to the genocidal white violence depicted in Yusef Iman's "Love Your Enemy." Baraka also patterns his musical language on Yusuf Rahman's in "Transcendental Blues" by composing phrases like "soft voice chanting," "indigo whispers," "voice warm and sliding simmering snaky blues."⁶⁹ The jihad of these poems (published by Jihad Productions) assumes a mystical tenor, an expansive vision of a future realized through the impending birth of the child, harmony with Amina, and the refuge of their neighborhood community in Newark—"our love is here" and "our hearts from Be have become what they must be."⁷⁰

"Love Is the Presence of No Enemy" is also a rejoinder to "Black Art," one of the first poems Baraka published with Jihad Productions, while he was still LeRoi Jones. Recited to music on Sunny Murray's album *Sonny's Time Now*, the poem says, "Let there be no love poems written / Until love can exist freely and / Cleanly. Let Black people understand / That they are the lovers and the sons of warriors and sons / of warriors are poems."⁷¹ *Spirit Reach* foresees love existing freely and cleanly: lovers that are both the offspring of the struggle and poems. Their son Obalaji's name means God's warrior, or the King's (LeRoi's) warrior, Baraka writes in the *Autobiography*.⁷² "Black Art," written and recited months before LeRoi Jones met Sylvia Wilson, seemed to again anticipate or lay out a path that he envisioned for himself and the future, one that found its culmination in *Spirit Reach* and Spirit House.

THE "BE(AT)ING" HEART OF ISLAMIC POETICS

The imagery of the Newark uprising in "From the Book of Life" is of violence, with Baraka describing the "pop, pop, pop of what sounded like a .22" from someone shooting into the prison. This is not a pacifist vision—the protesters are rebelling, looting, and resisting by dancing, running, smashing, destroying, wheeling, breaking, standing, fleeing, screaming. "From the Book of Life," though, speaks through a mystical language of a universal and pluralistic God consciousness of human unity, as Baraka uses multiple names for God-Allah, writing about the "natural follow of life force—from spirit to spirit. We are the universal energy transforming itself. Allah Krishna Chakra Obatala Vowels of Life. The thousand names of Divinity. Ism-Al-Azam! . . . All beings come from Allah-God. All beings are the consciousness of Allah-God. There is nothing except it ride the energies of all creation. Part of the Whole." Baraka writes about a black-yellow-white continuum reflecting cycles of life and death, birth and rebirth. Devils, evil, and injustice "fuel the flames of righteousness."⁷³ Baraka calls for a "gentle singer of songs" to "scream down the bastions of Evil. . . . All must be harnessed. All love all energy all passion must be harnessed and directed so that we may all re-enter the City of God." He describes growing stronger evolving "into his soul's spirit, as a spirit being. We have a living expanding Holy essence. The essence of our creator PEACE (AND LIFE) BE WITH YOU!"[74]

Baraka later describes "From the Book of Life" as "full of Islamic and other metaphysical symbolism."[75] Though depicting the personal hell of being beaten in the riots, he turns this imagery of "beating" into imagery of "vibration The heart's pulse."[76] Instead of the ninety-nine names of God in Islam, he refers to the "thousand names of Divinity" using the term *Ism al-Azam*, the greatest name of God in Arabic, but he also talks about the "universal energy" of Allah Krishna Chakra Obatala Vowels of Life. The "Pop! pop! pop!" of the devil's screaming red eye (gunfire) is converted through these very vowels of life, through these words and sounds, into now the "vibration The heart's pulse" that is not just a beat, but the expression of life. The heart's pulse is also a way of speaking the truth, of saying "only what you know Clearly & freely & swiftly, as it comes Springing from the heart!"[77] The imagery in the essay plays on the range of signification of the word "beating"—of the heart, the police, the music—imagery Baraka took up in the poetry in *Spirit Reach* (1972). The volume opens with a poem playing on these multiple meanings of beating that translate—but also transcend—racial terror through a kinship rooted in the heart, forged by passing through the bloodstained gate evoked in the writings of Frederick Douglass, Baraka, Saidiya Hartman, and Fred Moten. It's where the scream turns into a song.

Opening *Spirit Reach* is the poem "Deranged gutbucket pigtongue clapper heart," with a beat that doubles as heartbeat and the gutbucket beat of the music, as much as a punishing injunction toward deliverance. Baraka calls for a kind of collective transcendence, partly through an appeal to group solidarity symbolized through a pluralistic god consciousness that encompasses the Islamic Allah and the Yoruba Obatala and Olorun—creator of life, origin of morality and virtue. Drawing on a pluralistic understanding of God consciousness, the poem connects the beating inflicted on the outside by brutal conditions to the beating of the heart on the inside. "Deranged gutbucket pigtongue clapper heart" rhythmically suggests a drum like chant threaded through a Black musical vernacular: "cause allah be beatin be beatin be beatin . . . olorun be beatin and allah he be beatin obatala be beatin / and burnin he be all they all be beatin all all all / be beatin / allah, olorun, ra, obatala, they all be beatin."[78] It is what Baraka calls, in the same poem, "boplution . . . we will become what we are inside moving to be," a synthesis between bebop and evolution.

In the poem, titled "The Evolver," Baraka returns to the be-bop evolution, the "boplution," of the prior poem, writing about "the power of John Coltrane" and the "power of God:"

an unmanifest being
a manifest consciousness
a be-at-ing
a human be(at)ing

The poem connects a mystical God consciousness with the music of John Coltrane, Sun Ra, and Pharoah Sanders, a beat that Baraka riffs on, transforming the be-at-ing into a human being and into the beating of the human heart. The poem includes a diagram that approximates the "Coltrane circle" included in Yusef Lateef's 1967 *Repository of Scales and Melodic Patterns*. In Baraka's version, he puts the letters L I V E around a circle, which also makes L O V E with the circle as an "o," writing the letters GOOD (or God) inside radiating outward. Coltrane, Baraka writes, is "spirit incarnate," drawing on the sense of "spirit" as breath blowing through the horn, "shaping the blow of all feelings and spirit." Coltrane is "translator . . . of the many gods' GOD."[79]

In *Spirit Reach* Baraka conceives of himself as a "black holy man," "a black magician," on the "cosmic stage, spinning in my appointed orbit, giving orders to my dreams, ordering my imagination that the world it gives birth to is the beautiful quranic vision."[80] His poem "Study Peace" uses a mystical, Platonic vision of "the first prophet" as a "five pointed being of love," illuminated by the star, of which dreams, shadows, and the world of imagination is but a refraction or a reflection, cast by fires on the wall. We are just beings of the star's mind, images cast against the eternally shifting heavens." Some of these poems are like prayers, addressed to OAllah, as in his poem "Preachment." They are intertwined with Islamic references to Allah and the Qur'an, but also to Nation of Islam teachings about devils. In a 1969 interview "Islam and Black Art" published in *Negro Digest*, Baraka refers to himself as a "Muslim soothsayer," writing that his mission is "to reveal, to manifest Divinity that man can understand, to make marks, to make symbols, to make signs, to make sounds, to make images that reveal Divinity, that reveal the presence of the One Force that animates everything. . . . The artist's words, the signs, the symbols, the artifacts are magic things, they're supposed to be able to suggest the presence of Allah (God). Just by hearing them (words), showing them, they're supposed to place you in close contact with the Divinity; they're supposed to make you come face to face with the Divinity."[81]

Baraka operates precisely through an Islamic unorthodoxy vis-à-vis a Sunni (orthodox) perspective. In the "Islam and Black Art" interview conducted by Marvin X and Faruk, Baraka analyzes the power dynamic between Sunni practice and Black American Islam, talking about Sunni Muslims "jealously guarding" Islamic knowledge to gain "power over other people who don't have these facts," as well as denying acknowledgment of the practical application of Black American Islam for the context of the Black freedom struggle.[82] He does this, consciously or unconsciously, through reference to other orthodox unorthodoxies within Islam (like mysticism, magic, dreams, and signs), but also through his practice of an Islamic poetry innovating on the tradition of Islamic poetry.[83] He references Ibn 'Arabi, the Sufi mystical poet and theologian known as *al-shaykh al-akbar* (the greatest shaykh) of Islam, speaking to poetic unorthodoxies in the heart of Islamic orthodoxy, but also invoking Ibn 'Arabi as the poet of divine love, of the oneness of existence (*wahdat al-wujud*), and of pluralistic visions of the different paths to God.[84] Alongside the Black nationalist leanings in "From the Book of Life" and Nation of Islam–inflected language, Baraka's imagery is of a universal, what Sun Ra might call "cosmic" race (or "rays"), informed by an Islamic mysticism articulated through poetry.

BLACK FEMINISM AND THE BLACK ARTS

In *The Black Woman* (1970), edited by Toni Cade Bambara, Ann Cook posed the following question in "Black Pride? Some Contradictions": "Why really do we embrace Islam?"[85] Josef Sorett's analysis of her essay argues that "the attraction to an idea of Islam . . . imbued claims of racial authenticity with spiritual authority. . . . These religious visions also underwrote a specific gender order."[86] Amiri Baraka admits as much in the *Autobiography* and elsewhere, ultimately abandoning what he characterized as the chauvinistic dimensions of his Islam, its association with an Arab ethnic identity, and the "specific gender order" in the Black Power movement. Yet BAM artists negotiated that gender order, reconfiguring it discursively, in the institutions that they built, and in everyday practice.

Baraka would respond to *The Black Woman* in his own essay, "Black Woman," published in *Black World* in 1970, writing about his relationship with Amina and Spirit House as a microcosm of the Black nation, describing family and home as a kind of homeplace. In the essay he also discusses Black Power ideas about male leadership, women's natural roles, the importance of family bonds, and reproduction as a bulwark against genocide. "You, who I call my house, because there is no house without a man and his wife, . . . you are essential, to the development of any life in the house, because you are that house's completion, . . . by being the nation, as the house, the smallest example of how the nation should be. So you are my 'house,' I live in you, and together we have a house, and that must be the microcosm, by example, of the entire Black nation. 'Our nation is our selves.'"[87] In her 1981 book *Ain't I a Woman*, bell hooks launched a scathing critique of Baraka's essay and the patriarchal dimensions of the Black Power Movement, calling out Amiri in particular for relegating "black women to a subordinate position both in the political sphere and in home life" and for interpreting the "black male-dominated household with its inherently anti-woman stance as if it were a positive reaction against white racist values."[88]

Later hooks would revisit this analysis in her famous essay "Homeplace (a site of resistance)," reformulating her sense of home as a place of political solidarity. "Whatever the shape or direction of black liberation struggle (civil rights reform or black power movement) its structure was defined less by whether or not black women and men were conforming to sexist behavior norms and more by our struggle to uplift ourselves as a people, our struggle to resist racist domination and oppression." She argued that Black women should have "collectively sustained attempts to develop the latent feminism expressed by their willingness to work equally alongside black men in the black liberation struggle." That feminism was practiced, embodied, and lived by Amina Baraka through sustained political commitments, community organizing, and cultural work; Amina helped create what hooks calls "a revolutionary vision of black liberation that has a feminist dimension."[89] Amina Baraka labored "to create radical sanctuary for Black life" through her political, intellectual, and creative work in the Black Power, Black Arts, and Black feminist movements.[90] This was not just the symbolic labor of literary representation, but on the ground organizing making Black products and groceries available through the co-op, providing community child care, creating Black Studies reading groups, and teaching in the African Free School.[91] Home work as an ethic of care often remains invisible, largely erased—something Amina struggles with in her own poetry—despite having created real institutions with tangible impact on community life. The Barakas' home was a conceptual locus of the BAM and of Black Power politics, but also a real-life locale for coping with everyday survival.

In the introduction to the 1997 edition of his *Autobiography*, Amiri paid tribute to Amina, writing that her role in the "political organization that came out of the Spirit House would never have happened in the ways that it did without her.... The initial internal organization of CAP owes a great deal to Amina's insight and hard work; ... the African Free School, which at one time was our crowning achievement, was brought about largely through her efforts, organizational and theoretical. The insidious characterization of her as some silent, male-dominated anonymity has continuously outraged her."[92]

The Barakas—and Amina specifically—played key roles in constructing spaces for Black study in Newark. Amina organized women's study groups like the United Sisters, which later merged with the Sisters of Black Culture to create the Committee for Unified Newark (CFUN).[93] The Women's Division of CFUN became its "largest and most diverse subunit, ... devising the innovations that increased the functionality and reach of the cultural nationalist group ... and helped transform CFUN into an exemplar of Black Power organizing," Farmer observes. One of CFUN's main aims was electing Black candidates in Black majority Newark. But the Women's Division also established the African Free School, in addition to managing the day care center, food coop, and publishing house Jihad Productions, translating "ideology into tangible community building initiatives."[94]

Amiri's 1968 film *The New-Ark* showed Amina, holding baby Obalaji, calling neighborhood children to the African Free School as they lined up clapping and singing. Inside she teaches the Black Power ABCs: "Love, Man, Natural, One, Pride, Queen, Righteousness, Strength, Truth, Unity, Victorious, Wisdom, X=Negro." A 1969 feature article in *Ebony* similarly included images of Amina teaching, of the United Sisters study group, and of the Baraka family with Wanda, Vera, Obalaji, and the newborn Ras. But the article is about Amiri, titled "Ameer (LeRoi Jones) Baraka."[95]

Amiri's "Black Woman" essay paid tribute to the African Free School, saying that "to teach the children, to educate the children, is to make our future predictable, and positive. Our children are our future."[96] Later that year, Amina emphasized this point in a panel discussion devoted to the "Black Woman" on the television program *Black Journal*. She joined Vertamae Smart-Grosvenor, author of *Vibration Cooking*; Jean Fairfax, NAACP Legal Defense lawyer; Martha Davis of the Harlem Drug Fighters Union; Marion-Etoile Watson, producer for Metromedia Television; and Joan Harris, host of NBC's "Positively Black." Identified only as Mrs. LeRoi Jones, Amina talks about children as the future of the Black community and the importance of raising consciousness through education, referencing her work in the African Free School and the Committee for Unified Newark. The program deploys poetics to talk about Black women and Black study, with Nikki Giovanni reciting "Adulthood," a poem that calls out the "bourgeois intellectual pretentions" of institutions of higher education versus learning "through involvement ... functioning commitments"—lectures on Black history, writing books, staging theater productions, and finding love.[97] The episode also features Sonia Sanchez—who taught with Amiri at San Francisco State in the first Black Studies program while Amina was pregnant with Obalaji. Sanchez is reciting "Queens of the Universe" at Reverend Albert

Cleage's Shrine of the Madonna, a poem published earlier that year in one of the inaugural issues of *The Black Scholar*. The poem calls for being "guerrilla / fighters for our children's / minds. we mussssSSSST begin basement schools in our homes," a specific reference to Amina teaching "blkness":

> sistuh/Queens (Ameena Baraka for one)
>   moven in sun/wrapped/beauty . . .
>   teachen blkness. wherever the desire for freedom bes"[98]

Sanchez plays the etymological connection of Amina's name to the word "belief." These "true/believers (mumininas)" bring people together "to meet/answer these needs/screeeeeeams of liven."[99]

In her book *Remaking Black Power*, Ashley Farmer chronicles Amina's contributions. The women leaders of CFUN, the Mumininas (meaning "Believers" in Swahili and Arabic) published a booklet *Mwanamke Mwananchi (The Nationalist Woman)* through Jihad Productions. It served as a kind of handbook for the practice of Black Power, affirming Kawaida doctrine about men's natural leadership roles. Although the Congress of African People (CAP) and Kawaida understood "the African woman as an activist who induced cultural revolution through child rearing and education," the women, Farmer observes, "developed their own definition of the African Woman that challenged patriarchal definitions." They envisioned women's revolutionary role as "an activist who advocated for black women's equal participation in black liberation as a critical step in the cultural emancipation of African peoples all over the world."[100] Black nationalist women "challenged male advocates' patriarchal interpretations of women's roles and asserted their primacy in cultural-nationalist organizing, . . . [to] push organizational leaders to adopt more equitable organizing frameworks" and to practice "a gender-inclusive form of cultural nationalism."[101] The Combahee River Collective Statement issued in 1977, however, directly critiqued *Mwanamke Mwananchi* as an example of Black Power conceptions of gendered inequality:

> We understand that it is and has been traditional that the man is the head of the house. He is the leader of the house/nation because his knowledge of the world is broader, his awareness is greater, his understanding is fuller and his application of this information is wiser. . . . After all, it is only reasonable that the man be the head of the house because he is able to defend and protect the development of his home. . . . Women cannot do the same things as men—they are made by nature to function differently. Equality of men and women is something that cannot happen even in the abstract world. Men are not equal to

other men, i.e. ability, experience or even understanding. The value of men and women can be seen as in the value of gold and silver—they are not equal but both have great value.[102]

Amina Baraka issued a roaring retort. *Song for the Masses* (1978) is a poetry collection that reads like a manifesto, published under her birth name Sylvia and her married name Jones. The collection calls for struggle against oppression in all its forms, specifically economic inequality, poverty, and class oppression. The first poem in the collection, "Dedication," begins by stating who the poems are *not* meant for, a long list that includes Black nationalists (and an implicit critique of her own husband). "These poems are not meant for . . . hip black intellectuals who hate black women and themselves, . . . these poems are not meant for bourgeois nationalists who think wearing a dashiki or a buba and selling African art will liberate the Afro-American Nation." Another poem, "Warning," says to "run for your life" from "witchdoctors" who prescribe duties like those described in *Mwanamke Mwananchi*, "witchdoctors" who subscribe to a "narrow nationalism."

> when today's witchdoctors come at the women
> arm the women
> when they scream and sing their chants
> not to fight against oppression
> to
> only inspire the men
> only educate the children
> only take care of the home
> do not take that prescription
> it has proven to be a death drug

In what might be a reference to the Combahee River Collective Statement, "Dedication" says that "these poems are for Harriet Tubman and Sojourner Truth, . . . these poems are in particular for the women and men and oppressed nationalities."[103]

"SORTIN-OUT"

Amina Baraka formed cadres of women leaders that effectively put into practice some of Black Power's most important objectives: on-the-ground political organizing, economic self-determination, youth education, and cultural revolution.

FIGURE 7.3 Portrait of the Barakas in *Ebony* magazine showing Amina holding newborn Ras and Amiri holding two-year-old Obalaji, with Amina's daughters Vera sitting and Wanda standing on the back porch of Spirit House.

National Museum of African American History

Despite her role in this gender activism, her own writings were not included in the important anthologies of Black women's writings published in the 1970s and 1980s, nor were her earlier contributions to women's self-determination in the movement for Black liberation thoroughly chronicled—with a few notable exceptions.[104] Despite her pioneering work in the BAM and the Black Power movement, she was absent from the flood of Black feminist anthologies in the 1970s and 1980s: Bambara's *The Black Woman* (1970); Rashida Ismaili and Louis Reyes Rivera's *Womanrise* (1978); Erlene Stetson's *Black Sister: Poetry by Black American Women, 1746–1980* (1981); Sandra M. Esteves, Cherríe Moraga, and Gloria E. Anzaldúa's *This Bridge Called My Back* (1981); Akasha Gloria Hull, Patricia Bell-Scott, and Barbara Smith's *All the Women Are White, All the Blacks are Men, But Some of Us Are Brave* (1982), as well as her *Home Girls: A Black Feminist Anthology* (1983).

Attention to Amiri's public life and literary presence nearly eclipsed Amina's substantial work within both the Black Power movement and the BAM, her own years of labor remarkably unacknowledged. Despite concerted efforts on behalf of Newark's creative life and political future, scholarship has paid scant heed to her years of work—how she built cultural organizations like the Jazz Arts Society, Spirit House, and Kimako Blues Café, and community organizations like the African Free School, United Sisters ("a nationalist women's study group"), the grocery cooperative Duka Ujamaa, and Shani Baraka Women's Resource Center, all while bearing and raising seven children. Recent scholarship like Farmer's chronicles Amina's formative role in the Congress of African People (CAP), with careful attention to how her work organizing the women's groups served as a model for the larger organization. Farmer details how women occupied a central place in the Black Power movement, through political activism and cultural production, reshaping gendered roles in the process. As Zenzele Isoke writes of Black women activists in Newark, Amina "created political spaces to confront contemporary social marginality, . . . physical, symbolic, and relational spaces that . . . politicize and transform communities." Isoke calls these activists "alchemists of resistance" who work across the lines of oppressed communities to combat structural discrimination.[105]

Despite the labor Amina devoted to institution building, much of that work remained "unaccounted for," she says in her own poem "Sortin-Out." Published below one of Amiri's poems in the *Black American Literature Forum*, "Sortin-Out" reflects on her struggle to write and the writing of her struggles, as she tries to jot down her thoughts and ideas before the children got home from school. The poem describes a "Kubla Khan" moment: "Tryin not to forget what she was saying / more important what was on her mind." But then her son comes in from a half day and everything begins to "fade away." The poem asks why her life, like the poem, remains unwritten. The poem also answers that question: "pregnant at sixteen, married at seventeen / working in factories . . . she never made it to her dreams / was it being born to a 15 year old child / or was it being raised on Howard Street / or was it being raped at 14 / or having to drop out of school pregnant . . . more than not it was the Poet, the Monkish One / the famous one, the one she married . . . / to end-up standing before this window / & with this clipboard and pen."[106] "Sortin-Out" may be the closest thing we have to an autobiography of Amina Baraka, defying generic convention—just as so much of her life defied generic convention. Yet it does not completely account for her life: as the flotsam and jetsam, bits and pieces of experience flow through her poem, dimensions of her life difficult to capture. Amina published "Sortin-Out" in autumn 1982 while Amiri was writing his *Autobiography*—what would become a nearly 500-page volume. He wrote the book while spending weekends serving time in a Harlem halfway house, sentenced for resisting arrest after a fight with Amina. Amiri wrote the *Autobiography* during those weekends while Amina was at home with their five children. "Sortin-Out" was also written during this time, exploring the gendered politics of cultural work and specifically, the gendered labor of constructing a homeplace for the BAM and the Black Power movement. As Amina stands at the window trying to write, the words escape her—with Amiri, even in detention, free to write.

"Sortin-Out" later reappeared in *Confirmation: An Anthology of African American Women* (1983), which she and Amiri coedited. Its publication situated Amina among the important Black women writers of her generation, with her contribution placed among theirs. *Confirmation* came out amid a critical surge of Black women's writings and publications in books, anthologies, and journals, partly catalyzed by Barbara Smith's Kitchen Table Press founded in 1980. *Confirmation* opened a space for Amina "to speak what was on her mind" following—in alphabetical order—prominent Black women writers like Johari M Amini, Maya Angelou, Toni Cade Bambara, and followed by Gwendolyn Brooks, Jayne Cortez, Alexis de Veaux, and Mari Evans. But here was Amiri's name ahead of hers on the cover, most likely a publisher's decision—even in an anthology of African American women's writings. His birth name LeRoi Jones is given in parentheses, recognizing his status as a widely published author and creating a representational imbalance on the cover—Amiri listed first even though in alphabetical order her name comes first. Amina's writing was mainly published alongside Amiri's—often with her as second, not as coauthor: in *Confirmation*, in their volume *The Music: Reflections on Jazz and Blues*, and the poetry collection *5 Boptrees*. They are literary comrades, though this comradery is not evenly reflected either in their joint publications or in Amiri's writings.

THE BARAKAS' LEGACY

Both Amina and Amiri ultimately abandoned their commitments to Islam, instead embracing communism in the mid-1970s, though they kept their Muslim names and their son Ras is Muslim. Cultural and political aspects of their commitments survived, like their dedication to Black sovereignty and political self-determination. In the interview "Islam and Black Art," Amiri responds to a question Marvin X asks about "Islam [as] a political ideology" for the Black community. Islam functions, Baraka responds, as a "unifying principle—the collectivizing principle—to withstand the deathblows that white America is seeking to put on him; ... the onslaught of white America, ... these are the things that will mean survival."[107] This chapter details their "labor to create radical sanctuary for Black life," or what Toni Cade Bambara calls the "daily ritual of group validation in a liberated zone."[108]

In bell hooks's famous essay "Homeplace" she calls for consciously remembering Black women's "radically subversive political" efforts to construct home as "a community of resistance," and for "honoring their struggle." By documenting Baraka's extensive contributions to the movement/s—and by foregrounding her "intellectual labor and political visionary work, this chapter aims to honor her struggle but also to "struggle against forgetting" (as hooks says).[109] (In "Sortin-Out," Amina is "tryin not to forget" by writing down her life.) Amina Baraka's political activism, her creative and intellectual work, and her construction of a literary homeplace at the heart of Newark became a critical epicenter of the Black Arts Movement. Oftentimes this work was not considered part of the BAM, though Black women were "significant artistic contributors to the Black Arts oeuvre," sharing mutual commitments to "radical politics, radical rhetoric, claiming of the public, and the establishment of alternative cultural institutions and venues." Yet they remained "underrepresented and misrepresented" through an intentional "erasure."[110]

Today the Barakas' homeplace is a living archive of Black art and Black power, but also a testament to Black feminist labor constructing alternative institutions and spaces for Black life. Every inch of their home is covered in the history that they both lived and forged; every surface contains Black art and artifacts; shelves, benches, and floors are lined with books; posters adorn walls and are rolled up in baskets. The piano in the living room was bought for Nina Simone to play when she stayed at their house. Outside the kitchen hangs a hand-typed, signed copy of Langston Hughes's "Backlash Blues" (1967), which Simone sang at Harlem's 1969 Summer of Soul. On the wall opposite the poem hangs a dual portrait that Diego Rivera painted of himself and Frida Kahlo. In the pantry are more posters: of Lenin ("Long Live the Dictatorship of the Proletariat!), Robert F. Williams ("Self-Respect, Self-Defense, and Self-Determination"), and Che Guevara ("Si Ud. es capaz de temblar de indignación cada vez que se comete una injusticia en el mundo, somos compañeros"). Over the refrigerator hangs Emory Douglas's portrait of Amiri. The Baraka home is a teaching and learning space documenting the movement/s, but it is also the living space of the "mother of the movement," as Shani Baraka's friend Crystal Neville called Amina.

Vertamae Smart-Grosvenor's *Vibration Cooking* opens with a quote from Amiri's "Answers in Progress," a hymn to the Barakas' partnership and their political vision of common humanity: "love all the things that make you strong, /

FIGURE 7.4 Emory Douglas's portrait of Amiri, hanging over the refrigerator in the Barakas' kitchen.

Photo by author

be lovers, / be anything / for all the people of / earth."¹¹¹ "Answers in Progress" is an Afrofuturist vision of Black space created through Black art—a space that was also a home—where the Barakas both created and lived the future that they envisioned.¹¹² The Barakas were dedicated to the cultural flourishing of Newark and Black self-determination in the face of a political system in the 1960s in which the Black majority was governed by a white minority. The election of Ras as mayor is one of the fruits of their political labors and their home life as an epicenter of Newark community life. His generation is also the fruit of their cultivation of Black study and the Black Arts. Ras, a former schoolteacher, performs as the teacher taking roll and talking to students on *The Miseducation of Lauryn Hill* (1998), an album that pays tribute to Carter Woodson's *The Mis-Education of the Negro* (1933). He also raps on Sister Souljah's "Umbilical Cord to the Future" ("You must teach them! You must teach them! If you do not teach the children, they will not know.") This cultural production—and democratic political representation of the Black majority in Newark—is part of the legacy of the Baraka household, the BAM, and the longue durée of Black Studies that they helped further through their labor. Amina Baraka's work and activism is part of "black feminism's long labor of love-politics," a "black feminist political tradition" transforming love "into a theory of justice."[113] As the poem "Black Art" says, they are lovers, warriors, and poems.

CHAPTER 8

"BLK/VISIONS FOR BLK/LIVES"

Sonia Sanchez's Rebirth in Islam

for we have
        hearrrd   Malcolmmmmmm's
blood/
    letten/
        words   and
been born a gine.

—Sonia Sanchez, "words for our children," in *We A BaddDDD People*

The Nation gave me a place to develop the confidence that I needed.
It was a womb that got me ready to come out into the world.

—Linda, quoted in Dawn-Marie Gibson and Jamillah Karim's *Women of the Nation: Between Black Protest and Sunni Islam*

In "Belly of the World: A Note on Black Women's Labors," Saidiya Hartman writes about how "gestational language has been key to describing the world-making and world-breaking capacities of racial slavery. What it created and what it destroyed has been explicated by way of gendered figures of conception, birth, parturition, and severed or negated maternity. To be a slave is to be 'excluded from the prerogatives of birth.'"[1] This chapter chronicles how Sonia Sanchez uses gestational language to describe her conversion to Islam in the early 1970s as a delivery from "slave/mentalities," and as a "womb" from which she was reborn. In her poetry of the time, she describes Elijah Muhammad as midwife to the process: "within Elijah's hands / giving birth to ourselves."[2] Her poetry and writings in the period are replete with imagery of labor pains and birthing, of planting seeds in fertile soil, metaphorically deployed as a field for cultivating Black life outside of and in opposition to a history of alienation in white America.[3] In Hortense Spillers's essay "Mama's Baby, Papa's Maybe: An American Grammar," she writes about how Black liberation urgently seeks rupture with an American grammar of motherhood to make a new syntax, partly through authoring narratives that introduce new semantic fields. Sanchez deploys the imagery of parturition, birthing, and gestation not only to speak of giving life to new kinds of imaginaries to sustain Black life but also to bring into being new epistemologies for the project of African-American liberation. Sanchez introduces "a new semantic field/fold more appropriate to his/her own historic movement," one that she performs as a poet forging a new kind of poetry, a single mother of three, and a professor pioneering Black Studies in the university.[4]

The Nation of Islam—and Islamic—tropes and motifs that Sanchez deploys in her early poetry use gendered language to describe women's life-giving potential, semantics that expand to denote a power to give life to words. She cultivates an aesthetics that redefines the "controlling images" of Black reproductive labor by connecting its life-giving potential to Black women's poetic, intellectual, and political activism.[5] Citing Ngugi wa Thiong'o and Frantz Fanon,[6] she engages in "a struggle over the relations of representation,"[7] creating what bell hooks calls "spaces of agency ... for black people, wherein we can both interrogate the gaze of the Other but also look back, and at one another, naming what we see."[8] In articulating her reasons for joining the Nation of Islam, Sanchez talks about the "respect" she received as a Black woman, in bell hooks's sense of "looking back"—that is, looking at (*spect*) again (*re*)—by redirecting the gaze, and formulating a grammar, vocabulary, and system of signs for "naming what we see." Sanchez comments specifically on how people would "see" and "look at" sisters who joined the NOI, and her poetry similarly describes a politics of seeing and looking, of moving on past the mirror.[9]

Sanchez also uses Islamic motifs to give expression to the creative power of language to sustain community—partly through pedagogies focusing on Black youth and, by extension, the future of the Black community. She consistently directed her writing and poetry to children and children's education, developing poetic pedagogies that were also celebrations of communal visions of Black life. Reclaiming—and reshaping—the *imago* of Black womanhood was critical not only to reshaping popular discourses around Blackness, but also to the lived, embodied experiences of being and ways of seeing that Sanchez vividly describes.[10] We've co-opted this language, she says in an interview with Samy Alim in *B Ma: The Sonia Sanchez Literary Review*, "and we've made it live. We've given this language life, a life that is unbelievable, you know.... And what it does is that it makes it breathe. It gives it life. It gives it color.... We have given words life."[11]

In this chapter I look closely at the explosion of Sanchez's writings in the late 1960s and early 1970s—leading up to her conversion to Islam, during the time that she identified as Muslim and was a practicing member of the Nation of Islam until late 1975. Sanchez joined the NOI during a time of intense contestation over the issue of women's reproductive self-determination, during legal struggles over abortion and increased access to birth control, in the midst of national media attention to the forced sterilization of Black women, and among intensified national focus on the Black family and Black mothers. Much scholarship characterizes Sanchez's feminist advocacy of reproductive self-determination as being at odds with her membership in the NOI, with its strict regulation of women's bodies and fertility. Elijah Muhammad and the Nation of Islam fiercely criticized birth control and abortion as a eugenics campaign to destroy the Black race. Although Sanchez's writing embraces gestational language and images of rebirth, she also talks about her advocacy of reproductive self-determination as part of her contribution to the Nation of Islam—an advocacy she articulates in both interviews and her poetry. Sanchez worked in tandem with Sister Clotelle Scott (Ameenah Rasul), who developed contraceptive methods within the NOI in collaboration with Malcolm X.[12] She sings hymns to Sister Clotelle in her poetry, describing her as "directing the hunger of black women until they become magical" in her poem "Ima Talken Bout the Nation of Islam."[13] In "It's a New Day," the title poem of her poetry collection for children, Sanchez situates Sister Clotelle's contribution alongside Sojourner Truth, civil rights activist Fannie Lou Hamer, and the poetry of Gwendolyn Brooks. She pays tribute to Minister Louis Farrakhan, Elijah Muhammad, imprisoned SNCC chairman H. Rap Brown (Jamil Abdullah al-Amin), and the anticolonial president of Tanzania Julius Nyerere. "It's a New Day" also asserts her intention to be Muslim:

>   we gon be some
>   beautiful/black/women
>   gon move like the queens we be
>   gon be full/
>   time MUSLIM women
>   gon be strong as sojourner

> gon be gentle as
> > sister clotelle's smile
> gon be the poetry of gwendolyn's words
> gon be the green south of fannie lou hamer[14]

In the late 1960s and early 1970s Sanchez developed poetic imagery of cultivating and nurturing new life. During that time she was a single mother of three, having recently given birth to twin boys, divorced her husband, the Black Arts Movement poet Ethridge Knight, and moved from teaching Black Studies at San Francisco State College to the University of Pittsburgh (1969–70), Rutgers (1970–71), Manhattan Community College (1971–73), Amherst (1972–75), the University of Pennsylvania (1976–77), and then, Temple University.[15] She describes writing until 3 a.m., getting up at 6 to make her children breakfast, taking them to the babysitter, and then spending nearly twelve hours in the office before heading home. When she began teaching a course on "The Black Woman" at the University of Pittsburgh in 1969, her twin boys were only a year old.[16] Her play *Sister Son/ji*, published earlier in 1969, just after the twins were born, speaks of an intense anxiety about the forces threatening her pregnant body and the promise of life inside. The play talks about white violence menacing Black life in the womb, in an image strikingly evocative of the "Nightmare," the opening chapter of Malcolm X's *Autobiography*. The violence is actual and discursive, physically threatening the woman with child(ren) but also silencing her voice. It is both political and embodied, what Jennifer Nash calls "Black maternal politics as practices of survival, forms of advocacy, and strategies developed for safeguarding Black maternal and child life, making visible how obstetric violence is a form of state violence, . . . political projects that are necessarily Black feminist."[17] The play pleas for putting into practice a Black feminist articulation of Black Power politics: "Let us start building true blk/lives—let our family be a family built on mutual love and respect," as Sister Son/ji faces the terrors of the night—the "crackers" and "honkies" with their "pocketful of guns." With child, she feels the baby moving "against this silence. he kicks against my silence" in the face of the threat of "wite/amurica" that kills those "who try to fulfill their destiny."[18] Sister Son/ji calls out: "u, death. i'm calling yr / name . . . stay away from my family . . . for our tomorrows will be full of life/living/births."[19]

Sanchez describes the NOI as a "beacon" and a "haven" for her and her children, as a place of "protection . . . for, I suppose, surcease from a lot of turmoil in my life and in the movement."[20] She writes about her intense concern for raising her children in a safe and nurturing environment, giving them a place where they could "grow," get an education, and build a "foundation for this so-called blackness that we have now, because you will not survive unless you have a foundation."[21] She joined the NOI, she says, "because the public school situation was really pathetic. The Nation was one of the places to receive a good education at the time; it was a place to go for some kind of protection. It was also doing some very interesting things in terms of attempting to build businesses and schools."[22] In her writings and interviews in the Nation of Islam newspaper *Muhammad Speaks*, as well as in her poetry, Sanchez repeatedly talks about the NOI as an organization providing a framework for actualizing Black Power objectives around children's education and Black study. She weaves the NOI's insistence on a Black Studies education into her poetry, like in her 1970 poem "let us begin the real work (for Elijah Muhammad who has begun)." The poem calls for taking Black children out of white schools and teaching them "the work of / centuries. untold" and "what is to be / learnnnnned bout themselves."

> let us
> honestlee begin
> nation/hood
> builden.
> for our children.
> with our
> minds/hands/souls.
> with our blk/visions
> for blk/lives.[23]

An assemblage of discursive structures within the Nation of Islam informed Sonia Sanchez's poetry and helped shape her pioneering work in establishing Black Studies in the university and decolonizing Black children's schooling and education. Her poetics and activism also *influenced* discourses within the NOI and its mission to cultivate the education of Black children—during a time of intensified awareness about educational policies and their effect on children of color. In this chapter I examine how Sanchez's commitment to Black education underpins her writings, poetry, and children's books and is interwoven with her commitment to promoting and supporting Black women's pursuit of knowledge, study, and training. She saw it as a way of putting into action these commitments to Black Studies at a grassroots level, moving beyond what she calls rhetoric and writing and into a way of being, moving, and acting.[24]

Critical discussions of Sanchez's identification with Islam, as well as with Black nationalism, describe how it "conflicted with her nascent ideas of feminist responsibility," creating a "philosophical schism" stemming from "contradictory

FIGURE 8.1 "Poet, activist, and scholar Sonia Sanchez was the first African-American woman to join the faculty at Amherst College. She arrived as a visiting professor in 1972 and left for a position at Temple University in 1975," writes Amherst archivist Mike Kelly in "Black Lives of Amherst College." Sanchez was the chairperson of the Black Studies Department.

Amherst Archives

agendas of feminism, nationalism, and religion."[25] In Farah Jasmine Griffin's article on Malcolm X's gender politics, she discusses what she calls the "price" of the patriarchal promise for protection, which is possession, submission, and inequality.[26] This "protection" stood in opposition to the abuse African American women suffered throughout history, like the idea of homeplace that bell hooks talks about as a site of resistance. "It does not matter," hooks writes, "that sexism assigned them this role. It is more important that they took this conventional role and expanded it to include caring for one another, for children, for black men, in ways that elevated our spirits, that kept us from despair, that taught some of us to be revolutionaries able to struggle for freedom."[27] Griffin observes that women accepted traditional notions of patriarchy because the mother and wife role was "politically necessary for black people's survival."[28] Griffin eloquently testifies to another dimension of the appeal of the Nation of

Islam, an aesthetics of Blackness and a respect for Black womanhood that countered degrading images bombarding Black women on a daily basis.[29] Sanchez cites this "common ground of respect" as one of her main reasons for joining the Nation. This is the reason, she says, that people moved en masse into the NOI.

In her book *Being Muslim: A Cultural History of Women of Color in American Islam*, Sylvia Chan-Malik writes about Sanchez's "affective insurgency" against racist and sexist categories imposed on women of color in the United States. Islam becomes a "spiritual landscape and vehicle for Black women's liberation," giving expression to "the embodied and metaphysical nature of Black Muslim womanhood."[30] Chan-Malik's analysis and understanding of insurgency builds theoretically on earlier writing on insurgent Black life by scholars like bell hooks, Cornel West, Hortense Spillers, and Dylan Rodríguez. Spillers calls not for "joining the ranks of gendered femaleness," but for "gaining the *insurgent* ground as female social subject."[31] Though Sanchez situates her writing within gendered femaleness discussed by Spillers, the historically powerful "cultural synthesis long evaporated—the law of the Mother," she also transforms the field of signification and representation of "'motherhood' as a female blood-rite/right."[32] Sanchez theoretically understands her care as resistance and protest, as what Chan-Malik calls an affective insurgency against "the death function in the economy of biopower" (in Alexander Weheliye's words).[33] Her struggle is against the specter of death haunting Black children, "unborn malcolms" and "blk/martyrs," but also *for* "tomorrows . . . full of life/living/births."[34] She uses biological images of sex and gender, illuminating them as racializing assemblages rooted in a violent history, calling for a discursive break through the construction of new modes of being. She effects this transformation of the field of signification through her poiesis, and also through her commitments to her own children, to the education of Black children in America more broadly, and to the crystallization of Black Studies in higher education.

Sanchez's writings during this time provide a map for understanding how her identification with Islam infused her poetics and an aesthetics of blackness, as a form of knowledge of the "rich and varied cultural heritage" of the global African diaspora.[35] In an interview in *Muhammad Speaks* with Sister Minister Sharolyn at Muhammad's Temple No. 2, Sanchez identifies the Nation of Islam as the "source" of Black Arts and Black Power consciousness about class and racial oppression in the United States. In this conversation Sanchez talks about meeting people writing about Blackness in the late 1960s but searching for something more, for an origin, a source, but also a path forward to advance the cause of truth beyond rhetoric. Before her conversion, Sanchez saturated her writing with Nation of Islam language, references, and teachings, paying tribute to women in the NOI, to Elijah Muhammad and Malcolm X, and to the NOI newspaper *Muhammad Speaks*. I explore the traces of her nascent identification with Islam in her early collections of poetry: *Home Coming* (1969) and *We a BaddDDD People* (1970), dedicated to the "sistuhs in THE NATION OF ISLAM"; the broadsheet *Ima Talken Bout the Nation of Islam* (1971); the album *A Sun Lady for All Seasons* (released by Smithsonian Folkways in 1971), and also in 1971 a collection of children's poetry *It's A New Day* ("As-Salaam-alaikum (a greeting of peace) / for how else should we begin the day / save with peace for our people in a new land. / we be a new people in a new land"). These works explore NOI ideas about blackness, bodily and spiritual disciplines, the pursuit of knowledge of self and history, and the toxicity of whiteness. After her conversion, she authored an illustrated children's book *The Adventures of Fathead, Smallhead, and Squarehead* (1973) about three friends on pilgrimage to Mecca through the Sudan, a work that contributed to the formation of a critical body of literature directed at Black children in the 1970s. I contextualize these writings through extensive interviews conducted with Sanchez: in *Muhammad Speaks*; by scholars and academics (Joyce Ann Joyce and Susan Kelly); for the television documentary *Eyes on the Prize* along with the WGBH TV's program *Say Brother*; and in my own conversations with her during visits to her home in Philadelphia. Sanchez left the NOI in late 1975, constricted by the limitations its members put on her poetry, her movement, and her vision as they chaffed against her bringing poets like Gwendolyn Brooks and scholars like Shirley Graham Du Bois to speak.[36] Though she left the NOI and Islam, her legacy lives on in feminist hermeneutics of scholars like amina wadud, who took a writing class with Sanchez in the 1970s, in hip hop pedagogies, Black Studies, and the reformulation of an Islamic poetics by new generations of Muslim poets.[37]

A Blues Book for Blue Black Magical Women (1974) represents the culmination of these Islamic writings and perhaps the fullest expression of Sanchez's Islamic commitments, as she bears witness in her creative production, expressing a kind of biopolitics, or a life drive of (Black) art. *A Blues Book* expresses the full flower of Sanchez's Islamic period, a book length poem that she structures as a "REBIRTH" into a "FUTURE" self. Sanchez writes about tasting the

> seasons of my birth...
> tremble like a new/born/child troubled
> with new breaths
>   and my singing
> becomes the only sound of a

OBAC celebrants include (l-r) Sister Fatima Ali, education director, Nation of Islam; Laila Mannan; writer Shirley Graham Du Bois; OBAC member Angela Jackson, and Val Gray Ward, KUUMBA Workshop founder.

FIGURE 8.2 Organization of Black American Culture Writers Workshop meeting on November 27, 1975, with Sister Fatima Ali, the Education Director of the Nation of Islam; Sonia Sanchez (then Laila Mannan), Co-director of the Office of Human Development in the Nation of Islam; Shirley Graham Du Bois, author, playwright, composer, activist, and widow of W. E. B. Du Bois; poet Angela Jackson; and Val Gray Ward, Kuumba Workshop founder.

National Museum of African American History

> blue/black/magical/woman. walking.
> womb ripe. walking. loud with mornings. walking.
> making pilgrimage to herself. walking.[38]

The poem depicts rebirth both within the Black Arts trope of black magic, combined with the "blues matrix" described in Houston Baker's work on the Black Aesthetic. There is an ecstatic celebration of a creative force of regeneration, rooted in traditions scattered through the book-length poem—like her sense of spiritual pilgrimage into the self. Elijah Muhammad again appears as a midwife to this process, "opening the / door of the world" to "poets and soothsayers / rappers and raconteurs / politicians and activists, / writers and teachers." Sanchez deploys graphically explicit imagery of wombs and seeds, labor pains and birthing, doing so as a means of reclaiming "motherhood as the female bloodrite/right" and cultivating "representational potentialities" of this historically ordained discourse as "the founding term of a human and social enactment."[39] Hartman calls this the "black heart of our social poesis, of making and relation."[40]

MALCOLM'S WORDS AND BEING BORN AGAIN

In an essay on Malcolm X and "some possible feminist implications of his legacy," Angela Davis reflects on a "tradition [that] would bring together the historical movements for Black liberation and for women's liberation." Sanchez is what Davis describes as one of the "political descendants" of Malcolm X.[41] These are not biological descendants, but suggest a discursive community built through modes of collective representation that are both political and aesthetic. Sanchez's poem "malcolm" describes the effects of the systemic violence against Black lives as a miscarriage of justice in literal terms. In this poem, Sanchez is the child in the womb, the would-be descendant of Malcolm X's vision and dream.

> what might have been
> is not for him/or me
> but what could have been
> floods the womb until i drown.

The poem describes Malcolm X as a "dreamer," something usually associated with the legacy of Martin Luther King Jr. and his words.

> this dreamer,
> thick lipped with words
> will never speak again . . .

Sanchez describes the labor of continuing the legacy of his voice, articulated in specifically gendered terms as birth pains giving new life to the movement. She uses imagery of lips, words, the womb, miscarriage, labor, and hopeful rebirth. The final verses are put in Malcolm's "mouth" through quotation marks:

> "nothing
> is sacred now . . .
> until some voices
> squat with spasms."[42]

Sanchez calls on the capacity of words to breathe life into the movement they animate, with direct reference to Malcolm X's words and how his life was extinguished, giving birth to a movement through his thick lips. Another poem in *Home Coming*, titled "for unborn malcolms," revisits the motif of gestation that permeates this poetry. Speaking of the specter of death haunting future Black boys, Sanchez elegizes "blk/martyrs" Malcolm, Bobby Hutton, Denmark Vesey, reciting a long genealogy of lives lost in protest. Sanchez's "Malcolm" poem was first published in Dudley Randall and Margaret Burroughs's *For Malcolm* (1967), a book of elegies divided into sections on "Life" and "Death" and culminating with the eulogy Ossie David delivered at Malcolm X's funeral. The collections was inspired by Margaret Walker's reading of her own elegy for Malcolm at the Fisk University Writers' Conference in 1966.[43] Sanchez would republish "malcolm" in her first collection of poetry *Home Coming*.

These poems speak of the power of Malcolm X's words and speeches, but also of the aesthetics of Blackness that he cultivated. Sanchez first met Malcolm X at a CORE rally in Harlem, in front of Lewis H. Michaux's African National Memorial Bookstore, remembering the warmth of his smile versus what she had seen on television ("he was scary").[44] In "poem (for dcs 8th graders—1966–67)" also published in *Home Coming*, Sanchez gives a sense of how Malcolm X transformed her (self) perception: "look at me . . . i am black / beautiful. i have a / man who looks at / my face and smiles . . .

>   on my face
>   is malcolm
>   spitting his metal seeds[45]

The "spitting metal seeds" image develops the sense of words as weapons, weapon imagery borne out on *Home Coming*'s cover, with Black Panther artist Emory Douglas's design of an African girl carrying a spear. But Sanchez also imparts a vivid sense of the fertile power of the words "to plant seeds"—what would become a reigning motif in her poetry. "We were seditious," Sanchez says in her *B. Ma* interview with Samy Alim, "because of how we would plant seeds."[46] The metal seeds invoke the bullets in Malcolm X's famous 1964 "The Ballot or the Bullet" speech, where he sought to join forces with the civil rights movement on the issue of the Black vote in the South but threatened violence if fair elections were not held. Sanchez transforms these "metal seeds" into other kinds of images of words planting seeds in fertile soil, like her 1971 poem "a black/woman/speaks:"

>   i am deeeeeEEEP
>   blue / black / soil . . .
>   as i bring forth green / songs . . .
>   i am deep / red / soil
>   fo our emerging / black / nation."[47]

During the *Eyes on the Prize* television documentary, the interviewer asks Sanchez about Malcolm X's sexism, and she responds by saying that women were "queens of the universe"—but not in the sense of sitting on a throne and doing nothing. "It was a queen that worked, a queen that taught, a queen that led. A queen that was very much involved with the movement, you see." We weren't expected to keep quiet, she says, but to go out and spread the message and to use our minds.[48] Sanchez echoes Malcolm X's "who taught you to hate the color of your skin" speech, repeating his questions, but she also talks about different tones, the brownness, yellowness, blackness, blue-blackness, and "brownberryness of it all."[49] That is precisely what the Black Arts, Black Culture, Black Consciousness Movement set out to do and "that's what we tried to change," she says, so that never again would anyone walk the planet Earth and hate "what they are, what they be."[50]

In the same speech Malcolm X called the Black woman the most disrespected woman in America, the most unprotected person in America, the most neglected person in America. "As Muslims," he says, "the honorable Elijah Muhammad teaches us to respect our women."[51] Sanchez cites this respect as one of her main reasons for joining the NOI. Yes, there were problems, Sanchez says, and there were restrictions in the Nation of Islam and there were restrictions that were problems. But sisters were respected. And they felt safe. "There was a common ground of respect and, and, and love for each other. . . . You can't fight that. And, that was a very real kind of movement there." In *Ain't I a Woman*, hooks trenchantly critiques this notion of respect for Black women as shoring up the movement's "patriarchal base" where women were given protection in exchange for submission, seeing the "respect" as a reversal of the elevation of white women and the debasement of Black women. When hooks critiques the NOI, however, she reproduces the language from Malcolm X's speech almost verbatim, writing that "Black women are one of the most devalued female groups in American society."[52] The speech continues to have enduring cultural currency, as in Beyoncé's "Don't Hurt Yourself" on *Lemonade* and Megan Thee Stallion's 2000 performance on *Saturday Night Live*. Both performances sampled this Malcolm X speech: "The most disrespected woman in America is the black woman," he says. "The most unprotected woman in America is the black woman. The most neglected woman in America is the black woman."[53] Malcolm X's words and voice helped give birth to a new generation of Black aesthetics in the fight over representation in the public sphere.

Samy Alim and James Spady pay tribute to Sanchez as a poetic descendant of Malcolm X in Sonia Sanchez's literary journal *B. Ma* in a special issue titled "360 Degreez of Sonia Sanchez, Hip Hop, Narrativity, Iqhawe, and Public Spaces of Being"; the issue is dedicated to the memory of Dudley Randall, the publisher of

Broadside Press, one of the first independent Black presses that also published many of Sanchez's works.[54] Drawing on Geneva Smitherman's early, groundbreaking work on African American vernaculars in the Black Arts Movement, Alim traces a linguistic genealogy of the influence of BAM poetic language and Islamic consciousness on the hip hop nation.[55] One of those descendants is Kendrick Lamar, whose "The Blacker the Berry" recalls Sanchez's "blk/berry/face" as well as Harlem Renaissance author Wallace Thurman's *The Blacker the Berry: A Novel of Negro Life* (1923). Lamar's metaphors reference an age of digital media and a new era battling for control of representation, both political and aesthetic. Like "Queens of the Universe," the track plays on the "controlling images," but here of Black manhood, with the sexualized imagery of shooting recalling Black Arts imagery of words as weapons. The song is also a commentary on aiming high, as much as on "making a killing" off Blackness. Lamar's gendered imagery contrasts with—and complements—Sanchez's of gestation and rebirth. "The Blacker the Berry" directly references Malcolm X's "who taught you to hate the color of your skin" speech. Lamar asks: "You hate me don't you? You hate my people, your plan is to terminate my culture, ... you vandalize my perception." Like Sanchez, he sings about "blk/martyrs" and "unborn malcolms," but for Kendrick Lamar, the martyr is Trayvon Martin.

A QUEEN THAT WORKED, THAT TAUGHT, THAT LED

In her 1970 poem "Queens of the Universe," Sonia Sanchez writes about negative stereotypes—"controlling images" about Black women—in a list of names: "foxes, matriarchs, whores, bougie / bitches, sweet mommas, blk / bitches, sapphires, sistuhs and recentlee queens." We must discard colonizing names, she writes, "for our own survival" to build "our emerging blk/nation." She uses another name, the Swahili word *muminina*, meaning "believer," a loan word from the Arab and Islamic word *mu'minin*: "true / believers (mumininas) ... moven in human / nationalistic / revolutionary ways toward each other."[56] The term had an institutional basis, referring to a cadre of women leaders and activists in the Black Power movement, the Mumininas of Maulana Karenga's US Organization in California and Amiri and Amina Barakas' Committee for a Unified Newark in New Jersey, women who were in charge of the social and educational development of the community.[57] Sanchez uses the term to articulate her awakening Islamic consciousness during this period, in poetry that talks about moving toward nation building and teaching Blackness.[58]

In Farah Jasmine Griffin's essay about Malcolm X, "Ironies of the Saint," she argues that the queen image is fundamentally "antidemocratic" and representative of "a very problematic gender politics."[59] In interviews, Sanchez consistently declines to pit the Nation of Islam against her feminism, in contrast to other Black feminist critiques of the NOI like those of Griffin, as well as bell hooks, Patricia Hill Collins, Barbara Ransby, and Tracye Matthews, among others.[60] The Combahee River Collective Statement, for example, specifically critiqued the *mumininas* for their embrace of unequal power relations between men and women.[61] But Ashley Farmer, in her book *Remaking Black Power*, reassesses the central, mobilizing role of *muminina* women in the Black Power movement, arguing that they "developed the organizational infrastructure advocates needed to lead the community in their goal of cultural education."[62] Study, learning, and teaching, Farmer observes, were key components of this cultural nationalist activism, leading to the establishment of these schools "focusing on teaching children about their culture, heritage, and struggle.... Through the school curriculum, these women created empowering songs and activities for children that taught them black history, an appreciation of their culture, and tools to combat white cultural hegemony."[63] The *muminina* designation was used in the Committee for a Unified Newark (CFUN), which developed the African Free School, run by Amina Baraka, with the goal of translating "ideology into tangible community building initiatives," similar to the US organization's School of Afroamerican Culture, an independent community education center in Los Angeles.[64] The NOI already had a network of schools under the guidance and tutelage of Elijah Muhammad's wife Sister Clara Muhammad. Alongside these pedagogies, the US Organization and CFUN developed a set of specific disciplines for Black nationalist women, outlined in a pamphlet published by the Mumininas of CFUN through Jihad Productions.[65] The booklet has several different sections, outlining the role of the Black family, institutions for children's education, social development, and nutrition.

"Queens of the Universe" was originally published in a special double issue of *The Black Scholar* focused on Black women, motherhood, and family—a retort to Patrick Moynihan's 1965 report *The Negro Family*.[66] The Moynihan report problematized Black women's strengths and successes in education, employment, and heading households as a "tangle of pathology," along with a "delinquent" Black youth. Instead of pointing to underserved schools and lack of job opportunities, the Moynihan report blamed Black children for the "problem" of the Black family. Laughably calling white families "equalitarian," the report asserts that the matriarchal structure of the Black family "seriously retards the progress of the group as a whole," calling it "the principal source of the most aberrant, inadequate, or anti-social behavior that... now serves to perpetuate the cycle of poverty and deprivation."[67]

The *Black Scholar* special issue responded to these charges, leading with an article by Robert Staples, "The Myth of the Black Matriarchy." Another article by Alice Walker focused on how she developed a Black History curriculum for the Child Development Group of Mississippi (an article later incorporated into *In Search of Our Mother's Gardens*). The issue included an article on Harriet Tubman, lyrics to a Bessie Smith song, a "Black is Beautiful" print, and an article titled "Racism and Anti-feminism" by Shirley Chisholm; it closed with Sojourner Truth's "Ain't I a Woman" speech. In stark contrast to the reductive tone of the Moynihan report, the political and activist material in this *Black Scholar* issue was musical, poetic, and visual, creating a site of multimedia creative foment and protest, with "Queens of the Universe" as one of its interventions. The special issue was dedicated to W. E. B. DuBois whose own edited conference proceedings, *The Negro American Family* (1908), explored the effects of economic and social pressures on home life—a volume that was republished in the aftermath of the Moynihan report by several different presses.[68] Sanchez had included Moynihan's report on the syllabus of "The Black Woman," a course she taught in fall 1969 at the University of Pittsburgh.[69] The double issue's attention to women, children, motherhood, and the family in African American life anticipated the surge in Black feminist writings in the 1970s and 1980s that sought to redefining the "controlling images" of white definitions. Sanchez's poetics—alongside Chisholm's campaign for president, Walker's curriculum, Staples's research, and the legacies of Truth, Tubman, and Smith—did this work.

In "Queens of the Universe" the matriarchs of the Moynihan report are transformed into teachers and leaders but also into wordsmiths and culture makers, as Sanchez embraces what Saidiya Hartman calls the "brilliant and formidable ethic of care" paradoxically "produced through violent structures of slavery, anti-black racism, virulent sexism, and disposability."[70] The poem returns to the birth motif from the "Malcolm" poem, but now ecstatically framed as deliverance, rather than miscarriage. Her "brown, bamboo / colored, blk/berry/face, will spread itself over / this western hemisphere":

>   and the world
>   shaken by
>   my blkness
>   will channnnNNGGGEE
>   colors. & be
>   reborn.
>   blk. again.[71]

Sanchez is working toward a revolutionary understanding of what Alexander Weheliye calls "the centrality of blackness to the creation of the occident... necessary for the particular decolonizing critique developed within black studies." The centrality of Blackness—and Islam—to "the history of Western civilization" is essential to decolonizing the occident and its epistemologies, but also to disassembling the coloniality of being in Western modernity.[72] Not just the language of the NOI, but also its institutional infrastructure—and especially its commitment to Black study—helped provide a framework for this decolonization. But Sanchez also sees its organizational infrastructure as a space of refuge from white violence (epistemological and actual) for herself and her children.

Sanchez published "Queens of the Universe" before joining the NOI, but it anticipates the Islamic commitments articulated in her poetry after her conversion. She included the last stanza in her dedication to the "sistuhs in THE NATION OF ISLAM" in her collection *We A BaddDDD People* (1970). "Queens of the Universe" was reproduced, in its entirety, as the introduction to *A Blues Book for Blue Black Magical Women* (1974)—her book-length poem that represents the full flower of her Islamic commitments. The book unfolds as a spiritual journey depicting Sanchez's conversion as a rebirth and Elijah Muhammad as midwife: "WE ARE MUSLIM WOMEN / triumphant before Allah / flooding the earth like emeralds . . . within Elijah's hands / giving birth to ourselves."[73] *A Blues Book* envisions rebirth out of the humus and decay of history's violence and death—and a legacy of white violence against Black lives—through gendered imagery of the earth as a mother giving birth:

> sing me my history O earth mother
> about tongues multiplying memories . . .
> pull me from the throat of mankind
> where worms eat . . .
> tellLLLLLL me. earth mother
> for i want to rediscover me. the secret of me
> the river of me . . .
>
> rise up earth mother
> out of rope-strung-trees . . .
> let your mouth spill me forth . . .
> light up my mind.[74]

Sanchez uses the "gestational language" that Saidiya Hartman describes to draw attention to the "world-making" centrality of Blackness—but also of women to the "ontological ground for the Western order of things, ... the Western world order" and especially for defining "the category of Man" of the human.[75]

"GUERILLA/FIGHTERS FOR OUR CHILDREN'S MINDS"

In an interview with Joyce Ann Joyce in *Black Studies Is Human Studies*, Sanchez talks about her role pioneering Black Studies, helping found the first Black Studies program at San Francisco State College where she taught courses between 1966 and 1968. The aim, she says,

> was to interrupt and invade the study in the universities of American of White Studies, ... to bring into those spaces the study of African-Americans, of Black folk, and the impact that they had in the country and the world. So we, as writers, professors, educators began to insert African-Americans, people of color, on the world stage and we said, look we have contributed in such a fashion that you cannot teach history in a vacuum of European and White aesthetics. You've got to deal with the history and herstory of Africans in the diaspora.[76]

After Malcolm X's death in 1965, Sanchez retreated to Mexico but was called back to teach at SFSC. Jimmy Garrett, of the Black Student Union, met with Amiri Baraka and Sanchez to present the idea—"and we sat there that night and practically decided we would be part of this period." Askia Touré came out to teach as well and Dr. Nathan Hare was later hired, but they also established Black House as an alternative space, where people would line up to "listen to this culture, this culture that was going on" off campus.[77]

Sanchez's teaching, activism, commitments, and engagement with the Nation of Islam was central to decolonizing Western epistemologies through new/old, lost/found epistemologies. When she began teaching writers like W. E. B. Du Bois, Richard Wright, Langston Hughes, Frederick Douglass, and Samuel Delany, the students did not recognize their names. She began to realize that she was being monitored for teaching what is seen as "seditious" literature, while she thought she was just teaching "only literature" and "cultural things." Her contributions to Black Studies were not just in "invad[ing] the study in the universities of America of White Studies" and helping create alternative spaces of Black Study like Black House, but also formulating new pedagogies directed at the education and teaching of children, both in childrearing and in schooling.[78] These commitments to her teaching both at the university and at home overlap—and she describes the material conditions of making that work, of sitting in her office at the University of Pittsburgh until nine o'clock, having already been there for twelve hours and going home to relieve a babysitter from childcare. She describes reading to her children at night and making up stories that she would publish as *The Adventures of Fathead, Smallhead, and Squarehead* (1973), falling asleep with them, getting up and cleaning up their messes, washing clothes, washing dishes, grading papers. "Then, after I did that, I did my own writing," she says, going to bed around three in the morning and getting up at six to fix the children's breakfast.[79]

In "Queens of the Universe," Sanchez calls for becoming

> guerilla
> fighters for our children's
> minds. we mussssSSSST begin basement schools in our homes. or take
> over existen schools.

"Wite/schools teach blk/children to hate themselves"—contaminating their minds and bodies. Again referencing Malcolm X's "who taught you to hate the color of your skin," she writes that "the devil has superimposed on our minds." Using imagery of the white devil, she juxtaposes Nation of Islam language with Fanonian concepts of decolonization and national culture, talking about moving past the "whiteness of our minds" and the colonization of "body and soul" by becoming "true believers" who will move in revolutionary ways, cultivating "new ideas" and "new thoughts."[80]

Sanchez began developing her own body of children's literature just after the birth of her twin boys, works that crystalize a vision of her emerging commitments to the NOI. Her collection of poetry *It's A New Day (poems for young brothas and sistuhs)* helped develop the pedagogies of the movement through poetry composed with children in mind. The first poems are dedicated to her own children Morani and Mungu Weusi, whose names mean "black warrior" and "black god" in Swahili, and to her daughter Anita from her marriage to Albert Sanchez. She opens the first poem greeting her twins:

> As-Salaam-Alaikum my black princes
> the morning awaits u.
>   the world
> awaits yo/young/blackness
> sun/children

of our tomorrow.
Here is my hand
black/warriors of
our dreams.[81]

It's A New Day is structured as four sets in a musical composition, or a double album, unfolding as stages toward an envisioned future for the "children of our tomorrow."[82] Set 1 is titled "Cuz we be black women lovers of children" and set 2 "and we be singen teachen new songs to our children." Set 3 is a journey/safari to a "Black Beginnen" and set 4 references being a "new people in a new land." The final section includes a tribute to the paperboys selling copies of *Muhammad Speaks*; they are selling not just newspapers, she says, but "knowledge of self and truth." Their routes are "the mind of blk people." "Blk/praises to Elijah Muhammad," she writes, are "blk/love for our selves." Sanchez calls for moving toward Reverend Cleage (who founded the black nationalist Shrine of the Black Madonna Church), Minister Farrakhan, Imamu Amiri Baraka, and Elijah Muhammad, along with Sojourner Truth, Fannie Lou Hamer, Gwendolyn Brooks, Amina Baraka, and Sister Clotelle. The collection culminates in an embrace of the "original talk" of Islam: as-Salaam-alaikum, "holy words" giving praise to Allah and the "truth of Islam."[83]

Sanchez engages in translating color and color consciousness through reference to different linguistic codes and cultural traditions recovering and reconstructing different tones. The collection is permeated by elaborations on color and sound, as she talks about the blues and blueness ("all soul/shades of blackness"), "the blue/nite that covered yo/blackness" for her twin sons, and "high/yellow/black/girl walken like the sun u be" for her daughter Anita. She juxtaposes these color tones with sound tones from the music of Curtis Mayfield, Roberta Flack, John Coltrane, Nina Simone, James Brown, blues, jazz, and even an early "rap" reference, as she writes about the "Black Rhythm of Life." She formulates an aesthetics of color and sound, music and visual art woven into her poetic language, referring to her poetry as her song and her music, "a cascading sound" of rhythms and poems. These are the many shades, the many tones, of Blackness in her poetry.

In 1975, Sanchez would become the director of culture as well as codirector of the Office of Human Development in the Nation of Islam, writing the women's page and the children's page in *Muhammad Speaks*, beginning by publishing a series of articles about "Islam and the Rebirth of Women as Participants in Civilization." At the same time she was commissioned to write a series of children's books for the NOI. During this time in the early 1970s, there was increasing awareness of a dearth of literature for African American children, despite a long ("one hundred year") history of authors working toward creating such a literature reflecting the Black experience in the United States. The 1970s mark a definitive shift toward what Rudine Sims calls the creation of "a body of Afro-American literature for children," "culturally conscious books" that celebrate black culture in narrative, language, and settings.[84] These writing emerged in tandem with pioneering work by scholars like Geneva Smitherman writing on Black English, in her first journal publication "English teacher, why you be doing the thangs you don't do?" and in her later book *Talkin and Testifying: The Language of Black America*, which "intends to celebrate the community that gave me birth and to educate those in the community charged with molding the next generation. My work seeks to blend the Black Intellectual Tradition with the wisdom and wit of testifiers."[85]

During Sanchez's tenure at *Muhammad Speaks*, there was increased attention to Black children's education. The July 4, 1975, issue (titled "Religion is Alive") launched Sanchez's "New Frontiers" section. It included a number of articles on Black children and education and "the Black child in the 1970s" as "victims of behavioral experiments," examining "racist texts" and "textbook distortions" in US classrooms, and on children's literature promoting "positive images for youth."[86] An article "how to rear a healthy black child in America" reviewed the recently released *Black Child Care: How to Bring Up a Healthy Black Child in America, A Guide to Emotional and Psychological Development* by James P. Comer and Alvin F. Poussaint, professors at Yale and Harvard.[87] Editorials by the psychologist Dr. Na'im Akbar talk about the "misdirection of Western education," the "education of the black child," and how children "should see their 'historical' identity." By December of that year, *The Black Scholar* would follow suit with their own special issue titled "Black Youth," guided by the clear vision of Sister Sonia 5X Sanchez, now with the name Laila Mannan. The issue included articles by Brent Staples ("To Be Young, Black and Oppressed") and Daphne Muse ("Black Children's Literature: Rebirth of a Neglected Genre"), as well as a section featuring the poetry of Muslim children studying at the University of Islam.[88]

Sanchez's writings worked to create pedagogies for the movement that would be passed on to future generations, through a process of teaching, leading, and working for change in a body of literature as much as in a system of education. *The Adventures of Fathead, Smallhead, and Squarehead*, illustrated by Taiwo Shabazz, tells the story of children on pilgrimage to Mecca, traveling first through the Sudan. The story is a version of the tortoise and hare fable, a race between unequal contestants—with Smallhead and Squarehead being fast at everything "so they thought that they were better." Fathead arrives first, however, and the illustrations show him on the last pages with his hands gesturing in *du'a* (prayer) in the direction of Mecca. Sanchez calls it a silly story that made her children laugh, but it nevertheless addresses the struggle of learning in the face of unequal odds and charting an alternative path. The illustrations show the children building blocks with Arabic letters on them, an activity Sanchez woke up to one morning after falling asleep while reading to her children. This was one of the alphabets developed during that time to teach children—in the African Free School in Newark, the Uhuru Sasa School in Brooklyn, the US school of Afroamerican Culture in Los Angeles, and the Sister Clara Muhammad schools in the Nation of Islam. *The Weusi Alfabeti*—"the Black alphabet"—book developed for the Uhuru Sasa School by Black arts poet Yusef Iman is designed to teach children through a lexicon of Black power words, like what we see Amina Baraka using to teach in the film *The New-Ark* in the African Free School.

Sanchez's "New Frontiers" section of *Muhammad Speaks*, targeted at women and children, included a series of articles on the theme of "Islam and the Rebirth of Women as Participants in Civilization." The youth section of the newspaper then became incorporated into the main body of the newspaper, leading to a noticeable shift in attention to the well-being and education of Black children, building on increased scholarly attention to the issue. Sanchez's articles appear alongside a series of articles on "Education of the Black Child" written by the Afrocentric clinical psychologist Dr. Na'im Akbar, who would go on to author *Breaking the Chains of Psychological Slavery* (1996). In her first article for the new section "Respect for Wisdom," Sanchez writes about seeking knowledge to control and direct one's own life as well as to positively influence the environment and the lives of others. "Women under the thundering sun of wisdom," Sanchez writes, "will bring forth light for the dark lives of our people and return them to lives again that taste the waters of the Tigris; and touch the everlasting stone of Mecca. Drawn forth from the harvest of wisdom, we women will forsake hunger and grow like buds from this seedbed called the universe."[89]

Sanchez developed a body of literature—and a field of study—for Black Studies, Black children, and new generations of students facing integration into a white educational system in the aftermath of *Brown v. the Board of Education*. Sanchez talks about having brought her children into the Nation of Islam to give them a "foundation" in blackness, because otherwise, she says of her children, "you will not survive."[90] The Nation of Islam was the place to receive a good education, with their commitments to building schools and giving children an

FIGURE 8.3 Sanchez's children's book *The Adventures of Fathead, Smallhead, and Squarehead* was illustrated by the Weusi artist Taiwo DuVall Shabazz. This image shows the building blocks of knowledge written in Arabic letters.

Hortense "Bunnie" DuVall

education at a time that the schools were not teaching Black History, Black English, and Black Sociology.[91] This literature, this knowledge of self, this learning becomes for Sanchez the building blocks of life, what Hartman calls an ethic of life-giving care that shapes the refusal of and resistance to a "history of alienation in this country."[92] Sanchez also describes it as the building blocks of a civilization, spreading out over the Western hemisphere and changing the "artificial humanism" of white supremacy, so that the world will be "reborn. black. again."

FIGURE 8.4 Taiwo DuVall Shabazz's illustrations of Sanchez's *Fathead, Smallhead, and Squarehead* shows a child on the path to Mecca praying, holding his hands in *du'a* or supplication.

Hortense "Bunnie" DuVall

Sanchez discursively, aesthetically, pedagogically, and institutionally combats what Alexander Weheliye calls racializing assemblages—racism that "justifies the death function in the economy of biopower."[93] In a June 13, 1975, interview in the Nation of Islam newspaper *Muhammad Speaks*, Sanchez talks about "always moving knowledge; ... as long as we live we are constantly being made. We are constantly moving, that's how we stay alive. Once that learning ceases, we are for all purposes dead."[94]

A BLUES BOOK FOR BLUE BLACK MAGICAL WOMEN

Islamic references and Nation of Islam ideas, language, and imagery infuse *A Blues Book* in both form and content. The book opens with verses 96:1–5 of the Qur'an expressive of the poem's themes of rebirth. Known as the chapter of the "embryo," the verses compare the Qur'an to the creation of the human being and see reading and reciting as a process of teaching knowledge through the pen. Understood to be the first verses to come down to the Prophet Muhammad, the chapter is also known as Surat Iqra' (Chapter "Read!" or, "Recite!"). For the *Blues Book*'s cover, the artist Ademola Olugebefola (from the Weusi Collective) painted a watercolor of a woman situated in a keyhole niche framing a celestial blue sky. The color shines through her eyes, and layered shades of blue emanate through her head covering. Her African mask-like face has a star on the forehead, a circle sun / God's eye is positioned at her throat, and an Egyptian pyramid shapes her chest. In the copyright, Sanchez thanks Olugebefola as "a superbly gifted and talented artist who constantly amazes me with his progress and devotion. May Allah bless you my brother." Sanchez is shown at the end of the book wearing a Nation of Islam head covering in a photo taken by Olugebefola's fellow Weusi artist Ed Sherman ("your photography is poetry my brother," writes Sanchez). In the photograph, Sanchez is flanked her two sons in Nation of Islam bow ties. The book closes with the place, New York City, and the date in the Black Muslim Calendar (15,059), the Islamic *hijri* calendar (1391), and the Gregorian calendar (1973), a "translation" of time into three systems. The book is dedicated "with Love" to "my spiritual FATHER, THE HONORABLE ELIJAH MUHAMMAD, Messenger of ALLAH."

With *A Blues Book for Blue Black Magical Women*, Sanchez creates a futuristic space of becoming that suggests prophecy. Dreaming of and hoping for an envisioned future, her language functions as a portal to a new world, a space to freely live, breathe, and be. The book-poem's repeated motif of "giving birth to ourselves" harkens back to the "Malcolm" poem and the sad, frozen image of the miscarriage / abortion of justice juxtaposed with the hopeful imagery of the sacred labor of giving birth to words. The image is threaded through "Queens of the Universe," reiterated in multiple ways as "a breakfast of births let your mouth spill me forth," "earth mother . . . the day is turning in my thighs. and you are born BLACK GIRL," "i gave birth to myself . . . became myself," "i taste the seasons of my birth."[95] This is done partly through sliding off a mask of whiteness (the "whiteness of our minds," "slave mentalities," "the

FIGURE 8.5 Photograph of Sonia Sanchez and her twins, Mungu and Morani Weusi, on the back of *A Blues Book of Blue Black Magical Women*, with Sanchez wearing an Islamic headscarf and her children dressed in Nation of Islam bowties.

Sonia Sanchez

living mask . . . peels like picasso's planes.") But she also articulates this vision through a black vernacular, Islamic motifs, Nation of Islam precepts, and Qur'anic language, as she "vomits out the European words that handcuffed me," and begins "moving to the rhythm of Black womanhood."[96]

A Blues Book for Blue Black Magical Women is a structured journey through time that is personal, poetic, and political, beginning with the introduction, proceeding through sections PAST and PRESENT and punctuated by a REBIRTH before the final section FUTURE. FUTURE is divided into shorter parts that read like the shorter Meccan suras of the Qur'an, revealed during the earlier part of Muhammad's prophethood. These chapters are more lyrical and apocalyptic in tone, with images of turning the world upside down, weighing deeds in the scales of justice, the day of accounting (reparations?), and heaven and hell as garden and fire. All these are present in the FUTURE section of the *Blues Book*, with structure, rhythm, and thematics that echo the Qur'an, referring to the upending of the natural order through a series of oaths. But there are also elements specific to the Nation of Islam, of the divinity of Fard Muhammad and Elijah Muhammad as messenger (as "Lord of Almighty words"). Her Qur'anic style raises a number of issues about the distinction between the Qur'an and poetry—and the "false prophets" who are challenged to produce a verse like that of the Qur'an. This has been at the crux of debates over the Qur'an's singular literary style and specifically, its "inimitability" indicative of its miraculous nature.[97] Through this poetry, Sanchez sits at the edge of an Islamic tradition—and an Islamic orthodoxy—that has grappled explicitly and extensively with the relationship between the Qur'an and poetry.[98] But it also situates Sanchez firmly in a genealogy of creative elaboration of the Qur'an through the medium of poetry—whether in ascetic, mystical, wine, or love poetry—through what has been a vibrant element of the Islamic intellectual tradition. This poetry also calls up a long history of Islamic mystical poetry that draw on Qur'anic motifs, seeking to emulate the Qur'an through the very process of citation, recitation, and elaboration.[99] This kind of poetry, and these kind of poets, have sometimes stood in tense relation to Islamic orthodoxy for the creative license taken in their poems. But such creative liberties, particularly in the Sufi tradition, have been of central importance to the dissemination—and interpretation—of Islamic practice and scripture in widely varying historical, geographical, and cultural contexts.

The politics of Sanchez's Islamic poetry is part of this poetic tradition in Islam, yet in opposition to various (un)orthodoxies that include what Sherman Jackson calls the "protoIslam" of the Nation of Islam, as much as the Sunni "resurrection" within the Black Muslim community, which was dawning just as Sanchez left the NOI,[100] and was connected to the influx of Muslims immigrants following the Immigration Act of 1965. Many of these immigrants judged the Nation of Islam and Black Muslims as un-Islamic, partly as a result of the cultural biases of their own culturally inflected Islam, but also because of the racial biases that they assimilated in American society. Though earlier scholarship largely considered the Nation of Islam as a social movement rather than a religious group,[101] more recent work understands the Nation of Islam as one interpretation of Islam in a long history of reinterpreting Islamic forms—forms existing within different historical, geographical, and cultural contexts, including Sunni Arab Islam. This more recent scholarship specifically recognizes how Islamic signs, symbols, rituals, beliefs, scripture, and texts were interpreted within the American context.[102] It became a way of recuperating a past that freed the lost-found nation from white racism by relocating it in a place and time predating white European hegemony and its concomitant racial crimes of colonialism and the slave trade. Sanchez asserts her allegiance to the Black nationalism of the Nation of Islam—and this Black Muslim world view shapes her poetry during this time, what some in the Muslim world were calling an Islamic way of seeing and representing (*taswir*).[103] She does so through embracing or even producing what might be called a Nation vernacular of Islam—as a religion, a culture, and a language.

In creating a poetics of the NOI, Sanchez situates herself within the orthodoxy of unorthodoxy in the Islamic tradition. Through her emulation of Qur'anic style, she is not necessarily claiming a divinity for herself in the "we" of "WE ARE MUSLIM WOMEN," as the NOI does for Fard as "divine man." But she is experimenting with prophetic style, as an emulation and an internalization of the Qur'an's mode of discursive production, an internalization and an embodiment that has been a critical part of the Islamic tradition.[104] In this, Sanchez evokes other Muslim women around this time—talking about making a pilgrimage into the true self, living the "articulated" Qur'an, and experiencing an awakening and a rebirth.[105] In *A Blues Book*, Sanchez goes from writing about the "devil in my soul" to

> let me turn inside myself
> and sit down with ALLAH
> i have become like a temple
> i have made my form from
> HIS form and I am trying to be worthy[106]

The question of the human divine is seen as being one of the most problematic aspects of the Nation of Islam's doctrines, developed in all its ecstatic fringe unorthodoxy by the Five Percenters who celebrated Black man as gods.[107] But glorying in the divine through reciting the divine word goes far back in the Islamic tradition—not just through those seeking to produce a verse like it (Quran 2:23, 52:30)—but also through the Sufi tradition and especially Sufi poetry. It also can be found in contemporary works of Islamic feminism that cite Sufi hagiography as discursive models for their own paths of spiritual becoming, self-realization, and rebirth.[108]

However ironically—and tragically—for the Nation of Islam, Sanchez cites her poetry as one of the reasons for ultimately leaving the NOI. Elijah Muhammad was known for executing control over artistic production, as when he banned Farrakhan from singing and performing. But he was also deeply wary of competing visions and narratives, as the example of Malcolm X shows. *A Blues Book* has been scrubbed of the *mu'minina* references to the CFUN and US Organizations, along with a reference to Amina Baraka and Amiri Baraka's Republic of New Afrika (RNA) in favor of exclusive reference to the Nation of Islam and Elijah Muhammad. This control is clear particularly in the *Blues Book* language, from the changes to the original *Black Scholar* version of "Queens of the Universe," which uses Black English spellings, raw language, and slang vernaculars. In the *Blues Book* introduction, the experimental Black English spellings have been "standardized," as has the language, which probably speaks to NOI aspirations, as well as the organization's politics of respectability. These unfortunate "correctives" to the poetic beauty of Sanchez's Black language stymie what was becoming one of her most important poetic contributions—particularly at a time of increasing awareness and consciousness about Black English: as a language and a culture, and as a key to schooling and education.[109] But Sanchez also talks movingly about how people of all colors and stripes ("Black, White, green, purple, blue") told her "This is not proper English so it's not proper poetry." Yet the sound and beauty of her grandmother in her psyche drew her near. "And I loved it and I loved those words and I knew those words loved me. . . . Here it be. This is what this is really all about."[110]

Sanchez situates *A Blues Book for Blue Black Magical Women* in a blues matrix, combining the sense of the blues as a shade of color, an emotion, a skin tone, and a musical or linguistic sound. Olugebefola's blue watercolors and the poem's references to "blue song" fashion a multisensory, multimedia poetic experience. In her chapter on skin tones, language, and racialization, Rey Chow writes about how the process of naming (slave names and slave mentalities versus Islamic names and Islamic mentalities) "establishes the 'community' (or . . .'connectivity') in which the named object is given a life." Uncannily evoking Sanchez's language, Chow characterizes this as "a magical community" writing about naming, which "conjures a divine notion of creativity," "religious mysticism," and "revolutionary utopianism," through the "magical guise of touching and corresponding with the other."[111]

WOMEN OF THE NATION OF ISLAM

Sanchez's work stands alongside, within, and in creative tension with a body of vibrant Black feminist and womanist intellectual and cultural production that flourished in the early 1970s with the publication of Toni Cade Bambara's edited volume *The Black Woman: An Anthology* (1970), Mari Evans's poetry collection *I Am A Black Woman* (1970), Toni Morrison's *The Bluest Eye* (1970), Alice Walker's *In Search of Our Mother's Gardens* (1974), and Gerda Lerner's *Black Women in White America: A Documentary History* (1972). Sanchez was the first college professor to offer a seminar on literature by African American women—the course she taught on "The Black Woman" at the University of Pittsburgh in 1969—yet her writing was not included in *The Black Woman*, though it would be included in later anthologies like *Sturdy Black Bridges: Visions of Black Women in Literature* (1979).[112] Her writing in the early 1970s pays tribute to the different and sometimes divergent strands of Black feminism at the time, like in her dedication in *We a BadddDDD People* to 114 women in the Black Arts Movement (ameena [*sic*] baraka, gwendolyn brooks, sarah fabio, abbey lincoln, naima, furaha, kimako baraka, johari amini, carolyn rodgers, barbara ann teer, nina simone, evelyn neal, barbara llorens, margaret t. burroughs, margaret walker, ruby dee, trixie bullins, paule marshall, sarah wright, maya angelou, among others), women campaigning for Black Studies at San Francisco State College and at the University of Pittsburgh, and sisters in the Nation of Islam. She also includes her daughter Anita and her mother Lena Jones. Critical texts that followed, like the Combahee River Collective Statement and bell hooks's *Ain't I a Woman*, included fierce critiques of sexism within the Nation of Islam, the Black Power movement, and the BAM.[113]

The regnant interpretation of the Nation of Islam's attitude toward women, both scholarly and popular, is that it was sexist and patriarchal. These analyses consistently characterize Black nationalism—as well as the Black Power movement and the BAM—as promoting Black unity that conflicted with "a specifically black *feminist* consciousness."[114] In *The Feminist Avant-Garde in American Poetry*, Elizabeth Frost asserts that Black nationalism "impeded Sanchez from asserting a feminist agenda."[115] In her book on women's participation in the Black Power movement, however, Ashley Farmer warns against positioning Black feminism and Black nationalism as oppositional, arguing that such an approach ignores how women's extensive contributions shaped the Black Power movement, as much as Black Power concepts shaped Black feminism. In her book *Remaking Black Power*, Farmer invites us " to rethink the relationship between black feminism and Black power" by looking particularly at how "black women's formulations of black womanhood indicate that they consistently simultaneously identified as nationalist and feminist."[116] More recent scholarship on Sanchez urges us to situate her Black feminist commitments within her Black Arts one, talking about her "rigorous feminist attitude" as a "vocal womanist/humanist critic that privileged women's questions."[117] But if the movements of Black Power and its "sister" Black Arts have been understood as antithetical to feminism and women's liberation, both Islam in general and the Nation of Islam are seen as beyond the pale in this respect, in both scholarship and in popular imagination.[118] These theories are rooted in assumptions of misogyny long projected onto Islam. Despite arguing that Sanchez's Black nationalist commitments dovetailed with her womanist ones, Forsgren describes her joining the NOI "despite her womanist sensibilities"[119] New scholarship on women in the Nation of Islam, as well as on Muslim women and Islamic feminism, understands women's membership in the Nation of Islam beyond just women "participating in their own oppression,"[120] but as political interventions that work within and against extant models to embrace alternative modes of political community.[121] These alternative models often entail redefining gender relations—sometimes in ways that respond to, mirror, and reflect the structures they are trying to challenge, combat, and overturn. As Smethurst observes in his text *The Black Arts Movement*, to claim that these movements were "unusually sexist" distorts the "legacy of black women (and some men) in those movements as well as their contributions to the rise of second-wave feminism."[122]

Theorists of intersectionality like Kimberlé Crenshaw and Nira Yuval-Davis recognize that the "naturalizing discourses" of identity politics function as modes of resistance, political empowerment, and social reconstruction. Yuval-Davis calls for paying attention to the conditions producing these group categories and how these modes of signification are appropriated, subverted, reinterpreted, and used as weapons against already existing modes of domination and oppression. Sanchez's poetry can be situated at this nexus: where race and gender discrimination act as compounding forms of oppression, but also as sites of mobilization, revitalization, and resignification within and against dominant discourses of racism and sexism. Yuval-Davis describes the "representational forms" of social divisions as "expressed in images and symbols, text and ideologies." Sanchez's poetry taps into what Yuval-Davis calls " 'creative imagination' that underlies the linguistic and social categories of signification" and the "construction of categories of signification."[123] Sanchez engages in a process of translating these categories through references to a symbolic system of many tones, colors, sounds, ethnicities, geographies, and histories instead of the violent, abusive history of racism in the United States.

Islamic nationalism—and Islamic feminism—have been critical to decolonization movements, as well as political struggles against modes of secular authoritarianism. Islamic nationalism has not simply created Islamic feminism toward its own ends. But Islamic feminism has similarly instrumentalized Islamic nationalism toward "social empowerment and reconstruction" in the face repressive state violence, as well as colonial and neocolonial interventions. Colonial attempts to dismantle, reorder, and control the Islamic family resulted in a focus on family and community as a mode of resistance against this violence. Shoring up this unit became critical to regrouping and establishing grassroots community bonds resistant to Euro-colonial predations, as much as the violence of the secular state.[124] Women's writings and literature on this subject see and understand this as a political issue. Yet they also describe these Islamic solidarities on a visceral ontological/existential/affective level that is transformative, resulting in a kind of delivery from an exploitive order into another order in harmony with the moral arc of the universe. The productive confluence of these overlapping, intersectional identity politics is vividly articulated in Sanchez's writings. In the *Eyes on the Prize* interview, Sanchez talks about "the double and a triple oppression that we all had at the very beginning."[125]

Women in the NOI, writes Ula Taylor in *The Promise of Patriarchy*, "loved the Nation of Islam, despite its shortcomings. It offered them hope, stability, protection, and freedoms on their own terms, . . . women who gave so much with the purest intention to build a black nation filled with love and possibility."[126] She hopes that they see a "glimmer" of themselves in her account. Writings by Taylor, Gibson, Karim, and Farmer recognize that women claimed their freedom, leadership, and self-determination within—and through—the restrictive norms of the Nation of Islam and the Black Power movement. The glimmer of NOI women's experiences shines through in Sanchez's poetry, which intertwines feminism with Black nationalism, womanhood and Blackness, partly through Islamic words, motifs, signs, symbols, and scripture.

360°

Sanchez's poetry draws on what Carolyn Fowler calls "the notion of survival, since it has been so important in our historical evolution as a people, may remain part of the Black Aesthetic, emplanted as a myth, as a symbol encapsulating hundreds of years of Black history."[127] In "Mama's Baby, Papa's Maybe," Spillers interrogates this as a "kind of hieroglyphics of the flesh," asking if these markings " 'transfer' from one generation to another, finding its various symbolic substitutions in an efficacy of meanings that repeat the initiating moments.... This body whose flesh carries the female and male to the frontiers of survival bears in person the marks of a cultural text," a cultural text that she calls "an American grammar."[128] In Evie Shockley's *Renegade Poetics*, in her chapter on Sanchez, she comments on Fowler's quote, also quoted in Spady's *B.Ma* essay. "In other words, the artist could address the very real threats to African American survival through direct action or through the creation of art that would better enable African Americans to better understand and resist those threats."[129]

An anthology titled *three hundred and sixty degrees of blackness comin at you*, which Sanchez collected from a writers workshop she led at the Countee Cullen Library in Harlem in 1970, would be performed in July 2020—in the midst of Black Lives Matter protests against the deaths of Ahmaud Arberry, George Floyd, Breonna Taylor, Elijah McClain, and Rayshard Brooks, and in the middle of the COVID-19 pandemic that disproportionately affected Black, Hispanic, Native Americans, and Native Alaskans. The performer, filmmaker, and photographer Melissa Alexander staged an interpretation of Sanchez's anthology that she first came across at For Keeps Bookstore on Auburn Avenue in Atlanta, gathering a group of performers to stage the writings and bring the words (back) to life off the page. The performance opened with Dorothy Randall's "Black Mayflower," an imagining of what Spillers calls "the life of women, children, and infants in the 'Middle Passage' and ... the fate of the pregnant female captive and the unborn."[130] Randall imagines the horrors of the slave ship as a miscarriage in its hold, with "white ghosts of death" hovering over "this cold, dark womb, ... my belly strangely still."

> This floor heaves up and down,
> And side to side as if in labor,
> But there is no life in my body ...
> And in my womb, my little nation kicks no more.
>
> What foreign child shall this ship give birth to?
> What strange infant shall grow from
> The seeds of my raped motherland?
> I do not know.
> But they cannot have my manchild,
> And they will not have my soul.[131]

Randall would go on to author the book *Soul Between the Lines: Freeing Your Creative Spirit Through Writing* and become a poet in residence at Hunter College.

In "360 Degreez of Sonia Sanchez," from a special issue of *B. Ma: The Sonia Sanchez Literary Review*, James Spady and Samy Alim pay tribute to what they call a "narrative continuum" between the Black Arts Movement and hip-hop, between the language Sanchez developed in her poetry and the hip-hop generation, as a movement of continuity and change, or the "changing same." The special issue is dedicated to her as "Teacher, Mother, Poet, Dramatist, Activist, and Global Citizen. . . . Sonia Sanchez understands the power of knowledge and discourse in the realm of space and time. Her Black Womanist Aesthetic, valorization of Black language, history, and culture and ideological stance enables her to come to terms with the very power inherent in representation."[132]

Alim talks about "the power of the word in human life," and in his interviews with Sanchez, she says, "We are an extension of each other. Or we are a continuation of each other."[133] Her use of 360° refers to the tenth principle of the Supreme Mathematics of the Five Percenters, "the Cipher: completion of the circle." The other nine principles are: 1. knowledge, 2. wisdom, and 3. understanding, with the man, woman, and child, move into a culture of 4. freedom, 5. truth, and 6. equality, with Allah 7. at its center, 8. building destroying, and 9. being born and "bringing into existence a mental birth of self."[134] The title of Sanchez's *Love Poems*, published after she first joined the NOI, is written in the shape of a seven, referring (in Supreme Mathematics) to Allah, "the all and all is 360 degrees." Though Sanchez had not officially entered into the Nation of Islam when she taught this workshop at Countee Cullen Library in 1970 and 1971, the hand typed anthology is published by "5X Publishing," referring to her Nation of Islam name Sonia 5X. With Melissa Alexander's performance, the continuum comes full circle, bringing Sanchez's language alive for a new generation of poets and protests.

CODA

360° OF ISLAMIC AUDIOVISUALITIES

Revolution and Evolution

the circle runs complete as it is in the storm of peace, the all embraced embracing in the circle complete as in a peaceful storm . . . the holy world that we long for, knowing how to live, and what life is, and who God is, and the many revolutions we must spin through . . . vibration holy nuance beating against itself, a rhythm a playing.

—LeRoi Jones, "Black People: This is Our Destiny," *Black Art* (1966)

Left earth on a new birth
In space, out space, our place . . .
Vibrating, educating, stimulating
Young and old as a whole
Those who know jazz is prose

—The Last Poets, "Jazzoetry"

Black futures transcend history, but history is their essential matter. If we go back to move forward, is anything really lost? Isn't this also revolution?

—Alicia J. Lochard, *Space-Time Collapse I: From the Congo to the Carolinas*

This book is about the Islamic consciousness of the Black Arts Movement, its sons and daughters, its poetic antecedents, and the reverberations of Muslim ancestors. BAM artists revived and resurrected

Islamic knowledge through creative imagination conceived of as ritual that conjured the dead. They reinvigorated an Islam already present in Black American life and culture, tapping into the frequencies of Islamic soundscapes and languages and into Muslim codes through signs, symbols, and practices that revivified and reconfigured what white America sought to bury. BAM artists orchestrated this revival as Black art or black magic, necromancy or raising the dead, calling up its creative and transformational possibilities. The performances of Islamic commitments in BAM writings, music, poetry, visual art, clothes, practices, and language forged new selves, partly by retracing their roots and trans-Atlantic routes, transforming them into spiritual journeys.

In *What is Islam?* Shahab Ahmed grapples with scholarly interpretations of Islam's universal versus local dimensions—specifically, Islam's theological and legalistic aspects understood as closer to its core or essence in contrast to its local cultural manifestations. His chapter "Culture, Meaning, Symbol System, Core and Nucleus, Whatever-Muslims-Say-It-Is, Discursive Tradition, Orthodoxy, Process" explores the semiotic construction of religious meanings, analyzing Islam as a system of signification, what John R. Bowen calls "Muslims through discourse." This book examines how artists in the BAM drew on Islamic discourses to construct a "continent of meaning,"[1] envisioning an other/worldly existence and creating institutions of Black space to foster its realization. Islam was a system (among other systems) of "African signs and spirit writing" that structured a moral and ethical universe with the ability to resist what Amiri Baraka called the "deathblows of white America."[2] This Islamic cultural production reread and resuscitated a buried past for the Black Power era through a process of "critical fabulation" that reenvisioned Islamic commitments for the context of Black struggle in the 1960s and 1970s. It took different forms, alternately interpreted as territorial nationalisms, political geographies, Black space, international solidarities with other decolonial struggles, and other worlds; these imaginaries were able to psychically construct links, connections, and spaces through Black creative freedom alternately envisioned as transcendental, surreal, supernatural, speculative, insurrectionary, and Afrofuturist.[3] In talking about Islam as a "continent of meaning," Ahmed argues that to understand Islam is "to conceptualize how that continent is elaborated, articulated, constructed, conceived, and experienced as an undulating whole, even when its parts present themselves in and as apparently distinct and disconnected topographies."[4] In the BAM, this undulating whole was conceived in both topographical and temporal terms, as a past informing a present to shape a future as a nation, world, or space. BAM artists described this undulation as "thought waves" and "vibrations"—"all paths that lead to God," as John Coltrane wrote in the liner notes to *A Love Supreme*.[5] It is what Askia Muhammad Touré called

"Allah's Love vibrating in the Sunrise" in his poem "Tauhid," named for Pharoah Sanders's album *Tauhid*.[6]

BAM artists like Amiri Baraka, Amina Baraka, and Sonia Sanchez eventually abandoned the Nation of Islam because of restrictions on artistic expression. Sanchez became a minister of education and culture in the NOI in 1975, inviting Gwendolyn Brooks and Shirley Graham Du Bois to speak, something that raised objections from within the organization. Amina Baraka left the NOI after Malcolm X's assassination, but also because she understood her artistic commitments as being at odds with the NOI. Marvin X was admonished for his poetry by Elijah Muhammad himself, and at one point was kicked out of the NOI. Even Malcolm X was expelled from the NOI, only to expand his Muslim commitments. Farrakhan remained in the NOI but also retained his commitment to his art and music, deepening his knowledge of the Qur'an, though remaining faithful to Elijah Muhammad's conceptualization of Islam as a Black religion. Leaders like Elijah Muhammad tried to control the aesthetic production of the organization, as different Islamic orthodoxies have throughout Islamic history. (Black) Muslim aesthetics have proliferated beyond the rules, regulations, and guidelines erected by Elijah Muhammad or by any other Muslim sect, group, or orientation (like Sunni, Shi'a, or Sufi). The twenty-first century witnessed the "generative and expansive" nature of Black Muslim cultural production but was not always bound by particular interpretations of Islam or kinds of Islamic affiliation or belonging; it mingled instead with historical forms of Islam in the Americas. As Michael Gomez observes in *Black Crescent*, Islam "underwent cultural transmogrification to survive. Even so, the continuation and progression of Islam did not come to a halt in the United States; rather the Islamic heritage was in fact strengthened as a result of an ideological restructuring."[7]

"ALLAH'S LOVE VIBRATING IN THE SUNRISE"

The BAM reverberated in time and space, looking both to the past and the future, even while addressing struggles in the present; it was locally situated in grassroots organizing, but reached across the globe to connect to other struggles.[8] Margo Natalie Crawford writes about the "vibratory shock" of the BAM that broke out of a linear sense of Black aesthetics, conceiving of Black Art as a space of possibility that resonated back and forth in time and space. Crawford took the concept of "vibratory shock" from an advertisement in the BAM journal *Soulbook* that described rhythm as "the force which, through our sense, grips us at the root of our being." Through visual art, poetry, music, and dance, rhythm turns "all these concrete things toward the light of the spirit."[9] Crawford, calling for a "skepticism about any fixed notion of black art," argues instead for a sense of a cyclic motion, describing a "circularity of black aesthetic traditions, . . . the nonlinear, back-and-forth, black radical tradition of continuity and rupture," as "tidalectics" that ebb and flow but also suggest passages, ruptures, and returns.[10] She reflects on BAM's roots in the Harlem Renaissance, on how the BAM anticipated twenty-first century cultural production (particularly the hip-hop nation), and on the longer roots of the BAM in the aesthetic traditions of the African diaspora. In analyzing the "circularity of black aesthetic traditions" Crawford writes about Amiri Baraka's 1966 essay "The Changing Same," a 1966 essay by Baraka (then still publishing under the name LeRoi Jones), in which he writes about Black musical forms breaking out of the "strait jacket of American expression" through "the vibrations of a feeling, of a particular place, a conjunction of world spirit."[11] Baraka is specifically discussing the beboppers' embrace of Islam and their "self-conscious concern about God," a "Black Life Force" seeking clarity, seeking religion, seeking freedom. He calls John Coltrane, Albert Ayler, Sun-Ra, and Pharoah Sanders "God-seekers" whose "Wisdom Religion . . . The New Black Music, is toward change. It is change. It wants to change forms."[12] "The Changing Same," like his *Blues People*, is Baraka's "Sorrow Songs," what Deborah McDowell describes as "an archeological effort" and "a project of excavation" into how words and music convey veiled messages of an older theology and the "strange world of an unknown tongue."[13]

BAM poets like Askia Muhammad Touré understood music as channeling the call to Islam. In his poem "The Sound of Allah's Horn" he interprets the new music as a means of "Evolving, moving East, Mooooving Eastwards on the Winds from Mecca, on the Spirits of our Ancestors." He frames John Coltrane blowing his horn as a call to Allah, a legacy he passed down to his acolyte Pharaoah Sanders.

> ALLAH is calling! ALLAH is calling!
> ALLAH is calling! ALLAH is calling!
> . . . the star-filled Cosmos is vibrating in tune with the flame in
> Malcolm's voice, the love in 'Retha's heart, Ray Charles is grooving
> with James Brown both blowing Black and Proud joined by Black
> Magicians to blow your MIND Blackman, to expand your SOUL
> Blackwoman . . . and refill you with Allah.[14]

Touré's poetry plays on Islamic language: his collection *Juju (Magic Songs for the Black Nation)* begins with a section titled "The Opening," suggesting *al-fatiha* "The Opening" of the Qur'an. Touré's "Opening" pays tribute to Black leaders and musicians like Marcus Garvey and W. E. B. Du Bois, Langston Hughes and Booker T. Washington, Bessie Smith and Satchmo, Bird and Lady Day, Malcolm and Elijah, Otis Redding and Aretha Franklin—and John Coltrane. This opening is a kind of channel or a conduit to Islamic consciousness and Islamic knowledge. Meta DuEwa Jones writes about the jazz prosody of the Coltrane poem as a "vehicle for resurrecting black bodies from the deafening, deadening clutches of historical erasure," describing the "formal, cultural, and historical saturation within the Coltrane poem's graphic and sonic modalities."[15] Other scholars chart the Islamic inflections of Coltrane's *A Love Supreme* as Allah Supreme or Allahu Akbar; the liner notes' echoes of *al-fatiha* or the opening of the Qur'an ("God . . . is gracious and merciful" / "there is no other" / "Glory to God" / "all paths lead to God"); and Coltrane's connections to Ahmadiyya Islam through his relationship with his wife Naima and adopted daughter Syeeda.[16] His disciple Pharoah Sanders, who played on key albums like *Ascension* (1965) and *A Love Supreme* (1965), is described by Baraka and Touré as taking up Coltrane's mantle, in his horn-blowing bebopping, but also in his music's Islamic references, in his albums *Tauhid* ("Oneness" 1967), *Jewels of Thought* with its track "Hum-Allah Hum-Allah Hum-Allah" (1970), and *Summun Bukmun Umyun* (Deaf Dumb Blind, 1971).[17] *Ascension* and *A Love Supreme* were recorded in the months following Malcolm X's death, speaking to the albums as elegiac forms of mourning. The Coltrane poem, argues Meta DuEwa Jones, "often performs as a vehicle for hearing the dead speak." If Coltrane was elegizing Malcolm, so the BAM poets elegize Malcolm and Coltrane and a longer history of loss through soundscapes and wordscapes that "remember, revive, and riff"—on not just Malcolm's words and Coltrane's music, but also on their (re)visions of Islam for the context of Black struggle in the United States.[18]

Touré signs the opening poem of *Juju* with his full Muslim name Askia Muhammad Abu Bakr El-Touré, dating it 1387 (~1967) according to the *hijri* calendar, closing the poem writing, "my Heart my Soul my ALL vibrating." Here he riffs on Coltrane writing ALL in capitals in his original manuscript of the liner notes of *A Love Supreme* ("no road is an easy one but they ALL lead to God), which became in the published version "all vibrations-all paths lead to God."[19] Touré closes the poem repeating the words "A LOVE SUPREME" in caps seven times, riffing on the "typographic, orthographic, and just plain graphic features" of the BAM's jazz prosody.[20] Touré dedicates the following poem "Tauhid" to Pharoah Sanders, the poem named for Sanders's album *Tauhid*, a word that refers to the "oneness" of God in Islam, but also to Sufi mystical concepts of the oneness of existence.

> Reach with hungry Black minds towards that bright
> >   Crescent Moon
> glowing in the depth of Malcolm's eyes . . .
> Cosmic Rhythms
> >   flowing
> in the sound of Pharoah's horn . . .
> find your Afro-Soul, that holy part of you connecting
> >   Harlem to the roots of Timbuctoo . . .
> Allah's Love vibrating in the Sunrise.[21]

BAM poetry takes Coltrane's music—and *A Love Supreme* in particular—as a critical point of reference, as a "generative and expansive" interpretation of the language of Islam in a musical idiom; the album title (and lyrics chanted in the first track "Acknowledgement") is thought to refer to *Allahu akbar* or Allah Supreme. The Islamic language of Coltrane's musical idiom is reinforced in the poem that he includes as the liner notes, with multiple expressions doubling as translations or approximations of Islamic expressions, especially those used in prayer.[22]

What Crawford describes as vibrations, Tina Campt interprets as "the centrality of sonic and visual frequency to the work of Black contemporary artists"—sonic and visual frequencies that were also key to the multimedia nature of the BAM, with its invocations of sound, song, music, musicians, and instruments—and collaborations with visual artists from the Weusi Collective and AfriCOBRA. Campt's book *A Black Gaze: Artists Changing How We See* "offers a free-flowing and open-ended meditation on the musical/poetic dimensions of the artworks."[23] The Islamic imagery coded into the Black art of the BAM and its aesthetic descendants in the twenty-first century reorients the Black gaze toward alternative non-Western spaces, languages, and cultures, but also adapts a sense of presumed (Orientalist) foreignness toward alternative modes of belonging, new creative avenues of (self) expression, and cultural connections beyond the "strait jacket of American expression" or the "narrow national orbit."[24]

Even as the Islamic invokes Black difference, and also alienation, it becomes a means of understanding "Black alienation not as isolation but as . . . both generative and expansive."[25] What Crawford describes as "vibratory shock," Campt calls "the centrality of sonic and visual frequency to the work of Black contemporary artists."[26] Crawford describes this audiovisuality in her analysis of the mixed media of the BAM "that accentuates the flows *and* ruptures between the visual, sonic, and written staged as a meta-language" and also a "pedagogical mission."[27] Meta DuEwa Jones describes this as the "spiritual syntax" of the prosody of jazz poetry that has "musical, visual, and oral dimensions."[28] Jones focuses mainly on jazz poetry, while Campt examines the sonic and visual frequencies of contemporary fine art—the two scholars themselves operating in dialogue in a kind of multimedia approach. Though Campt argues that "no innovative Black art . . . preceded or informed the current moment," the BAM definitely "anticipated" the Black gaze in contemporary fine art and particularly the multimedia sensory dimensions of sight and sound. Crawford analyzes Amiri Baraka and Fundi (Billy) Abernathy's collaboration *In Our Terribleness* (1970) as "an attempt to find a black gaze"—with its mirrored frontispiece—what they call an "IMAGE STORY IN MOTION" ("LOOK AT THEM, at YOU / The living force.") One of the poems "IMAGE" puns on the word "organ" as vital organ and as instrument and reflects on images as both giving life and stopping life. The poem speaks of the organ (of the voice? the music? the heart?) as carrying religion through time to where we are at now: "our sight" / site. "Our / Place. Where we plays." Then the poem's imagery becomes of Black revolutionary *fellaheen*, African Muslims, and Moors.

> The Images are *stops* of the organ life.
> Carry the religion through years to our sight. Our
> Place. Where we plays It is all a play, of
> Illusion and memory God remembering . . .
> As we circle always toward light A shape of energy ur memory of him us
> Bloods
> The Blood
> The fellahs   (een there
>   Fellaheen
>   Bedouin
>   Black Arab
>   Hamitic Arab
>   Moor
>   Muslim
>   African[29]

Baraka generatively uses this vital sonic imagery of organs to imagine other kinds of representation of Blackness, as brotherhood and kinship, revolutionary uprising (the *fellah* and *fellaheen*, the peasant revolutionaries in the

Algerian war of independence), migratory (as Bedouin), Moorish or "Black Arab" (or "Moroccan" and African), and Muslim. *In Our Terribleness* expands definitions of Blackness through Baraka's sonic references to Black music ("organ life") and through Abernathy's photographic visual art. Abernathy's portraits of everyday Black life anticipate the photography of the artist Dawoud Bey; other portraits of the women of the NOI and the Fruit of Islam (FOI) pay tribute to the photography of Gordon Parks. Both the visual and the poetic aspects of *In Our Terribleness* weave expressions of Islam into the landscape of everyday African American life—portraits and poetics that also generate a new landscape of Islamic expression, expanding on an Islamic aesthetics and poetics that exceed what has gone before, even as they invoke core dimensions of the Islamic tradition.

The *Tauhid* of Pharoah Sanders—who was Coltrane's disciple and played on Coltrane's *A Love Supreme* as well as his *Ascension* (1965)—refers to the oneness of God, or oneness of existence (*wahadat al-wujud*). These albums exemplify the generative and expansive dimensions of the Black Muslim aesthetic, embraced and channeled even by those who do not officially or formally become Muslim or join Islamic organizations (like Sun Ra, Larry Neal, Fundi Abernathy, Gordon Parks, John Coltrane, Lauryn Hill, and Jenn Nkiru among others). They tap into the Islamic dimensions of the Black past, African American life and culture, and the Afrofuturist imaginary. Rather than a formal Islamic aesthetics bound by the Arab world or the Middle East or Sunni orthodoxy, these artists realize a more expansive Islamic aesthetics, an Islamic art that migrated across different cultural, historical, and political terrains. This expansive vision was partly realized through the platforms developed by the Black Shriners (and their interpretations of Islam in the aftermath of the World's Fair in Chicago), the Moorish Science Temple (and their vision of an Asian and African Islam), the Nation of Islam (and the concept of Islam as Asiatic and as the religion of Black people in the United States), but also the artists. Baraka's "IMAGE" poem plays on place as "plays" partly through homophonic punning, as Coltrane does in *A Love Supreme* and Pharoah Sanders does in "Hum-Allah." It plays on the Arabic, the Islamic expression, and equivalencies in English—as well as on other religions, like the concept of God's mercy, of the "ascension" in Coltrane's *Ascension* (as Jesus's ascension but also Muhammad's night journey), or the "prince of peace" in "Hum-Allah" (as both Jesus and possibly Amiri Baraka as a Muslim "prince"—an amir).

Achille Mbembe observes that "cultural history of Islam in Africa is marked less by critical exactitude than by an extraordinary power of imitation and an unparalleled talent for producing resemblances on the basis of different signs and languages," a religious identity "constructed by gathering together words that signify different things in different languages and ordering them around a central signifier that functions at once as image and mirage, parable and allegory. Because it manages to weave onomatopoeic relationships between writing and language, Islam constitutes the most perfect archive of resemblance in the history of identity formation in Africa."[30] Mbembe describes this as "a response of creative assimilation," leaving "open the question of what truly constituted an Islamic society or government." This openness was "a refusal to foreclose on new encounters," giving "ample space to the arts of healing and divination, or to the interpretation of dreams—in sum, to the resources of mysticism and the great orphic knowledge of local traditions."[31] Baraka invokes the Yoruban Olorun and Shango alongside Allah, but also Black Jesus, Black Moses, Black Egypt, Black Aesop. Rather than diluting the Islam in his poems, he underpins its transnational dimensions—and its dialogues with other religions and traditions. Rather than stopping the organ life, he plays it as an instrument, an aesthetic that plays with place, where Mecca is Mecca but is also Harlem but also Chicago. And the orientation is toward the East, toward Mecca, but also toward Songhai and Timbuctoo, Morocco and Egypt, Africa and Asia. The "Mid-East" is also a branch of the Brooklyn cultural institution "The East" in Brownsville.

BAM poets embraced a vision of African Muslim spirituality as a "star-filled Cosmos vibrating in tune with the flame in Malcolm's voice"—as Askia Muhammad Touré wrote in "The Sound of Allah's Horn"—evoking Mbembe's understanding of the cultural history of African Islam as creative assimilation and openness to "the resources of mysticism and the great orphic knowledge of local traditions."[32] "The Sound of Allah's Horn" was published in the anthology *Black Arts*, edited by Ahmed Alhamisi and Harun Kofi Wangara, who call the artists "spiritual warriors." Included in the anthology is Marvin X and Faruk's interview "Islam and Black Art," in which Baraka talks about getting "serious about Islam in terms of a spiritual philosophy" and studying "the root and history of Islam and associated philosophies" as a "spiritual key."[33] Baraka's collection *Spirit Reach* (1972) explored this period of "mystical focus" in his life through an Islamic lens.[34] Alongside poems like "The Evolver," "All in the Street," "Study Peace," and "Love is the Presence of No Enemy," his "Somebody's Slow is Another Body's Fast (Preachment)" onomatopoeically experimented with a cosmic vision of human unity connected through sonic frequencies, riffing on the oneness of Pharoah Sanders's *Tauhid*.[35]

> Can we raise ourselves. Increase the vibration. The cycle of life to constant frequency.
> All is

> none is
> constant.
> It is all vibration
> The swing of endless pendulum.
> I want we
> We as the two extremes oned.
> Atone.
> A Z one strike forever claaaaaaannnnnnng
> Clang in us
> A Z oned atone ...
> We are nation, great body, collect the fragments of the milky way, aswirl a top our heads.

The poem creates unity through the "A Z oned atone"—a tone at/one as both color and sound harmonized through the collections of fragments of the milky way into one body. The clang raises (or "races") "the cycle of life." They are "beautifuling chords of black life . . . ripples of eternal water." Baraka weaves the alphabet into these images, the A and the Z, the beee, the see, and the ooooooo, an alphabet in the same tradition as the Black Power alphabet taught by Amina at the African Free School and by Yusef Iman at the Uhuru Sasa Schule, rendered through punning and homophones. "The one, ooooooo, alll, the circle, what, see, you can we are, the bee the beee, to beee, the all, the all, oooooooo, spirit spirit spirit . . . And what is left is moving constant tremble lifes alive."[36] Baraka plays with vibration as a sound frequency—a sound that has a specific kind of tone—a tone that is also is a color and a race ("raise"). The sound/tone/frequency reverberates through time, as suggested in the swing of the pendulum (of a clock? a metronome?), but also creates a kind of unity "oned." Baraka puns on—and transforms—"owned" into "oned," turning the Black nation into a great body and a cosmic unity, collected fragments of the milky way, united by tone.

MECCAN OPENINGS

This musical poetic tradition is "rooted in Afro-diasporic expressive cultures" that "traveled on routes far beyond its origins," Su'ad Abdul Khabeer writes *Muslim Cool: Race, Religion, and Hip Hop in the United States*. To these roots and routes she adds the loop that "extends and returns, not in a closure but in a cypher . . . the loop is a metaphor for the linkages between Islam, hip-hop, and Blackness in the twenty-first century that create Muslim Cool: Islam, as practiced in US Black American communities, shaped hip-hop, which in turn shapes young twenty-first-century Black and non-Black US Muslims who return to Blackness and Islam as a way of thinking and a way of being Muslims—as Muslim Cool. Like a looped musical sample defined by sonic repetition and variation, Muslim Cool is a site of critical continuity and change."[37] The title of Sonia Sanchez's anthology *three hundred and sixty degrees of blackness comin at you* (1970) speaks of the cypher—and the metaphor of the loop—the 360° referring to "the Cipher: completion of the circle" in the Supreme Mathematics of the Five Percenters.[38] Sister Souljah's album *360 Degrees of Power* sampled Sanchez's language—and the language of the Five Percenters—in the album's title track, as she rapped about 360 degrees: "My brain is blazing strong and uprising / My mind is thinking faster than my eyes be blinking / Check out the science of me, and my chemistry / Aesthetic, altruistic, thought flow endlessly... Ancestors blessed me with the power of spirits."[39] The album and the song pay tribute to the "circularity of black aesthetic traditions," something the scholar Samy Alim riffs on and samples in his article "360 Degreez of Black Art Comin at You: Sista Sonia Sanchez and the Dimensions of a Black Arts Continuum," his own tribute to Sonia Sanchez. In Alim's interview with Sanchez, she says of the new generation of hip-hop artists: "We are an extension of each other or we are a continuation of each other. We continue the tradition and we bring an innovation to it each time, ... we've made it live. We've given this language life, a life that is unbelievable, you know; ... what it does is that it makes it breathe. It gives it life. It gives it color."[40]

Scholars like Geneva Smitherman, Samy Alim, and James Spady situate the roots of hip-hop in the jazz prosody, spoken-word performances, and jazzoetry of BAM poets, forms that had their own roots in the jazz and blues poetry of the Harlem Renaissance.[41] The Break Beat poets, who edited multiple anthologies of writings, cite BAM poets as progenitors of their spoken-word poetry. Other contemporary poets like Amir Sulaiman, Tariq Touré, Sasa Aakil, and Saadiya Bashir pay tribute to BAM poets like Amiri Baraka and Sonia Sanchez in their work. Twenty-first-century anthologies like Saleemah Abdul-Ghafur's *Living Islam Out Loud: American Muslim Women Speak* (2005); Kevin Coval, Quraysh Ali Lansana, and Nate Marshall's *The BreakBeat Poets: New American Poetry in the Age of Hip-Hop* (2015); Jamila Woods, Mahogany L. Browne, Idrissa Simmonds, and Patricia Smith's *Black Girl Magic* (2018); and Fatima Asghar and Safia Elhillo's *Halal if You Hear Me* (2019) bring together creative and artistic collectives that build on the work done in BAM anthologies by Dudley Randall, Margaret Burroughs, Amiri Baraka, Larry Neal, Ahmed Alhamisi, Harun Kofi

Wangara, John Henrik Clarke, and Addison Gayle—building what Alim calls "a deep understanding of the relationship between all of the Black Arts Movements."[42] These writers helped formalize an episteme through spiritual and intellectual collectives, creating communities of diverse voices that spoke in different media and genres and from different ideological perspectives.

The contemporary poet and hip-hop artist Amir Sulaiman draws on both "the resources of mysticism and the great orphic knowledge of local traditions" through his own experimentations with visual and audio poetry—what Sun Ra might call "tone poems" or "sound images."[43] His 2011 spoken-word album *Meccan Openings* pays tribute to the Sufi poet and theologian Muhi ad-Din Ibn al-ʿArabi, the "great shaykh of Islam" whose own *al-Futuhuat al-Makkiyya* (ca. 1240) is "a detailed symbolic map of the process of spiritual realization."[44] Sulaiman paid tribute to Ibn ʿArabi again in his 2020 visual poem *Laying Flowers, Setting Fires*, a short film about the Black Lives Matter movement as both protest and commemoration. *Laying Flowers, Setting Fires* is also a love poem, a ghazal, a gnostic form Ibn ʿArabi himself experimented with as an expression of devotion. Sulaiman's "trueandlivingmedia" refers to the film as a "poetic view into black love and the ever-present threat of violence and actual violence leveled against black people in America. It is both love poem and eulogy."[45] The film begins as a funeral, with women and girls dressed in white emerging from a coffin adorned with flowers, speaking to a resurrection or revival, but also of living ancestors. The film pays tribute (laying flowers) to those who have gone before, even while setting fires of protest.

Laying Flowers, Setting Fires charts a chain of poetic transmission, a spiritual and intellectual genealogy through the film's visual imagery of two books stacked one on top of the other in the poet's room: Claude Addas's *Quest for the Red Sulphur: The Life of Ibn ʿArabi* (1993) and Amiri Baraka's collected poems, *SOS: Poems 1961–2013*.[46] Ibn ʿArabi and Baraka are different (kinds of) ancestors in the Islamic poetic tradition, resurrected through Sulaiman's visual and poetic tribute, but also through the film's imagery of revival. Next to the books is a framed prayer written in Maghrebi script, the "prayer of the opener" recited by followers of the Tijani Sufi *tariqa* in the Maghreb and West Africa—a Sufi order whose doctrines and practices were deeply influenced by Ibn ʿArabi's mystical and theological writings. Hanging on the walls of the poet's room alongside the framed prayer are a photograph of the poet next to the Kaaba in Mecca, a prayer shawl, and a small drawing on a piece of notebook paper of a spaceship taking off into the sky. Sulaiman engages in a broad range of citational and re-citational practices, sonically and visually summoning the Islamic tradition in Black space, opening the film/poem with the Arabic letter *baa* that stands for the *basmallah*, the invocation of God's name, and Sulaiman whispering the *basmallah*. The basmallah—and the citational and recitational practices—signals Sulaiman's intention with respect to the poem, the film, and the art, ritualistically situating it in his Islamic commitments. The basmallah itself is an opening, marking a (new?) beginning, grounding the poem in an Islamic ethos. The visual and sonic dimensions of Sulaiman's poem grow out of the mixed media poetics of the BAM, reenvisioned in the digital era, formulated in the aftermath of the murder of George Floyd in May 2020, and circulated during the pandemic.

Sulaiman's 2011 album *Meccan Openings*, along with his other albums *Medinan Openings* and *The Opening* (the latter referring to *al-fatiha* or the opening of the Qur'an), are poetry collections, hip-hop albums, mystical allegories, and declarations of faith, drawing on the Sufi tradition, Islamic language, and references to the Qur'an. *Meccan Openings* opens with a Sufi *dhikr*, a ritualized "remembering" of God through "mentioning" God's ninety-nine names, reciting the Qur'an, and repeating prayers. Then we hear footsteps approaching (the listener? the poet?), greeting us with *as-salaamu alaykum wa rahamatuh* (peace and God's mercy on you all), as the listener (or the poet?) boards a (subway?) train known as the "transport." At various points of the album we hear train tracks speaking of the journey (or a poetic pilgrimage) that the "tracks" are taking us on. *Meccan Openings* was inspired while Ibn 'Arabi was on pilgrimage in 1202, traveling from al-Andalus across North Africa to Mecca. This mystical-theological treatise was written during his travels over the next twenty years, his magnum opus composed alongside other works like *Tarjuman al-Ashwaq* (the translator of desires), which uses love poetry or *ghazal* to talk about the divine—like Sulaiman in his poetry collection *Love, Gnosis, & Other Suicide Attempts* (2012).[47] Sulaiman seems to be taking us on a spiritual journey through time and space, but via a different poetic vehicle. Like Ibn 'Arabi, he uses key Arabic terms "with a polyvalence close to musical chords" in a field of intertextual references that has shifted profoundly in time and space.[48] Yet some things remain the same: the primary references to the "opening" of the Qur'an; the "Meccan openings" of the early community's jihad against persecution in Mecca; and Mecca as spiritual center, pilgrimage site, and direction of prayer. Sulaiman's *dhikr*, his remembering or mentioning of Mecca, the Qur'an, and Ibn 'Arabi, serves as its own conduit or vehicle of transport across time and space.

In the introduction to Ibn 'Arabi's *Meccan Openings*, James W. Morris writes that Ibn 'Arabi uses terminology from the Islamic scriptural tradition in ways "unfamiliar, and sometimes intentionally provocative, even to his original readers." Ibn 'Arabi plays with "often very different meanings and registers of key Arabic terms (especially from the Qur'an), which in his writings are normally close in their polyvalence to musical chords." Morris talks about the "allusive cross-references to other writings," as a "textual and referential poly-vocality so difficult to translate."[49] The phrase *futuhat makkiyya* itself has multiple meanings, referring first to the early Muslim community's reconquest of Mecca after the hijra or migration to Madina in 622. It also has spiritual connotations of revelations rooted in Mecca as the spiritual epicenter of the Muslim community. The "openings" also have erotic overtones implicit in ghazal poetry, where the divine becomes an object of desire that the poet accesses through the path of love. This is a hallmark of Ibn 'Arabi's poetry in particular, and of Sufi mystical poetry in general, but also of the Arabic and Islamic poetic tradition. In the *nasib*, the erotic opening of the qasida, the poet returns to his abandoned land (the campsite); reflects over the traces of what has been lost (the beloved); recreates his poetic vision via fragments of memory that fade in the distance; and embarks on a new poetic journey, abandoning the old, setting out to make a new life. These ritualistic contours of pre-Islamic poetry would inform both (more secular and profane) Arabic poetics and (more religious and devotional) Islamic poetics over centuries, becoming a frame for innovation and invention within the structure of ancient poetic conventions. *Meccan Openings*—like Sulaiman's other poetic, visual, and sonic work—ruminates on the traces of these older Islamic poetic forms, but innovates on them and reinvents them, making them real and relevant for a journey through a different land. This poetics of innovation also reflects on questions of tradition and change in the Islamic community, as Arabic literary criticism has through time.

Sulaiman's *Love, Gnosis* reads like a Sufi ghazal that merges eros with union with the divine—where the overt erotic meaning (*al-zahir*) contains inner spiritual meanings. The poem "isra: yusra" draws on Qur'an verse 94:5 beginning with these erotic lines: "her mouth could martyr me / between her parted lips is / a house of God." The poem's other references—to pasture, parish, and eyelashes—suggest the imagery of Ibn 'Arabi's most famous poem, where the divine is found in a women's gaze but also under the "skirts" (*kiswa*) of the Kaaba.[50] The collection speaks of other influences with epigraphs quoting the Sufi poet Farid al-Din Attar and his own collection of ghazal poetry, as well as (the mystical, ecstatic) Walt Whitman. Sulaiman brings his own polyvocality to this poetry, even as he grounds the work in his Islamic commitments. "My investment," Sulaiman says, "is in this Ummah and in the cause of the human being everywhere."[51]

While Ibn 'Arabi interpreted and reinterpreted core Islamic precepts and terminology in startling new ways, so Sulaiman uses religious language and theological-mystical frameworks for his poetry, music, and film, also in startlingly original ways. Although he addresses audiences of vastly different historical, literary, and linguistic contexts, he connects them via a shared vocabulary as well as a shared set of textual referents and ritual practices. In an interview with Yahsmin Mayaan Binti Bobo, Sulaiman says, "Some of my influences are from the Black Arts Movement of the Sixties and Seventies. People like Amina Baraka and Sonia Sanchez certainly influenced my craft. However, Hip Hop lyricism was more influential . . . even more than Hip Hop the language of the Qur'an, even in translation, colored my speech and gave me the high concepts with plain language."[52]

Sulaiman's references to Mecca embed his work in both the Islamic and the African American literary and poetic traditions, with echoes of "Harlem: Mecca of the New Negro" and of Gwendolyn Brooks's *In the Mecca* (1968). *In the Mecca* famously marked Brooks's radicalization in the 1960s and includes one poem about Malcolm X's assassination and another dedicated to Ron Karenga. *In the Mecca* is dedicated to Langston Hughes, James Baldwin, LeRoi Jones, and the educator Mike Alexandroff—like Sulaiman himself pays tribute to Baraka and Baldwin in *Laying Flowers, Setting Fires*. Brooks and Baraka participated in key writers' conferences together: the University of California at Berkeley Extension Program in Asilomar State Park in August 1964 and the Second Fisk Writers Conference in 1966, both forming the basis of the anthology *For Malcolm* (1967). Brooks's reference to the Mecca Flats in her own poetry evokes other historical layers—the Mecca Flats, an apartment complex designed to foster a new form of urban living, housed visitors to the 1893 World's Fair in Chicago, with an exhibition that featured a mosque, imams, and the call to prayer on "Cairo Street." It was also at the fair where "African Americans formed their own version of the Shriners" calling their organization "the Ancient Egyptian Arabic Order of Nobles of the Shrine" and using Islamic, Arabic, and Orientalist imagery that the Moorish Science Temple later drew on.[53] The Mecca Flats later became a site of resistance against the destruction of Black space in the 1950s, when residents protested its demolition by the Illinois Institute of Technology to build its College of Architecture.[54]

Sulaiman's work performs a poetics of citation and re-citation characteristic of BAM poetry that interprets and reinterprets earlier poetic and musical forms. He draws on the Qur'an, Ibn 'Arabi, Attar, Baraka, Sonia Sanchez, and hip-hop, charting an Islamic poetics that transcends doctrinal, racial, historical, geographical, linguistic, and cultural differences. It is a militant kind of plurality that emphasizes common humanity, but also a common Islam across the racial geographies of East, West, Asia, and Africa. In *Laying Flowers, Setting Fires* Sulaiman references Baraka and Ibn 'Arabi and samples Malcolm X, Dave Chappelle, James Baldwin, Toni Morrison, and Martin Luther King Jr.—tying common threads or cords/chords between these creatives. The video artist and cinematographer Arthur Jafa, who worked on John Akomfrah's *Seven Songs for Malcolm* and Julie Dash's *Daughters of the Dust*, coined a term that he calls "polyventiality," meaning "multiple tones, multiple rhythms, multiple perspectives, multiple meanings, multiplicity," a word that resonates with Morris's understanding of a polyvalence close to musical chords.[55]

This process of citation and re-citation performs tribute to those who have gone before but also becomes a means of archiving and reviving. Re-citations and rerecordings make it possible to surpass the problem of the fragment and the trace, healing fractured histories through genealogies reimagined and reconstructed, as forms of critical fabulation rooted rhizomically in the Muslim, African, and African American cultural and aesthetic traditions. In her own practice of critical fabulation, Saidiya Hartman rerecords the historical record in her rewriting of traces of the Black past—creating new records—in ways that have become emblematic of twenty-first century post-Black Black aesthetics as in the work of artists like Kehinde Wiley and Awol Erizku. In her book *The Muse Is the Music*, Meta DuEwa Jones writes about how poets and musicians "renovate tradition's rituals of recital as powerful sites of alterability; . . . poets read, revise, and recite works by their artistic ancestors in order to maintain connections to the past while taking pleasure in their returns to and revisions of historical memory."[56] Jones emphasizes the ritualistic dimensions of these performances, deploying "a riff on *records of recital* and *rituals of recital* to harness the distinct yet interrelated aspects of performance, and its archival practices, that the words *record*, *ritual*, and *recital* denote within this idiom. . . . These artists' vocal instrumentality, their performative methods of recital, crucially affects how their poems work formally and visually, both individually and as collaborative performances." Jones's attention to the visual and aural contours of these performances suggest what Michael Sells refers to as "sound vision" in his own analysis of ritualistic recitation of the Qur'an, the importance of vocal instrumentality, the Qur'an's own lyricism, and the scriptural evocation of that vision in the Islamic art of Qur'an manuscripts. Jones writes about how adaptations translate the "audible moment of performance into a legible trace in the revision, 'looking at it again.' "[57] Sulaiman's art—and the art of new Muslim poets, visual artists, and musicians—look again and again at the Islamic tradition, interpreting and reinterpreting it, revitalizing its traces in African American culture, and piecing together those fragments as a total way of life. This living Islam survives and thrives despite a Eurocentric secular Western world still fundamentally hostile to expressions of Islamic spirituality, however central Islam has been to the construction of the Western world.

Sulaiman's *Meccan Openings* is both album and spoken-word poetry, performing its own kind of polyvocality as a tone poem or a sound image. *Meccan*

Openings also pays tribute to the Islamic mystical tradition and its poetry, rewritten, reinterpreted, and revived in another time and place. Like Ibn 'Arabi, Sulaiman draws on key Arabic terms in the Islamic tradition that assume different registers in the context of African American spoken-word poetry rapped on an album to music. He taps into the Islamic substratum of African American cultural life that manifests in conscious and unconscious ways. He also creates "new beginnings" that destabilize linear genealogies, even as he traces his poetics to Baraka, Ibn 'Arabi, and the early Muslim community.[58]

In *Meccan Openings*, Sulaiman deploys—in the poetic modus operandi of the great shaykh of Islam Ibn 'Arabi—"allusive cross-references" to other kinds of Islamic writings in ways "unfamiliar and sometimes intentionally provocative."[59] He does so by situating varieties of the African American Islamic tradition directly in the Islamic tradition and vice versa. Midway through the album, in the section "Where Should I Begin," the train "track" drops us off at Terminal 9, suggesting another kind of mystical territory. In the *Supreme Mathematics* of the Five Percenters, no. 9 is "being Born: to bring into existence a mental birth of self."[60] The next track opens with the *Allahu akbar* of the call to prayer and Sulaiman juxtaposes NOI rhetoric about devils with Qur'anic language from Sura 114 about the whisperings of the devil (*wiswas al-khinas*). This work grows out of several religious, poetic, literary, and spiritual traditions, but it is also clearly, legibly Islamic, with the Islamic greeting *as-salaamu alaykum*, call to prayer, *Allahu akbar*, *basmallah*, and references to Mecca, jihad, *al-fatiha*, and Qur'an. Yet Sulaiman weaves together complex metatextual references to the African American literary tradition, spoken word poetry, and hip hop in ways that both renew and reinterpret the Islamic poetic tradition in the face of a history of white racial terror that suppressed indigenous forms of African religion, language, culture, and identity.[61] Like BAM poets (Baraka, Sanchez, Touré, Marvin X, and Rahman), Sulaiman navigates between Sunni, Sufi, and African American Islam, returning, reviving, rereading, revising, and renovating works by artistic ancestors "in order to maintain connections to the past."[62] There is a celebratory revivification—or resurrection—for the living present and imagined Afro-future of this work. Sulaiman's train gestures toward steampunk and esoteric underground railroads that are both poetic pilgrimages and journeys into a different kind of future.

The vitality of this world is visually depicted in *Laying Flowers, Setting Fires*. A woman dressed all in white walks through a thick forest, reaching a clearing with a coffin richly garlanded in the middle of what should be a scene of grief. Women and girls young and old, one by one, rise up out of the coffin, broad smiles on their faces. This revival is clearly a ritual—the women dressed all in white—like a Muslim funeral or Santería rites. Sulaiman seems also to be referencing slave rebellions through artistic representations like the gathering in the Bois Caiman at the start of the Haitian revolution in 1791. The "Black religious roots" of the "New Black Music" are "as old as Black religious gatherings in the forests of the West" and summoned through forms "signifying and rhythm pounding," Baraka writes in "The Changing Same."[63] Sulaiman's gathering in the forest clearly shows a celebration with the women dancing and gazing serenely at the camera. The film samples a 1977 interview with Toni Morrison, as Sulaiman lays flowers at the feet of other ancestors, drawing on sonic fragments from the more recent past. In the PBS Chicago interview, Morrison talks about music and literature as a form of bearing witness and about Black art as a kind of alchemy turning the dross of existence into love. "The truth lies in our myths, in our songs, that's what the seeds are," Morrison says. "It's not possible to constantly home in on the crisis. You have to have the love and you have to have the magic. That's also life.... I regard my responsibilities as a Black writer as someone who must bear witness. Someone who must record the way it used to be."[64]

THE CALL

The call to prayer provides a key point of reference for the audiovisual landscapes of the BAM and its creative descendants, like the call in Sulaiman's *Meccan Openings*; Askia Muhammad Touré's poem "The Call (A Solo from the West)" in *Songhai!*; the artist Abdul Rahman's illustrations of a muezzin performing the call to prayer (accompanying Touré's "The Call"); and the call to prayer opening Amiri Baraka's documentary film *The New-Ark*. These sonic, visual, and poetic renditions of the call, alongside other literary and cinematic representations, draw on longer histories of Muslim ritual practice of prayer in the Americas that the BAM reclaimed and resurrected. Alex Haley's *Roots* (1976) opens with Kunta Kinte's birth just before the dawn call to prayer, and Julie Dash's *Daughters of the Dust* (1991) begins with Bilali Muhammad, hands lifted in prayer, reciting the call to prayer at dawn on the St. Simons Island, off the coast of Georgia. The character and the scene refer to Bilali Muhammad (ca. 1770s–1859) of the nearby Sapelo Island, an enslaved Muslim who transcribed what is thought to be a fragment of Ibn Abi Zayd al-Qayrawani's jurisprudence text *al-Risala* (ca. 945). *Al-Risala* focuses on ablutions (*wudu'*), the call to prayer (*adhan*), and prayer (*salat*), a kind of instruction manual of how to perform ritual prayer in the hostile context of the antebellum South.[65] *Daughters of the Dust* shows the character

Bilali washing in the water, performing ablutions, and praying, with the pages of a text written in Arabic (the Qur'an? *Al-Risala*?) before him, channeling the visual image of Bilali Muhammad as ancestor as well as the sonic dimensions of the call to prayer.[66] These representations of the legacy of Bilali Muhammad, but also of the first muezzin Bilal (late sixth century) suggested by the name, is a way of calling to all those who do not know or hear the message, an invitation to join a

FIGURE 9.1 Abdul Rahman's illustration of the call to prayer opposite Askia Muhammad Touré's poem "The Call," from *Songhai!*.

Sultanah Rahman

community that Dash portrays in the film, Abdul Rahman in his visual art, Touré in his poetry, Baraka in his documentary, Haley in his novel, and Sulaiman in his music. As Hanif Abdurraqib writes, "The call to prayer is one of the sweetest songs that can hang in the air."[67]

This art draws on the sonic dimensions of the call to prayer, but Dash's film invokes the ritual and scriptural aspects of Islamic practice in the Americas through her visual representation of the prayer, the dawn, and the water—implicitly the direction of Mecca. Baraka juxtaposes the call to prayer emanating out of Spirit House with footage of actors practicing the lines to his play *A Black Mass* in front of Spirit House—juxtaposing two very different Islamic traditions. Touré opens *Songhai!* with an image of a muezzin. The video artist and cinematographer Arthur Jafa, who worked on *Daughters of the Dust*, said that he strives to make "Black images vibrate in accordance with certain frequential values that exist in Black music"—not just Aretha Franklin's lyrics "*but how she sang them*" and not just John Coltrane's sequence of notes, "*but the tone itself*."[68] He wants his films' visual imagery to find a way to carry "the weight of the sheer tonality in Black song."[69] He said these words at the "Black Popular Culture" conference organized by Michele Wallace at the Studio Museum in Harlem—just after *Daughters of the Dust* premiered in 1991. These visual and auditory representations "vibrate in accordance with certain frequential values that exist" in the call to prayer, visual imagery that carries its "sheer tonality," tones that were also coded into field hollers, yodels, and the blues, as Sylviane Diouf argues in "What Islam Gave the Blues."[70]

Ayanna Sharif's own short film *WUDU* (2019) shows a Black woman wearing a headscarf walking serenely at peace through the woods, a scene evoked almost identically in *Laying Flowers, Setting Fires*. Sharif shows the woman performing ablutions (*wudu'*) in a stream and performing the prayer. There is no call to prayer, however, but instead, Nina Simone singing "Blackbird" (1963), a song that Simone described as having "a Black trance mood that set the spirit for this tune."[71] This is Jafa's "idea of Black visual intonation," but through the call to prayer; a sonic frequency ritualistically connecting the Muslim community through time and space. In *A Black Gaze*, Tina Campt interprets Jafa's "idea of Black visual intonation" as a vibration or an oscillation—"an unstable temporality which produces complex forms of repetition that, rather than reproducing or replicating what came before it, creates new beginnings instead." These "cycles of return ... create new formations and new points of departure."[72] Alexander Weheliye builds on Campt's argument in *Feenin* (2023), writing about the "oscillation of different historical frequencies" in these sonic vibrations like the swinging pendulum and clanging tone of Baraka's "Preachment," the "ancestor faces form on the film of our brains" in Larry Neal's "Narrative of the Black Magicians" ("form your face with searing waves of sound"), or Sonia Sanchez asking if you can "hearrrRRRR" and "seeeEEE" the "black muslim/insurrection."[73] These poetic interventions fashion new aesthetic formations in Islam, but also new spiritual ones, renovating, renewing, and reviving religious practice and ritual worship. Coming full circle, it creates a "revolution in values," as King commented in a 1967 interview on Black Power sampled in Sulaiman's *Laying Flowers, Setting Fires*.[74]

The poet Tariq Touré performs his own interpretation in "The Call," his own "tone poem" or "sound image" that is also a short film. Although not related by blood to Askia Touré, his poem echoes Askia Touré's earlier poem "The Call," but reinterpreted in the aftermath of the killing of George Floyd, during the Black Lives Matter protests, and in the midst of the pandemic—like *Laying Flower, Setting Fires*. Touré recites the poem almost as a form of prayer as the call to prayer is recited over the poem and the camera shows the poet praying in a mosque next to the minbar, Allah written in green neon. The poem invokes Bilal, the first muezzin, the first caller to prayer, drawing a kind of genealogical line back to the early Muslim community and specifically, this early (earliest?) Muslim from the African diaspora: "The Prophet could have chose any of those to plant the seed / But the son of the enslaved rose to mention He / until the end of time in Holy Symphony." The film cuts to a scene of the poet wading into the water, suggesting religious ritual (and baptism), facing East toward Mecca for the prayer, return, and also the Middle Passage.[75]

Daughters of the Dust closes with a scene of the matriarch Nana: she sews up a talisman and ties it to a Qur'an. Inside the talisman, she places a lock of her own hair alongside a lock of her mother's hair, reconnecting herself to her enslaved mother who was sold away when Nana was a child. The spiritual, familial, and historical genealogy is tied to (and through?) the Qur'an, a tie (a cord/chord?) connecting them through time and space. "There must be a bond, a connection," Nana says, "Between those who are here and those who are across the sea. A connection. We are as two people in one body. Us that are old and the first of the new.... We must survive." But this cord/chord also creates something new, a film that resonates with sonic frequencies reconfigured for newer generations and changing contexts of both creativity and Black struggle. In the film, Nana is played by Vertamae Grosvenor—author of *Vibration Cooking, Or, the Travel Notes of a Geechee Girl* (1970), which blazed its way into the BAM and Black feminist cultural consciousness in the

1970s—and one of the literary mothers of the movements. The vibrations in *Vibration Cooking* are not just sonic and visual, but are food that feeds the spirit: "It don't matter if it's Dakar or Savannah, . . . Just turn on the imagination, be willing to change your style and let a little soul food in, . . . good food and good vibrations."⁷⁶

Under brutal conditions that oppressed overt signs of Islam during slavery and in its aftermath, Muslims found alternative ways to express forms of Islamic allegiances, engaging in a process of renewal (*tajdid*) and reinterpretation of the Islamic tradition and creating new kinds of Islamic identities in the process. The BAM helped envision the revival of Islam not just for Black nationalism, but also for a creative ethos striving to reimagine new forms of belonging, citizenship, and being—rooted in Afro-Asian epistemologies, ontologies, and theologies that were also American. These artists, poets, writers, and musicians revived Islamic words, language, and expressions; Muslim practices; and cultural signifiers of Islam for the BAM. They also created new forms of Islamic art and poetry in the West—ones that coded calls for racial justice into their very fabric—calls for racial justice that were then read back into the very foundations of the Islamic community, through processes of interpretation and reinterpretations within the format of this new Islamic art.

In a public conversation, part of a six-year project on Muslim American music and poetry sponsored by the Doris Duke Foundation for Islamic Art Building Bridges program, the singer, songwriter, musician, and actor Maimouna Youssef talked about the relationship between her art and being Muslim. Youssef, who grew up Muslim, is also part Choctaw and honed her craft chanting in the pow-wows. "I stand at that crossroads," she said, "I speak for all of those people who were unspoken for. The way you express your connection with your God, your language, your community, is through your tongue." A sweat lodge is a womb like space, she says, "to go in and rebirth yourself," something she likens to the *masjid*, the mosque, as another kind of space of rebirth. Youssef talked about the "power in the *fajr*," the dawn, the time of the first prayer of the day. Elijah Muhammad talked about this kind of rebirth or resurrection, she said, "specific to the needs of Black Americans, reclaiming a culture that wasn't given to us through slavery." (Re)claiming Islam was "decolonization." "Rebirth yourself brand new, as spiritual beings," she urged the audience of community members, "Go tell it on the mountain." Youssef referred to her singing as "raising the vibration on the planet and healing all of God's creatures." Singers have not been "allowed to be thinkers," but if you sing in a "tonal way," she says, "you're going to find the truth everywhere. The truth the way it feels, that vibration, that is God. Don't let them muddy your vibration," she says, "focus on the connectedness." It's "just doing God's work."[77]

NOTES

PRELUDE: الإطلال (AL-ATLAL)

1. Alexander G. Weheliye, "Black Studies and Black Life," *The Black Scholar: Journal of Black Studies and Research* 44, no. 2 (2014): 5–10; "[and Muslim]" is my insertion.
2. Meta DuEwa Jones, *The Muse Is Music: Jazz Poetry from the Harlem Renaissance to Spoken Word* (University of Illinois Press, 2013), 7, 19, 21.
3. Tina M. Campt, *A Black Gaze: Artists Changing How We See* (MIT Press, 2021), 81.
4. Sylviane A. Diouf, *Servants of Allah: African Muslims Enslaved in the Americas* (New York University Press, 1998), 251.
5. Aldon Lynn Nielsen, *Black Chant: Languages of African-American Postmodernism* (Cambridge University Press, 1997), 37.
6. John Akomfrah, dir., *The Last Angel of History* (Icarus, 1996).
7. Diouf, *Servants of Allah*, 56, 71.
8. James C. Scott, *Domination and the Arts of Resistance: Hidden Transcripts* (Yale University Press, 1990); Harryette Mullen, "African Signs and Spirit Writing," in *The Black Studies Reader*, ed. Jacqueline Bobo et al. (Routledge, 2004); Michael A. Gomez, *Black Crescent: The Experience and Legacy of African Muslims in the Americas* (Cambridge University Press, 2005), 200; Robert Farris Thompson, *Flash of the Spirit: African & Afro-American Art & Philosophy* (Random House, 1983); Laura Marks, "Monad, Database, Remix: Manners of Unfolding in *The Last Angel of History*," *Black Camera* 6, no. 2 (2015): 114; Margo Natalie Crawford, *Black Post-Blackness: The Black Arts Movement and Twenty-First-Century Aesthetics* (University of Illinois Press, 2017), 17; Frédéric Neyrat, "The Black Angel of History: Afrofuturism's Cosmic Techniques," *Angelaki: Journal of the Theoretical Humanities* 25, no. 4 (2020): 125; Mark Anthony Neal, *Black Ephemera: The Crisis and Challenge of the Musical Archive* (New York University Press, 2022), 151, 158.
9. Manning Marable and Hishaam D. Aidi, "Introduction," in *Black Routes to Islam* (Palgrave, 2009), 4.
10. Peter Lamborn Wilson, *Sacred Drift: Essays on the Margins of Islam* (City Lights Books, 1993), 22.
11. Stephen C. Finley, Margarita Simon Guillory, and Hugh Page Jr., "Introduction: Africana Esoteric Studies: Mapping a New Endeavor," in *Esotericism in African American Religious Experience: "There Is a Mystery . . .*", ed. Stephen, Finley, Margarita Simon Guillory, and Hugh Page Jr. (Brill,

2015), 13; R. A. Judy, *Sentient Flesh: Thinking in Disorder, Poiesis in Black* (Duke University Press, 2020), 266.

12. Jaroslav Stetkevych, *Zephyrs of Najd: Poetics of Nostalgia in the Classical Arabic Nasib* (University of Chicago Press, 1993); Lorenzo Thomas, "Askia Muhammad Touré: Crying Out the Goodness," *Obsidian* 1, no. 1 (1975): 36, 39; David Grundy, "Songs for the Future: Askia Touré's Songhai!," *Paideuma: Modern and Contemporary Poetry and Poetics* 48 (2022): 10. Both Thomas and Grundy situate Touré's poetry in "the tradition of Islamic verse, as well as the Afro-American folk tradition . . . in the manner of the great Islamic poets of the Arabic language," as Thomas observes.

13. James W. Morris, "Spiritual Imagination and the 'Liminal' World: Ibn 'Arabi on the Barzakh," *Postdata* 15, no. 2 (1995): 42–49.

14. Lorenzo Thomas, *Don't Deny My Name: Words and Music and the Black Intellectual Tradition* (University of Michigan Press, 2008), 116; Solayman Idris, *Star Logic (a Collection of Poiesis)* (Lumifont, 2020), 116. Also see the other works in Idris's "Times of the Signs" Trilogy: Solayman Idris, *Dusk Orientalis: ex Chrysalis* (Lumifont, 2020); and Solayman Idris, *The Sunrise in the West: On Amer-African Statecraft* (Lumifont, 2020).

15. Soyica Diggs Colbert, Douglas A. Jones Jr., and Shane Vogel, "Introduction: Tidying Up after Repetition," in *Race and Performance after Repetition*, ed. Soyica Diggs Colbert et al. (Duke University Press, 2020), 8.

16. Diouf, *Servants of Allah*, 251; Sherman A. Jackson, *Islam and the Blackamerican: Looking Toward the Third Resurrection* (Oxford University Press, 2005), 40; Marable and Aidi, "Introduction," 4.

17. Angela Davis, "Meditations on the Legacy of Malcolm X," in *Malcolm X: In Our Own Image*, ed. Joe Wood (St. Martin's Press, 1992), 44.

18. Amiri Baraka and Larry Neal, eds., *Black Fire: An Anthology of Afro-American Writing* (Black Classic Press, 2013), xvii.

19. Julius Lester, "The Singing Is Over: The Angry Children of Malcolm X," *Sing Out!* [magazine], October/November 1966, 120; Mark Whitaker, *The Afterlife of Malcolm X: An Outcast Turned Icon's Enduring Impact on America* (Simon & Schuster, 2025), 168.

20. Sofia Samatar, "Toward a Planetary History of Afrofuturism," *Research in African Literatures* 48, no. 4 (2017): 177; Jacob S. Dorman, *The Princess and the Prophet: The Secret History of Magic, Race, and Moorish Muslims in America* (Beacon Press, 2020), 6, 8. Dorman calls this process of reinvention and reinterpretation "polycultural bricolage."

21. Elijah Muhammad, *Message to the Blackman in America* (Secretarius Memps Publications, 1965), 215; Noble Drew Ali, "The Divine Origin of the Asiatic Nations," chap. 45 in *The Holy Koran of the Moorish Science Temple of America* (1927). The Circle 7 Koran, for example, calls the "Asiatic nations": "The Moorish, who were ancient Moabites, and the founders of the Holy City of Mecca. The Egyptians who were the Hamathites, and a direct descendant of Mizraim, the Arabians, the seed of Hagar, Japanese and Chinese. The Hindoos of India, the descendants of the ancient Canaanites, Hittites, and Moabites of the land of Canaan. The Asiatic nations of North, South, and Central America: the Moorish Americans and Mexicans of North America, Brazilians, Argentinians and Chileans in South America. Colombians, Nicaraguans, and the natives of San Salvador in Central America, etc. All of these are Moslems. The Turks are the true descendants of Hagar."

22. Stephen Finley, *In and Out of This World: Material and Extraterrestrial Bodies in the Nation of Islam* (Duke University Press, 2022), 2.

23. Weheliye, "Black Studies and Black Life," 5. Su'ad Abdul Khabeer similarly argues that Muslims are not "outsiders who navigate assimilation but rather actors whose lives and experiences are critical to the production and reproduction of the contemporary United States and the 'West' more broadly." Su'ad Abdul Khabeer, *Muslim Cool: Race, Religion, and Hip Hop in the United States* (New York University Press, 2016), 9.

24. Edward E. Curtis IV, *The Call of Bilal: Islam in the African Diaspora* (University of North Carolina Press, 2014); Rudolph T. Ware III, *The Walking Qur'an: Islamic Education, Embodied*

Knowledge, and History in West Africa (University of North Carolina Press, 2014); Mustafa Briggs, *Beyond Bilal: Black History in Islam* (Mustafa Briggs & Co. Publishing, 2022).

25. David Morgan, "Religion and Media: A Critical Review of Recent Developments," *Critical Research on Religion* 1, no. 3 (2013): 347–48.
26. Charles Hirschkind and Brian Larkin, "Media and the Political Forms of Religion," *Social Text* 26, no. 3 (2008): 2.
27. Crawford, *Black Post-Blackness*, 82.
28. Sun Ra, "Preparation for Outer Space," in *Jazz By Sun Ra* (Transition, 1957); Sun Ra and his Arkestra, *Jazz in Silhouette*, El Saturn, 1959; Sun Ra, *Immeasurable Equation* (Ihnfinity Inc. / Saturn Research, 1972), 7, 11, 70.
29. John F. Szwed, *Space Is the Place: The Lives and Times of Sun Ra* (Pantheon, 1997), 105–06; Graham Lock, *Blutopia: Visions of the Future and Revisions of the Past in the Work of Sun Ra, Duke Ellington, and Anthony Braxton* (Duke University Press, 1999), 47; John Corbett, *The Wisdom of Sun-Ra: Sun Ra's Polemical Broadsheets and Streetcorner Leaflets* (WhiteWalls, 2006), 5; Brent Hayes Edwards, *Epistrophies: Jazz and the Literary Imagination* (Harvard University Press, 2017), 140; William Sites, *Sun Ra's Chicago* (University of Chicago Press, 2020), 101.
30. Michael Sells, *Approaching the Qur'an: The Early Revelations* (White Cloud Press, 1999), 31.
31. Rey Chow, *Not Like a Native Speaker: On Languaging as a Postcolonial Experience* (Columbia University Press, 2014), 8.
32. W. E. B. Du Bois, *The Souls of Black Folk* (A. C. McClurg & Co., 1903).
33. Su'ad Abdul Khabeer, "Africa as Tradition in U.S. African American Muslim Identity," *Journal of Africana Religions* 5, no. 1 (2017): 39.
34. Talal Asad, *Genealogies of Religion: Discipline and Reasons of Power in Christianity and Islam* (Johns Hopkins University Press, 1993); Shahab Ahmed, *What Is Islam?: The Importance of Being Islamic* (Princeton University Press, 2016). I particularly draw on chapter 2, "Islam as Law, islams-not-Islam, Islamic and Isalmicate, Religion and Culture, Culture and Civilization," and chapter 4, "Culture, Meaning, Symbol System, Core and Nucleus, Whatever-Muslims-Say-It-Is, Discursive Tradition, Orthodoxy, Process."
35. John R. Bowen, *Muslims Through Discourse: Religion and Ritual in Gayo Society* (Princeton University Press, 1993), 8; Ahmed, *What Is Islam?*, 248–49.
36. Julian Mayfield, "Into the Mainstream and Oblivion," in *The American Negro Writer and His Roots: Selected Papers*, ed. John Aubrey Davis Sr., First Conference of Negro Writers 1959 (American Society of African Culture, 1960), 32; Amiri Baraka [LeRoi Jones], "The Changing Same (R&B and New Black Music)," in *Black Music* (William Morrow, 1967), 209.
37. Michelle D. Commander, *Afro-Atlantic Flight: Speculative Returns and the Black Fantastic* (Duke University Press, 2017), 26, 38; Michael Lieb, *Children of Ezekiel: Aliens, UFOs, the Crisis of Race, and the Advent of the End of Time* (Duke University Press, 1998), 155–57; Stephen Finley, "The Meaning of 'Mother' in Louis Farrakhan's 'Mother Wheel:' Race, Gender, and Sexuality in the Cosmology of the Nation of Islam's UFO," *Journal of the American Academy of Religion* 80, no. 2 (2012): 434–65. NOI theology about the Mother Plane function much like the fantastic flights that Commander discusses in her book, a redemptive transport to another world.
38. Saidiya Hartman, "Venus in Two Acts," *Small Axe: A Journal of Criticism* 12, no. 2 (2008): 11; Alexander G. Weheliye, *Feenin: R&B Music and the Materiality of BlackFem Voices and Technology* (Duke University Press, 2023), 7.
39. Weheliye, *Feenin*, 7; Hartman, "Venus in Two Acts"; Tavia Nyong'o, "Unburdening Representation," *The Black Scholar: Journal of Black Studies and Research* 44, no. 2 (2014): 70–80; Tavia Nyong'o, *Afro-Fabulations: The Queer Drama of Black Life* (New York University Press, 2019), 169; Jackson, *Islam and the Blackamerican*, 99–128. Sherman Jackson's chapter on "Black Orientalism" critiques Blackamerican understanding of the Muslim world as "a precursor and the imitator of the West in the latter's history of anti-blackness. . . . The Muslim world is rendered not only the

source of anti-black racism but of the most toxic reaction to this" (100). This "Black Orientalism," Jackson argues, portrays Blackamerican Muslims as cultural and racial apostates.

40. Crawford, *Black Post-Blackness*, 1; Campt, *A Black Gaze*, 78, 79, 81.
41. Lynn Swartz Dodd and Ran Boytner, "Filtering the Past: Archaeology, Politics, and Change," in *Controlling the Past, Owning the Future: The Political Uses of Archaeology in the Middle East* (University of Arizona Press, 2010), 3.
42. Alexander G. Weheliye, *Habeas Viscus: Racializing Assemblages, Biopolitics, and Black Feminist Theories of the Human* (Duke University Press, 2014), 111; Nyong'o, *Afro-Fabulations*, 168, 174.
43. Weheliye, *Habeas Viscus*, 18; Nyong'o, *Afro-Fabulations*, 169, 180. Emphasis in the original.
44. Geneva Smitherman, "Malcolm X: Master of Signifyin'," in *Malcolm X's Michigan Worldview: An Exemplar for Contemporary Black Studies*, ed. Rita Kiki Edozie and Curtis Stokes (Michigan State University Press, 2015).
45. Graeme Abernethy, *The Iconography of Malcolm X* (University of Kansas Press, 2013); Joseph McLaren, "Malcolm-Esque: A Black Arts Literary Genre," in *Malcolm X's Michigan Worldview: An Exemplar for Contemporary Black Studies*, ed. Rita Kiki Edozie and Curtis Stokes (Michigan State University Press, 2015).
46. Abdul Khabeer, "Africa as Tradition," 39.
47. Dudley Randall and Margaret G. Burroughs, eds., *For Malcolm: Poems on the Life and the Death of Malcolm X* (Broadside Press, 1967); John Henrik Clarke, ed., *Malcolm X: The Man and His Times* (Macmillan, 1970); James Smethurst, "Malcolm X and the Black Arts Movement," in *Cambridge Companion to Malcolm X*, ed. Robert E. Terrill (Cambridge University Press, 2010); Patrick D. Bowen, *A History of Conversion to Islam in the United States, Volume 2: The African American Islamic Renaissance, 1920–1975* (Brill, 2017), 559–63. On the "Malcolm poem," see Howard Rambsy, *The Black Arts Enterprise and the Production of African American Poetry* (University of Michigan Press, 2011), 101–24; on the "Coltrane poem," see Jones, *The Muse is Music*, 85–128.
48. Agadem Lumumba Diara, *Islam and Pan-Africanism* (Agascha Productions, 1973); Bowen, *African American Islamic Renaissance*, 563–64.
49. Jackson, *Islam and the Blackamerican*, 47–48. In his groundbreaking work *Islam and the Blackamerican*, Sherman Jackson writes about how these writers connected Islam "with the masses of Blackamericans via the creation of a long-sought alternative modality of American blackness" and in the process, "Blackamerican popular culture was profoundly reshaped."
50. Woodie King Jr., dir., *Death of a Prophet: The Last Day of Malcolm X*, movie, 1981; Spike Lee, dir., *Malcolm X* (Warner Brothers, 1992); John Akomfrah, dir., *Seven Songs for Malcolm X* (Black Audio Film Collective, 1993); Orlando Bagwell, dir., *Malcolm X: Make It Plain* (PBS, 1994); James H. Cone, *Martin & Malcolm & America: A Dream or a Nightmare* (Orbis Books, 1991); Clayborne Carson, *Malcolm X: The FBI File* (Caroll & Graf, 1991); Joe Wood, ed., *Malcolm X: In Our Own Image* (St. Martin's Press, 1992); Karl Evanzz, *The Judas Factor: The Plot to Kill Malcolm X* (Thunder's Mouth Press, 1992); James Gwynne and Amiri Baraka, eds., *Malcolm X: Justice Seeker* (Steppingstones Press, 1993); Heshaam Jaaber, *I Buried Malcolm (Haj Malik El-Shabazz): The Final Chapter...* (New Mind Productions, 1993); Michael Eric Dyson, *Making Malcolm: The Myth and Meaning of Malcolm X* (Oxford University Press, 1996).
51. Recitation: Jones, *The Muse Is Music*, 19, 21; reclamation: Samatar, "Toward a Planetary History of Afrofuturism," 177; reinterpretation, renovation, restoration: Colbert et al., "Tidying Up after Repetition," 8.
52. Larry Neal, "The Black Arts Movement," *The Drama Review: TDR* 12, no. 4 (1968): 30.
53. Joseph D. Eure and James G. Spady, eds., "Defiant Giants," in *Nation Conscious Rap* (PC International Press and Umum Museum Publishers, 1991), 203–4, as quoted in H. Samy Alim, *Roc the Mic Right: The Language of Hip Hop Culture* (Routledge, 2006), 20.
54. Robin D. G. Kelley, *Freedom Dreams: The Black Radical Imagination* (Beacon Press, 2002); Fred Moten, *In the Break: The Aesthetics of the Black Radical Tradition* (University of Minnesota Press,

2003); Komozi Woodard, *A Nation within a Nation: Amiri Baraka (LeRoi Jones) and Black Power Politics* (University of North Carolina Press, 2005); James Smethurst, *The Black Arts Movement: Literary Nationalism in the 1960s and 1970s* (University of North Carolina Press, 2005); Thomas, *Don't Deny My Name*; Rambsy, *The Black Arts Enterprise and the Production of African American Poetry*; Jones, *The Muse Is Music*; Carter Mathes, *Imagine the Sound: Experimental African American Literature After Civil Rights* (University of Minnesota Press, 2015); Crawford, *Black Post-Blackness*.

55. Aminah Beverly McCloud, *African American Islam* (Routledge, 1995); Richard Brent Turner, *Islam in the African-American Experience* (Indiana University Press, 1997); Edward E. Curtis IV, *Islam in Black America* (State University of New York Press, 2002); Jackson, *Islam and the Blackamerican*; Edward E. Curtis IV, *Black Muslim Religion in the Nation of Islam, 1960–1975* (University of North Carolina Press, 2006); Michael Muhammad Knight, *Blue-Eyed Devil* (Autonomedia, 2007); Marable and Aidi, "Introduction;" Zain Abdullah, *Black Mecca: The African Muslims of Harlem* (Oxford University Press, 2013); Zareena Grewal, *Islam Is a Foreign Country: American Muslims and the Global Crisis of Authority* (New York University Press, 2013); Bowen, *African American Islamic Renaissance*; Sylvia Chan-Malik, *Being Muslim: A Cultural History of Women of Color in American Islam* (New York University Press, 2018); Finley, *In and Out of This World*.

56. Sohail Daulatzai, *Black Star, Crescent Moon: The Muslim International and Black Freedom beyond America* (University of Minnesota Press, 2012); Michael Muhammad Knight, *The Five Percenters: Islam, Hip-Hop and the Gods of New York* (Oneworld Publications, 2013); Hisham Aidi, *Rebel Music: Race, Empire, and the New Muslim Youth Culture* (Vintage, 2014); Abdul Khabeer, *Muslim Cool*; Jeanette Jouili, "Islam and Culture: Dis/Junctures in a Modern Conceptual Terrain," *Comparative Studies in Society and History* 60, no. 1 (2019): 207–37; Richard Brent Turner, *Soundtrack to a Movement: African American Islam, Jazz, and Black Internationalism* (New York University Press, 2021).

57. Daulatzai, *Black Star, Crescent Moon*, 106.

58. Bowen, *African American Islamic Renaissance*, 564, 547–90 passim.

59. Daulatzai, *Black Star, Crescent Moon*, xiii.

60. Daulatzai, *Black Star, Crescent Moon*, 106; James T. Stewart, "The Development of the Black Revolutionary Artist," in *Black Fire: An Anthology of Afro-American Writing*, ed. LeRoi Jones and Larry Neal (William Morrow, 1968), 10; James T. Stewart, "The Development of the Black Revolutionary Artist," in *Black Arts: An Anthology of Black Creations*, ed. Ahmed Alhamisi and Harun Kofi Wangara (Black Arts Publications, 1969).

61. Moustafa Bayoumi, "East of the Sun (West of the Moon): Islam, the Ahmadis, and African America," in *Black Routes to Islam*, ed. Manning Marable and Hishaam D. Aidi (Palgrave Macmillan, 2009); Fatimah Fanusie, "Ahmadi, Beboppers, Veterans, and Migrants: African American Islam in Boston, 1948–1963," in *The African Diaspora and the Study of Religion* (Palgrave, 2007).

62. Ronald A. T. Judy, *(Dis)Forming the American Canon: African-Arabic Slave Narratives and the Vernacular* (University of Minnesota Press, 1993), 9; Judy, *Sentient Flesh*, 13.

63. Abdul Khabeer, *Muslim Cool*, 7.

1. "CONSTANT CONSCIOUS STRIVING"

1. Frantz Fanon, "De la violence," in *Les damnés de la terre* (Paris: F. Maspero, 1961), 1. "Libération nationale, renaissance nationale, restitution de la nation au people, Commonwealth . . . la décolonisation est toujours un phénomène violent." For the centrality of Fanon to Black Power and Black Arts, see Komozi Woodard, *A Nation within a Nation: Amiri Baraka (LeRoi Jones) and Black Power Politics* (University of North Carolina Press, 2005), 43, 50, 116.

2. Rolland Snellings, "Afro American Youth and the Bandung World," *Liberator* 5, no. 2 (1965): 4–7; Robin D. G. Kelley, *Freedom Dreams: The Black Radical Imagination* (Beacon Press, 2002), 60–109.
3. Lorenzo Thomas, "Askia Muhammad Touré: Crying Out the Goodness," *Obsidian* 1, no. 1 (1975): 31–49; Lorenzo Thomas, "The Shadow World: New York's Umbra Workshop & Origins of the Black Arts Movement," *Callaloo*, no. 4 (1978): 53–72; Lorenzo Thomas, *Extraordinary Measures: Afrocentric Modernism and 20th-Century American Poetry* (University of Alabama Press, 2000), 128–29; Kalamu ya Salaam, *The Magic of Juju: An Appreciation of the Black Arts Movement* (Third World Press, 2016), 19; David Grundy, *A Black Arts Poetry Machine: Amiri Baraka and the Umbra Poets* (Bloomsbury Publishing, 2019).
4. Fahamisha Patricia Brown, *Performing the Word: African American Poetry as Vernacular Culture* (Rutgers University Press, 1999); Carmen Kynard, *Vernacular Insurrections: Race, Black Protest, and the New Century in Composition-Literacies Studies* (State University of New York Press, 2013), 121. See Brown's chapter 3, "The Poetry of Preachment: Didacticism in African American Poetry"; Kynard's chapter 3, on the Black Arts Movement and Black Studies, argues that the poetry helped develop both a language and an institutional infrastructure for Black Studies.
5. Abu al-A'la al-Maududi, *al-Jihad fi-l-Islam* (Markazi Maktaba-yi Islami, 1927); Hasan al-Banna, *Risalat al-Jihad: Wa Jihadu fi Allah Haqqa Jihadihi* (Dar al-Kitab al-'Arabi, 1950s); Sayyid Qutb, *Milestones* (Islamic Book Service, 2006); Ruhollah Khomeini, *al-Jihad al-Akbar, Ya Mubaraza ba Nafs* (Mu'assasah-'i Intisharat-i Amir Kabir, 1978) Ali Shariati, "Jihad & Shahadat," https://www.shariati.com/english/jihadand.html.
6. Amiri Baraka [Ameer Baraka], "Foreword," in *Black Fire: An Anthology of Afro-American Writing*, ed. Amiri Baraka [LeRoi Jones] and Larry Neal (William Morrow, 1968); see note 11 below, which explains the alternate use Ameer, Amiri, and LeRoi Jones, as well as my method for citing works for a person who used an Islamic name after conversion. Gaston Neal, "Personal Jihad," in *Black Fire: An Anthology of Afro-American Writing*, ed. Amiri Baraka [LeRoi Jones] and Larry Neal (William Morrow, 1968); Larry Neal, "Jihad," in *Black Boogaloo (Notes on Black Liberation): Poems* (Journal of Black Poetry Press, 1969); Amiri Baraka [LeRoi Jones], *A Black Mass*, in *Four Black Revolutionary Plays: All Praises to the Black Man* (Bobbs-Merrill, 1969); Askia Muhammad Touré, "Jihad!: Toward a Black National Credo," *Negro Digest*, July 1969, 10–17.
7. Ni'mat Sidqi, *al-Jihad fi Sabil Allah* (Dar al-I'tisam, 1975); Zaynab al-Ghazali and 'Abd al-Hayy Faramawi, *Nazarat fi Kitab Allah* (Dar al-Shuruq, 1994); Sonia Sanchez, *Ima Talken Bout the Nation of Islam* [broadsheet] (New Pyramid Productions, 1971); amina wadud, *Inside the Gender Jihad: Women's Reform in Islam* (Oneworld Academic, 2006).
8. Francee Covington, "Are the Revolutionary Techniques Employed in *The Battle of Algiers* Applicable to Harlem?," in *The Black Woman*, ed. Toni Cade Bambara (Washington Square Press, 1970); Drucilla Cornell, "The Secret Behind the Veil: A Reinterpretation of 'Algeria Unveiled,'" *Philosophia Africana* 4, no. 2 (2001): 27–35.
9. H. Samy Alim, *Roc the Mic Right: The Language of Hip Hop Culture* (Routledge, 2006), 35.
10. Richard Brent Turner, *Islam in the African-American Experience* (Indiana University Press, 1997), 5, 25, 184, 201; Juan M. Floyd-Thomas, "A Jihad of Words: The Evolution of African American Islam and Contemporary Hip-Hop," in *Noise and Spirit: The Religious and Spiritual Sensibilities of Rap Music*, ed. Anthony B. Pinn (New York University Press, 2003), 49–70; H. Samy Alim, "Re-Inventing Islam with Unique Modern Tones: Muslim Hip Hop Artists as Verbal Mujahidin," *American Foreign Policy Interests* 8, no. 4 (2006): 45–58; Alim, *Roc the Mic Right*, 20–50; Keisha Hicks, "The Multifarious Jihads of Malcolm X: From Malcolm Little to El Hajj Malik El-Shabazz: 'I Am All That I Have Been'" (MA thesis, Cornell University, 2009).
11. The first editions of the book carry the name LeRoi Jones. But Jones, who had changed his name to Amiri Baraka after the Newark uprisings in 1967, signs the foreword with the name Ameer Baraka, given to him by the Hajj Heshaam Jaaber, known for mentoring, and burying Malcolm X. The

name Ameer (prince) (or Amiri) approximates the name LeRoi (the king), also suggesting a relationship to Malcolm "al-Malik" (the king). Throughout *Black Arts, Black Muslims*, I try to indicate what name the author, poet, or musician uses at the time of their work's creation—to be faithful to how they self-identify vis-à-vis the art, especially with their turn to Islam. Baraka continued to use his literary name LeRoi Jones for about five years after he took his new name, sometimes in parentheses. When discussing the titles of the works I try and honor any unconventional typography chosen by the author. But in the notes and bibliography I systemize writings under one name, with the name used at publication in brackets, and the titles of the works in conventional title case.

12. Baraka, "Foreword," xvii; Josef Sorett, *Spirit in the Dark: A Religious History of Racial Aesthetics* (Oxford University Press, 2016), 176–77.
13. wadud, *Inside the Gender Jihad*, 10.
14. Achille Mbembe, "Necropolitics," trans. Libby Meintjes, *Public Culture* 15, no. 1 (2003): 11–40.
15. Fanon, "De la violence," 2.
16. Sylvia Chan-Malik, *Being Muslim: A Cultural History of Women of Color in American Islam* (New York University Press, 2018), 9–10.
17. Larry Neal, "The Black Arts Movement," *The Drama Review: TDR* 12, no. 4 (1968): 29.
18. Cornel West, "The Dilemma of the Black Intellectual," *Cultural Critique* 1 (Autumn 1985): 112.
19. Katherine McKittrick, *Demonic Grounds: Black Women and the Cartographies of Struggle* (University of Minnesota Press, 2006), 13; Amiri Baraka [LeRoi Jones], "State/Meant," in *Home: Social Essays* (William Morrow, 1966), 281. "Black geographical togetherness and community ties also identify, for example, the sociocultural pull *away from* what bell hooks describes as terrifying and deathly representations of whiteness, or, the sociocultural pull *into* black spaces, such as familial-based migrations, cultural commitments, safe spaces, and the locations of churches [and mosques and temples!], entertainment venues, and community and political organizations," writes McKittrick. Poets like Baraka, Touré, Sanchez, and Neal represents whiteness as deathly, as in Jones's poem "state/meant": "The fair are / fair, and death / ly white."
20. Michael Muhammad Knight, *The Five Percenters: Islam, Hip-Hop and the Gods of New York*. Oneworld Publications, 2007, 43; Patrick Bowen, *A History of Conversion to Islam in the United States, Volume 2: The African American Islamic Renaissance, 1920–1975* (Brill, 2017), 122.
21. Amiri Baraka and James E. Hinton, dirs., *The New-Ark* (Harlem Audio Visual, 1968). Harvard Film Archive, James E. Hinton Collection.
22. Marvin X and Faruk, "Islam and Black Art: An Interview with LeRoi Jones," *The Negro Digest* 18, no. 3 (January 1969): 6; Marvin X and Faruk, "Islam and Black Art: An Interview with Ameer Baraka (LeRoi Jones)," in *Black Arts: An Anthology of Black Creations*, ed. Ahmed Alhamisi and Harun Kofi Wangara (Black Arts Publications, 1969).
23. Amiri Baraka and Sun Ra and his Myth Science Arkestra, *A Black Mass*, Jihad Productions, 1968; Baraka [Jones], *A Black Mass*, 39.
24. Melani McAlister, "One Black Allah: The Middle East in the Cultural Politics of African American Liberation, 1955–70," *American Quarterly* 51, no. 3 (1999): 641; Melani McAlister, *Epic Encounters: Culture, Media, and U.S. Interests in the Middle East since 1945* (University of California Press, 2005), 108.
25. Sohail Daulatzai, *Black Star, Crescent Moon: The Muslim International and Black Freedom Beyond America* (University of Minnesota Press, 2012), 106.
26. Amiri Baraka [LeRoi Jones], "Apple Cores #5—The Burton Greene Affair," *DownBeat* 33, no. 17 (1966), 21; Amiria Baraka [Imamu Amiri Baraka], *Black Music* (William Morrow, 1968), 136.
27. Baraka [Jones], *A Black Mass*, 34; Mbembe, "Necropolitics."
28. Lorrie Smith, "Black Arts to Def Jam: Performing Black 'Spirit Work' Across Generations," in *New Thought of the Black Arts Movement*, ed. Lisa Gail Collins and Margo Natalie Crawford (Rutgers University Press, 2006), 350.

29. Touré, "Jihad!," 11, 12.
30. Touré, "Jihad!," 16.
31. Touré, "Jihad!," 13.
32. Thomas, "Askia Muhammad Touré"; James Smethurst, *The Black Arts Movement: Literary Nationalism in the 1960s and 1970s* (University of North Carolina Press, 2005).
33. Touré, "Jihad!," 11, 12.
34. Touré, "Jihad!," 11, 12.
35. Taylor Branch, *Parting the Waters: America in the King Years, 1954–63* (Simon and Schuster, 1988), 166; Peniel E. Joseph, *The Sword and the Shield: The Revolutionary Lives of Malcolm X and Martin Luther King Jr.* (Basic Books, 2020), 166. Peniel characterizes Malcolm X as envisioning "the Black revolution as a sword cutting through centuries of oppression with political self-determination that would upend long-standing injustice."
36. Elijah Muhammad, *The Supreme Wisdom, Volume I: Solution to the So-Called Negroes's Problem* (MEMPS Publications, 1957), 13, 14. In the chapter "There Can Be No Love For an Enemy," Muhammad writes: "It is against the very nature of God, and man and all life, to love their enemies."
37. Muhammad, *Supreme Wisdom*; Malcolm X, "God's Angry Men," *New York Amsterdam News*, April 27, 1957.
38. Martin Luther King Jr., "'Give Us the Ballot,' Address Delivered at the Prayer Pilgrimage for Freedom," in *The Papers of Martin Luther King, Jr. Volume IV: Symbol of the Movement, January 1957–December 1958*, ed. Clayborne Carson et al. (University of California Press, 1957).
39. Martin Luther King Jr., "Loving Your Enemies: Sermon Delivered to the Dexter Avenue Baptist Church," Montgomery, Alabama, November 17, 1957, https://kinginstitute.stanford.edu/king-papers/documents/loving-your-enemies-sermon-delivered-dexter-avenue-baptist-church; Martin Luther King, Jr., *Strength to Love* (Harper & Row, 1963), 49–57.
40. James H. Cone, *Martin & Malcolm & America: A Dream or a Nightmare* (Orbis Books, 1991); Joseph, *The Sword and the Shield*.
41. Susan E. Cahan, *Mounting Frustration: The Art Museum in the Age of Black Power* (Duke University Press, 2016), 24–25. Iman's poem would be one of the only artworks by an African American identified by name, something inconceivable in the wake of the Harlem Renaissance and in the midst of the BAM. The exhibit was widely criticized for anthropologizing Harlem life, featuring a series of photographs plastered on the walls, rather than identifying key artists.
42. King, *Strength to Love*, 49–57.
43. Yusef Iman, Weusi Iman, and Job Mashariki, *The Pictorial Biography of a Great Renaissance Man: Kasisi Yusef Iman* (n.p., 1987), 3.
44. Malika Iman, *Intimate with the Ultimate: Memoirs and Tribute to Family and Political, Cultural, Spiritual Activists* (Malika Iman, 2018), 28–29. The Imans' children performed on television as "Young Spirit House Movers and Players," with Iman interviewed by Lenny Kravitz's mother Roxie Roker.
45. Yusef Iman, *Praise the Lord, but Pass the Ammunition* (Jihad Productions, 1967); The Jihad, *Black & Beautiful, Soul & Madness* (Jihad Productions, 1968); Yusef Iman, *Poetry for Our Beautiful Black Women* (Jihad Productions, 1969); Yusef Iman, ed., *The Young Black Poets of Brooklyn*. (Black News, 1970); Yusef Iman and Ben Caldwell, *Yesterday, Today, Tomorrow* (Weusi Kuumba Troupe, 1974); Iman et al., *A Great Renaissance Man*.
46. This is the kind of film that cinematographer Arthur Jafa said he would like to make, before he worked on John Akomfrah's *Seven Songs for Malcolm* (1993). Arthur Jafa, "69," in *Black Popular Culture: A Project by Michele Wallace*, ed. Gina Dent, Dia Center for the Arts: Discussions in Contemporary Culture #8 (Bay Press, 1992), 251; Woodie King, dir., *Death of a Prophet: The Last Day of Malcolm X*, TV movie, 1981; John Akomfrah, dir., *Seven Songs for Malcolm X* (Black Audio Film

Collective, 1993); Lebert Bethune, dir., *Malcolm X: Struggle for Freedom*, documentary film (Paris, 1964). *Death of a Prophet* includes footage that Jamaican Lebert Bethune filmed of Malcolm X on his 1964 visit to Paris, just months before his assassination.

47. Yusef Iman, "Love Your Enemy," in *Something Black Dedicated to Millions of Brothers and Sisters in the West* (Jihad Productions, 1966); Yusef Iman, "Love Your Enemy," in *Black Fire: An Anthology of Afro-American Writing*, ed. Amiri Baraka [LeRoi Jones] and Larry Neal (William Morrow, 1968), 368; Yusef Iman, *Love* (The East, 1972). These citations show the publishing trajectory of the poem, eventually shortened to *Love* and issued in pamphlet form.

48. Other works published in Egypt at this time, like Sayyid Qutb's 1949 *Social Justice in Islam*, comment at length on issues of race equality in Islam with reference to the situation of racial discrimination in the United States. In his "pillar of social justice in Islam" "Human Equality," he observes that "there can be no race or people that is superior by reason of its origin or its nature. Yet there are some races that to the present day insist that there does exist such a superiority"—calling out both racial apartheid in South Africa and the genocide, or "eradication," of the Native Americans in the United States. Qutb asserts that Islam is free of racial loyalties. Sayyid Qutb, *Social Justice in Islam* (Islamic Publications International, 2000), 70–71. Ahmad A. Galwash, *The Religion of Islam: A Standard Book* [first published in *al-Azhar* magazine] (Hafner Publishing Company, 1940), 80.

49. Galwash, *The Religion of Islam*, 86–87.
50. Galwash, *The Religion of Islam*, 86–87.
51. Russell Rickford, *We Are an African People: Independent Education, Black Power, and the Radical Imagination* (Oxford University Press, 2016), 13; Zenzele Isoke, *Urban Black Women and the Politics of Resistance* (Palgrave Macmillan, 2013).
52. Rickford, *We Are an African People*, 16.
53. Ula Yvette Taylor, *The Promise of Patriarchy: Women and the Nation of Islam* (University of North Carolina Press, 2017); Jarvis Givens, *Fugitive Pedagogy: Carter G. Woodson and the Art of Black Teaching* (Harvard University Press, 2021).
54. Carrie Rosefsky Wickham, *Mobilizing Islam: Religion, Activism, and Political Change in Egypt* (Columbia University Press, 2002); Asef Bayat, *Making Islam Democratic: Social Movements and the Post-Islamist Turn* (Stanford University Press, 2007); Ellen McLarney, *Soft Force: Women in Egypt's Islamic Awakening*, Princeton Studies in Muslim Politics (Princeton University Press, 2015).
55. Rickford, *We Are an African People*, 71.
56. Rickford, *We Are an African People*, 72.
57. Kwasi Konadu, *A View from The East: Black Cultural Nationalism and Education in New York City* (Syracuse University Press, 2009), 46.
58. Kasisi Yusef Iman, *Organize and Unify, Unify and Organize, Unify or Die, Die* (The East, 1972); Kasisi Yusef Iman, *Nation Time or N***** Time* (The East, 1972); Kasisi Yusef Iman, *Our Nation: What Will It Be?* (The East, 1972); Kasisi Yusef Iman, *Extermination or Unification* (The East, 1972); Kasisi Yusef Iman, *Annihilation or Separation* (The East, 1972); Kasisi Yusef Iman, *Genocide or Unify* (The East, 1972).
59. Iman, *Genocide or Unify*.
60. Iman, *Intimate with the Ultimate*, 77.
61. Rolland Snellings, "Song of Fire," *Umbra*, no. #2 (December 1963); Malcolm X, "God's Judgement of White America," in *The End of White World Supremacy: Four Speeches*, ed. Benjamin Karim (Arcade Books, 1971).
62. Malcolm X, "God's Judgement of White America."
63. Snellings, "Song of Fire"; Rolland Snellings, "Song of Fire," in *Black Fire: An Anthology of Afro-American Writing*, ed. LeRoi Jones and Larry Neal (William Morrow, 1968), 325.
64. Jones, *The Muse Is Music*, 85–86, 90.

65. Askia Muhammad Abu Bakr el-Touré, *Juju (Magic Songs for the Black Nation)* (Third World Press, 1970), 13.
66. Amiri Baraka, *The Autobiography of LeRoi Jones* (Lawrence Hill Books, 1997), 337.
67. Touré, *Juju*, 3; James T. Stewart, "Revolutionary Black Music in the Total Context of Black Distension," *Cricket*, no. 3 (1969): 13–14.
68. Touré, *Juju*, 20.
69. Thomas, "Askia Muhammad Touré," 34.
70. Wayne Shorter, *JuJu* (Blue Note Records, 1964); Archie Shepp, *The Magic of Ju-Ju* (Impulse!, 1967); Gary Bartz and NTU Troop, *Juju Street Songs* (Prestige, 1972).
71. Bethune, *Malcolm X: Struggle for Freedom*; Lebert Bethune, *Juju of My Own* (Union, 1965).
72. Frank Hives, *Ju-Ju and Justice in Nigeria*, with Gascoigne Lumley (John Lane, 1930); James H. Neal, *Ju-Ju in My Life* (Harrap, 1966).
73. Touré, *Juju*, 16.
74. Touré, *Juju*, 17; Pharoah Sanders, *Tauhid*, Impulse! Records, 1967.
75. Thomas, *Don't Deny My Name*, 30. Like "Song of Fire," his poem "Sunrise," also published in *Black Fire*, talks about "This Cry, this Call is the Song of the Race—through the years/ through the Veil," repeatedly urging: "SING out our Destiny . . . SING with your soul! SING of the Sun!"
76. Crawford, *Black Post-Blackness*, 83; Fred Moten, *In the Break: The Aesthetics of the Black Radical Tradition* (University of Minnesota Press, 2003), 66, 77. Moten also discusses a "old-new language" that "is not only its own metalanguage but its own truth."
77. Samatar, "Toward a Planetary History of Afrofuturism," 177–78.
78. See the special issue of *Paideuma* on *Songhai!* and especially David Grundy's astute observations about Touré's evocation of the call to prayer. Grundy, "Songs for the Future: Askia Touré's *Songhai!*," 10.
79. Wickham, *Mobilizing Islam*, 102, 120, 134; Bayat, *Making Islam Democratic*, 136–38; Yasmin Moll, "The Idea of Islamic Media: The Qur'an and the Decolonization of Mass Communication," *International Journal of Middle East Studies* 52 (2020): 623–42.
80. Amiri Baraka [LeRoi Jones], "S.O.S.," in *Black Art* (Jihad Productions, 1966). Jihad Productions' first publication was Sunny Murray's album *Sonny's Time Now* in which Jones recited his poem "Black Art" to music; its second publication was Iman's *Something Black*; and the third was Jones's poetry collection *Black Art*.
81. Jones, *The Muse Is Music*, 7.
82. Alim, *Roc the Mic Right*, 33.
83. Sanchez, *Ima Talken Bout the Nation of Islam*; Sonia Sanchez, "Ima Talken Bout the Nation of Islam," on *A Sun Lady for All Seasons Reads Her Poetry* (Smithsonian Folkways Records, 1971).
84. The Last Poets, *This Is Madness*, Mediasound, 1971; Askia Muhammad Touré, *Songhai!* (Songhai Press, 1972).
85. Ayi Kwei Armah, "Fanon: The Awakener," *Negro Digest*, October 1969, 4–9; Sonia Sanchez, "To Fanon," in *We a BaddDDD People* (Broadside Press, 1970); Sonia Sanchez, "To Fanon," in *Sun Lady for All Seasons* (Smithsonian Folkways, 1971).
86. Frantz Fanon, "On Violence," in *The Wretched of the Earth*, trans. Richard Philcox (Grove Press, 2004), 2; Aimé Césaire, *Discourse on Colonialism*, trans. Joan Pinkham (Monthly Review Press, 2000), 35–36.
87. Neal, "The Black Arts Movement," 35.
88. Frantz Fanon, *Toward the African Revolution: Political Essays*, trans. Haakon Chevalier (Grove Press, 1967), 53; Camille Robcis, *Disalienation: Politics, Philosophy, and Radical Psychiatry in Postwar France* (University of Chicago Press, 2021), 49.
89. Fanon, *The Wretched of the Earth*, 143.
90. Ademola Olugebefola, *Cover Artwork: "Ima Talken Bout the Nation of Islam"* (New Pyramid Productions, 1971); Gordon Parks, "Wake Up, Clean Up, Stand Up," *Life Magazine* 54, no. 22 (1963):

26–27. The pyramid composition of the artwork parallels Gordon Parks's photos of the women of the NOI in *Life* magazine, even as it evokes Egyptian, Afro-Asian cultural signs and imagery, operating simultaneously on several geographical and temporal registers, superimposing them.

91. Kalamu ya Salaam, "Sonia Sanchez," in *Dictionary of Literary Biography: Afro-American Poets Since 1955* (Gale, 1985), 41:298; "Discipline and Craft: An Interview with Sonia Sanchez," *African American Review* 34, no. 4 (2000): 683; James Spady, "Introduction: 360 Degreez of Sonia Sanchez, Hip Hop, Narrativity, Iqhawe, and Public Spaces of Being," *B. Ma: The Sonia Sanchez Literary Review* 6, no. 1 (2000): vi–1; La Donna Forsgren, *In Search of Our Warrior Mothers: Women Dramatists of the Black Arts Movement* (Northwestern University Press, 2018), 161.

92. Sonia Sanchez, *Three Hundred and Sixty Degrees of Blackness Comin at You: An Anthology of the Sonia Sanchez Writers Workshop at Countee Cullen Library in Harlem* (5X Publishing Co., 1971).

93. Salaam, "Sonia Sanchez," 298; "Discipline and Craft," 683; Spady, "Introduction: 360 Degreez of Sonia Sanchez, Hip Hop, Narrativity, Iqhawe, and Public Spaces of Being;" Forsgren, *In Search of Our Warrior Mothers*, 161.

94. Clarence 13X "Allah the Father," "Supreme Mathematics," *The Five Percenter Lessons*, n.d., https://fivepercenterlessons.wordpress.com/mathematics/; God Supreme Allah, ed., *Supreme Lessons of the Gods and Earths: A Guide for 5 Percenters to Follow As Taught by Clarence 13x Allah* (African American Bookstore, 1993); Felicia M. Miyakawa, *Five Percenter Rap: God Hop's Music, Message, and Black Muslim Mission* (Indiana University Press, 2005), 62–63.

95. Sonia Sanchez, "To Morani/Mungu," in *It's A New Day (Poems for Young Brothas and Sistuhs)* (Broadside Press, 1971); Sonia Sanchez, "We're Not Learnen to Be Paper Boys (for the Young Brothas Who Sell Muhammad Speaks)," in *It's A New Day (Poems for Young Brothas and Sistuhs)* (Broadside Press, 1971).

96. amina wadud, email communication with author, May 2024.

97. wadud, *Inside the Gender Jihad*, 262.

98. John L. Esposito and John O. Voll, *Islam and Democracy* (Oxford University Press, 1996).

99. wadud, wadud e-mail communication with author.

2. NATION IN A NATION IN A NATION

1. Frantz Fanon, *Les damnés de la terre* (F. Maspero, 1961), 195; Franz Fanon, *The Wretched of the Earth*, trans. Richard Philcox (Grove Press, 2004), 145. The translation of this quote is mine.

2. Fanon, *The Wretched of the Earth*, 151, 154.

3. Achille Mbembe, *Critique of Black Reason*, trans. Laurent DuBois (Duke University Press, 2017), 95; Youssef Carter, "Critiquing Black Muslim Reason: What Good Is Critical Race Theory for Muslims?," *Maydan: Islamic Thought*, February 5, 2020, https://themaydan.com/2020/02/critiquing-black-muslim-reason-what-good-is-critical-race-theory-for-muslims/. Drawing on Mbembe, Carter argues that "Black Muslim Reason is a unique site" where "people have struggled for their own human dignity."

4. Stuart Hall, "New Ethnicities," in *Stuart Hall: Critical Dialogues in Cultural Studies*, ed. David Morley and Kuan-Hsing Chen (Routledge, 1996), 441. "The term 'black' was coined as a way of referencing the common experience of racism and marginalization in Britain and came to provide the organizing category of a new politics of resistance, among groups and communities with, in fact, very different histories, traditions and ethnic identities. 'The black experience' . . . became 'hegemonic' over other ethnic/racial identities. . . . Culturally, this analysis formulated itself in terms of a critique of the way black were positioned as the unspoken and invisible 'other' of predominantly white aesthetic and cultural discourses."

5. Tavia Nyong'o, *Afro-Fabulations: The Queer Drama of Black Life* (New York University Press, 2019), 170; Arthur Huff Fauset, *Black Gods of the Metropolis: Negro Religious Cults of the Urban North* (University of Pennsylvania Press, 1944); Edward E. Curtis IV and Danielle Brune Sigler, eds., *The New Black Gods: Arthur Huff Fauset and the Study of African American Religions* (Indiana University Press, 2009). Fauset's *Black Gods of the Metropolis* is a deep dive into these alternative modes of religious belonging that emerged around the time of the Harlem Renaissance.
6. Claude McKay, "Sufi Abdul Hamid and Organized Labor," in *Harlem: Negro Metropolis* (Harcourt Brace Jovanovich, 1940); Ian Duffield, "Dusé Mohamed Ali and the Development of Pan-Africanism 1866–1945" (PhD Thesis, Edinburgh University, 1971); Patrick D. Bowen, "Abdul Hamid Suleiman and the Origins of the Moorish Science Temple," *Journal of Race, Ethnicity, and Religion* 2, no. 13 (2011): 1–54; Patrick D. Bowen, *A History of Conversion to Islam in the United States, Volume 2: African American Islamic Renaissance* (Brill, 2017), 117–30; Richard Brent Turner, *Islam in the African-American Experience* (Indiana University Press, 1997). Both Bowen and Turner engage in extensive explorations of the relationship of the UNIA to Muslim groups and leaders.
7. McKay, "Sufi Abdul Hamid and Organized Labor," 185.
8. McKay, "Sufi Abdul Hamid and Organized Labor," 186, 210; regarding "do for self," also see the chapter "A Nation of Our Own" in Elijah Muhammad, *Message to the Blackman in America* (Secretarius Memps Publications, 1965), 229–30.
9. Ishmael Reed, *Mumbo Jumbo* (Scribner, 1972), 38.
10. McKay, "Sufi Abdul Hamid and Organized Labor," 211.
11. Mbembe, *Critique of Black Reason*, 85, 95.
12. Richard J. Powell, *Black Art and Culture in the 20th Century* (Thames and Hudson, 1997), 41.
13. Margo Natalie Crawford, *Black Post-Blackness: The Black Arts Movement and Twenty-First-Century Aesthetics* (University of Illinois Press, 2017), 19, 21.
14. Crawford, *Black Post-Blackness*, 21.
15. Julian Mayfield, "Into Mainstream and Oblivion," in *The American Negro Writer and His Roots: Selected Papers*, ed. John Aubrey Davis Sr. First Conference of Negro Writers 1959 (American Society of African Culture, 1960), 32; Komozi Woodard, *A Nation Within a Nation: Amiri Baraka (LeRoi Jones) and Black Power Politics* (University of North Carolina Press, 2005. See, in particular, Woodard's exploration of the role of Black cultural nationalism and the cultural approach to Black Power through the figure of Amiri Baraka.
16. Richard Brent Turner, "Edward Wilmot Blyden and Pan-Africanism: The Ideological Roots of Islam and Black Nationalism in the United States," *The Muslim World* 87 (April 1997): 169; Turner, *Islam in the African-American Experience*, 47; Curtis, *Black Muslim Religion in the Nation of Islam, 1960–1975* (University of North Carolina Press, 2006), 21–44.
17. "Harlem: Mecca of the New Negro," in *Survey Graphic* (1925); Alain Locke, ed., *The New Negro: An Interpretation* (Albert and Charles Boni, 1925).
18. Just after the founding of the Mecca Temple in DC, the founders of the White Shriners, Walter Fleming and William Patterson, published a book *Mecca Temple: Ancient Arabic Order of the Nobles of the Mystic Shrine, Its History and Pleasures*, perhaps staking their claim, with orientalist imagery using Islamic words, expressions, and concepts, some of them written in Arabic script with the shaky hand of a nonnative student of Arabic, misspelling *as-salaamu alaykum* in Arabic.
19. Turner, *Islam in the African-American Experience*, 80–90; Zareena Grewal, *Islam Is a Foreign Country: American Muslims and the Global Crisis of Authority* (New York University Press, 2013), 85; Bowen, *A History of Conversion to Islam in the United States, Volume 2*, 12–13, 82. Bowen writes that "Islam was able to thrive only after it was legitimized in the black community in the early 1920s by Marcus Garvey's institution-changing black nationalist movement; ... it had a lingering presence in virtually all the Muslim groups of this period."

2. NATION IN A NATION IN A NATION

20. David G. Hackett, *That Religion in Which All Men Agree: Freemasonry in America* (University of California, 2014), 6–7.
21. Peter Lamborn Wilson, *Sacred Drift: Essays on the Margins of Islam* (City Lights Books, 1993); Aminah Beverly McCloud, *African American Islam*, 9–40; Turner, *Islam in the African-American Experience* (Routledge, 1995), 71–108; Curtis, *Black Muslim Religion*, 45–62; Bowen, "Abdul Hamid Suleiman"; Grewal, *Islam Is a Foreign Country*, 85–91; Fathie Ali Abdat, "Before the Fez: The Life and Times of Drew Ali, 1886–1924," *Journal of Race, Ethnicity, and Religion* 5, no. 8 (2014): 1–39; Bowen, *A History of Conversion to Islam in the United States, Volume 2*, 194–98; Dorman, *The Princess and the Prophet: The Secret History of Magic, Race, and Moorish Muslims in America* (Beacon Press, 2020).
22. Curtis and Sigler, *New Black Gods*, 4.
23. Sherman A. Jackson, *Islam and the Blackamerican: Looking Toward the Third Resurrection* (Oxford University Press, 2005), 39.
24. Curtis and Sigler, *New Black Gods*, 6–9.
25. Sherman A. Jackson, *Islam and the Problem of Black Suffering* (Oxford University Press, 2009).
26. Gayraud S. Wilmore, *Black Religion and Black Radicalism: An Interpretation of the Religious History of African Americans* (Orbis Books, 1998), 163, 196.
27. Turner, *Islam in the African-American Experience*, 124.
28. Turner, *Islam in the African-American Experience*, 99; McCloud, *African American Islam*, 15.
29. Manning Marable and Hishaam D. Aidi, "Introduction," in *Black Routes to Islam* (Palgrave, 2009); Su'ad Abdul Khabeer, *Muslim Cool: Race, Religion, and Hip Hop in the United States* (New York University Press, 2016), 7, 29–30.
30. Jackson, *Islam and the Blackamerican*, 47–48; Grewal, *Islam Is a Foreign Country*, 112–13.
31. Sohail Daulatzai, *Black Star, Crescent Moon: The Muslim International and Black Freedom Beyond America* (University of Minnesota Press, 2012).
32. Michael A. Gomez, *Black Crescent: The Experience and Legacy of African Muslims in the Americas* (Cambridge University Press, 2005), 159; Herbert Berg, *Elijah Muhammad and Islam* (New York University Press, 2009), 11–12.
33. Gomez, *Black Crescent*, 200.
34. Gomez, *Black Crescent*, 204.
35. Nancy Fraser, "Rethinking the Public Sphere: A Contribution to the Critique of Actually Existing Democracy," in *Habermas and the Public Sphere*, ed. Craig Calhoun (MIT Press, 1992); Michael Warner, *Publics and Counterpublics* (Zone Books, 2002); Charles Hirschkind, *The Ethical Soundscape: Cassette Sermons and Islamic Counterpublics* (Columbia University Press, 2009).
36. Mufti Muhammad Sadiq, ed., *The Moslem Sunrise* 1, no. 1 (1921).
37. Michael C. Dawson, *Black Visions: The Roots of Contemporary African-American Political Ideologies* (University of Chicago Press, 2001), 27–28.
38. Eric King Watts, "Cultivating a Black Public Voice: W. E. B. Du Bois and the 'Criteria of Negro Art,'" *Rhetoric & Public Affairs* 4, no. 2 (2001): 181–201.
39. James Baldwin et al., "The Negro in American Culture," *CrossCurrents* 11, no. 3 (1961): 205–24; Jennifer Lynn Stoever, *The Sonic Color Line: Race and the Cultural Politics of Listening* (New York University Press, 2016).
40. Darby English, *How to See a Work of Art in Total Darkness* (MIT Press, 2007), 45. But he critiques "this sharply circumscribed location" and the policing of the boundaries of Black art, confining it to what he calls a narrow set of possibilities. English sees this as restricting Black artists' range of forms and tropes resulting in "an unequivocally ethnic art," circumscribing Black art to a limited repertoire of referents.
41. George S. Schuyler, "The Negro-Art Hokum," *The Nation*, June 16, 1926, 662–63.
42. Langston Hughes, "The Negro Artist and the Racial Mountain," *The Nation*, June 23, 1926, 692–93. Hughes's characterization anticipates Malcolm X's later parable of the house slave versus the field slave.

43. Hughes, "The Negro Artist"; Fred Moten and Stefano Harney, "The University and the Undercommons: Seven Theses," *Social Text* 22, no. 2 (2004): 101–15; Douglas Jones, "'The Black Below': Minstrelsy, Satire, and the Threat of Vernacularity," *Theater Journal* 73, no. 2 (2021): 129–46.
44. Schuyler, "The Negro-Art Hokum."
45. Fauset, *Black Gods of the Metropolis*.
46. Schuyler, "The Negro-Art Hokum."
47. Schuyler, "The Negro-Art Hokum."
48. Hughes, "The Negro Artist."
49. For a discussion of "i-*magi*-nation," see Ameer Baraka, "Foreword," in *Black Fire: An Anthology of Afro-American Writing*, ed. LeRoi Jones and Larry Neal (William Morrow, 1968); Askia Muhammad Touré, "Jihad!: Toward a Black National Credo," *Negro Digest*, July 1969, 10–17. For "the alchemy of Black," see Powell, *Black Art and Culture in the 20th Century*, 7.
50. Eduardo Mendieta, "Decolonizing Blackness, Decolonizing Theology: On James Cone's Black Theology of Liberation," *The CLR James Journal* 27, no. 1/2 (2021): 101.
51. Amiri Baraka and Sun Ra and his Myth Science Arkestra, *A Black Mass*, Jihad Productions, 1968; Larry Neal, "The Narrative of the Black Magicians," in *Black Fire: An Anthology of Afro-American Writing*, ed. Amiri Baraka and Larry Neal (Black Classic Press, 2013), 314; Mendieta, "Decolonizing Blackness, Decolonizing Theology," 101.
52. Neal, "The Narrative of the Black Magicians," 314.
53. Neal, "The Narrative of the Black Magicians," 314.
54. Crawford, *Black Post-Blackness*, 57.
55. Neal, "The Narrative of the Black Magicians," 314.
56. Mathes, *Imagine the Sound*, 113.
57. Mathes, *Imagine the Sound*, 113.
58. Mathes, *Imagine the Sound*, 113.
59. William J. Harris, *The Poetry and Poetics of Amiri Baraka: The Jazz Aesthetic* (University of Missouri Press, 1986); T. J. Anderson III, *Notes to Make the Sound Come Right: Four Innovators of Jazz Poetry* (University of Arkansas Press, 2004); Meta DuEwa Jones, *The Muse Is Music: Jazz Poetry from the Harlem Renaissance to Spoken Word* (University of Illinois Press, 2013).
60. Lorenzo Thomas, *Don't Deny My Name: Words and Music and the Black Intellectual Tradition* (University of Michigan Press, 2008), 105.
61. James Smethurst, *The Black Arts Movement: Literary Nationalism in the 1960s and 1970s* (University of North Carolina Press, 2005), 22; Lorenzo Thomas, "'Communicating by Horns': Jazz and Redemption in the Poetry of the Beats and the Black Arts Movement," *African American Review* 26, no. 2 (Summer 1992): 295–97; Lorenzo Thomas, *Extraordinary Measures: Afrocentric Modernism and 20th-Century American Poetry* (University of Alabama Press, 2000), 130–31. Also see Sylvia Chan-Malik's inspirational writings on the role of blues, jazz, and hip hop in articulating a Muslim-American arts in the United States. Sylvia Chan-Malik, "Cultural and Literary Production of Muslim America," in *The Cambridge Companion to American Islam*, ed. Juliane Hammer and Omid Safi (Cambridge University Press, 2013), 279–98; Sylvia Chan-Malik, "Islam in the Arts in the USA," in *Routledge Handbook of Islam in the West*, ed. Roberto Tottoli (Routledge, 2014).
62. LeRoi Jones, "The Changing Same," in *Black Music* (William Morrow, 1967), 203–04.
63. LeRoi Jones, "The Changing Same," 188.
64. Du Bois, *The Souls of Black Folk*, 257.
65. Neal, "The Narrative of the Black Magicians," 313.
66. Daulatzai, *Black Star, Crescent Moon*, 49–74.
67. Dudley Randall and Margaret G. Burroughs, *For Malcolm: Poems on the Life and the Death of Malcolm X* (Broadside Press, 1967); Baraka and Neal, *Black Fire*; Addison Gayle, "The Black Aesthetic," in *The Black Aesthetic*, ed. Addison Gayle (Doubleday, 1972).

68. Malcolm X, *The Speeches of Malcolm X at Harvard*, ed. Archie Epps (William Morrow, 1968), 30, 32.
69. John Henrik Clarke, "The New Afro-American Nationalism," *Freedomways* 1, no. 3 (1961): 285–95; C. Eric Lincoln, *The Black Muslims in America* (Beacon Press, 1961); E. U. Essien-Udom, *Black Nationalism: A Search for an Identity in America* (University of Chicago Press, 1962).
70. Clarke, "The New Afro-American Nationalism," 288. "To the Black Muslims the American promise and the American dream have grown sour without fulfillment. They have lost faith in the United States as a democratic nation."
71. Grundy, *A Black Arts Poetry Machine*.
72. Amiri Baraka [LeRoi Jones], "'Black' Is a Country," in *Home: Social Essays* (William Morrow, 1966), 104.
73. Amiri Baraka [LeRoi Jones], *Home: Social Essays* (William Morrow, 1966), 125.
74. Amiri Baraka [LeRoi Jones], "The Legacy of Malcolm X, and the Coming of the Black Nation," in *Home: Social Essays* (William Morrow, 1966), 267.
75. Baraka [Jones], "The Legacy of Malcolm X, and the Coming of the Black Nation," 271.
76. Amiri Baraka [Imamu Amiri Baraka], *It's Nation Time* (Third World Press, 1970), 23; Imamu Amiri Baraka, *It's Nation Time: African Visionary Music*, Motown: Black Forum, 1972; McAlister, "One Black Allah: The Middle East in the Cultural Politics of African American Liberation, 1955–70."
77. Larry Neal, "An Afterword: And Shine Swam On," in *Black Fire: An Anthology of Afro-American Writing*, ed. Amiri Baraka [LeRoi Jones] and Larry Neal (William Morrow, 1968), 645, 647.
78. Neal, "Afterword," 639.
79. Malcolm X, *Malcolm X at Harvard*, 30, 32.
80. Martin Robison Delany, *The Condition, Elevation, Emigration, and Destiny of the Colored People of the United States, Politically Considered* (Martin Robison Delany, 1852), 12–13.
81. W. E. B. Du Bois, "A Negro Nation Within the Nation," *Current History*, June 1, 1935, 268–70.
82. Du Bois, "A Negro Nation within the Nation," 268–70.
83. Neal, "The Black Arts Movement," 39.
84. Neal, "The Black Arts Movement," 29, 39.
85. Neal, "The Black Arts Movement," 30, 39. Neal quotes Etheridge Knight: "Unless the Black artist establishes a 'Black aesthetic' he will have no future at all. To accept the white aesthetic is to accept and validate a society that will not allow him to live."
86. Du Bois, "A Negro Nation Within the Nation," 268–70.

3. SCIENCE'S FICTIONS

1. Southern Poverty Law Center, Louis Farrakhan, accessed July 19, 2023, https://www.splcenter.org/fighting-hate/extremist-files/individual/louis-farrakhan. The blog post has since been revised to call the Yakub teaching the NOI's "'theology' [in scare quotes]—or more appropriately, its mythology," dropping the words "bizarre and fundamentally antiwhite."
2. "Myth," Oxford Languages.
3. Elijiah Muhammad, *Message to the Blackman in America* (Secretarius Memps Publications, 1965), 103–22.
4. Steven Finley, *In and Out of This World: Material and Extraterrestrial Bodies in the Nation of Islam* (Duke University Press, 2022), 16. Italics in the original.
5. Graham Baker, "Christianity and Eugenics: The Place of Religion in the British Eugenics Education Society and the American Eugenics Society, c. 1907–1940," *Social History of Medicine* 27, no. 2 (2014): 281–302.

6. Isiah Lavender, *Afrofuturism Rising: The Literary Prehistory of a Movement* (Ohio State University Press, 2019).
7. Finley, "The Meaning of 'Mother' in Louis Farrakhan's 'Mother Wheel:' Race, Gender, and Sexuality in the Cosmology of the Nation of Islam's UFO," *Journal of the American Academy of Religion* 80, no. 2 (2012): 436, 460; Michael Lieb, *Children of Ezekiel: Aliens, UFOs, the Crisis of Race, and the Advent of the End of Time* (Duke University Press, 1998), 3–5.
8. Finley, *In and Out of This World*, 24; Claude A. Clegg III, *Life and Times of Elijah Muhammad* (University of North Carolina Press, 2014), 43; Patrick D. Bowen, *A History of Conversion to Islam in the United States, Volume 2: African American Islamic Renaissance, 1920–1975* (Brill, 2017), 263.
9. Jamika Ajalon, dir., *Locations of the M/othership: Black Women as Future Archetype of Resistance*. Third World Newsreel, 2009.
10. Alondra Nelson, "A Black Mass as Black Gothic: Myth and Bioscience in Black Cultural Nationalism," in *New Thoughts on the Black Arts Movement*, ed. Lisa Gail Collins and Margo Natalie Crawford (Rutgers University Press, 2006); Safiyah Cheatam, "From Counter-Memory to Counter-Culture: Black Islam in the U.S. through a Mundane Afrofuturist Lens," (MFA thesis, University of Maryland, 2021), 4; Samatar, "Toward a Planetary History of Afrofuturism," *Research in African Literatures* 48, no. 4 (2017): 177.
11. Finley, "Farrakhan's 'Mother Wheel,'" 460; Amiri Baraka [LeRoi Jones], "An Explanation of the Work," in *Black Magic: Collected Poetry, 1961–1967* (Bobbs-Merrill, 1969).
12. Malcolm X and John Henrik Clarke, "Organization of Afro-American Unity: A Statement of Basic Aims and Objectives," in *Malcolm X: The Man and His Times*, ed. John Henrik Clarke (Africa World Press, 1990), 341.
13. Larry Neal, "An Afterword: And Shine Swam On," in *Black Fire: An Anthology of Afro-American Writing*, ed. Amiri Baraka [LeRoi Jones] and Larry Neal. William Morrow, 1968; Larry Neal, "The Black Arts Movement," *The Drama Review: TDR* 12, no. 4 (1968): 29–39.
14. Neal, "Afterword."
15. Amiri Baraka [Le Roi Jones], *A Black Mass*, in *Four Black Revolutionary Plays: All Praises to the Black Man* (Bobbs-Merrill, 1969), 17, 24, 29.
16. Finley, "Farrakhan's 'Mother Wheel,'" 460.
17. Baraka [Jones], *A Black Mass*, 17.
18. Amiri Baraka, *The Autobiography of LeRoi Jones* (Lawrence Hill Books, 1997), 298.
19. John Szwed, *Space Is The Place: The Lives And Times Of Sun Ra* (Pantheon, 1997), 112; Rey Chow, *Not Like a Native Speaker* (Columbia University Press, 2014), 8. In writing about language and racialization (and on naming and identity), Chow talks about the "visual and audial significations of the word tones" that operates "at the border between shade and sound" ("an epidermalization of naming and calling").
20. Szwed, *Space Is The Place*, 155. Szwed writes about how Sun Ra wanted to title the liner notes "Preparation for Outer Space."
21. Amiri Baraka [LeRoi Jones], "Apple Cores #5—The Burton Greene Affair," *DownBeat* 33, no. 17 (August 25, 1966). For a riff on this idea of an Afrofuturist afterlife, see Vanessa Taylor, "Take Me From My Plight: On Afrofuturism, the Afterlife, and a Black Future," *Medium*, December 18, 2017, https://medium.com/@BaconTribe/take-me-from-my-plight-564b77132de6.
22. Amiri Baraka and Sun Ra and the Myth Science Arkestra, *A Black Mass*, Sonboy Records, September 6, 1999, https://www.forcedexposure.com/Catalog/baraka-leroi-jones-the-sun-ra-myth-science-arkestra-amiri-a-black-cd/SONBOY.001CD.html.
23. Baraka and Sun Ra and the Myth Science Arkestra, *A Black Mass*.
24. Lavender, *Afrofuturism Rising*, 7.
25. Finley, "Farrakhan's 'Mother Wheel,'" 443.

26. Britt Rusert, *Fugitive Science: Empiricism and Freedom in Early African American Culture* (New York University Press, 2017), 5–6; Michel Foucault, *The Order of Things: An Archaeology of the Human Sciences* (Pantheon, 1971), 378.
27. Rusert, *Fugitive Science*, 5–6; Foucault, *The Order of Things*, 378.
28. Neal, "Afterword"; Neal, "The Black Arts Movement."
29. Neal, "The Black Arts Movement," 30.
30. Bruce Dain, *A Hideous Monster of the Mind: American Race Theory in the Early Republic* (Harvard University Press, 2003), vii.
31. Paul Gilroy, *The Black Atlantic: Modernity and Double-Consciousness* (Harvard University Press, 1993), 73, 74. Its allegorical nature enables it to express inexpressible horrors, what Paul Gilroy calls "a topos of unsayability produced from . . . experiences of racial terror."
32. Isiah Lavender, *Race in American Science Fiction* (Indiana University Press, 2011), 6–7.
33. Finley, *In and Out of This World*, 24; Clegg, *Life and Times of Elijah Muhammad*, 43; Bowen, *A History of Conversion to Islam in the United States, Volume 2*, 263.
34. Lavender, *Race in American Science Fiction*, 6–7.
35. James Weldon Johnson, *Autobiography of an Ex-Colored Man* (Alfred A. Knopf, 1927); Nella Larsen, *Passing* (Alfred A. Knopf, 1929). *Black No More* includes some of the motifs of Johnson's *Autobiography*, both culminating in graphic accounts of white racial terror.
36. Margo Natalie Crawford, *Black Post-Blackness: The Black Arts Movement and Twenty-First-Century Aesthetics* (University of Illinois Press, 2017), 19.
37. For a discussion of French eugenics practices of forced abortion in the colonies, see Françoise Vergès, "The Island of Dr. Moreau," in *The Wombs of Women: Race, Capital, Feminism*, trans. Kaiama Glover (Duke University Press, 2020).
38. Elof Carlson, *Scientific Origins of Eugenics*, Ethical, Legal, and Social Implications Research Program, National Human Genome Research Institute, Archive on the American Eugenics Movement (Dolan DNA Learning Center, Cold Spring Harbor Laboratory, n.d.), http://www.eugenicsarchive.org/html/eugenics/essay2text.html.
39. Jeffrey Alan Hodges, "Euthenics, Eugenics and Compulsory Sterilization in Michigan, 1897–1960" (MA thesis, Department of History, Michigan State University, 1995), 59; Lutz Kaelber, "Michigan," *Eugenics: Compulsory Sterilization in 50 American States*, 2012, https://www.uvm.edu/~lkaelber/eugenics/MI/MI.html.
40. Campbell Gibson and Kay Jung, *Historical Census Statistics on Population Totals by Race, 1790 to 1990, and by Hispanic Origin, 1970 to 1990, for the United States, Regions, Divisions, and States*, Working Paper No. 56, Population Division (Washington, DC, 2002).
41. Hodges, "Euthenics, Eugenics and Compulsory Sterilization in Michigan, 1897–1960," 36–37.
42. Herbert Berg, *Elijah Muhammad and Islam* (New York University Press, 2009), 33–34. After converting, Fard renamed him Elijiah Kerriem.
43. Bowen, *A History of Conversion to Islam in the United States, Volume 2*, 252; Michael Muhammad Knight, "'I Am Sorry, Mr. White Man, These Are Secrets That You Are Not Permitted to Learn:' The Supreme Wisdom Lessons and Problem Book," *Correspondences*, Special Issue: Islamic Esotericism, vol. 7, no. 1 (2019): 170. Bowen and Knight discuss how the content of the "Lost Found Muslim Lessons" differs (Bowen) and concurs in fragments reproduced in several early texts: in the *Detroit Free Press* in 1932, an article about the NOI by Erdmann Beynon published in 1938, and a copy obtained by the FBI in 1942 when Elijah Muhammad was arrested for draft evasion (included in an internal 2/21/57 memo about the NOI).
44. Knight, "Secrets You Are Not Permitted to Learn," 171. Michael Muhammad Knight, *The Supreme Wisdom Lessons: A Scripture of American Islam* (Equinox, 2024), 123.
45. Knight, "Secrets You Are Not Permitted to Learn," 169.
46. Knight, "Secrets You Are Not Permitted to Learn," 183.

47. Ethan Blue, "The Strange Career of Leo Stanley: Remaking Manhood and Medicine at San Quentin State Penitentiary, 1913–1951," *Pacific Historical Review* 78, no. 2 (2009): 228.
48. Leo Stanley and Evelyn Wells, *Men at Their Worst* (D. Appleton, 1940), 110; Blue, "Strange Career of Leo Stanley," 232.
49. Blue, "Strange Career of Leo Stanley," 233; L. L. Stanley, "An Analysis of One Thousand Testicular Substance Implantations," *Endocrinology* 6, no, 1 (1922): 789.
50. August Weismann, *The Germ-Plasm: A Theory of Heredity*, trans. William N. Parker and Harriet Rönnfeldt (Scribner's, 1983).
51. Madeline Bowen, *San Quentin State Prison, Building 22*, Historic American Buildings Survey (National Park Service, US Department of the Interior, 2009); Peter Matthews Wright, "A Box of Self-Threading Needles: Epic Vision and Penal Trauma in the Fugitive Origins of the Nation of Islam" (MA thesis, University of North Carolina, 2004). In his MA thesis, Wright argues that Fard's "penal trauma" while incarcerated in San Quentin between 1926 and 1929 may have influenced the formulation of NOI doctrines.
52. H. G. Wells, *A Short History of Mankind* (Macmillan, 1925). "The early priest was really not so much a religious man as a man of applied science" and "astronomical science," he writes in the chapter "Primitive Thought / Beginnings of Cultivation / Primitive Neolithic Civilizations."
53. Wells, *A Short History of Mankind*.
54. Wells, *A Short History of Mankind*.
55. H. G. Wells, *The Science of Life* (Doubleday, Doran & Company, 1930), 288–90.
56. Aaron Gillette, *Eugenics and the Nature-Nurture Debate in the Twentieth Century* (Palgrave Macmillan, 2007), 123–24.
57. Michael Yudell, *Race Unmasked: Biology and Race in the 20th Century* (Columbia University Press, 2007), 89–90.
58. Lavender, *Race in American Science Fiction*, 8.
59. Nelson, "Myth and Bioscience," 148.
60. Hideyo Noguchi, "A Cutaneous Reaction in Syphilis," *Journal of Experimental Medicine* 14 (1911): 565; Susan Eyrich Lederer, "Hideyo Noguchi's Luetin Experiment and the Antivivisectionists," *Isis* 76, no. 1 (1985): 36; Adam Cohen, *Imbeciles: The Supreme Court, American Eugenics, and the Sterilization of Carrie Buck* (Penguin, 2016), 2, 111.
61. Bowen, *A History of Conversion to Islam in the United States, Volume 2*, 253, 261, 263. According to Bowen, texts like Thomas Nelson's *Mosaic Law in the Light of Modern Science* (1926), for example, puts forth the argument that "God's law is in fact a 'science,' and that Moses, therefore, was a great 'scientist;' Fard's teachings present Islam as a science and the wisest men in ancient times were also said to be scientists" (261).
62. Lavender, *Race in American Science Fiction*, 6; Finley, *In and Out of This World*, 16.
63. *New York Times*, "Biologist Asserts He Can Remold Man: Reports Changing Color, Method Will Enable Him to Transform Infant 'to Order,'" *New York Times*, October 25, 1929.
64. "Racial Metamorphosis Claimed by Scientist: Japanese Says He Can Change Black Skin into White," *Pittsburgh Courier*, November 2, 1929; Jane Kuenz, "American Racial Discourse, 1900–1930: Schuyler's *Black No More*," *A Forum on Fiction* 30, no. 2 (1997): 170n2. The *Courier* article says that Noguchi could make Blacks white using "sun rays, ultraviolet rays, special diets and glandular treatments."
65. George S. Schuyler, *Black No More: An Account of the Strange and Wonderful Workings of Science in the Land of the Free* (Macaulay, 1931), 4; Ida White-Duncan, "Kink-No-More," *The New York Age*, January 13, 1916, 2.
66. Ernest Allen, "Satokata Takahashi and the Flowering of Black Messianic Nationalism," *The Black Scholar* 24–21 (1994): 31; Berg, *Elijah Muhammad and Islam*, 33.

67. David Palter, "Testing for Race: Stanford University, Asian Americans, and Psychometric Testing in California, 1920–1935" (PhD diss., University of California, 2014), 22. Other scholars similarly observe the absurdity of eugenics claims, such as Dain, *Hideous Monster of the Mind*, viii ("illogical and absurd") and Rusert, *Fugitive Science*, 3 ("the absolute absurdity of that position, as well as the program of research behind it").
68. Schuyler, *Black No More*, 20, 72.
69. F. G. Crookshank, *The Mongol in Our Midst: A Study of Man and His Three Faces* (Kegan Paul, Trench & Trubner, 1924); Michael Kohlman, "Today and Tomorrow: To-Day and To-Morrow Book Series," Social Sciences and Humanities Research Council of Canada, *Eugenics Archive*, n.d., https://eugenicsarchive.ca/discover/timeline/546d00a8dabeefbb1a000001.
70. Kohlman, "Today and Tomorrow."
71. Lavender, *Race in American Science Fiction*, 6–7; Ernest Allen, "Satokata Takahashi and the Flowering of Black Messianic Nationalism," 31.
72. H. G. Wells, *Island of Dr. Moreau* (Penguin, 1896). For following terms see their respective pages "simian," 41, 54; black- and brown-faced, 13, 14, 24, 40; devils, 15, 16, 17; negroid, 54, 144.
73. Charles D. Martin, *The White African American Body: A Cultural and Literary Exploration* (Rutgers University Press, 2002), 62–74.
74. Schuyler, *Black No More*, 12, 28, 39.
75. Jeffrey Stanton, "Freaks and Side Shows," in *Coney Island History* (1997), https://www.westland.net/coneyisland/.
76. Hasan Kwame Jeffries, *Bloody Lowndes: Civil Rights and Black Power in Alabama's Black Belt* (New York University Press, 2009), 143; John Jennings and Stacey Robinson, "Connections," in *Black Kirby: In Search of the Motherboxx Connection* (Black Kirby Collective, 2013).
77. Zakiyyah Iman Jackson, *Becoming Human: Matter and Meaning in an Antiblack World* (New York University Press, 2020), 1–2; Claire Jean Kim, *Dangerous Crossings: Race, Species, and Nature in a Multicultural Age* (Cambridge University Press, 2014); Bénédicte Boisseron, *Afro-Dog: Blackness and the Animal Question* (Columbia University Press, 2018).
78. Kathryn Talalay, *Composition in Black and White: The Life of Philippa Schuyler* (Oxford University Press, 1995), 221–30, 251. Talalay argues that Philippa was influenced by her parents' "eugenic agenda" and ultimately sought an abortion for a child conceived with Georges Apedo-Amah, the Minister of Foreign Affairs of Togo, because he was Black.
79. Tressie McMillan Cottom, *Twitter Post*, October 5, 2016, https://twitter.com/tressiemcphd/status/783528151242727425; A. J. Muhammad, "'Get Out' Reading and Viewing List," Schomburg Center for Research in Black Culture, The New York Public Library, July 19, 2017, https://www.nypl.org/blog/2017/07/19/get-out-list. A number of astute observers noted Peele's erudite literary allusions to Amiri Baraka's [LeRoi Jones's] *Dutchman*, like Schomburg Library for Research in Black Culture librarian A. J. Muhammad. Tressie McMillan Cottom called *Get Out* "Dutchman + BLM aesthetic" on Twitter, saying "I'm surprised every horror movie isn't about racism because it's right there." But *Get Out* also drew on Yakub motifs about eugenics, white supremacy, brainwashing, and scientific racism.
80. Lavender, *Race in American Science Fiction*, 6; Martin, *White African American Body*, 153. Discussing the novel Martin writes that "whiteness and blackness become clearly arbitrary fluid fictions . . . unsettl[ing] racial construction until race itself is dismantled."
81. Susan Grubar, *Racechanges: White Skin, Black Face in American Culture* (Oxford University Press, 1997), 18, 19; Martin, *White African American Body*, 149.
82. Gilroy, *The Black Atlantic*, 73, 74.
83. Lavender, *Race in American Science Fiction*, 50, 51.
84. Werner Sollors, *Amiri Baraka / LeRoi Jones: The Quest for a "Populist Modernism"* (Columbia University Press, 1978); McAlister, *Epic Encounters: Culture, Media, and U.S. Interests in the Middle East since 1945* (University of California Press, 2005); Nelson, "Myth and Bioscience."

85. Alondra Nelson, "A Black Mass as Black Gothic: Myth and Bioscience in Black Cultural Nationalism, " in *New Thoughts on the Black Arts Movement*, ed. Lisa Gail Collins and Margo Natalie Crawford (Rutgers University Press, 2006), 138; Alondra Nelson, *Body and Soul: The Black Panther Party and the Fight against Medical Discrimination* (University of Minnesota Press, 2011); Alondra Nelson, *The Social Life of DNA: Race, Reparations, and Reconciliation After the Genome* (Beacon Press, 2016).
86. Alondra Nelson, "Afrofuturism," *Social Text* 20, no. 2 (2002): 1–15; Nelson, "Myth and Bioscience;" Nelson, *Body and Soul*; Nelson, *The Social Life of DNA*.
87. Nelson, "Myth and Bioscience," 138, 139, 148.
88. Edward E. Curtis IV, "Science and Technology in Elijah Muhammad's Nation of Islam: Astrophysical Disaster, Genetic Engineering, UFOs, White Apocalypse, and Black Resurrection," *Nova Religio: The Journal of Alternative and Emergent Religions* 20, no. 1 (2016): 15.
89. Stefan Kühl, *The Nazi Connection: Eugenics, American Racism, and German National Socialism* (Oxford University Press, 1994); Edwin Black, *War Against the Weak: Eugenics and America's Campaign to Create a Master Race* (Four Walls Eight Windows, 2003); Dorothy Roberts, *Killing the Black Body: Race, Reproduction, and the Meaning of Liberty* (Vintage, 2014); Alexandra Minna Stern, *Eugenic Nation: Faults and Frontiers of Better Breeding in Modern America* (University of California Press, 2016).
90. Curtis, "Science and Technology," 15.
91. Bowen, *A History of Conversion to Islam in the United States, Volume 2*; Knight, "Secrets You Are Not Permitted to Learn."
92. Muhammad, *Message to the Blackman*, 64–65; McAlister, *Epic Encounters*, 107; Ula Yvette Taylor, *The Promise of Patriarchy* (University of North Carolina Press, 2017), 115–17.
93. Curtis, "Science and Technology," 16; Nelson, "Myth and Bioscience," 148.
94. Roberts, *Killing the Black Body*, 84, 141; Jennifer Nelson, *Women of Color and the Reproductive Rights Movement* (New York University Press, 2003), 85–112; Alexandra Minna Stern, "Forced Sterilization Policies in the US Targeted Minorities and Those with Disabilities—and Lasted into the 21st Century," *The Conversation*, August 26, 2020, https://theconversation.com/forced-sterilization-policies-in-the-us-targeted-minorities-and-those-with-disabilities-and-lasted-into-the-21st-century-143144. Research by the Sterilization and Social Justice Lab shows that "sterilization rates for Black women rose as desegregation got underway.... The backlash involved the reassertion of white supremacist control and racial hierarchies specifically through the control of Black reproduction and future Black lives by sterilization."
95. Roberts, *Killing the Black Body*, 142; Baraka [Jones], *Autobiography*, 426. Roberts (like Alexandra Stern in *Eugenic Nation*) argues for differentiating between covert attempts by family-planning programs to prevent Black women from reproducing and Black women's own voluntary control over their reproductive rights—a stance Toni Cade Bambara, Frances Beal, and other Black feminists would voice and that Baraka would later adopt. ("We should not confuse birth control, which is voluntary, with enforced sterilization, which the imperialists practice on oppressed people.")
96. Muhammad, *Message to the Blackman*, 103.
97. Césaire, *Discourse on Colonialism*, 35–37, 41, 43.
98. Baraka [Jones], *A Black Mass*, 28, 30.
99. Baraka [Jones], *A Black Mass*, 2, 5, 11.
100. Baraka [Jones], *A Black Mass*, 29.
101. Mbembe, "Necropolitics," 22–23.
102. Mbembe, "Necropolitics," 17.
103. Muhammad, *Supreme Wisdom*, 21.
104. Muhammad, *Message to the Blackman*, 309.

105. Henry Dumas and Sun Ra, *The Ark and the Ankh: Sun Ra/Henry Dumas in Conversation, 1966, Slug's Saloon NYC* (Ikef Records, 2002), https://sunramusic.bandcamp.com/album/the-ankh-and-the-ark; Mathes, *Imagine the Sound: Experimental African American Literature After Civil Rights* (University of Minnesota Press, 2015); Harmony Holiday, "Disappearing Archives: Sun Ra and Henry Dumas, Recorded in Conversation," *Lit Hub*, June 10, 2019, https://lithub.com/disappearing-archives-sun-ra-and-henry-dumas-recorded-in-conversation/.
106. Art Sato, interview with John Gilmore, *Be-Bop and Beyond*, April 1986; John Corbett, *The Wisdom of Sun-Ra: Sun Ra's Polemical Broadsheets and Streetcorner Leaflets* (WhiteWalls, 2006), 66.
107. Szwed, *Space Is The Place*, 105–06; Graham Lock, *Blutopia: Visions of the Future and Revisions of the Past in the Work of Sun Ra, Duke Ellington, and Anthony Braxton* (Duke University Press, 1999), 47; Corbett, *Wisdom of Sun Ra*, 5; Brent Hayes Edwards, *Epistrophies: Jazz and the Literary Imagination* (Harvard University Press, 2017), 140; William Sites, *Sun Ra's Chicago* (University of Chicago Press, 2020), 101; Ellen McLarney and Solayman Idris, "Black Muslims and the Angels of Afrofuturism," *The Black Scholar* 53, no. 2 (2023): 30–47.
108. Sonny signed some of his early broadsheets "El Ra," gesturing, alongside the "El" in El Saturn Research, toward MSTA names that use "El" to express a Moorish identity, in addition to the "Ra" of Egyptian cosmology. Sun Ra and his band wore red fezzes and MSTA colors, red and green, until someone "warned them to never wear fezzes again." Promotional photographs from the 1950s show Sun Ra wearing fezzes, evoking identification with either or both the MSTA and/or the Black Shriners. See "Sun-Ra and His Modern Jazz Band," sec. 53:11, *Chicago Defender*, July 13, 1957; Alton Abraham, *Collection of Sun Ra*, Series VIII: Audio-Visual, Subseries 1: Photographs, Box 59 (University of Chicago Library); Szwed, *Space Is The Place*, 143; Sites, *Sun Ra's Chicago*, 95, 97.
109. Noble Drew Ali, *Koran Questions for Moorish Children*, 1/31 (Moorish Science Temple of America, 1931), vault.fbi.gov; Sites, *Sun Ra's Chicago*, 36.
110. Ali, *Koran Questions*; Szwed, *Space Is The Place*, 106; Corbett, *Wisdom of Sun Ra*, 66; Edwards, *Epistrophies*, 143.
111. Corbett, *Wisdom of Sun Ra*, 66; Sites, *Sun Ra's Chicago*, 99–103.
112. Szwed, *Space Is The Place*, 106.
113. Neal, "Afterword," 655.
114. Dumas and Sun Ra, *Sun Ra/Henry Dumas in Conversation*.
115. Neal, "The Black Arts Movement," 28.
116. Michael Muhammad Knight, *Magic in Islam* (Penguin Random House, 2016), 164, 166.
117. Neal, "Afterword," 655. "This sense of being separate, especially within a racist society with so-called democratic ideas," he writes, "this sense of the 'separate' moves through much of today's black literature; . . . a profound sense of a unique and beautiful culture; and a sense that there are many spiritual areas to explore *within* this culture. . . . There is a kind of peace in the separation. This peace may be threatened by the realities of the beast-world, but yet, it is lived as fully as life can be lived. This sense of a haven in blackness is found most often in the poetry."
118. Sylvia Wynter, "The Pope Must Have Been Drunk, the King of Castile a Madman: Culture as Actuality, and the Caribbean Rethinking Modernity," in *Reordering of Culture: Latin America, the Caribbean, and Canada in the Hood*, ed. Alvina Ruprecht and Cecilia Taiana (Carleton University Press, 1995); Jacob S. Dorman, *The Princess and the Prophet: The Secret History of Magic, Race, and Moorish Muslims in America* (Beacon Press, 202), 23. This quote opens Dorman's chapter "Oriental Magic" about Noble Drew Ali's work as a magician.
119. Paul Youngquist, "The Space Machine: Baraka and Science Fiction," *African American Review* 37, no. 2/3 (2003): 339.
120. Meta DuEwa Jones, *The Muse Is Music: Jazz Poetry from the Harlem Renaissance to Spoken Word* (University of Illinois Press, 2013), 7.

121. Travis Jackson, *Blowin' the Blues Away: Performance and Meaning on the New York Jazz Scene* (University of California Press, 2012), 369 quoted in Jones, *The Muse Is Music*, 7.
122. Jones, *The Muse Is Music*, 6.
123. Jones, *The Muse Is Music*, 5 ("ceremonial and communal function"); 6 ("rituals of recital"); 7 ("riffs, revisions, and remembrances...".
124. Finley, *In and Out of This World*, 22.
125. Soyica Diggs Colbert, Douglas A. Jones Jr., and Shane Vogel, "Tidying Up after Repetition," in *Race and Performance after Repetition*, ed. Soyica Diggs Colbert, Douglas A. Jones Jr., and Shane Vogel (Duke University Press, 2020), 8, 10.
126. Colbert et al., "Tidying Up after Repetition," 8, 10.
127. Sun Ra, "The Sound Image," in *Immeasurable Equation* (Ihnfinity Inc. / Saturn Research, 1972).
128. Baraka [Jones], "An Explanation of the Work."
129. Amiri Baraka and James E. Hinton, dirs., *The New-Ark*. Harlem, Audio Visual, 1968, Harvard Film Archive, James E. Hinton Collection; Amiri Baraka [Imamu Amiri Baraka], *Raise, Race, Rays, Raze: Essays Since 1965* (Random House, 1971); Sun Ra, *The Immeasurable Equation*, Ihnfinity Inc. / Saturn Research, 1972; Szwed, *Space Is The Place*, 209.
130. Sun Ra, "The Black Rays Race," in *The Immeasurable Equation*, 8.
131. Edwards, *Epistrophies*, 125.
132. Sun Ra, *Immeasurable Equation*, 13.
133. Sun Ra, "Preparation for Outer Space," in *Jazz By Sun Ra*, Transition, 1957.
134. Muhammad, *Message to the Blackman*, 42, 50, 65, 95, 108, 249.
135. Sun Ra, "Preparations"; Sun Ra and his Arkestra, *Jazz in Silhouette*, El Saturn, 1959; Sun Ra, *Immeasurable Equation*, 7, 11, 70.
136. Rey Chow, *Not Like a Native Speaker*, 8.
137. Baraka, *Raise, Race, Rays, Raze: Essays Since 1965*, 98.
138. Vanessa Taylor, "Take Me From My Plight: On Afrofuturism, the Afterlife, and a Black Future." *Medium*, December 18, 2017, https://medium.com/@BaconTribe/take-me-from-my-plight-564b77132de6.
139. Renee Cox, *The Signing*, 2017, Los Angeles Contemporary Museum of Art; Kevin Strait and Kinshasha Holman Conwill, eds., *Afrofuturism: A History of Black Futures* (Smithsonian Books, 2023).
140. Muhammad, *Message to the Blackman*, 233.
141. Elijah Muhammad, Black Velvet and Jeweled Kofia, the Interior Embroidered with "Elijah Muhammad, Our King, Messenger of Allah" (Heritage Auctions, 1970s), https://historical.ha.com/itm/general-historic-events/elijah-muhammad-black-velvet-and-jeweled-kofia-the-interior-embroidered-with-elijah-muhammad-our-king-messenger-of-allah-/a/6172-43244.s#; Bowen, *A History of Conversion to Islam in the United States, Volume 2*, 265. The kofia was embroidered with gold, diamonds, sapphires, rubies, emeralds, onyx, amethyst, and pearls.

4. MUSIC IN THE MESSAGE

1. Ralph Ellison, *Invisible Man* (Random House, 1952), 451–55; Jubilee Singers (Fisk University), *Many Thousand Gone*, American Missionary Association (Biglow and Main, 1872), 27.
2. Elizabeth Hinton, *America on Fire: The Untold History of Police Violence and Black Rebellion Since the 1960s* (Norton, 2021); Amiri Baraka, *The Autobiography of LeRoi Jones* (Lawrence Hill Books, 1997), 305.
3. Manning Marable and Garrett Felber, eds., *The Portable Malcolm X Reader: A Man Who Stands for Nothing Will Fall for Anything* (Penguin Classics, 2013), 81; Garrett Felber, *Those Who Know*

Don't Say: The Nation of Islam, the Black Freedom Movement, and the Carceral State (University of North Carolina Press, 2020), 85.

4. Malcolm X and Alex Haley, *The Autobiography of Malcolm X* (Ballantine Books, 2015), 247.
5. Hortense J. Spillers, "Fabrics of History: Essays on the Black Sermon" (PhD diss. University of Michigan, 1974).
6. Amiri Baraka [LeRoi Jones], "The Changing Same (R&B and New Black Music)," in *Black Music* (William Morrow, 1967), 204.
7. Malcolm X, "God's Angry Men," *New York Amsterdam News*, April 27, 1957.
8. Ellison, *Invisible Man*, 453; Malcolm X, "God's Angry Men," April 27, 1957, 18.
9. Louis X, "A White Man's Heaven Is a Black Man's Hell" (Muhammad's Mosque No. 32, 1960). See Abdul Basit Naeem, "Cites October 19th Benefit Concert As Example of New Outlook on Music," *Muhammad Speaks* 7, no. 5 (October 20, 1967): 10; and the liner notes for Prince Buster, *Africa-Islam-Revolution, Kingston, Jamaica 1966–72* (Earth Sound, 2019). Sources like these assert 1958 as the year that the track was recorded, but all copies seem to date to 1960. Naeem puts a question mark by the date. Its release on the label "A Moslem Sings" out of Phoenix Mosque No. 32, where Elijah Muhammad lived, suggests that proceeds would have gone in that direction. But it was also a Black label at a time that the recording industry was largely white-owned.
10. Nat Hentoff, "Elijah in the Wilderness," *The Reporter*, August 4, 1960, 37–40; James Baldwin, "Letter from a Region in My Mind," *New Yorker*, November 17, 1962; Nat Hentoff, "Remembering Malcolm," *Village Voice*, February 26, 1985; Nat Hentoff, *Speaking Freely: A Memoir* (Knopf, 1997). In his *Village Voice* article Hentoff recalls the song playing on repeat as he waited for an hour to interview Malcolm ("only one song played"). He asserts that it was the mid-1950s, before the NOI was in the white press, but the actual date of the article was 1960, a year after the documentary "The Hate that Hate Produced" premiered in July 1959.
11. W. E. B. Du Bois, "A Negro Nation within the Nation," *Current History*, June 1, 1935, 265–69; Elijiah Muhammad, *Message to the Blackman* (Secretarius Memps Publications, 1965), 230–32; Michael C. Dawson, *Black Visions: The Roots of Contemporary African-American Political Ideologies* (University of Chicago Press, 2001), 27–28; Warner, *Publics and Counterpublics* (Zone Books, 2002); Hirschkind, *Ethical Soundscape: Cassette Sermons and Islamic Counterpublics* (Columbia University Press, 2009).
12. Louis Farrakhan and Henry Louis Gates Jr., "Farrakhan Speaks," *Transition*, no. 70 (1996): 148–49.
13. Manning Marable, *Malcolm X: A Life of Reinvention* (Penguin Books, 2011), 132.
14. Farrakhan and Gates, "Farrakhan Speaks," 149.
15. James Weldon Johnson, *God's Trombones: Seven Negro Sermons in Verse* (Viking Press, 1927), 5.
16. Spillers, "Fabrics of History: Essays on the Black Sermon," 4–5. Though she analyzes Farrakhan's preaching, alongside her discussion of the musical cadences in the preaching of C. L. Lincoln, Spillers does not discuss Farrakhan as a musician.
17. Meta DuEwa Jones, *The Muse Is Music: Jazz Poetry from the Harlem Renaissance to Spoken Word* (University of Illinois Press, 2013), 7, 19. Jones writes about the process of citation in the recitation of the African American literary and poetic tradition, through an "aesthetics of riffs, remembrance, and improvisatory revision" on standards as an "overarching metaphor for ... cross-disciplinary forms of inter-artistic exchange and cultural expressivity" (23–24).
18. Aisha Khan, "Realising a Muslim Atlantic," AbuSulayman Center for Global Islamic Studies, George Mason University, *Maydan*, July 16, 2020, https://themaydan.com/2020/07/realising-a-muslim-atlantic/; S. A. Bonebakker, "Ibn Al-Mu'tazz and Kitab al-Badi'," in *'Abbasid Belles-Lettres*, ed. Julia Ashtiany et al. (Cambridge University Press, 1990); Ibn al-Mu'tazz, *Kitab Al-Badi'* (Maktabat al-Muthanna, 1979).

19. Sylviane Diouf, *Servants of Allah: African Muslims Enslaved in the Americas*. New York University Press, 1998, 251.
20. Farrakhan and Gates, "Farrakhan Speaks," 154. He includes Garvey among "all of these great men that preceded us, Dr. Gates, we are standing on their shoulders today." Describing a picture of Garvey on his uncle's wall, he said, "From there came this spirit, of a nationalistic love of black people and a desire for the black man to be what we believe God intended for us to be."
21. Malcolm X, "God's Angry Men," June 1, 1957, 20.
22. Jocelyne Guilbault, *Governing Sound: The Cultural Politics of Trinidad's Carnival Musics* (University of Chicago Press, 2007), 29, 39. Guilebault writes about calypso "as a crucible of unequal power and transcultural encounter," a "terrain on which power hierarchies and politics of exclusion were enacted," and "historical sediments fused ... with the histories of struggle and memories of community shared by enslaved Africans."
23. Paul Gilroy, *"There Ain't No Black in the Union Jack": The Cultural Politics of Race and Nation* (Hutchinson, 1987), 229, 236.
24. Malcolm X and Haley, *The Autobiography of Malcolm X*, 86; Robin D. G. Kelley, "The Riddle of the Zoot: Malcolm Little and Black Cultural Politics During World War II," in *Malcolm X: In Our Own Image* (St. Martin's Press, 1992).
25. Malcolm X, "Letter from Prison: 'Music, Brother, Is Ours,'" March 9, 1950, https://www.rrauction.com/auctions/lot-detail/345605706310161-malcolm-x-autograph-letter-signed/?cat=328.
26. Malcolm X, "Letter from Prison: 'Music, Brother, Is Ours.'"
27. John Coltrane, *A Love Supreme*, Van Gelder, 1965.
28. Jones, *The Muse Is Music*, 95.
29. Hazrat Inayat Khan, *Notes from the Unstruck Music from the Gayan of Hazrat Inayat Khan* (AE E Kluwer, 1948).
30. Malcolm X and Haley, *The Autobiography of Malcolm X*, 377; Malcolm "Shorty" Jarvis and Paul D. Nichols, *The Other Malcolm—"Shorty" Jarvis*, ed. Cornel R. West (McFarland & Company, 2001), 55, 125.
31. Jarvis and Nichols, *The Other Malcolm*, 55; Richard Brent Turner, *Soundtrack to a Movement: African American Islam, Jazz, and Black Internationalism* (New York University Press, 2021), 67–68, 86.
32. Garrett Felber, "Reconsidering Malcolm X and Islam," African American Intellectual History Society, *Black Perspectives*, February 8, 2016, https://www.aaihs.org/reconsidering-malcolm-x-and-islam/#_ftn3.
33. Malcolm X, "Letter from Prison: 'The Blacker a Man Is, the Holier He Is Inside,'" March 12, 1950, https://catalogue.swanngalleries.com/Lots/auction-lot/MALCOLM-X-Letter-from-prison-one-of-his-first-to-use-his-new?saleno=2471&lotNo=255&refNo=742749.
34. Malcolm X, "Letter from Prison: 'Music, Brother, Is Ours.'"
35. Malcolm X, "Letter from Prison: 'Music, Brother, Is Ours'"; Hisham Aidi, "The Music of Malcolm X," *New Yorker*, February 28, 2015, https://www.newyorker.com/culture/culture-desk/the-music-of-malcolm-x.
36. Turner, *Soundtrack to a Movement*, 120.
37. Allan Grant, "Mohammedan Leanings," *Life*, October 11, 1948, 142. No self-respecting Muslim would confuse Gillespie's shirtless, cross-legged pose with a Muslim prayer, but the public may not have properly differentiated.
38. Sonny Stitt, *All God's Children (Got Rhythm)*, Prestige, December 11, 1949; Malcolm X, "Letter from Prison."
39. Fatimah Fanusie, "Ahmadi, Beboppers, Veterans, and Migrants: African American Islam in Boston, 1948–1963," in *The African Diaspora and the Study of Religion*, ed. Theodore Louis Trost (Palgrave, 2007); Turner, *Soundtrack to a Movement*, 96.

40. Marable, *Malcolm X*, 71.
41. Aidi, *Rebel Music*, 113; Turner, *Soundtrack to a Movement*, 1. Turner ruminates at length on the influence of jazz on Malcolm X and Malcolm X's influence on jazz, beginning his book with a quote by Archie Shepp: "I equate Coltrane's music very strongly with Malcolm's language.... And I believe essentially what Malcolm said is what John played. If Trane had been a speaker, he might have spoken somewhat like Malcolm. If Malcolm had been a saxophone player, he might have played somewhat like Trane." Shepp does talk about the "rhetorical power of Malcolm X" on the Pushkin podcast "Archie Shepp: Activist of the Avant-Garde," https://www.pushkin.fm/podcasts/broken-record/archie-shepp-activist-of-the-avant-garde.
42. Turner, *Soundtrack to a Movement*, 114-15.
43. Farrakhan and Gates, "Farrakhan Speaks," 140, 145.
44. Naeem, "New Outlook on Music." Naeem says that "White Man's Heaven Is a Black Man's Hell" was released in "1958 (or 1957)." But the first recording on vinyl was issued in 1960, rather than in 1957 or 1958.
45. Naeem, "New Outlook on Music," 10; Turner, *Soundtrack to a Movement*, 158.
46. Aidi, "The Music of Malcolm X."
47. Richard Lei, "Louis Farrakhan, Calypso Charmer," *Washington Post*, October 15, 1995, https://www.washingtonpost.com/archive/lifestyle/1995/10/14/louis-farrakhan-calypso-charmer/40613502-02c1-48c0-8cde-8c0024d06015/.
48. Lei, "Louis Farrakhan, Calypso Charmer"; Pharoah Sanders, *Hum-Allah-Hum-Allah-Hum-Allah*, Jewels of Thought, Impulse! Records, October 20, 1969.
49. Su'ad Abdul Khabeer, *Muslim Cool: Race, Religion, and Hip Hop in the United States* (New York University Press, 2016), 6.
50. Malcolm X, "God's Angry Men," April 27, 1957, 34
51. *New York Amsterdam News*, "Mr. X Tells What Islan [sic] Means," April 20, 1957.
52. *New York Amsterdam News*, "The Real Harry Belafonte Story," April 20, 1957.
53. Malcolm X, "God's Angry Men," April 27, 1957, 34. An article Malcolm X wrote for the very first issue of *Muhammad Speaks* criticizes African American public figures like singers and writers for their interracial relationships. See Malcolm X, "Who Speaks for the Negro?," *Muhammad Speaks*, October 1, 1961, 1:1 edition.
54. Malcolm X, "God's Angry Men," June 1, 1957, 20.
55. Carter Mathes, *Imagine the Sound: Experimental African American Literature After Civil Rights* (University of Minnesota Press, 2015), 107.
56. Jonathan Curiel, "Muslim Roots of the Blues: The Music of Famous American Blues Singers Reaches Back through the South to the Culture of West Africa," *San Francisco Chronicle*, August 15, 2004, https://www.sfgate.com/opinion/article/Muslim-roots-of-the-blues-The-music-of-famous-2701489.php; Sylvia Chan-Malik, "Cultural and Literary Production of Muslim America," in *The Cambridge Companion to American Islam*, ed. Juliane Hammer and Omid Safi (Cambridge University Press, 2013), 281, 283–84; Sylviane A. Diouf, "What Islam Gave the Blues," *Renovatio: The Journal of Zaytuna College*, June 17, 2019, https://renovatio.zaytuna.edu/article/what-islam-gave-the-blues.
57. Malcolm X, "God's Angry Men," June 1, 1957, 20.
58. Martin Luther King Jr., "'Give Us the Ballot,' Address Delivered at the Prayer Pilgrimage for Freedom," in *The Papers of Martin Luther King, Jr. Volume IV: Symbol of the Movement, January 1957–December 1958*, ed. Clayborne Carson et al. (University of California Press, 1957).
59. *Life*, "Fervent Faces Amid a Gathering of Pilgrims," June 3, 1957, 14–15; Mahalia Jackson, *I've Been Buked and I've Been Scorned (Live in Prayer Pilgrimage for Freedom 1957)*, https://www.youtube.com/watch?v=FuQX33a9p44.

60. King, Jr., "Loving Your Enemies: Sermon Delivered to the Dexter Avenue Baptist Church." Montgomery, AL, November 17, 1957. https://kinginstitute.stanford.edu/king-papers/documents/loving-your-enemies-sermon-delivered-dexter-avenue-baptist-church.
61. Malcolm X, "God's Angry Men," June 1, 1957, 20.
62. Robert Darden, *Nothing but Love in God's Water: Black Sacred Music from the Civil War to the Civil Rights Movement* (Pennsylvania State University Press, 2014), 97, 129; Harry Belafonte, "Steal Away," *My Lord What a Mornin'* (RCA Victor, 1960).
63. Givens, *Fugitive Pedagogy: Carter G. Woodson and the Art of Black Teaching* (Harvard University Press, 2021).
64. Fisk University Jubilee Singers, *Steal Away*, vol. 2, 1915–1920, Fisk University Jubilee Singers, Document Records; Soul Stirrers, *Steal Away*, Aladdin, 1946; Mahalia Jackson and Nat King Cole, *Steal Away to Jesus*, Nat King Cole Show, NBC, November 12, 1957; Sam Cooke, *Steal Away*, Keen, 1960.
65. W. E. B. Du Bois, *The Souls of Black Folk* (A. C. McClurg & Co., 1903).
66. Ula Yvette Taylor, *The Promise of Patriarchy* (University of North Carolina Press, 2017), 154.
67. Taylor, *The Promise of Patriarchy*, 26.
68. Blind Willie Johnson ("The Blind Pilgrim"), "Motherless Children," Anchor, 1927; Blind Willie Johnson, "Mother's Children Have a Hard Time," in *His Story*, Folkways, 1957.
69. Samuel B. Charters, *The Country Blues* (Da Capo, 1959), 156; Malcolm X and Haley, *The Autobiography of Malcolm X*, 40–88.
70. Malcolm X, "God's Angry Men," June 1, 1957, 36; Elijah Muhammad, *The Supreme Wisdom, Volume I: Solution to the So-Called Negroes' Problem* (Secretarius Memps Publications, 1957), 11; Muhammad, *Message*, 42, 50, 65, 95, 108, 249.
71. Cliff Barrows, *Billy Graham Crusade Songs* (Billy Graham Evangelistic Association, 1957); Edith Blumhofer, "Singing to Save: Music in the Billy Graham Crusades," in *Billy Graham: American Pilgrim*, ed. Andrew Finstuen (Oxford, 2017).
72. Carl Smith Trio, "When the Roll Is Called Up Yonder," Columbia Records, 1957; Jimmy Dean, "When the Roll Is Called Up Yonder," in *Hour of Prayer*, Columbia Records, 1957; Singing Time in Dixie, "When the Roll Is Called Up Yonder," https://www.youtube.com/watch?v=kT9rlGi54yo; James R. Goff, *Close Harmony: A History of Southern Gospel* (University of North Carolina Press, 2002), 172.
73. James Milton Black. ed., "When the Roll Is Called," in *Sacred Praise* (Jennings and Graham, 1913); James Milton Black, "When the Roll Is Called Up Yonder," Edison Blue Amberol, 1913.
74. Louis X, "A White Man's Heaven Is a Black Man's Hell."
75. Malcolm X and Haley, *The Autobiography of Malcolm X*, 251; Marable, *Malcolm X*, 97.
76. Malcolm X and Haley, *The Autobiography of Malcolm X*, 252; Robert Darden, *People Get Ready!: A New History of Black Gospel Music* (Continuum, 2004), 196–220. I would like to acknowledge Michael West for drawing my attention to this passage in the *Autobiography*. Darden refers to Tharpe, Ward, and Jackson as the "three divas" in his chapter focusing on their contributions to Black gospel music.
77. Malcolm X, "God's Angry Men," June 1, 1957.
78. William Francis Allen, Charles Pickard Ware, and Lucy McKim Garrison, eds., "My Father, How Long?," in *Slave Songs of the United States* (A. Simpson & Co., 1867).
79. Du Bois, *The Souls of Black Folk*, 207; Mathes, *Imagine the Sound*, 11.
80. Diouf, "What Islam Gave the Blues."
81. Malcolm X, "God's Angry Men," *New York Amsterdam News*, May 25, 1957, 9; Louis X, "A White Man's Heaven Is a Black Man's Hell."
82. Peniel E. Joseph, *The Sword and the Shield: The Revolutionary Lives of Malcolm X and Martin Luther King Jr.* Basic Books, 2020, 43.
83. Peniel E. Joseph, *Waiting 'til the Midnight Hour: A Narrative History of Black Power in America* (Henry Holt and Co., 2006), 7; Joseph, *The Sword and the Shield*, 45; Smethurst, "Malcolm X and

the Black Arts Movement," in *Cambridge Companion to Malcolm X*, ed. Robert E. Terrill (Cambridge University Press, 2010).
84. Louis Farrakhan, "The Swan Song," Saviours' Day Address, Mosque Maryam, Chicago (February 27, 2022).
85. Jones, *The Muse Is Music*, 19.
86. Jones, *The Muse Is Music*, 7.
87. Travis Jackson, "'Always New and Centuries Old': Jazz, Poetry, and Tradition as Creative Adaptation," in *Uptown Conversation: The New Jazz Studies*, ed. Brent Hayes Edwards, Farah Jasmine Griffin, and Robert O'Meally (Columbia University Press, 2004), 489; Diouf, "What Islam Gave the Blues."
88. Marable and Aidi, "Introduction," 4.
89. Jones, *The Muse Is Music*, 7.
90. Curiel, "Muslim Roots of the Blues;" Chan-Malik, "Cultural and Literary Production of Muslim America," 281, 283–84; Diouf, "What Islam Gave the Blues."
91. Malcolm X, "God's Angry Men," April 27, 1957, 18.
92. Patrick Bernard analyzes the concept of call and response in Thomas W. Talley's 1922 work on Black folk rhymes, drawing on Bakhtin's concept of the dialogic. "Call and response" has been key to scholars' characterization of the African American literary tradition. See Patrick S. Bernard, "A 'Cipher Language:' Thomas W. Talley and Call-and-Response during the Harlem Renaissance," *African American Review* 52, no. 2 (2019): 126; Richard Powell, *African and Afro-American Art: Call and Response*, African Insights: Sources for Afro–American Art and Culture (Field Museum of Natural History, 1984); John F. Callahan, *In the African-American Grain: Call-and-Response in Twentieth-Century Black Fiction* (Wesleyan University Press, 1990); Patricia Liggins Hill et al., eds., *Call and Response: The Riverside Anthology of the African American Literary Tradition* (Houghton Mifflin, 1998); Henry Louis Gates Jr. and Jennifer Burton, eds., *Call and Response: Key Debates in African American Studies* (Norton, 2011). More recently, scholars like Sylviane Diouf have connected this feature of Black music to the Islamic musical tradition of West Africa. See: Diouf, "What Islam Gave the Blues."
93. T. J. Anderson III, *Notes to Make the Sound Come Right: Four Innovators of Jazz Poetry* (University of Arkansas Press, 2004), 14.
94. Aldon Lynn Nielsen, *Black Chant: Languages of African-American Postmodernism* (Cambridge University Press, 1997), 37.
95. Henry Louis Gates Jr., *The Signifying Monkey: A Theory of African American Literary Criticism* (Oxford University Press, 1988), 70.
96. Anderson, *Notes to Make the Sound Come Right*, 13.
97. Megan Thee Stallion, "Savage," in *Saturday Night Live*, with Beyoncé (2020), https://www.youtube.com/watch?v=CTpilDQXYr0; Megan Thee Stallion, "Why I Speak Up for Black Women," *New York Times*, October 13, 2020, https://www.nytimes.com/2020/10/13/opinion/megan-thee-stallion-black-women.html. A week after the SNL performance, she published the video Op-Ed in the *New York Times*, reiterating her protest in another medium.
98. Amiri Baraka, "A New Introduction," in *Black Fire: An Anthology of Afro-American Writing*, ed. Amiri Baraka and Larry Neal (Black Classic Press, 2013).
99. Heather Augustyn, *Ska: The Rhythm of Liberation* (Scarecrow Press, 2013), 29.
100. Abdul Khabeer, *Muslim Cool*, 8; Aisha Khan, *Far from Mecca: Globalizing the Muslim Caribbean* (Rutgers University Press, 2020), 135–36. Prince Buster and Jimmy Cliff were establishing in Jamaica what Khan describes as Muslim activists and musicians' performance of a "postcolonial Muslim Caribbean place of Islamic immanence that is a belonging to the land, and thus a belonging to the nation that proposes a citizenship not dependent upon religious or racial creolization" in Trinidad.
101. Mathes, *Imagine the Sound*, 10.

102. Joseph D. Eure and James G. Spady, eds., *Nation Conscious Rap*, (PC International Press, 1991); H. Samy Alim, *Roc the Mic Right: The Language of Hip Hop Culture* (Routledge, 2006); Richard Brent Turner, "Malcolm X and Youth Culture," in *The Cambridge Companion to Malcolm X* (Cambridge University Press, 2010), 101–12; Sohail Daulatzai, *Black Star, Crescent Moon: The Muslim International and Black Freedom Beyond America* (University of Minnesota Press, 2012), 89–136; Graeme Abernethy, *The Iconography of Malcolm X* (University of Kansas Press, 2013), 168–216; Hisham Aidi, *Rebel Music: Race, Empire, and the New Muslim Youth Culture* (Vintage, 2014); Zaheer Ali, "Curating the Malcolm X Mixtape Project," paper presented at The Legacy of Malcolm X: Afro-American Visionary, Muslim Activist, Duke University, February 16, 2015; Abdul Khabeer, *Muslim Cool*.
103. Public Enemy, "White Heaven/Black Hell," in *Muse Sick-n-Hour Mess Age*, Def Jam Recordings, 1994.
104. Dylan Rodríguez. "Black Studies in Impasse." *The Black Scholar* 44, no. 2 (2014): 37–49.
105. Malcolm X, "Message to the Grassroots," Afro-American Broadcasting and Recording Co., Northern Negro Leadership Conference, Detroit, MI, November 10, 1963; Public Enemy, "Fight the Power," on *Fear of a Black Planet*, Def Jam Recordings, 1990; Frank Kofsky, *Black Nationalism and the Revolution in Music* (Pathfinder, 1970), 258; Sohail Daulatzai, *Black Star, Crescent Moon: The Muslim International and Black Freedom beyond America* (University of Minnesota Press, 2012), 106.
106. Malcolm X, *On Afro-American History* (Merit Publishers, 1997), 22.
107. Ellison, *Invisible Man*, 454; Malcolm X, "Letter from Prison: 'Music, Brother, Is Ours.'"

5. "FLAME FEEDING FLAME"

1. Malcolm X and Alex Haley, *The Autobiography of Malcolm X* (Ballantine Books, 2015), 3.
2. Saidiya V. Hartman, *Scenes of Subjection: Terror, Slavery, and Self-Making in Nineteenth-Century America* (Oxford University Press, 1997), 3.
3. Malcolm X and Haley, *The Autobiography of Malcolm X*, 6.
4. Malcolm X and Haley, *The Autobiography of Malcolm X*, 4.
5. Marable Manning and Garrett Felber, eds., *The Portable Malcolm X Reader: A Man Who Stands for Nothing Will Fall for Anything* (Penguin Classics, 2013), 250.
6. Malcolm X, "Twenty Million Black People in a Political, Economic and Mental Prison," in *Malcolm X: The Last Speeches*, ed. Bruce Perry (Pathfinder, 1989), 72; Robin D. G. Kelley, "House Negroes on the Loose: Malcolm X and the Black Bourgeoisie," *Callaloo* 21, no. 2 (1998): 419–35.
7. Malcolm X, "God's Angry Men," *New York Amsterdam News*, June 1, 1957, 20.
8. Malcolm X, "Young Moslem Leader Explains the Doctrine of Mohammadanism," *Herald-Dispatch* (Los Angeles), July 18, 1957.
9. James Baldwin, *The Fire Next Time* (Vintage, 1993), 94.
10. Peniel E. Joseph, *Waiting 'til the Midnight Hour: A Narrative History of Black Power in America* (Henry Holt and Co., 2006), 7; Peniel E. Joseph, *The Sword and the Shield: The Revolutionary Lives of Malcolm X and Martin Luther King Jr.* (Basic Books, 2020), 45; James Smethurst, "Malcolm X and the Black Arts Movement," in *Cambridge Companion to Malcolm X*, ed. Robert E. Terrill (Cambridge University Press, 2010).
11. Joseph, *The Sword and the Shield*, 43.
12. Ossie Davis, "*Eyes on the Prize II: America at the Racial Crossroads 1965–85*, Telephone Pre-Interview Transcript," interview by Madison Davis Lacy, Jr. and Blackside, Inc., July 6, 1989, Washington

University Film and Media Archive, Henry Hampton Collection, http://digital.wustl.edu/e/eii/eiiweb/dav5427.0777.0370ssiedavis.html.

13. Maya Angelou, *Heart of a Woman* (Random House, 1981), 5–6; Kevin K. Gaines, *American Africans in Ghana* (University of North Carolina Press, 2006), 179–209; Paule Marshall, *Conversations with Paule Marshall* (University Press of Mississippi, 2010), 181. Angelou would describe Malcolm X in that meeting as "too bright.... A hot desert storm eddied around him and rushed to me.... Up close he was a great red arch through which one could pass to eternity. His hair was the color of burning embers and his eyes pierced."

14. John Henrik Clarke, *Malcolm X: The Man and His Times* (Macmillan, 1970), 341.

15. James Baldwin et al., "Negro in American Culture," *CrossCurrents* 11, no. 3 (1961): 205–24; Lorraine Hansberry, James Baldwin, and Langston Hughes, contribs., "The Negro Writer in America," *The Negro in American Culture*, WBAI Radio, January 1, 1961, Walter J. Brown Media Archives & Peabody Awards Collection at the University of Georgia, https://americanarchive.org/catalog/cpb-aacip-526-901zc7ss52; Robert Nemiroff, dir., *Lorraine Hansberry Speaks Out: Art and the Black Revolution* (Harper Audio / Caedmon, 1972).

16. Malcolm X and Bayard Rustin, *A Choice of Two Roads* (1960), http://corenyc.org/omeka/items/show/332; Malcolm X, "Bayard Rustin Debate," *Malcolm X Files*, November 1960, http://malcolmxfiles.blogspot.com/2013/05/bayard-rustin-debate-november-1960.html.

17. Baldwin, "A Negro Assays the Negro Mood," *New York Times*, March 12, 1961. https://www.nytimes.com/1961/03/12/archives/a-negro-assays-the-negro-mood-the-rise-of-independent-africa-he.html; James Baldwin, *Nobody Knows My Name* (Vintage, 1992), 72.

18. Imani Perry, *Looking for Lorraine: The Radiant and Radical Life of Lorraine Hansberry* (Beacon Press, 2018), 123, 126.

19. Dylan Rodríguez, "Black Studies in Impasse," *The Black Scholar* 44, no. 2 (2014): 39–40.

20. Hasan X, "Malcolm X—Debate with James Baldwin," *YouTube*, https://www.youtube.com/watch?v=sVNVb7sKwoU, last accessed September 2020; see also Ellen McLarney, "James Baldwin and the Power of Black Muslim Language," *Social Text* 37, no. 1 (2019), 59; Ellen McLarney, "The Burning House: Revolution and Black Art," *Souls: A Critical Journal of Black Politics, Culture, and Society* 23, no. 3–4 (2022), 187.

21. Timothy Tyson writes about "arson as black protest" during slavery, World War II, and the postwar black freedom movement. Timothy B. Tyson, "Burning for Freedom: Black Power and White Terror in Oxford, North Carolina" (MA thesis, Duke University, 1990); Timothy B. Tyson, *Radio Free Dixie: Robert F. Williams and the Roots of Black Power* (University of North Carolina Press, 1999), 262–63, 351n3.

22. Patrick S. Bernard, "A 'Cipher Language:' Thomas W. Talley and Call-and-Response during the Harlem Renaissance," *African American Review* 52, no. 2 (2019): 126; Richard Powell, *African and Afro-American Art: Call and Response*, African Insights: Sources for Afro–American Art and Culture (Field Museum of Natural History, 1984); John F. Callahan, *In the African-American Grain: Call-and-Response in Twentieth-Century Black Fiction* (Wesleyan University Press, 1990); Patricia Liggins Hill et al., eds., *Call and Response: The Riverside Anthology of the African American Literary Tradition* (Houghton Mifflin, 1998); Henry Louis Gates Jr. and Jennifer Burton, eds., *Call and Response: Key Debates in African American Studies* (Norton, 2011). More recently, scholars like Sylviane Diouf have connected this feature of Black music to the Islamic musical tradition of West Africa. See: Sylviane A. Diouf, "What Islam Gave the Blues," *Renovatio: The Journal of Zaytuna College*, June 17, 2019, https://renovatio.zaytuna.edu/article/what-islam-gave-the-blues.

23. Houston A. Baker Jr., "Critical Memory and the Black Public Sphere," in *The Black Public Sphere*, ed. Black Public Sphere Collective (University of Chicago Press, 1995); Michael C. Dawson, *Black Visions: The Roots of Contemporary African-American Political Ideologies* (University of Chicago Press, 2001); Michael C. Dawson, "The Black Public Sphere and Black Civil Society," in *The Oxford*

Handbook of African American Citizenship, 1865–Present, ed. Henry Louis Gates Jr. and et al. (Oxford University Press, 2012).

24. Jesmyn Ward, *The Fire This Time: A New Generation Speaks about Race* (Scribner, 2017); Amir Sulaiman, dir., *Laying Flowers, Setting Fires*, 2020, https://sapelosquare.com/2020/11/24/laying-flowers-setting-fires-amir-sulaiman, and https://www.youtube.com/watch?v=fYogdFvotho; Kim McMillon and Kofi Antwi, eds. *Black Fire This Time* (Willow Books, 2022); Meshell Ndegeocello, "No More Water / The Fire Next Time: The Gospel According to James Baldwin" (Symphony Space, New York, February 26, 2022).

25. Amiri Baraka, "A New Introduction," in *Black Fire: An Anthology of Afro-American Writing*, ed. Amiri Baraka [Le Roi Jones] and Larry Neal (Black Classic Press, 2013), xvii.

26. Orlando Edmonds, "Why James Baldwin's The Fire Next Time Still Matters," *Daily*, November 2, 2016, https://daily.jstor.org/feature-james-baldwin-fire-next-time/; Nicholas Powers, "Trapped in a Burning House," *TruthOut*, July 30, 2017, https://truthout.org/articles/trapped-in-a-burning-house-a-review-of-i-am-not-your-negro/; Sharif El-Mekki, "MLK's 'Burning House,' " *The Philadelphia Citizen*, January 19, 2018, https://thephiladelphiacitizen.org/mlks-burning-house/; Kendi King, "America Is Still A Burning House," *The North Star*, August 2, 2021, https://www.thenorthstar.com/p/america-is-still-a-burning-house.

27. Christen A. Smith et al., "Cite Black Women: A Critical Praxis (A Statement)," *Feminist Anthropology* 2, no. 1 (2021): 12.

28. Dylan Rodríguez, "Black Studies in Impasse," *The Black Scholar* 44, no. 2 (2014): 38; West, "The Dilemma of the Black Intellectual." This is what West describes, in an earlier article, as "insurgent creative activity on the margins of the mainstream ensconced within bludgeoning new infrastructures" (112).

29. Sun Ra, "Saga of Resistance," in *Black Fire: An Anthology of Afro-American Writing*, ed. Amiri Baraka and Larry Neal (William Morrow, 1968).

30. Henry Louis Gates Jr., *The Signifying Monkey: A Theory of African American Literary Criticism* (Oxford University Press, 1988), 70.

31. Malcolm X and Rustin, *A Choice of Two Roads*, 1960, http://corenyc.org/omeka/items/show/332; James Baldwin, Malcolm X, and Laverne McCummings, contribs., *Black Muslims vs. the Sit-Ins*, with James Baldwin et al., aired April 25, 1961, on WBAI, Pacifica Radio Archives (BB5322); Malcolm X, "Eleanor Fischer Interviews Malcolm X," 1961, WNYC, https://www.wnyc.org/story/87636-remembering-malcolm-x-rare-interviews-and-audio; Malcolm X, *El-Hajj Malik El-Shabazz Malcolm X: Collected Speeches, Debates, and Interviews (1960–65)*, ed. antihostile. n.d., http://malcolmxfiles.blogspot.com/2015/02/the-complete-malcolm-x-40-hours-of.html, 32.

32. Smethurst, "Malcolm X and the Black Arts Movement," 88.

33. Amiri Baraka, "A Wiser Play Than Some of Us Knew," *Los Angeles Review of Books*, March 22, 1987; Perry, *Looking for Lorraine*, 101; Soyica Diggs Colbert, *Radical Vision: A Biography of Lorraine Hansberry* (Yale University Press, 2021), 116.

34. Perry, *Looking for Lorraine*; Colbert, *Radical Vision*, 15.

35. Perry, *Looking for Lorraine*, 12–13.

36. Baraka, "A Wiser Play Than Some of Us Knew"; Amiri Baraka, *A Critical Reevaluation: A Raisin in the Sun's Enduring Passion* (New American Library, 1987).

37. Orlando Bagwell, dir. *Malcolm X: Make It Plain*. PBS, 1994; John Henrik Clarke, Malcolm X's collaborator in writing the charter for the OAAU, spoke about Malcolm X: "He was saying something over and above that of any other leader of that day. While the other leaders were begging for entry into the house of their oppressor, he was telling you to build your own house."

38. Hughes, "The Negro Artist and the Racial Mountain," *The Nation*, June 23, 1926, 692–93; W. E. B. Du Bois, "Criteria of Negro Art," *The Crisis* 32 (October 1926): 290–97.

39. Baldwin et al., "Negro in American Culture," 217.

40. Baldwin et al., "Negro in American Culture," 217.
41. Baldwin et al., "Negro in American Culture," 219; Hughes, "The Negro Artist." Hentoff references Hughes's earlier essay about the nature of Black art.
42. Perry, *Looking for Lorraine*, 121–22.
43. Baldwin et al., "Negro in American Culture," 220; Perry, *Looking for Lorraine*, 122; Baldwin, *The Fire Next Time*, 88. The audio (although misdated and with a different title) gives a sense of the quick-witted banter between Baldwin and Hansberry, the call and response that Perry references in her own quotation of the passage.
44. Kobena Mercer, *Welcome to the Jungle: New Positions in Black Cultural Studies* (Routledge, 1994), 240; Tavia Nyong'o, "Unburdening Representation," *The Black Scholar: Journal of Black Studies and Research* 44, no. 2 (2014): 73.
45. Baldwin et al., "Negro in American Culture," 220. Italics are mine.
46. Colbert, *Radical Vision*, 34.
47. Mayfield, "Mainstream and Oblivion," 220.
48. Baldwin et al., "Negro in American Culture," 206.
49. Baldwin et al., "Negro in American Culture," 218. They reject the idea of "socialist realism," arguing that art is not so much the truth reflecting the time and place of the book's writing, but the "past, the present, and the future. No book, either [the black writer's] book or the white man's book, can satisfy him about the truth. Because the truth is not only about what he has and what he is, but what he wants to become, and he wants America to become." Baldwin replies, "I accept the proposition that perhaps we are not so much reflecting life as trying to create it."
50. Baldwin et al., "Negro in American Culture," 209–10.
51. Baldwin et al., "Negro in American Culture," 209–10.
52. Joel Whitney, "Lorraine Hansberry Was an Unapologetic Radical," *Jacobin*, December 2020, https://www.jacobinmag.com/2020/12/lorraine-hansberry-raisin-in-the-sun-playwright.
53. Langston Hughes, "Testimony of Langston Hughes (Accompanied by His Counsel, Frank D. Reeves) before the Senate Permanent Subcommittee on Investigations of the Committee on Government Operations," *NPR*, March 24, 1953, https://legacy.npr.org/programs/atc/features/2003/may/mccarthy/hughes.html.
54. Mayfield, "Mainstream and Oblivion," 33. Italics are mine.
55. Baldwin et al., "Negro in American Culture"; Mayfield, "Mainstream and Oblivion."
56. Mary Helen Washington, *The Other Blacklist: The African American Literary and Cultural Left of the 1950s* (Columbia University Press, 2015), 241. The conference was also covered by the CIA, FBI, and Harold Cruse who was working undercover "to monitor and contain black radicalism," particularly its relationship to protest movements abroad. Expressions of cultural solidarity were carefully choreographed with the aim of surveillance and containment of dissident revolutionary elements that were variously anticolonial, socialist and communist, and sometimes Islamic. These distinct strands were not commensurate but had overlapping agendas and aims partly expressed through loose coalitions and solidarities built between different organizations in the Black Liberation Movement both at home and abroad.
57. Baldwin et al., "Negro in American Culture"; Washington, *The Other*, 239–65.
58. Julian Mayfield, "Into the Mainstream and Oblivion," in *The American Negro Writer and His Roots: Selected Papers*, ed. John Aubrey Davis Sr. First Conference of Negro Writers 1959 (American Society of African Culture, 1960), 33.
59. Martin Luther King Jr., "After Civil Rights: Black Power," interview by Sanders Vanocur, May 8, 1967, NBC News, https://www.nbcnews.com/video/martin-luther-king-jr-speaks-with-nbc-news-11-months-before-assassination-1202163779741.
60. Julian Mayfield, "Author Says Cuba Has Solution to Race Problem," *Fair Play*, October 25, 1960, 1.
61. Edith Sampson, a black delegate to UNESCO, disassociated herself from the United States' vote.

62. Julian Mayfield, "Castro's Visit to Harlem," letter, 1960, Julian Mayfield papers, Sc MG 339, box 7, folder 7. Schomburg Center for Research in Black Culture. Manuscripts, Archives and Rare Books Division, The New York Public Library; Mayfield, "Author Says Cuba Has Solution to Race Problem"; Tyson, *Radio Free Dixie*, 221; William Jelani Cobb, "Castro: A Friend to Americans of Color?," interview by Ed Gordon, August 25, 2006, National Public Radio, https://www.npr.org/templates/story/story.php?storyId=5709613; Garrett Felber, "A Bandung Conference in Harlem: The Meaning of Castro's Visit Uptown," Africa, *AAIHS*, December 1, 2016, https://www.aaihs.org/a-bandung-conference-in-harlem-the-meaning-of-castros-visit-uptown/.
63. Tyson, *Radio Free Dixie*, 237. Tyson is characterizing Williams's late 1960 and early 1961 speeches in Harlem for Fair Play for Cuba.
64. Lorraine Hansberry, "The Negro Writer and His Roots: Toward a New Romanticism," *The Black Scholar* 12, no. 2 (1981): 6.
65. Malcolm X, "Harlem Freedom Rally," New York, NY, July 1960, http://malcolmxfiles.blogspot.ca/2013/05/harlem-freedom-rally-1960.html.
66. Baldwin et al., "Negro in American Culture."
67. Perry, *Looking for Lorraine*, 152.
68. Malcolm X and Rustin, *A Choice of Two Roads*; Malcolm X, "Bayard Rustin Debate."
69. Malcolm X and Rustin, *A Choice of Two Roads*; "Islam Advancing in West Africa: Christians Worried by Gains—Simple Mosel Tenets Credited for Appeal," *New York Times*, October 6, 1960, https://www.nytimes.com/1960/10/09/archives/islam-advancing-in-west-africa-christians-worked-by-gains-simple.html.
70. Malcolm X and Rustin, *A Choice of Two Roads*; Malcolm X, "Eleanor Fischer Interviews Malcolm X." In the Rustin debate, Malcolm X criticizes Black leaders for making "the Negro masses used to thinking in terms of second-class citizenship, of which there is no such thing. We who follow the Honorable Elijah Muhammad believe that a man is either a citizen or he is not a citizen." In the Eleanor Fischer interview a few months later, he uses similar imagery to criticize Black leaders who make "the white man think that our people are satisfied to sit in his house and wait for him to correct these conditions. He is misrepresenting the thinking of the black masses, ... making the white man be more complacent than he would be if he knew the dangerous situation that is building up right inside his own house."
71. Kevin Gaines, "African American Expatriates in Ghana and the Black Radical Tradition," *Souls* 1, no. 4 (1999).
72. Malcolm X, *El-Hajj Malik El-Shabazz Malcolm X: Collected Speeches*, 13, 14, 15, 35; Muhammad, *Message to the Blackman in America* (Secretarius Memps Publications, 1965), 230.
73. Rafael Rojas, *Fighting Over Fidel: The New York Intellectuals and the Cuban Revolution*, trans. Carl Good (Princeton University Press, 2016), 166–67.
74. Tyson, *Radio Free Dixie*, 145, 344n74.
75. Julian Mayfield, "Letter to Arthur P. Davis," April 4, 1981, Julian Mayfield papers, Sc MG 339, box 4, folder 12. Schomburg Center for Research in Black Culture. Manuscripts, Archives and Rare Books Division, The New York Public Library; Julian Mayfield, "Letter to Lorraine Hansberry," April 5, 1961, Sc MG 680, box 63, folder 15. Schomburg Center for Research in Black Culture. Manuscripts, Archives and Rare Books Division, The New York Public Library; Rebeccah Welch, "Black Art and Activism in Postwar New York, 1950–1965" (PhD thesis, New York University, 2002), 2; Perry, *Looking for Lorraine*, 155. In Mayfield's April 1961 letter to Hansberry, he writes, "Ossie and I have been thinking that a few of us ought to get together one afternoon to knock around some of the problems that are bound to face us in the near future: Africa, Sit ins, Passive resistance, etc."
76. Davis, "*Eyes on the Prize II* ... Pre-Interview Transcript"; Malcolm X, "Who Speaks for the Negro?," *Muhammad Speaks*, October 1, 1961. 1:1 Edition.

77. David Tyroler Romine, "'Into the Mainstream and Oblivion:' Julian Mayfield's Black Radical Tradition, 1948–1984" (PhD thesis, Duke University, 2018), 148.
78. Malcolm X, *El-Hajj Malik El-Shabazz Malcolm X: Collected Speeches*, 205.
79. David Grundy, *A Black Arts Poetry Machine: Amiri Baraka and the Umbra Poets* (Bloomsbury, 2019), 35.
80. Baldwin, "A Negro Assays the Negro Mood"; Malcolm X, "Eleanor Fischer Interviews Malcolm X."
81. Baldwin, "A Negro Assays the Negro Mood"; Baldwin, *Nobody Knows My Name*, 72; Malcolm X, "Eleanor Fischer Interviews Malcolm X."
82. Malcolm X, *The Speeches of Malcolm X at Harvard*, ed. Archie Epps (William Morrow, 1968), 120, 127. Malcolm X, *El-Hajj Malik El-Shabazz Malcolm X: Collected Speeches*, 30, 32.
83. Malcolm X, *El-Hajj Malik El-Shabazz Malcolm X: Collected Speeches*, 13, 15, 34; Muhammad, *Message to the Blackman*, 229. Malcolm X talks about reading Du Bois while in prison, see Malcolm X and Haley, *The Autobiography of Malcolm X*, 201. At the Harlem Freedom Rally and at Queen's College, both in 1960, he talked about "a nation within a nation," as well as at Harvard the following year.
84. Bagwell, *Make It Plain*.
85. Baldwin, *The Fire Next Time*, 94.
86. Malcolm X and James Farmer, "Separation or Integration: A Debate," *Dialogue* 2, no. 3 (1962); Malcolm X and James Farmer, "Malcolm X v. James Farmer: Separation v. Integration," in *Negro Protest Thought in the Twentieth Century*, ed. Francis L. Broderick and August Meier (Bobbs-Merrill, 1965), 363; Marable and Felber, *Portable Malcolm X*, 198.
87. Malcolm X and Farmer, "Separation or Integration"; Malcolm X and Farmer, "Malcolm X v. James Farmer"; Marable and Felber, *Portable Malcolm X*, 198.
88. James H. Cone, *Martin & Malcolm & America: A Dream or a Nightmare* (Orbis Books, 1991).
89. Baldwin, *The Fire Next Time*, 89.
90. Muhammad, *Message to the Blackman*, 87.
91. Kelley, "House Negroes on the Loose."
92. Malcolm X, "Political, Economic and Mental Prison," 72.
93. Malcolm X, *El-Hajj Malik El-Shabazz Malcolm X: Collected Speeches*, 139.
94. Andrew Hill, *Black Fire* (Blue Note Records, 1964); Archie Shepp, "Malcolm, Malcolm Semper Malcolm," in *Fire Music*, Impulse!, 1965.
95. Turner, *Soundtrack to a Movement: African American Islam, Jazz, and Black Internationalism* (New York University Press), 2021, 1.
96. Ashley D. Farmer, "The Many Women Mentors of Malcolm X," *Black Perspectives*, May 3, 2016, https://www.aaihs.org/the-many-women-mentors-of-malcolm-x/.
97. Amiri Baraka, *The Autobiography of LeRoi Jones* (Lawrence Hill Books, 1997), 272, 274.
98. Baraka, "A New Introduction," xvii.
99. Askia Muhammad Touré [Rolland Snellings], "Song of Fire," *Umbra*, no. #2 (December 1963).
100. Lorenzo Thomas, "Askia Muhammad Touré: Crying Out the Goodness," *Obsidian* 1, no. 1 (1975): 32.
101. Lorenzo Thomas, "The Shadow World: New York's Umbra Workshop & Origins of the Black Arts Movement." *Callaloo*, no. 4 (1978): 53–72; Smethurst, "Malcolm X and the Black Arts Movement," 82; Grundy, *A Black Arts Poetry Machine*, 35.
102. Welch, "Black Art and Activism," 2–5.
103. Askia Muhammad Touré [Rolland Snellings], "Malcolm X as International Spokesman," *Liberator* 6 (February 1966): 6; Thomas, "The Shadow World," 61.
104. Marvin X [Marvin Jackmon], "Burn, Baby, Burn," *Soulbook: The Quarterly Journal of Revolutionary Afroamerica* 1, no. 3 (1965): 153; Marvin X [Marvin E. Jackmon], "Burn, Baby, Burn," in *Black*

Fire: An Anthology of Afro-American Writing, ed. Amiri Baraka [LeRoi Jones] and Larry Neal (William Morrow, 1968).
105. Marvin X [Marvin E Jackmon], "Burn, Baby, Burn"; Jerry Cohen and William S. Murphy, "There's Still Hell to Pay in Watts: Burn, Baby, Burn," *Life Magazine*, July 15, 1966, 34–64; Jimmy Collier and Frederick Douglass Kirkpatrick, *Burn, Baby, Burn*, The Best of Broadside 1962–1988: Anthems of the American Underground from the Pages of Broadside Magazine, Smithsonian Folkways, 2001, https://folkways.si.edu/the-best-of-broadside-1962-1988-anthems-of-the-american-underground-from-the-pages-of-broadside-magazine/folk/music/album/smithsonian.
106. Göran Hugo Olsson, dir., *The Black Power Mixtape 1967–1975*, IFC Films, 2011.
107. Amy Abugo Ongiri, *Spectacular Blackness: The Cultural Politics of the Black Power Movement and the Search for a Black Aesthetic* (University of Virginia Press, 2009), 107–11. See, in particular, Ongiri's chapter 3, "Black Power, Black Intellectuals, and the Search to Define a Black Aesthetic," which talks about the importance of anthologies for BAM.
108. Rodríguez, "Black Studies in Impasse," 39.
109. Joseph, *Waiting 'til the Midnight Hour*, 7.
110. Rodríguez, "Black Studies in Impasse," 39–40.
111. Gerald Horne, *Fire This Time: The Watts Uprising and the 1960s* (University Press of Virginia, 1995); Taylor Branch, *Pillar of Fire: America in the King Years, 1963–65* (Simon & Schuster, 1998); Sean Patrick O'Rourke and Leslie K. Pace, eds., *Like Wildfire: The Rhetoric of the Civil Rights Sit Ins* (University of South Carolina Press, 2020).
112. Kelley, "House Negroes on the Loose."
113. James Baldwin, "How to Cool It," *Esquire*, July 1968.
114. Jineea Butler, "Integrating into a Burning House," *The Final Call*, December 12, 2014.
115. Harry Belafonte and Michael Shnayerson, *My Song: A Memoir* (Knopf, 2011), 329.
116. King, "After Civil Rights."
117. Cornel West, *Restoring Hope: Conversations on the Future of Black America*, ed. Kelvin Shawn Sealey (Beacon Press, 1997), 24; Anthony V. Alfieri, "Integrating into a Burning House: Race- and Identity-Conscious Visions in Brown's Inner City," *Southern California Law Review* 84 (2011): 541–604; Autodidact 17, "Dr. Martin Luther King Jr: 'I Fear I Am Integrating My People into a Burning House,'" *New York Amsterdam News*, January 12, 2017, http://amsterdamnews.com/news/2017/jan/12/dr-martin-luther-king-jr-i-fear-i-am-integrating-m/; El-Mekki, "MLK's 'Burning House.'"
118. Sulaiman, *Laying Flowers, Setting Fires.*
119. Audre Lorde, *Sister Outsider: Essays and Speeches* (Ten Speed Press, 1984), 112.
120. Angela Davis, "Meditations on the Legacy of Malcolm X," in *Malcolm X: In Our Own Image*, ed. Joe Wood (St. Martin's Press, 1992), 44.

6. "FLY TO ALLAH"

1. Marvin Jackmon, *Flowers for the Trashman*, in *Black Fire: An Anthology of Afro-American Writing*, ed. Amiri Baraka [LeRoi Jones] and Larry Neal (William Morrow, 1968). In 1972 a "toned down" Nation of Islam version of the play entitled *Taking Care of Business* was performed at UC Berkeley's Zellerbach Hall accompanied by Sun Ra and his Arkestra. Both Marvin X and Sun Ra were teaching at Berkeley at the time, in their Ethnic Studies program, with Sun Ra as an "artist in residence" teaching a course "The Black Man in the Cosmos." Marvin X, interview with author, "Black History Poetry Reading Tour," February 7, 2020.
2. Carter Mathes, *Imagine the Sound: Experimental African American Literature After Civil Rights* (University of Minnesota Press, 2015), 30.

3. Robin D. G. Kelley, "Black Study, Black Struggle," *Ufahamu* 40, no. 2 (2018): 166.
4. Stefano Harney and Fred Moten, *The Undercommons: Fugitive Planning & Black Study* (Minor Compositions, 2016).
5. Mark Anthony Neal, *What the Music Said* (Routledge, 1998), 3.
6. Marvin X, *Notes of an Artistic Freedom Fighter* (Black Bird Press, 2019).
7. Marvin X, Juneteenth interviews by the author, June 19, 2019, in Oakland, Marin City, Berkeley, San Francisco; Harney and Moten, *The Undercommons*.
8. Marvin X and Faruk, "Islam and Black Art: An Interview with LeRoi Jones," *Negro Digest* 18, no. 3 (January 1969): 6.
9. Larry Neal, "The Black Arts Movement," *The Drama Review: TDR* 12, no. 4 (1968): 39; also see Alexander G. Weheliye, "Black Studies and Black Life," *The Black Scholar: Journal of Black Studies and Research* 44, no. 2 (2014): 5.
10. Mohja Kahf, "Teaching Diaspora Literature: Muslim American Literature as an Emerging Field," *Journal of Pan African Studies* 4, no. 2 (2010): 164, 167.
11. Kahf, "Teaching Diaspora Literature," 167. See also an excellent discussion of Kahf's analysis of Marvin X's contributions in Sylvia Chan-Malik, "Cultural and Literary Production of Muslim America," in *The Cambridge Companion to American Islam*, ed. Juliane Hammer and Omid Safi (Cambridge University Press, 2013), 286, 289–90.
12. J. Griffith Rollefson, *CIPHER: Hip Hop Interpellation* (University College Cork, 2018).
13. Carmen Kynard, *Vernacular Insurrections: Race, Black Protest, and the New Century in Composition-Literacies Studies* (State University of New York Press, 2013), 8; Sylviane A. Diouf, *Servants of Allah: African Muslims Enslaved in the Americas* (New York University Press, 1998), 161.
14. Larry Neal, "The Black Arts Movement," *The Drama Review: TDR* 12, no. 4 (1968): 29, 31. Talal Asad, *Formations of the Secular: Christianity, Islam, Modernity* (Stanford University Press, 2003), 25, 222.
15. Marvin X [Nazzam Al Sudan], *Sudan Rajuli Samia / Black Man Listen* (Al Kitab Sudan, 1967), 2–3.
16. Su'ad Abdul Khabeer, "Black Arabic: Some Notes on African American Muslims and the Arabic Language," in *Black Routes to Islam*, ed. Manning Marable and Hishaam D. Aidi (Palgrave Macmillan, 2009), 170–71.
17. Neal, "The Black Arts Movement," 38.
18. Aldon Lynn Nielsen, *Black Chant: Languages of African-American Postmodernism* (Cambridge University Press, 1997), 16–17.
19. Harryette Mullen, "African Signs and Spirit Writing," in *The Black Studies Reader*, ed. Jacqueline Bobo, Cynthia Hudley, and Claudine Michel (Routledge, 2004), 288.
20. Elijah Muhammad, *Message to the Blackman in America* (Secretarius Memps Publications, 1965), 12, 18, 50, passim. Elijah Muhammad referred to "the resurrection of the mentally dead so-called Negroes" and the "resurrection of the black nation, who are mentally dead to the knowledge of truth; the truth of self" (96). "The mentally dead are awakening," says Elijah Muhammad, "The slave masters have deceived you. They want you to remain deceived."
21. Nathan Hare, "Introduction," in Marvin X, *How to Recover from the Addiction to White Supremacy: A Pan African 12-Step Model for a Mental Health Peer Group* (Black Bird Press, 2008).
22. Marvin X, *Somethin' Proper* (Blackbird Press, 1998), 94.
23. See Sonia Sanchez's dedication in her collection of poetry *We A BaddDDD People*, to "marianna X waddy" among many others "for blk/wooomen: the only queens of the universe." Sonia Sanchez, *We A BaddDDD People* (Broadside Press, 1970), 5.
24. Marvin X, *Somethin' Proper*, 97.
25. Jacqueline Bobo, Cynthia Hudley, and Claudine Michel, eds., *The Black Studies Reader* (Routledge, 2004), 2.

26. Martha Biondi, *The Black Revolution on Campus* (University of California Press, 2014), 46–47; Charles P. Henry, *Black Studies and the Democratization of American Higher Education* (Palgrave Macmillan, 2016); Fabio Rojas, *From Black Power to Black Studies* (Johns Hopkins University Press, 2010), 45–91.
27. Henry, *Black Studies and the Democratization of American Higher Education*, 47.
28. Marvin X, *Somethin' Proper*, 102, 107.
29. Robert Allen, "Politics of the Attack on Black Studies," *The Black Scholar* 6, no. 1 (1974): 2–7; Henry, *Black Studies and the Democratization of American Higher Education*, 48.
30. Nathan Hare, "The Battle for Black Studies," *The Black Scholar* 3, no. 9 (1972): 32–47.
31. Nathan Hare, "A Conceptual Proposal for a Department of Black Studies," in *Shut It down! A College in Crisis: San Francisco State College, October 1968–April 1969; a Report to the National Commission on the Causes and Prevention of Violence*, by William H. Orrick, Jr. (Supt. of Docs., U.S. Govt. Print. Off., 1969), 160; Jarvis Givens, "Literate Slave, Fugitive Slave: Note on the Ethical Dilemma of Black Education," in *The Future Is Black: Afropessimism, Fugitivity, and Radical Hope in Education*, ed. Carl A. Grant, Michael J. Dumas, and Ashley N. Woodson (Routledge, 2020).
32. Hare, "A Conceptual Proposal for a Department of Black Studies," 163.
33. *The Black Scholar* devoted special issues to the subject in 1970 (2, no. 1), 1974 (6, no. 1), 1979 (11, no. 1), 1988 (19, no. 6), 2014 (44, no. 2).
34. Nathan Hare and Julia Hare, *The Miseducation of the Black Child—The Hare Plan: Educate Every Black Man, Woman and Child* (Black Think Tank, 1991).
35. Marvin X Jackmon, "Notes of an Artistic Freedom Fighter," 360 Poetry with Justice, Newark, NJ (February 7, 2020).
36. When Marvin founded the Black Arts West Theater, the building was being used by Nasser Shabazz Nasser, "a Muslim brother who was outside the Nation of Islam, but basically followed its teaching," a trajectory that Marvin would eventually follow as well. Later, in 1972, Marvin founded another institution the Black Educational Theatre in the same area. Marvin X, interviews with the author, June 19, 2019; Marvin X, "Dr. Akinyele Umoja Interviews Marvin X," *Black Bird Press News & Review*, August 24, 2012, https://blackbirdpressnews.blogspot.com/2012/08/dr-akinyele-umoja-interviews-marvin-x.html; Harry Justin Elam, *Taking It to the Streets: The Social Protest Theater of Luis Valdez and Amiri Baraka* (University of Michigan Press, 2001), 46.
37. Scott, *Domination and the Arts of Resistance: Hidden Transcripts* (Yale University Press, 1990), 124.
38. Marvin X, "Notes from an Artistic Freedom Fighter," 360 Poetry Night with Justice, Newark, NJ (February 7, 2020).
39. Sylvia Wynter, "A Black Studies Manifesto," *Forum N. H. I.: Knowledge for the 21st Century* 1, no. 1 (1994), 3-11; Christina Sharpe, "Black Studies: In the Wake," *The Black Scholar* 44, no. 2 (2014): 59.
40. Marvin X, *Somethin' Proper*, 126.
41. Marvin X, "Back to Black Arts Movement Guru Alonzo Batin," *Black Bird Press News & Review*, June 6, 2005, https://blackbirdpressnews.blogspot.com/2015/06/human-earthquake-hits-sacramento.html.
42. James Baldwin, *The Fire Next Time* (Vintage, 1993), 71; Marvin X, *Somethin' Proper*, 129.
43. Marvin X, *Somethin' Proper*, 122. On March 9, 1966, at the height of the war, Ali's draft status was revised to make him eligible to fight in Vietnam, leading him to say that as a Muslim he was a conscientious objector, and would not enter the US military. In an interview with the WABC New York television program *Like It Is*, he said: "My conscience won't let me go shoot my brother, or some darker people, or some poor hungry people in the mud for big powerful America. And shoot them for what? They never called me n*****, they never lynched me, they didn't put no dogs on me, they didn't rob me of my nationality, rape and kill my mother and father.... Shoot them for

what? How can I shoot them poor people? Just take me to jail." "Muhammad Ali on the Vietnam War-Draft," *Like It Is*, WABC-TV New York (1967), https://www.youtube.com/watch?v=HeFMyrWlZ68.

44. Yusef Iman, "Love Your Enemy," in *Something Black Dedicated to Millions of Brothers and Sisters in the West* (Jihad Productions, 1966), 4.
45. Henry Louis Gates Jr., *The Signifying Monkey: A Theory of African American Literary Criticism* (Oxford University Press, 1988), 23.
46. Marvin X, *Somethin' Proper*, 129; Marvin X, *Black Man Listen* (Broadside, 1969), 7.
47. Marvin X, *Fly to Allah* (Al Kitab Sudan, 1969), 19.
48. Jarvis R. Givens, *Fugitive Pedagogy: Carter G. Woodson and the Art of Black Teaching* (Harvard University Press, 2021); Jarvis Givens, "Fugitive Pedagogy in the Jim Crow Classroom: The Case of Carter G. Woodson," Hutchins Center for African and African American Research, Harvard University, October 31, 2018; Givens, "Literate Slave, Fugitive Slave."
49. Rey Chow, *Not Like a Native Speaker* (Columbia University Press, 2014), 8.
50. Muhammad al-Faruque, "Emigration," in *Encyclopaedia of the Qur'an*, ed. Jane Dammen McAuliffe (Brill, 2005).
51. Kelley, "Black Study, Black Struggle"; Weheliye, "Black Studies and Black Life," 7. "Neither black life nor black studies was meant to survive in mainstream institutions of higher learning, they still do, albeit precariously," writes Weheliye.
52. Diouf, *Servants of Allah*; João José Reis, *Slave Rebellion in Brazil: The Muslim Uprising of 1835 in Bahia*, trans. Arthur Brakel (Johns Hopkins University Press, 1995); Richard Brent Turner, *Islam in the African-American Experience* (Indiana University Press, 1997).
53. Terry Alford, *Prince Among Slaves* (Oxford University Press, 1977); Allan D. Austin, *African Muslims Antebellum America* (Routledge, 1997), 65-84.
54. Marvin X [Nazzam Al Sudan], *Sudan Rajuli Samia / Black Man Listen*, 1.
55. Marvin X, *Somethin' Proper*, 144.
56. Marvin X, *In the Crazy House Called America: Essays by Marvin X* (Black Bird Press, 2002).
57. Givens, "Fugitive Pedagogy in the Jim Crow Classroom"; Givens, "Literate Slave, Fugitive Slave"; Carl A. Grant, Michael J. Dumas, Ashley N. Woodson, eds., *The Future is Black: Afropessimism, Fugitivity, and Radical Hope in Education* (Routledge, 2020).
58. Marvin X [Nazzam Al Sudan], "Al Fitnah Muhajir," in *Sudan Rajuli Samia / Black Man Listen*, 16.
59. Sherman A. Jackson, *Islam and the Blackamerican: Looking Toward the Third Resurrection* (Oxford University Press, 2005), 44.
60. Marvin X, *Fly to Allah*, 19. Verse 4:100 would open the article about Muhammad Ali that did eventually appear in *Ramparts*, not Marvin X's interview, an article by Gene Marine titled "Nobody Knows My Name," playing on James Baldwin's 1961 collection of essays. Marine, "Nobody Knows My Name," 11.
61. Kynard, *Vernacular Insurrections*, 8.
62. Marvin X [Nazzam Al Sudan], *Sudan Rajuli Samia / Black Man Listen*, 7–10; Marvin X, *Fly to Allah*, 6–9; Muhammad, *Message to the Blackman*, 50, 52, 55, 65, 66. "Why the so-called Negroes (members of the Great Asiatic Nation of the Tribe of Shabazz) refuses to accept his own in because of being made blind, deaf, and dumb to the knowledge of self and kind by the devils when they were babies under slavery" (51). See the discussion of "Fly to Allah" in Chan-Malik, "Cultural and Literary Production of Muslim America," 290.
63. Marvin X [Nazzam Al Sudan], *Sudan Rajuli Samia / Black Man Listen*, 12. On connections between revolutionary Cuba and the Muslim International, see the exhibit Sohail Daulatzai, *Revolutionary Poster Art and the Muslim International* (Medina, 2014).
64. Abdul Khabeer, "Black Arabic," 170.

65. Fred Moten, *In the Break: The Aesthetics of the Black Radical Tradition* (University of Minnesota Press, 2003), 62–63, 65.
66. Moten, *In the Break*, 77; Scott, *Domination and the Arts of Resistance*, 115.
67. Ashley D. Farmer, *Remaking Black Power: How Black Women Transformed an Era* (University of North Carolina Press, 2017), 101–19.
68. Marvin X, "Harlem Queen," in *Fly to Allah*.
69. Abdul Khabeer, "Black Arabic," 169.
70. For an exploration of Islamic language in Black American culture see the chapter on "verbal mujahidin" in Samy Alim, *Roc the Mic Right: The Language of Hip Hop Culture* (Routledge, 2006), 20–51. For the influence of Black American culture on the Muslim world see the chapters titled "Ghettos in the Sky" and "The Jazz Caliphate" in Hisham Aidi, *Rebel Music: Race, Empire, and the New Muslim Youth Culture*. Vintage, 2014. He has also written extensively on the influence of Malcolm X on the Muslim world. See Aidi, "The Political Uses of Malcolm X," *Nka Journal of Contemporary African Art* 2018, nos. 42–43 (2018): 212–21.
71. Marvin X, "The Origin of Blackness," *Black Man Listen* (Broadside Press, 1969), 26–27.
72. Gates, *The Signifying Monkey*.
73. Nielsen, *Black Chant*, 37.
74. Marvin X, *Somethin' Proper*, 142. At the time, al-Shahristani was studying chemical engineering at the University of Toronto and in 2012 would later become the deputy Prime Minister of Iraq.
75. Marvin X, *Somethin' Proper*, 143–44.
76. Jackson, *Islam and the Blackamerican*, 47.
77. Marvin X, *Somethin' Proper*, 129.
78. Moten, *In the Break*, 64; Amiri Baraka [LeRoi Jones], "The Changing Same (R&B and New Black Music)," in *Black Music* (William Morrow, 1968), 206; for "*sans* blackness" see Marvin X, *Somethin' Proper*, 142.
79. Marvin X, "Oh, Ancestors Speak to Me! Digame Por Favor," *Black Bird Press News & Review*, May 4, 2018, https://blackbirdpressnews.blogspot.com/2018/11/oh-ancestors-speak-to-me-digame-por.html.
80. Amiri Baraka [LeRoi Jones], "Ka 'Ba," in *Black Magic: Collected Poetry, 1961–67* (Bobbs-Merrill, 1969), 146; see also Muhyiddin Ibn 'Arabi, "Gentle Now, Doves," in *Translator of Desires: Poems*, trans. Michael Sells (Princeton University Press, 2021), 36. Ibn 'Arabi's poem about the Ka'ba is similarly pluralistic: "My heart can take on any form/ For gazelles a meadow / A cloister for monks / A temple for idols, / pilgrim's Ka'ba."
81. Marvin X, "Al Hajj Harlem," in *Fly to Allah* (Al Kitab Sudan, 1969), 24.
82. Marvin X, *Somethin' Proper*, 108, 116, 132, 142.
83. Marvin X, "Back to Black Arts Movement Guru Alonzo Batin."
84. Marvin X, *The Black Bird: A Parable for Black Children* (Al Kitab Sudan, 1968). Malcolm X, "Twenty Million Black People in a Political, Economic and Mental Prison: January 23, 1963" in *Malcolm X: The Last Speeches*, ed. Bruce Perry (Pathfinder, 1989), 28.
85. Nina Simone, "Blackbird," Colpix Records, 1963; Clarence Bernard Jackson and James Hatch, "Fly Blackbird," in *Fly Blackbird*, Mercury, 1962 [cast recording; the musical was performed in Los Angeles, 1961, and off-Broadway in New York, 1962]; Malcolm X, "America's Gravest Crisis Since the Civil War" in *Malcolm X: The Last Speeches*, ed. Bruce Perry (Pathfinder, 1989), 60.
86. Malcolm X, "Message to the Grassroots" in *Malcolm X Speaks*, ed. George Breitman (Grove, 1965), 11; Malcolm X, "Political, Economic and Mental Prison," 37.
87. See chapter 5 for a full discussion of these debates; see also Lorraine Hansberry, James Baldwin, and Langston Hughes, *The Negro in American Culture*, WBAI TV, January 10, 1961, recording/bb3297; James Baldwin, Emile Capouya, Lorraine Hansberry, et al., "Negro in American Culture,"

CrossCurrents 11, no. 3 (1961): 205–24; Robert Nemiroff, dir. *Lorraine Hansberry Speaks Out: Art and the Black Revolution*. Harper Audio / Caedmon, 1972.
88. Baldwin, *Nobody Knows My Name*, 100.
89. Marvin X [Marvin Jackmon], "Burn, Baby, Burn," *Soulbook* 1, no. 3 (1965): 153; Marvin X [Marvin E. Jackmon], "Burn, Baby, Burn," in *Black Fire: An Anthology of Afro-American Writing*, eds. Amiri Baraka [LeRoi Jones] and Larry Neal (William Morrow, 1968), 269; Cornel West and Christa Buschendorf, *Black Prophetic Fire* (Beacon Press, 2014).
90. Julian Mayfield, "Into the Mainstream and Oblivion," in *The American Negro Writer and His Roots: Selected Papers*, ed. John Aubrey Davis Sr. First Conference of Negro Writers 1959 (American Society of African Culture, 1960), 29, 32–33.
91. Marvin X, *The Black Bird*.
92. Gates, *The Signifying Monkey*, 28. Is Gates himself signifying upon Larry Neal's "Malcolm X—An Autobiography"? The poem is written in the first person from the perspective of Malcolm X. While listening to the music of Lester Young and Billie Holliday, Malcolm says, "I understand the/ mystery of the signifying monkey,/ in a blue haze of inspiration, I reach to the totality of Being." Larry Neal, "Malcolm X—An Autobiography," in *Black Fire: An Anthology of Afro-American Writing*, ed. Amiri Baraka [LeRoi Jones] and Larry Neal (William Morrow, 1968), 316.
93. Maya Angelou, *I Know Why the Caged Bird Sings* (Random House, 1969); Lyman B. Hagen, *Heart of a Woman, Mind of a Writer, and Soul of a Poet: A Critical Analysis of the Writings of Maya Angelou* (University Press of America, 1996), 54.
94. Paul Laurence Dunbar, "Sympathy," in *Lyrics of the Hearthside* (Dodd, Mead, 1899).
95. Alice Dunbar, "The Poet and His Song," *African Methodist Episcopal Church Review*, October 1914.
96. Paul Laurence Dunbar, *Oak and Ivy* (Press of United Brethren, 1893).
97. Gates, *The Signifying Monkey*, 26.
98. Carolyn Rodgers, *Songs of a Blackbird* (Third World Press, 1969); Angelou, *I Know Why the Caged Bird Sings*.
99. Henry Louis Gates Jr., *Thirteen Ways of Looking at a Black Man* (University of Michigan, 1997); Morgan Parker would make this her own in "13 Ways of Looking at a Black Girl" (see Morgan Parker, *There Are More Beautiful Things Than Beyoncé* (Tin House Books, 2017), 29; Antonio Lopez, "13 Ways of Looking at a Paloma Negra," *Permafrost* 39, no. 2 (2017).
100. Marvin X, *Somethin' Proper*, 196.
101. Marvin X, interview with author, "Black History Poetry Reading Tour," February 7, 2020.
102. Marvin X, *Somethin' Proper*, 199.
103. Moten and Harney, *The Undercommons*, 96–97.
104. Wynter, "A Black Studies Manifesto," 5.
105. Ed Bullins, *Salaam, Huey Newton, Salaam* (Farber, 1993), 10, 13.
106. Marvin X, Juneteenth interviews by the author, June 19, 2019; Marvin X, *Somethin' Proper*, 109.
107. Giorgio Agamben, *Homo Sacer: Sovereign Power and Bare Life*, trans. Daniel Heller-Roazen (Stanford University Press, 1998), 88.
108. The Honorable Minister Louis Farrakhan, "Crack-Cocaine: The Great Conspiracy to Destroy the Black Male," delivered at Mosque Maryam in Chicago (November 3, 1996), *The Final Call* (April 5, 2014), https://www.finalcall.com/artman/publish/Minister_Louis_Farrakhan_9/article_101889.shtml.
109. Marvin X, *One Day in the Life* (Alice Arts Theatre, 1996), 32–33.
110. Marvin X, *One Day in the Life*, 26.
111. Elijah Muhammad, *Message to the Blackman*, 12, 18, 19, 50, 96.
112. Hare, Nathan, "Introduction," in *Somethin' Proper* (Black Bird Press, 1998), iii.
113. Marvin X, *Resurrection of the Dead* (Al Kitab Sudan, 1969).

114. Marvin X, *Somethin' Proper*, 11–12, 14; Marvin X, "My Life in the Global Village—Notes of an Artistic Freedom Fighter," *Black Bird Press News & Review*, January 16, 2017.
115. Moten and Harney, *The Undercommons*, 96–97.
116. Marvin X, *Notes of an Artistic Freedom Fighter*, 54, 240.
117. Anne Bardwell, "Project Breakthrough Appears Right Approach at Right Time," *Daily Independent Journal* (San Rafael), November 1, 1968.
118. "Sausalito Boycott: Freedom Class in Marin City," *Sausalito News* 79, no. 21 (1964): 1.
119. Inyoung Kang, "Sausalito Marin City Schools to Desegregate After State Inquiry," *The New York Times*, August 12, 2019.
120. Marvin X, Juneteenth Interviews by the author, June 19, 2019.
121. Marcus Garvey, "Emancipate Yourselves from Mental Slavery," *The Black Man: A Monthly Magazine of Negro Thought and Opinion* 3, no. 10 (July 1938).

7. THE BARAKAS IN NEW ARK

1. I use "Jones" to refer to LeRoi Jones in the period leading up to the aftermath of the Newark uprisings when he takes the name Ameer Baraka (later becoming Amiri Baraka). I use "Baraka" to refer to him throughout the period after he takes his new name, to distinguish between these periods and how it affected not just his life and his consciousness, but also his authorship, aesthetics, and cultural production. "Imamu Amiri Baraka (LeRoi Jones)" is how the name is written on the cover of *Spirit Reach*, with the honorific Imamu, the chosen Arabic/Swahili name, and his birth name.
2. Amiri Baraka, *The Autobiography of LeRoi Jones* (Lawrence Hill Books, 1997), 374.
3. Frederick Douglass, *Narrative of the Life of Frederick Douglass*, 1945 edition (Millenium Publications, 2014), 6; Saidiya Hartman, *Scenes of Subjection: Terror, Slavery, and Self-Making in Nineteenth-Century America* (Oxford University Press, 1997), 3–4; Fred Moten, *In the Break: The Aesthetics of the Black Radical Tradition* (University of Minnesota Press, 2003).
4. Moten, *In the Break*, 213.
5. Garrett Felber, *Those Who Know Don't Say: Nation of Islam, the Black Freedom Movement, and the Carceral State* (University of North Carolina Press, 2020), 1, 121, 225n8.
6. Max Roach, "Triptych: Prayer, Protest, Peace," in *We Insist! Max Roach's Freedom Now Suite*, with Abbey Lincoln, Candid, 1960; Moten, *In the Break*, 36–37. Moten writes that the echo of Aunt Hester's scream in the *Narrative of Frederick Douglas* "haunts" Ayler's "Ghosts," as it does Abbey Lincoln's vocal performance.
7. Baraka, *Autobiography*, 363; Ron Porambo, *No Cause for Indictment: An Autopsy of Newark* (Holt, Rinehart and Winston, 1971); Junius Williams and Tom Hayden, *Unfinished Agenda: Urban Politics in the Era of Black Power* (North Atlantic Books, 2014).
8. Baraka, *Autobiography*, 375.
9. Marvin X and Faruk, "Islam and Black Art: An Interview with LeRoi Jones," *The Negro Digest* 18, no. 3 (January 1969): 6.
10. Baraka, *Autobiography*, 378.
11. Amiri Baraka and James E. Hinton, dirs., *The New-Ark*. Harlem Audio Visual, 1968. Harvard Film Archive, James E. Hinton Collection.
12. Amina Baraka, interview with author, Newark, New Jersey, August 4, 2019.
13. Baraka, *The New-Ark*; Komozi Woodard, *A Nation Within a Nation: Amiri Baraka (LeRoi Jones) and Black Power Politics* (University of North Carolina Press, 2005), 2.
14. John Szwed, *Space Is the Place: The Lives And Times Of Sun Ra* (Pantheon, 1997), 183–86; Wilson, *Sacred Drift*, 26; Michael Muhammad Knight, *The Five Percenter: Islam, Hip-Hop and the Gods*

of New York (Oneworld Publications, 2007), 43; Patrick D. Bowen, *A History of Conversion to Islam in the United States, Volume 1: White American Muslims before 1975* (Brill, 2015), 122.

15. Melani McAlister, *Epic Encounters: Culture, Media, and U.S. Interests in the Middle East since 1945* (University of California Press, 2005), 91; Chan-Malik, "Cultural and Literary Production of Muslim America," in *The Cambridge Companion to American Islam*, ed. Juliane Hammer and Omid Safi (Cambridge University Press, 2013); Ammar Abduh Aqeeli, *The Nation of Islam and Black Consciousness* (Peter Lang Inc., 2019).

16. Baraka, *Autobiography*, 365, 375; Marvin X, and Faruk, "Islam and Black Art"; Amiri Baraka, "Islam and Black Art," in *Black Arts: An Anthology of Black Creations*, ed. Ahmed Alhamisi and Harun Kofi Wangara (Black Arts Publications, 1969).

17. Katherine McKittrick, *Demonic Grounds: Black Women and the Cartographies of Struggle* (University of Minnesota Press, 2006), 7, 18, 21; bell hooks, "Homeplace (a site of resistance)," in *Yearning: Race, Gender, and Cultural Politics* (South End Press, 1990).

18. Zenzele Isoke, *Urban Black Women and the Politics of Resistance* (Palgrave Macmillan, 2013), 1; Rhonda Y. Williams, "Black Women, Urban Politics, and Engendering Black Power," in *The Black Power Movement: Re-Thinking the Civil Rights-Black Power Era* (Routledge, 2006), 80.

19. Larry Neal, "The Black Arts Movement," *The Drama Review: TDR* 12, no. 4 (1968): 30, 39.

20. McKittrick, *Demonic Grounds*, 9. These were some of the "key ways black geographies ... are produced in landscapes of domination ... black imaginations and mappings [that] are evidence of the struggle over social space."

21. Moten, *In the Break*, 27–28.

22. Moten, *In the Break*, 130; Daniel Matlin, *On the Corner: African American Intellectuals and the Urban Crisis* (Harvard University Press, 2013), 125–26. The chapter in the *Autobiography* describing his return to Newark is titled "Home" and just after his return to Newark, he published the collection *Home: Social Essays* (1966).

23. Baraka, *Autobiography*, 231.

24. Baraka, *Autobiography*, 238. Italics mine.

25. Baraka, *Autobiography*, 277.

26. Baraka, *Autobiography*, 277, 288, 293; Baraka Amiri [LeRoi Jones], *Dutchman and The Slave: Two Plays* (William Morrow, 1964).

27. Baraka, *Autobiography*, 259.

28. Amina Baraka, interview with author, August 4, 2019.

29. Amina Baraka, interview with author, August 4, 2019; Baraka, *Autobiography*, 339. Rahman was a teacher at the Newark Arts High School that Amina had attended. In the biographical notes in *Black Fire*, Rahman calls himself "once slaved-named ronald stone re-incarnated to eternal life as a most willing slave of Allah, University and Almighty."

30. Yusuf Rahman, *Alhomdullilah!* (Am God Pub. Co., 1968).

31. Yusef Rahman, "Transcendental Blues," in *Black Fire: An Anthology of Afro-American Writing*, ed. Amiria Baraka [LeRoi Jones] and Larry Neal (William Morrow, 1968), 369–73.

32. Amiri Baraka [LeRoi Jones], "Apple Cores #4," *DownBeat* 33, no. 3 (1966): 15; Amiri Baraka [LeRoi Jones], "Apple Cores #4," in *Black Music* (William Morrow, 1968), 132–36. Just after the assassination of Malcolm X, Brown and Sanders had participated in a fundraiser for the Black Arts Repertory Theatre School, a concert later released as the album *The New Wave in Jazz* and which included Sun Ra and the Myth-Science Arkestra, Albert Ayler, Sonny Murray, and Archie Shepp. In August of that year, Sanders and Brown also played on John Coltrane's *Ascension*, recorded at the Van Gelder studios in Englewood, an album released in February 1966.

33. Baraka [Jones], "Apple Cores #4," 1966; Moten, *In the Break*, 35. Writing about Aunt Hester's scream, and Abbey Lincoln's remembering of the scream in her vocal performance, Moten calls this "the phonography of the very screams that open the way into the knowledge of slavery and the knowledge of freedom—operat[ing] as a kind of anacrusis (a note or beat or musicked word

34. Baraka, *Autobiography*, 339–40.
35. Baraka, *Black Music*, 121.
36. McKittrick, *Demonic Grounds*, 20–21.
37. Mathes, *Imagine the Sound*, 30, 217n40.
38. Amiri Baraka [LeRoi Jones], *A Black Mass*, in *Four Black Revolutionary Plays: All Praises to the Black Man* (Bobbs-Merrill, 1969).
39. Amiri Baraka [LeRoi Jones], "Apple Cores #5—The Burton Greene Affair," *DownBeat* 33, no. 17 (1966); Amiri Baraka [Imamu Amiri Baraka], *Black Music* (William Morrow, 1968), 157–60; Moten, *In the Break*, 152–82.
40. Baraka, *Autobiography*, 365. They named him Obalaji Malik Ali, meaning "God of the King's Warrior": Malik for Malcolm, and Ali after Muhammad Ali," echoing the "king" in LeRoi as much as the "king" in Malik, referring to Malcolm X's Arabic name.
41. Amina Baraka, interview with author, August 4, 2019; Amina Baraka, interview with author in Newark, New Jersey, June 20, 2022; Baraka, *Autobiography*, 378.
42. Baraka, *Autobiography*.
43. Amiri Baraka [LeRoi Jones], "Newark—Before Black Men Conquered," *Black Newark*, April 1968; Amiri Baraka [Imamu Amiri Baraka (LeRoi Jones)], *Raise, Race, Rays, Raze: Essays Since 1965* (Random House, 1971), 73, 75.
44. Baraka [Jones], "Apple Cores #4," 1966; Baraka [Jones], "Apple Cores #5—The Burton Greene Affair"; Baraka, *Black Music*, 157–60; Moten, *In the Break*, 152–82.
45. Pharoah Sanders, "Hum-Allah-Hum-Allah-Hum-Allah," *Jewels of Thought*, Impulse! Records, October 20, 1969; Askia Muhammad Touré, "Black Magic Music / A Love Ritual," in *Songhai!* (Songhai Press, 1972), 30–31. In the "Jihad! (spiritual fire/ritual)" "side" of Askia Muhammad Touré's 1972 poetry collection *Songhai!* his poem "Black Magic Music / A Love Ritual" ends with Leon Thomas's chant, but rewritten/miswritten as "OM! ALLAH, OM! ALLAH, OM! ALLAH, OM! ALLAH, OM! ALLAH, OM! ALLAH, OM! ALLAH" in a kind of meditation prayer. The poet asks, "Have you really duuug Pharoah, dug him bear down and screeeeeeeam—his eagle-soul soaring upwards through seven layers of the Cosmos to reach the Living Truth."
46. Su'ad Abdul Khabeer, "Africa as Tradition in U.S. African American Muslim Identity." *Journal of Africana Religions* 5, no. 1 (2017): 42.
47. Baraka, *Autobiography*, 370.
48. Baraka, *Autobiography*, 371.
49. Baraka, *Autobiography*, 374.
50. Baraka, *Autobiography*, 376.
51. Baraka, *Autobiography*, 374.
52. Baraka, *Autobiography*, 375.
53. Civil Rights Congress, *We Charge Genocide: Petition to the United Nations for Relief from the Crime of the United States Government Against the Negro People* (New York, 1951); Baraka, *Autobiography*, 374.
54. Amiri Baraka [Imamu Amiri Baraka (LeRoi Jones)], "From the Book of Life," in *Raise, Race, Rays, Raze: Essays Since 1965* (Random House, 1971), 53.
55. Malcolm X and Alex Haley, *The Autobiography of Malcolm X* (Ballantine Books, 2015), 180.
56. Muhammad, *Message to the Blackman in America* (Secretarius Memps Publications, 1965), 161.
57. Muhammad, *Message to the Blackman*, 6.
58. Elijah Muhammad, *Police Brutality* (Secretarius Memps, 1964); Frederick Knight, "Justifiable Homicide, Police Brutality, or Governmental Repression? The 1962 Los Angeles Police Shooting

of Seven Member of the Nation of Islam," *Journal of Negro History* 79, no. 2 (1994): 182–96; Claude A. Clegg III, "Nation Under Siege: Elijah Muhammad, the FBI, and Police-State Culture in Chicago," in *Police Brutality: An Anthology* (Norton, 2000); Gerry Spence, *Police State: How America's Cops Get Away with Murder* (St. Martin's Press, 2015); Clarence Taylor, *Fight the Power: African Americans and the Long History of Police Brutality in New York City* (New York University Press, 2018); Felber, *Nation of Islam, the Black Freedom Movement, and the Carceral State*.

59. Muhammad, *Message to the Blackman*, 204.
60. James Baldwin, *The Fire Next Time* (Vintage, 1993), 47–49; James Baldwin, "Letter from a Region in My Mind," *New Yorker*, November 17, 1962, 59-144.
61. Amiri Baraka [Imamu Amiri Baraka], "All in the Street," in *Spirit Reach* (Jihad Productions, 1972), 11.
62. Baraka, "All in the Street."
63. Yusef Iman, *Something Black Dedicated to Millions of Brothers and Sisters in the West* (Jihad Productions, 1966), 33.
64. Yusef Iman [Kasisi Yusef Iman], *Extermination or Unification* (The East, 1972). Kasisi is a type of honorific that in Swahili means priest.
65. #Brooklynology, "Black News," *Brooklyn Public Library, Center for Brooklyn History*, February 14, 2011, https://www.bklynlibrary.org/blog/2011/02/14/black-news.
66. Kasisi Yusef Iman, *Genocide or Unify* (The East, 1972).
67. Amiri Baraka [Imamu Amiri Baraka], "Love Is the Presence of No Enemy," in *Spirit Reach* (Jihad Productions, 1972), 16.
68. Baraka, "Love Is the Presence of No Enemy," 16.
69. Baraka, "Love Is the Presence of No Enemy," 16–17.
70. Baraka, "Love Is the Presence of No Enemy," 16–17.
71. Amiri Baraka [LeRoi Jones], "Black Art," in *Sonny's Time Now*, with Sunny Murray et al. (Jihad Productions, 1965).
72. Baraka, *Autobiography*, 365.
73. Baraka [Jones], "From the Book of Life," 52.
74. Baraka, *Autobiography*, 373; Baraka [LeRoi Jones], "From the Book of Life," 54.
75. Baraka, *Autobiography*, 372.
76. Baraka [Jones], "From the Book of Life," 51.
77. Baraka [Jones], "From the Book of Life," 51.
78. Amiri Baraka [Imamu Amiri Baraka], "Deranged Gutbucket Pigtongue Clapper Heart," in *Spirit Reach* (Jihad Productions, 1972), 1.
79. Amiri Baraka [Imamu Amiri Baraka], "The Evolver," in *Spirit Reach* (Jihad Productions, 1972), 2-3.
80. Amiri Baraka [Imamu Amiri Baraka], "Study Peace," in *Spirit Reach* (Jihad Productions, 1972), 4.
81. Baraka, Marvin X, and Faruk, "Islam and Black Art."
82. Baraka, Marvin X, and Faruk, "Islam and Black Art."
83. Jamal Eddine Bencheikh, *Poetique Arabe: Essai sur les voies d'une création* (Éditions Anthropos, 1975); S. A. Bonebakker, "Religious Prejudice against Poetry in Early Islam," *Medievalia et Humanistica* 7, nos. 77–99 (1976); Th. Emil Homerin, "Preaching Poetry," *Arabica* 38 (1991): 87–101; Jaroslav Stetkevych, *Zephyrs of Najd: Poetics of Nostalgia in the Classical Arabic Nasib* (University of Chicago Press, 1993).
84. Marvin X and Faruk, "Islam and Black Art"; Baraka, *Autobiography*, 371.
85. Ann Cook, "Black Pride?: Some Contradictions," in *The Black Woman*, ed. Toni Cade Bambara (Washington Square Press, 1970), 195.
86. Josef Sorett, *Spirit in the Dark* (Oxford University Press, 2016), 195.
87. Amiri Baraka [Imamu Amiri Baraka], "Black Woman," *Black World* 19, no. 9 (1970): 8.
88. bell hooks, *Ain't I A Woman: Black Women And Feminism* (Pluto Press, 1981), 94–95.

89. bell hooks, "Homeplace," 188–89.
90. Jennifer Nash, *Black Feminism Reimagined* (Duke University Press, 2019), 5; Jennifer Nash, *Birthing Black Mothers* (Duke University Press, 2021), 20.
91. Farmer, *Remaking Black Power*, 94.
92. Baraka, *Autobiography*, xxv.
93. Farmer, *Remaking Black Power*, 107.
94. Farmer, *Remaking Black Power*, 109.
95. David Llorens, "Ameer (LeRoi Jones) Baraka," *Ebony* 24, no. 10 (1969): 78–79.
96. Baraka, "Black Woman," 9.
97. Nikki Giovanni, "Adulthood (for Claudia)," in *Black Feeling, Black Talk, Black Judgement* (William Morrow, 1970), 68.
98. Sonia Sanchez, *The Black Scholar: In Memoriam: W. E. B. Du Bois* 1, no. 3/4 (1970): 30.
99. Sonia Sanchez, "Queens of the Universe," 30.
100. Farmer, *Remaking Black Power*, 94.
101. Farmer, *Remaking Black Power*, 110, 113.
102. Combahee River Collective, *Combahee River Collective Statement* (1977); Combahee River Collective, "A Black Feminist Statement," in *Words of Fire: An Anthology of African-American Feminist Thought*, ed. Beverly Guy-Sheftall (The New Press, 1995).
103. Amina Baraka [Sylvia Jones], "Dedication," in *Songs for the Masses* (n.p., 1978). *Song for the Masses* lists no publisher and no page numbers. It was most likely published through Jihad Productions, but Amina distances herself from the religious dimensions of Black struggle and instead embraces a materialist analysis of Black liberation as class struggle.
104. Farmer, *Remaking Black Power*, 104–09; Michael Simanga, "Amina Baraka and the Women of the Congress of African People," in *Amiri Baraka and the Congress of African People: History and Memory* (Palgrave Macmillan, 2015), 79–81; James Edward Smethurst, *Brick City Vanguard: Amiri Baraka, Black Music, Black Modernity* (University of Massachusetts Press, 2020), 40–52.
105. Zenzele Isoke, *Urban Black Women and the Politics of Resistance* (Palgrave Macmillan, 2013), 1–2.
106. Amina Baraka [Sylvia Jones], "Sortin-Out," *Black American Literature Forum* 16, no. 13 (1982): 106; Amina Baraka, "Sortin-Out," in *Confirmation: An Anthology of African American Women*, ed. Amiri Baraka (LeRoi Jones) and Amina Baraka (William Morrow, 1983), 74.
107. Marvin X and Faruk, "Islam and Black Art"; Amiri Baraka, "Islam and Black Art."
108. Jennifer Nash, *Birthing Black Mothers*, 20; Toni Cade Bambara, *Deep Sightings and Rescue Missions: Fiction, Essays, and Conversations* (Pantheon Books, 1996), 95.
109. bell hooks, "Homeplace," 42; Jennifer Nash, *Black Feminism Reimagined* (Duke University Press, 2019), 5.
110. Cheryl Clarke, *"After Mecca": Women Poets and the Black Arts Movement* (Rutgers University Press, 2004), 52–53; Winifred Breines, *The Trouble Between Us: An Uneasy History of White and Black Women in the Feminist Movement* (Oxford University Press, 2006), 62; Kimberly Springer, "Black Feminists Respond to Black Power Masculinism," in *The Black Power Movement: Re-Thinking the Civil Rights-Black Power Era*, ed. Peniel E. Joseph (Routledge, 2006), 113; Cherise A. Pollard, "Sexual Subversions, Political Inversions: Women's Poetry and the Politics of the Black Arts Movement," in *New Thoughts on the Black Arts Movement*, ed. Lisa Gail Collins and Margo Natalie Crawford (Rutgers University Press, 2006); Evie Shockley, *Renegade Poetics: Black Aesthetics and Formal Innovation in African American Poetry* (University of Iowa Press, 2011).
111. Amiri Baraka, "Answers in Progress," in *Tales: Short Stories* (Grove Press, 1967); Amiri Baraka and Vertamae Smart-Grosvenor, "Answers in Progress," in *Vibration Cooking, Or, The Travel Notes of a Geechee Girl* (1970, 1970), ix.
112. Paul Youngquist, "The Space Machine: Baraka and Science Fiction," *African American Review* 37, no. 2/3 (2003): 333–43.

113. Jennifer Nash, "Practicing Love: Black Feminism, Love-Politics, and Post-Intersectionality," *Meridians* 11, no. 2 (2011): 2, 19.

8. "BLK/VISIONS FOR BLK/LIVES"

1. Saidiya Hartman, "The Belly of the World: A Note on Black Women's Labors," *Souls* 18, no. 1 (2016): 166.
2. Sonia Sanchez, *A Blues Book for Blue Black Magical Women* (Broadside Press, 1974), 57; "A Shahada Rebirth Celebration," *American Muslim Journal*, July 17, 1992, 1; Marcia Hermansen, "Conversion to Islam in Theological and Historical Perspectives," in *The Oxford Handbook of Religious Conversion*, ed. Lewis R. Rambo and Charles E. Farhadian (Oxford University Press, 2014).
3. Hortense J. Spillers, "Mama's Baby, Papa's Maybe: An American Grammar Book," *Diacritics* 17, no. 2 (1987): 79. Spillers writes about how the project of liberation has found urgency in the motivation to rupture with the laws of an American grammar of motherhood to make a new syntax possible, partly by authoring narratives that introduce new semantic fields.
4. Spillers, "Mama's Baby, Papa's Maybe," 79.
5. Patricia Hill Collins, *Black Feminist Thought: Knowledge, Consciousness, and the Politics of Empowerment* (Routledge, 2008), 69.
6. Sonia Sanchez, *We A BaddDDD People* (Broadside Press, 1970), 50; Henry Hampton, dir., *Eyes on the Prize II: America at the Racial Crossroads 1965–85*, "Sonia Sanchez Interview," aired March 7, 1989, on PBS, Blackside.
7. Stuart Hall, "New Ethnicities," in *Black Film, British Cinema*, ed. Kobena Mercer (Institute of Contemporary Arts, 1987).
8. bell hooks, "The Oppositional Gaze: Black Female Spectators," in *Movies and Mass Culture*, ed. John Belton (Rutgers University Press, 1996), 248.
9. Sonia Sanchez, "Poem (for DCs 8th Graders—1966–67)" in *Home Coming* (Broadside Press, 1969), 22 ("look at me . . . / i am black/beautiful"); Sonia Sanchez, "A/Needed/Poem for My Salvation," in *We A BaddDDD People* (Broadside Press, 1970), 49 ("am gonna loooook in a / mirror each time i pass one. / smile at my image . . . / but mooooove/beautifullee on passsst it. / keep on holden yo/ head higher"). In Hampton, *Eyes on the Prize II*, Sanchez talks about the respect given to the sisters in the NOI.
10. George Yancy, *Black Bodies, White Gazes: The Continuing Significance of Race* (Rowman & Littlefield, 2008), 105.
11. H. Samy Alim, "360 Degreez of Black Art Comin At You: Sista Sonia Sanchez and the Dimensions of a Black Arts Continuum," *B. Ma: The Sonia Sanchez Literary Review* 6, no. 1 (2000): 24.
12. Leroy Baylor, "Ameenah Rasul, Leader of Women in the Nation of Islam, Dies at 90," *Amsterdam News* (New York City), July 17, 2014, http://amsterdamnews.com/news/2014/jul/17/ameenah-rasul-leader-women-nation-islam-dies-90/; Ula Yvette Taylor, *The Promise of Patriarchy: Women and the Nation of Islam* (University of North Carolina Press, 2017), 117.
13. Sonia Sanchez, "Ima Talken Bout the Nation of Islam," on *A Sun Lady for All Seasons Reads Her Poetry* (Smithsonian Folkways Records, 1971); Sonia Sanchez, *Ima Talken Bout the Nation of Islam* [broadsheet] (New Pyramid Productions, 1971).
14. Sonia Sanchez, "It's A New Day," in *It's A New Day (Poems for Young Brothas and Sistuhs)* (Broadside Press, 1971), 17.
15. Kalamu ya Salaam, "Sonia Sanchez," in *Dictionary of Literary Biography: Afro-American Poets Since 1955* (Gale, 1985), 41:298; Mike Kelly, "Black Lives of Amherst College," *The Consecrated Eminence*, March 17, 2015, https://consecrateddeminence.wordpress.amherst.edu/2015/03/17/black-lives-of

-amherst-college-non-alumni-edition/; La Donna Forsgren, *In Search of Our Warrior Mothers: Women Dramatists of the Black Arts Movement* (Northwestern University Press, 2018), 161.
16. Susan Kelly, "Discipline and Craft: An Interview with Sonia Sanchez," *African American Review* 34, no. 4 (2000): 683.
17. Jennifer Nash, *Birthing Black Mothers* (Duke University Press), 5–7.
18. Sonia Sanchez, "Sister Son/ji," in *I'm Black When I'm Singing, I'm Blue When I Ain't and Other Plays* (Duke University Press, 2010), 40–42; Sonia Sanchez, "Sister Son/ji," in *New Plays from the Black Theatre: An Anthology*, ed. Ed Bullins (Bantam Books, 1969), 104–06. Sonia Sanchez, "Malcolm/Man Don't Live Here No Mo," in *I'm Black When I'm Singing, I'm Blue When I Ain't and Other Plays* (Duke University Press, 2010), 56–57. "i am wite/amurica & i kill" is from the play *Malcolm/Man*.
19. Sanchez, Sonia, "Sister Son/ji," in *I'm Black When I'm Singing*, 42.
20. Hampton, *Eyes on the Prize II*; Forsgren, *In Search of Our Warrior Mothers*, 76; Sylvia Chan-Malik, *Being Muslim: A Cultural History of Women of Color in American Islam* (New York University Press, 2018).
21. Sister Minister Sharolyn, "A Conversation with Sis. Sonia 5X Sanchez," *Muhammad Speaks*, June 13, 1975, S3.
22. Kelly, "Discipline and Craft," 683.
23. Sonia Sanchez, "Let Us Begin the Real Work (for Elijah Muhammad Who Has Begun)," *We A BaddDDD People*, 65.
24. Sister Minister Sharolyn, "Conversation with Sis. Sonia 5X," S3–4.
25. Algernon Austin, "Theorizing Difference within Black Feminist Thought: The Dilemma of Sexism in Black Communities," *Race, Gender & Class* 6, no. 3 (1999): 52–66; Elisabeth A. Frost, *The Feminist Avant-Garde in American Poetry* (University of Iowa Press, 2005), 65; Jennifer Ryan, *Post-Jazz Poetics: A Social History* (Palgrave Macmillan, 2010), 53, 58, 59; Forsgren, *In Search of Our Warrior Mothers*, 76. Joyce's understanding of Sanchez's Islamic commitments as enriching her poetry is an exception to these interpretations that see the Nation of Islam as antithetical to womanist concerns: Joyce Ann Joyce, *Ijala: Sonia Sanchez and the African Poetic Tradition* (Third World Press, 1996), 80–87. Joyce specifically talks about "Islamic and African" conceptions of the family and its role in the larger community.
26. Farah Jasmine Griffin, "'Ironies of the Saint:' Malcolm X, Black Women, and the Price of Protection," in *Sisters in the Struggle: African-American Women in the Civil Rights-Black Power Movement*, ed. Bettye Collier-Thomas and V. P. Franklin (New York University Press, 2001), 216.
27. bell hooks, "Homeplace (A Site of Resistance)," in *Yearning: Race, Gender, and Cultural Politics* (South End Press, 1990), 385.
28. Barbara Omolade, "Hearts of Darkness," in *Words of Fire: An Anthology of African American Feminist Thought*, ed. Beverly Guy-Sheftal (The New Press, 1995), 352.
29. Griffin, "Ironies of the Saint," 216.
30. Chan-Malik, *Being Muslim*, 8.
31. Cornel West, "The Dilemma of the Black Intellectual," *Cultural Critique* 1 (Autumn 1985): 109–24; Spillers, "Mama's Baby, Papa's Maybe," 80; Dylan Rodríguez, "Black Studies in Impasse," *The Black Scholar* 44, no. 2 (2014): 37–49; bell hooks and Cornel West, *Breaking Bread: Insurgent Black Intellectual Life* (Routledge, 2016).
32. Spillers, "Mama's Baby, Papa's Maybe," 80.
33. Michel Foucault, *"Society Must Be Defended:" Lectures at the Collège de France, 1975–1976*, trans. David Macey (Picador, 2003), 255, 258; Alexander G. Weheliye, *Habeas Viscus: Racializing Assemblages, Biopolitics, and Black Feminist Theories of the Human* (Duke University Press Books, 2014), 56; Chan-Malik, *Being Muslim*, 8.
34. Sanchez, Sonia, "Sister Son/ji" in *I'm Black When I'm Singing*, 42.

35. Evie Shockley, *Renegade Poetics: Black Aesthetics and Formal Innovation in African American Poetry*. University of Iowa Press, 2011, 2–3.
36. Sonia Sanchez, conversation with the author, June 27, 2024.
37. amina wadud, email communication with the author," May 2024; amina wadud, *Inside the Gender Jihad: Women's Reform in Islam* (Oneworld Academic, 2006); Alim, "360 Degreez of Black Art"; H. Samy Alim, *Roc the Mic Right: The Language of Hip Hop Culture* (Routledge, 2006).
38. Sanchez, *A Blues Book for Blue Black Magical Women*, 42.
39. Spillers, "Mama's Baby, Papa's Maybe," 80.
40. Hartman, "The Belly of the World," 171.
41. Angela Davis, "Meditations on the Legacy of Malcolm X," in *Malcolm X: In Our Own Image*, ed. Joe Wood (St. Martin's Press, 1992), 37, 44, 45.
42. Sonia Sanchez, "Malcolm" in *For Malcolm*, ed. Dudley Randall and Margaret G. Burroughs (Broadside Press, 1967), 38–39; Sanchez, "Malcolm," *Home Coming*, 16.
43. Melba Joyce Boyd, *Wrestling with the Muse: Dudley Randall and the Broadside Press* (Columbia University Press, 2004), 143; Howard Rambsy, *The Black Arts Enterprise and the Production of African American Poetry* (University of Michigan Press, 2013), 54. "The anthology suggests that Malcolm X was a major source of creative and political inspiration for black poets."
44. Hampton, *Eyes on the Prize II*; Orlando Bagwell, *Malcolm X: Make It Plain* (PBS, 1994).
45. Sanchez, "Poem (for DCs 8th Graders—1966–67," in *Home Coming*, 22.
46. Alim, "360 Degreez of Black Art," 27–28.
47. Sonia Sanchez, "A Black/Woman/Speaks," on *A Sun Lady for All Seasons Reads Her Poetry* (Smithsonian Folkways Records, 1971).
48. Hampton, *Eyes on the Prize II*.
49. Malcolm X, "Who Taught You to Hate the Color of Your Skin?," Los Angeles, May 5, 1962, https://www.youtube.com/watch?v=kboP3AWCTkA.
50. Hampton, *Eyes on the Prize II*.
51. Malcolm X, "Who Taught You to Hate the Color of Your Skin?"
52. bell hooks, *Ain't I a Woman: Black Women and Feminism* (Pluto Press, 1981), 108.
53. Malcolm X, "Who Taught You to Hate the Color of Your Skin?"; Beyoncé, "Don't Hurt Yourself," in *Lemonade*, with Jack White (Jungle Studios, 2014); Megan Thee Stallion, "Savage," in *Saturday Night Live*, with Beyoncé (2020), https://www.youtube.com/watch?v=CTpilDQXYro.
54. Davis, "Meditations on the Legacy of Malcolm X," 44; James G. Spady, "The Centrality of Black Language in the Discourse Strategies and Poetic Force of Sonia Sanchez and Rap Artists," *B. Ma: The Sonia Sanchez Literary Review* 6, no. 1 (2000): 47–72; Alim, "360 Degreez of Black Art."
55. Geneva Smitherman, "The Power of the Rap: The Black Idiom and the New Black Poetry," *Twentieth Century Literature* 19, no. 4 (1974): 259–74; Geneva Smitherman, *Talkin and Testifyin: The Language of Black America* (Wayne State University Press, 1977).
56. Sonia Sanchez, "Queens of the Universe," *The Black Scholar: Journal of Black Studies and Research, In Memoriam: W. E. B. Du Bois* 1, no. 3/4 (February 1970): 29. In Patricia Hill Collins's chapter "Mammies, Matriarchs, and Other Controlling Images," she begins with a similar list of stereotypes, quoting Trudier Harris, *From Mammies to Militants* (69); Trudier Harris, *From Mammies to Militants: Domestics in Black American Literature* (Temple University Press, 1982), 4.
57. Ashley D. Farmer, *Remaking Black Power: How Black Women Transformed an Era* (University of North Carolina Press, 2017), 109–14.
58. Sanchez, "Queens of the Universe," 29.
59. Griffin, "Ironies of the Saint," 223; Saidiya Hartman, *Lose Your Mother: A Journey Along the Atlantic Slave Route* (Farrar, Straus and Giroux, 2008), 234.
60. hooks, *Ain't I a Woman*; Patricia Hill Williams, "Learning to Think for Ourselves: Malcolm X's Black Nationalism Reconsidered," in *Malcolm X: In Our Own Image*, ed. Joe Wood (St. Martin's

Press, 1992); Barbara Ransby and Tracye Matthews, "Black Popular Culture and the Transcendence of Patriarchal Illusions," in *Words of Fire: An Anthology of African American Feminist Thought*, ed. Beverly Guy-Sheftall (New Press, 1995).

61. Mumininas of Committee for Unified NewArk, *Mwanamke Mwananchi (The Nationalist Woman)* (Jihad Productions, 1971); Combahee River Collective, *Combahee River Collective Statement* (1977).
62. Farmer, *Remaking Black Power*, 98.
63. Farmer, *Remaking Black Power*, 99.
64. Farmer, *Remaking Black Power*, 108.
65. Mumininas of Committee for Unified NewArk, *Mwanamke Mwananchi (The Nationalist Woman)*.
66. Sanchez, "Queens of the Universe," 29.
67. Daniel Patrick Moynihan, *The Negro Family: The Case for National Action* (Office of Policy Planning and Research, US Department of Labor, 1965), 29–30.
68. W. E. B. Du Bois, *The Negro American Family* (Atlanta University Press, 1908). In the aftermath of the Moynihan report, the book was republished by numerous presses, including the original publisher, Atlanta University, as well as Arno Press, Negro Universities Press, and MIT Press among others.
69. Forsgren, *In Search of Our Warrior Mothers*, 75.
70. Hartman, "The Belly of the World," 171.
71. Sanchez, "Queens of the Universe," 34.
72. Alexander G. Weheliye, "Black Studies and Black Life," *The Black Scholar: Journal of Black Studies and Research* 44, no. 2 (2014): 5.
73. Sanchez, *A Blues Book for Blue Black Magical Women*, 57. See the beautiful discussion of Sonia Sanchez's "We Are Muslim Women" in Chan-Malik, *Being Muslim*, 8.
74. Sanchez, *A Blues Book for Blue Black Magical Women*, 23.
75. Weheliye, "Black Studies and Black Life," 5; Hartman, "The Belly of the World," 166.
76. Joyce Ann Joyce, *Black Studies as Human Studies: Critical Essays and Interviews* (State University of New York Press, 2005), 153.
77. Joyce, *Black Studies as Human Studies*, 154–55.
78. Kelly, "Discipline and Craft," 685; Joyce, *Black Studies as Human Studies*, 154.
79. Kelly, "Discipline and Craft," 684.
80. Sanchez, "Queens of the Universe," 29–32. Also see Sanchez, *Blues Book*, 16.
81. Sanchez, *It's A New Day*, 7.
82. The title of the collection refers to Nina Simone's "Feeling Good" from her 1965 album *I Put A Spell on You*: "Freedom in mine / And I now how I feel / It's a new dawn / It's a new day / It's a new life for me / I'm feeling good." James Brown also released "It's A New Day" that same year and Will.i.am released his own "It's a New Day" upon the election of Baraka Obama November 7, 2008.
83. Sanchez, *It's A New Day*, 27–29. In my copy of the poem, the Islamic words As-Salaam-alaikum, Elijah, Islam, and Allah are crossed out and "RA" is written over the word Allah, speaking to further translation of these conceptions of Blackness, partly through the superimposition of reader reception, but also speaking to negative reactions to the Islamic content.
84. Rudine Sims, *Shadow and Substance: Afro-American Experience in Contemporary Children's Fiction* (National Council of Teachers of English, 1982), 49; Violet J. Harris, "African American Children's Literature: The First One Hundred Years," *The Journal of Negro Education* 59, no. 4 (1990): 550.
85. Geneva Smitherman, "English Teacher, Why You Be Doing the Thangs You Don't Do?," *English Journal*, January 1972; Geneva Smitherman, "White English in Blackface or, Who Do I Be?," *The*

8. "BLK/VISIONS FOR BLK/LIVES"   ❧   311

Black Scholar 4, no. 8/9 (1973): 32–39; Smitherman, "The Power of the Rap"; Smitherman, *Talkin and Testifyin*.

86. Lonnie Kashif, "Black Child in the '70s: Students Victims of Behavioral Experiments," *Muhammad Speaks*, July 4, 1975, 14:43 Edition; Joe Walker, "Racist Texts Standard in U.S. Classrooms: Textbook Distortions Revealed," *Muhammad Speaks*, July 4, 1975, 14:43 Edition; Doreen 2X, "Muhammad Ali Biography: Positive Image for Youth," *Muhammad Speaks*, July 4, 1975, 14:43 Edition.
87. Deloris Costello and Joe Walker, "How to Rear a Healthy Black Child in America," *Muhammad Speaks*, July 4, 1975, 14:43 edition; James P. Comer and Alvin F. Poussaint, *Black Child Care: How to Bring Up a Healthy Black Child in America—A Guide to Emotional and Psychological Development* (Simon & Schuster, 1975).
88. Robert Staples, "To Be Young, Black and Oppressed," *The Black Scholar* 7, no. 4 (1975): 2–9; Daphne Muse, "Black Children's Literature: Rebirth of a Neglected Genre," *The Black Scholar* 7, no. 4 (1975): 11–15. "Special thanks to Sister Laila Mannan (formerly Sonia 5X Sanchez) for her help in compiling the poetry in this section. Sister Laila edits a children's page in *Bilalian News* (formerly *Muhammad Speaks*)" (17).
89. Sister Sonia 5X Sanchez, "Respect for Wisdom," New Frontiers, *Muhammad Speaks*, August 29, 1975, 14:51 Edition.
90. Sister Minister Sharolyn, "Conversation with Sis. Sonia 5X," s3.
91. Kelly, "Discipline and Craft," 683.
92. Hartman, "The Belly of the World," 166; Sanchez, "Queens of the Universe," 32; Sanchez, *A Blues Book for Blue Black Magical Women*, 16.
93. Foucault, *"Society Must Be Defended,"* 255, 258, as quoted in Alexander G. Weheliye, *Habeas Viscus*, 56.
94. Sister Minister Sharolyn, "Conversation with Sis. Sonia 5X," s3.
95. Sanchez, *A Blues Book for Blue Black Magical Women*, 23, 24, 39, 42.
96. Sanchez, *A Blues Book for Blue Black Magical Women*, 12, 14, 22, 29, 32, 34.
97. Margaret Larkin, "The Inimitability of the Qur'an. Two Perspectives," *Religion and Literature* 20 (1988): 31–47; Y. Rahman, "The Miraculous Nature of Muslim Scripture. A Study of 'Abd al-Jabbar's I'jaz al-Qur'an," *Islamic Studies* 35 (1996): 409–24; Issa J. Boullata, "The Rhetorical Interpretation of the Qur'an. I'jaz and Related Topics," in *Approaches to the History of the Interpretation of the Qur'an*, ed. Andrew Rippin (Gorgias Press, 2012).
98. Wolfhart Heinrichs, "The Meaning of Mutanabbi," in *Poetry and Prophecy: The Beginnings of a Literary Tradition*, ed. James L. Kugel (Cornell University Press, 1990); Michael Zwettler, "A Mantic Manifesto: The Sura of 'The Poets' and the Qur'anic Foundations of Prophetic Authority," in *Poetry and Prophecy: The Beginnings of a Literary Tradition*, ed. James L. Kugel (Cornell University Press, 1990).
99. Jaroslav Stetkevych, *The Zephyrs of Najd: The Poetics of Nostalgia in The Classical Arabic Nasib* (University of Chicago Press, 1993).
100. Sherman A. Jackson, *Islam and the Blackamerican: Looking Toward the Third Resurrection* (Oxford University Press, 2005), 26–29.
101. C. Eric Lincoln, *The Black Muslims in America* (Beacon Press, 1961).
102. Michael Muhammad Knight, *Blue-Eyed Devil* (Autonomedia, 2007); Edward E. Curtis IV, *Islam in Black America* (State University of New York Press, 2002); Edward E. Curtis IV, *Black Muslim Religion in the Nation of Islam, 1960–1975* (University of North Carolina Press, 2006); Jackson, *Islam and the Blackamerican*.
103. Sayyid Qutb, *al-Taswir al-Fanni Fi al-Qur'an* (Dar al-Ma'arif, 1945); Tawfiq Muhammad Sab', *Nufus wa-Durus fi-Itar al-Taswir al-Qur'ani* (Majma' al-Buhuth al-Islamiyya, 1971);

Muhammad Abu Musa, *al-Taswir al-Bayani: Dirasa Tahliliya li-Masa'il al-Bayan* (Maktabat Wahba, 1980).

104. Saba Mahmood, *Politics of Piety: The Islamic Revival and the Feminist Subject* (Princeton University Press, 2005); Rudolph T. Ware, *The Walking Qur'an: Islamic Education, Embodied Knowledge, and History in West Africa* (University of North Carolina Press, 2014).

105. Ellen McLarney, *Soft Force: Women in Egypt's Islamic Awakening*, Princeton Studies in Muslim Politics (Princeton University Press, 2015), 143–79.

106. Sanchez, *A Blues Book for Blue Black Magical Women*, 49.

107. Felicia Miyakawa, *Five Percenter Rap: God Hop's Music, Message, and Black Muslim Mission* (Indiana University Press, 2005); Michael Muhammad Knight, *The Five Percenters: Islam, Hip-Hop and the Gods of New York* (Oneworld Publications, 2007).

108. McLarney, *Soft Force: Women in Egypt's Islamic Awakening*, 103–79.

109. Smitherman, *Talkin and Testifyin*.

110. Hampton, *Eyes on the Prize II*.

111. Rey Chow, *Not Like a Native Speaker: On Languaging as a Postcolonial Experience* (Columbia University Press, 2014), 5.

112. Kelly, "Discipline and Craft," 683.

113. hooks, *Ain't I a Woman*, 111, along with edited volumes *The Afro-American Woman: Struggles and Images* (1978), *This Bridge Called My Back* (1981), and *Sisters of the Spirit* (1986).

114. Frost, *The Feminist Avant-Garde in American Poetry*, 65; Austin, "Theorizing Difference within Black Feminist Thought." Austin asserts that "Black feminists utilizing a black nationalist analysis of black sexism could not develop a serious critique," effectively ignoring Black feminism's relationship to the Black power movement, despite its critiques.

115. Frost, *The Feminist Avant-Garde in American Poetry*, 66.

116. Farmer, *Remaking Black Power*, 17.

117. Jacqueline Wood, "'Shaking Loose:' Sonia Sanchez's Militant Drama," in *Contemporary African American Women Playwrights*, ed. Philip C. Kolin (Routledge, 2007); Mike Sell, *Avant-Garde Performance & the Limits of Criticism: Approaching the Living Theatre, Happenings/Fluxus, and the Black Arts Movement* (University of Michigan Press, 2008); Forsgren, *In Search of Our Warrior Mothers*, 69.

118. Griffin, "Ironies of the Saint"; Forsgren, *In Search of Our Warrior Mothers*.

119. Forsgren, *In Search of Our Warrior Mothers*, 76.

120. Mahmood, *Politics of Piety*; Gibson and Karim, *Women of the Nation: Between Black Protest and Sunni Islam*, 155.

121. Gibson and Karim, *Women of the Nation: Between Black Protest and Sunni Islam*; Taylor, *The Promise of Patriarchy*; Farmer, *Remaking Black Power*.

122. James Smethurst, *The Black Arts Movement: Literary Nationalism in the 1960s and 1970s* (University of North Carolina Press, 2005), 87.

123. Nira Yuval-Davis, "Intersectionality and Feminist Politics," *European Journal of Women's Studies* 13, no. 3 (2006): 198, 203.

124. Diane Singerman, *Avenues of Participation: Family, Politics, and Networks in Urban Quarters of Cairo* (Princeton University Press, 1996); Lila Abu-Lughod, "The Marriage of Feminism and Islamism in Egypt: Selective Repudiation as a Dynamic of Postcolonial Cultural Politics," in *Remaking Women: Feminism and Modernity in the Middle East*, ed. Lila Abu-Lughod (Princeton University Press, 1998); Omnia Shakry, "Schooled Mothers and Structured Play: Child Rearing in Turn-of-the-Century Egypt," in *Remaking Women: Feminism and Modernity in the Middle East*, ed. Lila Abu-Lughod (Princeton University Press, 1998); McLarney, *Soft Force: Women in Egypt's Islamic Awakening*; Jeanette S. Jouili, *Pious Practice and Secular Constraints: Women in the Islamic Revival in France and Germany* (Stanford University Press, 2015).

125. Hampton, *Eyes on the Prize II*.
126. Taylor, *The Promise of Patriarchy*, 184.
127. Carolyn Fowler, "A Contemporary Blackamerican Genre: Pamphlet/Manifesto Poetry," *Black World*, June 1974, 4.
128. Spillers, "Mama's Baby, Papa's Maybe," 68.
129. Shockley, *Renegade Poetics*, 62.
130. Dorothy Randall, "Black Mayflower," in *Three Hundred and Sixty Degrees of Blackness Comin at You: An Anthology of the Sonia Sanchez Writers Workshop at Countee Cullen Library in Harlem*, ed. Sonia Sanchez (5X Publishing Co., 1971); Spillers, "Mama's Baby, Papa's Maybe," 73; hooks, *Ain't I a Woman*, 18–19.
131. Randall, "Black Mayflower."
132. James Spady, "Introduction: 360 Degreez of Sonia Sanchez, Hip Hop, Narrativity, Iqhawe, and Public Spaces of Being," *B. Ma: The Sonia Sanchez Literary Review* 6, no. 1 (2000): vi.
133. Alim, "360 Degreez of Black Art," 17.
134. John Ali, *120 Lessons: Knowledge of Self for the Black Man* (KAH Publication, 2012), 1, 3.

CODA. 360° OF ISLAMIC AUDIOVISUALITIES

1. Shahab Ahmed, *What Is Islam?: The Importance of Being Islamic* (Princeton University Press, 2016), 247–97; John R. Bowen, *Muslims Through Discourse: Religion and Ritual in Gayo Society* (Princeton University Press, 1993); for "continent of meaning" see Clifford Geertz, *The Interpretation of Cultures* (Basic Books, 1973).
2. Amiri Baraka, Marvin X, and Faruk, "Islam and Black Art," *The Negro Digest*, January 1969; Amiri Baraka, "Islam and Black Art," in *Black Arts: An Anthology of Black Creations*, ed. Ahmed Alhamisi and Harun Kofi Wangara (Black Arts Publications, 1969); Harryette Mullen, "African Signs and Spirit Writing," in *The Black Studies Reader*, ed. Jacqueline Bobo, Cynthia Hudley, and Claudine Michel (Routledge, 2004).
3. See the following for individual quotes: "supernatural," Frantz Fanon, *Les damnés de la terre* (F. Maspero, 1961); "transcendental," Yusef Rahman, "Transcendental Blues," in *Black Fire: An Anthology of Afro-American Writing* (Black Classic Press, 1968); "surreal," Robin D. G. Kelley, *Freedom Dreams: The Black Radical Imagination* (Beacon Press, 2002); "critical fabulation," Saidiya Hartman, "Venus in Two Acts," *Small Axe: A Journal of Criticism* 12, no. 2 (2008): 1–14; "insurrectionary," Carmen Kynard, *Vernacular Insurrections: Race, Black Protest, and the New Century in Composition-Literacies Studies* (State University of New York Press, 2013); "speculative," Reynaldo Anderson and Clinton R. Fluker, eds., *The Black Speculative Arts Movement: Black Futurity, Art+Design* (Lexington Books, 2019).
4. Ahmed, *What Is Islam?*, 250.
5. Meta DuEwa Jones, *The Muse Is Music: Jazz Poetry from the Harlem Renaissance to Spoken Word* (University of Illinois Press, 2013), 92–93.
6. Askia Muhammad Abu Bakr el-Touré, *Juju (Magic Songs for the Black Nation)* (Third World Press, 1970), 17.
7. Michael A. Gomez, *Black Crescent: The Experience and Legacy of African Muslims in the Americas* (Cambridge University Press, 2005), 200; Tina M. Campt, *A Black Gaze: Artists Changing How We See* (MIT Press, 2021), 79. Campt uses the words "generative and expansive" to talk about a Black visual aesthetic that aspires "to deliver the force of Black music in a visual register. It is an effort to render its beauty as an aesthetic that exceeds words by augmenting the visual with the intensity of feeling that defines black music. It . . . resounds with the frequential depths and

spiritual capacity of Black music. It is a vision achieved through a technique [cinematographer Arthur Jafa] calls Black visual intonation."

8. Sohail Daulatzai, *Black Star, Crescent Moon: The Muslim International and Black Freedom Beyond America* (University of Minnesota Press, 2012).
9. "What Is Rhythm? (Advertisement for Black Power!)," *Soulbook* 2 (1967): 152, quoted in Margo Natalie Crawford, *Black Post-Blackness: The Black Arts Movement and Twenty-First-Century Aesthetics* (University of Illinois Press, 2017), 1.
10. Crawford, *Black Post-Blackness*, 1–3.
11. Crawford, *Black Post-Blackness*, 2. Amiri Baraka [LeRoi Jones], "The Changing Same (R&B and New Black Music)," in *Black Music* (William Morrow, 1967), 209.
12. Baraka [Jones], "The Changing Same," 193, 199; Amiri Baraka [LeRoi Jones], *Blues People: The Negro Experience in White America and the Music That Developed from It* (William Morrow, 1963). In "The Changing Same," Baraka extends his earlier meditations in *A Blues People* on the blues as one of captive Africans' "methods of worshipping... when his white captors declared that he could no longer worship in the old ways." The blues, he argues, combined "holdovers from African religions" and "lyrics, rhythms, and harmonies essentially of African derivation, subjected to the transformations of American life."
13. Deborah E. McDowell, *"The Changing Same": Black Women's Literature, Criticism, and Theory* (Indiana University Press, 1995), xiii; W. E. B. Du Bois, *The Souls of Black Folk* (A. C. McClurg & Co., 1903).
14. Askia Muhammad Touré, "The Sound of Allah's Horn," in *Black Arts: An Anthology of Black Creations*, ed. Ahmed Alhamisi and Harun Kofi Wangara (Black Arts Publications, 1969), 136–37.
15. Jones, *The Muse Is Music*, 86.
16. Moustafa Bayoumi, "East of the Sun (West of the Moon): Islam, the Ahmadis, and African America," in *Black Routes to Islam*, ed. Manning Marable and Hishaam D. Aidi (Palgrave Macmillan, 2009), 75–76; Hisham Aidi, *Rebel Music: Race, Empire, and the New Muslim Youth Culture* (Vintage, 2014), 112–15.
17. Pharoah Sanders, *Tauhid*, Impulse! Records, 1967; Pharoah Sanders, "Hum-Allah-Hum-Allah-Hum-Allah," *Jewels of Thought*, Impulse! Records, October 20, 1969; Pharoah Sanders, *Deaf Dumb Blind (Summun Bukmun Umyun)*, A&R Studios, 1970.
18. Jones, *The Muse Is Music*, 85–86.
19. Jones, *The Muse Is Music*, 92–93.
20. Touré, *Juju*, 16; Jones, *The Muse Is Music*, 91–93, 95; Meta Du Ewa Jones, "Jazz Prosodies: Orality and Textuality," *Callaloo* 24, no. 1 (2002): 66–91.
21. Touré, *Juju*, 17.
22. Bayoumi, "Islam, the Ahmadis, and African America"; Jones, *The Muse Is Music*, 91–93; Aidi, *Rebel Music*, 112–15; Moustafa Bayoumi, "Allah Supreme: How Pharoah Sanders Found Freedom and Rebellion in Islam," *The Guardian*, December 29, 2022.
23. Campt, *A Black Gaze*, 7, 18–19.
24. Baraka [Jones], "The Changing Same," 209; Julian Mayfield, "Into the Mainstream and Oblivion," in *The American Negro Writer and His Roots: Selected Papers*, ed. John Aubrey Davis Sr., First Conference of Negro Writers 1959 (American Society of African Culture, 1960), 32.
25. Campt, *A Black Gaze*, 79.
26. Campt, *A Black Gaze*, 19.
27. Crawford, *Black Post-Blackness*, 83.
28. Jones, *The Muse Is Music*, 86.
29. Amiri Baraka [Imamu Amiri Baraka] and [Billy Abernathy] Fundi, *In Our Terribleness (Some Elements and Meaning in Black Style)* (Bobbs-Merrill, 1970).

30. Achille Mbembe, *Critique of Black Reason*, trans. Laurent DuBois (Duke University Press, 2017), 100.
31. Mbembe, *Critique of Black Reason*, 97.
32. Touré, "The Sound of Allah's Horn," 136–37; Mbembe, *Critique of Black Reason*, 97; Ahmed, *What Is Islam?*, 247–97.
33. Baraka, "Islam and Black Art," 51.
34. Amiri Baraka, *The Autobiography of LeRoi Jones* (Lawrence Hill Books, 1997), 365.
35. The poem was published in *Spirit Reach* and in Woodie King's anthology *Black Spirits* that same year. Baraka also recited the poem on the Black Power television program *Soul!*. Amiri Baraka [Imamu Amiri Baraka], "Somebody's Slow Is Another Body's Fast (Preachment)," in *Spirit Reach* (Jihad Productions, 1972), 20–21; Amiri Baraka [Imamu Amiri Baraka], "Somebody's Slow Is Another Body's Fast (Preachment)," in *Black Spirits: A Festival of New Black Poets in America*, ed. Woodie King (Random House, 1972); Gayle Wald, *It's Been Beautiful: Soul! And Black Power Television* (Duke University Press, 2015), 172, 244n32.
36. Baraka, "Somebody's Slow Is Another Body's Fast (Preachment)," 20–21.
37. Su'ad Abdul Khabeer, *Muslim Cool: Race, Religion, and Hip Hop in the United States* (New York University Press, 2016), 7.
38. John Ali, *120 Lessons: Knowledge of Self for the Black Man* (KAH Publications, 2012), 1, 3.
39. Sister Souljah, *360 Degrees of Power*, Epic/SME Records, 1992; H. Samy Alim, "360 Degreez of Black Art Comin at You: Sista Sonia Sanchez and the Dimensions of a Black Arts Continuum," *B. Ma: The Sonia Sanchez Literary Review* 6, no. 1 (2000): 31n1.
40. Alim, "360 Degreez of Black Art," 17, 24. This book was partly inspired by Alim's article that he wrote two years before we first met as graduate students in Ramzi Salti's Arabic class at Stanford. From the inception of the project, I followed Alim's cues in this article.
41. The Last Poets, *Jazzoetry*, Douglas Records, 1967.
42. Alim, "360 Degreez of Black Art," 2000, 30; Saleemah Abdul-Ghafur, *Living Islam Out Loud: AMerican Muslim Women Speak* (Beacon Press, 2005); Kevin Coval, Quraysh Ali Lansana, and Nate Marshall, eds., *The BreakBeat Poets: New American Poetry in the Age of Hip-Hop* (Haymarket Books, 2015); Jamila Woods, Mahogany L. Browne, Idrissa Simmonds, and Patricia Smith, eds., *The BreakBeat Poets Vol. 2: Black Girl Magic* (Haymarket Books, 2018); Fatimah Asghar and Safia Elhillo, eds., *Halal If You Hear Me* (Haymarket Books, 2019).
43. Mbembe, *Critique of Black Reason*, 97; Sun Ra, "Preparation for Outer Space," in *Jazz By Sun Ra* (Transition, 1957); Sun Ra and his Arkestra, *Jazz in Silhouette*, El Saturn, 1959; Sun Ra, *Immeasurable Equation* (Ihnfinity Inc. / Saturn Research, 1972), 7, 11, 70.
44. James Winston Morris and Ibn al-'Arabi, "Introduction to The Meccan Revelations," in *The Meccan Revelations*, ed. Michel Chodkiewicz (Pir Press, 2002), https://ibnarabisociety.org/introduction-to-the-meccan-revelations-james-morris/; Amir Sulaiman, *The Meccan Openings*, 2011, http://www.amirsulaiman.com/meccan-openings.
45. Amir Sulaiman, dir., *Laying Flowers, Setting Fires* (True + Living Media, 2020), https://www.youtube.com/watch?v=fYogdFvotho.
46. Claude Addas, *Quest for the Red Sulphur: The Life of Ibn 'Arabi*, trans. Peter Kingsley (Islamic Texts Society, 1993); Amiri Baraka, *SOS: Poems 1961–2013* (Grove Press, 2014).
47. Muhyiddin Ibn 'Arabi, *Translator of Desires: Poems*, trans. Michael Sells (Princeton University Press, 2021); Amir Sulaiman, *Love, Gnosis, & Other Suicide Attempts* (Penmanship Publishing, 2012).
48. Morris and Ibn al-'Arabi, "Introduction to The Meccan Revelations."
49. Morris and Ibn al-'Arabi, "Introduction to The Meccan Revelations."
50. Michael Sells, *Stations of Desire: Love Elegies from Ibn 'Arabi and New Poems* (Ibis Editions, 2000), 24, 25; Ibn 'Arabi, *Translator of Desires*.

51. Yahsmin Mayaan Binti BoBo, "Mute Man Talking: Poetry Under Surveillance, Interview with Amir Sulaiman," *The Black Commentator*, no. 186 (June 2006), https://blackcommentator.com/186/186_mute_man.html.
52. BoBo, "Mute Man Talking."
53. Peter Lamborn Wilson, *Sacred Drift: Essays on the Margins of Islam* (City Lights Books, 1993), 6–7; Edward E. Curtis IV, *Islam in Black America* (State University of New York Press, 2002), 45.
54. William Hansell, "Gwendolyn Brook's 'In the Mecca:' A Rebirth into Blackness," *Negro American Literature Forum* 8, no. 2 (1974): 199–209; Daniel Bluestone, "Chicago's Mecca Flat Blues," *Journal of the Society of Architectural Historians* 57, no. 4 (1998): 382–403; Daniela Kukrechtová, "The Death and Life of a Chicago Edifice: Gwendolyn Brook's 'In the Mecca,'" *African American Review* 43, no. 2/3 (2009): 457–72.
55. Arthur Jafa, "69," in *Black Popular Culture: A Project by Michele Wallace*, ed. Gina Dent, Dia Center for the Arts: Discussions in Contemporary Culture #8 (Bay Press, 1992), 253.
56. Jones, *The Muse Is Music*, 7.
57. Jones, *The Muse is Music*, 19; Michael Sells, *Approaching the Qur'an: The Early Revelations* (White Cloud Press, 1999), 31.
58. Campt, *A Black Gaze*, 31; Alexander G. Weheliye, *Feenin: R&B Music and the Materiality of Black-Fem Voices and Technology* (Duke University Press, 2023), 10, 12. Weheliye writes about "the oscillation of different historical frequencies" and about "synchronic and diachronic frequencies that present . . . a plethora of possible pasts and yet-to-comes."
59. Morris and Ibn al-'Arabi, "Introduction to The Meccan Revelations."
60. Sulaiman, *The Meccan Openings*; God Supreme Allah, ed., *Supreme Lessons of the Gods and Earths: A Guide for 5 Percenters to Follow As Taught by Clarence 13x Allah* (African American Bookstore, 1993); Felicia M. Miyakawa, *Five Percenter Rap: God Hop's Music, Message, and Black Muslim Mission* (Indiana University Press, 2005), 26–27, 55–57.
61. John O. Voll, "Renewal and Reform in Islamic History: Tajdid and Islah," in *Voices of Resurgent Islam*, ed. John L. Esposito (Oxford University Press, 1983).
62. Jones, *The Muse Is Music*, 7.
63. Baraka [Jones], "The Changing Same," 204.
64. Toni Morrison, "Toni Morrison Interview with John Callaway," *WTTW*, aired 1977, on PBS; *Laying Flowers, Setting Fires*.
65. Ronald A. T. Judy, *(Dis)Forming the American Canon: African-Arabic Slave Narratives and the Vernacular* (University of Minnesota Press, 1993), 209–83. See Judy's brilliant analysis of the Bilali Muhammad manuscript as breaking out of the literary canon of African American slave narratives.
66. Jafa, "69," 253.
67. Hanif Abdurraqib, *A Little Devil in America: In Praise of Black Performance* (Random House, 2021), 3.
68. Jafa, "69," 253.
69. Jafa, "69," 253.
70. Sylviane A. Diouf, "What Islam Gave the Blues," *Renovatio: The Journal of Zaytuna College*, June 17, 2019, https://renovatio.zaytuna.edu/article/what-islam-gave-the-blues.
71. Nina Simone, "Blackbird," in *World of Folk Music #107* (WNBC, 1964); Ayanna Sharif, dir., *WUDU: A Short Film*, 2019, https://www.youtube.com/watch?v=kDCebx8wuSs.
72. Campt, *A Black Gaze*, 81.
73. Weheliye, *Feenin*, 12; Larry Neal, "The Narrative of the Black Magicians," in *Black Fire: An Anthology of Afro-American Writing*, ed. Amiri Baraka and Larry Neal (Black Classic Press, 2013); Sanchez, *Ima Talken Bout the Nation of Islam*; [broadsheet] (New Pyramid Productions, 1971). Baraka, "Somebody's Slow Is Another Body's Fast (Preachment)."

74. Martin Luther King Jr., "After Civil Rights: Black Power," interview by Sanders Vanocur, May 8, 1967, NBC News, https://www.nbcnews.com/video/martin-luther-king-jr-speaks-with-nbc-news-11-months-before-assassination-1202163779741.
75. Tariq Touré, *The Call* (2020), https://www.youtube.com/watch?v=hr8lP2hDISQ.
76. Vertamae Smart-Grosvenor, *Vibration Cooking, Or, The Travel Notes of a Geechee Girl* (Doubleday, 1970), 83. One of those evenings that Grosvenor describes is a "soul in" with Sun Ra and the Solar Myth Science Arkestra, saying that "everybody was there, Larry and Evelyn Neal, Hettie Jones, LeRoi Jones, Sylvia Wilson, Rap Brown, and Mary Lyerly. (Lyerly was Coltrane's cousin and his composition, 'Cousin Mary' on *Giant Steps*, was written for her. Smart-Grosvenor says, "she has such good vibrations . . . I guess beautiful vibrations run in that family."
77. Maimouna Youssef, "Music, Art, and Being Muslim," Doris Duke Foundation for Islamic Art, Building Bridges: Muslims in America, The Ruby, Duke University, September 19, 2019.

BIBLIOGRAPHY

PRINT SOURCES

#Brooklynology. "Black News." *Brooklyn Public Library, Center for Brooklyn History*, February 14, 2011. https://www.bklynlibrary.org/blog/2011/02/14/black-news.

13X "Allah the Father," Clarence. "Supreme Mathematics." *The Five Percenter Lessons*, n.d. https://fivepercenterlessons.wordpress.com/mathematics/.

"A Shahada Rebirth Celebration." *American Muslim Journal*, July 17, 1992, 1.

Abdat, Fathie Ali. "Before the Fez: The Life and Times of Drew Ali, 1886–1924." *Journal of Race, Ethnicity, and Religion* 5, no. 8 (2014): 1–39.

Abdul Khabeer, Su'ad. "Africa as Tradition in U.S. African American Muslim Identity." *Journal of Africana Religions* 5, no. 1 (2017): 26–49.

Abdul Khabeer, Su'ad. "Black Arabic: Some Notes on African American Muslims and the Arabic Language." In *Black Routes to Islam*, ed. Manning Marable and Hishaam D. Aidi. Palgrave Macmillan, 2009.

Abdul Khabeer, Su'ad. *Muslim Cool: Race, Religion, and Hip Hop in the United States*. New York University Press, 2016.

Abdul-Ghafur, Saleemah. *Living Islam Out Loud: American Muslim Women Speak*. Beacon Press, 2005.

Abdullah, Zain. *Black Mecca: The African Muslims of Harlem*. Oxford University Press, 2013.

Abdurraqib, Hanif. *A Little Devil in America: In Praise of Black Performance*. Random House, 2021.

Abernethy, Graeme. *The Iconography of Malcolm X*. University of Kansas Press, 2013.

Abraham, Alton. *Collection of Sun Ra*. Series VIII: Audio-Visual, Subseries 1: Photographs, Box 59. University of Chicago Library, n.d.

Abu-Lughod, Lila. "The Marriage of Feminism and Islamism in Egypt: Selective Repudiation as a Dynamic of Postcolonial Cultural Politics." In *Remaking Women: Feminism and Modernity in the Middle East*, ed. Lila Abu-Lughod. Princeton University Press, 1998.

Abu Musa, Muhammad. *al-Taswir al-Bayani: Dirasa Tahliliya li-Masa'il al-Bayan*. Maktabat Wahba, 1980.

Addas, Claude. *Quest for the Red Sulphur: The Life of Ibn 'Arabi*, trans. Peter Kingsley. Islamic Texts Society, 1993.

Agamben, Giorgio. *Homo Sacer: Sovereign Power and Bare Life*, trans. Daniel Heller-Roazen. Stanford University Press, 1998.

Ahmed, Shahab. *What Is Islam?: The Importance of Being Islamic*. Princeton University Press, 2016.
Aidi, Hisham. *Rebel Music: Race, Empire, and the New Muslim Youth Culture*. Vintage, 2014.
Aidi, Hisham. "The Music of Malcolm X." *New Yorker*, February 28, 2015. https://www.newyorker.com/culture/culture-desk/the-music-of-malcolm-x.
Aidi, Hisham. "The Political Uses of Malcolm X." *Nka Journal of Contemporary African Art* 2018, nos. 42–43 (2018): 212–21.
Alfieri, Anthony V. "Integrating into a Burning House: Race- and Identity-Conscious Visions in Brown's Inner City." *Southern California Law Review* 84 (2011): 541–604.
Alford, Terry. *Prince Among Slaves*. Oxford University Press, 1977.
Ali, John. *120 Lessons: Knowledge of Self for the Black Man*. KAH Publication, 2012.
Ali, Muhammad. "Muhammad Ali on the Vietnam War-Draft," *Like It Is*, WABC-TV New York 1967, https://www.youtube.com/watch?v=HeFMyrWlZ68.
Ali, Noble Drew. *Koran Questions for Moorish Children*. 1/31. Moorish Science Temple of America, 1931. vault.fbi.gov.
Ali, Zaheer. "Curating the Malcolm X Mixtape Project." Paper presented at The Legacy of Malcolm X: Afro-American Visionary, Muslim Activist conference. Duke University, February 16, 2015.
Alim, H. Samy. "360 Degreez of Black Art Comin at You: Sista Sonia Sanchez and the Dimensions of a Black Arts Continuum." *B. Ma: The Sonia Sanchez Literary Review* 6, no. 1 (2000): 15–35.
Alim, H. Samy. "Re-Inventing Islam with Unique Modern Tones: Muslim Hip Hop Artists as Verbal Mujahidin." *American Foreign Policy Interests* 8, no. 4 (2006): 45–58.
Alim, H. Samy. *Roc the Mic Right: The Language of Hip Hop Culture*. Routledge, 2006.
Allah, God Supreme, ed. *Supreme Lessons of the Gods and Earths: A Guide for 5 Percenters to Follow As Taught by Clarence 13x Allah*. African American Bookstore, 1993.
Allen, Ernest. "Satokata Takahashi and the Flowering of Black Messianic Nationalism." *The Black Scholar* 24–21 (1994): 23–46.
Allen, Robert. "Politics of the Attack on Black Studies." *The Black Scholar* 6, no. 1 (1974): 2–7.
Allen, William Francis, Charles Pickard Ware, and Lucy McKim Garrison, eds. "My Father, How Long?" In *Slave Songs of the United States*. A. Simpson & Co., 1867.
Anderson, Reynaldo, and Clinton R. Fluker, eds. *The Black Speculative Arts Movement: Black Futurity, Art+Design*. Lexington Books, 2019.
Anderson. T. J. III. *Notes to Make the Sound Come Right: Four Innovators of Jazz Poetry*. University of Arkansas Press, 2004.
Angelou, Maya. *Heart of a Woman*. Random House, 1981.
Angelou, Maya. *I Know Why the Caged Bird Sings*. Random House, 1969.
Aqeeli, Ammar Abduh. *The Nation of Islam and Black Consciousness*. Peter Lang Inc., 2019.
Armah, Ayi Kwei. "Fanon: The Awakener." *Negro Digest*, October 1969, 4–9.
Asad, Talal. *Genealogies of Religion: Discipline and Reasons of Power in Christianity and Islam*. Johns Hopkins University Press, 1993.
Asghar, Fatimah, and Safia Elhillo, eds. *Halal If You Hear Me*. Haymarket Books, 2019.
Augustyn, Heather. *Ska: The Rhythm of Liberation*. Scarecrow Press, 2013.
Austin, Algernon. "Theorizing Difference within Black Feminist Thought: The Dilemma of Sexism in Black Communities." *Race, Gender & Class* 6, no. 3 (1999): 52–66.
Austin, Allan D. *African Muslims Antebellum America*. Routledge, 1997.
Autodidact 17. "Dr. Martin Luther King Jr: 'I Fear I Am Integrating My People into a Burning House.'" *New York Amsterdam News*, January 12, 2017. http://amsterdamnews.com/news/2017/jan/12/dr-martin-luther-king-jr-i-fear-i-am-integrating-m/.
Baker, Graham. "Christianity and Eugenics: The Place of Religion in the British Eugenics Education Society and the American Eugenics Society, c. 1907–1940." *Social History of Medicine* 27, no. 2 (2014): 281–302.

Baker, Houston A., Jr. "Critical Memory and the Black Public Sphere." In *The Black Public Sphere*, ed. Black Public Sphere Collective. University of Chicago Press, 1995.
Baldwin, James. *The Fire Next Time*. Vintage, 1993.
Baldwin, James. "How to Cool It." *Esquire*, July 1968.
Baldwin, James. "Letter from a Region in My Mind." *New Yorker*, November 17, 1962.
Baldwin, James. "A Negro Assays the Negro Mood." *New York Times*, March 12, 1961. https://www.nytimes.com/1961/03/12/archives/a-negro-assays-the-negro-mood-the-rise-of-independent-africa-he.html.
Baldwin, James. *Nobody Knows My Name*. Vintage, 1992.
Baldwin, James, Emile Capouya, Lorraine Hansberry, Nat Hentoff, Langston Hughes, and Alfred Kazin. "The Negro in American Culture." *CrossCurrents* 11, no. 3 (1961): 205–24.
Bambara, Toni Cade. *Deep Sightings and Rescue Missions: Fiction, Essays, and Conversations*. Pantheon Books, 1996.
Banna, Hasan al-. *Risalat al-Jihadi: Wa Jihad fi Allah Haqqa Jihadihi*. Dar al-Kitab al-'Arabi, 1950.
Baraka, Amina [Sylvia Jones]. "Dedication." In *Songs for the Masses*. N.p. 1978.
Baraka, Amina [Sylvia Jones]. *Songs for the Masses*. N.p. 1978.
Baraka, Amina. [Sylvia Jones]. "Sortin-Out." *Black American Literature Forum* 16, no. 13 (1982): 105–06.
Baraka, Amina. "Sortin-Out." In *Confirmation: An Anthology of African American Women*, ed. Amiri Baraka [LeRoi Jones] and Amina Baraka. William Morrow, 1983.
Baraka, Amina [Sylvia Jones]. "Warning." In *Songs for the Masses*. N.p. 1978.
Baraka, Amiri [Imamu Amiri Baraka], "All in the Street." In *Spirit Reach*. Jihad Productions, 1972.
Baraka, Amiri. "Answers in Progress." In *Tales: Short Stories*. Grove Press, 1967.
Baraka, Amiri [LeRoi Jones]. "Apple Cores #4." *DownBeat* 33, no. 3 (1966): 15.
Baraka, Amiri [LeRoi Jones]. "Apple Cores #4." In *Black Music*. William Morrow, 1968.
Baraka, Amiri [LeRoi Jones]. "Apple Cores #5—The Burton Greene Affair." *DownBeat* 33, no. 17 (1966).
Baraka, Amiri. *The Autobiography of LeRoi Jones*. Lawrence Hill Books, 1997.
Baraka, Amiri [LeRoi Jones]. "'Black' Is a Country." In *Home: Social Essays*. William Morrow, 1966.
Baraka, Amiri [LeRoi Jones]. *A Black Mass*. In *Four Black Revolutionary Plays: All Praises to the Black Man*. Bobbs-Merrill, 1969.
Baraka, Amiri [Imamu Amiri Baraka]. *Black Music*. William Morrow, 1968.
Baraka, Amiri [Imamu Amiri Baraka]."Black Woman." *Black World* 19, no. 9 (1970): 7–11.
Baraka, Amiri [LeRoi Jones]. *Blues People: The Negro Experience in White America and the Music That Developed from It*. William Morrow, 1963.
Baraka, Amiri [LeRoi Jones]. "The Changing Same (R&B and New Black Music)." In *Black Music*. William Morrow, 1967.
Baraka, Amiri. *A Critical Reevaluation: A Raisin in the Sun's Enduring Passion*. New American Library, 1987.
Baraka, Amiri [Imamu Amiri Baraka]. "Deranged Gutbucket Pigtongue Clapper Heart." In *Spirit Reach*. Jihad Productions, 1972.
Baraka, Amiri [LeRoi Jones]. *Dutchman and The Slave: Two Plays*. William Morrow, 1964.
Baraka, Amiri [LeRoi Jones]. "An Explanation of the Work." In *Black Magic: Collected Poetry, 1961–1967*. Bobbs-Merrill, 1969.
Baraka, Amiri [Ameer Baraka]. "Foreword." In *Black Fire: An Anthology of Afro-American Writing*, ed. Amiri Baraka [LeRoi Jones] and Larry Neal. William Morrow, 1968.
Baraka, Amiri [Imamu Amiri Baraka (LeRoi Jones)]. "From the Book of Life." In *Raise, Race, Rays, Raze: Essays Since 1965*. Random House, 1971.
Baraka, Amiri [LeRoi Jones]. *Home: Social Essays*. William Morrow, 1966.
Baraka, Amiri [Imamu Amiri Baraka]. *It's Nation Time*. Third World Press, 1970.
Baraka, Amiri [Imamu Amiri Baraka]. *It's Nation Time: African Visionary Music*. Motown: Black Forum, 1972.

Baraka, Amiri [LeRoi Jones]. "Ka 'Ba." In *Black Magic: Collected Poetry, 1961–67*. Bobbs-Merrill, 1969.
Baraka, Amiri [LeRoi Jones]. "The Legacy of Malcolm X, and the Coming of the Black Nation." In *Home: Social Essays*. William Morrow, 1966.
Baraka, Amiri [Imamu Amiri Baraka], "Love Is the Presence of No Enemy." In *Spirit Reach*. Jihad Productions, 1972.
Baraka, Amiri [LeRoi Jones]. "Newark—Before Black Men Conquered." *Black Newark*, April 1968.
Baraka, Amiri. "A New Introduction." In *Black Fire: An Anthology of Afro-American Writing*, ed. Amiri Baraka and Larry Neal. Black Classic Press, 2013.
Baraka, Amiri [Imamu Amiri Baraka (LeRoi Jones)]. *Raise, Race, Rays, Raze: Essays Since 1965*. Random House, 1971.
Baraka, Amiri [LeRoi Jones]. "S.O.S." In *Black Art*. Jihad Productions, 1966.
Baraka, Amiri. *SOS: Poems 1961–2013*. Grove Press, 2014.
Baraka, Amiri [Imamu Amiri Baraka]. "Somebody's Slow Is Another Body's Fast (Preachment)." In *Black Spirits: A Festival of New Black Poets in America*, ed. Woodie King. Random House, 1972.
Baraka, Amiri [Imamu Amiri Baraka]."Somebody's Slow Is Another Body's Fast (Preachment)." In *Spirit Reach*. Jihad Productions, 1972.
Baraka, Amiri [Imamu Amiri Baraka]. *Spirit Reach*. Jihad Productions, 1972.
Baraka, Amiri [LeRoi Jones]. "State/Meant." In *Home: Social Essays*. William Morrow, 1966.
Baraka, Amiri. "A Wiser Play Than Some of Us Knew." *Los Angeles Review of Books*, March 22, 1987.
Baraka, Amiri [Imamu Amiri Baraka] and [Billy Abernathy] Fundi. *In Our Terribleness (Some Elements and Meaning in Black Style)*. Bobbs-Merrill, 1970.
Baraka, Amiri [LeRoi Jones], and Larry Neal, eds. *Black Fire: An Anthology of Afro-American Writing*. William Morrow, 1968.
Baraka, Amiri, and Larry Neal, eds. *Black Fire: An Anthology of Afro-American Writing*. Black Classic Press, 2013.
Baraka, Amiri, and Vertamae Smart-Grosvenor. "Answers in Progress." In *Vibration Cooking, Or, The Travel Notes of a Geechee Girl*. Doubleday, 1970.
Bardwell, Anne. "Project Breakthrough Appears Right Approach at Right Time." *Daily Independent Journal* (San Rafael), November 1, 1968.
Barrows, Cliff. *Billy Graham Crusade Songs*. Billy Graham Evangelistic Association, 1957.
Bayat, Asef. *Making Islam Democratic: Social Movements and the Post-Islamist Turn*. Stanford University Press, 2007.
Baylor, Leroy. "Ameenah Rasul, Leader of Women in the Nation of Islam, Dies at 90." *Amsterdam News* (New York City), July 17, 2014. http://amsterdamnews.com/news/2014/jul/17/ameenah-rasul-leader-women-nation-islam-dies-90/.
Bayoumi, Moustafa. "Allah Supreme: How Pharoah Sanders Found Freedom and Rebellion in Islam." *The Guardian*, December 29, 2022.
Bayoumi, Moustafa. "East of the Sun (West of the Moon): Islam, the Ahmadis, and African America." In *Black Routes to Islam*, ed. Manning Marable and Hishaam D. Aidi. Palgrave Macmillan, 2009.
Belafonte, Harry, and Michael Shnayerson. *My Song: A Memoir*. Knopf, 2011.
Bencheikh, Jamal Eddine. *Poétique Arabe: Essai sur les voies d'une création*. Éditions Anthropos, 1975.
Berg, Herbert. *Elijah Muhammad and Islam*. New York University Press, 2009.
Bernard, Patrick S. "A 'Cipher Language': Thomas W. Talley and Call-and-Response during the Harlem Renaissance." *African American Review* 52, no. 2 (2019): 121–42.
Bethune, Lebert. *Juju of My Own*. Union, 1965.
Biondi, Martha. *The Black Revolution on Campus*. University of California Press, 2014.
Black, Edwin. *War Against the Weak: Eugenics and America's Campaign to Create a Master Race*. Four Walls Eight Windows, 2003.

Black, James Milton, ed. "When the Roll Is Called." In *Sacred Praise: For Use in Gospel Meetings, Evangelistic Services, Sunday Schools, Prayer Meetings, and Young People's Societies*. Jennings and Graham, 1913.

Blue, Ethan. "The Strange Career of Leo Stanley: Remaking Manhood and Medicine at San Quentin State Penitentiary, 1913–1951." *Pacific Historical Review* 78, no. 2 (2009): 210–41.

Bluestone, Daniel. "Chicago's Mecca Flat Blues." *Journal of the Society of Architectural Historians* 57, no. 4 (1998): 382–403.

Blumhofer, Edith. "Singing to Save: Music in the Billy Graham Crusades." In *Billy Graham: American Pilgrim*, ed. Andrew Finstuen, Grant Wacker, and Anne Blue Wills. Oxford, 2017.

Bobo, Jacqueline, Cynthia Hudley, and Claudine Michel, eds. *The Black Studies Reader*. Routledge, 2004.

BoBo, Yahsmin Mayaan Binti. "Mute Man Talking: Poetry Under Surveillance, Interview with Amir Sulaiman." *The Black Commentator*, no. 186 (June 2006). https://blackcommentator.com/186/186_mute_man.html.

Boisseron, Bénédicte. *Afro-Dog: Blackness and the Animal Question*. Columbia University Press, 2018.

Bonebakker, S. A. "Ibn Al-Mu'tazz and Kitab al-Badi'." In *'Abbasid Belles-Lettres*, ed. Julia Ashtiany, T. M. Johnstone, J. D. Latham, and R. B. Serjeant. Cambridge University Press, 1990.

Bonebakker, S. A. "Religious Prejudice against Poetry in Early Islam." *Medievalia et Humanistica* 7, nos. 77–99 (1976).

Boullata, Issa J. "The Rhetorical Interpretation of the Qur'an. I'jaz and Related Topics." In *Approaches to the History of the Interpretation of the Qur'an*, ed. Andrew Rippin. Gorgias Press, 2012.

Bowen, John R. *Muslims Through Discourse: Religion and Ritual in Gayo Society*. Princeton University Press, 1993.

Bowen, Madeline. *San Quentin State Prison, Building 22*. Historic American Buildings Survey. National Park Service, US Department of the Interior, 2009.

Bowen, Patrick D. "Abdul Hamid Suleiman and the Origins of the Moorish Science Temple." *Journal of Race, Ethnicity, and Religion* 2, no. 13 (2011): 1–54.

Bowen, Patrick D. *A History of Conversion to Islam in the United States, Volume 1: White American Muslims before 1975*. Brill, 2015.

Bowen, Patrick D. *A History of Conversion to Islam in the United States, Volume 2: The African American Islamic Renaissance, 1920–1975*. Brill, 2017.

Boyd, Melba Joyce. *Wrestling with the Muse: Dudley Randall and the Broadside Press*. Columbia University Press, 2004.

Branch, Taylor. *Parting the Waters: America in the King Years, 1954–63*. Simon & Schuster, 1988.

Branch, Taylor. *Pillar of Fire: America in the King Years, 1963–65*. Simon & Schuster, 1998.

Breines, Winifred. *The Trouble Between Us: An Uneasy History of White and Black Women in the Feminist Movement*. Oxford University Press, 2006.

Briggs, Mustafa. *Beyond Bilal: Black History in Islam*. Mustafa Briggs & Co. Publishing, 2022.

Briggs, Mustafa. *Beyond Bilal: Black Muslims in the East*. Mustafa Briggs & Co. Publishing, 2023.

Brown, Fahamisha Patricia. *Performing the Word: African American Poetry as Vernacular Culture*. Rutgers University Press, 1999.

Bullins, Ed. *Salaam, Huey Newton, Salaam*. Farber, 1993.

Butler, Jineea. "Integrating into a Burning House." *The Final Call*, December 12, 2014.

Cahan, Susan E. *Mounting Frustration: The Art Museum in the Age of Black Power*. Duke University Press, 2016.

Callahan, John F. *In the African-American Grain: Call-and-Response in Twentieth-Century Black Fiction*. Wesleyan University Press, 1990.

Campt, Tina M. *A Black Gaze: Artists Changing How We See*. MIT Press, 2021.

Carlson, Elof. *Scientific Origins of Eugenics*. Ethical, Legal, and Social Implications Research Program, National Human Genome Research Institute. Archive on the American Eugenics Movement. Dolan

DNA Learning Center, Cold Spring Harbor Laboratory, n.d. http://www.eugenicsarchive.org/html/eugenics/essay2text.html.
Carson, Clayborne. *Malcolm X: The FBI File*. Caroll & Graf, 1991.
Carter, Youssef. "Critiquing Black Muslim Reason: What Good Is Critical Race Theory for Muslims?" *Maydan: Islamic Thought*, February 5, 2020. https://themaydan.com/2020/02/critiquing-black-muslim-reason-what-good-is-critical-race-theory-for-muslims/.
Césaire, Aimé. *Discourse on Colonialism*, trans. Joan Pinkham. Monthly Review Press, 2000.
Chan-Malik, Sylvia. *Being Muslim: A Cultural History of Women of Color in American Islam*. New York University Press, 2018.
Chan-Malik, Sylvia. "Cultural and Literary Production of Muslim America." In *The Cambridge Companion to American Islam*, ed. Juliane Hammer and Omid Safi. Cambridge University Press, 2013.
Chan-Malik, Sylvia. "Islam in the Arts in the USA." In *Routledge Handbook of Islam in the West*, ed. Roberto Tottoli. Routledge, 2014.
Charters, Samuel B. *The Country Blues*. Da Capo, 1959.
Cheatam, Safiyah. "From Counter-Memory to Counter-Culture: Black Islam in the U.S. through a Mundane Afrofuturist Lens." MFA thesis, University of Maryland, 2021.
Chow, Rey. *Not Like a Native Speaker: On Languaging as a Postcolonial Experience*. Columbia University Press, 2014.
Civil Rights Congress. *We Charge Genocide: Petition to the United Nations for Relief from the Crime of the United States Government Against the Negro People*. New York, 1951.
Clarke, Cheryl. *"After Mecca:" Women Poets and the Black Arts Movement*. Rutgers University Press, 2004.
Clarke, John Henrik. "The New Afro-American Nationalism." *Freedomways* 1, no. 3 (1961): 285–95.
Clarke, John Henrik, ed. *Malcolm X: The Man and His Times*. Macmillan, 1970.
Clegg, Claude A., III. *Life and Times of Elijah Muhammad*. University of North Carolina Press, 2014.
Clegg, Claude A., III. "Nation Under Siege Elijah Muhammad, the FBI, and Police-State Culture in Chicago." In *Police Brutality: An Anthology*. Norton, 2000.
Cohen, Adam. *Imbeciles: The Supreme Court, American Eugenics, and the Sterilization of Carrie Buck*. Penguin, 2016.
Cohen, Jerry, and William S. Murphy. "There's Still Hell to Pay in Watts: Burn, Baby, Burn." *Life Magazine*, July 15, 1966, 34–64.
Colbert, Soyica Diggs. *Radical Vision: A Biography of Lorraine Hansberry*. Yale University Press, 2021.
Colbert, Soyica Diggs, Douglas A. Jones Jr., and Shane Vogel. "Introduction: Tidying Up after Repetition." In *Race and Performance after Repetition*, ed. Soyica Diggs Colbert, Douglas A. Jones Jr., and Shane Vogel. Duke University Press, 2020.
Collins, Lisa Gail, and Margo Natalie Crawford, eds. *New Thoughts on the Black Arts Movement*. Rutgers University Press, 2006.
Collins, Patricia Hill. *Black Feminist Thought: Knowledge, Consciousness, and the Politics of Empowerment*. Routledge, 2008.
Combahee River Collective. "A Black Feminist Statement." In *Words of Fire: An Anthology of African-American Feminist Thought*, ed. Beverly Guy-Sheftall. The New Press, 1995.
Combahee River Collective. *Combahee River Collective Statement*. 1977.
Comer, James P., and Alvin F. Poussaint. *Black Child Care: How to Bring Up a Healthy Black Child in America—A Guide to Emotional and Psychological Development*. Simon & Schuster, 1975.
Commander, Michelle D. *Afro-Atlantic Flight: Speculative Returns and the Black Fantastic*. Duke University Press, 2017.
Cone, James H. *Martin & Malcolm & America: A Dream or a Nightmare*. Orbis Books, 1991.
Cook, Ann. "Black Pride?: Some Contradictions." In *The Black Woman*, ed. Toni Cade Bambara. Washington Square Press, 1970.

Corbett, John. *The Wisdom of Sun-Ra: Sun Ra's Polemical Broadsheets and Streetcorner Leaflets*. White-Walls, 2006.
Cornell, Drucilla. "The Secret Behind the Veil: A Reinterpretation of 'Algeria Unveiled.'" *Philosophia Africana* 4, no. 2 (2001): 27–35.
Costello, Deloris, and Joe Walker. "How to Rear a Healthy Black Child in America." *Muhammad Speaks*, July 4, 1975. 14:43 edition.
Cottom, Tressie McMillan. *Twitter Post*. October 5, 2016. https://twitter.com/tressiemcphd/status/783528151242727425.
Coval, Kevin, Quraysh Ali Lansana, and Nate Marshall, eds. *The BreakBeat Poets: New American Poetry in the Age of Hip-Hop*. Haymarket Books, 2015.
Covington, Francee. "Are the Revolutionary Techniques Employed in *The Battle of Algiers* Applicable to Harlem?" In *The Black Woman*, ed. Toni Cade Bambara. Washington Square Press, 1970.
Covington-Ward, Yolana, and Jeanette S. Jouili, eds. *Embodying Black Religions in Africa and its Diasporas*. Duke University Press, 2021.
Cox, Renee. *The Signing*. 2017. Los Angeles Contemporary Museum of Art.
Crawford, Margo Natalie. *Black Post-Blackness: The Black Arts Movement and Twenty-First-Century Aesthetics*. University of Illinois Press, 2017.
Crookshank, F. G. *The Mongol in Our Midst: A Study of Man and His Three Faces*. Kegan Paul, Trench & Trubner, 1924.
Curiel, Jonathan. "Muslim Roots of the Blues: The Music of Famous American Blues Singers Reaches Back through the South to the Culture of West Africa." *San Francisco Chronicle*, August 15, 2004. https://www.sfgate.com/opinion/article/Muslim-roots-of-the-blues-The-music-of-famous-2701489.php.
Curtis, Edward E., IV. *Black Muslim Religion in the Nation of Islam, 1960–1975*. University of North Carolina Press, 2006.
Curtis, Edward E., IV. *The Call of Bilal: Islam in the African Diaspora*. University of North Carolina Press, 2014.
Curtis, Edward E., IV. *Islam in Black America*. State University of New York Press, 2002.
Curtis, Edward E., IV. "Science and Technology in Elijah Muhammad's Nation of Islam: Astrophysical Disaster, Genetic Engineering, UFOs, White Apocalypse, and Black Resurrection." *Nova Religio: The Journal of Alternative and Emergent Religions* 20, no. 1 (2016): 5–31.
Curtis, Edward E., IV, and Danielle Brune Sigler, eds. *The New Black Gods: Arthur Huff Fauset and the Study of African American Religions*. Indiana University Press, 2009.
Dain, Bruce. *A Hideous Monster of the Mind: American Race Theory in the Early Republic*. Harvard University Press, 2003.
Darden, Robert. *Nothing but Love in God's Water: Black Sacred Music from the Civil War to the Civil Rights Movement*. Pennsylvania State University Press, 2014.
Darden, Robert. *People Get Ready!: A New History of Black Gospel Music*. Continuum, 2004.
Daulatzai, Sohail. *Black Star, Crescent Moon: The Muslim International and Black Freedom Beyond America*. University of Minnesota Press, 2012.
Davis, Angela. "Meditations on the Legacy of Malcolm X." In *Malcolm X: In Our Own Image*, ed. Joe Wood. St. Martin's Press, 1992.
Davis, Ossie. "Eyes on the Prize II: America at the Racial Crossroads 1965–85, Telephone Pre-Interview Transcript." Interview by Madison Davis Lacy, Jr. and Blackside, Inc. July 6, 1989. Washington University Film and Media Archive, Henry Hampton Collection. http://digital.wustl.edu/e/eii/eiiweb/dav5427.0777.0370ssiedavis.html.
Dawson, Michael C. *Black Visions: The Roots of Contemporary African-American Political Ideologies*. University of Chicago Press, 2001.
Dawson, Michael C. "The Black Public Sphere and Black Civil Society." In *The Oxford Handbook of African American Citizenship, 1865–Present*, ed. Henry Louis Gates Jr. et al. Oxford University Press, 2012.

Delany, Martin Robison. *The Condition, Elevation, Emigration, and Destiny of the Colored People of the United States, Politically Considered*. Martin Robison Delany, 1852.
Diara, Agadem Lumumba. *Islam and Pan-Africanism*. Agascha Productions, 1973.
Diouf, Sylviane A. *Servants of Allah: African Muslims Enslaved in the Americas*. New York University Press, 1998.
Diouf, Sylviane A. "What Islam Gave the Blues." *Renovatio: The Journal of Zaytuna College*, June 17, 2019. https://renovatio.zaytuna.edu/article/what-islam-gave-the-blues.
Dodd, Lynn Swartz, and Ran Boytner. "Filtering the Past: Archaeology, Politics, and Change." In *Controlling the Past, Owning the Future: The Political Uses of Archaeology in the Middle East*. University of Arizona Press, 2010.
Doreen 2X. "Muhammad Ali Biography: Positive Image for Youth." *Muhammad Speaks*, July 4, 1975. 14:43 Edition.
Dorman, Jacob S. *The Princess and the Prophet: The Secret History of Magic, Race, and Moorish Muslims in America*. Beacon Press, 2020.
Douglass, Frederick. *Narrative of the Life of Frederick Douglass*. 1945 Edition. Millenium Publications, 2014.
Du Bois, W. E. B. "Criteria of Negro Art." *The Crisis* 32 (October 1926): 290–97.
Du Bois, W. E. B. *The Negro American Family*. Atlanta University Press, 1908.
Du Bois, W. E. B. "A Negro Nation within the Nation." *Current History*, June 1, 1935.
Du Bois, W. E. B. *The Souls of Black Folk*. A. C. McClurg & Co., 1903.
Duffield, Ian. "Dusé Mohamed Ali and the Development of Pan-Africanism 1866–1945." PhD thesis, Edinburgh University, 1971.
Dunbar, Alice. "The Poet and His Song." *African Methodist Episcopal Church Review*, October 1914.
Dunbar, Paul Laurence. *Oak and Ivy*. Press of United Brethren, 1893.
Dunbar, Paul Laurence. "Sympathy." In *Lyrics of the Hearthside*. Dodd, Mead, 1899.
Dyson, Michael Eric. *Making Malcolm: The Myth and Meaning of Malcolm X*. Oxford University Press, 1996.
Edmonds, Orlando. "Why James Baldwin's The Fire Next Time Still Matters." *Daily*, November 2, 2016. https://daily.jstor.org/feature-james-baldwin-fire-next-time/.
Edwards, Brent Hayes. *Epistrophies: Jazz and the Literary Imagination*. Harvard University Press, 2017.
Elam, Harry Justin. *Taking It to the Streets: The Social Protest Theater of Luis Valdez and Amiri Baraka*. University of Michigan Press, 2001.
Ellison, Ralph. *Invisible Man*. Random House, 1952.
English, Darby. *How to See a Work of Art in Total Darkness*. MIT Press, 2007.
Esposito, John L., and John O. Voll. *Islam and Democracy*. Oxford University Press, 1996.
Essien-Udom, E. U. *Black Nationalism: A Search for an Identity in America*. University of Chicago Press, 1962.
Eure, Joseph D., and James G. Spady, eds., *Nation Conscious Rap*. PC International Press and Black History Museum Umum Publishers, 1991.
Evanzz, Karl. *The Judas Factor: The Plot to Kill Malcolm X*. Thunder Mouth's Press, 1992.
Fanon, Frantz. *Les damnés de la terre*. F. Maspero, 1961.
Fanon, Frantz. "De la violence." In *Les damnés de la terre*. F. Maspero, 1961.
Fanon, Frantz. *Toward the African Revolution: Political Essays*, trans. Haakon Chevalier. Grove Press, 1967.
Fanon, Frantz. *The Wretched of the Earth*, trans. Richard Philcox. Grove Press, 2004.
Fanusie, Fatimah. "Ahmadi, Beboppers, Veterans, and Migrants: African American Islam in Boston, 1948–1963." In *The African Diaspora and the Study of Religion*, ed. Theodore Louis Trost. Palgrave, 2007.
Farmer, Ashley D. "'Abolition of Every Possibility of Oppression:' Black Women, Black Power, and the Black Women's United Front, 1970–1976." *Journal of Women's History* 32, no. 3 (2020): 89–114.
Farmer, Ashley D. *Remaking Black Power: How Black Women Transformed an Era*. University of North Carolina Press, 2017.

Farmer, Ashley D. "The Many Women Mentors of Malcolm X." *Black Perspectives*, May 3, 2016. https://www.aaihs.org/the-many-women-mentors-of-malcolm-x/.

Farrakhan, Louis, The Honorable Minister, "Crack-Cocaine: The Great Conspiracy to Destroy the Black Male," delivered at Mosque Maryam in Chicago (November 3, 1996), *The Final Call*, April 5, 2014, https://www.finalcall.com/artman/publish/Minister_Louis_Farrakhan_9/article_101889.shtml.

Farrakhan, Louis, and Henry Louis Gates, Jr. "Farrakhan Speaks." *Transition*, no. 70 (1996): 140–67.

Faruque, Muhammad al-. "Emigration." In *Encyclopaedia of the Qur'an*, ed. Jane Dammen McAuliffe. Brill, 2005.

Fauset, Arthur Huff. *Black Gods of the Metropolis: Negro Religious Cults of the Urban North*. University of Pennsylvania Press, 1944.

Felber, Garrett. "A Bandung Conference in Harlem: The Meaning of Castro's Visit Uptown." Africa. *AAIHS*, December 1, 2016. https://www.aaihs.org/a-bandung-conference-in-harlem-the-meaning-of-castros-visit-uptown/.

Felber, Garrett. "Reconsidering Malcolm X and Islam." African American Intellectual History Society. *Black Perspectives*, February 8, 2016. https://www.aaihs.org/reconsidering-malcolm-x-and-islam/#_ftn3.

Felber, Garrett. *Those Who Know Don't Say: The Nation of Islam, the Black Freedom Movement, and the Carceral State*. University of North Carolina Press, 2020.

Finley, Stephen C., Margarita Simon Guillory, and Hugh Page Jr. "Introduction: Africana Esoteric Studies: Mapping a New Endeavor." In *Esotericism in African American Religious Experience: "There Is a Mystery . . . "*, ed. Stephen C. Finley, Margarita Simon Guillory, and Hugh Page Jr. Brill, 2015.

Finley, Stephen. *In and Out of This World: Material and Extraterrestrial Bodies in the Nation of Islam*. Duke University Press, 2022.

Finley, Stephen. "The Meaning of 'Mother' in Louis Farrakhan's 'Mother Wheel:' Race, Gender, and Sexuality in the Cosmology of the Nation of Islam's UFO." *Journal of the American Academy of Religion* 80, no. 2 (2012): 434–65.

Floyd-Thomas, Juan M. "A Jihad of Words: The Evolution of African American Islam and Contemporary Hip-Hop." In *Noise and Spirit: The Religious and Spiritual Sensibilities of Rap Music*, ed. Anthony B. Pinn. New York University Press, 2003.

Forsgren, La Donna. *In Search of Our Warrior Mothers: Women Dramatists of the Black Arts Movement*. Northwestern University Press, 2018.

Foucault, Michel. *The Order of Things: An Archaeology of the Human Sciences*. Pantheon, 1971.

Foucault, Michel. *"Society Must Be Defended:" Lectures at the Collège de France, 1975–1976*, trans. David Macey. Picador, 2003.

Fowler, Carolyn. "A Contemporary Blackamerican Genre: Pamphlet/Manifesto Poetry." *Black World*, June 1974, 4–19.

Fraser, Nancy. "Rethinking the Public Sphere: A Contribution to the Critique of Actually Existing Democracy." In *Habermas and the Public Sphere*, ed. Craig Calhoun. MIT Press, 1992.

Frost, Elisabeth A. *The Feminist Avant-Garde in American Poetry*. University of Iowa Press, 2005.

Gaines, Kevin. "African American Expatriates in Ghana and the Black Radical Tradition." *Souls* 1, no. 4 (1999).

Gaines, Kevin K. *American Africans in Ghana: Black Expatriates in the Civil Rights Era*. University of North Carolina Press, 2006.

Galwash, Ahmad A. *The Religion of Islam: A Standard Book*. Hafner Publishing Company [first published in *al-Azhar* magazine], 1940.

Garvey, Marcus. "Emancipate Yourselves from Mental Slavery." *The Black Man: A Monthly Magazine of Negro Thought and Opinion* 3, no. 10 (July 1938).

Gates, Henry Louis, Jr., *The Signifying Monkey: A Theory of African American Literary Criticism*. Oxford University Press, 1988.

Gates, Henry Louis, Jr., and Jennifer Burton, eds. *Call and Response: Key Debates in African American Studies.* Norton, 2011.
Gayle, Addison, ed. "The Black Aesthetic." In *The Black Aesthetic.* Doubleday, 1972.
Geertz, Clifford. *The Interpretation of Cultures.* Basic Books, 1973.
Ghazali, Zaynab -al, and 'Abd al-Hayy Faramawi. *Nazarat fi Kitab Allah.* Dar al-Shuruq, 1994.
Gibson, Campbell, and Kay Jung. *Historical Census Statistics on Population Totals by Race, 1790 to 1990, and by Hispanic Origin, 1970 to 1990, for the United States, Regions, Divisions, and States.* Working Paper No. 56. Population Division. Washington, DC, 2002.
Gibson, Dawn-Marie, and Jamillah Karim. *Women of the Nation: Between Black Protest and Sunni Islam.* New York University Press, 2014.
Gillette, Aaron. *Eugenics and the Nature-Nurture Debate in the Twentieth Century.* Palgrave Macmillan, 2007.
Gilroy, Paul. *The Black Atlantic: Modernity and Double-Consciousness.* Harvard University Press, 1993.
Gilroy, Paul. *"There Ain't No Black in the Union Jack": The Cultural Politics of Race and Nation.* Hutchinson, 1987.
Giovanni, Nikki. "Adulthood (for Claudia)." In *Black Feeling, Black Talk, Black Judgement.* William Morrow, 1970.
Givens, Jarvis R. *Fugitive Pedagogy: Carter G. Woodson and the Art of Black Teaching.* Harvard University Press, 2021.
Givens, Jarvis. "Fugitive Pedagogy in the Jim Crow Classroom: The Case of Carter G. Woodson." Hutchins Center for African and African American Research, Harvard University, October 31, 2018.
Givens, Jarvis. "Literate Slave, Fugitive Slave: Note on the Ethical Dilemma of Black Education." In *The Future Is Black: Afropessimism, Fugitivity, and Radical Hope in Education*, ed. Carl A. Grant, Michael J. Dumas, and Ashley N. Woodson. Routledge, 2020.
Goff, James R. *Close Harmony: A History of Southern Gospel.* University of North Carolina Press, 2002.
Gomez, Michael A. *Black Crescent: The Experience and Legacy of African Muslims in the Americas.* Cambridge University Press, 2005.
Grant, Allan. "Mohammedan Leanings." *Life*, October 11, 1948, 142.
Grant, Carl A., Michael J. Dumas, and Ashley N. Woodson, eds. *The Future Is Black: Afropessimism, Fugitivity, and Radical Hope in Education.* Routledge, 2020.
Grewal, Zareena. *Islam Is a Foreign Country: American Muslims and the Global Crisis of Authority.* New York University Press, 2013.
Griffin, Farah Jasmine. "'Ironies of the Saint:' Malcolm X, Black Women, and the Price of Protection." In *Sisters in the Struggle : African-American Women in the Civil Rights-Black Power Movement*, ed. Bettye Collier-Thomas and V. P. Franklin. New York University Press, 2001.
Grubar, Susan. *Racechanges: White Skin, Black Face in American Culture.* Oxford University Press, 1997.
Grundy, David. *A Black Arts Poetry Machine: Amiri Baraka and the Umbra Poets.* Bloomsbury, 2019.
Grundy, David. "Songs for the Future: Askia Touré's Songhai!" *Paideuma: Modern and Contemporary Poetry and Poetics*, A Tribute to Askia M. Touré, vol. 48 (2022): 3–28.
Guilbault, Jocelyne. *Governing Sound: The Cultural Politics of Trinidad's Carnival Musics.* University of Chicago Press, 2007.
Gwynne, James, and Amiri Baraka, eds. *Malcolm X: Justice Seeker.* Steppingstones Press, 1993.
Hackett, David G. *That Religion in Which All Men Agree: Freemasonry in America.* University of California, 2014.
Hagen, Lyman B. *Heart of a Woman, Mind of a Writer, and Soul of a Poet: A Critical Analysis of the Writings of Maya Angelou.* University Press of America, 1996.
Hall, Stuart. "New Ethnicities." In *Black Film, British Cinema*, ed. Kobena Mercer. Institute of Contemporary Arts, 1987.

Hall, Stuart. "New Ethnicities." In *Stuart Hall: Critical Dialogues in Cultural Studies*, ed. David Morley and Kuan-Hsing Chen. Routledge, 1996.
Hansberry, Lorraine. "The Negro Writer and His Roots: Toward a New Romanticism." *The Black Scholar* 12, no. 2 (1981): 2–12.
Hansberry, Lorraine. *Raisin in the Sun*. Random House, 1959.
Hansell, William. "Gwendolyn Brook's 'In the Mecca': A Rebirth into Blackness." *Negro American Literature Forum* 8, no. 2 (1974): 199–209.
Hare, Nathan. "The Battle for Black Studies." *The Black Scholar* 3, no. 9 (1972): 32–47.
Hare, Nathan. "A Conceptual Proposal for a Department of Black Studies." In *Shut It down! A College in Crisis: San Francisco State College, October 1968–April 1969; A Report to the National Commission on the Causes and Prevention of Violence*, by William H. Orrick, Jr. Superintendent of Documents., US Government Printing Office, 1969.
Hare, Nathan. "Introduction." In *Somethin' Proper*. Black Bird Press, 1998.
Hare, Nathan, and Julia Hare. *The Miseducation of the Black Child—The Hare Plan: Educate Every Black Man, Woman and Child*. Black Think Tank, 1991.
"Harlem: Mecca of the New Negro." In *Survey Graphic*. 1925.
Harney, Stefano, and Fred Moten. *The Undercommons: Fugitive Planning & Black Study*. Minor Compositions, 2016.
Harney, Stefano and Fred Moten. "The University and the Undercommons: Seven Theses." *Social Text* 22, no. 2 (2004): 101–15.
Harris, Trudier. *From Mammies to Militants: Domestics in Black American Literature*. Temple University Press, 1982.
Harris, Violet J. "African American Children's Literature: The First One Hundred Years." *The Journal of Negro Education* 59, no. 4 (1990): 540–55.
Harris, William J. *The Poetry and Poetics of Amiri Baraka: The Jazz Aesthetic*. University of Missouri Press, 1986.
Hartman, Saidiya. "The Belly of the World: A Note on Black Women's Labors." *Souls* 18, no. 1 (2016): 166–73.
Hartman, Saidiya. *Lose Your Mother: A Journey Along the Atlantic Slave Route*. Farrar, Straus and Giroux, 2008.
Hartman, Saidiya V. *Scenes of Subjection: Terror, Slavery, and Self-Making in Nineteenth-Century America*. Oxford University Press, 1997.
Hartman, Saidiya. "Venus in Two Acts." *Small Axe: A Journal of Criticism* 12, no. 2 (2008): 1–14.
Heinrichs, Wolfhart. "The Meaning of Mutanabbi." In *Poetry and Prophecy: The Beginnings of a Literary Tradition*, ed. James L. Kugel. Cornell University Press, 1990.
Henry, Charles P. *Black Studies and the Democratization of American Higher Education*. Palgrave Macmillan, 2016.
Hentoff, Nat. "Elijah in the Wilderness." *The Reporter*, August 4, 1960.
Hentoff, Nat. "Remembering Malcolm." *Village Voice*, February 26, 1985.
Hentoff, Nat. *Speaking Freely: A Memoir*. Knopf, 1997.
Hermansen, Marcia. "Conversion to Islam in Theological and Historical Perspectives." In *The Oxford Handbook of Religious Conversion*, ed. Lewis R. Rambo and Charles E. Farhadian. Oxford University Press, 2014.
Hicks, Keisha. "The Multifarious Jihads of Malcolm X: From Malcolm Little to El Hajj Malik El-Shabazz: 'I Am All That I Have Been.'" MA thesis, Cornell University, 2009.
Hill, Patricia Liggins, et al., eds. *Call and Response: The Riverside Anthology of the African American Literary Tradition*. Houghton Mifflin, 1998.
Hinton, Elizabeth. *America on Fire: The Untold History of Police Violence and Black Rebellion Since the 1960s*. New York: Norton, 2021.

Hirschkind, Charles. *The Ethical Soundscape: Cassette Sermons and Islamic Counterpublics*. Columbia University Press, 2009.
Hirschkind, Charles, and Brian Larkin. "Media and the Political Forms of Religion." *Social Text* 26, no. 3 (2008): 1–15.
Hives, Frank. *Ju-Ju and Justice in Nigeria*. With Gascoigne Lumley. John Lane, 1930.
Hodges, Jeffrey Alan. "Euthenics, Eugenics and Compulsory Sterilization in Michigan, 1897–1960." MA thesis, Department of History, Michigan State University, 1995.
Homerin, Th. Emil. "Preaching Poetry." *Arabica* 38 (1991): 87–101.
hooks, bell. *Ain't I A Woman: Black Women and Feminism*. Pluto Press, 1981.
hooks, bell. "Homeplace (A Site of Resistance)." In *Yearning: Race, Gender, and Cultural Politics*. South End Press, 1990.
hooks, bell. "The Oppositional Gaze: Black Female Spectators." In *Movies and Mass Culture*, ed. John Belton. Rutgers University Press, 1996.
hooks, bell, and Cornel West. *Breaking Bread: Insurgent Black Intellectual Life*. Routledge, 2016.
Hughes, Langston. *Montage of a Dream Deferred*. Henry Holt, 1951.
Hughes, Langston. "The Negro Artist and the Racial Mountain." *The Nation*, June 23, 1926, 692–93.
Hughes, Langston. *Selected Poems of Langston Hughes*. Alfred A. Knopf, 1959.
Ibn al-Muʿtazz. *Kitab Al-Badiʿ*. Maktabat al-Muthanna, 1979.
Ibn ʿArabi, Muhyiddin. "Gentle Doves Now." In *Translator of Desires: Poems*, trans. Michael Sells. Princeton University Press, 2021.
Ibn ʿArabi, Muhyiddin. *Translator of Desires: Poems*, trans. Michael Sells. Princeton University Press, 2021.
Idris, Solayman. *Dusk Orientalis: ex Chrysalis*. Lumifont, 2020.
Idris, Solayman. *Star Logic (a Collection of Poiesis)*. Lumifont, 2020.
Idris, Solayman. *The Sunrise in the West: On Amer-African Statecraft (The Times of the Signs Trilogy)*. Lumifont, 2020.
Iman, Malika. *Intimate with the Ultimate: Memoirs and Tribute to Family and Political, Cultural, Spiritual Activists*. Malika Iman, 2018.
Iman, Yusef [Kasisi Yusef Iman]. *Annihilation or Separation*. The East, 1972.
Iman, Yusef [Kasisi Yusef Iman]. *Extermination or Unification*. The East, 1972.
Iman, Yusef [Kasisi Yusef Iman]. *Genocide or Unify*. The East, 1972.
Iman, Yusef [Kasisi Yusef Iman]. *Love*. The East, 1972.
Iman, Yusef. *Love Your Enemy*. The East, 1972.
Iman, Yusef. "Love Your Enemy." In *Something Black Dedicated to Millions of Brothers and Sisters in the West*. Jihad Productions, 1966.
Iman, Yusef. "Love Your Enemy." In *Black Fire: An Anthology of Afro-American Writing*, ed. Amiri Baraka [LeRoi Jones] and Larry Neal. William Morrow, 1968.
Iman, Yusef [Kasisi Yusef Iman]. *Nation Time or N***** Time*. The East, 1972.
Iman, Yusef [Kasisi Yusef Iman]. *Organize and Unify, Unify and Organize, Unify or Die, Die*. The East, 1972.
Iman, Yusef [Kasisi Yusef Iman]. *Our Nation: What Will It Be?* The East, 1972.
Iman, Yusef. *Poetry for Our Beautiful Black Women*. Jihad Productions, 1969.
Iman, Yusef. *Praise the Lord, but Pass the Ammunition*. Jihad Productions, 1967.
Iman, Yusef. *Something Black Dedicated to Millions of Brothers and Sisters in the West*. Jihad Productions, 1966.
Iman, Yusef, ed. *The Young Black Poets of Brooklyn*. Black News, 1970.
Iman, Yusef, and Ben Caldwell. *Yesterday, Today, Tomorrow*. Weusi Kuumba Troupe, 1974.
Iman, Yusef, Weusi Iman, and Job Mashariki. *The Pictorial Biography of a Great Renaissance Man: Kasisi Yusef Iman*. N.p., 1987.

"Islam Advancing in West Africa: Christians Worried by Gains—Simple Mosel Tenets Credited for Appeal." *New York Times*, October 6, 1960. https://www.nytimes.com/1960/10/09/archives/islam-advancing-in-west-africa-christians-worked-by-gains-simple.html.

Isoke, Zenzele. *Urban Black Women and the Politics of Resistance*. Palgrave Macmillan, 2013.

Jaaber, Heshaam. *I Buried Malcolm (Haj Malik El-Shabazz): The Final Chapter. . . .* New Mind Productions, 1993.

Jackmon, Marvin. See Marvin X.

Jackson, Sherman A. *Islam and the Blackamerican: Looking Toward the Third Resurrection*. Oxford University Press, 2005.

Jackson, Sherman A. *Islam and the Problem of Black Suffering*. Oxford University Press, 2009.

Jackson, Travis. "'Always New and Centuries Old:' Jazz, Poetry, and Tradition as Creative Adaptation." In *Uptown Conversation: The New Jazz Studies*, ed. Brent Hayes Edwards, Farah Jasmine Griffin, and Robert O'Meally. Columbia University Press, 2004.

Jackson, Travis. *Blowin' the Blues Away: Performance and Meaning on the New York Jazz Scene*. University of California Press, 2012.

Jackson, Zakiyyah Iman. *Becoming Human: Matter and Meaning in an Antiblack World*. New York University Press, 2020.

Jafa, Arthur. "69." In *Black Popular Culture: A Project by Michele Wallace*, ed. Gina Dent. Dia Center for the Arts: Discussions in Contemporary Culture #8. Bay Press, 1992.

Jarvis, Malcolm "Shorty," and Paul D. Nichols. *The Other Malcolm—"Shorty" Jarvis*. Ed. Cornel R. West. McFarland & Company, 2001.

Jeffries, Hasan Kwame. *Bloody Lowndes: Civil Rights and Black Power in Alabama's Black Belt*. New York University Press, 2009.

Jennings, John, and Stacey Robinson. "Connections." In *Black Kirby: In Search of the Motherboxx Connection*. Black Kirby Collective, 2013.

Jihad, The. *Black & Beautiful, Soul & Madness*. Jihad Productions, 1968.

Johnson, James Weldon. *Autobiography of an Ex-Colored Man*. Alfred A. Knopf, 1927.

Johnson, James Weldon. *God's Trombones: Seven Negro Sermons in Verse*. Viking Press, 1927.

Jones, Douglas. "'The Black Below': Minstrelsy, Satire, and the Threat of Vernacularity." *Theater Journal* 73, no. 2 (2021): 129–46.

Jones, LeRoi. See Baraka, Amiri.

Jones, Meta Du Ewa. "Jazz Prosodies: Orality and Textuality." *Callaloo* 24, no. 1 (2002): 66–91.

Jones, Meta DuEwa. *The Muse Is Music: Jazz Poetry from the Harlem Renaissance to Spoken Word*. University of Illinois Press, 2013.

Joseph, Peniel E. *The Sword and the Shield: The Revolutionary Lives of Malcolm X and Martin Luther King Jr.* Basic Books, 2020.

Joseph, Peniel E. *Waiting 'til the Midnight Hour: A Narrative History of Black Power in America*. Henry Holt, 2006.

Jouili, Jeanette. "Islam and Culture: Dis/Junctures in a Modern Conceptual Terrain." *Comparative Studies in Society and History* 60, no. 1 (2019): 207–37.

Jouili, Jeanette S. *Pious Practice and Secular Constraints: Women in the Islamic Revival in France and Germany*. Stanford University Press, 2015.

Joyce, Joyce Ann. *Black Studies as Human Studies: Critical Essays and Interviews*. State University of New York Press, 2005.

Joyce, Joyce Ann. *Ijala: Sonia Sanchez and the African Poetic Tradition*. Third World Press, 1996.

Jubilee Singers (Fisk University). *Many Thousand Gone*. American Missionary Association. Biglow and Main, 1872.

Judy, Ronald A. T. *(Dis)Forming the American Canon: African-Arabic Slave Narratives and the Vernacular*. University of Minnesota Press, 1993.

Judy, R. A. *Sentient Flesh: Thinking in Disorder, Poiesis in Black*. Duke University Press, 2020.
Kaelber, Lutz. "Michigan." *Eugenics: Compulsory Sterilization in 50 American States*, 2012. https://www.uvm.edu/~lkaelber/eugenics/MI/MI.html.
Kahf, Mohja. "Teaching Diaspora Literature: Muslim American Literature as an Emerging Field." *Journal of Pan African Studies* 4, no. 2 (2010).
Kang, Inyoung. "Sausalito Marin City Schools to Desegregate After State Inquiry." *The New York Times*, August 12, 2019.
Kashif, Lonnie. "Black Child in the '70s: Students Victims of Behavioral Experiments." *Muhammad Speaks*, July 4, 1975. 14:43 Edition.
Kelly, Susan. "Discipline and Craft: An Interview with Sonia Sanchez." *African American Review* 34, no. 4 (2000): 683.
Kelley, Robin D. G. "Black Study, Black Struggle." *Ufahamu* 40, no. 2 (2018): 153–68.
Kelley, Robin D. G. *Freedom Dreams: The Black Radical Imagination*. Beacon Press, 2002.
Kelley, Robin D. G. "House Negroes on the Loose: Malcolm X and the Black Bourgeoisie." *Callaloo* 21, no. 2 (1998): 419–35.
Kelley, Robin D.G. "The Riddle of the Zoot: Malcolm Little and Black Cultural Politics During World War II." In *Malcolm X: In Our Own Image*. St. Martin's Press, 1992.
Kelly, Mike. "Black Lives of Amherst College." *The Consecrated Eminence*, March 17, 2015. https://consecratedeminence.wordpress.amherst.edu/2015/03/17/black-lives-of-amherst-college-non-alumni-edition/.
Khan, Aisha. *Far from Mecca: Globalizing the Muslim Caribbean*. Rutgers University Press, 2020.
Khan, Aisha. "Realising a Muslim Atlantic." AbuSulayman Center for Global Islamic Studies, George Mason University. *Maydan*, July 16, 2020. https://themaydan.com/2020/07/realising-a-muslim-atlantic/.
Khan, Hazrat Inayat. *Notes from the Unstruck Music from the Gayan of Hazrat Inayat Khan*. AE E Kluwer, 1948.
Khomeini, Ruhollah. *al-Jihad al-Akbar, Ya Mubaraza ba Nafs*. Mu'assasah-'i Intisharat-i Amir Kabir, 1978.
Kim, Claire Jean. *Dangerous Crossings: Race, Species, and Nature in a Multicultural Age*. Cambridge University Press, 2014.
King, Kendi. "America Is Still a Burning House." *The North Star*, August 2, 2021. https://www.thenorthstar.com/p/america-is-still-a-burning-house.
King, Martin Luther, Jr. "'Give Us the Ballot,' Address Delivered at the Prayer Pilgrimage for Freedom." In *The Papers of Martin Luther King, Jr. Volume IV: Symbol of the Movement, January 1957–December 1958*, ed. Clayborne Carson et al. University of California Press, 1957.
King, Martin Luther, Jr. "Loving Your Enemies: Sermon Delivered to the Dexter Avenue Baptist Church." Montgomery, AL, November 17, 1957. https://kinginstitute.stanford.edu/king-papers/documents/loving-your-enemies-sermon-delivered-dexter-avenue-baptist-church.
King, Martin Luther, Jr. *Strength to Love*. Harper & Row, 1963.
King, Woodie, ed. *Black Spirits: A Festival of New Black Poets in America*. Random House, 1972.
Knight, Frederick. "Justifiable Homicide, Police Brutality, or Governmental Repression? The 1962 Los Angeles Police Shooting of Seven Member of the Nation of Islam." *Journal of Negro History* 79, no. 2 (1994): 182–96.
Knight, Michael Muhammad. *Blue-Eyed Devil*. Autonomedia, 2007.
Knight, Michael Muhammad. *The Five Percenters: Islam, Hip-Hop and the Gods of New York*. Oneworld Publications, 2007.
Knight, Michael Muhammad. "'I Am Sorry, Mr. White Man, These Are Secrets That You Are Not Permitted to Learn:' The Supreme Wisdom Lessons and Problem Book." *Correspondences*, Special Issue: Islamic Esotericism, vol. 7, no. 1 (2019): 167–200.
Knight, Michael Muhammad. *Magic in Islam*. Penguin Random House, 2016.
Knight, Michael Muhammad. *The Supreme Wisdom Lessons: A Scripture of American Islam*. Equinox, 2025.
Kofsky, Frank. *Black Nationalism and the Revolution in Music*. Pathfinder, 1970.

Kohlman, Michael. "Today and Tomorrow: To-Day and To-Morrow Book Series." Social Sciences and Humanities Research Council of Canada. *Eugenics Archive*, n.d. https://eugenicsarchive.ca/discover/timeline/546d00a8dabeefbb1a000001.

Konadu, Kwasi. *A View from The East: Black Cultural Nationalism and Education in New York City.* Syracuse University Press, 2009.

Kuenz, Jane. "American Racial Discourse, 1900–1930: Schuyler's *Black No More*." *A Forum on Fiction* 30, no. 2 (1997): 170–92.

Kühl, Stefan. *The Nazi Connection: Eugenics, American Racism, and German National Socialism.* Oxford University Press, 1994.

Kukrechtová, Daniela. "The Death and Life of a Chicago Edifice: Gwendolyn Brook's 'In the Mecca.'" *African American Review* 43, no. 2/3 (2009): 457–72.

Kynard, Carmen. *Vernacular Insurrections: Race, Black Protest, and the New Century in Composition-Literacies Studies.* State University of New York Press, 2013.

Larkin, Margaret. "The Inimitability of the Qur'an. Two Perspectives." *Religion and Literature* 20 (1988): 31–47.

Larsen, Nella. *Passing.* Alfred A. Knopf, 1929.

Lavender, Isiah. *Afrofuturism Rising: The Literary Prehistory of a Movement.* Ohio State University Press, 2019.

Lavender, Isiah. *Race in American Science Fiction.* Indiana University Press, 2011.

Lederer, Susan Eyrich. "Hideyo Noguchi's Luetin Experiment and the Antivivisectionists." *Isis* 76, no. 1 (1985): 31–48.

Lei, Richard. "Louis Farrakhan, Calypso Charmer." *Washington Post*, October 15, 1995. https://www.washingtonpost.com/archive/lifestyle/1995/10/14/louis-farrakhan-calypso-charmer/40613502-02c1-48c0-8cde-8c0024d06015/.

Lester, Julius. "The Singing Is Over: The Angry Children of Malcolm X." *Sing Out!* [magazine]. October/November 1966.

Lieb, Michael. *Children of Ezekiel: Aliens, UFOs, the Crisis of Race, and the Advent of the End of Time.* Duke University Press, 1998.

Life. "Fervent Faces Amid a Gathering of Pilgrims." June 3, 1957.

Lincoln, C. Eric. *The Black Muslims in America.* Beacon Press, 1961.

Llorens, David. "Ameer [LeRoi Jones] Baraka." *Ebony* 24, no. 10 (1969).

Lock, Graham. *Blutopia: Visions of the Future and Revisions of the Past in the Work of Sun Ra, Duke Ellington, and Anthony Braxton.* Duke University Press, 1999.

Locke, Alain, ed. *The New Negro: An Interpretation.* Albert and Charles Boni, 1925.

Lopez, Antonio. "13 Ways of Looking at a Paloma Negra." *Permafrost* 39, no. 2 (2017).

Lorde, Audre. *Sister Outsider: Essays and Speeches.* Ten Speed Press, 1984.

Mahmood, Saba. *Politics of Piety: The Islamic Revival and the Feminist Subject.* Princeton University Press, 2005.

Malcolm X. "America's Gravest Crisis Since the Civil War" in *Malcolm X: The Last Speeches*, ed. Bruce Perry. Pathfinder, 1989.

Malcolm X. "Bayard Rustin Debate." *Malcolm X Files*, November 1960. http://malcolmxfiles.blogspot.com/2013/05/bayard-rustin-debate-november-1960.html.

Malcolm X. "God's Angry Men." *New York Amsterdam News*, April 27, 1957.

Malcolm X. "God's Angry Men." *New York Amsterdam News*, May 25, 1957.

Malcolm X. "God's Angry Men." *New York Amsterdam News*, June 1, 1957.

Malcolm X. "God's Judgement of White America." In *The End of White World Supremacy: Four Speeches*, ed. Benjamin Karim. Arcade Books, 1971.

Malcolm X. *El-Hajj Malik El-Shabazz Malcolm X: Collected Speeches, Debates, and Interviews (1960–65)*, ed. antihostile. n.d. https://malcolmxfiles.com.

Malcolm X. "Harlem Freedom Rally." New York, NY, July 1960. https://malcolmxfiles.com.
Malcolm X. "Letter from Prison: 'The Blacker a Man Is, the Holier He Is Inside.'" March 12, 1950. https://catalogue.swanngalleries.com/Lots/auction-lot/MALCOLM-X-Letter-from-prison-one-of-his-first-to-use-his-new?saleno=2471&lotNo=255&refNo=742749.
Malcolm X. "Letter from Prison: 'Music, Brother, Is Ours.'" March 9, 1950. https://www.rrauction.com/auctions/lot-detail/345605706310161-malcolm-x-autograph-letter-signed/?cat=328.
Malcolm X, "Message to the Grassroots," Afro-American Broadcasting and Recording Co., Northern Negro Leadership Conference, Detroit, Michigan, November 10, 1963.
Malcolm X. *On Afro-American History*. Merit Publishers, 1967.
Malcolm X. *The Speeches of Malcolm X at Harvard*, ed. Archie Epps. William Morrow, 1968.
Malcolm X. "Twenty Million Black People in a Political, Economic and Mental Prison." In *Malcolm X: The Last Speeches*, ed. Bruce Perry. Pathfinder, 1989.
Malcolm X, "Who Speaks for the Negro?" *Muhammad Speaks*, October 1, 1961. 1:1 Edition.
Malcolm X, "Who Taught You to Hate the Color of Your Skin?," Los Angeles, May 5, 1962.
Malcolm X. "Young Moslem Leader Explains the Doctrine of Mohammadanism." *Herald-Dispatch* [Los Angeles], July 18, 1957.
Malcolm X and John Henrik Clarke. "Organization of Afro-American Unity: A Statement of Basic Aims and Objectives." In *Malcolm X: The Man and His Times*, ed. John Henrik Clarke. Africa World Press, 1990.
Malcolm X and James Farmer. "Malcolm X v. James Farmer: Separation v. Integration." In *Negro Protest Thought in the Twentieth Century*, eds. Francis L. Broderick and August Meier. Bobbs-Merrill, 1965.
Malcolm X and James Farmer. "Separation or Integration: A Debate." *Dialogue* 2, no. 3 (1962).
Malcolm X and Alex Haley. *The Autobiography of Malcolm X*. Ballantine Books, 2015.
Malcolm X and Bayard Rustin. *A Choice of Two Roads*. 1960. http://corenyc.org/omeka/items/show/332.
Marable, Manning. *Malcolm X: A Life of Reinvention*. Penguin Books, 2011.
Marable, Manning, and Hishaam D. Aidi. "Introduction." In *Black Routes to Islam*. Palgrave, 2009.
Marable, Manning, and Garrett Felber, eds. *The Portable Malcolm X Reader: A Man Who Stands for Nothing Will Fall for Anything*. Penguin Classics, 2013.
Marks, Laura. "Monad, Database, Remix: Manners of Unfolding in *The Last Angel of History*." *Black Camera* 6, no. 2 (2015): 112–34.
Marshall, Paule. *Conversations with Paule Marshall*. University Press of Mississippi, 2010.
Martin, Charles D. *The White African American Body: A Cultural and Literary Exploration*. Rutgers University Press, 2002.
Marvin X. "Back to Black Arts Movement Guru Alonzo Batin." *Black Bird Press News & Review*, June 6, 2005. https://blackbirdpressnews.blogspot.com/2015/06/human-earthquake-hits-sacramento.html.
Marvin X. *The Black Bird: A Parable for Black Children*. Al Kitab Sudan, 1968.
Marvin X [Marvin E. Jackmon]. "Burn, Baby, Burn." In *Black Fire: An Anthology of Afro American Writing*, ed. Amiri Baraka [LeRoi Jones] and Larry Neal. William Morrow, 1968.
Marvin X [Marvin Jackmon]. "Burn, Baby, Burn." *Soulbook: The Quarterly Journal of Revolutionary Afroamerica* 1, no. 3 (1965): 153.
Marvin X. "Dr. Akinyele Umoja Interviews Marvin X." *Black Bird Press News & Review*, August 24, 2012. https://blackbirdpressnews.blogspot.com/2012/08/dr-akinyele-umoja-interviews-marvin-x.html.
Marvin X [Nazzam Al Sudan]. "Al Fitnah Muhajir." In Sudan Rajuli Samia/Black Man Listen. Al Kitab Sudan, 1967.
Marvin X. *Fly to Allah*. Al Kitab Sudan, 1969.
Marvin X. "Harlem Queen." In *Fly to Allah*. Al Kitab Sudan, 1969.
Marvin X. *How to Recover from the Addiction to White Supremacy: A Pan African 12-Step Model for a Mental Health Peer Group*. Black Bird Press, 2008.
Marvin X. *In the Crazy House Called America: Essays by Marvin X*. Black Bird Press, 2002.

Marvin X. "My Life in the Global Village—Notes of an Artistic Freedom Fighter." *Black Bird Press News & Review*, January 16, 2017.

Marvin X. "Notes of an Artistic Freedom Fighter." 360 Poetry Night with Justice, Newark, NJ. February 7, 2020.

Marvin X. *Notes of an Artistic Freedom Fighter*. Black Bird Press, 2019.

Marvin X. "The Origin of Blackness." In *Black Man Listen*. Broadside Press, 1969.

Marvin X. "Oh, Ancestors Speak to Me! Digame Por Favor." *Black Bird Press News & Review*, May 4, 2018. https://blackbirdpressnews.blogspot.com/2018/11/oh-ancestors-speak-to-me-digame-por.html.

Marvin X. *One Day in the Life*. Alice Arts Theatre, 1996.

Marvin X. *Resurrection of the Dead*. Al Kitab Sudan, 1969.

Marvin X. *Somethin' Proper*. Blackbird Press, 1998.

Marvin X [Nazzam Al Sudan]. *Sudan Rajuli Samia/Black Man Listen*. Al Kitab Sudan, 1967.

Marvin X [Nazzam Al Sudan]. "The Underground Railroad Revisited." In *Fly to Allah*. Al Kitab Sudan, 1969.

Marvin X and Faruk. "Islam & Black Art: An Interview with Ameer Baraka (LeRoi Jones)." In *Black Arts: An Anthology of Black Creations*, ed. Ahmed Alhamisi and Harun Kofi Wangara. Black Arts Publications, 1969.

Marvin X and Faruk. "Islam and Black Art: An Interview with LeRoi Jones." *The Negro Digest* 18, no. 3 (January 1969): 6.

Mathes, Carter. *Imagine the Sound: Experimental African American Literature After Civil Rights*. University of Minnesota Press, 2015.

Matlin, Daniel. *On the Corner: African American Intellectuals and the Urban Crisis*. Harvard University Press, 2013.

Maududi, Abu al-'A'la -al. *al-Jihad fi-l-Islam*. Markazi Maktaba-yi Islami, 1927.

Mayfield, Julian. "Author Says Cuba Has Solution to Race Problem." *Fair Play*, October 25, 1960, 1.

Mayfield, Julian. "Castro's Visit to Harlem." Letter. 1960. Julian Mayfield Papers. Sc MG 339, box 7, folder 7. Schomburg Center for Research in Black Culture. Manuscripts, Archives and Rare Books Division, The New York Public Library.

Mayfield, Julian. "Into the Mainstream and Oblivion." In *The American Negro Writer and His Roots: Selected Papers*, ed. John Aubrey Davis Sr. First Conference of Negro Writers 1959. American Society of African Culture, 1960.

Mayfield, Julian. "Letter to Arthur P. Davis." April 4, 1981. Sc MG 339, box 4, folder 12. Schomburg Center for Research in Black Culture. Manuscripts, Archives and Rare Books Division, The New York Public Library.

Mayfield, Julian. "Letter to Lorraine Hansberry." April 5, 1961. Sc MG 680, box 63, folder 15. Schomburg Center for Research in Black Culture, Manuscripts, Archives and Rare Books Division, The New York Public Library.

Mbembe, Achille. *Critique of Black Reason*, trans. Laurent DuBois. Duke University Press, 2017.

Mbembe, Achille. "Necropolitics," trans. Libby Meintjes. *Public Culture* 15, no. 1 (2003): 11–40.

McAlister, Melani. *Epic Encounters: Culture, Media, and U.S. Interests in the Middle East since 1945*. University of California Press, 2005.

McAlister, Melani. "One Black Allah: The Middle East in the Cultural Politics of African American Liberation, 1955–70." *American Quarterly* 51, no. 3 (1999): 622–56.

McCloud, Aminah Beverly. *African American Islam*. Routledge, 1995.

McDowell, Deborah E. *"The Changing Same": Black Women's Literature, Criticism, and Theory*. Indiana University Press, 1995.

McKay, Claude. *Harlem: Negro Metropolis*. Harcourt Brace Jovanovich, 1940.

McKittrick, Katherine. *Demonic Grounds: Black Women and the Cartographies of Struggle*. University of Minnesota Press, 2006.

McLaren, Joseph. "Malcolm-Esque: A Black Arts Literary Genre." In *Malcolm X's Michigan Worldview: An Exemplar for Contemporary Black Studies*, eds. Rita Kiki Edozie and Curtis Stokes. Michigan State University Press, 2015.

McLarney, Ellen. "Beyoncé's Soft Power: Poetics and Politics of an Afro-Diasporic Aesthetics." *Camera Obscura: Feminism, Culture, and Media Studies* 34, no. 2 (2019): 1–39.

McLarney, Ellen. "The Burning House: Revolution and Black Art." *Souls: A Critical Journal of Black Politics, Culture, and Society* 23, no. 3-4 (2022): 185–210.

McLarney, Ellen. "James Baldwin and the Power of Black Muslim Language," *Social Text* 37, no. 1 (2019): 51–84.

McLarney, Ellen. *Soft Force: Women in Egypt's Islamic Awakening*. Princeton Studies in Muslim Politics. Princeton University Press, 2015.

McLarney, Ellen, and Solayman Idris. "Black Muslims and the Angels of Afrofuturism." *The Black Scholar* 53, no. 2 (2023): 30–47.

Mekki, Sharif, el. "MLK's 'Burning House.'" *The Philadelphia Citizen*, January 19, 2018. https://thephiladelphiacitizen.org/mlks-burning-house/.

Mendieta, Eduardo. "Decolonizing Blackness, Decolonizing Theology: On James Cone's Black Theology of Liberation." *The CLR James Journal* 27, no. 1/2 (2021): 101–20.

Mercer, Kobena. *Welcome to the Jungle: New Positions in Black Cultural Studies*. Routledge, 1994.

Miller, Rasul. "Bilal Abdurahman." *Sapelo Square*, February 23, 2016. https://sapelosquare.com/2016/02/23/profile-bilal-abdurahman/.

Miller, Rasul. *Black Muslim Cosmopolitanism: The Global Character of New York City's Black Muslim Movements, 1929–1990*. PhD thesis, University of Pennsylvania, 2019.

Miller, Rasul. "Black Muslim Racial Reimagining: Traditions of Racial and Religious Self-Making among Black Sunni Muslims in the US." *Journal of Africana Religions* 12 no. 2 (2024): 223–51.

Miyakawa, Felicia M. *Five Percenter Rap: God Hop's Music, Message, and Black Muslim Mission*. Indiana University Press, 2005.

Moll, Yasmin. "The Idea of Islamic Media: The Qur'an and the Decolonization of Mass Communication." *International Journal of Middle East Studies* 52 (2020): 623–42.

Morgan, David. "Religion and Media: A Critical Review of Recent Developments." *Critical Research on Religion* 1, no. 3 (2013): 347–56.

Morris, James W. "Spiritual Imagination and the 'Liminal' World: Ibn 'Arabi on the Barzakh." *Postdata* 15, no. 2 (1995): 42–49.

Morris, James W., and Ibn al-'Arabi. "Introduction to The Meccan Revelations." In *The Meccan Revelations*, ed. Michel Chodkiewicz. Pir Press, 2002. https://ibnarabisociety.org/introduction-to-the-meccan-revelations-james-morris/.

Moten, Fred. *In the Break: The Aesthetics of the Black Radical Tradition*. University of Minnesota Press, 2003.

Moynihan, Daniel Patrick. *The Negro Family: The Case for National Action*. Office of Policy Planning and Research, US Department of Labor, 1965.

Muhammad, A. J. "'Get Out' Reading and Viewing List." Schomburg Center for Research in Black Culture. The New York Public Library, July 19, 2017. https://www.nypl.org/blog/2017/07/19/get-out-list.

Muhammad, Elijah. Black Velvet and Jeweled Kofia, the Interior Embroidered with "Elijah Muhammad, Our King, Messenger of Allah." Heritage Auctions, 1970s. https://historical.ha.com/itm/general-historic-events/elijah-muhammad-black-velvet-and-jeweled-kofia-the-interior-embroidered-with-elijah-muhammad-our-king-messenger-of-allah-/a/6172-43244.s#.

Muhammad, Elijah. *Message to the Blackman in America*. Secretarius Memps Publications, 1965.

Muhammad, Elijah. *Police Brutality*. Secretarius Memps Publications, 1964.

Muhammad, Elijah. *The Supreme Wisdom, Volume I: Solution to the So-Called Negroes' Problem*. MEMPS Publications, 1957.

Mullen, Harryette. "African Signs and Spirit Writing." In *The Black Studies Reader*, eds. Jacqueline Bobo, Cynthia Hudley, and Claudine Michel. Routledge, 2004.
Mumininas of Committee for Unified NewArk. *Mwanamke Mwananchi (The Nationalist Woman)*. Jihad Productions, 1971.
Muse, Daphne. "Black Children's Literature: Rebirth of a Neglected Genre." *The Black Scholar* 7, no. 4 (1975): 11–15.
Naeem, Abdul Basit. "Cites October 19th Benefit Concert as Example of New Outlook on Music." *Muhammad Speaks* 7, no. 5 (October 20, 1967): 10.
Nash, Jennifer. *Birthing Black Mothers*. Duke University Press, 2021.
Nash, Jennifer. *Black Feminism Reimagined*. Duke University Press, 2019.
Nash, Jennifer. "Practicing Love: Black Feminism, Love-Politics, and Post-Intersectionality." *Meridians* 11, no. 2 (2011): 1–24.
Ndegeocello, Meshell. "No More Water / The Fire Next Time: The Gospel According to James Baldwin." Symphony Space, New York, February 26, 2022.
Neal, Gaston. "Personal Jihad." In *Black Fire: An Anthology of Afro-American Writing*, ed. Amiri Baraka [LeRoi Jones] and Larry Neal. William Morrow, 1968.
Neal, James H. *Ju-Ju in My Life*. Harrap, 1966.
Neal, Larry. "An Afterword: And Shine Swam On." In *Black Fire: An Anthology of Afro-American Writing*, ed. Amiri Baraka [LeRoi Jones] and Larry Neal. William Morrow, 1968.
Neal, Larry. "The Black Arts Movement." *The Drama Review: TDR* 12, no. 4 (1968): 29–39.
Neal, Larry. "Jihad." In *Black Boogaloo (Notes on Black Liberation): Poems*. Journal of Black Poetry Press, 1969.
Neal, Larry. "The Narrative of the Black Magicians." In *Black Fire: An Anthology of Afro-American Writing*, ed. Amiri Baraka [LeRoi Jones] and Larry Neal. William Morrow, 1968.
Neal, Larry. "New Space/The Growth of Black Consciousness in the Sixties." In *The Seventies*, ed. Floyd B. Barbour. Porter Sargent, 1970.
Neal, Mark Anthony. *Black Ephemera: The Crisis and Challenge of the Musical Archive*. New York University Press, 2022.
Neal, Mark Anthony. *What the Music Said*. Routledge, 1998.
Nelson, Alondra. "Afrofuturism." *Social Text* 20, no. 2 (2002): 1–15.
Nelson, Alondra. "A Black Mass as Black Gothic: Myth and Bioscience in Black Cultural Nationalism." In *New Thoughts on the Black Arts Movement*, ed. Lisa Gail Collins and Margo Natalie Crawford. Rutgers University Press, 2006.
Nelson, Alondra. *Body and Soul: The Black Panther Party and the Fight Against Medical Discrimination*. University of Minnesota Press, 2011.
Nelson, Alondra. *The Social Life of DNA: Race, Reparations, and Reconciliation After the Genome*. Beacon Press, 2016.
Nelson, Jennifer. *Women of Color and the Reproductive Rights Movement*. New York University Press, 2003.
Nelson, Jill, ed. *Police Brutality: An Anthology*. Norton, 2000.
Neuhaus, Richard John. *The Naked Public Square: Religion and Democracy in America*. Wm. B. Eerdmans Publishing, 1986.
New York Amsterdam News. "Mr. X Tells What Islan [sic] Means." April 20, 1957.
New York Amsterdam News. "The Real Harry Belafonte Story." April 20, 1957.
New York Times. "Biologist Asserts He Can Remold Man: Reports Changing Color, Method Will Enable Him to Transform Infant 'to Order.'" October 25, 1929.
Neyrat, Frédéric. "The Black Angel of History: Afrofuturism's Cosmic Techniques." *Angelaki: Journal of the Theoretical Humanities* 25, no. 4 (2020).
Nielsen, Aldon Lynn. *Black Chant: Languages of African-American Postmodernism*. Cambridge University Press, 1997.

Noble Drew Ali. *The Holy Koran of the Moorish Science Temple of America*. 1927.
Noguchi, Hideyo. "A Cutaneous Reaction in Syphilis." *Journal of Experimental Medicine* 14 (1911): 557–68.
Nyong'o, Tavia. *Afro-Fabulations: The Queer Drama of Black Life*. New York University Press, 2019.
Nyong'o, Tavia. "Unburdening Representation." *The Black Scholar: Journal of Black Studies and Research* 44, no. 2 (2014): 70–80.
Olugebefola, Ademola. *Cover Artwork: "Blues Book for Blue Black Magical Women."* Broadside Press, 1974.
Olugebefola, Ademola. *Cover Artwork: "Ima Talken Bout the Nation of Islam."* New Pyramid Productions, 1971.
Omolade, Barbara. "Hearts of Darkness." In *Words of Fire: An Anthology of African American Feminist Thought*, ed. Beverly Guy-Sheftal. The New Press, 1995.
Ongiri, Amy Abugo. *Spectacular Blackness: The Cultural Politics of the Black Power Movement and the Search for a Black Aesthetic*. University of Virginia Press, 2009.
O'Rourke, Sean Patrick, and Leslie K. Pace, eds. *Like Wildfire: The Rhetoric of the Civil Rights Sit Ins*. University of South Carolina Press, 2020.
Palter, David. "Testing for Race: Stanford University, Asian Americans, and Psychometric Testing in California, 1920–1935." PhD diss., University of California, 2014.
Parker, Morgan. *There Are More Beautiful Things Than Beyoncé*. Tin House Books, 2017.
Parks, Gordon. "Wake Up, Clean Up, Stand Up." *Life Magazine* 54, no. 22 (1963): 26–27.
Perry, Imani. *Looking for Lorraine: The Radiant and Radical Life of Lorraine Hansberry*. Beacon Press, 2018.
Pollard, Cherise A. "Sexual Subversions, Political Inversions: Women's Poetry and the Politics of the Black Arts Movement." In *New Thoughts on the Black Arts Movement*, ed. Lisa Gail Collins and Margo Natalie Crawford. Rutgers University Press, 2006.
Porambo, Ron. *No Cause for Indictment: An Autopsy of Newark*. Holt, Rinehart and Winston, 1971.
Powell, Richard. *African and Afro-American Art: Call and Response*. African Insights: Sources for Afro-American Art and Culture. Field Museum of Natural History, 1984.
Powell, Richard J. *Black Art and Culture in the 20th Century*. Thames and Hudson, 1997.
Powers, Nicholas. "Trapped in a Burning House." *TruthOut*, July 30, 2017. https://truthout.org/articles/trapped-in-a-burning-house-a-review-of-i-am-not-your-negro/.
Qutb, Sayyid. *Milestones*. Islamic Book Service, 2006.
Qutb, Sayyid. *Social Justice in Islam*. Islamic Publications International, 2000.
Qutb, Sayyid. *al-Taswir al-Fanni fi al-Qur'an*. Dar al-Ma'arif, 1945.
Rahman, Abdul. *Illustrations "Songhai!"* Songhai Press, 1972.
Rahman, Y. "The Miraculous Nature of Muslim Scripture. A Study of 'Abd al-Jabbar's I'jaz al-Qur'an." *Islamic Studies* 35 (1996): 409–24.
Rahman, Yusuf. *Alhomdullilah!* Am God Pub. Co., 1968.
Rahman, Yusef. "Transcendental Blues." In *Black Fire: An Anthology of Afro-American Writing*, ed. Amiri Baraka [LeRoi Jones] and Larry Neal. William Morrow, 1968.
Rambsy, Howard. *The Black Arts Enterprise and the Production of African American Poetry*. University of Michigan Press, 2011.
Randall, Dorothy. "Black Mayflower." In *Three Hundred and Sixty Degrees of Blackness Comin at You: An Anthology of the Sonia Sanchez Writers Workshop at Countee Cullen Library in Harlem*, ed. Sonia Sanchez. 5X Publishing Co., 1971.
Randall, Dudley, and Margaret G. Burroughs, eds. *For Malcolm: Poems on the Life and the Death of Malcolm X*. Broadside Press, 1967.
Ransby, Barbara, and Tracye Matthews. "Black Popular Culture and the Transcendence of Patriarchal Illusions." In *Words of Fire: An Anthology of African American Feminist Thought*, ed. Beverly Guy-Sheftall. New Press, 1995.

"Racial Metamorphosis Claimed by Scientist: Japanese Says He Can Change Black Skin into White." *Pittsburgh Courier*. November 2, 1929.
Reed, Ishmael. *Mumbo Jumbo*. Scribner, 1972.
Reis, João José. *Slave Rebellion in Brazil: The Muslim Uprising of 1835 in Bahia*, trans. Arthur Brakel. Johns Hopkins University Press, 1995.
Rickford, Russell. *We Are an African People: Independent Education, Black Power, and the Radical Imagination*. Oxford University Press, 2016.
Robcis, Camille. *Disalienation: Politics, Philosophy, and Radical Psychiatry in Postwar France*. University of Chicago Press, 2021.
Roberts, Dorothy. *Killing the Black Body: Race, Reproduction, and the Meaning of Liberty*. Vintage, 2014.
Rodgers, Carolyn. *Songs of a Black Bird*. Third World Press, 1969.
Rodríguez, Dylan. "Black Studies in Impasse." *The Black Scholar* 44, no. 2 (2014): 37–49.
Rojas, Fabio. *From Black Power to Black Studies*. Johns Hopkins University Press, 2010.
Rojas, Rafael. *Fighting Over Fidel: The New York Intellectuals and the Cuban Revolution*, trans. Carl Good. Princeton University Press, 2016.
Rollefson, J. Griffith. *CIPHER: Hip Hop Interpellation*. University College Cork, 2018.
Romine, David Tyroler. "'Into the Mainstream and Oblivion:' Julian Mayfield's Black Radical Tradition, 1948–1984." PhD thesis, Duke University, 2018.
Rusert, Britt. *Fugitive Science: Empiricism and Freedom in Early African American Culture*. New York University Press, 2017.
Ryan, Jennifer. *Post-Jazz Poetics: A Social History*. Palgrave Macmillan, 2010.
Sabʻ, Tawfiq Muhammad. *Nufus wa-Durus fi-Itar al-Taswir al-Qurʾani*. Majmaʻ al-Buhuth al-Islamiyya, 1971.
Sadiq, Mufti Muhammad, ed. *The Moslem Sunrise* 1, no. 1 (1921).
Salaam, Kalamu ya. *The Magic of Juju: An Appreciation of the Black Arts Movement*. Third World Press, 2016.
Salaam, Kalamu ya. "Sonia Sanchez." In *Dictionary of Literary Biography: Afro-American Poets Since 1955*, vol. 41. Gale, 1985.
Samatar, Sofia. "Toward a Planetary History of Afrofuturism." *Research in African Literatures* 48, no. 4 (2017): 175–91.
Sanchez, Sonia. *A Blues Book for Blue Black Magical Women*. Broadside Press, 1974.
Sanchez, Sonia. *Home Coming*. Broadside Press, 1969.
Sanchez, Sonia. *Ima Talken Bout the Nation of Islam* [broadsheet]. New Pyramid Productions, 1971.
Sanchez, Sonia. *It's a New Day (Poems for Young Brothas and Sistuhs)*. Broadside Press, 1971.
Sonia Sanchez, "Malcolm." In *For Malcolm*, ed. Dudley Randall and Margaret G. Burroughs. Broadside Press, 1967, 38-9.
Sanchez, Sonia. "Malcolm." In *Home Coming*. Broadside Press, 1969.
Sanchez, Sonia. "Malcolm/Man Don't Live Here No Mo." In *I'm Black When I'm Singing, I'm Blue When I Ain't and Other Plays*. Duke University Press, 2010.
Sanchez, Sonia. "A/Needed/Poem for My Salvation." In *We A BadddDD People*. Broadside Press, 1970.
Sanchez, Sonia. "Poem (for DCs 8th Graders—1966–67)." In *Home Coming*. Broadside Press, 1969.
Sanchez, Sonia. "Queens of the Universe." *The Black Scholar. In Memoriam: W. E. B. Du Bois* 1, no. 3/4 (1970): 29–34.
Sanchez, Sister Sonia 5X. "Respect for Wisdom." New Frontiers. *Muhammad Speaks*, August 29, 1975. 14:51 edition.
Sanchez, Sonia. "Sister Son/ji." In *I'm Black When I'm Singing, I'm Blue When I Ain't and Other Plays*. Duke University Press, 2010.

Sanchez, Sonia. "Sister Son/ji." In *New Plays from the Black Theatre: An Anthology*, ed. Ed Bullins. Bantam Books, 1969, 97-108.
Sanchez, Sonia. *Three Hundred and Sixty Degrees of Blackness Comin at You: An Anthology of the Sonia Sanchez Writers Workshop at Countee Cullen Library in Harlem*. 5X Publishing Co., 1971.
Sanchez, Sonia. "To Fanon." In *We a BaddDDD People*. Broadside Press, 1970.
Sanchez, Sonia. "To Morani/Mungu." In *It's a New Day (Poems for Young Brothas and Sistuhs)*. Broadside Press, 1971.
Sanchez, Sonia. "We Are Muslim Women." *Black World* 23, no. 3 (January 1974), 24.
Sanchez, Sonia. *We a BaddDDD People*. Broadside Press, 1970.
Sanchez, Sonia. "We're Not Learnen to Be Paper Boys (for the Young Brothas Who Sell Muhammad Speaks)." In *It's A New Day (Poems for Young Brothas and Sistuhs)*. Broadside Press, 1971.
Sato, Art. Interview with John Gilmore. *Be-Bop and Beyond*, April 1986.
"Sausalito Boycott: Freedom Class in Marin City." *Sausalito News* 79, no. 21 (1964): 1.
Schuyler, George S. *Black No More: An Account of the Strange and Wonderful Workings of Science in the Land of the Free*. Macaulay, 1931.
Schuyler, George S. "The Negro-Art Hokum." *The Nation*, June 16, 1926, 662–63.
Scott, James C. *Domination and the Arts of Resistance: Hidden Transcripts*. Yale University Press, 1990.
Sell, Mike. *Avant-Garde Performance & the Limits of Criticism: Approaching the Living Theatre, Happenings/Fluxus, and the Black Arts Movement*. University of Michigan Press, 2008.
Sells, Michael. *Approaching the Qur'an: The Early Revelations*. White Cloud Press, 1999.
Sells, Michael. *Stations Of Desire: Love Elegies from Ibn 'Arabi and New Poems*. Ibis Editions, 2000.
Shakry, Omnia. "Schooled Mothers and Structured Play: Child Rearing in Turn-of-the-Century Egypt." In *Remaking Women: Feminism and Modernity in the Middle East*, ed. Lila Abu-Lughod. Princeton University Press, 1998.
Shariati, Ali. "Jihad & Shahadat," https://www.shariati.com/english/jihadand.html.
Sharolyn, Sister Minister. "A Conversation with Sis. Sonia 5X Sanchez." *Muhammad Speaks* June 13, 1975, S3.
Sharpe, Christina. "Black Studies: In the Wake." *The Black Scholar* 44, no. 2 (2014): 59–69.
Shockley, Evie. *Renegade Poetics: Black Aesthetics and Formal Innovation in African American Poetry*. University of Iowa Press, 2011.
Sidqi, Niʿmat. *al-Jihad fi Sabil Allah*. Dar al-Iʿtisam, 1975.
Simanga, Michael. "Amina Baraka and the Women of the Congress of African People." In *Amiri Baraka and the Congress of African People: History and Memory*. Palgrave Macmillan, 2015.
Sims, Rudine. *Shadow and Substance: Afro-American Experience in Contemporary Children's Fiction*. National Council of Teachers of English, 1982.
Singerman, Diane. *Avenues of Participation: Family, Politics, and Networks in Urban Quarters of Cairo*. Princeton University Press, 1996.
Sites, William. *Sun Ra's Chicago*. University of Chicago Press, 2020.
Smart-Grosvenor, Vertamae. *Vibration Cooking, Or, The Travel Notes of a Geechee Girl*. Doubleday, 1970.
Smethurst, James. *The Black Arts Movement: Literary Nationalism in the 1960s and 1970s*. University of North Carolina Press, 2005.
Smethurst, James Edward. *Brick City Vanguard: Amiri Baraka, Black Music, Black Modernity*. University of Massachusetts Press, 2020.
Smethurst, James. "Malcolm X and the Black Arts Movement." In *Cambridge Companion to Malcolm X*, ed. Robert E. Terrill. Cambridge University Press, 2010.
Smith, Christen A., Erica L. Williams, Imani A. Wadud, Whitney N. L. Pirtle, and Cite Black Women Collective. "Cite Black Women: A Critical Praxis (A Statement)." *Feminist Anthropology* 2, no. 1 (2021): 10–17.

Smith, Lorrie. "Black Arts to Def Jam: Performing Black 'Spirit Work' Across Generations." In *New Thought of the Black Arts Movement*, ed. Lisa Gail Collins and Margo Natalie Crawford. Rutgers University Press, 2006.
Smitherman, Geneva. "English Teacher, Why You Be Doing the Thangs You Don't Do?" *English Journal*, January 1972.
Smitherman, Geneva. "Malcolm X: Master of Signifyin." In *Malcolm X's Michigan Worldview: An Exemplar for Contemporary Black Studies*, ed. Rita Kiki Edozie and Curtis Stokes. Michigan State University Press, 2015.
Smitherman, Geneva. "The Power of the Rap: The Black Idiom and the New Black Poetry." *Twentieth Century Literature* 19, no. 4 (1974): 259–74.
Smitherman, Geneva. *Talkin and Testifyin: The Language of Black America*. Wayne State University Press, 1977.
Smitherman, Geneva. "White English in Blackface or, Who Do I Be?" *The Black Scholar* 4, no. 8/9 (1973): 32–39.
Snellings, Rolland. See Touré, Askia Muhammad.
Sollors, Werner. *Amiri Baraka / LeRoi Jones: The Quest for a "Populist Modernism."* Columbia University Press, 1978.
Sorett, Josef. *Spirit in the Dark: A Religious History of Racial Aesthetics*. Oxford University Press, 2016.
Southern Poverty Law Center. Louis Farrakhan. https://www.splcenter.org/resources/extremist-files/louis-farrakhan/ (accessed July 19, 2023).
Spady, James G. "The Centrality of Black Language in the Discourse Strategies and Poetic Force of Sonia Sanchez and Rap Artists." *B. Ma: The Sonia Sanchez Literary Review* 6, no. 1 (2000): 47–72.
Spady, James G. "Introduction: 360 Degreez of Sonia Sanchez, Hip Hop, Narrativity, Iqhawe, and Public Spaces of Being." *B. Ma: The Sonia Sanchez Literary Review* 6, no. 1 (2000): vi–1.
Spady, James G. *Larry Neal: Liberated Black Philly Poet with a Blues Streak of Mellow Wisdom*. PC International Press and Black History Museum Umum Publishers, 1989.
Spence, Gerry. *Police State: How America's Cops Get Away with Murder*. St. Martin's Press, 2015.
Spillers, Hortense J. "Fabrics of History: Essays on the Black Sermon." PhD diss. University of Michigan, 1974.
Spillers, Hortense J. "Mama's Baby, Papa's Maybe: An American Grammar Book." *Diacritics* 17, no. 2 (1987): 65–81.
Springer, Kimberly. "Black Feminists Respond to Black Power Masculinism." In *The Black Power Movement: Re-Thinking the Civil Rights-Black Power Era*, ed. Peniel E. Joseph. Routledge, 2006.
Stanley, L. L. "An Analysis of One Thousand Testicular Substance Implantations." *Endocrinology* 6, no, 1 (1922): 789.
Stanley, Leo, and Evelyn Wells. *Men at Their Worst*. D. Appleton, 1940.
Stanton, Jeffrey. "Freaks and Side Shows." In *Coney Island History*. 1997. https://www.westland.net/coneyisland/.
Staples, Robert. "To Be Young, Black and Oppressed." *The Black Scholar* 7, no. 4 (1975): 2–9.
Stern, Alexandra Minna. *Eugenic Nation: Faults and Frontiers of Better Breeding in Modern America*. University of California Press, 2016.
Stern, Alexandra Minna. "Forced Sterilization Policies in the US Targeted Minorities and Those with Disabilities—and Lasted into the 21st Century." *The Conversation*, August 26, 2020. https://theconversation.com/forced-sterilization-policies-in-the-us-targeted-minorities-and-those-with-disabilities-and-lasted-into-the-21st-century-143144.
Stetkevych, Jaroslav. *The Zephyrs of Najd: The Poetics of Nostalgia in The Classical Arabic Nasib*. University of Chicago Press, 1993.
Stewart, James T. "The Development of the Black Revolutionary Artist." In *Black Arts: An Anthology of Black Creations*, ed. Ahmed Alhamisi and Harun Kofi Wangara. Black Arts Publications, 1969.

Stewart, James T. "The Development of the Black Revolutionary Artist." In *Black Fire: An Anthology of Afro-American Writing*, ed. Amiri Baraka [LeRoi Jones] and Larry Neal. William Morrow, 1968.

Stewart, James T. "Revolutionary Black Music in the Total Context of Black Distension." *Cricket*, no. 3 (1969): 13–14.

Stoever, Jennifer Lynn. *The Sonic Color Line: Race and the Cultural Politics of Listening*. New York University Press, 2016.

Strait, Kevin, and Kinshasha Holman Conwill, eds. *Afrofuturism: A History of Black Futures*. Smithsonian Books, 2023.

Sudan, Nazzam al. See Marvin X.

Sulaiman, Amir. *Love, Gnosis, & Other Suicide Attempts*. Penmanship Publishing, 2012.

Sun Ra. "The Black Rays Race." In *The Immeasurable Equation*. Ihnfinity Inc. / Saturn Research, 1972.

Sun Ra. *The Immeasurable Equation*. Ihnfinity Inc. / Saturn Research, 1972.

Sun Ra. "Preparation for Outer Space" [liner notes]. In *Jazz By Sun Ra* [album]. Transition, 1957.

Sun Ra. "Saga of Resistance." In *Black Fire: An Anthology of Afro-American Writing*, ed. Amiri Baraka [LeRoi Jones] and Larry Neal. William Morrow, 1968.

Sun Ra. "The Sound Image." In *Immeasurable Equation*. Ihnfinity Inc./Saturn Research, 1972.

"Sun-Ra and His Modern Jazz Band." *Chicago Defender*. Sec. 53:11. July 13, 1957.

Szwed, John F. *Space Is the Place: The Lives And Times Of Sun Ra*. Pantheon, 1997.

Talalay, Kathryn. *Composition in Black and White: The Life of Philippa Schuyler*. Oxford University Press, 1995.

Taylor, Clarence. *Fight the Power: African Americans and the Long History of Police Brutality in New York City*. New York University Press, 2018.

Taylor, Ula Yvette. *The Promise of Patriarchy: Women and the Nation of Islam*. University of North Carolina Press, 2017.

Taylor, Vanessa. "Take Me From My Plight: On Afrofuturism, the Afterlife, and a Black Future." *Medium*, December 18, 2017. https://medium.com/@BaconTribe/take-me-from-my-plight-564b77132de6.

Thomas, Lorenzo. "Askia Muhammad Touré: Crying Out the Goodness." *Obsidian* 1, no. 1 (1975): 31–49.

Thomas, Lorenzo. "'Communicating by Horns': Jazz and Redemption in the Poetry of the Beats and the Black Arts Movement." *African American Review* 26, no. 2 (1992): 291–98.

Thomas, Lorenzo. *Don't Deny My Name: Words and Music and the Black Intellectual Tradition*. University of Michigan Press, 2008.

Thomas, Lorenzo. *Extraordinary Measures: Afrocentric Modernism and 20th-Century American Poetry*. University of Alabama Press, 2000.

Thomas, Lorenzo. "The Shadow World: New York's Umbra Workshop & Origins of the Black Arts Movement." *Callaloo*, no. 4 (1978): 53–72.

Thompson, Robert Farris. *Flash of the Spirit: African & Afro-American Art & Philosophy*. Random House, 1983.

Touré, Askia Muhammad [Rolland Snellings]. "Afro American Youth and the Bandung World." *Liberator* 5, no. 2 (1965): 4–7.

Touré, Askia Muhammad. "Black Magic Music / A Love Ritual." In *Songhai!* Songhai Press, 1972.

Touré, Askia Muhammad. "Jihad!: Toward a Black National Credo." *Negro Digest*, July 1969, 10–17.

Touré, Askia Muhammad [Askia Muhammad Abu Bakr el-Touré]. *Juju (Magic Songs for the Black Nation)*. Third World Press, 1970.

Touré, Askia Muhammad [Rolland Snellings]. "Malcolm X as International Spokesman." *Liberator* 6 (February 1966).

Touré, Askia Muhammad [Rolland Snellings]. "Song of Fire." *Umbra*, no. 2 (December 1963).

Touré, Askia Muhammad [Rolland Snellings]. "Song of Fire." In *Black Fire: An Anthology of Afro-American Writing*, ed. Amiri Baraka [LeRoi Jones] and Larry Neal. William Morrow, 1968.

Touré, Askia Muhammad. *Songhai!* Songhai Press, 1972.
Touré, Askia Muhammad. "The Sound of Allah's Horn." In *Black Arts: An Anthology of Black Creations*, ed. Ahmed Alhamisi and Harun Kofi Wangara. Black Arts Publications, 1969.
Touré, Tariq. *2 Parts Oxygen: How I Learned to Breathe.* Touré Management, 2019.
Touré, Tariq. *Black Seeds: The Poetry and Reflections of Tariq Touré.* CreateSpace Independent Publishing, 2016.
Touré, Tariq. *The Call.* 2020. https://www.youtube.com/watch?v=hr8lP2hDISQ.
Turner, Richard Brent. "Edward Wilmot Blyden and Pan-Africanism: The Ideological Roots of Islam and Black Nationalism in the United States." *The Muslim World* 87 (April 1997): 169–81.
Turner, Richard Brent. *Islam in the African-American Experience.* Indiana University Press, 1997.
Turner, Richard Brent. "Malcolm X and Youth Culture." In *The Cambridge Companion to Malcolm X.* Cambridge University Press, 2010.
Turner, Richard Brent. *Soundtrack to a Movement: African American Islam, Jazz, and Black Internationalism.* New York University Press, 2021.
Tyson, Timothy B. "Burning for Freedom: Black Power and White Terror in Oxford, North Carolina." MA thesis, Duke University, 1990.
Tyson, Timothy B. *Radio Free Dixie: Robert F. Williams and the Roots of Black Power.* University of North Carolina Press, 1999.
Vergès, Françoise. "The Island of Dr. Moreau." In *The Wombs of Women: Race, Capital, Feminism*, trans. Kaiama Glover. Duke University Press, 2020.
Voll, John O. "Renewal and Reform in Islamic History: Tajdid and Islah." In *Voices of Resurgent Islam*, ed. John L. Esposito. Oxford University Press, 1983.
wadud, amina. *Inside the Gender Jihad: Women's Reform in Islam.* Oneworld Academic, 2006.
Wald, Gayle. *It's Been Beautiful: Soul! And Black Power Television.* Duke University Press, 2015.
Walid, Dawud. *Blackness and Islam.* Algorithm, 2021.
Walker, Joe. "Racist Texts Standard in U.S. Classrooms: Textbook Distortions Revealed." *Muhammad Speaks*, July 4, 1975. 14:43 Edition.
Ward, Jesmyn. *The Fire This Time: A New Generation Speaks about Race.* Scribner, 2017.
Ware, Rudolph T., III. *The Walking Qur'an: Islamic Education, Embodied Knowledge, and History in West Africa.* University of North Carolina Press, 2014.
Warner, Michael. *Publics and Counterpublics.* Zone Books, 2002.
Washington, Mary Helen. *The Other Blacklist: The African American Literary and Cultural Left of the 1950s.* Columbia University Press, 2015.
Watts, Eric King. "Cultivating a Black Public Voice: W. E. B. Du Bois and the 'Criteria of Negro Art.'" *Rhetoric & Public Affairs* 4, no. 2 (2001): 181–201.
Weheliye, Alexander G. "Black Studies and Black Life." *The Black Scholar: Journal of Black Studies and Research* 44, no. 2 (2014): 5.
Weheliye, Alexander G. *Feenin: R&B Music and the Materiality of BlackFem Voices and Technology.* Duke University Press, 2023.
Weheliye, Alexander G. *Habeas Viscus: Racializing Assemblages, Biopolitics, and Black Feminist Theories of the Human.* Duke University Press Books, 2014.
Weismann, August. *The Germ-Plasm: A Theory of Heredity*, trans. William N. Parker and Harriet Rönnfeldt. Scribner's, 1983.
Welch, Rebeccah. "Black Art and Activism in Postwar New York, 1950–1965." PhD thesis, New York University, 2002.
Wells, H. G. *Island of Dr. Moreau.* Penguin, 1896.
Wells, H. G. *The Science of Life.* Doubleday, Doran & Company, 1930.
Wells, H. G. *A Short History of Mankind.* Macmillan, 1925.

West, Cornel. "The Dilemma of the Black Intellectual." *Cultural Critique* 1 (Autumn 1985): 109–24.

West, Cornel. *Restoring Hope: Conversations on the Future of Black America*, ed. Kelvin Shawn Sealey. Beacon Press, 1997.

West, Cornel, and Christa Buschendorf. *Black Prophetic Fire*. Beacon Press, 2014.

"What Is Rhythm? (Advertisement for Black Power!)." *Soulbook* 2 (1967): 152.

Whitaker, Mark. *The Afterlife of Malcolm X: An Outcast Turned Icon's Enduring Impact on America*. Simon & Schuster, 2025.

White-Duncan, Ida. "Kink-No-More." *The New York Age*, January 13, 1916.

Whitney, Joel. "Lorraine Hansberry Was an Unapologetic Radical." *Jacobin*, December 2020. https://www.jacobinmag.com/2020/12/lorraine-hansberry-raisin-in-the-sun-playwright.

Wickham, Carrie Rosefsky. *Mobilizing Islam: Religion, Activism, and Political Change in Egypt*. Columbia University Press, 2002.

Williams, Junius, and Tom Hayden. *Unfinished Agenda: Urban Politics in the Era of Black Power*. North Atlantic Books, 2014.

Williams, Patricia Hill. "Learning to Think for Ourselves: Malcolm X's Black Nationalism Reconsidered." In *Malcolm X: In Our Own Image*, ed. Joe Wood. St. Martin's Press, 1992.

Williams, Rhonda Y. "Black Women, Urban Politics, and Engendering Black Power." In *The Black Power Movement: Re-Thinking the Civil Rights-Black Power Era*. Routledge, 2006.

Wilmore, Gayraud S. *Black Religion and Black Radicalism: An Interpretation of the Religious History of African Americans*. Orbis Books, 1998.

Wilson, Peter Lamborn. *Sacred Drift: Essays on the Margins of Islam*. City Lights Books, 1993.

Wood, Jacqueline. "'Shaking Loose:' Sonia Sanchez's Militant Drama." In *Contemporary African American Women Playwrights*, ed. Philip C. Kolin. Routledge, 2007.

Wood, Joe, ed. *Malcolm X: In Our Own Image*. St. Martin's Press, 1992.

Woodard, Komozi. *A Nation Within a Nation: Amiri Baraka (LeRoi Jones) and Black Power Politics*. The University of North Carolina Press, 1999.

Woodard, Komozi. *A Nation Within a Nation: Amiri Baraka (LeRoi Jones) and Black Power Politics*. University of North Carolina Press, 2005.

Woods, Jamila, Mahogany L. Browne, Idrissa Simmonds, and Patricia Smith, eds. *The BreakBeat Poets Vol. 2: Black Girl Magic*. Haymarket Books, 2018.

Wright, Peter Matthews. "A Box of Self-Threading Needles: Epic Vision and Penal Trauma in the Fugitive Origins of the Nation of Islam." MA thesis, University of North Carolina, 2004.

Wynter, Sylvia. "A Black Studies Manifesto." In *Forum N. H. I.: Knowledge for the 21st Century* 1, no. 1 (Fall 1994): 3–11.

Wynter, Sylvia. "The Pope Must Have Been Drunk, the King of Castile a Madman: Culture as Actuality, and the Caribbean Rethinking Modernity." In *Reordering of Culture: Latin America, the Caribbean, and Canada in the Hood*, ed. Alvina Ruprecht and Cecilia Taiana. Carleton University Press, 1995.

Yancy, George. *Black Bodies, White Gazes: The Continuing Significance of Race*. Rowman & Littlefield Publishers, 2008.

Youssef, Maimouna. "Music, Art, and Being Muslim." Doris Duke Foundation for Islamic Art, Building Bridges: Muslims in America. The Ruby, Duke University, September 19, 2019.

Youngquist, Paul. "The Space Machine: Baraka and Science Fiction." *African American Review* 37, no. 2/3 (2003): 333–43.

Yudell, Michael. *Race Unmasked: Biology and Race in the 20th Century*. Columbia University Press, 2007.

Yuval-Davis, Nira. "Intersectionality and Feminist Politics." *European Journal of Women's Studies* 13, no. 3 (2006): 193–209.

Zwettler, Michael. "A Mantic Manifesto: The Sura of 'The Poets' and the Qur'anic Foundations of Prophetic Authority." In *Poetry and Prophecy: The Beginnings of a Literary Tradition*, ed. James L. Kugel. Cornell University Press, 1990.

BIBLIOGRAPHY 345

RECORDINGS: MUSIC, POETRY, PLAYS

Baraka, Amiri [LeRoi Jones]. "Black Art." On *Sonny's Time Now*, with Sunny Murray, Albert Ayler, and Don Cherry. Jihad Productions, 1965.
Baraka, Amiri, and Sun Ra and his Myth Science Arkestra. *A Black Mass*. Jihad Productions, 1968.
Baraka, Amiri, and Sun Ra and the Myth Science Arkestra. *A Black Mass*. Sonboy Records, September 6, 1999. https://www.forcedexposure.com/Catalog/baraka-leroi-jones-the-sun-ra-myth-science-arkestra-amiri-a-black-cd/SONBOY.001CD.html.
Bartz, Gary, and NTU Troop. *Juju Street Songs*. Prestige, 1972.
Beyoncé. "Don't Hurt Yourself." On *Lemonade*, with Jack White. Jungle Studios, 2014.
Black, James Milton. "When the Roll Is Called Up Yonder." Edison Blue Amberol, 1913.
Collier, Jimmy, and Frederick Douglass Kirkpatrick. "Burn, Baby, Burn." On *The Best of Broadside 1962–1988: Anthems of the American Underground from the Pages of Broadside Magazine*. Smithsonian Folkways, 2001. https://folkways.si.edu/the-best-of-broadside-1962-1988-anthems-of-the-american-underground-from-the-pages-of-broadside-magazine/folk/music/album/smithsonian.
Coltrane, John. *A Love Supreme*. Van Gelder Studio, 1965.
Cooke, Sam and the Stars. "Steal Away." Keen, 1960.
Dean, Jimmy. "When the Roll Is Called Up Yonder." On *Hour of Prayer*. Columbia Records, 1957.
Dumas, Henry, and Sun Ra. *The Ark and the Ankh: Sun Ra/Henry Dumas in Conversation, 1966, Slug's Saloon NYC*. Ikef Records, 2002. https://sunramusic.bandcamp.com/album/the-ankh-and-the-ark.
Farrakhan, Louis [Louis X]. *A White Man's Heaven Is a Black Man's Hell*. Muhammad's Mosque No. 32, 1960.
Fisk University Jubilee Singers. *Steal Away*. Volume 2, 1915–1920. Fisk University Jubilee Singers, in Chronological Order. Document Records, n.d.
Hill, Andrew. *Black Fire*. Blue Note Records, 1964.
Jackson, Clarence Bernard, and James Hatch, "Fly Blackbird." On *Fly Blackbird*, Mercury, 1962.
Johnson, Blind Willie ["The Blind Pilgrim."] "Motherless Children." Anchor, 1927.
Johnson, Blind Willie. "Mother's Children Have a Hard Time." On *His Story*. Folkways, 1957.
Last Poets, The. *Jazzoetry*. Douglas Records, 1967.
Last Poets, The. *This Is Madness*. Mediasound, 1971.
Louis X. "White Man's Heaven Is a Black Man's Hell." On *A Muslim Sings*. Muhammad's Mosque No. 32. 1960.
Prince Buster. *Africa-Islam-Revolution, Kingston, Jamaica 1966–72*. Earth Sound, 2019.
Prince Buster. "White Man's Heaven." On *Africa-Islam-Revolution, Kingston, Jamaica 1966–72*. Earth Sound, 2019.
Public Enemy. "Fight the Power." On *Fear of a Black Planet*. Def Jam, 1990.
Public Enemy. "White Heaven / Black Hell." On *Muse Sick-n-Hour Mess Age*. Def Jam Recordings, 1994.
Roach, Max. "Triptych: Prayer, Protest, Peace." On *We Insist! Max Roach's Freedom Now Suite*, with Abbey Lincoln. Candid, 1960.
Sanders, Pharoah. *Deaf Dumb Blind (Summun Bukmun Umyun)*. A&R Studios, 1970.
Sanders, Pharoah. "Hum-Allah-Hum-Allah-Hum-Allah." On *Jewels of Thought*. Impulse! Records, October 20, 1969.
Sanders, Pharoah. *Tauhid*. Impulse! Records, 1967.
Sanchez, Sonia. "A Black/Woman/Speaks." On *A Sun Lady for All Seasons Reads Her Poetry*. Smithsonian Folkways Records. New York, 1971.
Sanchez, Sonia. "Ima Talken Bout the Nation of Islam." On *A Sun Lady for All Seasons Reads Her Poetry*. Smithsonian Folkways Records. New York, 1971.
Sanchez, Sonia. *A Sun Lady for All Seasons Reads Her Poetry*. Smithsonian Folkways Records. New York, 1971.

Sanchez, Sonia. "To Fanon." On *A Sun Lady for All Seasons Reads Her Poetry*. Smithsonian Folkways, 1971.
Shepp, Archie. "Malcolm, Malcolm Semper Malcolm." On *Fire Music*. Impulse!, 1965.
Shepp, Archie. *The Magic of Ju-Ju*. Impulse!, 1967.
Shorter, Wayne. *JuJu*. Blue Note Records, 1964.
Simone, Nina. "Blackbird." Colpix Records, 1963.
Simone, Nina. "Blackbird." On *World of Folk Music #107*. WNBC, 1964.
Singing Time in Dixie Choir, "When the Roll Is Called Up Yonder." https://www.youtube.com/watch?v=kT9rlGi54yo.
Sister Souljah. *360 Degrees of Power*. Epic/SME Records, 1992.
Smith, Carl. "When the Roll Is Called Up Yonder." *Sunday Down South*. Columbia Records, 1957.
Soul Stirrers. "Steal Away." Aladdin, 1946.
Stitt, Sonny. "All God's Children (Got Rhythm)." Prestige, December 11, 1949.
Sulaiman, Amir. *The Meccan Openings*. 2011. https://www.amirsulaiman.com/meccan-openings.
Sun Ra and his Arkestra. *Jazz in Silhouette*. El Saturn, 1959.

FILM, TELEVISION, AND RADIO

Ajalon, Jamika, dir. *Locations of the M/Othership: Black Women as Future Archetype of Resistance*. Third World Newsreel, 2009.
Akomfrah, John, dir. *The Last Angel of History*. Icarus, 1996.
Akomfrah, John, dir. *Seven Songs for Malcolm X*. Black Audio Film Collective, 1993.
Bagwell, Orlando, dir. *Malcolm X: Make It Plain*. PBS, 1994.
Baldwin, James, Malcolm X, and Laverne McCummings, contribs. *Black Muslims vs. the Sit-Ins*. Aired April 25, 1961, on WBAI. Pacifica Radio Archives (BB5322).
Baraka, Amiri, and James E. Hinton, dirs. *The New-Ark*. Harlem Audio Visual, 1968. Harvard Film Archive, James E. Hinton Collection.
Bethune, Lebert, dir. *Malcolm X: Struggle for Freedom*. Documentary film. Paris, 1964.
Cobb, William Jelani. "Castro: A Friend to Americans of Color?" Interview by Ed Gordon. August 25, 2006. National Public Radio. https://www.npr.org/templates/story/story.php?storyId=5709613.
Farrakhan, Louis. "The Swan Song." Saviours' Day Address, Mosque Maryam, Chicago (February 27, 2022).
Hampton, Henry. *Eyes on the Prize II: America at the Racial Crossroads 1965–85*. "Sonia Sanchez Interview." Aired March 7, 1989, PBS, Blackside.
Hansberry, Lorraine, James Baldwin, and Langston Hughes, contribs. *The Negro in American Culture*. WBAI TV, recording/bb3297. January 10, 1961.
Hansberry, Lorraine, James Baldwin, and Langston Hughes, contribs. "The Negro Writer in America." *The Negro in American Culture*. WBAI Radio, January 1, 1961. Walter J. Brown Media Archives & Peabody Awards Collection at the University of Georgia. https://americanarchive.org/catalog/cpb-aacip-526-901zc7ss52.
Holiday, Harmony. "Disappearing Archives: Sun Ra and Henry Dumas, Recorded in Conversation." *Lit Hub*, June 10, 2019. https://lithub.com/disappearing-archives-sun-ra-and-henry-dumas-recorded-in-conversation/.
Hughes, Langston. "Testimony of Langston Hughes (Accompanied by His Counsel, Frank D. Reeves) before the Senate Permanent Subcommittee on Investigations of the Committee on Government Operations." *NPR*, March 24, 1953. https://legacy.npr.org/programs/atc/features/2003/may/mccarthy/hughes.html.
King, Martin Luther, Jr. "After Civil Rights: Black Power." Interview by Sanders Vanocur. May 8, 1967. NBC News. https://www.nbcnews.com/video/martin-luther-king-jr-speaks-with-nbc-news-11-months-before-assassination-1202163779741.

King, Woodie, dir. *Death of a Prophet: The Last Day of Malcolm X*. TV movie, 1981.
Lee, Spike, dir. *Malcolm X*. Warner Brothers, 1992.
Malcolm X. "Eleanor Fischer Interviews Malcolm X." 1961. WNYC. https://www.wnyc.org/story/87636-remembering-malcolm-x-rare-interviews-and-audio.
Megan Thee Stallion. "Savage." In *Saturday Night Live*, with Beyoncé. 2020. https://www.youtube.com/watch?v=CTpilDQXYro.
Megan Thee Stallion. "Why I Speak Up for Black Women" [op-doc]. *New York Times*, October 13, 2020. https://www.nytimes.com/2020/10/13/opinion/megan-thee-stallion-black-women.html.
Morrison, Toni. "Toni Morrison Interview with John Callaway." *WTTW*. Aired 1977, on PBS.
Nemiroff, Robert, dir. *Lorraine Hansberry Speaks Out: Art and the Black Revolution*. Harper Audio / Caedmon, 1972.
Olsson, Göran Hugo, dir. *The Black Power Mixtape 1967–1975*. IFC Films, 2011.
Sharif, Ayanna, dir. *WUDU: A Short Film*. 2019. https://www.youtube.com/watch?v=kDCebx8wuSs.
Sulaiman, Amir, dir. *Laying Flowers, Setting Fires*. True + Living Media, 2020. https://www.youtube.com/watch?v=fYogdFvotho; https://sapelosquare.com/2020/11/24/laying-flowers-setting-fires-amir-sulaiman.

INDEX

360°, 237–39; *360 Degrees of Power* by Sister Souljah 250; "360 Degreez of Black Art" by Samy Alim, 250; 360° Poetry Night with Justice (Newark), 17, 157; as a cipher, 44; in the *Supreme Mathematics* of the Five Percenters, 44; *three hundred and sixty degrees of blackness comin at you* by Sonia Sanchez, 19, 44, 238

Abdul Hamid, Sufi: in *Harlem: Negro Metropolis*, 53; in Ishmael Reed's *Mumbo Jumbo* (as Abdul Sufi Hamid), 54

Abdul Khabeer, Suʻad, 31, 120, 121, 162, 164, 186

Abernathy, Fundi (Billy), 246, 247

Abraham, Alton, 91

adhan (call to prayer), 20, 40, 41, 257; "The Call (A Solo from the West)," by Askia Muhammad Touré, 257; "The Call," by Tariq Touré, 260; in *Daughters of the Dust* (film), dir. Julie Dash, 257–59; of Bilal ibn Rabah, 10, 15, 166; illustrations by Abdul Rahman, 39, 258; in *Meccan Openings* by Amir Sulaiman, 256, 257; in *The New-Ark* (film), dir. Amiri Baraka, 257; in *al-Risala* of Ibn Abi Zayd al-Qayrawani, 257; at the World's Fair in Chicago in 1893, 254; in *WUDU* (short film), dir. Ayanna Sharif, 259. *See also the individual artists*

aesthetics: African diasporic, 7; Black, 63, 215, 237, 243, 250, 260; Islamic, 58, 152; white, 55

African Free School, 33, 181, 197, 198, 199, 202, 227, 249

Afro-American Festival of the Arts, 65

Afrofuturism, 28, 72, 85, 87, 92, 96, 97; *Afrofuturism: A History of Black Futures* exhibit, 97; Black Kirby (Stacy Robinson and Jack Jennings), 85; Muhammad-Ali, Khaalidah, 97; Nafis, Angel, 97; Nelson, Alondra, 72, 82, 87; Samatar, Sofia, 8, 40; Taylor, Vanessa, 97; and Yakub teaching, 74; Youngquist, Paul, 94. *See also* Akomfrah, John; Baraka, Amiri; Black Panthers; Cheatam, Safiyah; Lavender, Isiah; Mothership; Sun Ra; Touré, Askia Muhammad

Ahmad, Muhammad (Max Stanford), 7; and the Revolutionary Action Movement (RAM), 23, 61, 155

Aidi, Hisham, 5, 16, 19, 109, 110, 117, 121

Aireen, Dara, 30, 34

Akomfrah, John: *The Last Angel of History* (film), 97; poet figure in *Last Angel*, 5; *Seven Songs for Malcolm*, 14–15, 256

Ali, Dusé Mohamed: Black Nationalism, 53; Pan-Africanism, 57

Ali, Muhammad, 97, 105, 155, 157, 158, 298n43

Ali, Noble Drew, 26, 53, 57, 58, 179

Ali, Zaheer, 18

Alim, Samy, 41, 121, 209, 217, 218, 250

Allahu akbar, 3, 6, 39, 40, 161, 164, 175, 244, 245; in John Coltrane illustration by Abdul Rahman, 39; in *Meccan Openings* by Amir Sulaiman, 256; in the Newark uprisings, 178, 187

al-Amin, Jamil Abdullah (H. Rap Brown), 209
Alhamisi, Ahmed Akinwole (Lawrence Edward Graham, Jr.), 3, 248, 250
Allah Temple of Islam. *See* Nation of Islam
The American Negro Writer and His Roots, 65, 134, 142
American Society of African Culture, 61, 65, 134
Ancient Arabic Order of the Nobles of the Mystic Shrine (white Shriners), 56, 274n18; Mosque of Mecca Temple in New York City, 55
Ancient Egyptian Arabic Order Nobles Mystic Shrine of North and South America and Its Jurisdictions (Black Shriners), 53, 55, 254; Mecca Temple (Washington, DC), 56, 274n18
Angelou, Maya, 66, 141, 203, 235; in Ghana, 126, 135, 291n13; *I Know Why the Caged Bird Sings*, 169, 170; UN protests, 126, 137
Apple Cores columns in *DownBeat*, 184, 185
Arabic, 3, 12, 25, 40, 43, 58, 74, 93, 107, 144, 151, 152, 153, 156, 199, 227, 228, 247, 251, 252, 253, 256, 258, 274n18. *See also* Jackmon, Marvin X
al-atlal (traces, remains), 3, 6
audiovisuality: in Islamic art, 247; in the mixed media of the BAM, 245–47; "sound vision," 11, 255; and Sun Ra's "sound images," 11, 96, 255, 260, 284n127
Ayler, Albert, 64, 183, 243

Baldwin, James, 126, 128, 138, 143, 144, 157, 189, 254; *The Fire Next Time*, 125, 127, 131, 138–39, 168; and Malcolm X, 138; and police brutality, 143; "A Negro Assays the Negro Mood" (UN protests 1961), 137–38; WBAI panel "The Negro in American Culture," 126, 129, 131–32, 133. *See also* Hansberry, Lorraine (burning house)
Bambara, Toni Cade, 196, 203, 204
Bandung (world/spirit), 23, 133, 135
al-Banna, Hasan, 24
Baraka, Amina (Sylvia Wilson), 3, 4, 156, 180, 181, 185, 186, 198, 220, 225, 227, 249, 254; author's interviews with, 18; *Black Journal* TV appearance, 199; feminism and Black Power, 197, 200–02; and Nation of Islam, 14, 180, 184, 234, 242; partnership with Amiri Baraka (LeRoi Jones), 18, 24, 73, 152, 179, 180, 182, 183–84, 187, 189, 192–93, 196–97, 198, 204, 219, 241; *Songs for the Masses*, 200, 306n103; "Sortin' Out," 202–03, 204–05. *See also* African Free School; Duka Ujamaa; Shani Baraka Women's Resource Center; United Sisters
Baraka, Amiri (LeRoi Jones, Ameer Baraka), 3, 12, 15, 22, 37, 38, 40, 41, 44, 64, 109, 130, 137, 143, 156, 163, 166, 180, 182, 186, 187, 190, 197, 203, 204, 219, 223, 225, 240, 246, 247, 250; Afrofuturism, 97; *The Autobiography of LeRoi Jones*, 140, 178–79, 182–83, 184, 186, 187, 193, 196, 198, 202–03; *A Black Mass*, 24, 26, 27, 30, 32, 33, 62, 72–75, 76, 77, 78, 82, 87, 89, 91, 93–95, 96, 174, 175, 179, 180, 183, 185, 186, 259; *Black Magic*, 95, 215, 241; "The Changing Same," 64, 103, 243, 257; "From the Book of Life," 193–94, 196; "Islam and Black Art," 152, 195–96, 203, 248; "Love is the Presence of No Enemy," 192, 193, 248; and Nation of Islam, 14, 242; *The New-Ark* (film), 26, 179, 181, 198, 257; Newark (also New Ark), 26, 27, 30, 33, 34, 44, 67, 73–75, 91, 96, 143, 178–82; *SOS: Poems 1961–2013*, 251; *Spirit Reach*, 178, 189, 190, 193, 194–95, 248. *See also* Black Arts Repertory Theatre School (BARTS); Baraka, Amiri, and Larry Neal, eds. (*Black Fire*); Jihad Productions
Baraka, Amiri, and Larry Neal, eds.: *Black Fire: An Anthology of Afro-American Writing*, 24, 25, 29, 35, 38, 65, 67, 73, 93, 124, 128, 140, 141, 142, 150, 168, 175, 184; *Black Fire* afterword by Neal, 73; *Black Fire* foreword (1968) by Baraka, 93; *Black Fire* new introduction (2013) by Baraka, 7
Baraka, Kimako, 235; Kimako Blues Café, 202
Baraka, Obalaji, 18, 156, 182, 186, 187, 192, 198, 199, 201, 304n40
Baraka, Ras, 180, 192, 198, 201, 203, 205
Baraka, Shani, 18, 204; Shani Baraka Women's Resource Center, 18, 181, 202
basmallah, 6, 256; in Amir Sulaiman's *Laying Flowers, Setting Fires*, 144, 251–52; in Amir Sulaiman's *Meccan Openings*, 252; in *dhikr* (remembrance or recitation), 252; letter *baa* standing in for, 144, 251; Marvin X's *Black Man Listen* [as *basmallah*], 164; in *The Moslem Sunrise*, 58. *See also* frontispiece image
bebop. *See* jazz

INDEX

Belafonte, Harry: and King, Martin Luther, Jr., 105, 111, 143–44; and the Montgomery Bus Boycott, 112; in the *New York Amsterdam News*, 110–11. *See also* calypso
Bey, Dawoud, 247
bioscientific/biomedical experimentation. *See* Yakub teaching
birth control, 192, 282n95; "Birth Control Death Plan," 88; and genocide, 34, 88–89; in *Muhammad Speaks*, 34; and the Nation of Islam, 83, 88–89, 209; and Sanchez, Sonia, 209; and Scott, Sister Clotelle (Ameenah Rasul), 209. *See also* eugenics
Black Arts Repertory Theatre School (BARTS), 23, 30, 44, 73, 141, 184
Black Arts West Theater. *See* Jackmon, Marvin X
black bird: "13 Ways of Looking at a Paloma Negra" by Antonio Lopez, 171; *The Black Bird* (parable by Marvin X), 33, 152, 167, 168, 170; Black Bird Press of Marvin X, 168; "Blackbird" by Beyoncé, 171; "Blackbird" by Nina Simone, 167, 170; *Fly Blackbird* musical, 167; *Songs of a Black Bird* by Carolyn Rodgers, 170; "Thirteen Ways of Looking at a Blackbird" by Wallace Stevens, 171. *See also* Angelou, Maya; Dunbar, Paul Lawrence
Black feminism, 196–97, 201, 204, 206, 235–36. *See also* Baraka, Amina
Black fire, 37, 127, 140, 142. *See also*: *Black Prophetic Fire*; *The Fire Next Time*
Black Fire: An Anthology of Afro-American Writing. See Baraka, Amiri and Larry Neals, eds.
Black Kirby, 85.
Black Lives Matter, 7, 121, 128, 143, 144, 238, 251, 260
Black magic, 37, 61, 62, 93, 195, 243; in "Black Magic Music/A Love Ritual" by Askia Muhammad Touré, 304n45; in *A Black Mass* by Amiri Baraka (LeRoi Jones), 89–90, 93, 95, 185; in *A Blues Book for Blue Black Magical Women* by Sonia Sanchez, 214–15; "Narrative of the Black Magicians" by Larry Neal, 62, 64, 260; as necromancy, 241
Black Magic (1969). *See* Baraka, Amiri
Black Magic (1928). *See* Morand, Paul
A Black Mass. See Baraka, Amiri. *See also under* Yakub teaching

Black NewArk (newspaper), 179, 186
Black No More. See Schuyler, George
Black Panther imagery: Black Panther film franchise, 85; Jack Kirby, 85; and the Lowndes County Freedom Organization, 85
Black Panthers (Black Panther Party), 42, 44, 151, 155, 157, 165, 166, 168, 172
Black Power, 157, 159, 163, 164, 165, 179, 180, 181, 182, 187, 196, 197, 198, 201, 202, 203. 204, 210, 211, 213, 219, 220, 235, 236, 237, 241, 249, 260
Black Prophetic Fire (Cornel West), 128
The Black Scholar: Journal of Black Studies and Research, 155, 156, 199, 220, 221, 226, 234
Black Student Union, 154, 223. *See also* Negro Students Association
Black World, 196. *See also Negro Digest*
Blakey, Art, 108; Art Blakey's Jazz Messengers, 37, 38, 108
Blount, Herman Poole. *See* Sun Ra
Bonner, Marita, and *The Purple Flower*, 54
Broadside Press, 26, 160, 219
Brown, Hubert Gerold (H. Rap Brown). *See* al-Amin, Jamil Abdullah
Brown, Marion, 27, 75, 183, 184, 185
Bureau for Social Hygiene. *See* eugenics
Burroughs, Margaret, 235, 250

Caldwell, Ben, "Islamic Vision," 37
call to prayer. See *adhan*
calypso: and Belafonte, Harry, 105; and Farrakhan, Louis (Louis Eugene Walcott), 103. *See also* ska
Canada, 151, 160, 166, 169, 177
Caribbean, 4, 9, 16, 24, 105, 119
Castro, Fidel, 134–35, 157, 294n62
Césaire, Aimé, 43, 76, 89
"Changing Same." *See* Baraka, Amiri
Cheatam, Safiyah, 72, 97
Chicago, 3, 10, 24, 53, 56, 91, 92, 125, 138, 157, 247, 248, 254
Clarke, John Henrik, 65, 141, 251; *Malcolm X: The Man and His Times*, 7–8, 14; "The New Afro-American Nationalism," 66; and Organization of Afro-American Unity (OAAU) charter, 126
Clay, Cassius. *See* Muhammad Ali
Cleaver, Eldridge, 154, 155, 156
Cliff, Jimmy, 120, 290n100

Coltrane, John, 37, 38, 39, 64, 109, 183, 195, 225, 243, 244, 259; *Ascension*, 184, 247; "Coltrane poem," 14; "A Love Supreme," 38; *A Love Supreme* and liner notes, 107, 241, 244, 245, 247; Abdul Rahman illustration of, 39
Combahee River Collective, 199, 220, 235
Committee for the Negro in the Arts, 61, 65, 134
Committee for a Unified Newark (CFUN), 180, 198, 199, 234. *See also* Mumininas
Congress of Black Writers and Artists, 51
Cordero, Dr. Ana Livia, 133, 169
countermemory, 72
counterpublic: Black, 52, 58, 59, 104, 127, 128, 133; Islamic, 33–34, 52, 58, 104
Countee Cullen Library, 44, 238, 239
Cox, Renée, 97
Crookshank, F. G., 83
Cuba, 61, 134, 136, 142, 162
Cultural Association for Women of African Heritage, 137
Curtis, Edward E., IV, xi, xiii, 72, 88

daʿwa (proselytization/call to Islam), 19, 20, 40, 41, 103, 106, 109
Dash, Julie: *Daughters of the Dust* (film), 255, 257–59, 260
Davis, Angela, 7, 88, 145, 171, 216
Davis, Miles, 183
Davis, Ossie, 30, 140–41; and *Death of a Prophet*, 30; and *Purlie Victorious*, 126, 136
Dee, Ruby, 126, 129, 140–41, 235
Delany, Martin, 53, 67, 68
Delany, Samuel, 97, 223
devil, 25, 86, 89, 165, 173, 174, 224, 233, 256; blue-eyed, 71; crack cocaine, 173; white, 27, 32, 37, 160
DiPrima, Diane, 183, 215, 242
Doris Duke Foundation for Islamic Art: Building Bridges, xiii, 17, 261
DownBeat, 27, 74, 184, 185
dream, American, 125, 131, 134, 136, 138–39, 142, 143, 277n70. *See also* nightmare
Du Bois, Shirley Graham, 126, 135, 214, 215, 242
Du Bois, W. E. B., 11, 37, 53, 54, 59, 68, 129, 130, 133, 135, 223, 244; "Criteria for Negro Art," 60; *The Negro American Family*, 221; "A Negro Nation within the Nation," 68, 69; at Second Pan-African Congress, 85; "The Sorrow Songs," 64, 116, 243; *The Souls of Black Folk*, 116
Duka Ujamaa, 181, 202
Dunbar, Paul Laurence, 59; "Sympathy" and caged bird image, 169–70
DuVall, Taiwo. *See* Shabazz, Taiwo DuVall

The East (cultural center), 34, 248; Weusi, Jitu (founder of), 34
Egypt, 12, 24, 28, 30, 44, 107, 142, 161, 165, 174, 248, 271n48
esoterica, 24, 80, 85, 94, 96, 256
eugenics, 59, 71, 77, 78, 80, 89, 281n67; in *A Black Mass*, 76, 87; British Eugenics Society, 81; Bureau for Social Hygiene (est. John D. Rockefeller), 82; Crookshank, F. G., 83; Eugenics Record Office, 81; and experimentation on human subjects, 72, 90; and the "germ plasm," 79, 81; Knight, Michael Muhammad, 80; and medical racism, 83; Morand, Paul, 84–85; in popular culture, 71–72, 76, 82, 86; as pseudoscience, 71, 72, 83, 90; and the "Race Betterment Foundation" of Dr. John Harvey Kellogg; Stanley, Dr. Leo, 80; and sterilization, 71, 82, 88, 90, 209; in the *To-day and To-morrow* series, 71, 83; and the Yakub teaching, 70, 71, 72, 77, 86, 88–89. *See also* birth control; genocide
Eurocentrism: in American school system, 9, 16, 22, 25, 95, 150, 152, 153, 155, 162; in pedagogies, 3, 28, 53, 155
Eyes on the Prize, 214, 218, 237

fabulation: *Afro-Fabulations* of Tavia Nyong'o, 13; critical fabulation of Saidiya Hartman, 12, 13, 241, 255, 313n3
Fanon, Frantz, 23, 25–26, 43, 65, 208; "the awakening of Islam," 52, 66; in *Black Fire*, 67–68; in Black Study groups, 156–57; and decolonization, 52; the language of the colonizer, 175; "On National Culture," 51–52; "On Violence," 43; and religion, 23; and "Song of Fire" by Askia Muhammad Touré, 36; "To Fanon" by Sonia Sanchez, 43; *Les damnés de la terre (The Wretched of the Earth)*, 51, 157
Farid, Bilal, 37, 44, 259; *Sun Lady for All Seasons* by Sonia Sanchez, 42; *This is Madness* by The Last Poets, 43
Farmer, James, 138

Farrakhan, Louis, 75, 103–06, 110, 115, 117, 118, 122, 139, 209, 225, 234, 242; "A White Man's Heaven is a Black Man's Hell," 30, 111, 114, 116, 118, 120, 123, 125, 162, 285n9; "Crack Cocaine: The Great Conspiracy," 173; Million Man March, 121; *Orgena*, 74, 103
Faruk, 152, 196, 248
al-fatiha (the opening), 26, 256; *The Opening* of Amir Sulaiman, 252; "The Opening" of Askia Muhammad Touré, 38, 244, 252; of the Qur'an, 26, 38, 244, 252
Fauset, Arthur Huff, 61
Fauset, Jessie, 78
fire. *See* Black fire
The Fire Next Time. See Baldwin, James
First Negro Writers Conference, 65, 134, 135
Five Percenters, 44, 233, 239, 250, 256
The Floating Bear, 183
frequency, 245, 248, 249, 259. *See also* vibration

Galwash, Ahmad A., 32
Garrett, Jimmy, 154, 223
Garvey, Marcus, 17, 30, 36, 37, 53, 56, 57, 66, 67, 68, 69, 105, 177, 244, 274n19, 286n20
Gayle, Addison, *The Black Aesthetic*, 65
genocide, 34, 71, 86, 192, 271n48. *See also* eugenics
Ghana, 14, 38, 126, 134, 135, 136, 169
al-Ghazali, Abu Hamid, 167
al-Ghazali, Zaynab, 24
Gilmore, John, 91
Graham, Lawrence Edward. *See* Alhamisi, Ahmed Akinwole
Great Migration, 56, 62
"God's Angry Men." *See* Malcolm X

Haley, Alex: *The Autobiography of Malcolm X* (coauthor), 106, 125; *Roots*, 177, 257, 259
al-hamdulillah, 3, 6, 37, 40, 44, 184, 186, 188, 187; in *The Autobiography of LeRoi Jones* by Amiri Baraka, 187; in *Alhomdullilah!* by Yusuf Rahman, 186; in "Hum-Allah-Hum-Allah-Hum-Allah" by Pharoah Sanders, 186; in "Ima Talken Bout the Nation of Islam" by Sonia Sanchez, 42
Hansberry, Lorraine, 65, 128, 130, 132, 141, 142; and Baldwin, James, 126, 137; and the burning house, 134, 138, 140, 143, 144, 145; and Malcolm X, 126, 127, 130, 135–36; *Raisin in the Sun*, 129, 130; WBAI panel "The Negro in American Culture," 126, 131, 133, 134
Hare, Nathan, 44, 154, 155, 176, 223
Harlem, 3, 18, 24, 38, 40, 55, 56, 101, 106, 109, 134, 135, 152, 166, 182, 183, 217, 248
Harlem Drug Fighters Union, 198
Harlem Freedom Rally, 135
Harlem Renaissance (the "New Negro Arts Movement" or the "Negro Renaissance"), 55, 59, 61, 63, 69, 71, 73, 78, 84, 97, 128, 143, 219, 243, 250
Harlem Writers Guild, 61, 126, 137, 141
Hartman, Saidiya, 178, 194, 207, 215, 221, 223, 228, 255
Hentoff, Nat, 101, 126, 131
hijra, 151, 159, 161; to Aksum, 15; *hijri* calendar, 3, 28, 37, 159, 230, 244; to Madina, 159, 253; in Marvin X's writings, 159; El Muhajir (etymological connection), 151, 159; in the Qur'an, 161–62
Hinton, Johnson X, 29, 102, 112, 122, 128
hip-hop, 16; Abdul Khabeer, Su'ad, 249–250; Alim, Samy 44, 239, 260; and the BAM, 24, 27; hip-hop nation, 243; pedagogies of, 214; and Spady, James, 121, 218, 239, 260
Holmes, Rayshon, 181
Howard University, 155
Hughes, Langston, 59, 60, 65, 106, 223, 244, 254; and Hansberry, Lorraine, 131; *Montage of a Dream Deferred*, 131, 134; "The Negro Artist and the Racial Mountain," 60; Schuyler-Hughes debate (*The Nation*), 60, 61; WBAI panel "The Negro in American Culture," 126, 129, 131–32, 133
Huxley, Aldous, 81
Huxley, Julian, 81

Ibn al-'Arabi, Muhi ad-Din (also Ibn 'Arabi), 253; in "From the Book of Life" by Amiri Baraka, 196; in "Islam and Black Art" interview with Amiri Baraka, 196; and *Laying Flowers, Setting Fires* by Amir Sulaiman, 251; *Meccan Openings*, 252; and *Meccan Openings* by Amir Sulaiman, 251; *Tarjuman al-Ashwaq* (Translator of Desires), 252
Ibn Sori, Abd al-Rahman Ibrahima, 160
I Know Why the Caged Bird Sings. See Angelou, Maya

ijtihad. See *jihad*
Iman, Yusef (Joseph Washington), 3, 18, 22, 30, 34, 35, 38, 227, 249; "Lord Make Me Understand," 191; "Love Your Enemy," 29, 36, 162, 193; *Something Black*, 29
"Islam and Black Art: An Interview with LeRoi Jones." See Baraka, Amiri; Faruk; Marvin X
isra' and *mi'raj* (the Prophet's night journey and ascension into heaven): in Louis Farrakhan's account, 75; in Samia Idroos's prayer rug, 72; and the Mother Plane, 72, 265n37

Jackmon, Darrel Patrick (Abdul Ibn El Muhajir), 161, 174
Jackmon, Marvin X, 3, 22, 24, 256; Academy of da Corner, 17, 149, 173, 176; addiction, 153–54, 172–74; Arabic language and writing, 151, 160–64, 166, 174; Black Arts West Theater, 150, 151, 156; *The Black Bird*, 152, 167, 168, 170; *Black Bird News & Reviews*, 167; Black Bird Press, 168, 170; Black Educational Theater (San Francisco), 175; *Black Man Listen*, 160, 164; Black Panthers, 18, 151, 157, 165, 166; "Burn, Baby, Burn," 142, 168; Canada (Toronto), 151, 159, 160, 165, 166, 169, 177; Cleaver, Eldridge, 154; as conscientious objector, 158–59; *Fly to Allah*, 152, 159, 160, 162, 166–67; "Islam and Black Art," 152, 195–96, 203, 248; Juneteenth event (Marin County, 2019), 17, 176–77; on Malcolm X, 170; Muhammad, Elijah, 14, 23, 29, 30, 36, 38, 65, 165, 242; Nation of Islam, 154, 156, 157–58, 165, 174, 202; as *Negro Digest* interviewer, 26; Newton, Huey, 154, 172, 173; *One Day in the Life*, 154, 173; poetry tour, 17; *Resurrection of the Dead*, 95, 152, 174; at San Francisco State College, 23, 44, 149, 159; *Somethin' Proper* (autobiography), 150, 154, 167, 172, 175, 176; *Sudan Rajuli Samia*, 160; and Sun Ra, 171
Jafa, Arthur: Black visual intonation, 259; polyventiality, 255
jazz, 16, 17, 37, 38, 64, 95, 104, 106, 109, 115, 117–19, 120, 121, 140, 169, 183, 184–85, 203, 225; bebop, 4, 33, 94, 108, 195, 243, 244; jazzoetry (*This Is Madness*, album by The Last Poets), 43, 240; prosody and poetry, 20, 33, 36, 41, 60, 62, 63, 94, 244, 250
Jazz Arts Society, 27, 75, 184, 185, 202
Jennings, Jack, 185. *See also* Afrofuturism
jihad, 3, 5, 27, 29, 32, 35, 40, 41, 46, 162, 252, 256; in *Black Fire*, Baraka and Neal, eds., 24, 25; *ijtihad* (independent reasoning or intellectual jihad), 25, 45, 47; in "Ima Talken Bout the Nation of Islam" by Sonia Sanchez, 24, 42–43; in *Inside the Gender Jihad* by amina wadud, 24, 45; *al-Jihad al-Akbar* [The Greater Jihad] by Ruhollah Khomeini, 24; *jihad bi-l-lisaan* (jihad of the tongue), 24; *jihad fi sabil Allah* (jihad on the path of God), 26; *jihad al-nafs* (jihad of the self or soul), 20, 23, 25, 26; *jihad al-qalam* (jihad of the pen), 20, 22, 25, 33, 158; in "Jihad!: Toward A Black National Credo" by Askia Muhammad Touré, 24
Jihad Productions, 24, 26, 29, 32, 33, 37, 40, 67, 73, 158, 168, 179, 180, 191, 193, 198, 199, 220
Johnson, James Weldon, 78, 104
Jolson, Al, and minstrelsy, 61
Jones, Hettie, 183
Jones, LeRoi. *See* Amiri Baraka
Jones, Meta DuEwa, 104, 107, 244, 246; "riffs, revisions, and remembrances," 94, 117; "rituals of recital," 104, 255

Karenga, Maulana Ron and the US Organization, 219, 254. *See also* Mumininas
Kawaida doctrine, 198, 199; US School of Afroamerican Culture, 33, 163
Khomeini, Ayatollah Ruhollah. *See under* jihad
Killens, John Oliver, 156; First Negro Writers Conference, 65; and Harlem Writers Guild, 141; and Organization of Afro-American Unity (OAAU) charter, 126
King, Martin Luther, Jr., 127; assassination, 60, 143; burning house imagery, 127, 128, 134, 143, 144; "Give Us the Ballot" speech, 29; Belafonte, Harry 105, 111, 143–44; "I Have a Dream" speech, 134; in *Laying Flowers, Setting Fires* by Amir Sulaiman, 254, 260; "loving your enemies," 29, 111–12; Malcolm X, 29, 100, 103, 110, 118, 138; Montgomery Bus Boycott, 29, 110; Prayer Pilgrimage for Freedom, 29, 112; *Strength to Love*, 29, 30
Kirby, Jack, 85
Knight, Etheridge, 44, 277n85
Knight, Michael Muhammad, 16, 72, 80, 93

Larsen, Nella (*Passing*, 1929), 78
The Last Poets, 34, 43, 240
Lateef, Yusef (*Repository of Scales and Melodic Patterns*, autobiography), 195
Lavender, Isiah, 81; *Afrofuturism Rising*, 75; "blackground," 77, 78, 97; *Race in American Science Fiction*, 77, 87; and science fiction, 84, 86, 87
Liberation Committee for Africa, 137
Lincoln, Abbey, 36, 66, 137, 169, 179, 183, 186, 235, 302n6, 303n33. *See also* Roach, Max
Little, Malcolm. *See* Malcolm X
"Lost Found Muslim Lessons," 78
Lowndes County Freedom Organization, 85
Louis X. *See* Louis Farrakhan
"Love Your Enemy." *See* Iman, Yusef
Lumumba, Patrice, 66, 126, 137, 141, 143, 157

Malaika, 163
Malcolm X, 7, 13, 14, 23, 25, 29, 37, 38, 62, 63, 65–66, 67, 92, 101, 114, 117, 128, 186, 212, 214, 219; assassination, 29, 30, 38, 60, 62, 73, 94, 139, 140, 141, 142, 180, 183, 242, 254; Baldwin, James, 126–27, 138; and censure by Elijah Muhammad, 116–17; Coltrane, John, 183; *Death of a Prophet: Last Day of Malcolm X* (dir. Woodie King), 14, 30, 38, 270–71n46; Du Bois, W. E. B., 65, 135; Farmer, James, 138; Farrakhan, Louis, 104, 105, 115, 118; as "fire prophet," 130, 142; *For Malcolm* (ed. Dudley Randall and Margaret Burroughs), 7, 14, 65, 142, 217, 254, 270; "God's Angry Men," *New York Amsterdam News* columns, 29, 102, 103, 105, 109, 110–13, 115–16, 118, 120, 122, 125, 135; "God's Judgement of White America" (speech), 36, 139, 141; Hansberry, Lorraine, 126–27, 130, 135, 140, 141; imagery related to master's house on fire, 125, 127, 135, 137–44, 167–68; Iman, Yusef, 30; and influence on music, poetry, and film 119, 120–23, 218, 254; Jarvis, Malcolm, 107; King, Martin Luther, Jr., 29, 111–12, 134, 144, 145; "the legacy of malcolm x, and the coming of the black nation" by LeRoi Jones, 67; letters from prison, 106–08; *Make it Plain* (film, dir. Orlando Bagwell), 14; *Malcolm X: In Our Own Image* (ed. Joe Wood), 8, 15; Malcolm X Project at Columbia, xiv, 8, 109; *Malcolm X: The Struggle for Freedom* (dir. Lebert Bethune), 38, 270–71n46; the "Malcolm poem," 14, 65, 221, 230, 266n47; Mayfield, Julian, 134, 136, 141; "Mr. X" (track) by Max Roach, 36, 109, 119; in prison, 65, 68; Rustin, Bayard, 127, 135; Sanchez, Sonia, 209, 216–17, 218, 219, 223–24, 234; *Seven Songs for Malcolm* (dir. John Akomfrah), 14–15, 256; "Twenty Million Black People in a Political, Economic and Mental Prison" (speech), 167; "White Man's Heaven Is a Black Man's Hell," 104, 105, 109, 115.
Malcolm X and Alex Haley, *The Autobiography of Malcolm X*, 115, 124–25, 130, 144, 188, 210
Marable, Manning, 5, 104, 109, 117
Martin, Trayvon, 7, 128, 219
Marvin X. *See* Jackmon, Marvin X
al-Maududi, Abu al-'Ala, 24
Mayfield, Julian, 12, 145, 169; Communist Party member, 134; exile in Ghana with Dr. Ana Livia Cordero, 133–34, 135, 136; First Negro Writers Conference, 65, 134; "Into the Mainstream and Oblivion," 133, 169; Malcolm X, 126, 136, 141; Williams, Robert F., 136
McKay, Claude, 53, 54, 61
Mecca, 3, 6, 12, 28, 32, 41, 108, 159, 166, 214, 227, 229, 243, 248, 252, 253, 256, 259, 260; "Harlem: Mecca of the New Negro," 56, 167, 254; *In the Mecca* by Gwendolyn Brooks, 254; Mecca Flats, 254; Mecca Temple, (Washington, DC), 56; Mosque of Mecca Temple (New York City), 55; "Road to Mecca" in Marvin X's *Somethin' Proper*, 154, 172
Meccan Openings. *See under* Ibn 'Arabi
Meccan Openings. *See under* Sulaiman, Amir
memory: collective memory, 82, 87; counter-memory, 97; historical memory, 4, 114, 117, 256; "riffs, revisions, and remembrances" of Meta DuEwa Jones, 4, 94, 117, 256; poetic memory, 6; tonal memory, 63, 116
mental death (white brainwashing), 151, 154
Message to the Blackman in America. *See under* Muhammad, Elijah
metalanguage, 163, 272n76
Montgomery Bus Boycott. 29, 110, 112
Moorish Science Temple of America (MSTA), 8, 55, 57, 91, 179, 247
Morand, Paul (*Black Magic*, 1928), 84–85
Moten, Fred, 60, 70, 150, 163, 166, 171, 175, 178–79, 182, 194

motherhood, 206, 213, 215, 220, 221, 307n3
Mother Plane, 71–72, 77, 84, 265n37
Mothership, 72, 97: "The Force is Female," (textile by Samira Idroos), 72; *Locations of the M/othership* (film dir. by Jamika Ajalon), 72; *Mothership: Voyage Into Afrofuturism* (Oakland exhibit), 72; Parliament's *Mothership Connection*, 72, 97. *See also* Afrofuturism
Muhammad, Sister Clara, 220; and University of Islam schools (later Sister Clara Muhammad schools), 183, 227
Muhammad, Elijah, 14, 36, 38, 45, 54, 57, 65, 67, 69, 75, 78, 79, 80, 83, 84, 90, 91, 93, 103, 104, 108, 109, 110, 113, 116, 117, 118, 125, 128, 135, 138, 139, 160, 165, 166, 188, 208, 209, 211, 214, 215, 218, 222, 225, 230, 232, 234, 242, 261; as Elijah Poole, 79; *Message to the Blackman in America*, 97–98, 120, 125, 128, 136, 174; *Pittsburgh Courier* column, "Mr. Muhammad Speaks," 83; *Supreme Wisdom*, 29, 91, 114; *Supreme Wisdom Lessons*, 80
Muhammad Speaks, 34, 88, 110, 138, 140, 166, 171; Sonia Sanchez column, 45, 211, 213–14, 225, 226, 227, 229
Muhammad, Wallace Fard, 53, 57, 75–81, 84, 85, 118, 159, 232, 233, 279n42, 280n51, 280n61
Muhammad-Ali, Khaalidah, 97
Mumininas: in the Committee for a Unified Newark (CFUN), 199; and the Combahee River Collective, 200, 220, 235; Kawaida doctrine, 199; *Mwanamke Mwananchi (The Nationalist Woman)* booklet, 199, 200; in "Queens of the Universe" by Sonia Sanchez, 219; in the US Organization, 219
Murray, Sunny, *Sonny's Time Now*, 193
myth science. *See* Sun Ra

Naeem, Abdul Basit, 109–10, 118
Nafis, Angel, 97
Nation of Islam (NOI): Allah Temple of Islam, 7; teachings, 22, 25, 30, 71, 72, 75, 77, 79–80, 82, 88, 91, 93, 95, 97, 113, 114, 195, 126, 162, 175. *See also under* Baraka, Amina; Baraka, Amiri; birth control; Jackmon, Marvin X; Malcolm X; resurrection
Ndegeocello, Meshell, 128
Neal, Larry, 16, 22, 23, 24, 25, 27, 64, 74, 76, 152, 247; "Black American Music" (unfinished ms.), 63; "Black Arts Movement" (essay), 43, 63, 67, 69, 73, 76, 93, 152, 153, 181; "Jihad," 22; "The Narrative of the Black Magicians," 62–64, 260. *See also* Baraka, Amiri, and Larry Neal, eds., *Black Fire*
necromancy, 37, 91, 93, 95, 241; necro (root word), 91–93, 154
necropolitics, 25, 27, 90–91
Negro Digest (became *Black World* in 1970), 26, 195
Negro Students Association, 154
Negro Renaissance. *See* Harlem Renaissance
The New-Ark. *See under* Baraka, Amiri
New Ark (Newark), 26, 96, 182, 183; and Newark, 3, 10, 17, 18, 24, 27, 30, 33, 67, 143, 152, 180, 182, 192–93, 198, 202, 204, 205, 206; in *The Autobiography of LeRoi Jones*, 187–88; uprising/rebellion (1967), 178–79, 184–85, 186, 190. *See also* Spirit House
The New Negro, 55, 60
New Negro Arts Movement. *See* Harlem Renaissance
Newark. *See* New Ark
New Pyramid Productions, 26, 42, 44
Newton, Huey, 18, 85, 154, 172, 173. *See also* Black Panther Party
New York Amsterdam News, 103, 112. *See also under* Malcolm X, "God's Angry Men" columns
nightmare, 138–39, 183; American, 29, 134, 136, 142; and Martin Luther King's dream, 29, 134, 144, 145; "Nightmare" in *The Autobiography of Malcolm X*, 124, 125, 130, 210
Nkrumah, Kwame, 157
Noguchi, Hideyo, syphilis injections, 82, 86, 87, 280n64
Noguchi, Yusaburo, pseudoscientific claims, 83, 86, 87

Oakland, 3, 10, 17, 18, 24, 72, 85, 149, 151, 152, 154, 165, 175
Olugebefola, Ademola, xii, 18, 37, 42, 43–44, 45, 46, 230
On Guard for Freedom, 137
The Opening. *See al-fatiha*
Organization of Afro-American Unity (OAAU), 7, 14, 30, 73, 126. *See also* Clarke, John Henrik; Killens, John Oliver; Malcolm X

Panther Woman (from *Island of Dr. Moreau*), 84, 85. *See also* H. G. Wells.
Parks, Gordon, 247
Peele, Jordan, *Get Out* (film), 86
Pittsburgh Courier. *See* Schuyler, George; Muhammad, Elijah
poiesis: in "Belly of the World" by Saidiya Hartman, 207; "in Black" of R. A. Judy, 5; Sanchez, Sonia, 213, 215; in *Star Logic (a Collection of Poiesis)* of Solayman Idris, 6; in Sun Ra, 96
Poole, Elijah. *See* Muhammad, Elijah
Prayer Pilgrimage for Freedom. *See* King, Martin Luther, Jr.
Présence Africaine, 134
Prince Buster (Cecil Bustamente Campbell), 105; as Ali, Muhammad Yusef, 120
Prince Hall, 56
public sphere (dominant white, Christian American), 55, 57, 60, 189; and the Black counterpublic, 128, 132–33, 218

queens (biblical, Qur'anic, Black power), 163. *See* "Queens of the Universe" under Sanchez; "Harlem Queens" under Marvin X
Qur'an, 3, 15, 25, 242; in *Blues Book* by Sonia Sanchez, 230, 232, 233; in *Daughters of the Dust* (dir. Julie Dash), 260; interpretations of verses, 22–23, 37, 25, 40, 114, 230, 232, 253, 256; in *Love, Gnosis* by Amir Sulaiman, 253–54; in Marvin X's poetry, 151, 158, 160, 161–64, 165, 166; Meccan suras, 231; in the Islamic poetic tradition, 232–33; recitation, 6, 11, 40, 41, 58, 62, 116, 117, 118, 232, 255; in "Study Peace," by Amiri Baraka, 195; Sura Iqra' (96), 166, 230. *See also al-fatiha* (the opening)
Qutb, Sayyid, 24, 271n48

Rahman, Abdul, 18, 37, 39, 40, 259; illustrations of Askia Muhammad Touré's *Songhai!*, 258
Rahman, Yusuf (Ronald Stone), 3, 303n29; *Alhomdullilah!*, 184, 186; "Transcendental Blues," 184, 192
Randall, Dudley, 7, 14, 65, 160, 217, 218, 250
rap, 4, 27, 225
Rasheed, Kameelah Janan, 18
recitation (in BAM aesthetic), 42, 117, 121. *See also under* Jones, Meta DuEwa; Qur'an in Islamic tradition, 15, 40, 104–05

re-citation, 4, 37, 116, 122, 144, 251, 254, 255
Reed, Ishmael (*Mumbo Jumbo*), 54, 70
resurrection, 4, 6, 7, 36, 53, 75, 93, 118, 144, 154, 176, 232, 251, 256, 262; from "mental death," 91, 98, 151; as the Nation of Islam's five principles of belief, 174; *Resurrection of the Dead* by Marvin X, 95, 152, 174–75
revolution: in Africa, Asia, Latin America, 23, 36; armed, 151; Black, 36, 68, 135, 138, 139, 140, 142, 143; Cuban, 127, 134, 137; cultural, 19, 22, 33, 66, 73, 126, 129, 151, 157, 199, 200; *Four Black Revolutionary Plays* by Amiri Baraka, 79; Franz Fanon on, 51; Marvin X on (2019), 127; "Message to the Grassroots" speech, 122; political, 117, 126; "Revolutionary Black Music" by Jimmy Stewart, 37; "Spiritual Internal Revolution," 28; in values, 14, 260
Revolutionary Action Movement (RAM), 23, 61, 155; and Max Stanford (Muhammad Ahmad), 7
Roach, Max, 30, 34, 183; "Däähoud," 109; "Mr. X," 36, 109; "Triptych: Prayer/Protest/Peace," (with Abbey Lincoln), 186; *We Insist: Max Roach's Freedom Now Suite*, 36, 186
Robinson, Stacy. *See* Afrofuturism
Robinson, Sylvia. *See* Amina Baraka
Rockefeller Institute for Medical Research. *See* eugenics
Rockefeller, John D., and Bureau for Social Hygiene. *See* eugenics
Rustin, Bayard, 112; and Malcolm X on WBAI, 127, 135

sacred: community, 4; *Sacred Drift* by Peter Lamborn Wilson, 5; sacred labor, 230; sacred mosques, 165; sacred music, 117; sacred words and texts, 45, 58, 118, 166
as-salaamu alaykum, 3, 256, 274n18; in "Harlem Queen" by Marvin X, 183; in Malcolm X's letters (as "As Salaam Alaikum"), 109; in *Meccan Openings* by Amir Sulaiman, 252; in *It's a New Day* by Sonia Sanchez ("As-Salaam-alaikum"), 214
San Francisco State College (SFSC), 23, 44, 141, 149, 151, 154, 155, 156, 171, 176, 199, 210, 223, 235
Sanchez, Sonia, 3, 18, 19, 22, 28, 64, 95, 152, 154, 156, 212, 231; *Blues Book for Blue Black Magical Women*, 199, 214, 222, 230–34; *Home Coming*, 44; "Ima Talken Bout the Nation of Islam,"

Sanchez, Sonia (*continued*)
24, 27, 42; *It's a New Day*, 45, 225; as Laila Mannan, 215, 226; in *Muhammad Speaks*, 214, 225, 227, 229; and Nation of Islam, 14, 45, 47, 208–09, 210–11, 213, 224, 225, 232–35, 238, 239; "Queens of the Universe," 199, 219, 221, 222, 224; *Sister Son/ji*, 210; as Sonia 5X, 226; *A Sun Lady for All Seasons Reads Her Poetry*, 43; three hundred and sixty degrees of blackness, 238, 250; *We a BaddDDD People*, 207, 222. See also under Malcolm X

Sanders, Pharoah, 27, 34, 38, 64, 75, 183, 184, 185, 195, 243; "Hum-Allah-Hum-Allah-Hum-Allah," 110, 186, 244, 247; *Jewels of Thought*, 244; *Tauhid*, 242, 244, 247, 248

Schuyler, George, 59; *Black No More*, 73, 77, 78, 82, 83–84, 86, 94, 97; "Negro Art-Hokum," 60–61; *Pittsburgh Courier* column, 83; Schuyler-Hughes debate (*The Nation*), 60, 61

Schuyler, Philippa Duke, 86

science fiction, 70; in analyses of Nation of Islam teachings, 72, 75–76; *Black No More* (George Schuyler), 77, 78; and Finley, Stephen, 71; as a hermeneutical necessity/tool, 71, 73. See also Lavender, Isiah; Wells, H. G.; Yakub teaching (and *A Black Mass*)

scream, as sonic signifier in BAM arts, 178–79, 184, 186, 187, 194

Seal, Bobby, 85

Sékou Touré, Ahmed, 33, 51, 52

Shabazz, Betty, 30

el-Shabazz, el-Hajj Malik. See Malcolm X

Shabazz, Taiwo DuVall, xi, xii, 18; illustrator of *The Adventures of Fathead, Smallhead, and Squarehead*, 226, 228, 229

Shani Baraka Women's Resource Center. See Baraka, Shani

Shariʻati, ʻAli, 24

Shepp, Archie, 34, 140, 183; *The Magic of Ju-Ju*, 37; "Malcolm, Malcolm Semper Malcolm," 119, 140; "Poem for Malcolm," 119

Shriners: Black Shriners. See Ancient Egyptian Arabic Order Nobles Mystic Shrine; White Shriners. See Ancient Arabic Order of the Nobles of the Mystic Shrine

Shorter, Wayne, and *Juju*, 37

Sidqi, Niʻmat, 24

ska, 4, 105, 109, 119, 120, 121

skin tone, 11; in Rey Chow's *Not Like a Native Speaker*, 234; Sanchez, Sonia, *A Blues Book*, 234; Jafa, Arthur, "Black visual intonation," 259

Smart-Grosvenor, Vertamae (*Vibration Cooking*), 198, 204, 261, 317n76

Snellings, Rolland. See Askia Muhammad Touré

social Darwinism, 71, 76, 77, 89

Songhai, 3, 12

Songhai! See Touré, Askia Muhammad

Le Sony'r Ra. See Sun Ra

Southern Poverty Law Center, 70, 75

Spillers, Hortense, 103, 104, 213; "Mama's Baby, Papa's Maybe," 238

Spirit House, 30, 33, 34, 44, 179, 180, 187, 193, 197, 198, 201, 202, 259

Spirit Reach. See Baraka, Amiri

Stanford, Max. See Muhammad Ahmad

Stanley, Leo, 80, 85–86

sterilization. See eugenics

Stokes, Ronald, 119, 128, 138, 143, 189

Stone, Ronald. See Rahman, Yusuf

Student Nonviolent Coordinating Committee (SNCC), 155, 209

Sulaiman, Amir, 17, 250, 254, 259; *Laying Flowers, Setting Fires*, 144–45, 257; *Love, Gnosis, and Other Suicide Attempts*, 252, 253; *Meccan Openings*, 251, 252, 255–56; *Medinan Openings*, 252; *The Opening*, 252

Suleiman, Abdul Hamid, 53

Sun Ra (Le Sony'r Ra), 27, 34, 64, 75, 91–92, 116, 171, 183, 195, 196, 243, 247, 296n1, 303n32, 317n76; collaboration on *A Black Mass*, 62, 74–75, 91, 78, 93, 94–96; collaboration on Marvin X's *Resurrection of the Dead*, 175; "myth science," 73, 74; sound image/tone poem, 11, 74, 96, 255, 260, 284n127; "Sun Ra songs," 89; Sun Ra's Myth Science Arkestra, 26, 72, 73, 179

Supreme Wisdom. See Muhammad, Elijah

tauhid, 37, 40; *Tauhid* (album) by Pharoah Sanders, 38, 186, 242, 244, 247, 248; "Tauhid" (poem) by Askia Muhammad Touré, 242, 244

Taylor, Vanessa, 97

Third World Strike, 153

Thomas, Leon, 186, 304n45

Thomas, Lorenzo, 6, 28, 37, 63, 141

Timbuktu (also Timbuctoo, Timbuctu), 3, 12, 38, 167, 245

Touré, Askia Muhammad (Rolland Snellings), 3, 22, 23, 28, 35, 36, 38, 56, 137, 141, 142; "The Call," 40, 61, 258, 260; "Jihad!: Toward A Black National Credo," 24, 27, 28; *Juju (Magic Songs for the Black Nation)*, 36–37, 38, 244; "The Opening," 38, 244; *Songhai!*, xiv, 22, 36, 39, 40, 43, 94, 257, 258, 259. *See also* Umbra Workshop
Touré, Tariq, 17, 149, 250; "The Call," 41, 260
Turner, Nat, 37, 67
Tuskegee syphilis experiments, 82
Tyner, McCoy, 34, 37

UFOs, 71, 72, 75. *See also* Mother Plane; Mothership
Uhuru Sasa School (also Shule), 33, 34, 191, 227, 249
Umbra Workshop, 23, 61, 141
umma (also Umma, Ummah), 15, 18, 123
undercommons, 60, 150; and fugitivity, 150, 175; and Marvin X, 150
Underground Railroad, 62; in Marvin X's poetry, 161, 169
United Sisters, 181, 198, 202
Universal Negro Improvement Association and African Communities League (UNIA-ACL), 30, 56
uprisings: Detroit, 179; Ferguson, 143; Harlem, 101–02; Newark, 179, 187, 189, 193; Watts, 142, 168, 179
US Organization. *See* Karenga, Maulana Ron
US School of Afroamerican Culture (Los Angeles). *See* Karenga, Maulana Ron

Vesey, Denmark, 37, 217
vibration, 11, 13, 194, 240, 248, 249, 259, 262; "vibratory shock," 242–43, 245. *See also* frequency
Vietnam, 134
Vietnam War, 144, 151, 152, 155, 157, 158, 159, 169, 175, 186, 298n43

vivisection, 80, 82, 84, 85
Voice of the People, 120

Wadi, Mar'yam (also Maryanna Waddy), 154
wadud, amina: *Inside the Gender Jihad*, 45; *Qur'an and Woman*, 45–47; Sanchez, Sonia, 45, 214
Walcott, Louis Eugene. *See* Farrakhan, Louis
Wangara, Harun Kofi, 248, 251
Washington, Joseph. *See* Yusef Iman
WBAI, 17; Malcolm X/James Baldwin debate, 125, 127, 129, 138; Malcolm X/Bayard Rustin debate, 127, 135; Marvin X interview, 17; "The Negro in American Culture" panel, 126, 129, 130–33, 137, 140, 144, 145
Weheliye, Alexander, 4, 13, 222, 229, 259
Wells, H. G.: *Island of Dr. Moreau*, 84; *Men Like Gods*, 81; *A Short History of Mankind*, 81; *War of the Worlds*, 84
Weusi Collective, 18; Weusi Nyumba Ya Sanaa Gallery, 40. *See also individual artists*: Farid, Bilal; Olugebefola, Ademola; Rahman, Abdul
Weusi, Jitu (Leslie Campbell). *See* The East
Williams, Robert F., 135, 136, 137, 204
Wilson, Sylvia. *See* Baraka, Amina
Wilson, Vera, 183, 198, 201
Wilson, Walter Vernon, 183
Wilson, Wanda, 183, 198, 201
Woodson, Carter, 17, 154, 156, 172, 177, 205
Wynn, Barry, 179

Yakub teaching, 72, 73, 74, 78, 79–81, 84, 85, 86, 88, 89, 90, 93, 277n1, 281n79; bioscientific/biomedical research, 72, 82, 86, 87, 89; in *A Black Mass*, 26, 32, 75, 76, 77, 87, 89, 94–95, 97, 174, 185; and science fiction, 71, 82–83, 86, 87

GPSR Authorized Representative: Easy Access System Europe, Mustamäe tee 50, 10621 Tallinn, Estonia, gpsr.requests@easproject.com

www.ingramcontent.com/pod-product-compliance
Lightning Source LLC
Chambersburg PA
CBHW031230290426
44109CB00012B/236